INSTRUCTOR'S MANUAL

Perrine's

Literature

Structure, Sound, and Sense

Ninth Edition

Thomas R. Arp
Southern Methodist University

Greg Johnson
Kennesaw State University

THOMSON

WADSWORTH

Australia • Canada • Mexico • Singapore • Spain • United Kingdom • United States

THOMSON
WADSWORTH

Instructor's Manual
Perrine's Literature: Structure, Sound, and Sense, Ninth Edition
Thomas R. Arp / Greg Johnson

Publisher: Michael Rosenberg
Acquisitions Editor: Aron Keesbury
Development Editor: Helen Triller-Yambert
Marketing Manager: Mary Jo Southern
Senior Project Manager, Editorial Production:
  Samantha Ross

Manufacturing Manager: Marcia Locke
Permissions Editor: Roberta Broyer
Compositor/Production Service: Graphic World Inc.
Cover Designer: Bill Reuter
Printer: West Group

Thomson Higher Education
25 Thomson Place
Boston, MA 02210-1202
USA

Asia (including India)
Thomson Learning
5 Shenton Way
#01-01 UIC Building
Singapore 068808

Australia/New Zealand
Thomson Learning Australia
102 Dodds Street
Southbank, Victoria 3006
Australia

Canada
Thomson Nelson
1120 Birchmount Road
Toronto, Ontario M1K 5G4
Canada

UK/Europe/Middle East/Africa
Thomson Learning
High Holborn House
50–51 Bedford Road
London WC1R 4LR
United Kingdom

ISBN 1-4130-0655-8

The material from *The Art of Total Relevance: Papers on Poetry* by Laurence Perrine was originally published by
Newbury House Publishers in Rowley, MA. These materials are now reprinted by permission granted by the estate of the author

Commentaries adapted for "Incident" by Countee Cullen, "Design" by Robert Frost, and "Mr. Flood's Party" by
Edwin Arlington Robinson from *100 American Poems of the Twentieth Century* by Laurence Perrine and James M.
Reid, copyright © 1966 by Harcourt, Inc., are reprinted by permission of the publisher.

Contents

Poetry The Elements of Poetry   93

Chapter One   What Is Poetry?   94

Chapter Two   Reading the Poem   104

Chapter Three   Denotation and Connotation   114

Chapter Twelve Rhythm and Meter   216

Chapter Thirteen Sound and Meaning   227

Poems for Further Reading   281

Drama   The Elements of Drama   373

Chapter One   The Nature of Drama   374

Chapter Two   Realistic and Nonrealistic Drama   380

Chapter Three   Tragedy and Comedy   387

Plays for Further Reading   403

Foreword

This Instructor's Manual includes commentary on all the stories, poems, and plays in *Perrine's Literature: Structure, Sound, and Sense*, Ninth Edition. In some discussions we have included bibliographical references to other analyses, but we have not done this uniformly or systematically. Instructors wishing to locate other discussions should consult critical books on the authors in question (especially those that have indexes), in addition to the basic bibliographic aids that direct the reader to individual explications and analyses.

Like the Ninth Edition of the textbook that it accompanies, this manual represents the work of three authors; the main author of each entry is identified by initials.

In an earlier edition, Laurence Perrine wrote:

> To the interpretations and judgments in this manual we should be foolish to expect universal consent; they will serve their purpose if they provoke more careful scrutiny of the works in question, and an intelligent dissent. . . . Certainly, the approach taken here to any selection is only one of various possible approaches. Apollo does not speak in any of these comments, but in the works themselves. The oracles that report him here are neither priests nor prophets, but fallible human beings like yourselves.

Thomas R. Arp
Greg Johnson

Fiction

The Elements
of Fiction

Chapter One

Reading the Story

Richard Connell **The Most Dangerous Game** (page 67)*

"The Most Dangerous Game" is an exciting suspense story, and students will like it. The kinds of conflict it embodies and its chief devices for arousing and maintaining suspense are discussed on page 105. Its use of name symbolism is briefly discussed on page 275, its structure on page 103, its point of view on page 228, and its irony on page 336. The trick in teaching it will be to draw from the students themselves, as subtly as possible, a perception of its limitations, for nothing turns students off faster than scoffing at something they like, or betraying a tendency to look down on it.

The improbabilities of the story are patent enough. There is, first of all, the implausibility of the "mystery" of Ship-Trap Island. In the opening conversation between Whitney and Rainsford, we are given to believe that very little is known of this "God-forsaken place"—only vague superstitions and ominous legends. Yet when Rainsford visits the place, we find out that the island is equipped with electricity and that General Zaroff, in his immense, well-maintained château, serves soup with whipped cream, imports his clothes and his champagne from overseas, and smokes perfumed cigarettes. It clearly takes a community of thousands to run this place, and there must be constant commerce between it and the rest of the world. It is hard to fathom how there can be much of a secret about it. But the author disguises this implausibility from us by showing us no human beings there except Zaroff and Ivan. Unless we stop to think, we regard the island as isolated and virtually uninhabited. The problem of social control—of how Zaroff runs this place and pursues his inhuman pleasures without inspiring rebellion (it would take a small private army)—is not addressed.

The character of Zaroff is equally implausible. Manufactured by the conjunction of contradictory traits—extreme savagery (he says that Ivan is "like all his race, a bit of a savage," and then adds, "He is a Cossack. . . . So am I") and extreme civility, Zaroff is an effective character for a story of this

---

*Unless otherwise specified, all page references in this Manual are to the text of *Perrine's Literature: Structure, Sound, and Sense*, Ninth Edition.

kind—that is, he is blood-chilling. But he adds nothing to our knowledge of human nature. Boredom with the tameness of hunting grizzlies, jaguars, and Cape buffalo (and, after all, a Cape buffalo did lay him up for six months) is hardly enough to explain his psychological aberration, nor is it probable that his psychological aberration should have no other symptom but scorn for "romantic ideas about the value of human life." Calm rationality marks everything that Zaroff does. Even so, his character is inconsistent. A gambler plays to win his bet, a hunter hunts to kill. There is no plausible reason why Zaroff should thrice turn back from the hunt after tracking down his game, except that the author arbitrarily wants to prolong the excitement. In short, Zaroff is not believable (contrast him with the delinquents in "The Destructors" and Dick Prosser in "The Child by Tiger"). He is, however, vivid. The little details of characterization ("Then he sat down, took a drink of brandy from a silver flask, lit a perfumed cigaret, and hummed a bit from *Madame Butterfly*") make him a much more memorable and substantial character than Rainsford. Rainsford is merely a stock adventure-story hero: tall, brave, strong, resourceful, virtuous (he is quick to condemn manhunts as "cold-blooded murder"). His one individualizing trait—the touch of unimaginativeness betrayed in his opening conversation with Whitney—is made no more of. The main conflict of the story is good versus evil, hero versus villain.

But the basic evidence that "The Most Dangerous Game" is a commercial story is its absence of organic unity and therefore of theme. This is discussed on page 372.

Should we care? It has been a good story—perhaps that is enough. But it is not enough if we never ask for anything more.

A British film based on this story is entitled *The Hounds of Zaroff*; an older full-length feature version using the original title fabricates a "love interest" for Rainsford.   LP

Tobias Wolff   Hunters in the Snow (page 86)

Wolff's story exemplifies the complex art of characterization in its portrayal of three men, their shifting alliances, and their Darwinian power struggle in the snowy wilderness of Washington State. Initially the obese Tub appears as a figure of fun and a "butt" (as his name spelled backwards implies) of jokes: empowered in their truck while Tub stands helpless in the snow, his "friends" Kenny and Frank, picking up Tub an hour late for the hunting trip, harass him by almost running him down. There is a context here, of course, of lively young men who enjoy practical jokes, but immediately there is an undercurrent of real malice in the way Kenny and Frank treat Tub. The kidding is not good-natured but hurtful, as when Kenny immediately makes fun of Tub's obesity to Frank: "He looks just like a beachball with a hat on, doesn't he?"

Wolff's use of detail lets us know that these are working-class men who live in a relatively lawless world: despite the bitter cold, they are using an unheated truck because "some juvenile delinquents" had vandalized it. James Hannah likewise observes that the story features a hostile environment and that we get little of the usual background information on the characters: "The three men appear isolated from the world. During the hunt, they move across a deserted landscape focusing the reader's attention on their interactions. The title itself, like the title of a painting, promises a minimalist portrayal of three men in pursuit of game in a world of whiteness that is lifeless and inhospitable. . . . [The] lack of background is like the snowscape, an empty environment." See Hannah's full discussion in *Tobias Wolff: A Study of the Short Fiction* (New York: Twayne, 1996) 7–9.

As the three men drive toward the hunting area, Wolff establishes the characters allied against Tub—especially Frank, the most villainous of the three. Not only is Frank, a married man with children, engaged in a sexual affair with a fifteen-year-old girl; he is also the type of man who fancies himself a philosopher, using phrases like "Tune in on that energy" and "Get centered." (Later in the story, the more plain-spoken Kenny chastises Frank for his "hippie bullshit.") Another telling detail is the pinky ring Frank wears "with a flat face and an 'F' in what looked like diamonds." Any discussion of the ring should proceed carefully (a surreptitious glance at students' pinkies can be helpful) but clearly Wolff means to suggest Frank's bad taste and his egocentricity, for what kind of man wears a ring emblazoned with his own initial in fake diamonds? The occasional counterculture "wisdom" he spouts is belied by this showy materialism and by his ongoing insults to Tub. Admiring his own ring, Frank says casually to Tub, "You haven't seen your own balls in ten years." Frank has slightly more education than his two friends (his vocabulary is more complex, and he alludes to a Shakespeare play later in the story), but like The Misfit in O'Connor's "A Good Man Is Hard to Find," he uses his intelligence purely for self-serving purposes.

"Hunters in the Snow" maintains an omniscient point of view, reporting the three men's actions from an objective stance and occasionally (but not obtrusively) commenting on them. For instance, the narrator emphasizes the lack of any real friendship among the three men with another small observation as they are getting past a barbed-wire fence: "Tub had trouble getting through the fences. Frank and Kenny could have helped him; they could have lifted up on the top wire and stepped on the bottom wire, but they didn't. They stood and watched him." Through its accretion of such observations and details, the story makes clear that each of the three men is wholly self-interested and that the balance of power among them could shift at any time, depending on circumstances.

Wolff continues to stress the suspension of ordinary laws governing human behavior. When, after hours of fruitless searching for deer, they find deer sign in a posted area, Frank insists they get permission to hunt there because "the people out here [don't] mess around," foreshadowing violent action.

Wolff orchestrates the next scenes with great deftness and economy. Kenny goes alone into the farmhouse to ask permission, while Tub and Frank stay in the truck. With Kenny gone, Tub tries to enlist Frank's sympathy and offers to hear about Frank's relationship with the babysitter: this brief conversation signals the shift in allegiance (Tub and Frank vs. Kenny instead of Frank and Kenny vs. Tub) that will dominate the second half of the story.

Even after the men get permission, the hunting is unsuccessful. In a foul mood, Kenny vents his anger by shooting at a fencepost: "'There,' Kenny said. 'It's dead.'" Inspired, Kenny also shoots a tree and then, to Frank's and Tub's shock, an aging dog belonging to the farmer. Just as he'd enjoyed scaring Tub by almost hitting him with the truck in the opening scene, he now points his gun at Tub as if to shoot him next, but Tub surprises Kenny by shooting him first, in self-defense.

The wounded Kenny, undone by his own practical joke, becomes the odd man out for the rest of the story. Some of the best moments include the macabre comedy of Frank and Tub attempting to "care" for Kenny by covering him with a blanket that keeps blowing off, and making hapless attempts to get him to a hospital. Only when Frank and Tub learn from the farm couple that they'd *asked* Kenny to shoot the dog does the full impact of Kenny's joke (which has backfired on him, literally) become clear.

Wolff's orchestration is particularly subtle as he moves Frank out of the room, to call the hospital, when the farmer tells Tub why Kenny shot the dog. Presumably Tub keeps the information to himself because he needs Frank to testify that Kenny's shooting at him was wholly unprovoked and his self-defensive shot justified. All these mechanics of the plot serve to underscore the essential self-centeredness of the three characters: each is struggling for dominance over the others with no real concern for the others' fates. After the farmer's wife gives Frank complicated written directions to the hospital, Wolff adds another small detail testifying to the essential lack of human empathy in this fictive world. It has grown dark outside, and the farmer says he has no flashlight to give them (surely not the truth), but that he will leave the porch light on; then he forgets, or declines, even to provide the porch light, and the three men struggle in darkness ("clashing by night," one might say) to load Kenny into the truck. First there is a brief scuffle between Tub and Frank; Tub asserts his physical size, demanding that Frank stop making sarcastic remarks about his weight and wresting an apology from him. The shift in power is complete; Frank and Tub are allied in the relatively warm truck cab, while the wounded, bleeding, freezing Kenny lies in the back of the truck at the mercy of the elements and his "friends."

While Tub seemed the most sympathetic character at the beginning, the reader may come to feel that Kenny is guilty, at most, of a callous, rascally disposition, while Frank and Tub are both self-centered literally to a murderous degree. Frank and Tub, a pedophile and a food addict, are accustomed to thinking only of their own appetites, so it isn't surprising that they leave the wounded Kenny in the truck while they stop for coffee, using the rationalization that if they "freeze," they'll never get Kenny to the hospital.

The final third of the story drifts into tragicomedy as Kenny, delirious with cold and loss of blood, is instructed by the others to repeat the mantra "I am going to the hospital." At this point, Tub realizes he left the written directions to the hospital back at the farmhouse, but by now Tub and Frank are forging, as they see it, a new bond by "confessing" to one another. Tub admits to his food addiction, Frank details his illegal affair with the young girl. In a classic scene of what psychologists call "enabling," Frank insists that Tub sit down and eat several huge plates of pancakes, butter, and syrup—an act, of course, unconsciously designed to make Frank feel better about his own indulgences.

In the final paragraph, Tub and Frank have grown so close that Tub finally confesses that Kenny had been asked to shoot the farmer's dog. They glance through the back window at Kenny, who is deliriously repeating "I'm going to the hospital," a statement undercut with devastating effect by the narrator in the final two sentences: "But he was wrong. They had taken a different turn a long way back."

The thematic bleakness of this story—in which people form symbiotic alliances purely to further their own gains and in which there is virtually no charity, love, or beauty—is mitigated to some degree by the humor of the dialogue and situation. While some readers may complain they "can't care" about any of these three characters, this story (like some of Hemingway's) seems to suggest that human beings, especially when isolated in a natural setting, can shed their socially constructed humane traits and become as primitive and predatory as the most unevolved natural creatures. In an interview, Tobias Wolff reported that three short films of "Hunters in the Snow" have been made, but that PBS refused to show any of them because of this bleakness: "it's such an ugly little story that they won't show it," Wolff remarked. (From Jay Woodruff, ed., *A Piece of Work: Five Writers Discuss Their Revisions* [Iowa City: U of Iowa P, 1991]; qtd. in Hannah, 124.)

Apart from its content, "Hunters in the Snow" bears comparison with "Interpreter of Maladies" and "How I Met My Husband" in its intricate, artful pattern of plot structure, characterization, and point of view, resulting in a consummately "well made" story.

The theme of this story is mentioned on page 193, and its ironies on pages 334 and 336.   GJ

Chapter Two

Plot and Structure

Graham Greene **The Destructors** (page 111)

"Destruction after all is a form of creation," the narrator tells us in what might well serve as a compact statement of the theme of the story. The creative instinct, unable to find a constructive outlet, turns to destruction and derives artistic and imaginative satisfactions from it. The protagonists of this story—the gang—work hard at destruction. They reject opportunities for personal gain that accompany it. Absorbed in their work, they forget personal rivalries. Blackie and Trevor cooperate fully: "The question of leadership no longer concerned the gang."

But the story has a social setting, which expands the theme. The members of the gang live in a blitzed world. Unconsciously they are taking revenge on a society that has betrayed them. This society is a class society, and all the values associated with it are fitly symbolized in the two-hundred-year-old house, built by a titled architect, Sir Christopher Wren. Partly these are snob values, as evidenced by Trevor's mother, who "considered herself better than her neighbors" though her husband had "come down in the world." Partly they are money values, as represented by the bank notes that Trevor and Blackie burn. But they are also such values as beauty, courtesy, love. "It's a beautiful house," says Trevor, who is later ridiculed when he says "Please." Trevor has turned against these values himself: "All this hate and love," he tells Blackie, "it's soft, it's hooey. There's only things." The symbolic identification of the house with the old social order and its values is established by the link between Blackie's meditation on the word "beautiful" and the lorry-driver's vision of the house at the end of the story. Blackie worries over the word "beautiful": it "belonged to a class world that you could still see parodied at the Wormsley Common Empire by *a man wearing a top hat* and a monocle, with a haw-haw accent" (italics LP). The lorry-driver cannot constrain his laughter: "One moment the house had stood there with such dignity between the bomb-sites like *a man in a top hat,* and then, bang, crash, there wasn't anything left—not anything" (italics LP).

There are additional brief comments on this story on pages 162–163, 193, 228, 275, 336.   LP

Alice Munro   How I Met My Husband (page 125)

Munro's story illustrates the way a writer may deploy the elements of plot and narrative structure. In many ways, "How I Met My Husband" adheres to a traditional structure: it begins *in medias res,* initiating suspense in the first line with the dramatic possibility of an airplane crashing into a house; it develops the background information and characterization through dramatic action and dialogue; it deftly overturns readers' expectations and builds suspense as the focus on the protagonist's erotic awakening and ultimate marriage intensifies; it employs several minor characters as "foils" to clarify the protagonist's characterization and lead to her emotional insight, or epiphany, in the last few paragraphs; and it features a classic example of a successful "surprise ending"—that is, one neither gimmicky nor predictable, but one that flows out of the preceding action in a way that is both inevitable and surprising, providing a satisfying and fully rounded closure.

The story's style is well-suited to the narrator and the subject matter, though the reader soon becomes aware that the Edie telling the story is wiser and more mature than Edie at age fifteen, when the story actually takes place. For instance, she mentions that she quit school partly because "they didn't make it nice for [her] or explain the way they do now" and notes that she was "slimmer at fifteen than anybody would believe who knows [her] now." Such remarks, along with the title itself, suggest a reminiscence told from the vantage point of a long-married woman.

Munro keeps the story dramatically immediate by using a plain, straightforward style that replicates the voice of an ordinary farm girl in rural Ontario, which Edie was as a teenager. (Moreover, the action is set shortly after World War II, an era when a naive farm girl like Edie would have been "innocent" and more insulated from popular culture than a girl of the same age today.) Like such disparate fictional protagonists as Jane Eyre or Huckleberry Finn, Edie wins the reader over quickly with her vulnerability, her loneliness, and her honesty. Munro introduces a foil character early on who helps clarify these traits: the obstreperous Loretta Bird, mother of seven children, who nonetheless spends her days gossiping at other people's farms and lounging around hotel coffee shops instead of staying home with what she calls her "yappers." Essentially a comic figure, Loretta also serves a plot function by providing information about the handsome barnstormer, Chris Watters, and by heightening the tension when she brings the genuinely malefic and emotionally unbalanced Alice Kelling onto the scene, precipitating the climax.

The veterinarian and his wife for whom Edie works as a "hired girl," Dr. and Mrs. Peebles, also contrast with Edie, since they have tried (with minimal success) to assume rural identities and values whereas Edie, with her peasant shrewdness, sees through them at once, noting that the Peebleses like to eat outside (a habit mystifying to farm people) and are unable to perform the domestic chores that are second nature to her.

Munro also heightens the tension when she highlights both Edie's secret life and her honesty: she does "deceptive" things like wear Mrs. Peebles's clothes when she's alone in the house, and though she occasionally tells lies, she admits these to the reader. This emphasis on her human foibles and her honesty in describing them adds to her reliability as a narrator. A key development in the plot, of course, occurs when Chris Watters comes to the house for water when Edie is gussied up in her employer's clothes. He indulges in mild, flirtatious banter with her, and Munro emphasizes Edie's vulnerability and youth once again: "I didn't know how to joke back then. I was too embarrassed." Watters, the mysterious aviator who has just returned from the war, represents a romantic hero to the cloistered Edie, and when she gets up the nerve to visit his tent at the nearby fairgrounds, she notes that "My heart was knocking away, my tongue was dried up." Unlike Edie at fifteen, the older narrator is preparing us for her first major infatuation, yet allowing us (primarily because of the title) to believe that her romantic fantasy might become a reality.

The next rise in tension comes, of course, with the arrival of Alice Kelling, who claims she is Chris Watters's fiancée. Her ignoble need to follow him around, evidently without his encouragement, hints at the truth (today, she would be called an "obsessive lover," even a "stalker"), as do the suggestions that Alice is considerably older than Watters.

Edie sees through Alice Kelling as she did Loretta Bird, and when she bakes Chris a cake and goes again to visit him, we aren't surprised when he decides to flee. In a subtle, beautifully cadenced scene, he and Edie have a romantic interlude in his tent (going beyond kissing, but stopping short of intercourse), and the good-natured but unreliable Watters promises he will write to her. Readers will have varied responses to Watters's character: some will see him as kindly and, in his own loneliness, sympathetic in not taking full advantage of Edie's naiveté; others, especially in today's political climate, will denounce him as a child molester. We must adhere to the text, however, which suggests that this is an important and primarily positive (if also painful) interlude in Edie's life, and one that leads, after all, to her meeting her actual husband, the mailman.

By encouraging the reader's own fantasies that Chris Watters might somehow be Edie's husband, Munro cleverly replicates for the reader the irrational hope and letdown that Edie herself experiences. As E. D. Blodgett remarks, Edie's function is "to show how we prefer our version of the truth to whatever the truth may be" (*Alice Munro* [Twayne: Boston, 1988] 77).

The conclusion is especially satisfying because after the passionate meeting between Edie and Watters is discovered and misinterpreted, and after Alice Kelling brands Edie a "country tramp," Mrs. Peebles expels both Alice and Loretta Bird from the bucolic farm setting and Edie returns to her fantasy of awaiting Watters's letter. The last paragraph includes a gentle irony in Edie's mentioning that her husband, Carmichael, believed Edie had been going "after him" by waiting near the mailbox every day. The kindhearted and newly wise Edie knows better than to disabuse him of his romantic fantasy. She has found her own happiness in making other people happy, an assertion that provides a bittersweet and entirely believable conclusion to this story. GJ

Jhumpa Lahiri   Interpreter of Maladies (page 141)

Lahiri's story is obviously quite different from Munro's "How I Met My Husband": "Interpreter of Maladies" uses third-person point of view rather than first; it is set in India rather than rural Ontario; it deals with entirely different subject matter. Yet Lahiri's story, too, exemplifies a superb use of plot and narrative structure to illustrate a theme and effect a change—in this case, a poignant one—in a fully characterized protagonist.

One major focus here, of course, is the "international theme": the disparity between the Americanized Das family and the older, more traditional Mr. Kapasi, their tour guide. He is experiencing what Americans call a "midlife crisis": his youthful dreams (inspired by his love of languages) of being an "interpreter for diplomats and dignitaries" were never realized; his domestic life is physically comfortable but spiritually unfulfilling and lacking in romance. (His wife does not even fully undress during sex.) Mr. Kapasi is a man of substance and imagination whose life seems unlikely to offer him the opportunity for full self-actualization: thus the aura of melancholy attached to him, and the admirable dignity with which he speaks, chooses his impeccable clothes, and fulfills his mundane duties as a tour guide and as a medical assistant in a doctor's office where he interprets the Gujarati dialect spoken by patients trying to explain their ailments to English-speaking physicians.

Suspense develops when Mrs. Das, a young woman Mr. Kapasi finds physically appealing, claims to find his interpreting job "romantic." This provides a dual excitement for Mr. Kapasi, enabling him to see himself as someone doing an important job and as a romantic figure in the lovely Mrs. Das's eyes. The narrator, and therefore the reader, can see a shallowness in Mrs. Das's conversation and behavior that the somewhat conventional, naive Mr. Kapasi (who is also blinded to a degree by his attraction to Mrs. Das) cannot yet perceive.

Lahiri conveys the situation through carefully selected details: Mrs. Das offers Mr. Kapasi a piece of gum, for instance, and when he bites into the gum "a thick sweet liquid [bursts] onto his tongue." He notices her "close-fitting blouse" and the strawberry-shaped "appliqué" in her cleavage (later, this may recall to some readers a scarlet letter). Similarly, "[h]e could smell a scent on her skin, like a mixture of whiskey and rosewater." To the dignified Mr. Kapasi, Mrs. Das represents a garden of earthly delights and erotic possibility; after a picture-taking session, Mrs. Das casually asks for his address so she can send him a photo and in doing so inadvertently encourages his fantasies. Though the Das family lives in New Jersey, he imagines initiating an intense, romantic correspondence of the kind Mrs. Das could never reciprocate. These imagined letters comport with the story's emphasis on language, text, and interpretation, for Mr. Kapasi does not entertain the expected lubricious fantasies of a sexual encounter, but instead a return to his youthful dreams of language: "As his mind raced, Mr. Kapasi experienced a mild and pleasant shock. It was similar to a feeling he used to experience long ago when, after months of translating with the aid of a dictionary, he would finally read a passage from a French novel, or an Italian sonnet, and understand the words, one after another, unencumbered by his own efforts. In those moments Mr. Kapasi used to believe that all was right with the world. . . ." Reflecting their different cultural preoccupations, Mrs. Das represents raw sexuality and superficial culture, whereas Mr. Kapasi is attracted to notions of idealistic romance and the artful, meaningful constructs of literary language.

Another plot element involves one of the Das family's three children, Bobby. Early on, we learn that he was "slightly paler than the other children," a bit of foreshadowing that prepares the reader for Mrs. Das's disclosure to Mr. Kapasi that Bobby is the product of a one-time sexual encounter with a friend of her husband's. Mrs. Das claims she has felt "pain" for eight years in her marriage and Mr. Kapasi (the wise interpreter) suggests she may actually be feeling guilt; the romantic fantasy is clearly over when Mrs. Das, offended, stalks away. And its hopelessness is signaled definitively at the end of the story, of course, when the slip of paper with Mr. Kapasi's address slips out of the careless Mrs. Das's purse.

Contrasting cultural values, the plot of "Interpreter of Maladies" seems strongly biased in favor of traditional Indian morality. As the title suggests, language itself conveys this theme: Mr. Kapasi's diction is precise, even scholarly, whereas the members of the Das family (including the adults, who are portrayed as overgrown children) use trite phrases like "Cool" and "Neat." The monkeys the group encounters in the climactic scene not only symbolize, in their Western connotations, the animality of Mrs. Das and her children but the culturally unevolved state of Mr. and Mrs. Das's sensibilities, for which "philistine" would be a kindly adjective. In Indian culture, however, the monkeys (called "hanuman") are venerated; the so-called "monkey god" for whom they are named plays an important role in the *Ramayana*. All Mrs. Das can say about the monkeys is that they "give [her] the creeps" and even Mr. Das, a teacher, is presented as wholly obtuse, absorbed in a guidebook produced outside of India and completely unaware of the complex, delicate exchanges between Mr. Kapasi and his wife. The different cultural meanings attached to monkeys in American and Indian culture are only one of the symbolic elements that help provide an entry into the relationship between the cultures dramatized in Mr. Kapasi's attraction to Mrs. Das, and his ultimate disillusionment with her.

With its clear yet subtly cadenced narrative style, "Interpreter of Maladies" unfolds as an ordinary day-trip in which a courtly Indian guide serves a crass American couple. But through the poignant insights into Mr. Kapasi's midlife sorrows and the disclosure of Mrs. Das's infidelity, compounded by her adult life spent conducting a dishonest marriage, the story achieves an extraordinary complexity for which the cultural backdrop provides additional levels of meaning. The ancient temples and monuments visited by the childlike Das family, in particular, help create the ironic contrast that the story as a whole exploits.

The delicate ending offers a satisfying denouement, since only Mr. Kapasi (and here the third-person limited viewpoint becomes crucial) observes the slip of paper with his address as it blows out of Mrs. Das's purse to be lost forever. There is no need, here, for the narrator to describe Mr. Kapasi's sadness and disillusionment. It is all there in that wonderfully sad moment when Mr. Kapasi observes, alone, the death of his fantasy and the likely continuation of the melancholy solitude he had hoped to escape—for a brief, naive while.   GJ

Chapter Three

Characterization

Alice Walker Everyday Use (page 166)

The theme of "Everyday Use" is mentioned on page 193, and its symbolism on pages 275 and 281.

The story presents its theme ironically by contrasting ideas of "heritage." Dee (self-named "Wangero"), dressed in African costume and scornfully bullying her mother and sister for their backwardness even while she plunders their house, has artificially, fictitiously created for herself a past that includes pride in an African origin and a nostalgia for the simplicity of her downtrodden kinfolk; the narrator has as her past what she can remember having lived and heard (Wangero's attempts to make her mother acknowledge that the name Dee originated with the white oppressors fails—for though the mother believes she *could* trace the name back to the days of slavery if she wanted to, she reacts to the bullying by saying she will go no further back than her own and her sister's time). Hakim, Wangero's companion (husband? wonders the mother), has his version of a past, captured in committing himself to Islam. Maggie's past is not only memory (she wouldn't need a quilt to remember Grandma Dee) but also a vital and active part of her present—for she can in fact make quilts herself, having been taught by her authentic ancestors the arts and crafts of making things for "everyday use" that her sophisticated sister considers artifacts of a quaint past.

The contrast between Maggie and Wangero is the battleground of the mother's spirit, and when the conflict focuses on the quilts that her educated daughter would snatch away and hang on the wall to display her heritage, the mother takes her stand: what has been promised to Maggie will be Maggie's, and Dee will not get her own way—for once. This climactic decision defines the dynamic characterization of the mother, not a temporary but a permanent change, for it has been working its way to the fore throughout the narration.

The preparation for this change has been embedded in the mother's continuing ambivalence about Dee, a woman both to be admired and to be feared, so headstrong as always to have managed "to stare down any disaster in her efforts," dangerous but strong. How dangerous she is may be indicated by the implication that she burnt down their house—and nearly burnt her sister to death—because of hatred for it (and perhaps, as the narrator once thought, hatred of her sister as well). The mother knows her well, knows that there should be limits on what she can get away with, yet until the climax has always found it better to yield. But she remembers, having been "hooked in the side in '49, [that] cows are soothing and slow and don't bother you, unless you try to milk them the wrong way." In this story, Dee finally tries "to milk" her mother "the wrong way" and discovers the limits of maternal indulgence.

Much can be taught about the subtleties of fiction with this story: the first-person narration, from the perspective of a woman who freely concedes lack of education and sophistication, lack of femininity and grace, displays an admirable economy in the selection of detail and meditation. Like the remark about cows, almost every reported thought has the double purpose of revealing character and advancing theme. For example, the mother's little "dream" of appearing on TV on "This Is Your Life" to greet her grateful, successful daughter discriminates between fiction and reality (she knows that all is rehearsed and prettified for the audience), but it also reveals a desire to be the glamorous, svelte, witty, and self-confident woman Dee would like her to be. The narrator is ignorant of the black movement and its varieties of expression—Wangero's allegiance to a tribal Africa in her name, her dress, her jewelry; Hakim's allegiance to a Muslim Africa and its Arabic traditions; and the "beef-cattle peoples down the road," apparently a black nationalist commune so unimaginable to her that the narrator "walked a mile and a half just to see the sight" of black men having rifles to protect themselves against racial assault. Yet her wonder at these things, and her simple naiveté in reporting them, comically reveal her balanced judiciousness in reacting to them. While it is not in her nature to judge outright (perhaps as a result of her religious faith), she is certainly a trustworthy observer of fads and fashions—and she remains honest about her feelings even when circumstances might elicit blanket condemnation: although she thinks Dee's dress outlandish, "so loud it hurts [her] eyes," when she sees her daughter walk in it she admits she likes its flowing looseness.

The central thematic contrast in the story pits the narrator's (and Maggie's) honesty and integrity against the posturing and artificiality of Dee, their self-sacrifice against her rapacity, their authentic relationship to a heritage of beautiful things made for "everyday use" against her ethnic pretentiousness. What is most remarkable about the mother, perhaps, is her patience and forbearance—how many of us would have sat through Dee's taking "picture after picture" of what she regards as squalid quaintness, photographing a tin-roofed duplicate of a house she may have destroyed out of hatred for it and what it stood for, but now to be recorded as evidence of her "heritage"? And all that before she puts her camera away for a condescending kiss of greeting!

A DVD dramatized adaptation of this story is available from Wadsworth, including an interview with the author. The adaptation "softens" the portrait of Dee/Wangero by omitting not only many of the narrator's evaluations of her but also several of the reported events—for example, Dee's previous refusal to take the quilts to college with her, and Dee's complicity in the fire that destroyed the old house and mutilated Maggie. Although these are not included in the dramatization, they form part of the analysis of character in the author's interview.

The DVD probably will be most useful in classroom discussions if the instructor draws attentions to omissions and changes, as well as to the important differences between first-person point of view and the dramatic point of view necessitated by a dramatization. A good starting point might be to ask students which significant remarks in the narrative have been represented by visual effects, and which of them have been dropped. What purpose is served, for example, by the omission of the narrator's report of her amazement at seeing the black men down the road protecting themselves from white violence "with rifles in their hands"?   TRA

Katherine Mansfield   Miss Brill (page 175)

The story's theme is briefly discussed on page 194, its plot on page 373, its point of view on page 229, and its symbolism and use of irony on pages 279–80, 335–36, and 338.

Katherine Mansfield's little masterpiece presents us with the pathetic moment in the life of an elderly and lonely spinster when she realizes for the first time that she is old and lonely. The setting is a French resort town, probably on the Riviera. Miss Brill is an Englishwoman who supports herself by tutoring the children of English families in the town and by reading the papers to an old invalid gentleman. We know that she is getting old because of her methodical ways and set habits. She keeps her fur wrapped in moth powder and repairs it with sealing wax. Every Sunday, in season and out, she goes to the park, always starting from home at exactly the same time, always sitting in her "special seat," always on the way back buying an almond cake for her Sunday treat. We know that Miss Brill has no friends, for she goes to the park alone, eats her Sunday meal alone, has no one to confide in except her pupils, has to make up surprises for herself. (When there is an almond in her cake, Miss Brill strikes her match in "quite a dashing way.") We never learn her first name, for no one ever calls her by it. The fact that she is a spinster and in a foreign country underlines her isolation. The title suits this story perfectly: it tells us that the protagonist is English, unmarried, and friendless.

At the beginning of the story, however, Miss Brill does not realize her loneliness, for she has developed a knack for projecting herself into the lives of people around her. She dramatizes her fur: "Dear little thing! . . . 'What has been happening to me?' said the sad little eyes. . . . Little rogue biting its tail just by her left ear." She dramatizes the band: out of season it "was like someone playing with only the family to listen." Especially she dramatizes people: she has become an expert in eavesdropping on conversations, "sitting in other people's lives just for a minute." The fur, the band, its conductor with his new coat, the other people in the park, the children—all become persons in Miss Brill's life. She doesn't realize that she's living entirely in her own imagination, in a world of her creation. Neither does she think of herself as old. At one point she makes a significant observation:

> Other people sat on the benches and green chairs, but they were nearly always the same, Sunday after Sunday, and—Miss Brill had often noticed—there was something funny about nearly all of them. They were odd, silent, nearly all old, and from the way they stared they looked as though they'd just come from dark little rooms or even—even cupboards!

This description is ironic, for, without Miss Brill's realizing it, it fits her perfectly. At the end of the story she is called "a stupid old thing," and she returns to her dark little room "like a cupboard."

The moment of insight is shattering for Miss Brill and poignant for the reader. It is so for two reasons. First, Miss Brill, however odd, old, and withdrawn she may appear on the outside, has been revealed as warm and gentle on the inside. There is nothing mean, cranky, or vindictive about her. She wants people to love one another. She would like to "shake" the English lady who keeps complaining to her sympathetic husband. She is distressed when a beautiful woman flings away her violets that a little boy has picked up for her. And she hears the drum beating "The Brute! The Brute!" when a man puffs smoke into the face of the lady in the ermine toque. (The "lady" in the ermine toque is clearly a prostitute soliciting trade, but Miss Brill, innocent and unworldly, does not realize this and sympathizes with her entirely.) Though Miss Brill's own need for love is frustrated and repressed, she desires love for other people. Second, the moment of disillusion contrasts sharply and ironically with the mood of joy which Miss Brill, and the reader, feel up until that shock. Joy rises steadily in the story from its opening sentence: "It was so brilliantly fine—the blue sky powdered with gold and great spots of light like white wine splashed over the Jardins Publiques," through Miss Brill's fancying that she is participating in a play, to the climax in which it seems to her that "in another moment all of them, all the whole company, would begin singing." Then come the cruel words, thrust like a dagger at her and her beloved fur.

What effect does the incident have on Miss Brill's life? Does she ever strike her match in "a dashing way" again? We know that she does not buy her usual almond cake that Sunday. And we know that an illusion has been destroyed for her. She will never be able to think of herself in quite the same way again. At the beginning of the story Miss Brill is in love with the world. At the end she has been rudely thrust out of it.

What are we to make of the last sentence? She puts her fur back in its box: "But when she put the lid on she thought she heard something crying."

In one respect Miss Brill has not changed. She still dramatizes the things around her, and her poor little fur piece has been insulted. The fur piece, of course, is a symbol for Miss Brill herself. It too comes out of a dark box, and goes back into a dark box. It too has been ridiculed. At the end of the story Miss Brill and the fur piece merge. It is herself that she hears crying.   LP

Mary Hood   How Far She Went (page 179)

The protagonist is a country woman in her fifties with a "secret, unforgivable, that not another good thing could ever make up for." The "secret," like so many past events in this story, is presented indirectly, even obliquely, but it appears to be this: she had been seduced by a man who deserted her, but "there was no love in the begetting" of her illegitimate daughter, only "the sinful fumble of flesh." When her child was born she had to lie on the birth certificate, but held no love for the baby who turned out "wild" and died young, after "sudden wedlock" and the birth in turn of her daughter. Now, at fifteen, the girl has been dumped on her grandmother by her father. To the grandmother, the whole sequence seems a "punishment" that will pass on from generation to generation.

The unnamed granddaughter is like her own mother "wild," defiant, angry, and emotionally wounded. She hates living in the country alone with her granny, but she seems to have no options. In boredom and resentment, and ashamed of "minding so much" that her father has abandoned her to this place, she walks away from the farm. Seeming to act as antagonist, she stands against her grandmother and all her ways, feeling no love from her and dismayed by the discovery that her father too does not love her. But as the title suggests, she goes too far when she accepts a ride from a drunken biker, the ultimately dangerous antagonist to both her and her granny.

The climactic scene occurs when the two women flee from the bikers to hide in the lake under the dock where the grandmother is forced to drown her little dog to keep him from giving them away. Again, the title is evoked, for this is how far *she* will go to protect them. Once the bikers withdraw and evening comes on, the two emerge from the lake and head for home. The final actions allow the two to sense the emotional ties that bind them: the grandmother has sacrificed the dog that was to her "as contrary and restless as a child," "like a baby," and then "like a dead child," in order to protect the girl. The girl, in turn, shows her ability to sympathize when she speaks respectfully to her grandmother and offers to carry the body of the dog. At that point, "they saw each other as well as they could in that failing light, in any light." Having exposed their emotions to each other, though still reticent in expressing them, the two wounded women walk home together, having at least for the time defended themselves from the ravages of abusive and faithless men.   TRA

Chapter Four

Theme

Toni Cade Bambara The Lesson (page 195)

The style of this story is mentioned on page 371, its point of view on page 230, and its irony on pages 334–35.

There are two Sylvias in the story, the adult reminiscing in the first para-graph, and the child narrating the action from the second paragraph onward. This shift in narration is signaled by the paragraph break but also by the switch from past to present tense and by the introduction of a particular in-cident after the generalized summary of the first paragraph. The adult per-spective is an essential component of the story because Sylvia's childhood re-sponse to the events of the day is not fully defined at the conclusion where she is still resisting Miss Moore's lesson, although she is preparing to "think [it] through." What the opening paragraph shows is that at least one aspect of the lesson has been learned: the girl who confidently thought that she knew more than the "old and stupid" or the "young and foolish" is viewed ironically by the mature adult that she became. Sylvia the sassy know-it-all resists Miss Moore (and the whole notion that an older woman might be more intelligent or informed than she), but by the end of the story, she is at least ready to think about the day's experience. The starting point of learn-ing is acknowledging that there may be something to learn, and that is what Sylvia does.

The incident reported is Miss Moore's rounding up the children on the block for an expedition to the most expensive toy store in New York—perhaps in the world. Her purpose is to teach the children a lesson about the haves and the have-nots, and to suggest to them that economic inequality might be a target for their future energies: her repeated lesson is "that poor people have to wake up and demand their share of the pie" (the children do not even know what kind of pie she's talking about).

It is important to see that Miss Moore is not focusing on the inequalities of racism. These, it must be assumed, are fully known and recognized by the children. When Sylvia suggests a more interesting activity for the day it includes leading Sugar in a terrorist attack on the "West Indian kids," and she sees Miss Moore filing that away for a future lesson on brotherhood. As black children transported from the south to New York, Sylvia feels her friends are superior to other blacks who don't share her language and customs. The only mention of the white race in the story comes when Sylvia comments on their craziness for wearing stockings and even furs on a hot summer day.

The trip to Fifth Avenue is eye-opening and even intimidating for Sylvia. Her emotional reaction is complex: she feels "shame" at the entrance to F. A. O. Schwarz, something like the awe that struck her in the Catholic church and squelched her plan to shock the congregation by tap dancing at the altar, and also some anger at Miss Moore for forcing her into the toy-store experience. That exposure to the luxuries of wealthy children mushrooms as the objects of fascination are increasingly more expensive—the $300 microscope, the $480 paperweight, and then the $1195 sailboat.

Miss Moore's lesson is concerned with economic inequality and the injustice of a democracy that rests on it. That is what Sugar learns and what she obediently voices, to Sylvia's disgust (her ally Sugar has betrayed their common bond of superiority to the ideas of the "old and stupid"). But Miss Moore is herself not entirely satisfied with Sugar's definition, looking "sorrowfully" to Sylvia for a further statement of the lesson. While we cannot know exactly what more she wants to hear, we might presume that it would have something to do with ways to rectify the situation—that she hopes to hear her brightest (and most resistant) pupil suggest solutions leading to actions, some way in which she could demand her share of the pie. But whatever it is that Miss Moore desires, Sylvia in effect withdraws for the moment into Sugar's simplistic and crass definition that "the dough" is what matters, and the two girls go off planning how to spend the four dollars that Sylvia has withheld from Miss Moore's taxi money. Later, Sylvia will begin grappling with what else she has learned this day.

Sylvia is a developing character, as is evidenced by the maturity displayed in the opening paragraph. But by the end of the story, she has not yet undergone that development. Rather, she has had an experience that will certainly lead to important changes in her attitudes and in her thinking. No doubt there will have to be other experiences added to the one on Fifth Avenue, but it seems to be an important starting point.

The theme of this story might be stated thus: one of the lessons to be learned on the road to maturity is that there are lessons to be learned—that an open mind and some humility may show the way out of smugness and complacency. So stated, the theme may thus comprehend both the conflict between mature wisdom and immature self-satisfaction (Miss Moore versus Sylvia) and the growth that may spring from a shocking exposure to the values of other people (Sylvia versus F. A. O. Schwarz).   TRA

Anton Chekhov   Gooseberries (page 202)

In her penetrating and admiring essay "Reality in Chekhov's Stories," Eudora Welty states the central paradox of Ivan Ivanovitch's experience at Alehin's farm: "he moves from the profundities of joy to the heights of despair" (*The Eye of the Story: Selected Essays and Reviews* [New York: Random, 1979] 76). The paradoxical phrasing is necessary in summarizing this story, for both in theme and in structure, Chekhov displays the complex self-contradictions of experience, a subject matter that any writer must approach with caution and with mastery of his art lest the result be merely self-contradictory.

Structurally, "Gooseberries" presents one example in this book of a "frame story," an extended narration by a character who is himself the subject of a narration (the other is Nadine Gordimer's "Once upon a Time," page 220). This "story within a story" technique opens up numerous possibilities as it permits the interplay of the narrator's ideas and attitudes with the materials of the narrated frame. Quickly one notices that Ivan Ivanovitch's story about his brother's ambition and then success as a landowner with a gooseberry patch is paralleled by the setting and situation in which the story is told, Alehin's prosperous but grimy farm that mixes the owner's filth, hard toil, and simple living habits with the luxury of his inherited surroundings—the white bathhouse, the elegance of the second-story rooms, the beauty of his young maidservant. As Welty puts it, "as Ivan talks, the farm, the day, the house with its encrustations of time, the seductive room with its beautiful attendant, its romantic portraits of ladies and generals around the walls, and the rain falling outside, all stand about the story he tells like screens of varying substance of reality and dream" (75). These materials provide a commentary on the values that Ivan Ivanovitch dismisses and on those he embraces.

From the very opening paragraph of the story, Chekhov indicates that we must recognize the possibility of self-contradiction and complexity in reactions to the scene. The day is "heavy . . . grey, dull . . . and one expects rain and it does not come," yet by the end of the paragraph this oppressive setting is interpreted as "mild and dreamy," evoking "love of [this] countryside" and this "great . . . beautiful land." And then within a few lines, the long-awaited and much desired rain begins to fall—and even the dogs perceive it as an ordeal to be avoided. The men take shelter at Alehin's, which from a distance presents them with a beautiful, inviting vista ("there was a gleam of the river, and the view opened onto a broad expanse of water with a windmill and a white bathhouse"). A little closer, and the mood reverses itself yet again: "it was damp, muddy, and desolate; the water looked cold and malignant."

But this is not merely a matter of appearance giving way to reality, of a closer view removing the attraction of the distant prospect—though that theme is part of the experience of the story. As a matter of fact, its opposite is equally present: what seems ugly in prospect may turn out to be beautiful, and what seems delightful may ultimately be a cause for despair. That is the complex paradox of Ivan Ivanovitch's story about his brother Nikolay, a story of a man whose obsession with possession and ownership (what he desires to own is a romanticized, self-gratifying notion of rural life) leads him morally downward as he gets closer and closer to his goal; and by the time he achieves that goal he and his household, servant, dog and all, have been transformed into pigs. The much-prized gooseberries are hard and tart—but not to him, for he has managed to crawl into his dream and refuses to perceive the reality. To Nikolay, this is beauty and perfection; to Ivan, the result is haunting, disgusting, and depressing.

In telling his tale, Ivan seems gradually to discover its "moral" in its contrast to Nikolay's counterpart, what Alehin has and is. Nikolay—vicious, selfish, money-grubbing materialist, finally a deluded, lazy, self-satisfied pig among his pigs; Alehin—generous, vigorous, unconcerned with appearances, unconscious of the bounty of inherited status, surrounded by delights and personally careless about himself. It is to him that Ivan addresses his discovery: "There is no happiness and there ought not to be; but if there is a meaning and an object in life, that meaning and object is not our happiness, but something greater and more rational. Do good!"

Ivan progresses from the joyous exhilaration of his swim (plunging over and over to the bottom as if to discover the ultimate dimensions of his world) to the anguish and despair of his final insight. What he sees is what the reality of the story has reiterated over and over: in happiness there lies pain, in agony the beauty of life may be felt, and in being alive each of us must be prepared to realize the immense complexity of life. Welty's paradox—"the profundities of joy . . . the heights of despair"—captures that theme, for joy may be found at the bottom of the darkest river, despair in the sweet and brilliant luxuriance of a drawing room.

Is Ivan Ivanovitch's outburst to Alehin the "moral" of Chekhov's story? The answer must be "neither yes nor no." It is what one human being has made of his observations and experience, and is therefore a true representation of a human truth. But this particular, realistic man is framed by Chekhov's story, the rain continues to fall, and for all his moralizing Ivan's story is disregarded by both Burkin and Alehin, to whom it (like the grey, dull day that has preceded it) is "dreary," having no direct bearing on *them* as individual human beings. And in an open-ended symbol, Ivan Ivanovitch's pipe reeks.

In addition to Welty's essay, the following provide valuable insights into this masterwork: Ronald Hingley, introduction to Anton Chekhov, *The Russian Master and Other Stories* (New York: Oxford UP, 1984) x-xi; Irina Kirk, *Chekhov* (Boston: Twayne, 1981) 107–10; Donald Rayfield, *Chekhov: The Evolution of His Art* (New York: Harper, 1975) 191–92; Mark Schorer, *The Story: A Critical Anthology* (New York: Prentice, 1950) 61–65; and the following articles collected in *A Chekhov Companion*, ed. Toby W. Clyman (Westport, CT: Greenwood, 1985): Andrew R. Durkin, "Chekhov's Narrative

Technique," 123–32; Ralph Lindheim, "Chekhov's Major Themes," 55–69; Donald Rayfield, "Chekhov and the Literary Tradition," 35–51. An invaluable research guide, for those wishing to go further, is K. A. Lantz, *Anton Chekhov: A Reference Guide to Literature* (Boston: Hall, 1985).   TRA

Eudora Welty   A Worn Path (page 212)

The symbolism of this story is analyzed on pages 275–78. Any discussion of this story should proceed from the author's own essay "Is Phoenix Jackson's Grandson Really Dead?" (*The Eye of the Story* [New York: Vintage, 1979] 158–62). There Welty makes two necessary points: first, the events in a story may have no meaning beyond the literal, or like life they may have multiple meanings (both literal and figurative), but they may not mean *other* than their literal meanings—that is, her story may have symbolic meanings, but these do not violate the reality of the events themselves; and second, the subject of the story, expressed through Phoenix's journey, is "the deep-grained habit of love."

Phoenix's journey is not quite allegorical (there is no one-to-one correspondence of event to antecedent meaning), but it is symbolic in the way Eudora Welty's fiction is symbolic: true-life incidents, perfectly comprehensible simply as the things that people do and have done to them, are revelations of human realities beyond the individual example. For Phoenix Jackson, the journey is repeated when necessary, whenever her grandson's throat requires the soothing medicine; its incidents are, as Welty says,

> passing adventures—some dreams and harassments and a small triumph or two, some jolts to her pride, some flights of fancy to console her, one or two encounters to scare her, a moment that gave her cause to feel ashamed, a moment to dance and preen . . . parts of life's uncertainty.

The story includes name symbolism: "Phoenix," the mythical bird of immortality, repeating in its life cycle the perpetuation of life; "Jackson," the name of two heroes (a general and a president), and the center and capital of the state. These slightly ironic comparisons are reverberative rather than explicitly symbolic, as are the "passing adventures" of Phoenix, the Christmas season, the mission of the journey itself, and the many references to antiquity and age. One would not say that Phoenix Jackson is everyman, that Christian salvation is a topic, that charity is extolled as the greatest of the virtues: these are all implied parts of the texture of the story, but all are supportive to the subject, "the deep-grained habit of love."

It is the word "habit" in the author's definition that sets this story off from allegory and symbol: Welty's point is that Phoenix Jackson is not immortal, not heroic, not even exceptional or special. She even forgets momentarily what the whole arduous trip has been for. She doesn't sentimentalize her invalid grandson, nor perceive anything special about herself besides her age. It is the *habit* of her love that moves her. It is certainly not Phoenix who notices connections and symbols in the various bird images, in the sequence of ordeals and trials she passes, nor in the life-giving sun. Rather, in her simple way, she reveals her unpretentious vision of heaven: in "a pearly cloud of mistletoe" she is offered a slice of marble-cake by a little boy, to whom she modestly says: "That would be acceptable." The understatement of that response captures the emotional tone of the story.

A valuable analysis of the story is Alfred Appel's in *A Season of Dreams: The Fiction of Eudora Welty* (Baton Rouge: LSU Press, 1965) 166–71.

Wadsworth has provided on DVD a dramatization of this story that is chiefly valuable for its visual presentation of characters and landscape; there is very little suggestion of the symbolic richness of "A Worn Path," and readers who have lived with and loved the story for a long time will feel disappointed. But for what it does do, the production can be of some use to beginning readers, and an interview with the writer that follows is of course interesting.   TRA

Nadine Gordimer   Once upon a Time (page 220)

The sample analysis in the Writing section discusses the relationship of the "frame" to the body of this story, and its value as literature is mentioned on page 373.

The story is rife with ironies, the most obvious and appalling being the destruction of the little boy by the wire coils installed for protection. Many lesser ironies anticipate that effect: the alarm systems (whimsically compared to a flock of animals exchanging "bleats and wails") create enough din for burglars to saw through bars and gain access to houses "under cover of the electronic harpies' discourse"; the boy uses the electronic gate receiver as a walkie-talkie to play "cops and robbers"; the installation of burglar bars to keep out intruders makes the family view "the trees and sky through bars," imprisoning them and leaving the burglars at large; the happy story of Sleeping Beauty leads the boy to emulate Prince Charming braving "the terrible thicket of thorns"—only to fall prey to the "DRAGON'S TEETH" of the wire coils.

In addition to these examples of situational irony, the point of view itself is ironic because of its resemblance to a children's story. The tone is created by the "once-upon-a-time" phrasing: "In a house, in a suburb, in a city, there were a man and his wife who loved each other very much and were living happily ever after." The man's mother is a "wise old witch" (the perspective here is no doubt the wife's) who bestows both gifts and advice, including the book of fairy stories that leads to the catastrophe and the warning against any dealings with the blacks in the streets. The simplifying tone reduces the emotional life of this family to two basic, complementary feelings:

fear of the blacks outside their house, and loving protectiveness of the family. All the actions of the story rest on those paired impulses, just as characters in children's stories are simply motivated and easily explained. The plot, therefore, contains no interior conflicts of any kind—no self-examinations or doubts about these paramount motives, no moral questioning, no concern for justice or fairness.

In the brief space of the story, the motive of fear grows in a steady sequence of actions, each new fear leading to a new protective action. That the members of the family acknowledge this process and yet approve of the efforts made to protect them is reflected in the decision to install the wire coils: "It was the ugliest but the most honest in its suggestion of the pure concentration-camp style, no frills, all evident efficacy." Their growing fears have led them step by step and open-eyed into imprisoning iron bars and then the isolation of a "concentration camp." But they are not hysterical about their fear (that is left to the trustworthy housemaid); they are almost cool and smug as they act on it. They are convinced that their way of coping with perceived danger is the correct way.

What they do *not* act upon or consider is the cause or source of the danger. The wife's charitable instinct, to feed the hungry beggars, is overruled by the housemaid and the protective husband, for the husband believes that charity will only "encourage them" and besides, "they are looking for their chance" to break in. The true needs and purposes of this intrusive crowd are covered over by fear of them. Trying to live in safety, the members of the family create for themselves an image of the nation they live in—a nation separated by extreme and cruel measures into islands of safety surrounded by need, want, and oppression. This "children's story" is a parable of the South African experience, and a warning about its consequences. From the white perspective, riots in the black quarters arouse no pity and bring no aid— "buses were being burned, cars stoned, and schoolchildren shot by the police in those quarters out of sight and hearing of the suburb," eliciting from the family only the response of fortifying *their* quarter, guarding *their* child.

The introductory frame defines the true issue and reveals honest fear. The writer who awakens fearing some personal threat from an intruder (in a world where there are murdering housebreakers and vengeful victims of injustice) discovers that *that* fear, while reasonable and justifiable enough, is less disturbing than the fear and pity she feels for the victims of a racist nation. To think of the interment "in the most profound of tombs" of the wage-slave gold miners is far more distressing than the fear of personal danger, for it confesses guilt for the complicity of living in a structure of "brick, cement, wood and glass" literally built on a foundation of cruelty and injustice.

The "children's story" ironically detaches itself from these realities, so that its fears seem wholly selfish and even unjustified. The horror with which it concludes ironically seals the theme of both story and frame: an unjust social system creates an environment of fear that can destroy both the oppressor and the oppressed.   TRA

Chapter Five

Point of View

Willa Cather **Paul's Case** (page 234)

In the first ten paragraphs of the story we see Paul principally as other people see him, especially his teachers. His drawing master voices their common feeling when he says, "There is something wrong about the fellow"—something that none of them understands. At the beginning of paragraph 11 ("As for Paul, he ran down the hill . . .") we are taken into Paul's inner world. The author lets us understand what it is that is "wrong" about Paul, and why he commits suicide. But she does not trace the origins of his trouble (the fact that his mother is dead is almost the only clue) nor give us a psychiatric diagnosis. Instead she lets us share Paul's experience, his apprehension of life.

Throughout the story Paul moves between two worlds—a world of drab reality, as represented by school and his home on Cordelia Street; and a world of glamour, lights, music, color, and luxury, as represented by Carnegie Hall and the stock theater, and later by New York and Europe. The first world oppresses him; the second attracts and draws him: he dreams about it and invents fictions about it. An abnormally sensitive boy—he cannot stand the yellow wallpaper—he is nevertheless not creative, or truly artistic. Symphonies as such mean nothing to him; a barrel-organ will touch him off as readily as an orchestra. He does not desire to be a musician or an actor. All he needs is "the spark," the stimulus, the release, that enables him to revel in daydreams. When he goes to the art gallery, paintings of Paris or Venice provide the "spark," allowing him to dream of luxurious, exotic worlds. Not the artistic merit of the paintings, but their subject matter, excites him. He does not stand and admire them, but sits before them and loses himself.

All of Paul's pleasures invoke an escape from the real world he lives in into a glittering unreal world of ease, style, fashion, and refinements. When one route of escape is cut off, he is forced to find another, more drastic and less rational. When the theater and the symphony hall are denied him, he embezzles money and goes to New York. When New York is threatened, he takes the ultimate escape in suicide.

Pittsburgh, known in Willa Cather's time as the "Smoky City," and New York, the modern Baghdad, have obvious symbolic value in terms of Paul's two worlds.   LP

Eric Roberts stars in a dramatized version of the story in the PBS television series "The American Short Story." The film is generally faithful to the story, so that a discussion of the difference between the points of view displayed in the two different media of drama and fiction can be very useful. TRA

Shirley Jackson   The Lottery (page 251)

The theme of the story may be expressed in some such form as this: essentially decent and kindly people may perform cruel, irrational actions through their unquestioning acceptance of traditions and customs that have lost their original meaning or ground for belief. The symbol of the lottery is obviously an open one and might accommodate a wide range of specific applications (social segregation? class distinction? racial and religious prejudice? hazing? capital punishment? nationalism? war?). The suggestion of specific applications is less important than the comment made on human nature. The main irony of the story lies in the discrepancy between the friendliness and goodwill of the community and the cruelty and meaninglessness of the practice it perpetuates.

Though Jackson has developed none of her characters, she has skillfully indicated a range of attitudes among them. Mr. Summers represents civic duty. He is reasonably progressive, has substituted slips of paper for chips of wood, would like to have a new box. But he doesn't question the ritual itself. He is a man of ignorant goodwill. Old Man Warner is the bigoted reactionary who complains that "People ain't the way they used to be" and is contemptuous of the younger generation. Ironically, he does not recognize his own inner contradictions. "Next," he says of the young folks, "they'll want to go back to living in caves," not realizing that he himself has never emerged from the cave. Mr. and Mrs. Adams are the liberals. They at least question the necessity of the lottery. "Some places have quit lotteries," they point out. But they do nothing to protest against the lottery or to change it. Mrs. Hutchinson is the self-centered individual, and perhaps the one in whom latent cruelty is most apparent. She accepts the lottery without concern until it falls on *her*; then she protests that it is unfair, and would eagerly shift her fate to someone else, even her own daughter. Mr. Summers becomes *her* scapegoat. The majority of the villagers simply accept the lottery without question.

Students who misread the story are likely to do so by overemphasizing the role of Mrs. Hutchinson or by seeing the story merely as a satire on the acceptance of tradition. The protagonist of the story is the whole community, not Mrs. Hutchinson. Mrs. Hutchinson, if she emerges as the central figure at the end of the story, is nevertheless significant only insofar as she is

representative of the community. The chief antagonist of the story is probably the villagers' own blind acceptance of tradition, but the horror of the
story arises from the fact that there is so little conflict. The antagonist wins
without a struggle. Nevertheless, the story is not an attack against the acceptance of tradition as such. Many traditions (for example, the exchange of
gifts at Christmastime as a symbol of love and concern) are beneficent and
enrich our lives. The thrust of the story is against the unquestioning acceptance of cruel, irrational traditions.

As a final comment, I quote one of my students: "Had the author left the
scapegoat custom in its primitive setting, the reader very likely would have
dismissed the story with a few complacent reflections on man's glorious conquest of ignorance and superstition. On the other hand, if the story had dealt
with an actual modern example of cruel traditional social custom, the tendency would have been to narrow the message of the story instead of suggesting by symbolism its many modern parallels."

In *Come Along with Me* (New York: Viking, 1968), Jackson has an amusing account of the to-do that followed the initial publication of this story in
The New Yorker. It is instructive in its revelation of the many ways in which
a writer's intentions may be misunderstood.

There are brief references to this story on pages 164 and 232.   LP

Katherine Anne Porter   The Jilting of Granny Weatherall
(page 260)

The life of an indomitable matriarch comes to an end in a confused ac-
counting of her fourscore years and an ambiguous prediction of her soul's destiny. Like Emily Dickinson's speaker in "Because I could not stop for Death,"
Granny Weatherall's busy life ends with an imagined journey "outward" with
no clearly defined destination.

The last day of Ellen Weatherall's life registers jaggedly and incoherently
on her consciousness, and the narration represents that psychological fact by
a skipping chronology, mistaken identities, and a selective memory that expresses in fragments the major events of her long life. This example of a
stream-of-consciousness narrative presents a sequence of thoughts at a critical moment in the character's life—in Granny's case, her dying day. (This
technique gives the impression of an "unedited" narration, switching topics,
losing and regaining threads of stories, and thus realistically implying the inconsistencies of the way we think and remember; but of course such a narration is highly structured and selected by the author, who is ordering her materials in order to create the sense of a mind in action.) That Ellen's
consciousness is represented by disorderly perceptions and recollections is
ironic, since she has for sixty years been devoted to neatness, cleanliness, and
order. She managed to "weather all" the adversities of a long life by keeping
it strictly under control.

Granny Weatherall's life has included three events of major consequence, spaced out at twenty-year intervals. When she was twenty, she was left waiting with the priest for a prospective husband who never turned up; at forty, she bore her last child (Hapsy), suffering greatly from thrombosis in her legs ("milk-leg") and then pneumonia; and at sixty, she made a circuit of her living children to bid them goodbye and ready herself for death, "made her will and came down with a long fever" (paragraph 18)—and then recovered to live twenty more years without any fear or sense of dying. The significance of these events to Ellen is that each of them led to redefinitions of her life and her faith. What the stream-of-consciousness technique permits is emphasis on events in the order of their relative importance to the character, to the exclusion of potentially more significant incidents. In this woman's case, for example, one might have expected some greater importance to be attached to her first childbirth, to the untimely death of her husband, or to the death of her favorite child, Hapsy. By her remembering the events that she does instead, those three remembered events are made to be the shaping incidents of her life.

The first, the jilt by her fiancé George, is the most important both in literal and symbolic senses. That was the day when "a whirl of dark smoke rose and covered" the orderliness of her life; "that was hell," and she knows that "remembering him" and "losing her soul in the deep pit of hell" were the same thing (paragraph 29). So she has willed herself, for sixty years, to forget him and to trust in her salvation through the intercession of "a few favorite saints who cleared a straight road to God for her" (paragraph 49). The emotional and spiritual shock of that event (notice that the story is titled after that event, not after its central event, the *dying* of Granny Weatherall) has led her to shape her life into the varieties of order and meaning available to a strong-willed woman—working by the sweat of her brow, raising a large family after their father's death, ministering to her livestock and her neighbors, caring for the sick and offering her services to the church. It is an exemplary life, but of course it lacks what it lost at the jilting: a beloved husband, a mate to do those things assigned by her religion to the male, an emotionally full life not only as mother and homemaker but as woman. That jilting was the event that turned her to self-sufficiency and to a smugness about her faith and her destiny that even now, at the time of death, display themselves in querulousness and a wish to be left alone to get ready for "tomorrow" in her own way.

The death of her last-born child, who had herself borne a son, is perhaps the oddest omission from Granny's recollection of climaxes. It is obvious that Hapsy is the child who matters most to her, the only one Granny calls for at the last, the one she mistakes the nurse for, "the one she had truly wanted" (paragraph 43). Her one vivid memory of Hapsy may account for this omission: she recalls "Hapsy standing with a baby on her arm. [Granny] seemed to herself to be Hapsy also, and the baby on Hapsy's arm was Hapsy and himself and herself, all at once . . ." (paragraph 41). This merging of identities of herself with both a child and his mother symbolically implies her faith in those "favorite" persons of her Catholic faith—in this case, clearly, her daughter and grandson are to her the Madonna and Christ. Hapsy is not dead, then, in Ellen's spiritual life. (What has become of Hapsy's son? The terms of the story and of religion suggest that he, too, is physically dead but divinely immortal.)

At the climax of the story—Granny's death—these symbols are finally focused and the title brought into a new light. What if Hapsy is not to be found, she wonders. That would define death as a bottomless sinking, "down and down . . . into endless darkness," so she pleads for God to give her a sign. With cosmic irony (and grim wit), she realizes: "For the second time there was no sign. Again no bridegroom and the priest in the house" (paragraph 61). Her hope for an earthly paradise ended with the jilting at the altar; are her hopes for heaven equally frustrated? Her consciousness, of course, cannot answer that question.

Much has been written about this story. Among the valuable discussions to which the present remarks are indebted are Joann P. Cobb,"Two Modern Losers" (repr. Harold Bloom, ed., *Katherine Anne Porter* [New York: Chelsea, 1986] 97–106); John Edward Hardy, *Katherine Anne Porter* (New York: Ungar, 1973) 89–96; Darlene Harbour Unrue, *Truth and Vision in Katherine Anne Porter's Fiction* (Athens, GA: U of Georgia P, 1985) 98–101 and passim; and Eudora Welty, "Katherine Anne Porter: The Eye of the Story," *The Eye of the Story; Selected Essays and Reviews* (New York: Vintage, 1979) 307–40.

Geraldine Fitzgerald is featured in "The American Short Story" adaptation of this story for PBS.   TRA

Ernest Hemingway   Hills Like White Elephants (page 268)

The whole story takes place during a forty-minute wait between trains. The couple's history is indicated by the labels on their bags and by a line or two of dialogue. What lies ahead of them is implied by the entire force and direction of the story. Within this forty-minute interval a decision is confirmed that will affect the whole quality of their future lives. The circumstances in which the decision is settled have symbolic force. The couple lose the chance to change directions. The man's refusal to accept the burden of parenthood, his wish to make the woman undergo an abortion so that they can be "just like [they] were before," represents a nonacceptance of change, a denial of growth and life, a movement toward sterility and emptiness, and this is what the future lives of the couple will hold. The child begun in the woman's womb is a "white elephant" for a man eternally unwilling to accept responsibility.

With this story and others like it Ernest Hemingway revolutionized the style of modern prose fiction. The third study question is thus perhaps the most important for thorough class discussion. The main force of the story lies in the tone and the changes of tone in the dialogue of the two characters, all indicated by the words they use. The story is much like a small play with the stage directions incorporated in the dialogue itself. Oral reading of portions of the story by members of the class may help to emphasize this point. Three pairs of students might be asked to read the same passage, followed by class discussion of their readings. Hemingway's contribution to prose style is well discussed, with particular reference to this story, by H. E. Bates in *The Modern Short Story* (Boston: Writer, 1941) 167–73.   LP

Chapter Six

Symbol, Allegory, and Fantasy

D. H. *Lawrence*   The Rocking-Horse Winner (page 285)

The opening sentence of the story tells us that the mother "had no luck." The boy's last words are "I am lucky." The first use of the word exemplifies verbal irony; the final use, dramatic irony. Both uses are literally true in the restricted sense that the mother gives for the word: "It's what causes you to have money." The boy's mistake about "filthy lucker" is at the thematic heart of the story, for the confusion of luck with lucre causes all the unhappiness of the story. (Such confusion is not rare, but almost universal, as demonstrable from the history of our language. Though the similarity of "luck" and "lucre" is accidental, the near synonyms "fortune" and "a fortune" link the two meanings in one word.)

It is an irony of situation that the woman who considers herself unlucky has been immensely lucky in a truer sense of the word. She is beautiful, she started with every advantage, she married for love, she has bonny children, and she has artistic talent. But all these gifts are negated by her inability to love, and by her need to live "in style," to "keep up" a social position, and to satisfy expensive tastes. Nevertheless, this mother is characterized differently from the greedy stepmothers of the fairy tales. She is not cruel. She is gentle and anxious for her children. Her heart is "curiously heavy" when she sees her son becoming tense and overwrought. At a big party in town, she feels such "rushes of anxiety" about him that she cannot suppress the impulse to leave the dance and to telephone home. But gentleness and anxiety are not love. Love puts love first always, and is willing to sacrifice for what it loves. Paul's mother subordinates love to social position and expensive tastes, which means that she doesn't love at all, for where is the willingness to sacrifice?

Paul feels the lack of the love he should be getting from his mother: he unconsciously realizes that the demands of the house for more money are connected with that lack, and he blindly tries to cure the condition by supplying the money. But the whispers of the house are only a symptom, not the cause, and Paul's remedy only makes things worse. Materialistic craving can never be satisfied. Paul's compulsive efforts to satisfy his mother's craving finally kill him. Riding the rocking horse is an effective symbol for material-istic pursuits, for it is a furious activity that gets one nowhere.   LP

A film of this story was made in 1950 (91 minutes, British).   TRA

Nathaniel Hawthorne   Young Goodman Brown (page 299)

To the question "Had Goodman Brown fallen asleep in the forest, and only dreamed a wild dream of a witch-meeting?" critics have proposed four basic answers: (1) yes, the whole experience was a nightmare induced in him by his own and/or his society's preoccupation with evil and sin; (2) no, he was indeed guilty of keeping an appointment with the devil, who showed him the evil in himself, in his wife, and in apparently just and godly citizens and churchmen, including his own forebears; (3) no, he had seen and heard the evidences of evil reported in the story, but they were delusions produced by the devil; (4) no, he had not slept but had experienced hysterical halluci-nations, the product of his own obsessive concern with sin and marital fidelity.

The necessity for answering the narrator's question rests on more than the fact that he asks it and then offers no answer but "Be it so, if you will." The nature of the question itself is implied throughout the story, for it asks "Is there a natural (as opposed to supernatural) explanation for what Brown underwent?" For Hawthorne not to resolve this issue is characteristic of a writer who often creates ambiguities out of such natural/supernatural con-flicts (readers of *The Scarlet Letter* will recall the question of the flaming "A" in the night sky during Dimmesdale's crisis, and the unresolved question of whether Dimmesdale does in fact have a scarlet letter on his own naked breast).

The ambiguity in "Young Goodman Brown" is created at many points in the story. Technically, it is almost entirely told from the limited third-person point of view—Brown's perception—and to the extent that it is so limited, it is impossible for a reader to discriminate between fact and Brown's imagination. But there are frequent moments in the course of the forest narration that expand the point of view to include an authorial voice even before the narrator poses his dream question. Such, for example, are the words and phrases *as it were, as if, perhaps, some affirm that, must have been an ocular deception,* and *doubted whether he had heard aught but the mur-mur of the old forest, whispering without a wind.* In addition, Hawthorne re-ports Brown's perceptions with *seem, appear, beheld,* and *fancied,* and the persons he sees are called *figure, form,* and *shape.* The cumulative effect of such language is to cast doubt on the literal reality of Brown's experience, to suggest that it might indeed have a natural explanation depending on the distortions of his imagination. The reader is not forced to believe liter-ally in witchcraft and the devil, but may if he is so inclined accept any of the four major explanations.

The ending of the story is not indeterminate—the whole of Brown's future is presented—but the theme is indeterminate, for Hawthorne's ambiguous narrative creates an issue even larger than the question of Brown's personal experience; that is, is the diabolical figure right when he pronounces that evil is the nature of mankind? Has Brown's forest journey, whatever its reality, revealed to him a truth? Typically, Hawthorne refuses to answer explicitly, but he does show the effect of Brown's belief—a life darkened with suspicion, mistrust and gloom, a mind poisoned by doubt (yet as some critics point out, his misanthropy is sporadic, the result of doubt rather than conviction: though he "often" shrank from his wife, he was the progenitor of "a goodly procession" of children and grandchildren).

The structure of the tale has been much praised. It has an archetypal familiarity: the young man undertaking a journey into the unknown, possessed by a desire for knowledge but aware that the knowledge is forbidden, who draws back time and again, yet moves forward until the climactic revelation that thenceforward changes his life (parallels to Adam, and to his relations with Eve, have been drawn). That Brown's "evil purpose" has to do with forbidden knowledge rather than with power seems clear from the promises of the devil at the interrupted baptismal ceremony: if they join in the communion, Brown and Faith will "be partakers of the mystery of sin, more conscious of the secret guilt of others, both in deed and thought, than they could be now of their own." Brown goes into the forest to meet the devil, but he claims that his "covenant" with him is fulfilled simply by meeting him; his intention has been to keep the appointment and thus confirm the devil's existence, but to return the next day still a good Christian, clinging to Faith and following her to heaven. The evidence presented to him to prevent his turning back systematically reveals that there is no such thing as a good Christian. But at the climax, apparently to protect his Faith from such knowledge, he exhorts her to rely on God and resist the devil, and this exhortation forestalls his own baptism into evil knowledge. He is left with doubt, the suspicion of the truth of the devil's pronouncement, based on the evidence he has seen and heard.

Until the climax, Goodman Brown repeatedly plans to leave the forest, and is repeatedly dissuaded by deepening visions of evil—the information that his father and grandfather were in league with the devil in their unjust and inhumane behavior; the appearance of "his moral and spiritual adviser" Goody Cloyse chatting amiably with the devil; the audible but invisible minister and Deacon Gookin on their way to the meeting; and finally the voices in the dark cloud, including Faith's, and the apparently material evidence of one of her pink ribbons. The result of this last is his frenzied rush toward the meeting-place, with the declaration "My Faith is gone! . . . There is no good on earth, and sin is but a name. Come, devil! for to thee is this world given." The satanic parody of a communion service is dispelled when he recognizes in "the slender form of a veiled female" his wife Faith and protectively stops her from joining.

The ambiguities of perception and theme focus the story not on theo-logical truth but on the psychological consequences of belief and doubt. One of Hawthorne's recurring themes is that dwelling on moral absolutes—good or evil, virtue or sinfulness—is destructive and dehumanizing, as demon-strated by the long life of gloom that resulted from Brown's forest journey in quest of a moral absolute. Taking a clue from the technical fact of a manipu-lated point of view, we may leave the ambiguities where Hawthorne so care-fully placed them, and recognize that ambiguity itself is part of the theme. We cannot know whether Brown had suffered a hallucination, or what might have induced it; there is evidence to support the devil's claim that mankind is devoted to evil, if we accept Brown's certainty that all apparent goodness is mere hypocrisy; but there is also evidence to suppose that he is wrong, if we judge the actions of the townspeople after his return. Judging by other works of Hawthorne, men are not inherently evil but are capable of evil ac-tions, chiefly actions that spring from excessive pride and intellectuality, and that victimize or exploit other people. An evil act may be done by an other-wise good person, and good consequences may be the result of willfully evil actions. For Hawthorne, all men are potentially evil—and potentially good. Moral ambiguity is a pervasive fact of life.

This is Hawthorne's most widely analyzed short story, chiefly because of its ambiguities; certainly no single analysis will satisfy all readers. The fore-going should be regarded as *an* analysis, to be supplemented by the following: Thomas E. Connolly, ed., *Nathaniel Hawthorne: Young Goodman Brown* (Columbus, OH: Merrill, 1968), which anthologizes twelve critiques; Robert W. Cochran, "Hawthorne's Choice: The Veil or the Jaundiced Eye," *College English* 23 (1962): 342–46. Consult also the extensive bibliography of articles about the story listed in *Twentieth-Century Short Story Explication, New Series* (1993).   TRA

Joyce Carol Oates   Where Are You Going, Where Have You Been? (page 311)

In this story, love assumes a forbidding guise, representing not a poten-tial communion between two people but an allegorical confrontation be-tween an innocent female and a demonic, sexually threatening male. Based on the case of an Arizona serial killer who preyed upon teenage girls and was dubbed "The Pied Piper of Tucson" in a *Life* magazine article, "Where Are You Going" is the most anthologized and most discussed of all Oates's stories. Interpreted variously as an inverted fairy tale, a tale of initiation, and an "ex-istential allegory," the story has generally been recognized as uniting Oates's greatest strengths as a short story writer. Although set in the "real world," a carefully rendered social and psychological context, the story also has a mythic, fairy tale dimension that gives the main character, fifteen-year-old Connie, the status of an allegorical figure. The story unites the psychological realism and gothic horror that are Oates's most characteristic and effective fictional modes. As these are combined here, the effect is chilling and unforgettable.

In many ways Connie is a typical middle-class American teenage girl; blond and pretty, she maintains a knowing, wisecracking exterior that conceals her insecurity and dreamy romanticism. Oates effectively portrays a teenager who haunts the shopping malls and hamburger joints with other girls just like her, who fights with her mother and feels contempt for her "plain and steady" older sister, and who spends her time "thinking, dreaming about the boys she met." The narrator stresses the atmosphere of humid summer nights and the "urgent insistent pounding" of rock music as one with Connie's developing sexuality. Despite her vanity and immaturity Connie is likable and sympathetic because she suffers the typical romantic delusions of extreme youth; even her sarcasm and small cruelties to her less popular peers are symptoms of innocence for girls like Connie and her friends, who enter a "bright-lit, fly-infested restaurant" with "faces pleased and expectant as if they were entering a sacred building that loomed up out of the night to give them what haven and blessing they yearned for." While the reader expects that Connie will suffer a disillusionment—at first, this seems to be a realistic and fairly ordinary "initiation" story—the narrative takes a sharp, unexpected turn when Connie is suddenly left alone, separated from her giggling friends and her stern but protective family. The story carefully sets the stage for an allegorical dream experience that universalizes the sexual and psychological fate of a girl like Connie and focuses on her terrifying rite of passage.

Soon after her family leaves for a Sunday barbecue and Connie begins sunbathing in the back yard, "dreaming and dazed with the warmth about her as if this were a kind of love, the caresses of love," the story moves from realism into an allegorical dream-vision. Recalling a recent sexual experience as "sweet, gentle, the way it was in movies and promised in songs," Connie opens her eyes and "hardly knew where she was." Shaking her head "as if to get awake," she feels troubled by the sudden unreality of her surroundings, unaware—though the reader is aware—that she has entered a new and fearsome world, one in which love is neither sweet nor gentle. In this world Connie's youthful romanticism will meet an abrupt and cruel end.

When the ironically named Arnold Friend first arrives at Connie's house, driving his sleazy gold jalopy and accompanied by a strange, ominously silent male sidekick, Connie deflects him with her usual pert sarcasms and practiced indifference. Throughout the long scene that follows, Connie's terror slowly builds. The fast-talking Arnold Friend insinuates himself into her thinking, attempting to persuade her that he's her "lover," his smooth-talking seductiveness finally giving way to threats of violence against Connie's family if she doesn't surrender to his desires. The story places Connie inside the kitchen and Arnold Friend outside with only a locked screen door between them. While Friend could enter by force at any time, the narrative emphasizes the seduction, the sinister sing-song of Friend's voice: a demonic outsider, he has arrived to wrest Connie from the protective confines of her family, her home, and her own innocence. The story makes clear that Friend represents Connie's initiation not into sex itself—she is already sexually experienced—but into sexual bondage; "I promise it won't last long," he tells her, "and you will like me the way you get to like people you're close to. You will. It's all over for you here." As feminist allegory, then, the story describes the beginning of a young and sexually attractive girl's enslavement within a conventional, male-dominated sexual relationship.

As Connie attempts to escape, her sexual hysteria has reached its peak, and she understands that "she was locked inside it the way she was locked inside this house." But, as Friend tells her, the house is "nothing but a cardboard box that I can knock down any time." Finally Connie's terror has sent her into a state of numbed acquiescence, so that her capitulation to Friend moves the story to its final state of terrified unreality. Now Connie's heart is "nothing that was hers . . . but just a pounding, living thing inside this body that wasn't really hers either." Defeated, depersonalized, Connie approaches a fate she "did not recognize except to know that she was going to it."

While in realistic terms, especially considering the story's source, Connie may be approaching her actual death, in allegorical terms she is dying spiritually, surrendering her autonomous selfhood to male desire and domination. Her characterization as a typical girl reaching sexual maturity suggests that her fate represents that suffered by most young women—unwillingly and in secret terror—even in America in the 1960s. As a feminist allegory, then, this is a cautionary tale, suggesting that young women are "going" exactly where their mothers and grandmothers have already "been": into sexual bondage at the hands of a male "Friend."

A 1986 film of this story, entitled "Smooth Talk" and available on VHS, was directed by Joyce Chopra and stars Laura Dern as Connie and Treat Williams as Arnold Friend. The director chose to radically alter the ending, the viewing of which in concert with reading the text can provoke fruitful discussions of the story's theme, the film's anticipated audience, and other issues. GJ

Gabriel García Márquez   A Very Old Man with Enormous Wings (page 327)

This story provides a brief introduction to García Márquez's world of "magical realism." It fuses the details of coastal village life with such fantastic elements as a winged old man and a woman changed into a spider for disobeying her parents.

Like the author's novel One Hundred Years of Solitude, the story is notable for its objective, dispassionate narrative voice, which relates mundane details of daily life and the most bizarre, fantastic events in the same tone. In effect, reality and fantasy are blended seamlessly together. If the first sentence, for instance, is wholly realistic in describing a rainstorm, the killing of crabs, and a sick infant, the second sentence lurches abruptly into a new perspective: "The world had been sad since Tuesday." This combination of fable-like allegory (an entire world, as opposed to an individual person, being "sad") and unapologetic specificity ("since Tuesday") conveys the nature of García Márquez's fictive arena, where the distinctions that most readers, especially student readers, take for granted—between reason and emotion, logic and irrationality, waking and dreams, the tangible and the impossible—are not acknowledged and are even denied.

Like Shirley Jackson's "The Lottery," García Márquez's story deals in part with the psychological contours of an entire community, showing how primitivism and spirituality coexist within human beings. Father Gonzaga's endless exchange of letters with papal officials satirizes the slowness and inefficacy of institutions, and the human need to categorize and label what cannot be explained. One of the key phrases early in the story describes the way Pelayo and his wife, after finding the old man with wings, "very soon overcame their surprise and . . . found him familiar." The phrase also sums up a reader's adjustment to the story: we suspend our disbelief and accept the narrative terms of a fantasy, so that we are no longer so surprised when the spider-woman (the size of a ram) appears, or when a leper's sores sprout sunflowers.

While some students, especially the most logically minded ones, will be intent on finding specific meanings for each fantastic image or turn of events, what should be stressed is not any putative flow of logic in the story or its "plot," but rather its strong flow of imagination and the absolute, deadpan conviction with which the narrator spins the tale. As Raymond L. William cautions, "The text offers no rational explanation for the enigmatic man. . . . [O]ne must take extreme care in attributing rational laws of cause and effect on innately irrational things. The story also affirms García Márquez's right of invention." See William's full discussion in *Gabriel García Márquez* (Boston: Twayne, 1984) 93–97. For a discussion placing the story within a cultural context, see Vera M. Kutzinski, "The Logic of Wings: Gabriel García Márquez and Afro-American Literature" in Robin Fiddian, ed., *García Márquez* (London and New York: Longman, 1995) 214–28.

In its larger contours, "A Very Old Man with Enormous Wings" dramatizes the human tendency to turn any spiritual reality to profit or, as it were, to convert gold into straw. Accustomed to miracles, Pelaya and Elisenda come to ignore the old man after their greed and materialism have led them astray. Elisenda's final vision of him struggling for flight (in a most ungainly, non-angelic way) and ultimately turning to "an imaginary dot on the horizon of the sea" is nonetheless quite moving. If Elisenda requires a spate of onion-cutting to inspire tears, the attentive reader may not. Once again, the supernatural and the mundane (an angel, aloft, and a spiritually coarsened woman preparing dinner) unite in a memorable tableau.   GJ

Chapter Seven

Humor and Irony

Frank O'Connor   The Drunkard (page 339)

Frank O'Connor's enchanting and hilarious story is one in which human insight accompanies and gives rise to the humor from beginning to end. In its account of Father's reactions to Mr. Dooley's death—of his motivations for attending the funeral; of his spiritual pride over teetotalism and its consequences; of the progress of his drunkenness; of Mother's attempt to use the son as a brake; of Father's bribing the son with lemonade and telling him to go play in the road; of the son's motivations in drinking the beer; of the progress of the son's drunkenness; of Father's reactions to his missing drink, and to the boy's sickness; of Father's embarrassment and shame on the way home; of the final ironic reversal in which Mother calls the son an "angel" for having got drunk—the story is continuously funny and continuously true. Even such a small detail as the narrator's remark about "the lonesomeness of the kitchen without a clock" presents an insight of poignant and absolute authenticity.

O'Connor's shrewd observation of human nature is nowhere better manifested than in his depiction of the ambivalent and mixed motivations of human beings. The shallow writer oversimplifies human motivation. The good writer realizes its full complexity. In his desire to attend his friend's funeral, for instance, Mr. Delaney is prompted partly by the Christian motivation of "Do as you would be done by" ("We'd be glad," he says, "if it was our own turn"). But he is also acutely aware of what other people may think ("'Twould be expected. . . . I wouldn't give it to say to them"). In addition, he *enjoys* funerals for their show ("Five carriages and sixteen covered cars!" he exclaims afterwards. "There's one alderman, two councillors and 'tis unknown how many priests. I didn't see a funeral like this from the road since Willie Mack, the publican, died"). Finally, of course, he looks forward to the celebration in the pub afterwards—a regular holiday outing. Undoubtedly the first two reasons are partly rationalizations for the latter two, but there is no reason not to regard them as genuine at the same time, for Mr. Delaney is a man of decent human impulses and of normal awareness of social opinion.

Students with a moralistic turn of mind (and there are surprisingly many of them) misread this story as a story of the Drunkard Reformed. The father is so acutely ashamed when his little boy gets drunk and he recognizes his own behavior in his son's, they claim, that he discovers the folly of his drinking and his guilt in causing his family to suffer. Thereafter he never takes another drink. Such a reading is unfortunate, for it turns the story into a tract. O'Connor is not writing about the Evils of Drink; the neatest twist in the story, in fact, lies in the son's being congratulated for getting drunk. O'Connor's story is about numerous human vanities and foibles; it is not directed against the existence of pubs. The misinterpretation may be countered with at least five lines of argument: (1) The father already knows the folly of drunkenness, and during his periods of abstinence he laughs at the folly of men who waste their money on liquor. (2) He does not consider himself to blame for his son's drunkenness; rather, he indignantly strives to absolve himself: "I gave him no drink. . . . He took it while my back was turned." (3) The chief emotion he feels over his son's drunkenness is social embarrassment, not moral shame. What acutely distresses him is being made a spectacle for the neighbors. (4) His regret is not over having gone to the pub but over having been denied his fun there: "Not one drop of drink crossed my lips the whole day. How could it when he drank it all? I'm the one to be pitied, with my day ruined on me, and I after being made a show for the whole road." This is not the language of contrition. (5) Finally, there is the narrator's response to Father's "Never again, never again, not if I lived to be a thousand!" "To this day," says the narrator, "I don't know whether he was forswearing me or the drink." If Father had successfully forsworn either one, the narrator would have known about it.   LP

Woody Allen   The Kugelmass Episode (page 348)

As fantasy this story falls in the category of realistic persons placed in an impossible situation. Kugelmass is an ordinary man who has an extraordinary experience. His personality is familiar Woody Allen territory: an unremarkable, even humdrum man whose life seems to be going nowhere, and who is beset with the cliches of modern urban life—two failed marriages, one ending in divorce and the other unbearable but unescapable, an analyst who offers little help, financial pressures, an unrewarding profession, and signs of the physical deterioration of middle age. What he longs for is an escape into romance and adventure—as would so many people in such situations.

In some unexplained way the Great Persky, a stage magician, has learned of Kugelmass's plight, and perhaps of his therapist's judgement that what Kugelmass wants is a magician, not an analyst. However he has come to know this, Persky makes the initial contact and introduces Kugelmass to the magic box that transports a person into a work of literature.

The romantic affair with Emma Bovary begins in a deeply satisfying way to both of them. He is an exciting exotic with wonderful (twentieth-century) clothes who tells her about life in New York, movies, shopping, luxurious hotels, and so forth. She is as ravishing as Flaubert made her, and Kugelmass is bowled over. Their relationship is thus gratifying to them both, beginning with the pastoral delights of walking in the French countryside, moving on to sex and what passes for love—but then they fulfill their mutual desire for Emma to come to New York, and the relationship gradually begins to pall. By the end of her visit, they are not even saying goodbye as Persky finally manages to make his cabinet work. Everything has soured, probably a reflection of the kinds of relationships Kugelmass has had with his first and second wives as the magic wears off and ordinariness sets in.

Kugelmass's first reaction is to swear off forever such literary time-travel, but in a short time he wants just one more fling. This time instead of romance he opts for erotica, perhaps because a simple sexual adventure will cause less emotional drain. But the cabinet fails one last time, and in a slapstick conclusion Persky drops dead, the cabinet burns, the whole building is consumed by fire, and poor Kugelmass is transported forever into a Spanish grammar book. The ending with all its improbable coincidences focuses the story as fantastic.   TRA

Albert Camus   The Guest (page 358)

"The Guest" reflects its author's existentialist philosophy that man's life is difficult and without ultimate meaning but that nevertheless a man defines himself during life by the quality of his moral decisions and his courage in acting on them.

The protagonist, Daru, a French Algerian who teaches Arab children in the middle of a bleak Algerian plateau where he was born and which he loves, is given the unwelcome "duty" of transmitting an Arab prisoner to police headquarters at a village some four hours' distant. It is not his job, but police shorthandedness in the face of an incipient Arab revolt has thrust it upon him. A sensitive, humane, and compassionate man, Daru treats his hostage as a human being rather than as a member of a subject race, as guest rather than as prisoner. Though he is a French civil servant, he is revolted by the notion of handing the Arab over to French authorities for trial.

The story centers on Daru's dilemma. Should he do what Balducci would consider his duty, obey orders and deliver the prisoner? Or should he follow his own human impulse and give the Arab his freedom? On the one hand, Daru is responsible for the prisoner. He has been given an order; he has signed a receipt. In addition, he is a Frenchman; he will fight against the Arabs if war is declared; for him, as for Balducci, the French are "us" and the Arabs are "them." Moreover, the Arab is a murderer; and Daru, a peaceable man, cannot repress his wrath against all men who wantonly kill, motivated by hate, spite, or blood lust. But on the other hand, the Arab is a human being, and it offends Daru's "honor" to treat him, however guilty, with anything less than human dignity. Such treatment demands that the Arab be judged by his own people, not by alien French masters.

The necessity of moral choice can be an almost intolerable burden, and Daru several times wishes he were free of it. He is filled with joy when, awakening from his nap, he thinks that "the Arab might have fled and that he [will] be alone with no decision to make." When the Arab gets up to urinate during the night, Daru at first thinks, "He is running away. . . . Good riddance!" In the morning he simultaneously curses "his own people who had sent him this Arab and the Arab who had dared to kill and not managed to get away." But the decision must be made.

Daru solves his dilemma by taking the Arab on a two-hour journey across the plateau to where two ways divide, by giving him money and food to last for two days, by pointing out the way to a prison, a two-hour walk, and the way to freedom, a day's journey to the pasturelands where the nomads will take him in and shelter him according to their law. When Daru looks back, later, he sees "with heavy heart" the Arab walking slowly on the road to prison. Still later, back in the classroom, he finds clumsily chalked up on the blackboard the words, "You handed over our brother. You will pay for this."

Camus's story is about the difficulty, the agony, the complexity, the necessity, the worth, and the thanklessness of moral choice. It tells us that moral choice may be difficult and complex, with no clear distinction between good and evil, and with both rational and irrational, selfish and unselfish claims justifying each course of conduct. It tells us that moral choice is a burden that man would willingly avoid if he could, but also that it is part of the human condition that man cannot evade and remain man. It shows us that man defines himself by moral choice, for Daru makes the choice that the reader wants him to make, and establishes his moral worth thereby. But the story also shows that moral decision has no ultimate meaning, for the universe does not reward it. Not only does the Arab fail to take the freedom offered him but, ironically, the Arab's tribesmen misinterpret Daru's action and threaten revenge.

In large terms, Daru is representative of moral man, and his desert is representative of the world. He is essentially alone in this world, which is "cruel to live in," and life has no overarching or transcendental meaning. "This is the way it was; bare rock covered three quarters of the region. Towns sprang up, flourished, then disappeared; men came by, loved one another or fought bitterly, then died. No one in this desert, neither he nor his guest, mattered." In Camus's world man lives alone, makes his moral decision alone, suffers alone, and dies alone. At the end of the story, in consequence of the very action by which Daru has affirmed his selfhood, he has cut himself off from those he had tried to aid. "In this vast landscape he had loved so much, he was alone." His aloneness is both literal and symbolic.

Four misconceptions of the story should be avoided:

1. The main conflict of the story is not between individual conscience and society or the state, between Daru and Balducci. Daru's own conscience

and loyalties are divided. What is required of Daru is not simply the courage to resist the pressures of society and do what is right; it is the courage to make a moral decision between alternatives, neither of which is entirely right.

2. The story does not concern the impossibility of isolating oneself from society and from human responsibility, as does, for instance, Conrad's *Victory*. Daru has fled neither responsibility nor mankind. He is an employee of the French government engaged in the responsible task of education. In times of drought he distributes wheat. If war comes, he will be a soldier. He has chosen this isolated region to live in because he loves it, not because he hates mankind.

3. Daru does not evade making a decision. True, by pointing out the two ways to the Arab he does shift some of the weight of decision from himself to the Arab—but only some. For Daru is not paralyzed by inaction. He does not simply wait in indecision till the authorities or the Arabs crash in on him. By putting the Arab two hours on his way and giving him money and food to last two days, Daru takes positive action. The decision to let the Arab make his own decision is itself a decision. In allowing the Arab to make his own choice, he has given the Arab the ultimate freedom—the only freedom, Camus might say, that men have.

4. The Arab does not choose the road to prison because of Daru's kindness. From the beginning the Arab is pictured as passive, uncomprehending, a little stupid. He at no point makes any motion toward attempting to escape. Some prior attempt to escape, or an act of rebellion, would be necessary to establish a change of attitude on the Arab's part after Daru's decision. Instead, his passivity is stressed throughout. He is anxious about his fate but also resigned to it. He is warmed by Daru's humanity, but his response is to want Daru to accompany him and Balducci to police headquarters. His final attempt to communicate with Daru—"Listen"—is best interpreted as a repetition of this earlier request. He doesn't want to be left alone in a hostile world. He wants the man to come with him who has treated him as a human being.

[An expanded version of this manual entry was published in *Studies in Short Fiction* 1 (1963): 52–58. A reply by John K. Simon was published in the same journal, 1 (1964): 289–91.]   LP

Chapter Eight

Evaluating Fiction

Exercise (page 375)

"A Municipal Report" and "A Jury of Her Peers" both present a situation in which a wife is oppressed by her husband. In each story the husband's tyranny eventuates in his being murdered. Each story directs the reader's sympathy toward rather than against the murderer. In each story the external sign of this is that the character from whose viewpoint the story is told conceals a crucial piece of incriminating evidence. These are the principal similarities between the two stories. The differences will be apparent from what follows.   LP

O. Henry   A Municipal Report (page 375)

"A Municipal Report" is one of the most celebrated stories of one of America's most celebrated writers. It has been reprinted in dozens of anthologies. It is nevertheless a contrived story. Written with O. Henry's usual verve, entertaining in its account of Nashville, it falsifies and sentimentalizes its human materials.

In plot the story is a tissue of coincidences. Hardly has the narrator arrived in Nashville—a city of over one hundred thousand people—than he independently encounters, quite by accident, first, the husband, and, second, the faithful former family retainer of the sequestered woman he has come to visit. In each encounter money changes hands. He observes Major Caswell paying for the drinks with silver money. He himself pays his carriage driver with two dollar bills, one of which is easily identifiable. A second pair of co-incidences lies in the fact that the crucial clues of the story—the patched dollar bill and the variegated coat with its single yellow horn button—are both uniquely identifiable. It is, of course, the patched dollar bill that Azalea Adair coincidentally draws forth to pay for tea, and that, coincidentally, the Major is on hand to intercept. That evening, back at his hotel, the narrator again coincidentally encounters the Major, who buys the drinks with the patched dollar bill. On his next visit to the house on Jessamine Street, the narrator is coincidentally present at Azalea Adair's hunger-faint (the narrator is always on hand for significant happenings) and leaves her a $50 advance. That evening he again encounters Uncle Caesar at his stand and notices the missing button (Caesar never has other customers when the story needs him). Coincidentally it is during the narrator's visit to Nashville that Caesar, after a long history of the Major's villainies, is finally moved to kill him. Coincidentally the narrator is present at the drugstore where the Major's body is brought, and later, at the hotel, he coincidentally overhears a man who had been coincidentally present when the Major had displayed fifty dollars that afternoon to people in the hotel. Some of these coincidences are large, some are small; all together, they are incredible.

The characters who enact this plot are the paper-thin cutouts of sentimental fiction. The Major is pure villain, differing from the waxed-mustache variety mainly in being clean-shaven and failing to say "Aha!" He is fully characterized as a blabbing rat, but, lest we miss the point, we are later told that he is "despicable" and "a drunken, worthless loafer." Azalea Adair is the dignified heroine, frail, white-haired, long-suffering, brave in poverty, too proud to accept charity from her friends though dying of hunger. (She is like the Kitty Morgan that she tells about: "The boiling oil was sizzling as high as her heart; but I wish you could have seen the fine little smile that she carried from table to table.") Old Caesar, the carriage driver, is the picturesque Negro retainer, descended from kings, absolutely loyal to the daughter of the man who owned his father. Thus, there are two characters with hearts of gold and one with a heart as black as night. But the narrator, too, has a heart of gold. Though a commercial agent, he nevertheless arranges a contract for Azalea at eight cents a word rather than the authorized two. None of these characters is substantial enough to bear psychological probing. Azalea, after an altercation with her husband that results in his taking both of her dollars, returns to her guest without signs of discomposure. Uncle Caesar, after murdering the Major "in terrific battle," returns to his street corner and his trade without discomposure: "Step right in suh. Fifty cents to anywhere in the city. . . ." And the narrator thinks, after disposing of the evidence, "I wonder what's doing in Buffalo!"

The theme of the story is that romance can happen anywhere—even in Nashville. This theme is stated in a kind of essay placed around the narrative proper (and is repeated in the conversation of Azalea Adair), and the narrative proper is meant to illustrate it. Abstractly, of course, the theme is perfectly true, but the narrative proper is too contrived to give it a true embodiment. And, if the essay were removed from the narrative, the theme would disappear also, or be greatly altered. It *ought* to have something to do with the psychology and ethics of murder. But the characters are so unreal that the murder becomes unreal.

If we read the story purely for humor, it is entertaining. But insofar as it appeals to our moral sympathies, it oversimplifies complex issues and gives us a false and facile view of life.   LP

Susan Glaspell   A Jury of Her Peers (page 389)

"A Jury of Her Peers," first published in 1917, was based on the original one-act play "Trifles," which Glaspell wrote for the Provincetown Players in 1916. Students interested in differences between dramatic and narrative techniques may wish to compare the two versions.

Like "A Municipal Report," "A Jury of Her Peers" has a specific locale—the American Midwest (knowing Glaspell's life and other writings, we can place it in Iowa). The hard conditions and lonesomeness of life in this locale have everything to do with the story. The setting is an accessory to the murder.

Though the murder is under investigation by the sheriff and the county attorney, the story is not a who-dun-it. The murderer is already in jail, suspicion is cast on no other person. The story focuses not on *who*—but on *why*. Its interest is psychological.

The husband in this story is not a villain. He is known among his neighbors as "a good man": he doesn't drink, he keeps his word, he works hard, he pays his debts. But the exigencies of a difficult existence have made him "a hard man"—taciturn, "close" with money. Having eliminated all frivolous pleasures from his own life, he is infuriated when he finds that his wife has spent hard-earned money on a canary—and he breaks its neck. Though hardly likable, he is understandable and believable.

Unlike Old Caesar in "A Municipal Report," who kills Major Caswell for injury done not to himself but to his father's master's daughter, Mrs. Wright has not committed a disinterested murder. Her injury is personal, her motivation more believable. She kills her husband in a cold passion. Her behavior after the killing is also more believable. She looks "queer . . . as if she didn't know what she was going to do next. And kind of—done up." Yet out of long household habit she has resumed her household tasks. Her worrying about her fruit—after being taken to jail—has the touch of absolute authenticity. (It is matched by Mrs. Hale's worrying—at the scene of the murder—whether her son is dressed warmly enough.) The lonesomeness of a hard life—without children, without company, without conversation, without song—has shaped Mrs. Wright as it has shaped her husband. Less hard than he, she cannot bear it.

But the foreground conflicts in this story are more important than those of the unseen murderer and her victim (or should we say, the murdered man and his victim?). They concern Mrs. Hale *versus* Mrs. Peters, Mrs. Hale and Mrs. Peters *versus* themselves, and the women *versus* the men. The story contrasts the men's world and the women's. Concerned with "important" matters, the men feel superior to the smaller world in which, they think, the women live. They minimize the difficulties of running a kitchen and keeping towels clean. They laugh at "the insignificance of kitchen things," at worry over preserves, at concern with the difference between quilting a quilt or just knotting it. Mr. Hale explains that "women are used to worrying over trifles" and questions whether they would "know a clue if they did come upon it." For all the gallantry of the county attorney's "what would we do without the ladies?" the men unconsciously patronize them. Ironically, of course, the women's very familiarity with "the insignificance of kitchen things," and their recognition of the true importance of these things, enables them to discover the evidence that the men cannot find. It is the men who would not "know a clue if they did come upon it."

But perhaps the true center of the story lies in what the women do with the evidence. Mrs. Wright is tried by "A Jury of Her Peers." The title has an ironic twist, for there is no formal trial in the story, and the "jury" consists not of twelve men but of two women—Mrs. Wright's "peers" in a stricter sense than usual (at the time of the story women were not called on for jury service nor were they allowed to vote). The implication of the story is that, if a motivation were supplied at the trial, Mrs. Wright would be found guilty and put to death. "The law is the law," and "the law has to punish crime," says Mrs. Peters before she makes her final decision; and the county attorney had said of Mrs. Wright, "I guess before we're through with her she may have something more serious than preserves to worry about." The central conflict of the story therefore comes to be between legalistic justice and the larger understanding and compassion of the two women. Who killed John Wright? In the eyes of the law, Mrs. Wright. But the evidence of the strangled canary, which is a symbol of the former Minnie Foster as well as a piece of evidence, is that John Wright killed Minnie Foster. And was this just one person killing another? "I know what stillness is," says Mrs. Peters, a statement later echoed by Mrs. Hale. And Mrs. Hale breaks out, "Oh, I *wish* I'd come over here once in a while! That was a crime! That was a crime! Who's going to punish that?" In other words, Mrs. Hale sees even herself, shaped by the conditions of *her* life, as accessory to the murder. The law would only oversimplify.

So the final conflict of the story, an internal one, belongs to the two women—and especially to Mrs. Peters. *Is* she "married to the law"—in both senses of that phrase? She decides she is not and conceals the evidence. Whether she did right or not is an arguable question, but the story is on her side. The strangled canary has paradoxically both convicted and exonerated Mrs. Wright before "a jury of her peers."   LP

Edith Wharton   Roman Fever (page 409)

This famous story is replete with ironic surprises, so pervasively that the "surprise ending" is consistent and even expected—at least, *some* sort of surprise is expected. Among the surprising ironies are these: Alida Slade and Grace Ansley are intimate friends, yet they know very little about each other and are in fact rival opponents; Mrs. Slade judges Grace to be "old New York" and thus feebly on the wane and categorizes herself as modern and energetic, yet it is Grace who has violated the codes of moral behavior and

Alida who has been a model of propriety; Mrs. Slade is physically more commanding and socially more "vivid," but in fact is insecure in her position and her accomplishments; Mrs. Slade presents herself as the superior, victorious rival, but is gradually revealed as the envious also-ran. It is thus not much of a surprise at all when Grace Ansley reveals the mortifying truth that Alida Slade's marital happiness and smug superiority are built on sand. The conclusion also opens up the ironic conflict between individual behavior and the social norms that are presumed to prevail. Under their veneer of polite New York social manners, both women are fierce combatants in the game of love.

We might add to the list of ironies a technical one: the story is predominantly presented from the point of view of Mrs. Slade, whose thoughts and musings are constantly on display, thus leading the reader to assume that she is the protagonist (and one might even say, heroine). By contrast, Mrs. Slade's impression of Mrs. Ansley as a "museum specimen of old New York," pallid and slightly withdrawn, is reinforced by the author's offering only the rarest of glimpses into Mrs. Ansley's thoughts. Yet the apparent protagonist is defeated both by her own envious contrivance and by the triumph of Grace Ansley over her. By the story's end, it would be more appropriate to designate the unassuming Grace as protagonist and pompous Alida as defeated antagonist.

While the action seems to arise from the coincidence of the two former neighbors' staying at the same hotel in Rome, no doubt their social status limits them to a narrow range of fine hotels; in any case, a coincidental meeting as the starting point of a plot is not unusual and falls within the devices employed in much fine fiction. It is certainly not so obviously a contrivance as two experienced big-game hunters encountering each other in a chateau on a mysteriously remote island.

The double plot of Wharton's story, presenting a set of actions in the present in Rome, and a recollected conflict a generation earlier, is balanced at several points, the most significant being that in both the past and the present, Alida supposes herself victorious over her rival, and in both it is Grace who unostentatiously triumphs. Grace has lived with the sentimental memory of the letter of invitation that she supposed was the only written evidence of Delphin Slade's desire for her, while Alida has lived with the guilty secret of her forgery; but both of them have kept the text of the burnt letter alive in memory through all these years, and each of them has secretly pitied the other's supposed defeat.

These two plots are also extended backward and forward in time. The legendary perfidy of Grace's great-aunt's destruction of her love-rival by means of Roman fever is a precursor (and it would seem, an inspiration) for Alida's luring Grace out into the dangerous damps of the Colosseum for a supposed tryst. And Babs and Jenny, as they are perceived by their mothers, are two more girls engaged in potentially amorous rivalry. In all the plots, as Mrs. Slade remarks, there are mothers who try to restrain and protect their daughters from their destructive impulses, and in all of them the mothers' efforts are fruitless as each generation plays out its willful roles. As one critic says, "this repeated story of female transgression is literally an old wives' tale" (Sweeney, cited below).

Meanwhile, the superficial narrative of this placid, indolent afternoon is bathed in the shifting lights and glories of the Roman landscape that is itself an ironic counterpoint to the action. For as the light wanes and each physical feature takes on a more meditative gloom, the fever within is rising. Mrs. Slade cannot restrain her increasing fury (any more than she could contain the "rage" that vented itself in the forged letter), and Mrs. Ansley's shock is unsettling enough to cause her knitting, her gloves, and her ornate bag to go tumbling to the ground "in a panic-stricken heap." The title reverberates throughout the story, for it ranges in implication from a simple reference to a malarial fever that no longer threatens to the feverishness with which the women engage in their final contretemps. The scene is both Roman—a "diffused serenity" traced through its many stages of diminishing beauty—and a fever of emotions rising as the cool damps rise.

Of the many critical treatments of this story, the following will repay examination: Dale Bauer, "Edith Wharton's 'Roman Fever': A Rune of History," *College English* 50 (1988): 681–93; Susan Goodman, *Edith Wharton's Women: Friends and Rivals* (Hanover: UP of New England, 1990) 154–55; R. W. B. Lewis, "A Writer of Short Stories," in *Edith Wharton: Modern Critical Views*, ed. Harold Bloom (New York: Chelsea, 1986) 27–28; Susan Elizabeth Sweeney, "Edith Wharton's Case of 'Roman Fever,'" in *Wretched Exotic: Essays on Edith Wharton in Europe*, ed. Katherine Joslin and Alan Price (New York: Peter Lang, 1993).   TRA

F. Scott Fitzgerald   A New Leaf (page 420)

This bittersweet tale of life in the "jazz age" is attractive chiefly for its simple romantic plot and its evocation of the superficiality of the people and the times. It presents those people honestly and without irony, so that their failures do not resonate with meanings that transcend the particulars. That is its greatest weakness, but also the source of its attraction, especially for twenty-first-century students who will readily "relate" to characters and situations that will remind them of contemporary soap operas.

Julia Ross is a well-bred and well-to-do woman of twenty-one who can apparently spend her time anywhere she chooses, being supported by parents and relatives. She has not attended college, but has lived a vibrant social life of parties, infatuations, and pursuit by "suitable" young men. Her destiny is marriage within her own social class. She has a conscience, but more potent is her sense of social propriety: she is willing to accept a luncheon date with handsome but disreputable Dick Ragland, but she hides his identity from her (presumably proper) aunt. She knows that her aunt would find him socially unacceptable, and so she resorts to mild deception to avoid her aunt's disapproval.

Julia is bowled over by Dick's marvelous good looks and by Paris in springtime, half-remembering a sensuous passage by Shelley; as a well-bred girl, she restrains her reaction to the setting and to his sexiness:

Julia trembled discreetly; she controlled herself; . . . She sat there, a well-behaved woman of twenty-one, and discreetly trembled.

Her initial meeting with Dick is shadowed by the warnings of her suitor Phil Hoffman—Dick has behaved so badly in Paris that he is no longer welcome anywhere (that is, at the homes of any people in their social circle). But Julia is smitten, admires Dick's pledge to turn over a new leaf and give up drinking on his twenty-eighth birthday, and accepts a lunch invitation.

When Dick appears, drunk and disheveled, she sends him away and refuses to meet him again. Her naiveté has been shattered: she thought "a heavy drinker was someone who sat up late and drank champagne and maybe in the small hours rode home singing," an amusing tippler. Dick is a disgusting, ugly mess—quite the opposite of both the charming champagne bibber and the gorgeous "archangel" she had seen in him.

However, when Dick has indeed gone on the wagon, Julia admits him back into her life, confident that he loves her and that she can be his strength, his savior, if his weakness should ever recur. With a certain amount of prudence, she delays their wedding until she can be sure of him, and even introduces a separation by going to visit her parents as an additional test. She has become certain that with her help, he can stay sober; she wants to discover if he can manage on his own.

Ironically, he manages to stay sober, but confesses to her that it was with the help of her friend Esther Cary during Julia's absence. He has proved that he can be sober—but has also proved that Julia is not his mainstay, that as she says, "'any woman can help [him].'" Julia gives up on him, again and completely, and marries steady, successful Phil, but still nurtures in her heart a love for him that she insists "wasn't just [for] his good looks."

In a sense, she's right about that, because her love for Dick was in part based on her confidence that she could be his strength in beating down the devils inside him. That is, her love was also self-love, a pride in her own abilities. Her final break with him may appear to him to be mere sexual jealousy because he has been unfaithful to her, but more than that, it is her disappointment that she was not the only one who could sustain his sobriety and responsibility. She has needed him to be both weak and dependent. Both of them display the emotional immaturity of self-centered people who cannot really love.

In contrast to "Roman Fever," "A New Leaf" has not only the shallowness of its characters, but also a shallowness or weakness of characterization. Over and over, the characters' emotional states are simply named or labeled rather than dramatized. This is a particular weakness when Julia is called upon to have conflicting feelings, or to display some complexity of personality. Paragraph 23 is a clear example of authorial intrusion, even editorializing, as it summarizes a variety of shortcomings in a woman "a little too good." It is also obvious in the example quoted above: she "trembled discreetly . . . discreetly trembled," which leaves one to wonder not only what that actually looked like, but how *indiscreet* trembling would appear.

This tendency to editorialize is reflected in the wavering point of view. The story is primarily told from Julia's perspective, particularly as she tries to understand and accommodate herself to her attraction to Dick. But she is also summarized and judged by an omniscient narrator who seems not to trust the reader to infer her weaknesses. Such authorial commentary replaces what might have been a meaningful irony balancing weaknesses of Julia's against those of Dick. The ironic judgment comes at the very end, when the omniscient voice enters the mind of her husband Phil to make an unspoken observation on Julia's idealized memory of Dick: "Better let it all alone in the depths of her heart and the depths of the sea [where Dick has drowned himself]." Both Julia and Dick fail to "turn over a new leaf," that is, to begin a new and better life for themselves by overcoming with their own strengths the weaknesses that their styles of life have encouraged.   TRA

Two Featured Writers:
James Joyce
and
Flannery O'Connor

James Joyce   Araby (page 437)

"Araby," one of the early, childhood stories in *Dubliners*, features perhaps the most famous example of the Joycean "epiphany." The story as a whole depicts an idealistic young boy's disillusionment when faced with the crassness and spiritual poverty of the real world.

Like other Joyce stories, "Araby" includes an artful combination of youthful and mature narrative voices. The first-person narrator is clearly recalling his experience of a childhood infatuation, or "puppy love," from the vantage point of a young adult (Joyce wrote the story in his early twenties). Therefore, although the narrator is describing his infatuation with his friend Mangan's sister in immediate, sensuous terms he also uses imagery that communicates the rather sordid reality in which the boy lived at the time.

In fact, the story achieves its effects largely through imagery. The setting is highly significant: the boy lives on a dead-end ("blind" is Joyce's term) street, and the narrator mentions such non-romantic elements as "ashpits," "dark odorous stables," and the "brown imperturbable faces" of the surrounding homes. The boy is a kind of romantic hero who, as he says, carried the beloved girl's image like a "chalice" (religious imagery also abounds in the story) through "places the most hostile to romance." Yet the boy clings to his romanticism: "My eyes were often full of tears (I could not tell why) and at times a flood from my heart seemed to pour itself into my bosom."

The boy's aunt and uncle further contribute to the non-romantic atmosphere within which the boy clings to his idealistic dream vision of Mangan's sister (who wears a silver bracelet, and is described as having a halo of light surrounding her face and hair). The boy goes with his aunt to do the marketing and encounters such items as "barrels of pigs' cheeks." "drunken men and bargaining women," and "the curse of laborers." Similarly, at home, the boy endures a visit from one Mrs. Mercer (whose name evokes the mercenary reality of these people's lives, which is again at odds with the boy's inner world of idealistic beauty), and when his uncle arrives home, the man is clearly drunk. In addition to the setting itself, the uncle is an antagonist because the possibility that he may withhold money the boy needs for his romantic quest to "Araby," the bazaar where he hopes to buy Mangan's sister a present, provides some of the story's suspense.

When the uncle finally relents and the boy is free to leave for the train station, it seems that his quest will succeed. There is a special train that will take him directly to the bazaar. However, because the uncle has delayed the narrator's quest, he arrives late, and the description of the bazaar prepares us for the disillusionment to come: "the greater part of the hall was in darkness. I recognized a silence like that which pervades a church after a service." In another religious/commercial image, the narrator recalls that "two men were counting money on a salver," which has suggested to some critics the betrayal of Christ by Judas for pieces of silver and a further adumbration of the betrayal of the boy's fondest dreams.

Students often miss the epiphanic moment of the story because of its extreme subtlety. The boy is listening vaguely to a conversation between the shopgirl he wants to help him and two young men. The dialogue among these three is entirely superficial and unremarkable; clearly, the girl is just passing the time in flirting with the young men until her shift at the bazaar is over. However, she finally asks the boy if he wants to buy anything and, to students' frequent surprise, he says "No, thank you." What has happened, of course, is that all the potential disillusionment of the various settings and his encounters with adults throughout the story have finally broken into consciousness during the shopgirl's inane conversation: the boy realizes that his quest is futile.

The closing paragraphs merely complete the boy's initiation into a frightful and dark adult world. Whereas Mangan's sister had been bathed in the light of the boy's idealism, the imagery now is of darkness: "the light was out. The upper part of the hall was now completely dark." The final sentence, with its emphatic alliteration and assonance, evokes the boy's immediate reaction to his epiphany: "Gazing up into the darkness I saw myself as a creature driven and derided by vanity; and my eyes burned with anguish and anger." The boy will return home empty-handed, robbed by an ugly and commercial world of his fondest romantic dreams.   GJ

James Joyce Eveline (page 442)

This story is put forward as an example of what Joyce called the "paralysis" of Dublin. It presents its protagonist at a crisis in her life, at the moment when she might take decisive action and (like Joyce himself) escape the constrictions of an ugly and dispiriting life.

The beginning scene, with Eveline sitting exhausted at the darkening window, breathing in the "odor of dusty cretonne," leads her to a nostalgic reminiscence of childhood where there was an open field for her to play in with her siblings and other children. Even though her father would beat them if he caught them at play, ". . . they seemed to have been rather happy then" (the phrasing suggests that it was not a carefree and joyous childhood—*seemed* and *rather* undercut that impression). This wistfulness for past pleasure is then abruptly stopped: childhood is gone, people have died, and Eveline herself is about to go away.

She then meditates on her present situation, on the dissatisfaction of her work, the hardship and growing threat of living with her father, the loneliness of her life at home. Her rescuer has come into her life in the form of Frank the sailor. Their brief courtship had its excitements and then aroused the animosity of her father, who protectively (and jealously?) forbade her to see Frank—"I know these sailor chaps." So they met furtively and planned an elopement to Buenos Aires where Frank has "a home waiting for her."

In the growing darkness, as she sits, Eveline hears a street organ and flashes back to the death of her mother after a "life of commonplace sacrifices" (like Eveline's) that closes "in final craziness." Terror-stricken, she rushes to Frank as her savior from such a life.

The moment of departure arrives, Eveline meets Frank at the quay, and in "a maze of distress, she [prays] to God to direct her, to show her what [is] her duty." Whether by God's direction, or by her own helplessness to act, she remains while Frank boards the ship.

As critics have shown, it is possible to view these incidents from at least two quite different perspectives—and it is not really possible to decide between them. Eveline may in the end collapse into the creature of habit, the passive, defeated drudge, who "like a helpless animal" cannot break out of its captivity. Or her excited, frenzied state may be rescuing her from an unprincipled seducer, at the last moment leading her back to safety and respectability. Frank is, after all, a "sailor chap" about whom she knows nothing and who may or may not be telling her the truth about their future. If his purposes are marriage and a home with her, why should the marriage be postponed until they have departed? Is there really a home waiting in Buenos Aires? If this is the future he dreams about, why is he willing to leave her behind? Her father may be motivated by his need for a housekeeper and her small wages, but he may also sincerely be trying to protect her from a seducer.

Whichever perspective one chooses, Eveline's fate is pathetic, for she has not escaped the dreariness of her life in Dublin, and she has lost what seemed to her the promise of a new and happy life. The future promises little but the sameness of her stifled, lonely life, with the additional growing threat of violence, from her father. If this is an escape from a possible danger, it is also a retreat into a known "life of commonplace sacrifices."

There are comments on this story on pages 338, 372, and 374.   TRA

James Joyce   The Boarding House (page 447)

"The Boarding House" is a story about the unspoken collusion between a mother and her daughter in trapping a husband for the daughter.

Mrs. Mooney is vulgar, coarse, shrewd, and capable in all matters concerning her self-interest. The fact that she is "a butcher's daughter" is a verbal clue to her character. Though butchers' daughters are actually no better or worse than other men's daughters, the connotations of the phrase suggest a certain coarseness. Mrs. Mooney "dealt with moral problems as a cleaver deals with meat." She puts up an outward show of respectability but has no inner possession of it. Her eye is always open for the main chance.

The initial clues to her character are provided by her own marriage. She acquires a husband (her father's foreman), discards him, and takes all of the assets. The visible facts make the failure of her marriage seem entirely the husband's fault. He drinks, he plunders the till and runs the shop into debt, quarrels with his wife in public, buys bad meat, and ruins the business. But silently we wonder, what was his provocation? *Why* did he go after his wife with a cleaver one night?

After discarding her husband, Mrs. Mooney discards the shop and acquires a boarding house. Her resident boarders call her *The Madam*, not because they regard the house as a brothel, but because she has the manners and abilities of a brothel keeper. She knows "when to give credit, when to be stern and when to let things pass." She knows, that is, when to demand payment and when to postpone such a demand. Her criterion is not based on concern for the merits or welfare of the boarder, but on concern for the ultimate profit-and-loss outcome to the house. Her son, moreover, has many of the qualities of a doorkeeper or "bouncer" for a brothel, and her daughter has some of the manners of a prostitute.

Clearly the mother treats her daughter as potentially either an economic asset or liability. She first sends Polly out to be a typist in an office, but when her ex-husband drops in daily to see their daughter, she brings Polly home again to do housework and "to give her the run of the young men." When she notices that something is "going on" between Polly and one of the eligible men, she watches but keeps her own counsel. In other words, she allows—even silently encourages Polly to "get into trouble," then pretends to be indignant when it happens. Her motive is to get her daughter "off her hands" (financially, that is). When she senses that things have gone far enough, she interviews Polly to confirm her suspicions. It is an awkward interview for both of them, for each is trying to deceive the other—not about *what* has happened, but about *how* it happened. Mrs. Mooney doesn't want Polly to suspect that she has actually connived in the seduction, and Polly doesn't want her mother to know that she had divined her mother's intention. Before summoning Mr. Doran, Mrs. Mooney reviews her position—or "counts her cards," as Joyce puts it. She is sure she will "win." She is an "outraged mother." She had mistakenly assumed Mr. Doran to be "a man of honor." But he had simply "taken advantage of Polly's youth and inexperience." All three of these last statements are heavy with dramatic irony. The truth is that she is a gratified mother, that she had foreseen that Mr. Doran could be victimized, and that she and Polly, working concertedly but without consultation, have "taken advantage" of Mr. Doran's inexperience and vulnerable situation. Mr. Doran has been weak but not designing. Mrs. Mooney and Polly have been designing. Only Mr. Doran feels remorse for what has happened. Mrs. Mooney has got a daughter "off her hands." Polly looks forward to being married.   LP

Flannery O'Connor   A Good Man Is Hard to Find (page 454)

Written in O'Connor's mid-twenties, "A Good Man Is Hard to Find" remains not only her most famous story but one of the touchstones of modern American fiction.

Both the major trademarks of O'Connor's fiction—the social comedy, which she termed "manners," and the religious theme, which she called "mystery"—are here, fused brilliantly in a narrative at once so enticing and so shocking that it sometimes polarizes a classroom. (See O'Connor's posthumously published essay collection *Mystery and Manners* [New York: Farrar, 1969] for her highly personal definition of these terms, which are key to understanding her fiction.) Some students respond to the comedy *and* the violence, while others become uncomfortable with the near-savage satire and the seemingly casual dispatch with which The Misfit and his gang murder six "innocent" members of a typical mid-century Southern family.

This story, like O'Connor's work generally, poses special interpretive problems, since few readers unversed in the author's background or her thinking will grasp the meaning she intends to convey. This problem, however, often sparks lively discussion: does O'Connor's art "fail" because it does not communicate her intended theme, or should we follow D. H. Lawrence's advice to heed not the teller, but the tale, allowing the story its independence from the so-called intentional fallacy? An especially interesting complexity develops when the same conservative-minded students shocked by the story's seeming disrespect of grandmothers and happy endings learn of the writer's deeply religious sensibility, sometimes deciding they "like" the story after all. Students who respond primarily to the satiric view of hypocritical behavior, on the other hand, may agree readily to the idea that O'Connor's Catholicism "doesn't matter": what matters is that she has written a great, memorable story.

Clarifying the nature of O'Connor's fiction at the outset helps to adjust the reader's expectations when confronting this idiosyncratic author. Joyce Carol Oates has summarized in a single brief paragraph both the thematic focus and the quality of O'Connor's achievement:

> Not meant to be realistic or naturalistic, her fiction should be read as a series of parables. Like the metaphysical poets . . . she yokes together sacred and secular images by violence; it is the artistic arrangement of these images, in themselves grotesque, that leads to the construction of a vision that is not grotesque but harshly and defiantly spiritual. Her death in the summer of 1964 marked not simply the end of the career of a powerful descendant of Faulkner whose individual achievements are at times superior to his, but the end of the career of one of the greatest religious writers of modern times. ("The Visionary Art of Flannery O'Connor," *New Heaven, New Earth: The Visionary Experience in Literature* [New York: Vanguard, 1974] 145.)

In "A Good Man Is Hard to Find," one of her funniest and most terrifying "parables," there are three major scenes. In the first, the grandmother and her family discuss the proposed trip and the escaped Misfit (whose exploits are publicized in the newspaper), and then start out for Florida in their car. In the second, they stop for a break at The Tower, a barbecue place run by

Red Sammy and his wife, where they discuss The Misfit and bewail the lack of good men in the modern world. In the third, their argument and car accident are followed by the encounter with The Misfit and the murder of the entire family. O'Connor skillfully weaves the three scenes together through foreshadowing, imagery, and point of view, achieving the effect of a seemingly ordinary, even commonplace tale that drifts ineluctably into horror.

In the first scene, the satire is bitingly funny. Reversing conventional expectations, the grandmother is the most naive and childlike character, while the young children are the most sophisticated and cynical. The grandmother's adult son, Bailey, and her unnamed daughter-in-law are virtual ciphers, representing what the author considers unredeemed natural creatures not yet humanized by grace. To this end, the animal imagery is relentless: Bailey's shirt is decorated with parrots, while his wife has a face as "broad and innocent as a cabbage" and a head scarf with "two points on the top like a rabbit's ears." (There are more than a dozen other animal images sprinkled through the story.) The grandmother is a more complex character: though hypocritical and manipulative, she is also basically good-hearted and full of life. Dressed as a "lady" for the trip, she tries to find something positive in everything and everyone, even in a foreshadowing glimpse of a cemetery containing "five or six graves."

The second scene expands the story to include Red Sammy and his wife, showing the grandmother's embarrassment at the children's inability to follow the Southern code of polite behavior. (The monkey outside The Tower is surely emblematic of the children's savage behavior—ironically, the monkey is much better-behaved—and of their spiritually unevolved state.) The scene signals a purgatorial interlude, since "The Tower" implies a place of suffering and torture, while the proprietor's name suggests a devilish figure. Moreover, Red Sammy gives the story its title: "'A good man is hard to find,' Red Sammy said. 'Everything is getting terrible. I remember the day you could go off and leave your screen door unlatched. Not no more.'"

This discussion of "goodness," in which Red Sammy and the grandmother hypocritically applaud their superior virtue in a world of vice, leads naturally to the final scene when the grandmother, back in the car with her family, tries to coax her son into visiting an old plantation she'd seen as a young woman. She enlists the children in her cause by making the plantation sound romantic and exciting, and she claims the side-trip would be "educational" for them. The grandmother's manipulative behavior leads to the family's tragedy, however, when Bailey, capitulating to her wishes, turns down a dirt road and overturns the car after the grandmother's cat, secreted in her valise because Bailey had forbidden her to bring it along, springs onto Bailey's shoulder. It is her fault, too, that The Misfit decides he must murder them, for she isn't crafty enough not to exclaim that she recognizes him from the newspaper photograph. The Misfit and his gang have arrived in a "hearse-like automobile," and this carefully orchestrated scene foregrounds the encounter between The Misfit and the grandmother, even as the reader is uncomfortably aware that the remaining family members are being taken by his gang into the woods and systematically murdered.

The Misfit, an atypical criminal with his "scholarly look" and his philosophical rationalization for his evil acts, personifies O'Connor's view of human depravity resulting from the rejection of Christ. Ironically, because of his intellectual probing of religious issues, O'Connor considered The Misfit to have a greater capacity for grace than the other characters; but like Satan in Milton's *Paradise Lost,* he has deliberately rejected grace and the entire purpose of human life by ascribing to the philosophy summarized in Satan's line "Evil, be thou my good."

As this final scene turns less funny and more wrenching, the grandmother becomes a pitiable figure, desperately clinging to her polite manners even as she pleads shrilly for her life. But her lifelong habits of deceit and self-interest drop away when O'Connor allows her to accept divine grace by reaching out to The Misfit and exclaiming selflessly, " 'Why you're one of my babies. You're one of my own children!' " This sudden conversion of the hypocritical grandmother into a "good woman" so frightens The Misfit that he kills her immediately, the diction suggesting a perverted sacramentalism when he shoots her "three times" and views her touch as the bite of "a snake." Though the grandmother dies in a state of grace, "her face smiling up at the cloudless sky," The Misfit continues to reverse the values of good and evil.

O'Connor achieves a brilliant closure when, necessarily eliminating the dead grandmother's point of view, she narrates in the laconically objective viewpoint of a camera lens observing the scene. Now The Misfit utters the story's most memorable line: " 'She would of been a good woman,' The Misfit said, 'if it had been somebody there to shoot her every minute of her life.' " At once funny and macabre, this line shows The Misfit's doleful recognition that the grandmother did finally become "good," which accounts for the changed appearance of his eyes, which are "red-rimmed and pale and defenseless-looking." At the story's close he remains an isolated figure of obdurate and unhappy evil, reprimanding one of his mindless sidekicks who seems to be enjoying the murders. " 'It's no real pleasure in life,' " The Misfit says. O'Connor leaves the reader stranded in a bleak, bloodstained landscape, the modern world without Christian grace. While some readers may see the grandmother as the victim of a tragedy, the author views her as saved and triumphant, having achieved her full selfhood and oneness with God.

O'Connor discusses her intentions in writing the story in *Mystery and Manners* and in her letters collected posthumously under the title *The Habit of Being,* ed. Sally Fitzgerald (New York: Farrar, 1979). Most of the dozens of book-length critical studies devoted to O'Connor offer interpretations, including the following noteworthy discussions: Richard Giannone, *Flannery O'Connor and the Mystery of Love* (Urbana and Chicago: U of Illinois P, 1989) 46–53; Frederick Asals, *Flannery O'Connor: The Imagination of Extremity* (Athens and London: U of Georgia P, 1982) 142–54; Martha Stephens, *The*

Question of Flannery O'Connor (Baton Rouge: Louisiana UP, 1973) 17–36; Miles Orvell, *Invisible Parade: The Fiction of Flannery O'Connor* (Philadelphia: Temple UP, 1972) 130–36; and Kathleen Feeley, *Flannery O'Connor: Voice of the Peacock* (New Brunswick: Rutgers UP, 1972) 69–76.   GJ

Flannery O'Connor Good Country People (page 468)

In this, one of O'Connor's funniest and most accomplished stories, the author presents two typical conflicts in the relationship between Mrs. Hopewell and her adult daughter, Joy/Hulga: the conflict between a prideful child and an anxious parent (such as we see between the sons and Mrs. May in "Greenleaf"); and that between an avowed intellectual, non-believing individual and a nominal (if rather hypocritical) Christian. As is almost always the case in her fiction, O'Connor depicts the sin of pride in her "hard-headed" characters (as she once described them) as something requiring a violent epiphany to bring them into the realm of Christian grace.

"Good Country People" begins and ends with a frame device that features Mrs. Hopewell and her indomitable subordinate on the farm, Mrs. Freeman. Mrs. Hopewell, as her name suggests, is a person who thinks of herself as a lady and an upright member of society, much like the grandmother in "A Good Man Is Hard to Find." By contrast, Mrs. Freeman is pure "country," the personification of the type named in the story's title. In the early part of the story, she is associated with heavy machinery, including an oncoming truck and a refrigerator; her imperturbable nature is a source of antagonism to Joy/Hulga, since the latter's intellectual pretensions are lost on Mrs. Freeman.

Joy/Hulga, the protagonist, has renounced her given name, "Joy," in favor of the ugly name "Hulga," one she has chosen largely because it displeases her mother. Disabled since the age of ten when a hunting accident cost her her leg, Joy/Hulga is now proud of her artificial leg, as she is proud of all the personal qualities that set her apart from the world of "normal" young women. She has no interest in young men, for instance, another fact that irritates Mrs. Hopewell. She has a Ph.D. in philosophy, which Mrs. Hopewell considers a pointless accomplishment, and sits around the house all day reading philosophical tomes and quoting atheistic philosophers in the successful effort to keep her mother in a constant state of upset and dismay.

When the other major character, a Bible salesman with the suggestive name Manley Pointer appears on the scene, Joy/Hulga initiates a mock-romance with him, believing him to be simple-minded and deciding she can flaunt her disbelief in his presence. What she does not know is that the Bible salesman is a con man whose own copy of the Bible is hollowed-out and filled with a flask of liquor, a set of pornographic playing cards, and a packet of condoms. After he maneuvers Joy/Hulga into a hayloft, Pointer uses his salesman's guile to talk Joy/Hulga into removing her wooden leg so that he can examine it. As O'Connor commented in one of her essays, the artificial leg has by this time become a literary symbol with much accumulated meaning. It represents everything to which Joy/Hulga attaches her overweening pride and has become an emblem of her very identity and her uniqueness in the world.

In the climactic scene, Pointer quickly inserts the leg into his valise and makes off with it, leaving Joy/Hulga, her face "churning" with emotion, in a state of complete and childlike vulnerability. As she has done throughout the story, O'Connor employs religious imagery here, portraying Pointer as a kind of perverse Christ figure who, through his chicanery, has unwittingly brought Joy/Hulga to her salvation. Although the story does not reach to this point, one may assume that Joy/Hulga, like the grandmother after her head "cleared for an instant" in her ultimate confrontation with The Misfit, achieves her own moment of grace after this destruction of her artificial and prideful ego.

In the final scene, the story returns to the foil characters Mrs. Hopewell and Mrs. Freeman, who unlike Joy/Hulga undergo no dynamic change: Mrs. Hopewell continues to repeat her airy clichés, while Mrs. Freeman remains obtuse and unflappable. Like so much of O'Connor's fiction with its rural settings and earthy characters, "Good Country People" illustrates the idea that even in the most unlikely of locales, the mystery of Christian redemption can be a part of daily life.   GJ

Flannery O'Connor   Greenleaf (page 486)

Mrs. May's family is on its way down. Her deceased husband had been a businessman in town. She has had to go to the country. Her sons, who represent respectively decadent materialism and sterile intellectualism, are unmarried. She has no grandchildren. The Greenleafs are a family on the way up. Mr. and Mrs. Greenleaf, who represent the family's primitive beginnings, have seven children. Their sons have educated themselves, are practical and productive, and are advancing in the world. The Greenleafs have six grandchildren, three by each son. While one family is dying on the vine, the other is growing and thriving. Mrs. May, whose consuming mental preoccupation is social status and who has an acute need to maintain belief in her own innate superiority, is exasperated by her sons' failure to support their "position" and by the prospect that the low-born, vulgar Greenleafs will usurp it. "In twenty years do you know what those people will be?" she asks her sons. "Society," she says blackly.

The two families are contrasted in many ways, perhaps most significantly in religion. Mrs. May's nominal religion is Christianity; her real religion is respectability. She has no deep religious beliefs, but she believes in going to church. Mrs. Greenleaf's religion is primitive and grotesque, but springs from genuine conviction. Her "prayer healing," however naive or superstitious, is motivated by a desire to help people totally unknown to her. The self-righteous Mrs. May is recurrently motivated by a desire to hurt people whom she knows.

Mrs. May wonders how she has put up with Greenleaf for fifteen years. The reader is more disposed to wonder how Greenleaf has put up with Mrs. May for so long. The two figures seem almost embodiments of impatience and patience. But Greenleaf's patience has its limits. When Mrs. May insists on Greenleaf's killing a bull belonging to his own sons, he finally loses his temper, though he continues to obey her orders. Mrs. May's most characteristic emotion throughout the story is anger. At this point Greenleaf also becomes angry.

The story makes use of all three kinds of irony. Scofield uses verbal irony, for instance, when he displays Mrs. May's delicate blue-veined little hand dangling from her wrist and yells out, "Look at Mamma's iron hand!" Most consistently the story depends on dramatic irony that results largely from the use of the limited third-person point of view with Mrs. May as the focal character. We continuously see the characters and the events of the story as reflected through Mrs. May's mind, but we see them in a quite different light than she does. When Mrs. May retires to bed thinking that "if the Greenleaf boys had risen in the world it was because she had given their father employment when no one else would have him," we see that she thinks of herself as deserving gratitude for her generosity, but when later we are told that "She had not fired him because she had always doubted she could do better," we plainly see that she has hired Greenleaf, and hung on to him, entirely from self-interest. When we are told of the Greenleaf boys that during the war they "had both managed to get wounded and now they both had pensions," we see that Mrs. May thinks of the wounds as something the boys had deliberately incurred from motives of self-interest, but we interpret them as evidences of bravery. Throughout the story the reader's judgments and Mrs. May's judgments are at variance, largely because Mrs. May is constantly reflecting on the shortcomings and deficiencies of other people, but is conscious of none in herself. When Mrs. May tells Mrs. Greenleaf, "Jesus would be *ashamed* of you," our chief response is to think that Jesus would be ashamed of *her*.

The story also makes repeated use of irony of situation. The most obvious example results from Mrs. May's imagining Greenleaf gored by the bull and thinking of it "almost with pleasure as if she had hit on the perfect ending for a story she was telling her friends." The actual ending of the story is perfect from a different point of view: it represents poetic justice for Mrs. May's fifteen years of persecuting Greenleaf and for trying to make him kill his sons' bull. Mrs. May's revenge boomerangs.

The symbolism of this story is complex, and the following discussion will attempt only a partial exploration of that complexity. The bull is a multiple symbol. It symbolizes, first of all, the Greenleafs. The bull is "gaunt and long-legged"; the Greenleaf boys are "long-legged and rawboned and red-skinned." The bull is a scrub bull—of inferior stock—yet it is healthy and hardy; the Greenleafs, as Mrs. May sees them, are "scrub-human," yet also healthy and hardy. The bull eats Mrs. May's hedges; Mrs. May dreams of something eating her farm, feels that the Greenleafs have lived off her for fifteen years, and fears that they may eventually get the farm. The bull comes "like some patient god" to woo Mrs. May; Greenleaf has been patient, or enduring, for fifteen years. The bull finally becomes angry and gores Mrs. May; Greenleaf finally becomes angry, and the bull, which belongs to his sons, is in a sense the agent of his revenge. But the bull, besides being a symbol of the human Greenleafs, also represents something divine. At the beginning of the story it has a hedge-wreath on its horns "like a menacing prickly crown." Bull-worship, according to Frazer's *Golden Bough*, was common in several ancient lands: bulls were considered symbols of the sun, types of reproductive energy or generative force, and emblems of the Father God. In Mrs. May's second dream, the bull is identified with the sun: the sun charges her, as the bull actually charges her later. The bull, the sun, and the Greenleafs in this story may all be taken as symbols of natural and divine forces, of reproductive energy, and of life itself, which Mrs. May attempts to pen up, shut out, or destroy. These forces seek Mrs. May's regeneration. The bull is said to be "like some patient god come down to woo her," "like an uncouth country suitor," and finally "like a wild tormented lover." But when Mrs. May persistently denies these forces, they destroy her. At the end Mrs. May has "the look of a person whose sight has been suddenly restored but who finds the light unbearable," and in death she seems "to be bent over whispering some last discovery" into the bull's ear. Mrs. May's revelation has come too late to be of any use.

There is an excellent discussion of the mythic dimensions of this story by Frederick Asals in *Studies in Short Fiction* 5 (1968): 317–30.   LP

Stories for
Further Reading

Chinua Achebe   **Civil Peace** (page 511)

QUESTIONS

1. Discuss the irony in "Civil Peace," beginning with the title.
2. Contributing to the irony is the third-person omniscient point of view. In which passages is the omniscient narrator's ironic viewpoint particularly noticeable? How does his attitude toward Jonathan's plight differ from Jonathan's own attitude toward it?
3. Discuss Jonathan's characterization. How has his character been formed, at least in part, by his environment and by historical events?
4. Jonathan lost his youngest son during a civil war, yet he considers himself "extraordinarily lucky." Is this attitude callous or admirable?
5. The thieves outside Jonathan's door are characterized solely through their dialogue. Discuss the unusual way in which they rob Jonathan of his money. How are they different from typical thieves in a developed country like the United States?
6. What is the meaning of the recurrent phrase "Nothing puzzles God"?

The plot of Achebe's "Civil Peace" is simple: after the Nigerian Civil War in the 1970s, an Ibo man returns to his village with his family (minus his youngest son, killed during the war); he makes money at various odd jobs and rebuilds his partly demolished hut; he turns the "rebel money" he makes in to the government and receives an "ex gratia" award of twenty pounds; and he then has the money stolen from him by a group of nocturnal marauders.

What makes the story distinctive is not the plot but the tone, which exploits an ironic distance between the protagonist, Jonathan, and the sophisticated omniscient narrator, who views Jonathan with a bemused detachment and admiration, while making clear to the reader what havoc the war has wrought on ordinary villagers.

The title itself is ironic, since the "civil peace" following the war is marked by anarchy, a political condition well-represented by the faceless thieves who visit Jonathan's hut late at night. Throughout this tale of family tragedy and loss, however, Jonathan himself maintains an upbeat mood that may strike some readers, especially well-fed Americans, as puzzling and even off-putting.

Achebe describes Jonathan's initial joy at having "five inestimable blessings"—namely his own head, his wife's, and, as the narrator says ironically, "the heads of three out of their four children." Jonathan apparently spends little time grieving over his son, but the story implies that grief is not a luxury he can afford: he must focus his considerable energies on providing for the family members who have survived. His use of an old bicycle as a makeshift "taxi," his rebuilding of his hut, his putting family members to work and his opening a palm-wine bar: all suggest the keen instincts for survival developed by a man who takes nothing for granted in his unstable and impoverished environment.

An American reader having grown up during decades of peace and prosperity may wonder at Jonathan's cheerfulness and lack of bitterness, but this is precisely Achebe's point: the daily reality of violence and loss makes someone like Jonathan happy simply to stay alive and keep his family together. Though Jonathan witnesses another man driven to "near-madness in an instant" after having his own ex-gratia award stolen by a "heartless ruffian," Jonathan keeps his sanity by focusing intently on accumulating money, on restoring a modicum of stability to his family's life, and perhaps most important, on looking forward rather than backward. His struggle for basic survival precludes self-pity. As one critic remarks, "The reader might well view the wit, energy, compassion and muted optimism of this story in the aftermath of the civil war with something of the admiring incredulity with which he or she responds to Jonathan Iwegbu's unfailing optimism as he counts his blessings after the devastation of war" (C. L. Innes, *Chinua Achebe* [Cambridge: Cambridge UP, 1990] 126).

Another discussion is in Donald B. Burness, "Solipsism and Survival in Achebe's 'Civil Peace' and 'Girls at War'," *Ba Shiru: A Journal of African Languages and Literature* 5 (1973): 64–67.

One of the most original passages is the exchange between Jonathan and the thieves in the night who come to steal his money. As Innes remarks,

> The second half of this story, the account of the robbery, suggests that Achebe might well, if he so wished, prove a dramatist. The episode mingles fear, suspense and hilariously grim comedy as the off-stage robber leader and his chorus of thugs introduce themselves, satirically join in the cries for assistance, offer to call for the "soja" when neither neighbours nor police respond, and reassure the frightened family. (126)

Instead of breaking the flimsy door down and bursting inside, the thieves knock in mock-politeness and ask that Jonathan turn over his much-needed twenty pounds. The story dramatizes the lack of a stable political and civil order through the brazenness of these thieves, who know there is no one to stop them. It is also likely they are not eager to harm anyone and are expressing, like the narrator, their own ironic sense of the chaotic world in which they live.

Even the loss of his money, however, does not seem to disturb Jonathan, who rationalizes the situation by thinking he did not even have the money the week before, so he has really lost nothing. His often-repeated refrain, "Nothing puzzles God," implies a cheerful acquiescence to fate, and it is clear to the reader that he will simply continue working and soon will replace the stolen money. Though the narrator's broader perspective allows us to empathize with Jonathan's plight, Jonathan himself simply continues forward, a human emblem of optimism and endurance.   GJ

Raymond Carver   Cathedral *(page 516)*

QUESTIONS

1. Describe the first-person narrator's voice. How does the style in which he tells his story help to characterize him? Is he likable or unlikable?
2. What does the narrator's wife contribute to the story? Are you sympathetic with her desire to maintain a friendship with Robert? Does this friendship threaten her marriage?
3. Discuss the complex characterization of the blind man. In what ways does he depart from our stereotypical ways of thinking about blind people? How is his characterization important to the narrator, and how does the relationship between them change as the story proceeds?
4. What is the symbolic significance of cathedrals? Why is their drawing of a cathedral together important, and what kind of epiphany does the narrator have during this experience?
5. What do the characters' indulgence in alcohol and marijuana say about them? Does their altered state of consciousness contribute to the climax of the story?

This story features Carver's famously spare, "minimalist" prose style at its best. It also deals with typical Carver characters: rather disaffected, middle-class Americans who seem vaguely unmoored in their lives and who seek solace through drinking and smoking marijuana.

The three major characters are a seemingly mean-spirited, unnamed narrator, his wistful and somewhat resentful wife, and a blind man, Robert, who had been a friend of the wife's before her marriage. The scene is quickly set: the couple has moved from Seattle to New York state, and the blind man is coming to visit them. We learn immediately that the narrator has a negative attitude toward the blind man's impending arrival: "A blind man in my house was not something I was looking forward to," he says, and he unkindly jokes to his wife that maybe he will take the blind man bowling. The wife, who has kept in touch with Robert through audiotapes mailed back and forth, is by contrast looking forward to Robert's visit and criticizes her husband for his attitude.

Robert's blindness is soon enough to be seen as metaphorical: it is actually the narrator who is blind to the possibility of friendship or commonality with a person different from himself. His wife remarks that he doesn't have any friends, and when he learns that the blind man's deceased wife was named Beulah, he dismissively says that Beulah was "a name for a colored woman." Numbed to reality by drugs, the narrator has defensively closed himself into his own claustral and friendless world, which as the story proceeds the blind man manages to puncture, allowing for the epiphany that occurs in the closing scene.

To the narrator's surprise, Robert when he arrives does not comport with his stereotypical notions of how a blind man should look and behave. Robert has a full beard and does not wear glasses to cover his eyes (clearly, the narrator would be more comfortable if he did wear glasses, since that would help him from direct confrontation with another person). The narrator is also shocked when he learns that Robert had met, married, and buried Beulah all without ever having seen what she looked like: "It was beyond my understanding," he says, a statement that hardly surprises the reader since the narrator himself is "blind" to the realities of people different from himself, those who do not share his biases and limitations.

When Robert arrives, the narrator is further surprised that the blind man, in shaking hands, "squeezed hard, held my hand," an emblem of Robert's outgoing, people-oriented nature. As this scene proceeds, and the three characters share drinks and then dinner together, the narrator is impressed by Robert's appetite for life: he loves to drink Scotch, he eats his dinner with gusto, and he is willing to try marijuana though he has never smoked dope before. The narrator's attitude toward Robert has begun to change: "I watched with admiration," he says, as the blind man tucks into his dinner. After the meal, when the wife leaves briefly to change clothes, and the narrator and Robert are left together, the narrator continues to warm to his guest, who is so kind-hearted and friendly that even the originally dour and caustic narrator has begun to relax and enjoy himself in the man's presence.

When the wife returns to the living room and the three begin to watch television together (the blind man joking that he can tell whether a set is color or black-and-white, an example of his self-effacing charm), they confront a documentary on cathedrals built in the Middle Ages. In the final scene, the narrator is motivated by a desire to help the blind man "see" what a cathedral looks like, since he reasons that the word "cathedral" means nothing to Robert. At this point, Robert has a typically creative idea, suggesting that the narrator get a piece of paper and pencil so they can draw a cathedral together, the blind man's hand atop the narrator's. As the narrator is drawing, Robert tells him to "close your eyes," an action that of course helps bring the narrator into Robert's sightless world. But in fact, the narrator is achieving a spiritual vision of communion, which the symbol of the cathedral aptly illustrates. Though Robert suggests, after a time, that the narrator can open his eyes again, the narrator voluntarily keeps them shut, enjoying his moment of epiphanic transcendence: "I had my eyes closed. I thought I'd keep them that way for a little longer. I thought it was something I ought to do." The narrator has clearly escaped the bounds of his previously stingy and self-enclosed world: "I was in my house," he says. "I knew that. But I didn't feel like I was inside anything."

Wadsworth has provided an excellent film version of this story, along with an interview with Tess Gallagher, Raymond Carver's widow. In the interview, Gallagher offers the biographical information that the story was written at a time when the alcoholic Carver had been sober for several years and was achieving a breakthrough in his life and work, and that "Cathedral" is the major story of this breakthrough period.   GJ

John Cheever   The Swimmer (page 529)

QUESTIONS

1. What is Neddy's reason for wanting to "swim across the county"? Is this presented as a plausible motivation? Is it more plausible in a man called "Neddy" than in a man named "Edward"?
2. The point of view of the story is omniscient, but is more or less limited to Neddy's consciousness. At what point in the story is it more strictly limited? How are those limitations related to the plot and theme?
3. Collect examples of Neddy's definitions and evaluations of himself, and of the social world around him. Is he consistent in his self-estimations? How do you account for his attitude toward (a) the Biswangers (b) the Hallorans, (c) the crowd at the public pool?
4. What is the social structure of Neddy's world? What are its rituals and customs? How does it contrast with the life at the public pool? Are there stratifications within it? Is Neddy typical or untypical of his social set? What about this social world is appealing, and what is judged satirically?
5. Is there a particular place where the story clearly begins employing fantasy? What nonrealistic distortions of time and its effect on weather are manifested? How old is the protagonist at the end of the story? What truth about Neddy and about his social world is manifested in the fantasy?
6. What incidents in Neddy's life must be inferred from the words and actions of other characters, because they are not registered directly in Neddy's consciousness? What does the psychological suppression of these incidents add to the characterization of Neddy?
7. In the second paragraph of the story, the narrator reports of Neddy that "he might have been compared to a summer's day." Do you recognize the literary allusion here? (Consult Shakespeare's Sonnet 18, "Shall I compare thee to a summer's day," and consider the relevance of the poem to Neddy Merrill's estimation of himself and his youth.)
8. Define the conflicts presented in the story. Do they include man-against-himself? Is Neddy a developing character? What theme is expressed by the plot of the story?

Neddy or Ned Merrill (not Edward, but only the boyish nicknames) undertakes a whimsical pilgrimage, a journey of exploration and discovery intended to lend support to his semi-heroic, self-satisfied feeling about himself, the first man to swim across the county. But the realistic narration, the matter-of-fact tone, and the limited third-person point of view create a somber fantasy satirizing both Neddy and his social world. At what point does the fantasy begin? It is really difficult to say: certainly after the welcomed but destructive thunderstorm, the time races through the day and through seasons, the warm midsummer becomes a chill autumn, the vigorous and virile protagonist is debilitated and sapped of strength and dignity. But even before these overt signals, the story has given a sense of its allegorical framework, as Neddy leaves a poolside party of the hungover and visits, in order, a party at the Grahams' just getting underway, a party at the Bunkers' in full swing, and the eerily deserted site of a party at the Levys'. Neddy's pilgrimage is not only geographical but also social, across a landscape familiar in its customs and in "the rigid and undemocratic realities" of its society.

As Cheever is renowned as the fictional explorer of suburbia, so Neddy's trek displays the attractive and unattractive features of that social landscape. This is a world of leisure, parties, overindulgence in food and drink, and material accumulation; yet it also worships sport, youth, vitality, friendliness. In its artificiality it has created a "river" of swimming pools that allows the protagonist to go exploring, though its denizens display a broad range of attitudes toward naturalness (including the eccentric nudists). Its morality is easy, condoning adultery and snobbery. Success, as displayed in possessions, seems its highest value.

Neddy's journey takes him not only across this social world but also through his own history, though there the landscape is less familiar, both to Neddy and to the reader. As Neddy asks himself, "Was his memory failing or had he so disciplined it in the repression of unpleasant facts that he had damaged his sense of the truth?" For Neddy has become so secure and confident in his relationships, so practiced in maintaining his youthful attitudes and outlook, and so incapable of self-examination that he has been unable to comprehend what has happened to him: his loss of fortune, stability, family, and health. As naturally as day passes to night or summer to autumn, Neddy has descended from his apex—but without recognizing the signs of it, so that each change seems a fresh and inexplicable shock of loss. The naiveté of his boyish charm is also a barrier to self-knowledge. His "determinedly original" mind is one that has not been shaped by experience, so like an adolescent he has a "vague and modest idea of himself as a legendary figure . . . a man with a destiny."

Cheever takes Neddy from the fullness of his complacency to the emptiness of his reality—and then leaves him there, shivering outside his locked and deserted house, leaves him with the potentiality of self-discovery but without any implication that Neddy will proceed to know himself. Will he, like Goodman Brown, live on as a bitter, poisoned pessimist? Will he, like Miss Brill, manage to put these experiences away in a box? Will he, like Fitzgerald's Dick Ragland, escape from his losses by an ultimate act of despair? Or will he revert to his old habits and find ways of rationalizing and shifting the responsibility from himself?

The allegory here moves symbolically from summer to chill, and from a fully supported social existence to desolation. In the second paragraph the narrator paraphrases Neddy's abundant good feeling about himself: "he might have been compared to a summer's day," alluding to Shakespeare's Sonnet 18, that lovely, extravagant proclamation of the triumph of youthful beauty over all the ravages of time. At the end Neddy is left in the condition of another Shakespeare creature, "unaccommodated man . . . a poor, bare, forked animal" suffering loneliness, desolation, and terror. Is Neddy Merrill ready now, finally, to explore the meaning of being human?

This story has received considerable critical attention. Among the most useful analyses are Robert M. Slabey's "John Cheever: The 'Swimming' of America," Eugene Chesnick's "The Domesticated Stroke of John Cheever," and Stephen C. Moore's "The Hero on the 5:42: John Cheever's Short Fiction," all collected in R. G. Colling, *Critical Essays on John Cheever* (Boston: Hall, 1982).

A Columbia Pictures adaptation of this story starring Burt Lancaster (1968) is available on DVD and videocassette. Although it devises more elaborate scenes of Neddy's encounters on his journey, it is faithful to the tone and meaning of the story.   TRA

Judith Ortiz Cofer   American History (page 539)

QUESTIONS

1. Discuss the social hierarchy outlined by this story. How do the people of differing races and social backgrounds interact? How is the different background of the narrator and Eugene significant?
2. Explore the significance of the title. Why is the very broad title appropriate to such a brief, personal tale?
3. Why is the story set around the time of John Kennedy's assassination? How does this historical context add meaning to the story?
4. How old is the narrator? How is her age important in establishing her characterization?
5. Discuss the story's use of symbolic detail.

This brief story deals with a young Puerto Rican girl, the narrator, who in ninth grade has an infatuation with one of her "Anglo" classmates, named Eugene. Written in the form of a fictional memoir, the first-person account carefully places this very private memory in the context of one of the most notorious historical events of the twentieth century, the assassination of President John F. Kennedy.

The narrator recounts a memory that all Americans of a certain age share: remembering where they were when they got news of Kennedy's death. The story richly details the narrator's home and school life during that autumn of 1963. Her neighborhood in Paterson, New Jersey, represents the American melting pot; her school has black, white, and Hispanic students; her apartment house, known as "El Building," houses Puerto Rican immigrants, while the only house in the neighborhood with a yard and trees has been occupied until recently by an elderly Jewish couple, on whose relatively affluent life the narrator has spied wistfully. In the present time of the story, Eugene and his family have moved into the Jewish couple's former residence, and the narrator dreams of getting to know Eugene.

When she finally gets up the nerve to introduce herself to him ("I was ready for rejection, snobbery, the worst"), she is pleasantly surprised that Eugene seems to like her. A quiet, studious boy, Eugene is viewed by the thoughtful narrator as a kind of soul-mate and potential boyfriend. (The narrator has just turned fourteen and has begun menstruating; her sexual awakening coincides with her infatuation with Eugene as well as with the much larger political change heralded by the assassination.) On the day Kennedy is killed, her rather ordinary plans to visit Eugene's house for the first time so they can study together initiate the story's painful epiphany.

Eugene's house has a green front door, which the narrator sees as a symbol of hope on this epochal day in American history. However, when she knocks on the door, she is confronted by Eugene's mother, an insensitive nurse who gestures callously toward El Building (which now looks to the narrator like "a gray prison") and asks if she lives there. The woman apparently associates her with a lower class of undesirable immigrants, for she refuses to let the narrator inside and tells her that Eugene doesn't want to study with her. (This moment of confrontation with an insensitive and "foreign" adult may be compared with the epiphany in Joyce's "Araby," when the boy overhears some Englishmen flirting with a shopgirl and experiences his own moment of romantic disillusionment.) The girl goes home and, her mother having stressed to her the importance of this day, lies in bed "trying to feel the right thing for our dead president." But, being only fourteen, she cannot grasp the historical ramifications of the assassination, being too wrapped up in her own private heartbreak. She closes with the symbolism of the snowfall, which the story has already set up as an emblem of purity that the air and grit of Paterson turns "gray," the hopeless color of her apartment building. Like the boy in "Araby," the narrator has suffered the painful loss of romantic idealism in a world whose idealized American hero, like her own hopes, has perished.   GJ

Stephen Crane   The Bride Comes to Yellow Sky (page 546)

QUESTIONS

1. Like many western stories and movies, this one has the classical confrontation of town marshal and desperado. In what way does it differ from the expected stereotype? Where does the interest of the story lie?
2. The story is built around a number of ironic contrasts. Explore each of these for what it contributes to the theme:
   a. Jack Potter's behavior on the train, especially as it approaches Yellow Sky: the contrast between his thoughts and feelings, and his actions and speeches.
   b. Scratchy Wilson's sense of his role, and his costume and actions.
   c. Mrs. Potter's attitude toward her puff sleeves and her view of her new position in life.
   d. The décor of the parlor car and the appearance of the main street in Yellow Sky.
3. Although written in the omniscient point of view, the story frequently presents visual details as they are perceived by one or another of the characters. Show how these moments of limited point of view are used to reveal character (include the barkeeper's dog).

4. What does the image in the last sentence of the story reveal about what has happened to Yellow Sky?

Time has run out for the old way of life in Yellow Sky. In the last sentence of the story, Scratchy Wilson's boot heels leave "funnel-shaped tracks in the heavy sand," the last vortex as the sands flow through the hourglass. But the story ironically and steadfastly refuses to sentimentalize either the rough masculinity of the old West or the domesticating femininity of the East, which is replacing it. Crane's comic irony consistently undercuts the expected stereotypes of both ways of life, providing detail after detail to demonstrate the shortcomings of both. "The dignity of motion" of "the great Pullman" in the first paragraph immediately sets up the central theme: as the train speeds westward the perspective of its passengers makes it seem that the "plains of Texas [are] pouring eastward"—not as one might have supposed, that eastern values are rushing west (as they certainly are) but that the West is rushing to easternize itself. This visual first impression is subsequently supported by the portraits of Jack Potter and his unnamed bride. He had traveled eastward, but not to the East, to fetch himself a wife from San Antonio. In the civilized sumptuousness of the parlor car, a glittering parody of elegance, surrounded by more worldly passengers and tyrannically highbrow railroad personnel, Potter is extremely ill at ease and yet proud of his transformation, and his bride, whose hands are probably as red as his (from cooking rather than from outdoor work), preens herself on her stylish "puff sleeves" at the same time that they embarrass her. These two self-conscious westerners have decked themselves out in eastern garb and are on their way to carry style into Yellow Sky country. To the blasé characters on the train they are a joke, two overdressed hicks posing as sophisticates; to themselves, although they are too shy to acknowledge it, they are terribly apprehensive about how Yellow Sky will react to the new roles they believe they have adopted.

The second section of the story backtracks chronologically, from 3:42 when the train arrives, to 3:21 when the action in Yellow Sky begins. Any expectations about the wildness of the Wild West are immediately overturned: the saloon is not the Golden Nugget or the Last Chance, but the "Weary Gentleman"; its patrons are not macho cowboys and gunslingers but a garrulous traveling salesman whose jokes fall flat, three taciturn locals, and two Mexican sheepherders; the rest of the town is dozing through the hot afternoon. While the townspeople may occasionally kick a dog on the boardwalk, showing the motiveless brutality associated with a frontier town, the processes of civilization have already taken root in "vivid green grass-plots" carefully nurtured in the inhospitable natural climate.

Only Scratchy Wilson remains as a vestige of the stereotypical gunslinger (and the bachelor Marshal Potter was his law-and-order counterpart, the only man who could master him). "About the last one of the old gang that used to hang out along the river," Wilson has come to town on one of his regular drunken sprees to shoot up Yellow Sky. But how wild is this last representative of the West? Tricked out in his garishly decorated boots and his maroon-colored flannel shirt from the garment district of New York City, he displays his prowess by terrifying the barkeeper's dog. In the final confrontation with the marshal, Scratchy uncomprehendingly surrenders to the fact that his nemesis is not only unarmed but married—the game between them, playing out those old western roles, is "all off now."

What Crane demonstrates throughout the story are the false assumptions that the characters have about their roles and how other people see them. With relentless but good-humored irony, he punctures one after another— the manly hero, the blushing bride, the vicious desperado, the blasé sophisticate, the witty drummer—but most of all, the readers' own assumptions about frontier life. All are subjected to the test of reality, and all collapse in a comic heap.   TRA

William Faulkner A Rose for Emily (page 556)

QUESTIONS

1. Can you establish a clear chronology for all the events in Emily's life in the order in which they occurred? How is the issue of chronology related to the larger thematic design of the story?
2. Discuss the physical descriptions of Emily Grierson at various points in the story. How do they help to characterize her? Do they also help to characterize the narrator?
3. Analyze the characterization of Homer Barron, and compare him to the character of Emily's father. Is Homer Barron's name significant? Is he a static or a developing character?
4. What is the effect of the final paragraph? How does it change the reader's attitude toward Emily and her fate?
5. What are the advantages of first-person plural point of view in this story? What would be lost if it were told in first-person singular, by one of the townspeople, or in third-person limited point of view?
6. How is the point of view related to the plot structure? What might be the rationale for dividing the story into five distinct sections and for violating narrative chronology?
7. In an interview, Faulkner said that "A Rose for Emily" was a kind of "ghost story." Compare it to other ghost stories you have read.

"Thus she passed from generation to generation—dear, inescapable, impervious, tranquil, and perverse" (paragraph 51): as a transitional sentence leading to the double surprise ending, this summary of Emily Grierson's life captures much of the ambivalence that the townspeople felt about her. Had the summary come after the discovery of Emily's ghastly secret, that she had continued well into her old age to lie with the decayed corpse of the man she poisoned, there might well have been other adjectives—"ghoulish, necrophiliac, insane," for example.

The suspense that comes from withheld information is one of the strategies of this gothic tale. Another is the apparently jumbled chronology, beginning with "when Miss Emily Grierson died" and then backtracking through the visible (or surmised) events of her observable life, but not moving consecutively from earlier to later. Section 1, after a symbolic, introductory generalization about her house, recounts two incidents involving her tax remission: in 1894, on the death of her father, courtly Colonel Sartoris used his mayoral prerogative to remit her taxes "into perpetuity"; in approximately 1926, thirty years after the town fathers tried to eliminate the stench of death from her premises by spreading lime, the new generation of officials tried to collect taxes from her but were rebuffed by her laconic repetition, " 'I have no taxes in Jefferson.' "

In Section 2, the episode of the smell of her rotting sweetheart is reported, reverting in time to 1896, two years after her father's death and when Miss Emily was in her thirties and beginning to elicit the sympathy of the townspeople for her spinsterhood. Her pitiable situation (as they saw it) reminds them of the first indication of an unbalanced mind, when in 1894 she refused to acknowledge her father's death, then "broke down" and permitted his corpse to be buried—an incident foreshadowing the surprise ending.

Section 3 turns to 1895 and the first appearance of Homer Barron and his courtship of Miss Emily. Once again, the pity of the town is aroused, this time not by her lonely unmarried condition but by the scandal of her taking up with a common Yankee laborer. And then once again the narrative returns to 1896, when beset by her Alabama cousins, Miss Emily buys the "rat poison" that puts the finish to Homer Barron and any chance of marriage.

The fourth section summarizes her preparation for marriage, the minister's wife's summoning of the cousins to prevent any further damage to her reputation from consorting with the Yankee, her preparations to marry despite their intervention, and Homer's last appearance alive, entering via the kitchen door. Except for a recollection of her china-painting lessons for a few years in the early 1900s, from this point on the chronology is straightforward as her seclusion deepens, her waist broadens, and her health gradually fails. Her death came at about the same time as the publication of the story, at the end of the 1920s. R.I.P. Emily Grierson, 1856?–1929?

But not quite at peace, of course, for the final section in the present opens up the bedroom that no one except Emily had seen in forty years, the time span from just before her father's death to the present. And there the townspeople make their gruesome discovery. Miss Emily had bought Homer his toiletries, his wedding suit, the nightshirt for the bridal bed, and then had murdered him; she had preserved his body in the bridal chamber; and she had even in her old age lain with that body.

The random chronology in reporting these unhappy and even disgusting events is a reflection of the attitude of the point-of-view characters, that plural "we" and "our" who tell the tale, and in part it reveals the underlying meaning of a sensational story. The narrative is structured like a gossip's story, with reminiscences to and fro in time clustered around a series of object lessons. It is the structure of effective moralizing, each of the five sections designed to elicit a judgment of Miss Emily. The first (the tax remission) shows her eccentric pertinacity overcoming changing values; the second (her spinsterhood and madness at her father's death) arouses some pity but intensifies the impression of oddness; the third (the courting of Homer Barron, the purchase of arsenic) elicits gasps of scandal and shows the same steely determination as the tax episode. In the fourth section, Miss Emily's pathetic situation as a jilted woman, her increasing seclusion, and then her demise make her a figure of sentimental sympathy that gradually moves out of the picture. Finally, in the last section, the narrator springs the trap, creating shudders of disgust and horror as the long-kept secrets are divulged.

This narrative method creates suspense and the final shock. It also justifies certain lingering mysteries, because what the townspeople don't know can't be told. And that is chiefly the question of what Miss Emily actually felt, the motives that can only be guessed from the biased report of her actions. To take just one example, what exactly went wrong between her and Homer? Which of them brought their affair to an end? Did she bow to the social pressures of her Alabama cousins and reject him, even after she had bought his wedding outfit? Did his implied preference for younger men, his avowal "that he was not a marrying man," lead her to an act of vengeance when he refused her? And how long had she been contemplating the use of poison? Its purchase (in the narration) precedes the purchase of the gifts for Homer, but she buys both the gifts and the poison while the cousins are in her house. Are they the potential targets? Could she have been considering suicide, as the narrator guesses?

These irresolvable mysteries contribute to the emotional effect of the story, and also reinforce the role of the first-person plural narration. What at first sounds like an authoritative, judgmental voice with its own sense of the meanings of the events is in fact limited in a very realistic way. It is the collective voice of observers who are not only limited by their attitudes but also by their literal inability to penetrate to the mysteries of Miss Emily's motives. When Faulkner referred to this as a "ghost story," he opened up another line of inquiry: who is the ghost here? Homer? Miss Emily? Or is the story itself like a ghost, haunting the imagination with its mysteries of personality? TRA

Zora Neale Hurston   The Gilded Six-Bits (page 564)

QUESTIONS

1. Describe as fully as you can the style of living of Missie May and Joe Banks. Are we asked to pity them for their socioeconomic situation, or to admire the way in which they have found happiness in their circumstances? What kind of value does Missie May place on gold?

2. Discuss the Saturday ritual of Joe's "chunking" money into his front door, and each character's behavior in the opening scene. What kind of playacting is going on, and what symbolic meaning does it have for them?
3. Characterize Otis D. Slemmons and the way the townspeople react to him. Why is he attractive to Joe and to Missie May? Why is Missie May skeptical about him?
4. Can you explain why Joe laughs when he discovers his wife in bed with Slemmons? Missie May expects Joe to desert her, but he doesn't. Why not? How is the conflict between them resolved?
5. Slemmons is undoubtedly the antagonist in the plot; is there as clear a sense of whether Joe or Missie May is the protagonist? After Slemmons departs, the Bankses are in conflict; can you identify protagonist/antagonist in their conflict?
6. How do you interpret the final action in the story, Joe's spending the gilded half-dollar on candy for Missie May and her baby? Are he and his wife developing characters?

This most-anthologized of Hurston's stories was also the last she published before concentrating on novels and folk studies. It has generally been praised critically, with one notable exception: in her introduction to a study of Nella Larsen, Deborah E. McDowell cites it as an example of stories whose protagonists retreat from the brink of independence and/or self-realization to return to a patriarchal order. She says of such fictional endings that they "sacrifice strong and emerging independent female identities to the most acceptable demands of literary and social history" (Introduction to Nella Larsen, *Quicksand* and *Passing* [New Brunswick: Rutgers UP, 1986], quoted by Adele S. Newson, *Zora Neale Hurston: A Reference Guide* [Boston: Hall, 1987] 76). Such an objection seems tendentious, however, wishing that Hurston had written a different story with a different protagonist, to satisfy the critic's desire for a story of female liberation. Hurston's story is rather more complex than that, for it presents a genuine puzzle about the identity of its protagonist. Can we so confidently say that Missie May Banks is the central character? Isn't there an equal claim to be made for Joe Banks? Certainly both of them experience inner conflicts about their roles in the marriage as well as the external conflict that separates them, and they share equally in the resolution of conflicts. One might as easily respond to McDowell that the ending is an unsatisfactory retreat by Joe from his potential independence.

For the story goes full circle, from the exuberance and playfulness of the role-playing that Missie May and Joe delight in, to a return to that same set of behaviors after the threat to their marriage gradually dissipates. It is not a plot based on developing characters, but on the loss and recovery of a prized and precious intimacy that is expressed in childlike pretenses. Once Missie May's strength returns, she promises that they can again share in the rough and tumble, tickling and teasing, that have been their characteristic means of expressing love.

In effect, the plot juxtaposes two social orders. One is that of Missie May and Joe, naive and unsophisticated, imitating in their adulthood many of the characteristics of adolescence and even childhood. The weekly game that they play on Joe's payday unconsciously defines two distinct male/female roles. On the one hand, the man throws money into the doorway as if he were buying love and attention (an archetype that evokes both King Lear and prostitution), and Missie May pretends to be angered by the cash-for-love implications. On the other hand, the man hides in his pockets candy, chewing gum, scented soap, and a handkerchief for the girl to discover and seize in their "friendly battle," as if he were her father and she a youngster who plays tickle and tussle with him. She has of course prepared for him all the delicious dinner treats that please him so, but at dinner they talk "very little, . . . that [talk] consist[s] of banter that pretend[s] to deny affection but in reality flaunt[s] it." This is very much the behavior of children or preteens for whom a declaration of affection is an embarrassment. It is not that Missie May and Joe are without a true and deep affection, but that in their simple code of behavior it must be expressed indirectly and ironically.

The other behavioral code is embodied in "Mister Otis D. Slemmons, of spots and places—Memphis, Chicago, Jacksonville, Philadelphia and so on," the sophisticated, womanizing braggart whose morality, like his gold pieces, is a sham. He is apparently the first of his kind encountered by Joe and Missie May, and in their innocence they are both gulled by him. Joe is plainly envious of him, with admiring hero-worship that makes him wish he had Slemmons's potbelly and his gold adornments as signs of affluence. Missie May is skeptical about him when she hears Joe's praise, but when she meets him she too wishes for the gold that marks his superiority—so that she might adorn Joe with it.

It is her desire to obtain the gold for Joe that leads her to prostitute herself with Slemmons, who promises to give it to her, causing the overt clash between the two behavioral codes. It isn't clear whether her tryst with Slemmons reached a climax, for the interruption of Joe's arrival sends Slemmons scurrying away in terror after trying to assuage Joe's anger with an offer of sixty-two dollars of "gold money." The upshot of Joe's struggle with Slemmons is that Joe gets the coin from the watch-chain, while Missie May's guilt leads to despair and depression because she has destroyed their marriage. Joe's behavior after the event expands upon the derisive laughter with which he discovered Slemmons and Missie May: rather than confront his wife with accusations or denunciations, he becomes aloof and detached. To her amazement, he doesn't desert her, but continues to depend on her for her household services.

Gradually Joe's coolness departs, and after three months he asks her to rub liniment on his aching back—and "before morning, youth triumphed and Missie exulted." Joe leaves her the gold coin, and she discovers that it is really only a gilded half-dollar—and is further depressed to think that Joe was now treating her like a fifty-cent whore. Joe repeats his pretense of an aching back every ten days or so, until after a few weeks he discovers her pregnancy, and Missie gives birth to a boy who is the "spittin' image" of Joe (as his mother even insists).

The last action of the story finally expunges Slemmons from their lives, as Joe spends the whole gilded half-dollar on the molasses kisses that Missie loves—a prodigious purchase, the shopkeeper thinks, and indeed it is a considerable amount of money for a man whose weekly wage ranges from nine to twelve dollars. The circular plot is completed when Joe returns home with the groceries, the candy, and genuine silver dollars for his wife. The protagonists have undergone a trial of their love, but at last resume the innocent honesty that had been threatened by sham and fraud.   TRA

Ha Jin   A Contract (page 575)

QUESTIONS
1. Explore the narrator's characterization. Is he an admirable character?
2. Based on your knowledge or research into recent Chinese history, what is the story depicting about the culture in which it is set?
3. What is the nature of the "contract"? What do its contents say about the narrator? What is the significance of Gu Gong's reaction to the contract?

Ha Jin grew up in China and served as a soldier in the Chinese army until moving to the United States to become a writer and a teacher of creative writing.

Though written in an unadorned and economical prose style, his stories and novels richly convey the late twentieth-century Chinese experience. In this very short piece, the narrator, Cheng, must deal with a subordinate who is lording it over his own subordinates and forcing them to perform menial tasks, such as emptying the basin in which he has washed his feet. The subordinate, Gu Gong, is thus disrupting military solidarity and attempting to establish an unacceptably demeaning hierarchical relationship among the soldiers.

Gu Gong insults Cheng and challenges him to a fight, an offer that Cheng, who is physically "not his match," wisely turns down. Instead he proposes that they engage in formal combat, with weapons, and he draws up a contract to seal the agreement. When he hears the contents of the contract, however, Gu Gong "turned shallow." Clearly, the narrator has been bluffing, but the bluff has paid off. Gu Gong returns to his bunk and "buried his head in his quilt," fearful of an honest, man-to-man encounter that does not allow him the advantage that his superior size would have given him in an ordinary fistfight.

The narrator closes by first fearing that he would be reprimanded for his creative solution to the problem with Gu Gong, but in fact he is praised for his effort and rewarded with a promotion, showing that a cool head and thoughtful strategy are superior to "manly" braggadocio in solving conflicts with others.   GJ

Herman Melville   Bartleby the Scrivener (page 579)

QUESTIONS

1. Identify the protagonist and define the kinds of conflict that make up the plot.
2. Characterize the staff at the Wall Street office before the arrival of Bartleby. How are they comic? Why does the lawyer not replace them?
3. Track the development of Bartleby's performance in his job at the office. Are there any verifiable reasons for his behavior? Is he a developing character?
4. How does the lawyer feel about Bartleby at the various stages of his story? Are his feelings clear to him? How do you feel about Bartleby as the story develops? Can you say for certain why he does what he does (or does not do what he does not)?
5. What kind of man is the lawyer? Is there any reason to disbelieve what he says about Bartleby or about himself and his reactions? Is he a good man? Is he a developing character?
6. What is tragic about Bartleby's story? What is comic about it? How are these emotions complementary?

As a narrative, this is a simple, straightforward story, with little plot complication, with a single external conflict that is fully resolved, and told by an observant and sensitive narrator. It is also profoundly enigmatic, and since the "rediscovery" of Melville early in the last century has aroused critical opinion of the widest divergence—not about its excellence, but about its theme. What does the simple story *mean*? To answer that, most have turned to an analysis of the characters of the protagonist/narrator and the antagonist/scrivener.

The interpretations cannot all be summarized or argued here, but this and the following paragraph contain a sampling of their points: the elderly lawyer who tells the tale is smug, obtuse, and unreliable, unable to understand either Bartleby or himself; he is defensive because he feels guilt for what happened to Bartleby; he is an exploitive representation of capitalism and business ethics who warps his clerks and destroys Bartleby; he is an exemplar of Christian forbearance and charity but is too cowardly or weak to act on these virtues; he is an ordinary man facing an extraordinary test, and does as much as could possibly be expected.

Bartleby is a Thoreauvian dissenter, using "passive resistance" to make a point about capitalist exploitation; he is a martyr whose death condemns the system represented by the lawyer; he is going insane; he is a writer who has learned that art is impossible because communication is impossible; he is a man who cannot cope with the complexity of human interaction, and withdraws into immobility and death.

For this note, two things need to be kept clear as an approach to the story: first, the character of Bartleby is enigmatic, and no amount of argument or research can penetrate it, for we can know only what the narrator knows, and Bartleby is an agonizing puzzle to him. Second, the narrator is a man who candidly confesses his puzzlement, who is jolted out of his complacency by the persistent truculence of Bartleby. He does his best to understand both the scrivener and his own reaction to him. He tries to discern the best course of action in a situation that baffles him, and therefore is constantly examining his possibilities and his motives.

The simple story is this: a pale and melancholy young man is given a job as a copyist in a law office on Wall Street and gradually refuses to perform his duties. Although he no longer works, he also refuses to leave the office and takes up residence there. The lawyer who has employed him vainly tries in various ways first to induce him to do his job, then to leave the premises. In frustration, the lawyer moves his establishment to another office, and the clerk is arrested by the new tenant of the Wall Street office, is imprisoned, and refusing to eat, dies.

The complication of the story arises from the lawyer's various attempts to cope with this unusual situation, and to search himself for an understanding of how he is responding and should respond. The lawyer is and remains ambivalent, for there is no way of explaining *why* Bartleby behaves as he does, nor can the lawyer figure out the best thing to do. His last exclamation ("Ah, Bartleby! ah, humanity!") reveals the depth of his anguish over what has happened to this young man, and what may happen to us all.

The story has that tragic dimension, the inexplicable self-destruction of a human being that touches so deeply. At the same time, it has its comic side, and readers are well advised not to overlook that, for the ambiguities of the theme are mirrored in the doubleness of its tone. Before the advent of Bartleby there is a Dickensian description of the other employees of the office, the odd three who have nicknamed each other Turkey, Nippers, and Ginger Nut. The first two of them have split personalities but together form a unity: Turkey is wonderfully efficient in the mornings until he has his lunchtime drinks, after which he is essentially incapable of good, steady work; Nippers is the opposite, except his problem seems not to be drink but perhaps an ulcer that pains him in the mornings until his midday meal. This complementary pair comically anticipate Bartleby's progress in the office, for at first he is marvelously efficient, and then he grows less and less useful. Ginger Nut, the office boy, does his chores with alacrity, and although he is ostensibly learning the law he seems to be only a typical twelve-year-old errand boy.

These caricatures are not however the type of comedy that reinforces the deeper ambivalences of the story. For that, we must look at some of the comic absurdities of the exchanges between Bartleby and the lawyer. Two examples (cited by McCall, below) will suffice. When the lawyer is desperately looking for something for Bartleby to do rather than stay on at the old office doing nothing, he suggests "going as a companion to Europe, to entertain some young gentleman with [his] conversation?" (paragraph 208)—a suggestion so incongruous as to be hilarious, for entertaining conversation is what Bartleby lacks altogether. In that same scene, as he approaches his old law office the lawyer comes upon Bartleby:

Going upstairs to my old haunt, there was Bartleby silently sitting upon the banister at the landing.

"What are you doing here, Bartleby?" said I.

"Sitting upon the banister," he mildly replied. (paragraphs 191–93)

This is deadpan humor, the statement of the literal fact as a response to a figurative question—the lawyer did not mean to ask what he was doing there, but why he was doing it. And Bartleby never answers "why" questions.

The famous " 'I would prefer not to' " which becomes Bartleby's only explanation shares in the kind of doubleness that the simultaneously tragic and comic story contains. "Prefer" has positive implications, a term used for those things we like or want or favor; it suggests desire *for* something. What Bartleby desires, however, is negative, "not to" do or have something. The key term thus has its own dimension of preposterousness, a simultaneous mingling of desire and denial, that makes Bartleby so inscrutably baffling.

I cite only one reference here (the standard bibliographical sources are available and daunting). Dan McCall in *The Silence of Bartleby* (Ithaca, NY: Cornell UP, 1989) presents a level-headed, sensible, and graceful account of the approaches taken by what he calls "the Bartleby Industry," and offers a sympathetic and sane interpretation of the story. His notes will guide the curious teacher into the labyrinth of other, more partial interpretations.

Two dramatized versions of this story are available on video, neither of them wholly satisfying but both of them suggestive enough for classroom use. A PBS production available from Films for the Humanities is entitled *Bartleby the Scrivener*, and is more faithful, even to the extent of having the unnamed narrator address the camera directly. The other, a feature film called simply *Bartleby*, adapts the story as a contemporary London drama, and has the advantage of two star actors, Paul Scofield and John McEnery. Either or both of these adaptations could provide interesting material for classroom discussion of the gains and losses involved in "translating" literary fiction to another medium.   TRA

Edgar Allan Poe The Cask of Amontillado (page 611)

QUESTIONS

1. Are there any clues to the motivation of Montresor's revenge beyond those in the opening sentence?
2. In carrying out his revenge, how does Montresor take advantage of (a) Fortunato's "one weakness," (b) the carnival season, (c) the catacombs? What similarity is there between the way he handles Fortunato and the way he handles his servants?
3. What kind of man is Montresor? Is he mad or sane? Rational or irrational? Emotional or unemotional? Explain.
4. What symbolic or ironic functions are served by (a) Fortunato's name; (b) his costume; (c) Montresor's name (in French, "my treasure"); (d) Montresor's coat of arms and family motto; (e) the carnival setting; (f) Montresor's account of his pleasure in meeting Fortunato on the street; (g) Montresor's reply to Fortunato's declaration, "I shall not die of a cough"; (h) Montresor's drinking "long life" to Fortunato; (i) Montresor's declaration that he too is a mason; (j) Montresor's

speech after fettering Fortunato,"Once more let me implore you to return"? Do you find any further examples?

5. Why and to whom is Montresor revealing his crime fifty years after he committed it?

6. Does Montresor's revenge satisfy his two criteria for perfect revenge? Why or why not?

Detective fiction and journalistic reportage are often concerned with the concept of "the perfect crime"—a murder or a train robbery so perfectly planned that its perpetrator is never apprehended or even identified. "The Cask of Amontillado" has most often been interpreted as the story of a perfect revenge. Montresor succeeds in making himself known to Fortunato, but to no one else, before taking Fortunato's life, and he plans the crime so successfully that it is still undiscovered after fifty years. Fortunato's death, moreover, is sufficiently lingering that he has time to meditate on his fate; his life is not instantly snuffed out as by a rifle shot. (The phrase "At length" in the story's first paragraph is open to two meanings.)

Many readers of the story feel, however, that in a psychological and spiritual sense the revenge has failed, that Montresor does not get from it the satisfaction he had anticipated, and that, ironically, Fortunato has in fact been taking revenge on Montresor for fifty years through the agency of Montresor's tormented conscience. The central interpretive issue of the story, then, is whether Montresor's revenge is, as judged by his own criteria, successful or unsuccessful.

When we reread carefully Montresor's two requirements for a successful revenge, we find that each is ambiguous. (1) "I must not only punish, but punish with impunity. A wrong is unredressed when retribution overtakes its redresser." Ambiguously, this statement does not tell us whether retribution by one's own conscience is included or excluded. (2) "[A wrong] is equally unredressed when the avenger fails to make himself felt as such to him who has done the wrong." The victim must know who killed him, and must recognize that the killing is an act of vengeance. Ambiguously, this principle does not tell whether the victim must know why he is being avenged, what he has done to provoke vengeance.

Those who view the revenge as unsuccessful state their case somewhat as follows: (1) Fortunato never understands what Montresor is doing, or why, but thinks it only "an excellent jest"; thus Montresor's second condition for a perfect revenge is never fully satisfied. (2) The key sentence of the story is Montresor's assertion   "My heart grew sick" in the final paragraph. Montresor's heartsickness is caused, not as he says by the dampness of the catacombs, but by a sudden nausea of guilt and hypocrisy. Thus Montresor's first condition for a perfect revenge is not satisfied. (3) Poe has taken pains to draw an ironic parallel between Montresor and Fortunato; both are from noble families; both are connoisseurs of wine; their names are similar in meaning; both wear carnival costumes; in different parts of the story each repeats the words of the other. The identification is completed when Montresor re-echoes the screams of Fortunato. "*Montresor. Fortunato.* Are these not synonymous?" asks one commentator. "Has not Montresor walled up himself in this revenge?" (Daniel Hoffman, *Poe Poe Poe* [New York: Random, 1985] 218–19, first published by Doubleday, 1972.) (4) The dead Fortunato, buried with Montresor's ancestors, may be said to have taken over the Montresor family motto, *Nemo me impune lacessit,* and to be punishing Montresor for his crime. (5) After fifty years of agonized mental torment, Montresor, very likely on his deathbed, feels compelled to confess his crime to his family priest. (6) Montresor's final words, "*In pace requiescat!*", are a plea for peace for himself—a peace he has not known for fifty years.

Most of the similarities noted in (3) above can be accounted for as well by the "successful revenge" theory as by the "failed revenge" theory. The similarity of names simply indicates that both are from noble, wealthy families. Both wear carnival costumes because it is the carnival season. Montresor imitates Fortunato's screaming to assure himself and to demonstrate to Fortunato that no one else is in hearing range. Only the first two points in (3) need more discussion.

Fortunato knows *who* is murdering him but doesn't know *why.* The evidence, in fact, suggests that he doesn't even know *how* he insulted Montresor, or even that he *has* insulted him; and Montresor is very careful not to let him know. "Neither by word nor deed," he says, "had I given Fortunato cause to doubt my good will." Indeed, Montresor throughout the story refers to Fortunato as his "friend," and, until the very end, treats him like one. Fortunato has no suspicion nor reason for suspicion that Montresor regards him as anything other than a friend.

What is the motivation for Montresor's action? Montresor claims that Fortunato has done him a "thousand injuries" and finally has "ventured upon insult." A "thousand" can be dismissed as overstatement, but what puzzles a contemporary American reader is the ranking of "insult" above "injury" as a motive for revenge. This story, written more than a century and a half ago, is set in Italy, where Old World families of noble descent were very much concerned with family "honor." For them an "insult," even a very slight one, might well be considered as worse than an injury, since the insult is aimed at family "honor," whereas an injury is more likely directed against family goods. Though neither the injuries nor the insult is specified in the story (possibly because Poe was after his "single effect" and wanted the reader to concentrate on the revenge and not upon its cause), there are some clues from which we may make inferences.

Shortly after they have entered the catacombs, Montresor proposes that they turn back: "You are rich, respected, admired, beloved; you are happy, as once I was." A short while later, in response to Fortunato's comment on the extensiveness of the vaults, Montresor replies, "The Montresors . . . were a great and numerous family." Fortunato says, "I forget your arms." Montresor replies, "A huge human foot d'or, in a field azure; the foot crushes a serpent rampant whose fangs are imbedded in the heel." "And the motto?" asks Fortunato. "*Nemo me impune lacessit.*" Montresor's use of present and past tenses in the remarks suggests that the Fortunato family is at the height of its power and prestige, while the Montresor family is in decline. That Fortunato has forgotten the Montresor arms reinforces this conclusion (and may constitute another such "insult," unconscious on Fortunato's part but perhaps as keenly felt by Montresor as the one that first provoked him). The family motto, "No one attacks me with impunity," recalls Montresor's first criterion for a successful revenge: "I must not only punish, but punish with impunity." In the coat of arms, as interpreted in this context, Fortunato's family is represented by the human foot and the Montresor family by the serpent. Putting all these considerations together, we may conclude that Montresor's revenge is motivated not necessarily by some personal insult but by some slight which in Montresor's mind impugns the family honor. Thus Montresor feels that he must perform the role of the snake in the family crest, else the motto will be a lie.

Possibly the most pointed questions one may ask in trying to decide whether Montresor's revenge is successful or unsuccessful concern the *tone* of the story and the identification of the person to whom it is told (addressed in the opening paragraph as "You, who so well know the nature of my soul"). Is this story a confession of guilt made to a father-confessor, by a man perhaps on his deathbed, who has been suffering agonies of conscience for the past fifty years? Or is it an account given to a kinsman or close friend of how the speaker preserved the integrity of the family motto? Although the four words "My heart grew sick" admittedly are a difficulty that interpreters favoring the successful-revenge theory must deal with, they seem to be a slight basis for positing fifty years of moral anguish; and, in fact, they offer an obstacle to the unsuccessful-revenge interpreters as well, for if the story is a "confession," why should Montresor explain this heartsickness as caused by "the dampness of the catacombs"? As to the *tone* of the story, I cannot find a word that expresses remorse or guilt or a pleading for forgiveness. I find, instead, a prideful voice that says, in effect, See how clever I was in preparing a niche for Fortunato in the catacombs, in assuring that my servants would not be present, in luring my enemy there, and, in fact, in managing the whole affair. The tone is boastful or gloating rather than contrite. And why that half century between the doing and the telling? It is a good round number. But if Montresor is suffering agonies of conscience, why should he not seek an earlier absolution? On the other hand, if he was seeking the perfect revenge, a condition of his definition (the avenger must "punish with impunity. A wrong is unredressed when retribution overtakes its redresser") requires a waiting period before it can be known whether this condition has been met. For this use, a good round number would be expected, and fifty years would seem more than ample. But Montresor is capable of patience, as he showed early on in the interval between the planning of his revenge and his execution of it.

I do not wish to referee this revenge dispute. The critics who have argued for the failed revenge have done so much more persuasively and more fully than I have been able to do for them here. And indeed their interpretation adds one more irony—a crowning one—to the pervasive ironies that any reading of the story must acknowledge. Rather than commit myself firmly to either side, I provide a selected list of critiques for further reading.

Successful revenge:
Kenneth Kempton, *The Short Story* (Cambridge: Harvard UP, 1947) 86–89; Joseph J. Moldenhauer, "Murder as a Fine Art: Connections Between Poe's Aesthetics, Psychology, and Moral Vision," *PMLA* 83 (1968): 284–97; Marvin Felheim, "The Cask of Amontillado," *Notes & Queries* 199 (1954): 447–48; Terence Martin, "The Imagination at Play," *Kenyan Review* 28 (1966): 195–98.

Unsuccessful revenge:
Robert Foulke and Paul Smith, *An Anatomy of Literature* (New York: Harcourt, 1972) 873, 876–80; James W. Gargano, "'The Cask of Amontillado': Masquerade of Motive and Identity," *Studies in Short Fiction* 4 (1967): 119–26; Charles A. Sweet, Jr., "Recapping Poe's 'Cask of Amontillado,'" *Poe Studies* 7 (June 1974): 10–12; Sam Moon, *Notes & Queries* 199 (1954): 448; Donald Pearce, "'The Cask of Amontillado,'" *Notes & Queries* 199 (1954): 448–49; Richard H. Fossum, "Poe's 'The Cask of Amontillado,'" *Explicator* 17 (1958): item 16.   LP

Elizabeth Tallent   No One's a Mystery (page 617)

QUESTIONS
1. Describe the characterization of the two principal characters. What details help to define their characters?
2. What is the significance of the girl's age? How would the story be different if she were either older or younger?
3. How does the setting contribute to the story's meaning? Contrast the setting with that in Hemingway's "Hills Like White Elephants."
4. Why is there a mention of the wife passing by in her Cadillac? What is the dramatic significance of this moment in the story?
5. Other than sexual enjoyment, what does each character gain from this relationship? Will the relationship, in the long run, turn out to have been an important one for the girl?
6. Explore the significance of the title.

This very short story economically portrays a romantic relationship between a teenager and her considerably older lover. There is a strong suggestion that the affair will not last much longer, since the couple has reached a crossroads in their relationship. For this reason, the story may be fruitfully compared with Hemingway's "Hills Like White Elephants" (page 268), a narrative of similar length that also dramatizes, mostly through dialogue, two lovers' very different views on the future of their romance.

Here the lovers are contrasted through their differing attitudes toward the affair, the narrator as an idealistic eighteen-year-old who fantasizes that her lover will ultimately leave his wife and marry her, leading to a blissful marriage with two idealized children, the lover a somewhat jaded older man who clearly has no intentions of divorcing and who seems to be encouraging his girlfriend to be more realistic about the frankly sexual and temporary nature of their relationship. The opening scene deftly portrays the power differential between the two: by pushing the girl down onto the floorboard of his truck, a degrading position where she is down among discarded beer pop-tops and his manure-covered boots, Jack demonstrates the girl's subjugated and undignified position in their romance. Their drinking of tequila and their need to hide the girl from view of his wife passing in her Cadillac further underscore the furtive and illicit behavior to which the couple is accustomed.

Jack has further emphasized the girl's youth and inexperience by giving her a five-year diary for her eighteenth birthday, a gift normally associated with much younger girls and one suggesting that he would like her to reflect, through diary entries, on her life and on the fact that she would be better off without Jack; he also implies that she is like a "little kid" in her naiveté. Students typically have differing reactions to Jack's characterization, which can lead to lively discussion: is he a complete cad and even a "pervert," since he has become involved with an underage girl (they have clearly been having sex long before the eighteenth birthday arrives); or is he to be admired for trying to shatter the girl's self-destructive idealism regarding their affair?

The setting—all the action takes place outside Cheyenne, Wyoming, in a truck moving down a heat-drenched highway—further suggests the transient nature of their doomed romance. (Here too there are similarities to the Hemingway story, which is set in a train station where the lovers and everyone around them are about to travel somewhere else.) The dialogue, in which the two characters argue in a light-hearted but meaningful way over what the girl will write in her diary, succinctly dramatizes their differing perspectives. While the girl imagines a marriage in which she will prepare gourmet meals for them to enjoy when Jack arrives home and she will have beautifully named children, Jack supposes that she will recall the affair with an "old guy" whose name she can't even remember. The last few lines of the dialogue portray the lovers as hopelessly at odds, with Jack's concluding salvo offering the girl a gentle insult that he hopes, presumably, will puncture her romantic daydreams about the future.

What is the significance of the title? They are listening to a song on the tape deck by Roseanne Cash entitled "No One's a Mystery": the song title is also appropriate for the story because we come to see so clearly, in approximately two pages of text, that the girl's infatuation is balanced perfectly against Jack's cynicism. The situation is clear and anything but mysterious to an objective observer—i.e., the reader. Both characters stand revealed as temporary lovers whose affair will someday be viewed by the girl, once she is thoroughly disillusioned, as a coming-of-age experience that marked her entry into a mature awareness of herself and of the bittersweet nature of adult relationships.   GJ

John Updike   A & P *(page 619)*

QUESTIONS

1. What characteristics of American society in the years leading up to the date of the publication of the story (1960) are represented here? How does Sammy feel about contemporary social values?
2. In what ways is Sammy a representation of those social values? Why does he contrast his family parties with what he imagines about the parties of Queenie's family? Would he prefer the latter?
3. How do the customers in the supermarket react to the appearance of Queenie and her friends? How does the manager Lengel react to them? How do other employees react to them?
4. Why does Sammy quit his job? Does he hope to gain anything from doing so?
5. Explain the last sentence of the story.
6. Why is the first-person narration of this story appropriate? Is Sammy a totally reliable narrator, or is there some irony directed at him?

The title refers to the supermarket chain (formally called The Great Atlantic and Pacific Tea Company) that was predominant in America at the time the story was written. It is probably necessary to inform students of that, and to provide them with some background about the 1950s when Sammy would have been forming his ideas—the "Eisenhower years" characterized by social conformity, consumerism, and the Cold War (it's to the last of these that Sammy alludes when he parodies the name of the supermarket with his prediction that in 1990 it will be "the Great Alexandrov and Petrooshki Tea Company" [9] when Soviet-style total conformity will have taken over).

Social conformity is central to the conflict, represented in various ways even before Sammy makes his rebellious gesture, and his attitude toward it is expressed in his remarks about the "sheep"-like customers of the store who stare at the half-naked girls and then when Sammy resigns knock against each other to avoid his check-out lane "like scared pigs in a chute" (30). Sammy himself has been enlisted into the flock of conformists by accepting his parents' pressures and donning the apron with his name on it and the bow-tie belonging to the A & P, but his resentment shows through the ironic way in which he describes the store and its customers. He is ready for a life-changing stance even before the girls' nonconformist appearance.

Sammy's overt motivation is driven by lust, of course. He dwells on the physical attractions of the girls—even the less-perfect companions of the girl he nicknames "Queenie." At nineteen, in late adolescence and with minimal responsibility, he is drawn to the girls and thus repulsed by Lengel's "policy." For Sammy, both the attraction and the repulsion function to drive him to his noble self-sacrifice. He chooses nonconformity over the narrow-minded judgmentalism of Lengel and the shoppers, and of course sides with the other men who appreciate and lust for the girls—the not-quite-domesticated Stokesie with his wife and two children, the ogling butcher McMahon who even evokes Sammy's pity for girls who don't know how they are arousing a lecher. Sammy is not so coarse in his admiration of them, but his hormones are just as active.

The act of rebellion is a response to the "Sunday-school-superintendent" lecturing of Lengel. It means that Sammy will no longer accept the restrictive values of this puritanical society, and will move on to develop his own more liberal values. But as the final line of the story acknowledges, he feels "how hard the world [is] going to be to [him thereafter]." Provoked by the unkind treatment of the girls and drawn by their appeal, he's taken a new and more difficult direction.

The DVD dramatization of the story available from Wadsworth (originally a part of the PBS American Short Story series of the mid-1980s) inevitably drops much of the first-person narration and expands on the descriptive materials. It stars Sean Hayes, a familiar actor from the television series *Will and Grace*, and is accompanied by an intelligent interview with John Updike.   TRA

Thomas Wolfe   The Child by Tiger (page 625)

QUESTIONS

1. Discuss the setting of the story (assuming for the purpose that the action takes place roughly twenty-five years before the first publication in 1937, as suggested by the first sentence). How important are time and place to the events and attitudes of various characters? How much do we learn about the town and its people? On what implicit premise are the black-white relationships in this town based? How does the use of offensive language contribute to your understanding of the characters and the time?
2. The story begins and ends with stanzas from William Blake's poem, "The Tiger." How does this poem relate to the theme of the story? If you are not familiar with it, look it up and read the whole poem. How is it related to the passage in the Bible to which Dick's Bible was left open (paragraphs 118-21)?
3. What kinds of mysteries does this story contain? To what extent are these resolved?
4. Dick Prosser's character consists of many contradictions. In his contradictions, is Dick completely unlike the people of the white community? Why does he "go crazy"? Is he a plausible character?
5. What feelings and considerations motivate the whites in tracking Dick down? What meaning has Dick's final gesture of removing his shoes and awaiting the

posse (paragraph 102)? How does this action contrast with the way his body is treated by the whites?

6. The story continues for several pages after its climactic event, Dick's death. Why? What theme is expressed in the final pages?

7. The narrator tells the story twenty-five years after its events took place. What importance does this removal in time have for the meaning of the story? Should we identify the author with the attitudes of the narrator as a boy? As a man?

Originally published in *The Saturday Evening Post* for September 11, 1937, and reprinted in *Post Stories of 1937* (Boston: Little, Brown, 1938), "The Child by Tiger" was afterward slightly altered and expanded by Wolfe for inclusion as Chapter 8 in his novel *The Web and the Rock* (New York: Harper, 1939). The earlier version is used here because, written to be a short story rather than part of a novel, it has a self-contained self-sufficiency that the later version lacks. The chief change between the two versions is an alteration in the point of view. The short story is told from the first-person point of view with the boy (named Spangler) as narrator. The novel uses the limited third-person point of view. The reason for the change is that the boy, who is only a minor character in the short story, becomes the central character of the novel (though, renamed "Monk" Webber, he remains an observer in this episode). For a story told from the angle of vision of an observer rather than a participant, first-person point of view is ideally adapted, for it has greater naturalness and immediacy than other points of view, and there is seldom need for the author to tell us more about the narrator than he can tell us about himself. Use of the limited third-person point of view, as pointed out in Chapter 5, is extremely rare when the viewpoint is that of a minor character. Wolfe shifted to this point of view for his novel probably for two reasons: first, with the minor character now his major character, he did need to tell us more about him than the protagonist could believably tell us; second, he wished as much as possible to avoid identification of the protagonist with himself, for which he had been criticized in his earlier novels.

Like "The Most Dangerous Game," "The Child by Tiger" is the story of a manhunt, complete with the use of hounds; but in setting, plot, character—in almost all respects—it is more credible, more complex, and more significant.

The most significant fact about the town that furnishes the setting of the story (in the novel it is called Libya Hill and is clearly a fictional version of Asheville, North Carolina, where Wolfe grew up) is that its social and economic structure is based on white dominance over blacks. It is a town where blacks work as chauffeurs, handymen, cooks, and Pullman porters, and where the mayor, the police, the professional men, and most of the shop owners are white. Blacks have a choice of living in basement rooms or in "Niggertown"; the best parts of town are reserved for whites. The spectrum of white inhabitants of the town extends from decent people like the Sheppertons, who are kindly to their colored help; to vicious types like Lon Everett, the sot who smashes Dick in the face after drunkenly running into him; to Ben Pounders, the ferret-faced, mongrel-mouthed "collector of usurious lendings to the blacks," who boasts of putting the first shot into Dick.

The conflicts of the story, however, do not just involve blacks against whites. Dick's maniacal outburst is triggered by conflict with a black man over possession of a black woman, and, when he goes berserk, he kills indiscriminately, black or white. The whites are also in conflict with one another. Mayor Will Hendershot, Hugh McNair, and one or two others make a heroic effort to protect Cash Eager's hardware shop and to keep the mob from lynch law.

Yet the origins of Dick's craziness, insofar as they are not part of the mystery of all human nature, lie clearly in the racial situation of the town and region. A man of superior abilities and gifts, Dick must take work tending the furnace and driving a car. A grown man of over thirty, he has learned to flatter the children of the white race by addressing them as "Cap'n" and "Mr." A highly religious man, he waits for his white employers on Sundays standing at the side door of the white church, "holding his chauffeur's hat respectfully in his hand." Unjustly struck in the face by a drunken white man, he knows that, to keep out of trouble, he must keep his hands at his sides and let himself be struck again. Discovered with a rifle in his room by the white boys, he knows that it may be taken away from him unless he gives an acceptable explanation for possessing it, and he does so by inventing a falsehood. In short, Dick functions constantly in situations that are an affront to his human dignity and abilities, and he constantly suppresses his instinctive reactions to such situations until suppression itself has become a kind of second instinct. The strain of these suppressions, shown only occasionally in a narrowing and reddening of his eyes, is what leads to Dick's homicidal outburst. Yet Dick is not conscious of being oppressed by a white society; he has merely adjusted, subconsciously, to what seems to him the natural order of things. His outbreak, therefore, does not take the form of turning against whites. He goes truly crazy: he turns against everybody.

The theme of the story has to do with the mysterious presence of violence, savagery, and evil in the human soul. Dick is a symbol of that destructive violence, as is the tiger in Blake's poem. From the beginning of the story, Dick is identified with that tiger or with the offspring of that tiger. He gathers up the football "in his great black paw," at boxing he is "as cunning and crafty as a cat," he moves softly and swiftly and "sometimes like a cat" leaps into view. At the end he is identified explicitly as "a tiger and a child." But Dick is not the symbol of black violence; he is the symbol of *human* violence. His savage outbreak is matched by the savage outbreak of the whites. There is a "blood note" in the ugly growl of the crowd that gathers in the square. In the sound of the baying hounds, there is "the savagery of blood" and "the savagery of man's guilty doom." It is significant that this savage excitement touches even the boys, who are Dick's friends and champions. Nebraska Crane's eyes, as he summons his friends, shine "with a savage sparkle." The whites, when they riddle Dick's body with bullets, have gone berserk just as

Dick went berserk. Dick is "night's child and partner, a token of the other side of man's dark soul . . . a symbol of man's evil innocence."

"The Child by Tiger" is not a suspense story like "The Most Dangerous Game," yet there is plenty of suspense in it. At first there is the mystery of Dick's character. Dick is declared by Mr. Shepperton to be "the best man he'd ever had." "And yet?" the narrator asks. "He went too softly, at too swift a pace . . . there was something moving in the night. . . ." The reader's curiosity is aroused by this mystery and by the sense of something to come. Then, as soon as the boys see the rifle in Dick's room, "blue-dull, deadly in its murderous efficiency," and especially when they hear the ringing of the fire bell in the city hall, the reader wants to know what will happen next. The excitement continues unabated until Dick's death.

What is the meaning of Dick's final gesture of removing his shoes and facing the mob, erect, on bare bleeding feet? It is something, the narrator says, "that no one ever wholly understood." It may be an act of humility as Dick prepares to meet his Maker (see Exodus 3.5 and Acts 7.33). Or it may be equally a gesture of human dignity, an assertion of manhood. Dick will no longer flee like a hunted animal. He is a man, and will face his death like a man.

Dick, in fact, is not only a man; he is ourselves.   LP

Poetry

The Elements
of Poetry

Chapter One

What Is Poetry?

Alfred, Lord Tennyson   **The Eagle** (page 647)

The first stanza presents what one sees looking at the eagle, perhaps looking up at him, with the sun above him and the blue sky around him. The second stanza is more concerned with looking down from the eagle's vantage point; it presents what *he* sees. The first stanza is more static (with "clasps," "Close," "stands"), the second stanza more dynamic (with "crawls," "watches," "falls"). These are small points, but they help to organize the poem. The expressions mentioned in the first study question are all figurative.   LP

William Shakespeare   **Winter** (page 650)

The words "merry" and "sings" are used *ironically* (see 760–761).   LP

Wilfred Owen   **Dulce et Decorum Est** (page 651)

The poem makes its bitter protest against the idea that dying for one's country is "sweet and becoming" by describing the agonizing death of one soldier caught in a gas attack during World War I. (We infer from the last two lines that the soldier is dead; what we witness in the poem is the anguish and horror of his dying.)

The speaker is a fellow soldier, a member of the same unit, and a witness of the dying. His account is given some time after the event (as measured by weeks or months), for he has reexperienced it in recurrent nightmares ever since (15–16). From our knowledge of World War I and of the poet's own experience, we may infer that the speaker is English, that the gas shells were German, and that the action occurred in France or Belgium. The speaker has probably been furloughed back to England at the time of his account, for the person he ironically addresses as "My friend" would seem to be an older man who is patriotically recruiting teenaged boys into the service of their country, or into readiness for such service (the word "children" is undoubtedly an overstatement of their youth).

The simile in line 1 compares the soldiers' packs to sacks carried by beggars. The word "softly" (8) is particularly sinister, for it connotes something gentle but here denotes something deadly. The phrase "sick of sin" (20) means "sick from sin." The most remarkable image in the poem is the simile in lines 13–14. The phosgene gas used in World War I was greenish in color, hence the man caught in it seems "As under a green sea . . . drowning." The under-ocean effect is enhanced by the fact that he is viewed by the other soldiers through the misty panes of their gas masks, which were like the goggles in the helmets used by deep-sea divers at the time. Finally, the man is literally drowning (being suffocated) in that his lungs are being deprived of oxygen; but the phosgene gas also corrodes the lungs, thus leading to the uglier imagery in lines 21–24.

The theme of the poem is obvious: It is *not* sweet and becoming to die for one's country in modern warfare.   LP

William Shakespeare   Shall I compare thee to a summer's day? (page 656)

This poem of praise begins and ends with references to the act and product of writing a poem about beauty and moderation. The speaker is therefore a poet conscious of his creation. The starting point is a simple question, almost an exercise or assignment: can I create a poem comparing you to a day in summer? The conclusion is triumphant: I have done so, and my poem will last forever and immortalize you.

Initially, the comparison has two points to make: the subject of the poem is more beautiful than a summer day, and is more "temperate." This word denotes a person who is not excessive or extreme in passion or action, someone who possesses forbearance and self-restraint, someone who is mild mannered. As a term applied to summer days it denotes a middle range of temperature and a lack of extreme weather conditions.

The structure of the comparison arising from the claim in line 2 introduces a third element that grows naturally from a discussion of day and season, and that is time and time's effects on beauty. In proving that the person is more "temperate" than summer, the speaker gives an example of one extreme of weather, the "[r]ough winds" that disturb the lovely appearance of youthful "buds of May," but he goes on in a metaphor to disparage the brevity of the summer season, an apparent digression from his main points. In line 5 the second quatrain returns to temperateness—sometimes the summer sun is extreme in its heat—and then takes up again the beauty of summer, reminding the listener that (in contrast to the excess of heat) the summer sun is often clouded over, dimmed and darkened, and therefore less lovely. The second half of the quatrain (7–8) draws together the three topics: all beauty at some time will decline because of the passage of time or the "changing course" that nature follows as it moves from extreme to extreme.

In line 9 the poem makes a turn as it drops the literal comparison to summer and instead uses summer as a metaphor for what is lovely in the person being addressed. The poet also moves away from his own moderate tone and theme by employing overstatement: your beauty will never be lost, nor will you succumb to time and mortality, because this poem will immortalize you. The couplet reiterates the point: as long as any person can read, your life will continue.

That turn in line 9 not only violates the poet's belief in moderation as a virtue, it also undercuts the literalness of his comparison. To that point, time in the poem has been real time, its effects real effects, and the subject of the poem has been credited with what are real superiorities: a temperament that is constant and moderate, a loveliness that is reliable and not wavering and changeable. But with the opening of the third quatrain the poet goes one step farther (too far, some might say): he lays claim to a superiority over time itself, and treats the metaphorical immortality of his subject as if it were literal. "You will not die, nor will your beauty fade"—flattering praise, but not true.

It was a commonplace in Renaissance poetry to make the claim that a poem immortalizes its subject, and Shakespeare is always a master at vivifying a commonplace. No one could escape being delighted by such praise as this, but the thoughtful reader will also acknowledge a sleight-of-pen trick as what is beautifully true yields to what is flatteringly (and self-flatteringly) untrue.   TRA

Robert Hayden   The Whipping (page 656)

This narrative poem—in the present tense, with a memory flashback in lines 13–18—strongly suggests that the speaker's assurance that "it is over now, it is over" is true only of this particular whipping of this particular boy. But as the concluding stanza clearly indicates, "hidings" have been the life-long story of the old woman's experience, were clearly part of the speaker's life, and are and will be the boy's experience. That is, physical punishment and its even more damaging counterpart, "hateful / Words," are persistent conditions of life.

There is little beauty in the experience of the poem, though one could make a case for the beauty of artistic arrangement, the precision of imagery, and the musicality of the language.   TRA

Emily Dickinson   The last Night that She lived (page 657)

The poem arises from the practice of the death-bed vigil so widespread in the nineteenth century, and thus runs the danger of joining a tradition of mawkish sentimentality or morbid curiosity. But as so often in Dickinson's poems that flirt with sentimental subjects, the details and the stance of the speaker avoid an excess of feeling, and the subject itself becomes fresh and surprising.

In the first place, the poem does not suggest that the dying woman is approaching eternal bliss, but is about to become "infinite"—out of time and space, but not into some supernal existence. The viewers' response (plural throughout, and thus not a plumbing of the emotions of one loving observer) is involved but analytical. The emotions are unexpected: the sense of a difference in "Nature," the new insight that suddenly "Italicize[s]" insignificant things, the slight projection of feelings onto the dying woman—blaming those who will live on—and even "Jealousy" of the woman who approaches infinity. These and others exclude banality and look with great honesty at confused but genuine emotions.

The actual moment of death is delicate and full of restraint. "She mentioned, and forgot" suggests the slight confusion of the woman, and then the simile of the reed bending gently to the pressure of flowing water implies only the lightest of resistance before she "Consented, and was dead" (21–24).

The final stanza most nearly approaches the morbidly tender offices afforded to the dead, rearranging the body for a more seemly viewing (to make it seem comfortably asleep). But the last two lines are shocking in an altogether different way. The mourners are left with an "awful" (awed, stunned) "leisure," having no other duties to the deceased, and must now begin "to regulate" their faith. The shock is that for all its matter-of-fact honesty about feelings, the poem has indeed steered away from the question of faith and the afterlife, only reaching that when the experience is over. Now, the speaker says, we must try to accommodate this "awful" event into a belief system. The task looks enormous. The death has aroused grief, but more it has cast doubt.   TRA

Dudley Randall   Ballad of Birmingham (page 658)

This moving poem displays many of the characteristics of a traditional folk ballad: it is a narrative poem with a large component of dialogue; it presents a contemporary event; it tells its story without overt analysis or explanation; and it employs simple metrical and stanzaic forms.

As in the ballads, the material *not* explicitly reported is significant—chiefly, in this case, the identity of the perpetrators, their motives and the motives of the police and others who suppressed freedom, the effect on the city of the bombing outrage, and the precise fate of the child (the poem refers only to the shoe, not to the child, though we might infer from lines 23–24 that the child was among the four who were killed: "that smile was the last smile / To come upon [the mother's] face"). These are the issues that would be included in a newspaper account, along with speculation about future consequences.

Instead, the poem focuses on just two people, the mother and child, and their motives and actions. The child, in a precocious show of social responsibility, wants to help "make our country free" (12). (Notice that the poem does not identify her race until line 19, and that her concern is stated in terms that encompass more than racial injustice in Alabama.) The child is willing to give up her "play" time for the larger cause. The mother, on the other hand, displays protective love and fear for her child's safety, and denies her daughter's twice-requested wish to participate in the Freedom March. In arguing against it, the mother carefully does not excite her daughter's animosity toward the police—their "clubs and hoses, guns and jails," and "fierce and wild" dogs are given an autonomy that makes them sound self-wielding. She does not say, "I am afraid the police will beat you, or set their dogs on you, or shoot you," nor in making her request does the child say, "I want to march so that unjust and brutal people will be forced to give up their power over us." This verbal reticence is part of the ballad tradition, and also serves to create additional sympathy for these two, who are not expressing hatred for the government or the police.

The images in the fifth stanza increase sympathy and respect for this child who wants to take on adult cares. We witness her "grown-up" preparation for going into a house of worship, we observe the care she takes with her beautiful "night-dark hair," we smell the sweetness of the scented soap of her bath, and we see the purity and delicacy displayed in her white gloves and white shoes. Given the racial situation, there is some dramatic irony in the contrasts of "night-dark," "brown," and "white" associated with the child (but we must resist reading too much into the child's choice of "white" articles—she is not trying to be like a white child, but is wearing what is appropriate to church). We can be sure that the pronoun "She" (17) refers to the child, since line 21 identifies "the mother" as a contrast to the "She." It is important that the child be the one who bathes and dresses and cares for her hair, for these are further signs of the "grown-up" competence that led her to want to join the Freedom March.

The central irony of the poem is of course that the "sacred place" of safety to which the mother guides her child is the place that destroys her. That irony also embodies the theme of the poem, for in this microcosm of mother and child the senseless brutality of the racial bigots is displayed at its worst: the bombing of children at prayer is a symbol of the viciousness and cowardice that lay behind racist suppression. In offering this single personal incident to represent that theme, Randall can achieve more in 32 lines of poetry than an orator might in an hour-long speech denouncing racial injustice.   TRA

Gwendolyn Brooks   Kitchenette Building (page 660)

Essentially the poem sets up contrasts between squalor and dream, and asks the question whether a dream could actually prevail in such surroundings. It conveys its ideas as much by imagery as by statement, and might be used as a preliminary exploration of sense images that evoke the constrictions and squalor of tenement or substandard housing and contrast them to images of freedom, escape, joy. Visual images of the gray walls, gray hair, and perhaps the gray pallor of the skin create feelings of drab monotony and exhaustion. These are intensified by the pungency of the olfactory images—the stale smells of "onion fumes" and "fried potatoes / And yesterday's garbage ripening in the hall."

The possibility of a "dream"—that is, a beautiful hope for some better life—replaces gray with "white and violet," and produces a "giddy sound" that would replace the mundane, leaden necessities of paying the rent or the meager, dutiful personal relationships ("feeding a wife," "satisfying a man") with fluttering and even operatic flights. But entertaining such unrealistic dreams is too great an effort, and is beaten down by the difficulties of working for their fulfillment. Nurturing a dream means "warm[ing] it, . . . keep[ing] it very clean," and hoping that it will bring the news of release and relief, but there is neither time nor opportunity for such nurture. The tactile imagery of warmth associated with dreaming gives way to the practical urgency of taking one's turn in the shared bathroom where there may yet be "lukewarm" water to bathe in.

The lives of the building's residents are indeed pitiable when even dreaming of escape and beauty is beyond their energies.   TRA

William Carlos Williams   **The Red Wheelbarrow** (page 661)

The simplicity of this free verse poem inevitably leads students to question "What *does* depend upon these things, and *how* much is 'so much'?" The answer is "human life," both as physical existence and as aesthetic experience.

Momentarily ignoring the visual details—"red," "glazed," and "white"—one might investigate the importance of the objects. A wheelbarrow is a basic farm implement associated with the most primitive stage of human toolmaking, only one step advanced beyond the use of sledges or unwheeled barrows for dragging heavy loads. Rainwater is obviously an essential for farming as for all life, and chickens provide two common foodstuffs in their flesh and their eggs. Thus, the objects can be seen as among the most basic in providing physical sustenance, and much therefore "depends / upon" them.

By contrast, the visual imagery is nonutilitarian. Although paint does protect against rot and rust, the color red has no specific usefulness. The glazing of rain (and the potential rotting of wood that it implies) is more potentially harmful than beneficial, and a chicken is an egg-layer and a source of meat whatever its color. These visual references thus run counter to the utilitarian functions of the objects they adorn. But they provide contrasts and harmonies of color, shape, and texture basic to aesthetic enjoyment. White

and red are clear contrasts, as are a shiny glaze contrasted to the downy softness of a chicken's feathers. While there is a contrast between the living and
nonliving objects, one may also see a vague similarity in the triangular shapes
of a wheelbarrow and a pecking chicken. (It helps students to see this if
chalkboard sketches are provided.)

The poem thus offers two distinct dependencies: we depend upon farmers
for our food (and they depend upon nature in producing it), and as sensitive
observers we depend upon visual perceptions to feed us aesthetically.   TRA

Langston Hughes   Suicide's Note (page 661)

Like the miller's wife in the last stanza of Robinson's "The Mill" (page
994), the fictitious writer of this brief "note" found in the "calm" look of the
water an attraction that makes suicide by drowning seem a reasonable and
desirable act. However, Hughes's suicide has no implied or suggested motive
for his desperate act beyond that apparently rational response to an invitation—that is, there is nothing to suggest the origin or cause for despair. The
note doesn't look backward or analyze why the writer came to the river, but
is limited to that momentary response to an imagined request. The psy-
chopathology of suicide is not the concern.

But the unbalanced state of mind, whatever its origins, is suggested both
by the writer's hearing the river speak to him and by his decision to respond
positively to what is so passionless an invitation. It is not quite normal to
imagine kissing a *person* whose request for a kiss issued from a "calm, / Cool
face," apparently a stranger who employs no seductive methods or gestures
but simply asks. This is emotionally a long distance from its allusive counterpart, the passionate desire of Narcissus whose adoration of what he sees on
the surface of the water leads to his drowning.

The *k* alliterations function doubly: they link the strange conjunction of
"calm" and "Cool" to "kiss," emphasizing its oddness, and by their harsh initial sounds they remind us that this moment of succumbing to an amorous
invitation was deadly.   TRA

A. E. Housman   Terence, this is stupid stuff (page 662)

Housman's poem compares the efficacy of three things for helping one
lead a satisfactory life: cheerful poetry, alcohol, and pessimistic poetry. The
first two, by making one "see the world as the world's not," arouse expectations that life can rarely fulfill. The result is disappointment and disillusionment. Pessimistic poetry, by truly picturing a world containing "much less
good than ill," prepares one for the troubles that are sure to come. Thus fortified, one can withstand their shock and lead a satisfying life.

In the first verse paragraph a friend playfully criticizes Terence (Housman) for the kind of poetry he writes and gives a delightful parody of it in the

two lines (7–8) about the cow. Reading his poetry, the friend claims in a humorous overstatement, is driving Terence's friends mad and causing them to die before their time. He pleads with Terence to write cheerful poetry instead.

Terence replies that if his friend wants gaiety and cheer, liquor is more efficacious than poetry. It makes the world seem a "lovely" place and oneself a "sterling" lad. The only trouble is that this picture is "all a lie." By implication, cheerful poetry likewise misrepresents the world. Liquor and optimistic poetry are for "fellows whom it hurts to think." Their effect is temporary and ultimately enfeebling. They offer escape, not a solution.

In the first six lines of the third section Terence sums up his philosophy. To train for ill is to prepare oneself for the world as it is. One can do this by reading the kind of poetry Terence writes. It will strengthen "heart and head" and prepare one's soul for adversity. Many students misread the poem at this point. They fail to see that "the stuff I bring for sale" is Terence's poetry, metaphorically compared to a bitter brew that "is not so brisk" (so intoxicating) as the literal ale of the second verse paragraph. Its "smack is sour" because it was wrung out of bitter experience.

In the final section Terence clinches his point by telling a parable. Mithridates immunized himself to poison by first taking a little and then gradually increasing the dosage. As a result, Mithridates lived a long and satisfactory life. Similarly, Terence implies, one can immunize oneself against the troubles of life by reading the kind of poetry Terence writes.   LP

Adrienne Rich   **Poetry: I** (page 664)

QUESTIONS

1. Vocabulary: *trope* (5), *vatic* (5), *glosses* (21).
2. According to this poem, what are the various reasons why people read poetry? How does a study of poetry repay the reader's effort?
3. The poem distinguishes between an experienced reader, embodied by the poem's speaker, and a beginning reader, the "someone young" (19). Describe these two kinds of readers and what the experience of poetry means for each.

In the first verse paragraph the poem presents a young man and woman who are studying poetry. One of them, the woman, is learning the history of poetry but yearns to hear "shreds of music" in it. The man is learning the fashionable jargon of criticism but yearns to find something with which he can identify and which will clarify for him his own identity. Both of them, then, are pursuing poetry intellectually and abstractly, and both of them feel the lack of an immediate, emotional experience. The speaker summarizes their problem: "They cannot learn without teachers"—that is, they are looking to the past, to traditions, history, and analysis, because these are what can be taught and learned. And as she says, that was where she and the person she addresses began their poetic journey.

But the intuitive need for *"More!"* (14), albeit faint and vague, presses on the young readers as it did upon the speaker and her listener in their early approaches to poetry. She recalls the time in youth when they, like the young readers, assumed the true teacher was poetry itself, that poets could teach them "how to live." Their hunger for deeper experience and wisdom in poetry has passed, but it is characteristic of the young that they all make such demands on poets, even if they do not know what questions to ask them. Poets, in turn, having matured and grown less frustrated and angry, write their lines of verse, and provide "glosses" on them, but the young continue to find the poem "wanting."

This poem thus draws its contrasts between the young and the experienced, the hungry and the satisfied. It does so by juxtaposing the two young people of the opening section to the mature poet, and by comparing the mature poet to her own younger self. There is an assumed process of growth that is recapitulated. Ironically, the result of that growth is a loss of intensity and the development of critical faculties that make it impossible for the young to comprehend the experience of the mature.   TRA

Archibald MacLeish   Ars Poetica (page 665)

The poet's philosophy of his art is summed up in the opening and closing lines of the poem's third section. A poem is concerned with experience, not with propositional statements. When it is successful, it is "equal" to the experience it creates; the reader properly responds to it by imaginatively "living" that experience, not by judging the content of the poem as right or wrong, true or false. To create experience, the rest of the poem tells us (and illustrates in its telling), the poem must rely on images and symbols.

"Ars Poetica" has three sections, each of which includes what seems a paradox or a violation of common sense. Section one declares that a poem should be "palpable" and "wordless." Yet if we run our fingers over this poem as printed on the page, the only palpable thing is the page; our fingers make no distinction between recipe, advertisement, poem, or blank sheet of paper. And does not MacLeish's statement that a poem should be "wordless" run directly counter to Wallace Stevens's (in "The Noble Rider and the Sound of Words," *The Necessary Angel*) that "Poetry is a revelation in words by means of the words"? No, I think not. What MacLeish means is that the "experience" or "revelation" created is wordless. When we read a poem, we must of course be acutely sensitive to the words, but the result of sensitive reading is that we are drawn into an imaginative experience in which we see "globed" peach or pear, or draw our thumb over an old medallion, or feel the soft moss and worn stone of an ancient casement ledge, or watch a flight of birds crossing the sky.

Section two asserts that a poem "should be motionless in time / As the moon climbs," which seems contradictory in itself, for how can something be "motionless" and yet climb? Yet the moon "climbs" so slowly that its motion is imperceptible except when it can be related to some earthly object, such as the horizon or "night-entangled trees," and watched for some time. What is this section saying about a poem then? That when we read it, we are so caught up in the experience created that we are unconscious of the passage of time? Or that the experience it creates lingers in the mind and fades from memory slowly and almost imperceptibly? An excellent case for the latter reading is made by Edwin St. Vincent, in *Explicator* 37 (Spring 1979): 14–16, through a detailed analysis of the difficult syntax of this section.

And so we come to the summary third section, which says that a poem should be "equal to: / Not true" and "should not mean / But be." Does this mean that a poem should be meaningless? No, only that its "meaning" (what we have called in Chapter 9 its "total meaning") is an *experience*, not an idea or propositional statement, and is expressed through images and symbols. The symbolic image of "An empty doorway and a maple leaf" (suggesting absence, loneliness, and the transitory quality of life) creates "all the history of grief," and the image of "leaning grasses and two lights above the sea" (suggesting perhaps a summer field where two lovers might lie overlooking the ocean) creates the experience of love.   LP

Chapter Two

Reading the Poem

Thomas Hardy   **The Man He Killed** (page 670)

The hesitations and repetitions of stanza 3 beautifully reflect the thought processes of the speaker. The pause after "because" (9) occurs because he is groping for an explanation. When he finds one, he must repeat the "because." He then has to convince himself that this answer is correct and sufficient. He does this (or tries to do it) by telling himself three times emphatically that it is (a) "Just so"; (b) "my foe of course he was"; (c) "That's clear enough." But despite this triple emphatic effort at self-assurance, we know that the attempt is unsuccessful, as it trails off into "although. . . ."   LP

Philip Larkin   **A Study of Reading Habits** (page 671)

Any reader should see that neither the language nor the attitudes of the speaker in this poem could possibly be those of a poet. To clinch the case, one can point out that Philip Larkin was by profession a librarian.

The speaker is a weak person, unable to face reality, who as boy and adolescent avoided it by reading "escape" fiction, either in pulp magazines or in paperbacks. As a boy (stanza 1), he identified himself with the virtuous hero, the man who overcomes villainy by physical force. As an adolescent (stanza 2), he vicariously engaged in sex escapades by identifying with the bold villain (Dracula type) or the picaresque hero (James Bond type). As a young man, he has reached a stage at which reading no longer conceals from him his own failures; he now recognizes himself in the weak secondary characters, and must find escape in alcohol.

Even better than Hardy's "The Man He Killed," this poem demonstrates that poetry need not be made of lofty, dignified, exquisite, or even original language. The language here is vulgar, slangy, and trite; yet it is perfectly chosen to express the intellectual poverty of its speaker. Good poets choose their words not for their beauty or elegance, but for their expressiveness—that is to say, their maximum appropriateness to subject, situations, and speaker. Trite language need not make a trite poem, as this piece effectively demonstrates. And even working within the limitations of deliberately trite language, Larkin achieves striking effects. The word "ripping" (10), for instance, has not only its slang meaning of "exciting" or "great" but also its literal meaning (here) of "ripping the clothes off of"—a duality of which the poet was probably aware and the speaker unaware.

In "Terence, this is stupid stuff" (page 662), Housman agrees with the speaker that "ale's the stuff to drink" for "fellows whom it hurts to think" and that one should "Look into the pewter pot / To see the world as the world's not"; but for wiser fellows, Housman recommends reading. However, Housman is recommending quite a different kind of reading from that engaged in by Larkin's speaker; he is recommending a kind in which one can "see the world" as the world *is*. Thus, Housman is in diametrical disagreement with Larkin's speaker, and probably in perfect agreement with Larkin himself.   LP

A. E. Housman   Is my team plowing (page 674)

The word "bed" (28) signifies literally the bed that the living man sleeps in, metaphorically the grave that the dead man lies in, and symbolically a lot in life, or condition of existence. The word "sleep" has corresponding meanings: of sleeping, of being dead, and of having a certain lot. In addition, it gathers up from the last stanza the meaning of sleeping with a woman, that is, of making love.

The poem at first seems cynical, suggesting, as it does, the transience of human loyalties. On reflection, however, few people expect a man or woman not to remarry after a first mate has died. (Housman's poem probably doesn't refer to marriage, but the principle is the same.) In general, Housman's poetry is pessimistic about our chances for happiness, but Housman is not cynical about human courage or human virtue.   LP

John Donne   Break of Day (page 677)

The situation presents two lovers in bed. The man has just remarked "It's day!" (or something of the sort) and has made a gesture toward getting up. The woman's reply is a protest against his leaving. In the three stanzas of the poem she suggests three reasons why he might be thinking of leaving (because it's light; because he fears to expose their relationship; and because he has business to attend to) and shows each in turn to be invalid. The second of these concerns shows that the lovers are unmarried.

The speaker is conclusively proved to be the woman by her use of the pronoun "him" in line 12. Additional evidence is offered by the following considerations: (a) it was the woman who, under the double standard of morality, risked her reputation ("honor") in an illicit relationship; (b) a man would have been more likely than a woman to be drawn away by "business";

(c) the speaker makes her complaint against "the busied man," not the busied *person*; (d) the speaker compares the offender to a "married man" who woos another, not a married *person*, married *woman*, or *wife*.

Lines 15–16 may be read as meaning either (a) love (personified as a sovereign) can admit the poor man, the foul man, even the false man into her province, but cannot admit "the busied man," or (b) the poor man, the foul man, and the false man can admit love into their lives, but "the busied man" cannot. We do not have to choose between these two readings. Both make sense.

The woman clearly has a scale of values that puts love at the top. She is not ashamed of her relationship with the man (as shown in the second stanza). She has committed herself to him and expects an equal commitment from him. His "business" threatens that commitment, and she is jealous of it as she would be jealous of any rival. Their love is as sacred to her as if legitimatized by marriage; he cannot have *two* mistresses: "business" and her.

Though the arguments of the three stanzas are logically discrete, they are verbally linked. Stanza 1 is connected to stanza 2 by the repeated image of "light"; stanza 2 is connected to stanza 3 by the contrast of her "being well" and his having (possibly) "the worst disease of love." The poem's title not only means *Morning* but suggests the threatened separation ("break") between the lovers.

Students may have to be guided through the figurative legerdemain of stanza 2. Light is personified (as a mute, unable to speak), it is metonymically linked with its source, the sun; and the sun is metaphorically compared to a large eye (which is in turn referred back as the sole anatomical feature of the personified Light). The sun may discover the two lovers in bed together but, having no tongue, it can spread no scandal; *even if it could* (the woman declares), she would not be shamed by anything it could say.   LP

Emily Dickinson   There's been a Death, in the Opposite House (page 678)

The speaker in this poem has not been informed of the death across the way and apparently does not know who has died. He (his sex is revealed in line 12) is not one of the neighbors who "rustle in and out." Probably he is a visitor in the house from which he watches. But he is no stranger to the ways of country towns: he knows by the signs immediately and intuitively that a death has occurred. He is a sensitive observer, able to report and to interpret precisely and imaginatively what he sees and to enter empathetically into the thoughts and feelings of the children who hurry past.

What he focuses on is the difference that the death makes in the ordinary life of a house. The house itself seems to have a "numb look," as if stunned by the unusual occurrence. Neighbors—mostly women, for their skirts "rustle"—come and go, offering help and sympathy. The sick room is ventilated, a mattress hung to air across the windowsill. The children hurry by, scared, for death to them is mysterious and vaguely terrifying: they can think of the corpse only as "it," not as a person, and they wonder if "it" died on the mattress they see. The minister enters "stiffly," not relaxed: this is a solemn occasion, and he will be the most important person in the funeral ritual. He immediately takes command. The milliner and the undertaker arrive to measure—between them—the corpse for the coffin, the mourners for black veils and other mourning apparel, and the house itself for getting the coffin in and out and perhaps for hanging with crepe bunting. (The word "house" is used, throughout the poem, as a metonymy to indicate not just the house itself, but the activity and the people around and within it, although the house itself seems to reflect this numbness in the way its window opens. Even the minister reflects it in his stiffness.) The speaker concludes with an account, not of what he sees, but of what he knows will soon be seen—the funeral procession of black coaches hung with tassels that will take the body and the mourners to the cemetery. He then generalizes his opening observation—how easy it is to tell when a death has occurred in a country town.

Some students will have difficulty with the tone of this poem, seeing it or the people in it as regarding death callously, impersonally, or coldly. The mistake may result from misinterpreting the role of the speaker (who is an observer, not a participant), or from misconceiving the "numb look" (which signifies not lack of emotion, but the stunned state following or accompanying too much emotion), or from identifying the attitude of the children toward the corpse with that of the adults or the observer. The poem focuses on the outside of the house, not on the dead person, because that is what the observer sees; but all of the activity he sees results from the presence of the dead person within. The tone of the poem reflects the awesomeness of death and its solemnity. Part of the speaker's attitude is revealed in his reference to the undertaker as "the Man / Of the Appalling Trade" (in the double sense of "horrifying" and "putting a pall on" a coffin) and to the funeral procession as a "Dark Parade" (dark literally because of the black badges of mourning but with the additional connotations of mystery and awesomeness).

Though written by a woman, this poem has a male speaker. Donne's "Break of Day," though written by a man, has a female speaker. An instructive point can be made from this juxtaposition. ·   LP

Mari Evans   **When in Rome** (page 679)

The first speaker is a white woman, the second her black maid. We are given only the unspoken thoughts of the second speaker, hence the inclusion of her words in parentheses.

Though the white employer's words take the outward form of affection and solicitude ("Mattie dear . . . take / whatever you like"), their tone, without her realizing it, is subtly patronizing. The invitation to take "whatever you like" is qualified by "don't / get my anchovies / they cost / too much!" And her utter ignorance of what the black servant likes to eat betrays the essential emptiness of her solicitude. The phrase "take / whatever you like / to eat" functions on two levels: *take whatever you wish to take*, and *take whatever you enjoy eating*. (There is almost nothing in the icebox that the black woman really *likes*.)

The black woman's attitude is one of repressed antagonism. Consciously or unconsciously, she knows she is being patronized, and though she is accustomed to speaking outwardly in terms of respect ("yes'm"), her resentment expresses itself through the use of irony: "what she think, she got— / a bird to feed?" and "yes'm. just the / sight's / enough!" The last phrase can be read in two ways.

The title and the conclusion are an allusion to the familiar saying "When in Rome, do as the Romans do." Rome in the poem serves as a metaphor for the white world, and the speaker is tired of having to eat what whites like to eat rather than what blacks like to eat.   LP

Sylvia Plath   Mirror (page 680)

Although the speaker is the personified mirror, who in the second stanza goes on to personify itself as a lake, the subject of the poem is the woman who looks into the mirror and learns the truth of the changes in her appearance that time brings. Like a person, the mirror looks outward, observing— and meditating about—the objects that come into view. But unlike a person, the mirror has no preconceptions; it does not distort its vision with emotional responses. It is godlike in its detached truthfulness, even if it is a little god with a limited area of observation.

As a lake (and perhaps like the pool into which Narcissus plunged in adoration of his own beauty), the mirror still will give only the truth about the surface of reflections, no matter how the woman might want to find a deeper truth. Candlelight and moonlight, which cast flattering dim gleams of romantic imagination are, by comparison with the mirror's faithful images, "liars."

What the searching woman finds in the truthful reflection is the sad fact of aging: the little girl that she was is now dead, and the old woman that she will become lurks in the depths of time, waiting to appear and terrify her.   TRA

William Blake   The Clod and the Pebble (page 680)

This miniature debate presents two opposing attitudes toward love, each side being given exactly six lines. The vulnerable, destructible clod of earth is crushed by the hooves of the cattle. But this loss of identity as the clod is "trodden" (6) into the earth is expressed as a song proclaiming that true love is selfless and sacrifices its own desires and comforts for the sake of the beloved. Such sacrifice, says the clod, creates a heavenly condition that thwarts the designs of hell.

The smooth, hard pebble resists the pressure of the brook's water that washes around it with a warbling sound, its identity intact. Its song advocates a wholly selfish, possessive love that even takes delight in the discomfort of the beloved. This act defies heaven and creates a hell.

If we take "Heaven" and "Hell" (4, 12) figuratively, as metonymies for God and the devil, or as symbols of goodness and evil, the poem takes on metaphysical meanings. Selfless love is the agency for promoting the goodness of God, while possessive love is allied with the wickedness of Satan.

Does the poem give any clues about the winner? Our first impulse probably is to say that heaven is assuredly better than hell, that concern for others is better than selfishness, and that we cannot doubt that goodness is preferable to evil. But the language of the poem tends to call these values into doubt. The clod sings, but the pebble "warble[s]." The pebble's song is in "meters meet" (8), that is, proper or fitting. In terms of connotative language, the pebble seems to have the edge.

Sound also contributes to meaning: the main musical device in the poem is alliteration. In lines 4 and 12, which might be called variant refrains, the concluding words "despair" and "despite" and the reversed positions of "Heaven" and "Hell" create the variation, but the lines probably reinforce the ambivalence of the poem because of their near-identity; they force us to restate the central question, which is better?

If euphony is a mark of superiority (that is, if the beauty of sound is significant), the pebble wins. The clod is presented in a triple alliteration on the "k" sound ("Clod of Clay . . . cattle's), with a reinforcement of "t" sounds ("little . . . Trodden . . . cattle's) (5–6). In contrast to these hard, harsh consonants, the pebble is characterized in four "b" sounds and two "m" sounds, softer and more mellifluous in their music ("But a Pebble of the brook, / Warbled . . . meters meet") (7–8). In addition, there is the assonance of the phrase "these meters meet" (8).

In addition to these subjective impressions, the pebble gets the last word.

So much for internal evidence. While students will, of course, rarely have heard of Blake's cosmology, we might also recall his frequent inversion of heaven and hell as representatives of repressive control and personal, independent freedom. For the beginning reader, perhaps the best strategy is to allow students to sense the ambivalence and to suggest that some sort of "negative capability," in which the mind can simultaneously entertain two contrasting ideas, might be appropriate to this poem. And while the ideas are in contrast, students might also be led to see that in either case, the definition requires the participation of its opposite: the clod needs the destructive force of the hoof to fulfill its purposes, and the pebble must have the forceful flow of the brook to achieve its. In effect, clods need pebbles and pebbles need clods.

For an analysis that places the poem in the context of Blake's *Songs of Experience,* see Nicholas Marsh, *William Blake: The Poems* (New York: Palgrave, 2001) 173–77.   TRA

Yusef Komunyakaa   Facing It (page 681)

This poem powerfully evokes the speaker's confrontation with one of the major cultural monuments of the twentieth century, the Vietnam Veterans Memorial in Washington, D.C. Throughout the poem, the speaker emphasizes his own "clouded reflection" (6) in the mirror-like surface of black granite. Unable to remain an objective, unemotional observer, he becomes one with what he sees: "I'm stone. I'm flesh." (5).

As the poem develops, the speaker's physical observation of the Memorial inspires an imaginative vision of the war and its participants. After touching one of the names, he sees "the booby trap's white flash" (18). Moreover, this line illustrates the way the speaker employs vivid colors to evoke the contrast between the Memorial and what the speaker sees reflected inside it. For instance, he sees an imagined "white flash" and the literal image of a white veteran reflected in the "black mirror" he is facing. The sight of "a red bird's / wings," suggesting vibrancy and movement, forms a marked contrast with the motionless "stare" of the speaker and the fixed nature of the Memorial itself.

The poem finally suggests the speaker's inability to "read" a Memorial whose predominant feature is textual, a listing of the 58,022 names of those who died in Vietnam. The speaker's vision constantly shifts, suggesting the complexity of what he sees and preventing a fixed and coherent vision. Appropriately the poem ends with an image of misreading: "In the black mirror / a woman's trying to erase names: / No, she's brushing a boy's hair" (29–31). These lines repeat a major irony evoked throughout the poem: life continues even in the "face," literally, of a memorial to the dead.   GJ

Edwin Arlington Robinson   Eros Turannos (page 682)

The first three stanzas present the ambivalent feelings of an older woman being courted by a younger man, as well as a few lines that reveal the man's true feelings. In the first stanza, she asks herself what drew her heart to a man whom she fears and mistrusts: the title gives one answer, the powerful erotic drive embodied in a magisterial god of love. Although she can judge rationally that her suitor's suspiciously "engaging mask" provides good enough "reasons to refuse him," she has another strong motive—a fear that if she does not accept him, her life will become merely a series of lonely, downward stages leading to old age and death, like drifting slowly down a river and being lost as it empties into the sea. The power of love added to the fear of loneliness is enough to overcome her clear reasoning.

The second stanza presents her decision as the result of being over-whelmed by a dimming of her wisdom and love's blinding her to the truth (that he is a Judas who has presumably already betrayed her, perhaps with a younger woman). And so she accepts him, with a swallowing of her pride.

The poem introduces the man's perspective in lines 15–20. In the con-clusion of the second stanza, recognizing that she has decided to accept him, he nonchalantly "waits [for her acceptance] and looks around him," leaving it to her to take the decisive step and, in effect, become his pursuer. The first four lines of the third stanza reveal why he has proposed marriage to a woman he does not love: her social position as the product of a rich and eminent family attracted him to her, and though he has some doubts or misgivings about marrying her, the "Tradition" embodied in herself and in her property both "Beguiles and reassures him." Although he will be entering into a love-less marriage, without the promise of joy or even contentment, he will sacri-fice those possibilities in exchange for the comforts provided by money and a distinguished family.

Line 21, in the middle of stanza 3, returns to the woman's point of view to reiterate that her fear of aging has overcome the doubts she has about his character, and so despite her prejudices against him, "she secures him." He, too, of course, has secured what he wants—which may, in a pun, be her se-curities as well as a secure position in her house. And those symbols of her wealth and position that "allure[d] him" are transformed in her imagination in the fourth stanza: that "sense of ocean and old trees" (17) is now to her "[t]he falling leaf" and "pounding wave" that signal confusion and disillu-sionment. The transformation of *his* symbols into *hers*, and their terrible ef-fect on her, strongly suggests that he has deserted her. Line 29 reports that her "passion lived and died" within her home (it is her "passion," necessarily, since he has had none), and as a consequence she has shut herself up in the family mansion and become the center of gossip in "town and harbor side."

The gossips of the town emerge, in stanza five, as the choric narrators of this pitiful story who at the end come forth to evaluate and interpret it. They tell "[t]he story as it should be," making from their limited experience the judgment that the secluded woman has now gone crazy, and was probably a little daft to begin with in accepting such a man (although they acknowledge that the full "story of a house" is probably beyond anyone's narrative powers). With a hint of cruelty, they mean to tear away the "kindly veil" that obscures her from their knowledge even while they confess that their interpretation of her is no more than guesswork. In this intent we may discover another re-flection of the prominence of the woman and her family: "we" townspeople are willing to invent motive and madness to denigrate this distinguished "house."

But finally, after all, the gossips are willing to acknowledge that despite their attitude toward her loss, something quite special and even heroic may have happened in that house. Having "striven" with the god of Love, she may have received from him more than the townspeople can comprehend—

some ineffable gift that in her fall has made her even more distant and mysterious to them. The gift of that god might even be his traditional blindness to the gradual deterioration as she passes down over the "foamless weirs / Of age" (7–8) like a "stairway to the sea." What she feared in stanza one—a long and lonely old age—may be quite a different experience in the wake of a passion that has died.

The relative obscurity of this poem arises chiefly from two sources, both contributing to its power. On the one hand, the poem omits details, and thus leaves readers with the same kind of guesswork that the townspeople indulge in. On the other hand, the poem has a richness of abstract vocabulary that elevates the story to a tragic level, as well as recurring and developing symbolism that seems to rise from elemental sources: ocean, tree, and river belong to a mythic world. While we lose precision and clarity, those details that the gossips would most love to have, we gain a kind of sublimity that comes from struggling with the gods.

Although written more than 40 years ago, two of the best critical analyses of this excellent poem are in Roy Harvey Pearce, *The Continuity of Poetry* (Princeton: Princeton UP, 1961) 261–64, and Louis O. Coxe, *E. A. Robinson* (Minneapolis: U of Minnesota P, 1962) 24–30.   TRA

Adrienne Rich   Storm Warnings (page 684)

QUESTIONS

1. This poem suggests an analogy between natural and emotional weather. Identify the lines and phrases in which this analogy is implied.
2. In stanza three, what are the "elements" (16) that "clocks and weatherglasses cannot alter" (17)? What meaning is suggested by the pun on "shutters" (21)?
3. What do we learn about the speaker of the poem? What is her attitude toward the coming storm?
4. Why does the speaker use the first-person singular pronoun in the opening stanzas and then change to first-person plural later in the poem (21, 26, 27)?
5. Discuss the multiple meanings—natural, social, political, personal—of the poem's final phrase, "troubled regions" (28).

This early Rich poem probes its central analogy between natural and emotional weather. The speaker, reading a book indoors, becomes aware of an incipient snowstorm and begins walking "from window to closed window" to observe the rising winds, the bending trees. Her aloneness is notable: like Emily Dickinson, who once wrote of her "polar privacy," Rich's speaker inhabits "a silent core of waiting," aware of the way in which time has traveled along "secret currents of the undiscerned / Into this polar realm."

In addition to inner and outer weathers, the poem is concerned with the way time brings inevitable change; our human "clocks and weatherglasses" may help predict change but can do nothing to avert it: "We can only close the shutters." Rich may intend a pun on "shutters," since the speaker's eye serves the function of a camera's observing lens (yet another example of human technology which, by preserving the moment, tries to elude time's passage), intently observing the landscape as it writhes and darkens.

In the final stanza, the speaker's "sole defense" against the storm's arrival is to draw the curtains and light candles "sheathed in glass" to protect them against the draft of wind coming through an unsealed keyhole. On the symbolic level, the image of the glass sheath may recall Sylvia Plath's "bell jar," a forced isolation; but in contrast to Plath's image of stifling, literally maddening isolation, Rich's glass wall protects the human light of warmth and domesticity, and by extension all the humane, civilizing values that separate the speaker from natural and psychic forces, those "troubled regions" of world and mind defined here as primitive, menacing, and potentially destructive.

Reinforcing this motive is the poem's calm, reasonable tone; though the speaker's voice seems edged with sadness, she exhibits neither panic nor anger. Instead her attitude is one of cautious pragmatism born of experience: "These are the things that we have learned to do." In its movement from the individual "I" leaving book and pillowed chair in the first stanza to the "we" and "our" of the final lines Rich broadens the significance of her central metaphor to encompass social and political "regions" in addition to those of the heart.

Alice Templeton asserts that "Storm Warnings" is one of several early Rich poems that echo "the rhythms, forms, and themes of modernist poets such as W. H. Auden and T. S. Eliot" (*The Dream and the Dialogue, Adrienne Rich's Feminist Poetics* [Knoxville: U of Tennessee P, 1995] 12). The poem is discussed in detail in Craig Werner, *Adrienne Rich: The Poet and Her Critics* (Chicago: American Library Association, 1988) 43–44.   GJ

Chapter Three

Denotation and Connotation

Emily Dickinson   **There is no Frigate like a Book** (page 686)

Miles suggests a measurable and therefore a lesser distance than "Lands"; also, it suggests distance only. "Lands" suggests not only distance but difference—not only far lands, but foreign lands, perhaps even fairy lands. The connotations of *cheap* are unfavorable; of "frugal," favorable. "[P]rancing," besides participating in the alliterative sequence of "a Page / Of prancing Poetry," brings to mind the metrical effects of poetry and the winged horse Pegasus, symbol of poetry in Greek mythology.   LP

William Shakespeare   **When my love swears that she is made of truth** (page 688)

Because of the pun on *lie,* students frequently misconceive the tone of this sonnet as light. It might better be called dark. The pun is grim, not merry. Trapped in a love affair he knows to be unworthy of him, too weak to break loose, the speaker cynically resigns himself to continuing it, though he knows his mistress is unfaithful. He cannot leave the honey pot; it has become a "habit."

The attraction of the affair is sensual, as shown by the two meanings of "lie"—conjunction at the physical level, separateness at the spiritual. Not only do the two lovers lie to each other, the speaker lies to himself, and *knows* that he lies to himself. He *pretends* to believe the woman's lies (2) in the hope that she will think him young and naive (3–4), and he makes himself think in one part of his mind that the deception works (5) though he knows in another part that it does not (6). A no-longer young man—one who is fully learned in "the world's false subtleties," including his own—he has ambivalent feelings toward his mistress and toward himself. Line 11 is not mature wisdom but rationalization. Love's *best* habit is trust, not *seeming* trust. Mature lovers can accept each other's faults without needing to lie to each other about them, and the speaker would not feel insecure about his age if he were confident of his mistress's love for him.

The speaker is a number of years older than the woman and is uneasy about the discrepancy. He cannot be really *old*, else he would have no chance even in his own mind of making her think him young.

"Simply" (7) carries its older meaning of "foolishly" (cf. the nursery rhyme "Simple Simon met a pieman"), while "simple" (8) means "plain" or "unadorned." "[V]ainly" (5) primarily means "futilely" (cf. "in vain") but with overtones of "in such a way as to please one's vanity." "[H]abit" (11) is a garment or clothing and also a customary practice. "[T]old" (12) means both "spoken" and "counted."   LP

Ellen Kay Pathedy of Manners (page 689)

Though it wittily satirizes certain modes of social behavior, this poem does not quite fit the literary category of "comedy of manners" because it has no happy ending; nor does it fit the category of "tragedy" because it does not dramatize the sudden "fall" from high to low estate of a protagonist of heroic stature. It is accurately labeled a "Pathedy of Manners" because it concerns the pathetic waste of life and talent by a woman whose false values made her prefer appearance to substance and choose manners over merit. Inasmuch as her false values are those of a class, the poem presents a form of social pathology.

Brilliant, beautiful, and wealthy, the woman of the poem wasted her gifts on inauthentic goals. She might have made some great and useful contribution to humanity; instead she chose to shine in fashionable society and expended herself in acquiring the superficial graces to make her successful there. She learned to distinguish authentic pearls from paste (in necklaces or cufflinks) and to tell real Wedgwood from fraud, but she let fashionable opinion ("cultured jargon") govern her artistic tastes rather than a truly formed and independent judgment. Back home from the obligatory trip abroad, she made an "ideal" marriage (that is, she married a man with impeccable social credentials) and had "ideal" (well-behaved, well-dressed, clean) but lonely children, in an "ideal" (fashionably situated and well-appointed) house. The thrice-repeated adjective exemplifies verbal irony.

Now at forty-three, her husband dead and her children grown, she is going through a middle-age crisis, reevaluating her life and regretting that it has not been more meaningful. She toys with the idea of taking a new direction, but it is too late. The phrase "kill time" (19) has a double meaning. She would like to destroy the time lost since her college years, but can only waste time by dreaming of doing so. Her dreams of taking up that lost opportunity are only an illusion, and she can only "re-wed" (another double meaning) these illusions. Unable to pursue an independent course of action, she can only fend off "doubts" (about the value of her present life) with "nimble talk." Though a hundred socially elite acquaintances call on her, she is without a single intimate friend. The poem ends with a brilliant combination of pun and paradox: "Her meanings lost in manners, she will walk / Alone in brilliant circles to the end." In terms of true intimacy she will be alone, although she will move in brilliant social circles to the end of her life; in terms of meaningful living she will walk in circles till the end of her life, not advance along a line of significant purpose.

The speaker is probably a college classmate of the protagonist, who has seen her the day before, roughly a quarter-century after their first acquaintance. This meeting has caused the narrator to reflect on the protagonist's life.   LP

EXERCISES (pages 691–692)

1. (a) steed, (b) king, (c) Samarkand.
2. (a) mother, (b) children, (c) brother.
3. (a) slender, thin, skinny, gaunt; (b) prosperous, affluent, moneyed, loaded; (c) intelligent, smart, brainy, eggheaded.
4. (a) having acted foolishly.
5. Denotations: fast *runner:* swift; fast *color:* permanent; fast *living:* reckless; fast *day:* abstinent. Connotations: the third is negative, the other three positive.
6. In the first example *white* suggests rare beauty; in the second it suggests extreme fear.

Henry Reed   Naming of Parts (page 692)

The poem presents a corporal or sergeant giving instruction to a group of army trainees. There are two "voices" in the poem, but their dialogue is conducted within the mind of one person, probably that of a recruit. The first three-and-a-fraction lines of all but the last stanza are the spoken words of the sergeant as heard by the recruit. The last two-and-a-fraction lines of these stanzas, and the whole of the final stanza, are the unspoken thoughts of the recruit. This interpretation can be disputed, for there is some ambiguity about the "speaker" in the poem. Exact determination, however, is unimportant. Whoever the "speaker" is, he is a sensitive person. His unspoken thoughts furnish a comment on the instruction he receives or is compelled to give.

The instruction takes place out of doors. It is spring. Not far off are gardens in blossom, with bees flying back and forth, cross-pollinating the flowers. The time apparently is just before or just after the outbreak of a war, during a period of rapid mobilization, for the equipment of the recruits is incomplete. Their rifles have no slings and no piling swivels.

The meaning of the poem grows out of the ironic contrast between the trainees and the gardens, both of which have symbolical value.

Besides lacking slings and piling swivels, the trainees have not got a "point of balance," in one sense the point on the rifle at which it balances on the finger, in another sense a psychological point of balance in their lives. Living in barracks, apart from wives and sweethearts, they are living an unnatural kind of life. Their lives are incomplete, like their equipment. By learning the parts of the rifle, they are preparing to kill and be killed. They are living a regimented life. Being raw recruits, they are awkward. Their lives are tedious, as expressed by the repetition of dull phrases. The rifle is a mechanical instrument, and their lives are likewise mechanical.

The gardens represent the natural, the free, the graceful, the beautiful, the joyous—everything that is missing from the lives of the trainees. The bees, by fertilizing the flowers, are helping to bring about new life. The trainees and the gardens thus symbolically represent a series of opposites: death versus life, incompleteness versus completeness, the mechanical versus the natural, regimentation versus freedom, awkwardness versus grace, drabness versus beauty, tedium versus joy—the list can be extended. Through this ironic juxtaposition, the poet indirectly makes a statement about the kind of life imposed on man by war and preparation for war.

The poem is heavy with sexual implications and, if handled with tact, discussion of these will open up a further dimension of meaning. If handled clumsily, such discussion will give this aspect of the poem a false emphasis and send students away thinking it a "dirty" poem. Men segregated from women tend to become obsessed with sex and to think of women as sexual objects rather than as persons. The absence of normal contacts between the sexes is one reason for the lack of a "point of balance" in the recruits' lives. Many words and phrases in the poem symbolically or connotatively suggest sexual "parts" or actions: "thumb," "bolt," "breech," "rapidly backwards and forwards," "assaulting and fumbling," "cocking-piece."

The language and rhythm of the poem beautifully support its central contrast. The words of the sergeant are prosy, and their rhythm is a prose rhythm, frequently faltering and clumsy. In the lines about the gardens, the words are beautiful and the rhythm flows. The abrupt change in rhythm from smooth to halt is especially striking in the middle of line 17.

The poem is discussed by Richard A. Condon in *Explicator* 12 (June 1954): item 54.   LP

Langston Hughes   Cross (page 693)

The speaker is a "cross" (literal) between black and white, and this is the "cross" (metaphorical) that he has to bear. There is also an overtone of the adjectival meaning "angry" in the title.   LP

William Wordsworth   The world is too much with us
(page 694)

This sonnet juxtaposes nineteenth-century Christian English faith in industrial development and mercantile values with a primitive faith in the pagan deities of nature. As one scholar puts it, it is in the traditional mode of

the conflict between Christ and Pan, but the conflict is exacerbated by identifying Christianity with modern materialism and urban insensitivity to nature. Wordsworth places his speaker at a fulcrum: he is forlornly identified
with the modern, and his own way of glimpsing natural vitality and harmony
is by wishing he could be a pagan—though he knows intellectually that the
beliefs of ancient Greece are "outworn."

The speaker stands in a grassy meadow on a calm moonlit night, in view
of the sea. This placid and unspectacular situation makes him forlorn as he
thinks of the worldliness that destroys emotional and imaginative response
to natural beauty. "We," including the speaker, have traded away the real
power of imagination that we possessed; we "get" wealth, but we "spend" our
hearts for it. Nature is no longer ours, nor we hers.

The opening quatrain abstractly generalizes, withholding the motive for
the generalizations. It contrasts the presumed power of trade with the internal power of the imagination, and declares that the real cost of a materialistic value system is our hearts.

The second quatrain begins to set the scene, establishing the time and
place: it is night, the sea is calm, the moon is bright, and the expected high
winds of the seaside are subdued. The speaker poetically personifies sea and
winds, an imaginative contrast to the philosophical generalizations of the
first quatrain, representing the speaker's attempt to display his own sensitive
image-making powers—but his images tend toward triteness, as lines 8–9
suggest by abruptly changing the tone to straightforward colloquialism. The
phrase "For this, for everything" reveals a loss of imaginative concreteness,
and the cliché "out of tune" emphasizes the speaker's failure either to feel or
to create. As a transition from octave to sestet, these lines appear to give up
the attempt to counter crass materialism with poetic originality.

Instead, beginning in line 9, the speaker swears (by his Christian God)
his preference for a pagan creed that would allow him to believe in such
mythical nature deities as Proteus and Triton as antidotes for his forlornness.
But in fact he was not "suckled" in such a creed and can summon up only a
glimpse of these nature gods, ironically created for him by great Christian
English poets of the past. "Pleasant lea" is quoted from Spenser's "Colin
Clouts Come Home Again," a description of Colin's first view of England
(line 283); the reference to Proteus alludes to Milton's *Paradise Lost*
(3.603–604); and line 14 refers again to "Colin Clout": "Triton blowing loud
his wreathèd horn" (line 245). Desiring to reach backward to a natural pa-
ganism, the speaker must rely on his Christian poetic heritage. Furthermore,
he realizes that he cannot actually hold such beliefs and is wistful about the
"outworn" but imaginative mythological personifications of sea and wind,
visible Proteus, audible Triton, representing a lost harmony between man
and nature.

For further discussion of the mythical and literary allusions, see Douglas
Bush, *Mythology and the Romantic Tradition in English Poetry* (Cambridge: Harvard UP, 1937) 58–59.   TRA

Adrienne Rich   "I Am in Danger—Sir—" (page 695)

QUESTIONS

1. Vocabulary: *snood* (4), *variorum* (6).
2. Analyze the connotations of the following words: "scraps" (3), "monument" (6), "pulsed" (11), "battered" (12), and "buzzing" (18).
3. In a letter to his wife, Higginson referred to Dickinson as "half-cracked." Does the poem suggest this as an appropriate description of Dickinson? Why or why not?
4. What are the multiple denotations of the final word of the poem, "premises" (24)? How does this pun provide an effective closure for the poem?

This poem is Rich's tribute to Emily Dickinson, about whom Rich has also written in the essay "Vesuvius at Home: The Power of Emily Dickinson." It is Dickinson's power as an artist that Rich also celebrates here, portraying Dickinson's incessant thinking as a battering ram: "your thought pulsed on behind / a forehead battered paper-thin" (11–12).

The poem's title is an enigmatic statement from one of Dickinson's letters to T.W. Higginson, the *Atlantic Monthly* editor with whom the poet corresponded for more than two decades. Yet Higginson wrote to his wife that he considered Dickinson "half-cracked," and Rich employs imagery of war to convey the difficult path Dickinson's work endured toward publication in the eccentric but powerful form in which Dickinson wrote her poems. Her *oeuvre* was a "battlefield" (3) for almost a century (by referring to Dickinson's short poems as "scraps" [3], Rich summons the connotation of a scrap as a fight), until the 1955 Thomas H. Johnson variorum edition became a "monument" (6) to her ultimate victory in the decades-long editorial wars.

Rich praises Dickinson for being "equivocal to the end" (7), paradoxically a woman yet "masculine / in single-mindedness" (13–14). According to Rich, one of Dickinson's signal achievements was her independent use of language, since the "spoiled language" (18) of the now-forgotten poetry popular in Dickinson's era sang of "Perjury" (20) in the poet's ears.

In tribute to Dickinson's well-known poetic traits, Rich employs brief four-line stanzas, dashes, and unexpected capitalization in her own poem. Her final stanza again praises Dickinson's independence, summoning up the poet's well-known love of solitude: "you chose / silence for entertainment, / chose to have it out at last / on your own premises" (21–24). The phrase "have it out" picks up the fighting metaphor initiated earlier in the poem, and the pun on "premises"—Dickinson's literal home, and her independently achieved intellectual premises—is another tribute to one of the older poet's own favorite techniques.

This poem is discussed at length in Claire Keyes, *The Aesthetics of Power: The Poetry of Adrienne Rich* (Athens: U of Georgia P, 1986) 81–83. Keyes observes: "Rich imagines Emily Dickinson's retreat from the world as being caused by an intense focus on language, as if Dickinson literally could not live with the 'spoiled language' about her and had to withdraw to a world shaped and sustained, the poem implies, by the language of her poetry" (81). See also Craig Werner, *Adrienne Rich: The Poet and Her Critics* (Chicago: American Library Association, 1988) 101–02.   GJ

Robert Frost   Desert Places (page 696)

Unlike "Stopping by Woods on a Snowy Evening" (page 793), this poem presents a speaker who observes a snow scene but who does not pause to consider his relationship to it; he is "going past" (2), and the first line suggests speed and urgency in doing so. Nevertheless, his observation draws him into a meditation in which the natural phenomenon is an analogue to his state of mind and spirit. The field is about to become smooth and empty as the snow will cover all evidence of growth, both cultivated crops and intrusive weeds, and has already obliterated traces of animal life. Very soon, the snow will in turn be completely obscured by the darkness. Despite his sense that this process is not directly related to him, this suggests to the human observer a loneliness of an extreme sort, a loneliness so profound that it implies cosmic emptiness and meaninglessness: the scene will become "A blanker whiteness [etymologically a redundant phrase] of benighted snow / With no expression, nothing to express" (11–12). The blanking out of all distinctions by the snow is to be followed by darkness so profound that it reminds the speaker of total moral or intellectual ignorance, as the double denotation of "benighted" implies.

This extreme vision of nothingness is expressed in rich and impressive diction that creates the rhetorical climax of the poem. It is followed by a deflating drop in tone and diction as the speaker attempts to deflect the seriousness of his insight. The childlike slanginess of "scare" comes at the point where we might anticipate *terrify* or *horrify,* but instead we hear some of the bravado of a frightened child, daring someone to scare him. This deflation of tone is extended by the usually comic double rhymes of the last stanza: *spaces–race is–places.* (That Frost intended this comic effect is suggested by his revision of the poem between its first publication in *American Mercury* 31 [1934] and its book publication in 1936. Line 14 originally read "on stars void of human races"; the revised version, by using two monosyllables to create the feminine rhyme, calls more attention to it.)

The speaker's strategy—to make little of the terror he has induced in himself by his thoughts about the snow scene—has the dismissive air of the endings of "Design" (page 796) and "Bereft" (page 716), and like them, ironically expresses feelings even more terrifying. Why worry about the infinite emptiness of the universe, he says, when one can find that quality of emptiness simply by examining one's own spirit. Understated and even jocular as it is, this concluding stanza is of course even more frightening than the observation of the snowfield.

The poem makes use of two important allusions. The title and concluding phrase are quoted from Hawthorne's *The Scarlet Letter,* chapter 18, where "desert places" are introduced as a simile to describe the "moral wilderness" into which Hester Prynne is free to wander as the result of her expulsion from society. "They" who cannot terrify the speaker (13) have been identified as astronomers, but also as followers of Blaise Pascal, who wrote, "The eternal silence of these infinite spaces terrifies me" (*Pensées*, 206).

This justly famous poem has drawn many interpreters. Among them there is some disagreement (as indeed this manual entry does not agree with all of them). See two essays in *Frost Centennial Essays* (Jackson: UP of Mississippi, 1974): Albert J. von Frank, " 'Nothing That Is': A Study of Frost's 'Desert Places,' " 121–32, and Edward Stone, "Other 'Desert Places': Frost and Hawthorne," 275–87. Other comments may be found in Reuben A. Brower, *The Poetry of Robert Frost: Constellations of Intention* (New York: Oxford UP, 1963) 108–10; Lewis H. Miller, Jr., "Two Poems of Winter," *College English* 28 (1967): 314–16; Seymour Chatman, *An Introduction to Poetry* (Boston: Houghton, 1968) 11–13; Charles B. Hand, "The Hidden Terror of Robert Frost," *English Journal* 58 (1969): 1166–68; Carol M. Lindner, "Robert Frost: Dark Romantic," *Arizona Quarterly* 29 (1973): 243–44; Frank Lentricchia, *Robert Frost: Modern Poetics and the Landscapes of Self* (Durham, NC: Duke UP, 1975) 95–99 and *passim*. In Norman Friedman and Charles A. McLaughlin, *Poetry: An Introduction to Its Form and Art* (New York: Harper, 1961), this poem is used in nine chapters as the central example for various approaches to analysis of poetry.   TRA

John Donne   A Hymn to God the Father (page 697)

According to Izaak Walton, Donne's first biographer, this poem was written during a severe illness in 1623. It is a *confession* of sin and a *prayer* for forgiveness; but by its acknowledgment of the power and mercy of God, it becomes a *hymn* as well.

The first two lines refer to *original sin*, the sin we are all guilty of by inheritance from Adam's sin in the Garden. Having "spun / My last thread" means roughly "having reached the end of my life." The image derives from the Greek myth of the three Fates—Clotho, who spun the thread of life; Lachesis, who twisted it; and Atropos, who cut it short—but Donne has effectively simplified the myth. The "shore" is the shore on *this* side of the river or water that one must cross to reach eternal life.

The poet puns on his own name in the penultimate line of each stanza. In the first two stanzas the first "done" means "finished"; the second means both "finished" and "Donne." In the third stanza the first "done" means "performed" (also in line 2), and the second again means both "finished" and "Donne."

In line 15 "thy Sun" is an obvious pun on "thy Son." It is particularly relevant because Jesus was God's agent to bring mercy to mankind, and this poem is a prayer for forgiveness.

In the final line of each stanza, the word "more" is a pun on the maiden name of Donne's wife. We must not think, however, that Donne regarded his marriage as a mistake or counted it among his sins. Rather, he subscribed to the "Neoplatonic belief that to rise to the love of God one must leave behind the love of 'creatures'"; thus his continuing love for Anne is an obstacle to his reaching heaven.

It is worthy of notice that this eighteen-line poem involves only two rhymes; and that the word "forgive" occurs four times, the word "sin" eight times, and the word "done" seven times. These repetitions, along with the two-line refrain, account for much of the poem's power.

Two worthy articles on this poem, especially as to the pun on *more*, are "John Donne's Terrifying Pun," by Harry Morris, in *Papers on Language and Literature* 9 (Spring 1973): 128–37; and "Donne's 'A Hymn to God the Father': New Dimensions," by David J. Leigh, in *Studies in Philology* 75 (1978): 84–92. My quotation comes from the first of these, p. 132.   LP

Elizabeth Bishop   One Art (page 698)

With a forced tone of nonchalance, the speaker in this modified villanelle insists that all losses can be faced stoically. She begins with insignificant losses—keys, a little time, memories of places and names—and proceeds to those of greater emotional value—a prized keepsake, loved houses. Hyperbolically, she reports the loss of realms, rivers, and a continent. The climax of the poem occurs in the final stanza, the loss of a beloved person, which too can be mastered—almost. The last line, with its parenthetic command to herself, reveals that the mastery of this loss requires a great exertion of will, if indeed it can be mastered at all.

Whimsically, the poem is presented as a lesson to the reader: "Lose something every day," until practice in mastering the sense of loss will render future losses less disastrous in their effects. The first three stanzas, in the second person, present the lesson; in the last three the speaker offers her own experience as supporting evidence. But with the increasing sense of regret and even pain, the ironic stance of the speaker is made clear: mastering the sense of loss is not "one art" that can be learned through coping with lesser losses.

The word "loss" is used both metaphorically and literally, undercutting the statement that all losses are equal. The inequalities are manifest when one questions whether or not the references to losing keys, losing time, and losing a beloved person employ the term "loss" in the same sense. What the poet achieves, in seeming to believe that the word is single in its meaning, is the statement that not all loss can be mastered.   TRA

Chapter Four

Imagery

Robert Browning　**Meeting at Night** (page 701)

Robert Browning　**Parting at Morning** (page 702)

The auditory imagery of "Meeting at Night" is strongly reinforced by onomatopoetic effects. In lines 5–6 the sound of the boat's hull grating against the wet sand of the beach seems echoed by the series of *sh*, *ch*, and *s* sounds in "pu*sh*ing . . . quen*ch* . . . *s*peed . . . *sl*u*sh*y *s*and." In line 9 the sharp *p* of the onomatopoetic "ta*p*" is repeated in "*p*ane," and the *-tch* of the onomatopoetic "scra*tch*" is partially anticipated in "*sh*arp" as well as repeated in the rhyme.

Both meanings suggested for the last line of "Parting at Morning" are applicable. The "world of men" does need the contributions of the male speaker to its daily labors; and the speaker himself—as Browning's answer implies—needs the companionship of men as well as the love of a woman.　　LP

EXERCISES (page 703)

1. Lines 7–8: auditory "hoots," with implications of derision; line 16: visual and organic; line 22: auditory and visual. All add to the disgust and revulsion the poem is evoking.
2. Line 3: tactile, kinesthetic, and visual, feeling the wind, sensing and observing the shaking, evoking a sense of pity and threat; line 5: tactile and visual; line 6: visual. All contribute to the essential contrasts between temperate and intemperate.
3. Line 17: visual; line 18, olfactory; line 29, tactile. The first two augment the pity and admiration for the girl; the last underscores the frantic terror and horror of the distraught mother.
4. Line 7, visual; line 27, visual and auditory; line 47, visual. All three water images contribute to the sense of an inevitable liquid progress toward dissolution.

Gerard Manley Hopkins　**Spring** (page 703)

Hopkins's poem is an Italian sonnet. The octave is descriptive; the sestet makes a religious application. The abstract statement of the first line is made concrete with rich particularized imagery in the rest of the octave, and this richness of imagery is supported throughout the poem by richness of sound—alliteration, assonance, consonance, interior rhyme, and end rhyme.

In the sestet, spring is compared to the Garden of Eden, and this in turn to childhood. The three things thus compared have at least three things in common: (a) they are characterized by abundant beauty, sweetness, and joy; (b) they each occur at the beginning of something—the year, human existence, individual life; (c) they are innocent, free of sin. But the mention of Eden reminds the poet that human beings were thrust out of paradise through the sin of Adam and Eve. He therefore exhorts Christ, the innocent "maid's child," to capture the minds of girls and boys before they too spoil their lives by sinning. The poem is—or ends in—a prayer.

The poem is as rich in associational connections as it is in imagery and sound. For example, blue, the color of thrush's eggs, is the color of the sky (and thus of heaven) and is also the Virgin Mary's color, symbolic of purity. White, the color of lambs and pear blossoms, symbolizes innocence, as do lambs themselves, which also have symbolic association with Christ. Thus religious connotations are already implicit in the octave, ready to be activated by the explicit references in the sestet.   LP

William Carlos Williams   The Widow's Lament in Springtime (page 704)

The most striking imagery in the poem occurs in the first five lines, when the widow is expressing her sorrow directly: "new grass / flames" combines (paradoxically) the color and freshness of springtime's first growth with the visual impression of flickering and leaping upward, and the tactile pain of fire. "[T]he cold fire / that closes round me" compacts the paradox into an oxymoron, combining two contradictory tactile sensations with the suffocating sensation of being closed in. After that point in the poem, the imagery is generalized and flat (in imitation of the widow's lack of responsiveness to what had formerly given her excitement through its visual impressions): the abstractly named colors ("white," "yellow," "red"), the indistinguishable "masses" (denoting quantity, connoting heaviness), even the flatly anonymous "some bushes" have little image-making vividness or specificity.

The widow's choice of her "yard" as the symbol of her grief is appropriate: a fenced, protected, nurtured, cherished space, specially arranged and created for its beauty (and in context, a beauty shared with her husband) has become for her a stifling, heavy, depressing enclosure. A yard, as an artificial arrangement of nature, is contrasted to natural meadows, woods, and marsh. Her son's suggestion is also apt: he wants to entice his mother to go out beyond the yard, to move gradually out of her grief. (The gradualness of the process is beautifully imitated in the periodic sentence structure that draws the attention outward through a series of prepositional phrases in lines 21–23.) For the widow, of course, there would only be one virtue in going out there, a place where she could fall downward into the flowering trees and sink into a literally suffocating marsh.

The tense shift in lines 18–19 is purposeful, though not grammatical or even logical. Now, in her grief, the widow can "notice" in the present tense (without her accustomed joyful response to spring), but even this uninvolved act of noticing feels to her like a past moment to be forgotten, not a present event to be experienced.   TRA

Emily Dickinson   I felt a Funeral, in my Brain (page 705)

A strange, powerful, highly original poem, "I felt a Funeral, in my Brain" is also a difficult one. It describes a funeral and burial service from the point of view of the person who is being buried. But is this funeral literal or metaphorical? If figurative, what is the literal term in the metaphor? If literal, where is the speaker? And why does she report her experience through only one of the traditional five senses—why tell us what she hears but not what she sees, smells, tastes, or touches? It is *not* strange that competent critics have disagreed about a proper reading of this poem.

The description of the funeral service is formal and exact. In stanza 1 the mourners view the body, which has been placed in an open coffin at the front of the church. In stanza 2 the mourners have taken their places in their pews while the preacher conducts the service with Bible readings and observations about the life of the departed. In stanza 3 the pallbearers carry the coffin from the church to the graveyard. In stanza 4 (but beginning with line 12) the dead person hears the church bell tolling for her death. Since they are now outside, the bell's tolling seems to fill the whole of space. Silence itself (personified) has been destroyed, along with the speaker, who has been silent throughout the poem. In stanza 5 the coffin is lowered into the grave.

The poem is confined to auditory imagery because the speaker is confined in her coffin. She cannot see through the coffin lid, and in any case her eyelids have been drawn down over her eyes, so she cannot see even in stanza 1, when the coffin is open. After it has been closed, hearing is the only sense available to her. That she *can* hear is one of those fictions that we must accept on poetic faith.

Is the burial metaphorical or literal? The critical consensus is that it is metaphorical. One interpretation sees the funeral service as a metaphor for spiritual suffering and pain. In the words of William H. Shurr (*The Marriage of Emily Dickinson* [Lexington: UP of Kentucky, 1983] 79), the poem expresses the "mental and nervous exhaustion" Dickinson felt during a crucial period of her life.

The majority of critics, however, read the poem as a metaphor for a mental breakdown—a psychotic episode in the speaker's life. The fact that the "Funeral" was felt in the speaker's "Brain" (not her soul), that she feels her "Sense . . . breaking through" and her "Mind . . . going numb," and especially the climactic assertion that "a Plank in Reason broke," plunging her rapidly down through successively lower states of irrationality until she finally ceases "knowing"—all point toward the funeral's being a metaphor for a progressive case of insanity. But these two interpretations are really not far apart (the second may be seen as including the first), and we need not spend much time debating them. By any standard or by either interpretation, this is a great poem.   LP

Adrienne Rich   Living in Sin (page 706)

QUESTIONS

1. Explain the grammatical structure and meaning of the sentence in lines 4–7. What are its subject and verb? What style of life do its images conjure up? To whom or what does "his" (7) refer? Why might these images induce the woman to move into the man's "studio"?
2. What contrasting connotations, both positive and negative, are contained in the title phrase?
3. On what central contrast is the poem based? What is the central mood or emotion?
4. Discuss the various kinds of imagery and their function in conveying the experience of the poem.

The central contrast of the poem is between glamorous expectation and realistic fulfillment. The central emotion is disillusionment. The woman had thought that "Living in Sin" with an artist in his studio would be romantic and picturesque. The phrase "living in sin" suggests (here) the free, unconventional bohemian life. The word "studio" connotes something appealing, not just a top-story room in a walk-up flat. The sentence in lines 4–7 gives the picture that had arisen in the woman's mind when he had urged her to come live with him. She had not foreseen that the apartment might be dirty, creaky, and bug-infested, with noises in the plumbing—that furniture would have to be dusted, windows cleaned, beds made, and dishes washed—and that her lover would not be romantic all the time. The irony of the situation is that "living in sin" with an artist in his studio proves not much different from marriage to a working man in a run-down apartment.   LP

Seamus Heaney   The Forge (page 707)

The poet pronounces his name SHAYmus HEEny.

The poem evokes the loss associated with the shift from hand-crafted horseshoes to rubber-tired automobiles. Its focus is on the forge of the blacksmith who made and repaired wagon parts (axles, iron hoops for wheels, and above all shoes for the horses that drew the wagons). The speaker claims to know no more than the "door into the dark," literally the door of the forge, figuratively the doorway into a past he has never personally lived. But his imagination—his image-creation—goes beyond merely seeing the darkened doorway and the useless, rusting remnants of an earlier age. He travels into the room, hears the ringing of the hammered anvil, is startled by the sight of the "unpredictable fantail of sparks" (4), hears the hissing of hot iron in water as a new shoe is annealed. He imagines the anvil "somewhere in the center" (6), so central to the smith's work as to be like an altar. And also, in a visual comparison, that anvil is single-horned at one end, like a "unicorn": mythological, romantic, perhaps pathetic, but certainly not to be found in a modern world.

Then the speaker looks again, literally, at the man, leaning out of the doorway (idle, without his old tasks to perform), and notices physical details that place him in the past—the leather apron, the unsightly virility of hairs growing out of his nose. He imagines what the smith must be thinking about: the lost "clatter / Of hoofs" (11–12) as horse-drawn wagons passed, replaced by the shining, quiet auto traffic "flashing in rows" (12). He concludes by imagining that the smith retreats into his forge (and into the past), slamming the door and flicking its latch, there to return to work that no longer needs to be done.

The imagery is excitingly vivid, and sets up meaningful contrasts between what is seen and what is heard. The auditory images evoke both past and present. The past: "anvil's short-pitched ring" (3), "hiss" (5), "clatter / Of hoofs" (11–12), imagery that is sharp and exciting; the present: the sound of his grunting disapproval, the "slam and flick" of shutting out the modern, and the wheezing of the bellows as he beats "real iron" (13–14). The visual imagery similarly is in two contrasting sets: "the dark" (1), "old axles and iron hoops rusting" (2), and the observed appearance of the smith (10–11), all subdued and obsolete, versus "the unpredictable fantail of sparks" (4), an imagined brilliance of the past, and the "traffic . . . flashing in rows" (12), vivid but monotonously mechanical.

The poem is in form an Italian sonnet with approximate or only vestigial rhymes. For example, *water/altar* and *center/square* are rhymed in the second quatrain of the octave, and the *cdcdcd* rhymes of the sestet employ exact rhyme for the *d*-rhymes (*nose/rows/bellows*) but have only the consonance of the *k*-sound for the *c*-rhymes (*music, clatter, flick*).

Thomas C. Foster, in *Seamus Heaney* (U of Michigan-Flint P, 1989, 24–25), offers a symbolic reading of the poem. For him, the distance between the smith and the speaker represents "the inaccessibility of artistic mystery to the nonartist." This interpretation seems to me to overlook the fact that the "nonartist" speaker is in fact a word-craftsman, and also ignores the contrasts between the modern and the obsolete.   TRA

Robert Frost   After Apple-Picking (page 708)

Let us be clear from the start about one thing: the speaker in this poem has had a richly satisfying experience. He may be "overtired," but it is that good kind of overtiredness that comes when a man has worked hard and long at a task he loves and does well. There may be two or three apples he has overlooked somewhere, but what is that to the thousands he has harvested?

No human task is done perfectly. The love he has felt for his task and the care he has put into doing it well are best expressed in lines 30–31: "There were ten thousand thousand fruit to touch, / Cherish in hand, lift down, and not let fall." His love and the care he takes with each apple are beautifully expressed by the grammatical pauses, which slow down the rhythm and divide line 31 into three infinitive phrases, and seem to divide the action itself into separate phases, emphasizing each. His love for the task shines out radiantly from the word "Cherish." His care and concern are indicated by the paradoxical phrase "lift down." His conscientiousness for the quality of his work is further shown by his sending "to the cider-apple heap" (35) every apple that falls to the ground, no matter how unblemished it appears on the outside. The whole harvesting experience is symbolized by the ladder which, one end planted firmly on Earth, points with the other end "Toward heaven." Like the speaker in Frost's "Mowing," this speaker can find in his work here on Earth an almost heavenly joy.

Repetitive labor brings repetitive dreaming. When the speaker tells what form his dreaming is about to take, his dream continues the labor of the day, but on a larger scale: "Magnified apples appear and disappear, / Stem end and blossom end, / And every fleck of russet showing clear." The dream experience blends into the working experience, so that in the lines that follow he is describing both. A rich use of imagery makes the experience vivid and exact: the visual imagery of the magnified apples; the tactile and kinesthetic image in "My instep arch not only keeps the ache, / It keeps the pressure of a ladder-round"; the kinetic image of "I feel the ladder sway as the boughs bend" (where the rhythm makes the line itself sway); the auditory image of "The rumbling sound / Of load on load of apples coming in." These figures of dream experience are one with the work experience. We are reminded again of "Mowing," where "The fact is / the sweetest dream that labor knows." Earlier in the poem we have the olfactory image of "The scent of apples" (8), together with the visual and tactile images of the thin ice skimmed from the drinking trough.

The time of the poem is the end of the day, the end of a season ("Essence of winter sleep is on the night"), and the end of the harvest. These endings, plus the drowsiness of the speaker and the six-times repeated reference to sleep, inevitably invite the reader to read symbolically. The symbolic implication is that sleep after a day's work represents death after a life's work. Four of the six references to sleep come in the last five lines of the poem where the speaker wonders whether his oncoming sleep ("whatever sleep it is") is like the woodchuck's sleep (hibernation) or "just some human sleep." The speaker does not answer the implied question, but insofar as the poem suggests an answer, it is that, if there is a life after death, it will not differ much from the life lived here on earth, perhaps only as much as his dream differs from his waking life. The speaker has fulfilled his life here, and does not need a future life to complete it. The poem does not *say* that; it suggests it.

The phrase "ten thousand thousand" (30) is overstatement. The phrase "just some human sleep" (42) is understatement. At the literal level, the woodchuck's hibernation lasts much longer than man's winter sleep, but the hibernation is a comatose, torpid, dreamless state. Human sleep is shorter, but dream-filled.

This poem is iambic in meter but with irregular line lengths (ranging from six feet in line 1 to one foot in line 32) and with irregular rhyming: every line in the poem rhymes with some other line, but without a fixed pattern. The longest separation of end rhymes is that of *heap* (35) and *sleep* (42), but internal rhymes in between help bridge the gap.

The following discussions of this poem are useful: Robert Penn Warren, "Themes of Robert Frost," *The Writer and His Craft: Hopwood Lectures, 1932–1952* (Ann Arbor: U of Michigan P, 1954) 218–33; Reuben A. Brower, *The Poetry of Robert Frost: Constellations of Intention* (New York: Oxford UP, 1964) 23–27; Robert Faggen, *Robert Frost and the Challenge of Darwin* (Ann Arbor: U of Michigan P, 1997) 313–17; and Jay Parini, *Robert Frost, A Life* (New York: Holt, 1999) 140–42.   LP

Robert Hayden   Those Winter Sundays (page 709)

The central images evoke coldness and heat, and are extended into the emotions reported and experienced by the speaker: his sense of cold indifference to his father in contrast to the emotional warmth expressed in the father's loving care, and in contrast to the warmth the speaker feels for his father now.

The father's actions all imply love: even on Sundays, when he need not rise early to work for his family's sustenance, he is the one who undertakes the task of driving coldness from the house. And he goes beyond the necessity of providing warmth, adding the care of his son's appearance (the "good shoes" that need to be polished for church).

The coldness is made especially vivid in the sensory images that describe it—"blueblack" (2) in the pre-dawn darkness, and so solid and brittle that its retreat from the heat causes it to splinter and break. But the physical warmth of the house cannot dispel the emotional chill: the speaker flatly asserts that "No one ever thanked him," and the household continues to suffer from "chronic angers" (5, 9).

The poem moves from past to present time, and from memory to self-castigation, with the repeated lament "What did I know, what did I know" (13). Thoughtless and indifferent childhood gives way before the mature knowledge "of love's austere and lonely offices" (14), and the poem ends in regret and remorse.   TRA

Jean Toomer   Reapers (page 710)

The plural title ambiguously captures the central contrast of this brief lyric: there are two sets of reapers, both identified as "[b]lack"—men in the first line and horses in the fifth. The contrast is developed between the human reapers with their sense of completeness (as well as the sense of tradition—"as a thing that's done" refers both to their satisfaction with the accomplishment of a sharpened scythe, and to their sense that this is the way the job is to be done) and the machinelike horses drawing the mechanical mower, insensitive to what they destroy, cutting both "weeds and shade," and slaughtering animals in their path.

There is, of course, a distortion in this contrast, since it does not pit the human reapers against the human driver of the mowing machine. Instead it pretends that the inhuman horses are the voluntary force in the use of the machine. The focus moves from the observed and admired human mowers of lines 1–4 to the observed and detested effects of mechanical mowing in lines 5–8. But do not human reapers also cut both weeds and "shade," and do they not kill field rats? Contrasting the effect of the mechanical mower to the attitudes of the human mowers is in its way unfair, thematically, for it compares not the acts of mowing, human or machine, but the feelings of the observer. He sees in the reapers a collective humanity that nevertheless maintains its individuality—although they act in unison, and in a traditional, inherited fashion, they start "one by one" (4). On the other hand, he does not see the driver of the horses drawing the mower; in fact, he credits the horses with driving.

It is tempting to see here a racial suggestion: to the white owners of the fields, black men and black horses are synonymous. But there is the further suggestion that the sensitive observer, pitying the bleeding rat, cannot see the driver of the mowing machine. Is he white? Is he driving horses now, as he drove black men formerly? And is the speaker of the poem black (as the poet was)?

However we answer such questions, we must at least recognize that the poem is clear in its preference for "[b]lack reapers" over "[b]lack horses," even to the extent of glossing over the distorted comparison that results from such a preference. The sound qualities of the poem reinforce the preference: in the first quatrain, the frequent alliteration of *s* and *st*, the assonance of long *e* sounds, and the lilting repetition of "one by one" create a musicality that harmonizes with the speaker's approving tone; in the second quatrain, the *s-* alliteration serves to emphasize not "silent swinging" (4) but startled-stained violence, and *b-* and hard *c-* alliteration lend weightiness and abruptness, while the long *e-* assonance turns up in words of negative connotation: "weeds," "field," "squealing," "bleeds."   TRA

George Gordon, Lord Byron   The Destruction of Sennacherib (page 710)

This poem uses lively, spirited imagery to convey the spirit and meaning of a biblical story: the destruction of an army led by the Assyrian king, Sennacherib, during an invasion of Jerusalem. Visual imagery predominates: the "purple and gold" (2) vision of the Assyrian army, the "sheen" (3) of the spears, the king's "steed with his nostril all wide" (13), the might of the army that has "melted like snow" (24).

Students will likewise respond to the rhythm of the poem, which evokes the violent energies of battle. Bernard Blackstone writes that the poem is "a brilliant metrical and theatrical *tour de force*. Cosmic imagery—stars on the sea, the blue wave rolling nightly, the leaves of the forest, the winds of Autumn, the rock-beating surf, the dew, the melting snow—emphasizes the ironic contrast between the Assyrians' wolfish might, apparently invincible, and the awesome power of 'the Angel of Death' who makes use of the winds to bring about the tyrant's destruction" (*Byron: A Survey* [London: Longman, 1975] 137).   GJ

John Keats To Autumn (page 711)

Opulently rich in imagery, "To Autumn" is also carefully structured. The first stanza deals with the ripening process, the second with harvesting activities, the third with natural sounds. Although each stanza blends various kinds of imagery, each gives prevalence to one kind. The first stanza is dominated by images of fullness and tension, a kinesthetic-organic imagery apparent in such words as "load," "bend," "fill," "swell," "plump," "budding," and "o'er-brimmed." The second stanza places greatest emphasis on visual imagery. The third stanza stresses auditory images, some of them onomatopoetic (*wailful, bleat, whistles, twitter*).

The poem is also structured in time, the three stanzas presenting a progression both in the season of the year and in the time of day. The first stanza presents early autumn: fruit and nuts are coming to ripeness. The second stanza presents mid-autumn: harvesting is in process. The third stanza presents late autumn: the harvest over, stubble-plains remain, and the swallows gather for their migration southward. In parallel movement, the first stanza presents morning: mists are on the fields and the sun is "maturing" (perhaps in the triple sense of climbing the sky, moving toward the winter solstice, and bringing the fruits to maturity). The second stanza presents midday and afternoon: the reaper, overcome by lassitude and the fume of poppies, sleeps on a "half-reaped furrow," and the worker at the cider press watches "the last oozings hours by hours." The third stanza presents evening: sunset streaks the clouds and touches the stubble-plains "with rosy hue," crickets and birds resume their songs.

This double movement in time toward endings, plus the question asked at the beginning of stanza 3, points to the theme of the poem—Keats's most persistent theme—that of transience. In this poem, however, Keats does not regard transience with the anguish manifested in "Ode on a Grecian Urn" (page 918) and "Ode to a Nightingale" (page 977). Autumn (symbolic of the latter part of life) has its beauty (its "music") as well as spring (symbolic of youth); and the images of the third stanza, though touched with melancholy (the day is "soft-dying," the small gnats "mourn," the light wind "lives or dies," the swallows gather to depart), are as lovely as those in the first (when one thinks "warm days will never cease"). The mildness and beauty of the images throughout the poem, the peacefulness especially of those in the third stanza, and the assurance that Autumn has its music too, all reveal a serene acceptance of passing life.

The poem is a sustained apostrophe, addressed to a personified Autumn. Though this personification is most explicit in the second stanza, where Autumn is pictured in various roles as a harvest worker, it is manifested also in the first stanza (where Autumn is "bosom-friend" of the sun, conspires with him, and blesses the vines) and in the third (where it is exhorted not to "[T]hink" of the songs of spring). The sun is also personified, and the fecundity of nature in stanza 1 results apparently from the union of female Autumn and male Sun.   LP

Chapter Five

Figurative Language I

Simile, Metaphor, Personification, Apostrophe, Metonymy

Frances Cornford   **The Guitarist Tunes Up** (page 715)

The guitarist is compared negatively to a "lordly conquerer" and positively to a lover or husband; but, since all three are men, the figurative element in this simile is slight. It is strong, however, in the other half of the comparison—that of a guitar to "a loved woman." Here there is no question of the essential unlikeness of the things compared. (The similarities exist in the curved shape, in the capacity to utter sweet sounds, in responsiveness to the man's touch, and, most of all, in the way they are approached by the man—with "attentive courtesy.")

The literal and figurative terms of the simile come together in the pun on the word "play"—meaning (a) to perform music and (b) to engage in sexual play.   LP

Robert Francis   **The Hound** (page 715)

The dual possibilities of the "hound's intent" are underscored by the poet's craftsmanship each of the three times they are mentioned: (a) the four-syllable word "Equivocal" occupies a whole line of the poem; (b) the opposed possibilities in lines 4–5 are given in a rhyming couplet (the only one in the poem) and by the exact duplication of the meter in the two lines (the only adjacent lines in the poem that match each other exactly); (c) in line 10 the two possibilities are designated by two alliterating monosyllabic nouns ("teeth," "tongue") naming parts of the dog that serve as metonymies respectively for a hostile or friendly intent.

The basic meter of the poem is iambic dimeter, though only lines 2, 7, and 10 are perfectly regular. All lines rhyme, but in an irregular pattern.   LP

Robert Frost   Bereft (page 716)

Time: a fall evening. Place: an isolated house with a wooden front porch (in disrepair) on a hillside overlooking a lake. The speaker has opened the front door to inspect the weather. A storm is coming up. The door tugs at his hand. The wind swirls the leaves up against his knee like a striking snake. Waves break in foam and spray against the shore of the usually placid lake.

There is "Something sinister" (11) in the tone of the poem as well as in the sound of the wind. The title, the imagery, the massed rhymes all give the poem such ominousness and weight as to overbear any comfort the speaker may hope to give himself in the last two words.

The sounds of the poem reinforce the oppressive tone. Although the poem is sixteen lines long, it uses only five rhyme sounds, almost only three. Ten lines end in rhymes containing long -o- sounds, reinforcing the onomatopoetic *roar* and the desolation of the twice-repeated *alone* (see discussion of phonetic intensives on page 865). Four lines end in rhymes with prominent -s- sounds reinforcing the onomatopoetic *hissed*. The two remaining lines end only in an approximate rhyme (*abroad–God*), further weakening the force of the last line to reassure the speaker or the reader. The onomatopoeia of *hissed* is supported not only by the rhymes, but by the repeated s-alliterations in the lines following; it is anticipated in the repeated -s- sounds of the lines preceding.

The wind in line 3 would seem to be compared to a wild beast. The "restive" (4) door is personified—as if it had a will of its own. The speaker's "life" (15) is like some habitation he lives in that is larger than his house— but no stronger.   LP

Emily Dickinson   It sifts from Leaden Sieves (page 717)

The subject of "It sifts from Leaden Sieves" is snow, though nowhere is this subject named. Instead, it is developed through a series of metaphors in which the literal term is represented by the pronoun "It." Most of these are metaphors of the third form in which only the figurative term is named ("Alabaster Wool," "Fleeces," "Celestial Veil"). In lines 1–2 and 17–18, however, not even the figurative term is named. In 1–2 it is flour; in 17–18 it is some kind of soft white cloth or lace. These are metaphors of the fourth form.

The "Leaden Sieves" refer to the darkened sky or clouds from which the snow is fallling (a metaphor of the third form). But kitchen sieves were ordinarily (during Emily Dickinson's time) tinware; hence another metaphorical process is involved in the substitution of "Leaden," with its connotations of heaviness and darkness in the weather, as opposed to the lighter, shinier connotations of tin. "Wool" as a figurative term for snow suggests softness and whiteness, but the introduction of "Alabaster" as an adjective brings in an additional comparison, making the snow whiter and giving it a surface crustiness or hardness.

"Face" is an appropriate metaphor for a natural surface (even a dead metaphor in such phrases as "the face of a cliff"), but faces are seldom "Even"—so this is a special face, a face compared to something having a smooth, flat surface. "Unbroken Forehead" works in a similar way: this is an unwrinkled or unfurrowed forehead. The harvested field of "Stump, and Stack—and Stem" is metaphorically compared to a room once inhabited (before the harvest) by a personified summer but now "empty" (no longer filled with growing grain). The "Artisans" are snowflakes, the ghostlike weavers of the fleeces, veils, ruffles, and laces. At the end of the poem the snowflakes stop falling, but their creation—the variegated designs of snow on the ground—remains.   LP

David Mason   Song of the Powers (page 719)

This poem employs a familiar children's game to make a statement about the destructive nature of power.

By personifying the stone, paper, and scissors, the poem conveys the rather obtuse viewpoints of egocentric elements that can only revel in their own powers without seeing the destructive nature of those powers. Diction such as "crush" (3), "smother" (9), and "gashing" (15) suggests this destructiveness, but each element's tone of self-congratulation predominates, as in the third stanza in which the scissors says, "nothing's so proper / as tattering wishes" (17–18).

In the last stanza, personification is dropped and the speaker addresses directly what the three elements have said. His primary emphasis is that "all end alone," a phrase that he uses twice (22, 27). His ironic advice that the reader should accumulate power in the form of paper, scissors, and stone somewhat cynically suggests that human beings will seek power at any cost, regardless of the aloneness that results from its destructive effects. The repetitive final line, "as you will, you will," creates a meaningful pun: the reader will seek power, the speaker implies, and that seeking is a result of the human being's blind "will." (The poem alludes here to Friedrich Nietzsche's phrase "the will to power.") The poem's use of a children's game as an emblem of power-seeking emphasizes that the will to power is innate in human beings, in childhood as well as in maturity.   GJ

John Keats   Bright Star (page 721)

One of Keats's finest sonnets, "Bright Star" makes complex use of apostrophe while also exemplifying the poet's superb lyricism.

The address to the star emphasizes its "steadfast" permanence in contrast to the speaker's cherished but fleeting moment of romantic happiness as he lies next to his sleeping lover. He insists he does not want to share the star's isolation as a kind of austere hermit (a "sleepless Eremite"); yet the lyrical beauty of language used to describe the star and its condition implies a measure of envy on the speaker's part. The brilliant second line with its supple alliteration of *l-* and *n-* sounds—"Not in lone splendor hung aloft the night"—emphasizes the majesty of the star's situation; similarly, lines 5–8 portray the star as a serene perceiver of a world purified by waters giving "ablution" to the shores and by snows providing a "new soft fallen mask" to mountains and moors alike.

In contrast to this chill yet beautiful vision, the speaker lies in a "sweet unrest," the poem's key phrase; it suggests both his creaturely happiness and his intellectual dissatisfaction with the knowledge that passion cannot last. His repetition of the words "forever" and "still" signals his keen awareness that his lover's "ripening breast" and "tender-taken breath"—both expressed in participial verb forms emphasizing process and change—can be enjoyed only in a world of time and flux. If the speaker cannot enjoy his passion forever, he would prefer to "swoon to death"—that is, to die during this most exquisite peak of his romantic happiness.

"Bright Star" is a condensed expression of Keats's major concerns as a poet and may be fruitfully compared with his theme of passion vs. permanence as developed more fully in "Ode on a Grecian Urn" (page 918) and "Ode to a Nightingale" (page 977). As Newell F. Ford observes in a lengthy discussion, the sonnet presents "in brief compass the whole of his poetic life, admirably balancing the opposing tendencies within him" (*The Prefigurative Imagination of John Keats* [Hamden, CT: Archon, 1966] 145). Another fine analysis that incorporates biographical considerations and a comparison of the final poem with an earlier version is in Walter Jackson Bate, *John Keats* (Cambridge: Harvard UP 1963) 618–20. Other discussions may be found in John Jones, *John Keats's Dream of Truth* (London: Chatto, 1969) 232–32; Aileen Ward, *John Keats: The Making of a Poet*, rev. ed. (New York: Farrar, 1986) 297–300; and Andrew Motion, *Keats* (New York: Farrar, 1997) 472–74.   GJ

EXERCISES (page 724)

1. Personification and metaphor: day = a man; sky = a blue urn; sunlight = fire. ("Ode")
2. Simile: words = sunbeams.
3. Personification: Joy, Temperance, Repose = persons.
4. Metonymy: pen = literature or persuasive writing; sword = armed might or armies. (*Richelieu*, 2.2)
5. Metaphor: oaths = straw; human desire or impulse = fire i' the blood. (*The Tempest*, 4.1)
6. Metaphor: conventional minds or souls = furnished rooms. (Nothing in a furnished room belongs to or is original with its occupant.) ("The Cambridge ladies . . .")
7. Literal.
8. Metaphor: the desert = a lion. ("Sister Songs" 2)

9. and 10. When asked the difference between these two statements, students usually say that the first expresses certainty, the second possibility. The real difference is that the first is metaphorical, the second is literal; that is, it is literally true that we *may* die tomorrow, but it is literally unlikely that we *shall* die tomorrow. Tomorrow = the day of death; the underlying metaphor is a *lifetime = one day*; and the meaning is "Life is very short; therefore we should enjoy it while we can." The imaginative force that shrinks the span of a lifetime to a single day is destroyed, and the statement rendered drab and prosaic, when this passage is misquoted, as it so often is. "Eat and drink," of course, is somewhat more than literal in both 9 and 10. The sense is "Let us be merry and enjoy ourselves" (we are being urged to drink wine, not water). Eating and drinking may be taken as a symbol, or a metonymy, for living the good life.

Richard Wilbur   Mind (page 725)

The first two stanzas extend the comparison of a mind at "purest play" to a bat flying alone in a pitch-dark cave. The meaning is that as a bat, by means of a physical faculty (its ability to emit high sounds and guide itself by their echoes), can fly freely in the darkest enclosure, so the human mind, with its intellectual capacity, can move freely through the darkness it inhabits—presumably, ignorance, the unknown, mental spaces not yet explored and understood. The qualifying phrases in this comparison are significant: this is the mind at *play*, not striving or reasoning or employing its trained thought processes. And this play of the mind is compared to "senseless wit" in the bat, a paradoxical phrase of multiple denotations. "[S]enseless" denotes both deprived of sensory perception (as a bat is unable to see) and mentally lacking, stupid, or meaningless. The word "wit" denotes the power of drawing surprising and amusing connections between ideas, and expressing those ideas in clever language—but it also denotes intelligence, sagacity, and understanding. Putting those four denotative implications together yields a number of witty combinations: stupid intelligence, blind cleverness, unconscious insight, and so forth. A "senseless wit" guides the blind bat, for without the sense of sight it flies perfectly and purposefully in its cave; that same kind of wit guides the human mind in playful flights that move as if instinctively, or unconsciously, into new areas of intelligence and understanding.

What the bat and the mind can *do* with this "senseless wit" is also brilliantly laid out in the pun in line 4: they can avoid destruction (physical for the bat, intellectual for the mind). The mind will draw no false conclusions, nor will its thinking process cease because of some impenetrable obstacle; the bat will not conclude its flight, nor its life, by colliding with a stone wall.

The last stanza turns to examine and evaluate the simile: has the poet been as witty as a bat in making his comparison? Yes, he answers, but (unlike the bat) the mind also can make mistakes, and some of those mistakes may alter the whole intellectual environment. There is another pun in the "happiest intellection," for *happy* means both delighted or pleased, and lucky or fortunate: the freely playing mind may by good luck come up with new insights that are delightful.   TRA

Emily Dickinson   I taste a liquor never brewed (page 725)

The poet's delight in nature is expressed through an extended metaphor in which ecstasy is likened to intoxication. The liquor on which the poet gets drunk is air and dew and all the beauty of summer. This liquor is natural: it has not been brewed; and "Not all the Vats upon the Rhine" (famous for its breweries) yield a comparable liquor. She drinks it from "Tankards scooped in Pearl" (cumulus clouds in summer skies by my interpretation, but other interpretations are possible). The "inns of Molten Blue" are summer skies, and "endless" is an overstatement modifying "days" or "summer" or both. Bees and butterflies (both of which take nectar from flowers) are her drinking companions, but the poet declares she will out-drink both—drink them under the table! Indeed she will make such a spectacle of herself and raise such a hullabaloo that seraphs and saints will run to the windows of heaven to investigate and, looking out, will see the poet leaning drunkenly against the celestial lamppost!

The fancifulness of the poem's metaphors keeps the poem bubbling with high-spirited fun. The alliteration of *Debauchee of Dew* (6) follows the vowel alliteration of line 5 (all vowels alliterate with each other), in which *every* syllable except one (*-bri-*) begins with a vowel, so that reading it is like taking continuous small sips of air. The trochaic substitution in the first foot of line 7 not only emphasizes the word *Reeling* but introduces a reeling movement into the line. (The basic metrical and rhyme pattern is iambic $x^4a^3x^4a^3$, but in line 15 a metrical pause replaces the last beat, giving emphasis to the delightful assonantal phrase "little tippler" by which the poet characterizes herself.)   LP

Sylvia Plath   Metaphors (page 726)

The speaker is a pregnant woman. The loaf is the growing fetus (an allusion to a slang expression for pregnancy, "she's got a loaf in the oven"). The "fat purse" is her belly, swollen as if she had eaten a bag of green apples. The "red fruit" (like the "yeasty rising" and the "new-minted" money) is the unborn child; "ivory" refers to its skin, "fine timbers" to its delicate bones.

The "train" is pregnancy; the "nine syllables" are the nine months of pregnancy. The poem has nine lines. Each line has nine syllables.   LP

Philip Larkin   Toads (page 727)

Toads are squat, cold-blooded, warty creatures, and, though they can be handled quite harmlessly, their warts do contain a poisonous fluid that oozes out when they are attacked and makes the attacking animal sick. The speaker in this poem, no doubt the poet himself, lugubriously but humorously complains that he is encumbered with *two* toads. The first, specifically identified as work, squats *on* his life, binding him down to a repetitious six-day routine, all for the sake of the weekly or monthly paycheck and an old-age pension. The second toad, left unidentified, squats *in* him, and represents those internal qualities that prevent his throwing over his job and using his wits to live a day-by-day existence, choosing the risky, free life over the safe, unfree one.

Why is the second toad not identified? Because it represents no single nameable quality but a combination of qualities that the speaker himself might find difficult to specify with any exactitude: timidity, prudence, middle-class morality, love of material comforts, perhaps even conscience (though the speaker would be slow to claim this last).

In the final stanza the speaker won't go so far as to say that the first toad embodies the second toad's spiritual truth, but neither does he deny it, and pretty clearly it at least comes close to doing so. That is why he will probably never rid himself of either toad. As so often in Larkin's poetry, the speaker finds himself in a dilemma, caught between alternative choices, neither one of which is fully attractive to him.

The poem is remarkable for its use of an expressive colloquial diction that can modulate through the plain, the slangy, and the vulgar ("Stuff your pension!") yet gracefully pun on that vulgarity with an allusion to one of Shakespeare's most exquisite passages—Prospero's speech in *The Tempest* that includes the lines ". . . We are such stuff / As dreams are made on, and our little life / Is rounded with a sleep" (4.1.156–58).

The phrasing "Lots of folk . . . Lots of folk" (*not* "Lots of folk . . . These folk") seems to indicate that the people mentioned in stanza 3 are not quite the same as those mentioned in stanzas 4–5. Those in stanza 3 "live on their wits" and probably make a fair go of it, perhaps even blarneying their way to fame or the girl or the money, if not all three. "Lecturers" seldom "live up lanes." The people in stanzas 4–5 are paupers, still they don't actually starve, and the toad *work* doesn't squat on their lives.   LP

Adrienne Rich   Ghost of a Chance (page 728)

QUESTIONS

1. Consider the meaning of the title. How is the title appropriate?
2. What does the speaker mean by the "old consolations" (8)?
3. The poem turns on a single simile beginning "like a fish" (10). What meaning does the poem attach to the images of the fish, the "wave" (17), and the "triumphant / sea" (18–19)?

This short poem begins bluntly: "You see a man / trying to think" (1–2). As the title implies, the odds are against him, primarily because he will likely succumb to "the old consolations" (8). In the context of Rich's frequently articulated gender politics, these consolations include all the perquisites of patriarchal power and privilege; it is surely significant that she has specified "a man" rather than a woman or simply a person.

The speaker compares the man trying to think originally and independently to a fish out of water, "half-dead from flopping / and almost crawling / across the shingle" (11–13). The fish simile leads the speaker to compare the man's accustomed element to the "triumphant / sea" (18–19), into which he will be pulled back "blind" (18).

Albert Gelpi sees the sea as a female image opposed to the man's intellectual seeking: "'Ghost of a Chance' pits a man's discriminating intellect against the backward suck of the female sea, undifferentiated and undifferentiating. The rhythms of the middle lines imitate the strained effort to emerge into air, and the monosyllable of the last word-line, climaxing the long drag of the previous line, suggests the satisfaction which comes from the oblivion of the sea's triumph—a satisfaction which makes resistance all the more urgent" ("Adrienne Rich: The Poetics of Change," in Barbara Charlesworth Gelpi and Albert Gelpi, eds., *Adrienne Rich's Poetry and Prose: Poems, Prose, Reviews and Criticism* [New York: Norton, 1975] 288).   GJ

John Donne   A Valediction: Forbidding Mourning (page 729)

Izaak Walton, Donne's first biographer, tells us that Donne wrote this poem to his wife and gave it to her before leaving on an embassy to the French court, a project that would separate them for two months. His wife, who was with child at the time, had been reluctant to let him go, as she feared some ill during his absence.

Without this biographical information, however, we can know that the speaker in the poem is not dying. In the famous simile that concludes the poem, it is the traveling foot that "comes home" to the fixed foot, not the fixed foot that follows after the traveling foot to join it in some other place (such as heaven). Students often get the wrong notion of this poem, partly because of the title, partly because of the death image in the first stanza. It should be pointed out to them that the dying "virtuous men" in this stanza belong to the figurative part of a simile, not to the literal referent. The sense is "Let us part from each other as silently and imperceptibly as a dying virtuous man parts from his soul."

The love of the true lovers (members of the "priesthood") is a love of souls and minds rather than primarily of senses; therefore they can never be truly parted, and they do not "carry on" (like "lay" lovers) when they are physically separated. Donne has skillfully managed his meter so as to force an equal accent on both syllables of "[a]bsence" (15), thus bringing out the pun. Absence, for the "laity," is literally *ab* + *sense*: to be away from sense, to be separated from "eyes, lips, and hands."

Three similes compare the parting of true lovers to the parting of virtuous men from life, to the expansion of gold beaten into gold leaf, and to the separation of the legs of a pair of drawing compasses. A metaphor compares it to the almost imperceptible "trepidation" (trembling) of the spheres (as contrasted to the gross movements of the earth—flood, tempest, and earthquake).   LP

Andrew Marvell   To His Coy Mistress (page 730)

Perhaps the greatest obstacle to student understanding of this poem is its title. The word "Mistress" has none of its most common modern meanings: the "lady" (2, 19) of the poem is, in fact, a virgin (28). Also, the word "coy" means no more than "modest" or "reluctant," without its usual modern connotations of teasing or playing hard-to-get. The lady is reluctant to accede to her lover's pleas because of "honor" (29), which requires that she preserve her virginity until marriage. But the young man is not proposing marriage. In short, this is a seduction poem. It is also a *carpe diem* poem. The speaker belittles the lady's "honor" as of no importance in the face of the brevity of life and the imminence of death. Life being so short, they must enjoy their pleasures *now*. He puts his argument into syllogistic form: (a) *if* we had time enough, your coyness would not be a crime; (b) *but* time rushes on, death comes quickly, and nothing follows; (c) *therefore* we should make love *now*.

The poetic force of the poem derives, not from the cogency of the syllogism, but from the fancy, wit, and imaginative force with which it is presented. First, the speaker elaborates the temporal with the spatial dimension. If they had "world enough, and time" (he says), not only could they stretch out his courtship from "ten years before the Flood" (an immeasurably distant time in the past) till "the conversion of the Jews [to Christianity]" (an inconceivably remote time in the future), but they could pass their time separated by oceans and continents (she looking for rubies along the river Ganges in India; he complaining, in verse or song, of her coldness by the river Humber in England). He could allow his "vegetable love" to grow "Vaster than empires, and more slow." (The phrase "vegetable love," suggesting a love bloodless and unimpassioned, capable only of growth, subtly makes such a prospect seem undesirable.) He could also spend the amount of time praising her beauty that each of its features deserves, and would end up praising her heart (implying that his love for her is more than physical, as he would be glad to demonstrate if he had time). The tone of this first section is fanciful and playful; it is appropriately the longest of the poem's three sections, for it depicts a state of nature in which there is no need to hurry.

At line 21 the tone changes dramatically. It becomes urgent. The speaker constantly feels "Time's wingèd chariot" about to overtake him. Time is at his back; and ahead (after death) he sees nothing but "Deserts of vast eternity" (eternity is a desert, a vast blank, a place without life). In the grave, she will lose her beauty; he will no longer be able to sing her love songs; she will lose her "long-preserved virginity" ("You're going to lose it anyway," the lover implies; "would you rather lose it to me—or the worms?"); her "quaint honor" will turn to dust (the word "quaint" has a slightly deprecatory connotation here, suggesting something without real importance; and a sexual pun buried beneath the word further trivializes the "honor" it is attached to); and, finally, his "lust" will turn to ashes (the speaker is quite frank here in confessing that his desires are physical). This section ends with a wry irony: the grave would seem a perfect place for making love—dark, quiet, private—but, strangely, no one makes love there.

Therefore, says the speaker, let us make love while we are young and eager, desiring and desirable. Let us love, not with a "vegetable love," but like "amorous birds of prey" (fiercely, like hawks or eagles). Let us devour time before time devours us. Rather than remaining as far apart as the Ganges and the Humber, "Let us roll all our strength and all / Our sweetness up into one ball" (a sphere is the most compact concentration of matter) "And tear our pleasures with rough strife / Thorough the iron gates of life." (There is considerable disagreement about the exact reference of the "gates of life" image, but the tone and meaning of the lines are clear enough. The tone is resolute and determined; the meaning is, Let us love, not passively and delicately, but passionately and actively.) Thus, though we cannot make time stand still (we cannot hold back death), we can make it seem to pass very quickly (excitingly, vitally, rather than dully or monotonously).

The poem concerns time more than love. It is perhaps the most intense, most urgent *carpe diem* poem in English. The poet has chosen love-making as a symbol for any activity that involves living intensely. As an argument for seduction, the poem is certainly specious. The lady, by waiting till she can fulfill her desires honorably, may save herself fifty years of misery. Conceived of, more generally, as an argument for spending one's hours in pleasurable, useful, or rewarding activities, the argument has greater force. The person who has to "kill time" out of boredom is a pitiful failure. The speaker is determined to master time rather than let it master him.   LP

Langston Hughes   Dream Deferred (page 732)

Specifically the "dream deferred" is that of full and equal participation of blacks with whites in the political and economic freedoms supposedly guaranteed by the Constitution. Metaphors, because more condensed, are (other things being equal) more "explosive" than similes. The metaphorical comparison of black frustration to a bomb (metonymically representing a race riot or even armed revolution) is therefore appropriately placed in the climactic position.   LP

Billy Collins   Introduction to Poetry (page 732)

This whimsical satire on beginning readers of poetry should probably not offend many students because of its exuberant wealth of apparently disconnected figures of speech. The speaker is a teacher (or perhaps a poet, or a poet/teacher) who wants to arouse his students to react to a poem as an experience rather than as a statement or message. He begins with the nearly-literal figure of simile, comparing a poem to "a color slide" (3) which can yield a little—but not much—when held up to the light, for a slide requires a slide-projector and a screen to make a full impact on the viewer. But as a starting place, the simile seems appropriate: it says that the full power of a poem is only barely sensed when it looks like a miniature picture. It requires projected light (insight? imagination?) and magnification (intense interest? curiosity?) to yield its experience. The simile suggests reader involvement but also implies some level of passivity, as if the poem were an external object to be viewed as a picture of reality. With proper projection and magnification, its surface meaning will be rewarding enough.

But in line 4 the speaker turns to a metaphor that demands more than passive observation. A poem is like a bee-hive, full of movement, a place of reproductive activity and stored sweetness, and it buzzes as a sign of the richness of its life. One must listen as well as look, and consider both interior and exterior signification.

The metaphors in lines 5–8 require a different kind of involvement with a poem. A poem can be like a maze with its twists and turns ultimately leading to freedom and release. It can be like a darkened room in which the reader gropes for some source of illumination that will suddenly make everything starkly clear. The metaphor in lines 9–11 again shifts to a more active reading, demonstrating the rush of excitement and pleasure, the exhilarating joy that comes from mastering balance and wave as one skis across the surface of a deep, sustaining body of water that is identified in the distance by the creator of that element.

Sadly, the slide/bee-hive/maze/room/lake give way to the final metaphor comparing the poem to a criminal suspect who won't talk and the reader to a brutal interrogator. All the liveliness of interplay and participation is cast aside. The poem is tied down and tortured and beaten because it will not state in plain terms "what it really means." The frustrated readers are looking for the key, the magic stone, the plum in Little Jack Horner's Christmas pie (see page 791), or what we have called the prose meaning. Not joy nor excitement, but information, is what these readers demand. Perhaps if they engage themselves sufficiently with "Introduction to Poetry" they can get beyond that stage.   TRA

Chapter Six

Figurative Language 2

Symbol, Allegory

Robert Frost   **The Road Not Taken** (page 734)

Since the publication (1970) of the second volume in Lawrance Thompson's three-volume biography of Frost, there have been an increasing number of different interpretations of "The Road Not Taken." These interpretations see the poem principally as an example of dramatic irony rather than of symbol. They are perhaps best summed up in Elaine Barry's discussion (in *Robert Frost* [New York: Ungar, 1973] 12–13) by her statement that "the poem is a gentle parody of the kind of person whose life in the present is distorted by nostalgic regrets for the possibilities of the past, who is less concerned for the road taken than for the 'road not taken.'" The impetus for these interpretations was provided by Thompson's revelation that Frost himself regarded the poem as a gentle spoof of his English friend Edward Thomas and thought of Thomas rather than of himself as the speaker in the poem (*Robert Frost: The Years of Triumph* [New York: Holt, 1970] 87–89, 544-48). After a careful review of the evidence, both external and internal, I find myself unable to accept these ironic interpretations. (I fall back on D. H. Lawrence's adage, "Never trust the artist. Trust the tale.") However, the instructor should know of the existence of these other interpretations, and may wish to raise them for discussion in the classroom.   LP

Walt Whitman   **A Noiseless Patient Spider** (page 736)

The situation of a man accepting the energies of a spinning spider as an example to himself should recall the famous story of the fourteenth-century Scottish king Robert the Bruce (Robert I), who in apparent defeat retired into a cave for refuge. There he watched the tireless efforts of a spider that despite repeated failure refused to give up spinning; the king resolved to continue in battle—and was victorious. By the nineteenth century this anecdote had become a moral exemplum of the virtue of pertinacity (a narrative version of "If at first you don't succeed, try, try again!").

In its earliest unprinted version this poem had as its theme the poet's sense of loneliness as he searches for love in a world of "fathomless latent souls of love." (See Gay Wilson Allen, *The Solitary Singer* [New York: New York UP, 1967] 342.) The present version transforms both the moral tale and the earlier unprinted poem, changing the subject to the soul's yearning for spiritual truth. "[I]n measureless oceans of space," the soul seeks security, an "anchor." Despite the traditional symbolism of an anchor as Christ or as the hope for salvation (see Hebrews 6.19), the poem does not openly suggest that Christianity is the answer to the speaker's problem. In fact, a "ductile anchor" attached to a "gossamer thread" suggests fragility and plasticity, rather than the security of a defined, systematic religion.

In Whitman's image, the spider resembles a fisherman, unreeling his lines as he launches them forth. The vocabulary of the poem tends to corroborate an implicit nautical or fishing context: "promontory," "launched," "unreeling," "oceans," "bridge," "anchor." Though the speaker seems not to be consciously aware of it, the imagery itself suggests a Christian solution to his problem—the anchor of Christian salvation, with the speaker's search evoking the church's role as a "fisher of men."

While the poem draws an explicit comparison between the spider's activity and that of the spiritually questing man, there are clearly implied contrasts as well: the contrast of size and perspective (a spider's promontory is indeed "little," and the area of exploration may seem to it to be a "vacant vast surrounding," but the range of "measureless oceans of space" inhabited by man is considerably grander); the spider's patience is in contrast to the "musing, venturing, throwing, seeking" of the man; the noiselessness of the spider may be contrasted to this verbal outpouring from the human being; and of course the spider's actions must be read literally, the man's metaphorically.

The poem should be examined for examples of alliteration, assonance, and consonance as poetic devices providing a replacement for regular rhythm and rhyme. Overstatement, particularly in the spatial references, emphasizes the need to recognize contrasts within the overt comparison.   TRA

William Blake   The Sick Rose (page 737)

The "night" and the "howling storm" are part of the symbolic design of the poem: they give it depth and resonance and they *may* be assigned a specific meaning. (The "howling storm" is materialism, say a couple of critics, and I have no objection.) In general, however, there is a danger that the student (and sometimes the professional critic), once the powers of symbolism have been discovered, will want to press down all the buttons, to find an equivalent for every noun in the story or poem. At this point, reading the poem becomes an exercise in ingenuity rather than one in understanding and enjoyment. Symbol-hunting is a practice no less bad, perhaps, than moral-hunting. The symbol-hunter tends to restrict rather than expand the meaning of a poem by converting a symbolic story into an allegory.   LP

Seamus Heaney   Digging (page 739)

The central symbol and metaphor are discussed in the text. Another area of exploration, as indicated in question 2, is the imagery. The poem abounds with sensory signals, most of them (of course) visual, since visual imagery is usually predominant. The first tactile image occurs in line 2, where the thickness of the pen between finger and thumb seems to fit the hand "snug as a gun" (with perhaps a glance at the phrase "the pen is mightier than the sword," and a gun is even mightier). The fourth verse paragraph is the richest in imagery (10–14), including the coarse appearance and feel of the boot, the feeling of a boot nestling on the surface of the spade's "lug," the pressure of the shaft of the spade "[a]gainst the inside knee," and the sensation of the spade being "levered firmly" in the soil. Then we see the strewing of the discarded potato plants, the "bright edge" of the spade disappearing into the earth, the new potatoes being scattered on the surface, and with the children we feel the "cool hardness" of the potatoes grasped in our hands as we gather them up.

The imagery in the second-to-last verse paragraph (25–28) is both full and recapitulative. The scene of the potato digging comes back as a "cold smell," the grandfather's peat digging is audible and tangible as a "squelch and slap / Of soggy peat," and the father's digging in the flower beds ("a clean rasping sound" in line 3) is both heard and felt in "the curt cuts of an edge / Through living roots." This array of sensations comes to life and awakens the poet, who in turn resolves to re-create the experience for others.

The study question asks what *emotions* are evoked by the images. The answer is not simple, just as the emotions of the poem are not simple. Merely one specific example may lead the reader toward the complexity of the issue: "the squelch and slap / Of soggy peat" (25–26) in any other context might be repugnant, for it evokes sound and touch that are unappealing. Yet these sensations are offered as part of the nostalgic pull exerted on the speaker. The men who lived those lives of digging were experts at doing unpleasant and arduous tasks; they did them because they needed to be done; while no one would willingly choose to work so hard as a labor of love, the speaker regrets that he himself has "no spade to follow men like them" (28).   TRA

Robert Herrick   To the Virgins, to Make Much of Time
(page 742)

The rosebuds in the first stanza symbolize pleasures. The general meaning of the poem is to enjoy life while one can, for life is short, and the capacity for enjoyment is progressively and sharply reduced in middle age and old age. The last stanza specifies one kind of pleasure—but an important kind: sexual fulfillment in marriage. In the title, the word "virgins" rather than *maidens* underscores the sexual significance.

The meaning of a symbol, like the meaning of a word, is largely controlled by context. Herrick's rosebuds are generalized by the author's emphasis on the swift passage of time, and by his use of the plural rather than the singular. *Gathering* rosebuds suggests getting as many as possible, and thus the rosebuds suggest a variety of pleasures—including, of course, the pleasure of gathering rosebuds.

"[S]miles" (3) personifies the flower that is dying, thus adding poignance to its death and preparing us for the idea that it is the death of persons, not of flowers, that Herrick is really concerned about. "[R]ace" (7) emphasizes swiftness. "[S]pent" (11) has the connotation of exhausted or wasted, whereas "use" (13) suggests making a profitable or worthy employment of a resource (in this case, time).   LP

George Herbert   Peace (page 743)

A mental quest in this poem is allegorically treated as a geographical search; that is, the literal question *How can I achieve peace of mind?* is translated into the figurative question *Where does Peace dwell?*

The "reverend good old man" (19) is a clergyman. The word "reverend" is skillfully used to suggest two meanings: worthy of being revered, and belonging to the clergy. His "garden" (37) is the Church. The "prince" (22) is Christ, "the Prince of Peace"; the "twelve stalks of wheat" (28) are the twelve apostles; the "grain" (37) is the Christian gospel. The first three stanzas have the general meaning of "I searched everywhere." But, more specifically, the secret cave suggests solitude; the rainbow, beauty; and the "gallant flower" (the "Crown Imperial"), the royal court.

The simplicity of language and the narrative plainness of this poem are beautifully supportive of its subject matter. The poem convinces us by its very manner (at least while we read) that the good life is to be found in plain living and a simple Christian faith, shared in a Christian community—not in the excitements or adornments of a life at court, or in straining after beauty, or in withdrawing from the world. Seldom is allegory more simple or more appealing.   LP

EXERCISES (page 745)

1. a. symbol.   b. literal.   c. metaphor   d. symbol   e. metaphor
2. Dickinson's "I heard a Fly buzz—when I died" symbolizes death by the fly (in ironic contrast to "the King," the expected manifestation of death). Shapiro's "The Fly" introduces several figurative comparisons, but its literal subject is a fly.
3. The symbolism of the tiger is discussed on pages 284–286 of this manual. The "lamb" in this poem is faintly symbolic of meekness, weakness, purity. It might

rather be considered an example than a symbol. Whatever symbolic force it has in this poem is allusive, derived from its traditional uses; this poem does not create that force. I would call it more literal than symbolic.
4. The following are symbolic: a, b, e, h, j, k; the literal poems are the remainder: c, d, f, g, i, l.

Robert Frost   Fire and Ice (page 746)

Scientists have made various predictions about how the world will end, most of them involving either a fiery or an icy terminus. At the time that Frost published this poem (December 1920), probably the two leading theories were (a) that, as the earth gradually loses momentum in its orbit, it will be drawn by gravity closer and closer to the sun, until finally it plunges into the sun and (b) that, as the sun gradually cools, or as the interior of the earth itself cools, the earth will get colder and colder, until finally all life is extinguished in a new ice age. Both theories still have many supporters.

Frost makes symbolic use of these theories. Fire becomes a symbol for desire or passion, ice a symbol for hate, the earth a symbol for human or civilized life ("world" means both physical and social world). The poet has experienced enough of desire and hate within himself to recognize that both passion (e.g., desire for sensual gratifications, possessions, or power) and hate (e.g., between nations, classes, or races) are forces strong enough to bring an end to mankind.

The last line is understatement. Instead of saying that desire or hate could ruin, wipe out, or annihilate mankind, Frost says only that either would "suffice."   LP

Alfred, Lord Tennyson   Ulysses (page 746)

Ulysses represents and recommends a life of continuous intellectual aspiration; he has an avid thirst for life and experience that finds fulfillment primarily in the life of the mind rather than in the life of the senses (his concluding injunction is "To strive, to seek, to find," not "to taste, to touch, to smell"). Geographical exploration in the poem symbolizes intellectual exploration. The key lines for this interpretation are lines 30–32: "And this gray spirit yearning in desire / To follow *knowledge* like a sinking star, / Beyond the utmost bound of human *thought.*" But throughout the poem are words and phrases that reinforce this reading. In line 5 Ulysses characterizes Ithacans as a savage race that "hoard, and sleep, and feed, and know not me" (that is, a people who live a materialistic and physical life and know not the excitement of the intellectual life). In line 13 he says, "Much have I seen and *known.*" In line 46 he addresses his mariners as souls that "have toiled, and wrought, and *thought* with me."

The westward journey has a double symbolism that is also congruent with this reading. In sailing westward (toward the setting sun), Ulysses is sailing toward death (going west is a traditional symbol for death); he is also sailing from what, for the Greeks, was the *known* world (the Mediterranean world) into what was for them the *unknown* world (the world of the Atlantic, beyond the Strait of Gibraltar). The meaning is that Ulysses will continue to seek new knowledge, new discovery, until his death. The continuing nature of this search is also indicated in the images of following knowledge "like a sinking star" (31) and of sailing "beyond the sunset, and the baths / Of all the western stars" (60–61). One cannot, of course, ever catch up with a sinking star or with the setting sun; no matter how far west one sails, they still set beyond a horizon still farther west. Likewise, no matter how much knowledge one gains, there is still further knowledge to be sought. Thus Ulysses's quest is truly one of continuing aspiration: his thirst for new knowledge will never be satisfied; he will continue to seek new knowledge until he dies. What will become of him *after* death, he does not know (62–64), but his program for life before death is clearly mapped out.

The image in lines 18–21 includes the idea of a horizon that is always to be sought, never to be reached—that is, the idea of knowledge that is never to be exhausted. Lines 26–29 tell us that every hour of life brings new experience, new knowledge. (Grammatically, the subject of "is saved" is probably to be construed as "something more," with "A bringer of new things" in apposition and "every hour" treated as an adverbial modifier; but the ambiguity of the construction suggests the wisdom of saving every hour possible from death, of living as long as possible in order to learn new things.) "[T]hunder" and "sunshine" (48) are symbols for adversity and good fortune. "[H]earts" and "foreheads" (49) are metonymies for wills and minds (the meaning is "We confronted the thunder and the sunshine with free wills and free minds"). The poem celebrates strength of will as much as it does the intellectual quest. The metaphor in line 23 compares a person to a sword or a shield.

"Ulysses" has commanded an enormous amount of critical attention. Major discussions of the poem may be found in A. Dwight Culler, *The Poetry of Tennyson* (New Haven: Yale UP, 1977) 224–30; Alastair W. Thomson, *The Poetry of Tennyson* (London: Routledge, 1986) 65–70; Linda K. Hughes, *The Manyfaced Glass: Tennyson's Dramatic Monologues* (Athens, OH: Ohio UP, 1987) 95–100; and Marion Shaw, *Alfred, Lord Tennyson* (New York: Harvester-Wheatsheaf, 1988) 63–65.

The relation of sound to meaning in the poem is discussed on pages 869–71 of the text.   LP

Alastair Reid   Curiosity (page 749)

In its own sardonic and humorous fashion, this poem has much the same theme as Tennyson's "Ulysses." Cats and dogs symbolize two different kinds of people: cats, the intellectually curious, the adventurous, and the unconventional; dogs, the incurious, the prudent, and the conventional. Though the parallel is not to be pressed too hard, Ulysses is a cat, Telemachus a dog. The poet's sympathies are with cats. (Tennyson regards Telemachus more favorably, however, than Reid regards dogs.)

The poem utilizes two folk sayings: "Curiosity killed the cat," and "Cats have nine lives." The poem says that curiosity is dangerous, but that one cannot really *live* without it. Curiosity leads to suffering and discomfort; nevertheless, it is the condition of being really alive. Intellectual curiosity is the kind in question.

"[D]eath" in line 3 means literal, physical death. "[T]o die" in line 16 means to die intellectually, emotionally, and spiritually; that is, to exist in a merely physical sense, like Tennyson's Ithacans—or like dogs. "[T]o die" in lines 34–35 means "to suffer," and "dying" in lines 41–42 means "suffering." Thus "to die" has exactly opposite meanings in lines 16 and 34–35, and these two opposite meanings, being both figurative, are in turn both opposite to the literal meaning of "death" in line 3. These contradictory meanings are not a sign of the author's confusion, as they would be in a logical treatise or in any discursive prose; they are what give life and interest to the poem. Manifested in metaphor, and resulting in paradox, they help the poet probe the real significance of living. He is firmly in control; he knows what he is doing.   LP

Richard Wilbur   The Writer (page 750)

The poem has a double subject, as the ambiguous reference of the title suggests. It concerns the speaker's daughter and the beginning of her career as a writer, and it concerns the speaker-as-writer, creating his poem about her. This situation is made clear at line 11, when the speaker hears in his daughter's typing pause her rejection of his "easy figure," so that he must find a more suitable figure of speech to express his wish for her future.

His first figure, elaborated through the first three stanzas, is in fact traditional, a metaphor comparing her life to a journey. He makes it more vivid and particular by specifying a sea voyage, and by propounding a variety of explicit comparisons: the house is her ship, and the light breaking over the house at the place where her room is located is like the water breaking at the prow of a ship. Her typewriter sounds to him "Like a chain hauled over a gunwale" (6) as she weighs anchor for her trip. The "stuff / Of her life" (7–8)—the weight of her past experiences that she must carry along as cargo (including perhaps his own fame as a writer)—is heavy. He brings the metaphor to a close by wishing her "a lucky passage" (9).

Then it is that he interprets her pause as a dismissal of his comparison, and she and he and the whole house then wait in stillness for his next attempt. His replacement springs to him out of his memory. It is not another metaphor, but a symbol, that of a starling trapped in her room, which after many exhausting attempts to escape, managed finally to find "a smooth course for the right window" and flew from the "world" of the house to its own free world (29, 30).

As a symbol for the girl attempting to become a writer, this is very apt: good writing takes hard work and many arduous attempts; it entails failures and battering. The writer may be able to see the goal but may be blocked, as by a window pane, from flying to it. When success finally comes it is like soaring into another world, and the "spirits" of readers will rise with the writer's. So, as he concludes, writing "is always a matter . . . / Of life or death" (31–32), not a simple forward progression through time and space like a sea voyage but hard work, frustration, and pain, which may be rewarded not with reaching a destination but with transcending the ordinary world.

The poem enacts this process, trying and rejecting a trite metaphor, and from that failure discovering in a memory an original and heartfelt symbol. The girl *may* become a writer; the speaker *is* one.   TRA

Adrienne Rich   Power (page 751)

QUESTIONS

1. What kind of "power" is symbolized by the amber bottle (3)? How does the poem suggest that its "tonic" (4) was not an authentic medication?
2. "Marie Curie" (6) was a Polish-born scientist (1867-1934) who studied in Paris, married the French chemist Pierre Curie, pioneered the study of radioactivity, and received two Nobel Prizes, in physics and in chemistry. Discuss the various meanings of "power" that are implied by the description of her.
3. What does "Marie Curie" symbolize? Is that symbol restricted to women scientists? How is "denying" (14, 16) a symbolic action?

The first line in this barely punctuated poem at first seems merely to be a clause introducing the first statement (lines 2–4), but the repeated "Today" (2, 6) suggests that both incidents, the discovery of the tonic bottle and reading about Marie Curie, are two types of "Living . . . history" (1) that the speaker is exploring, both of them representing varieties of "Power." The opening image of the "backhoe" (2) is yet another type of power, brute mechanical power that is capable of opening up the earth and disclosing its "earth-deposits" (1).

But what chiefly interests the poet in the first example are the mythical power attached to the charlatan's nostrum and the gullibility of those who bought a tonic that could cure either "fever   or melancholy."

Both the hope and the disappointment symbolized by that cure-all are suggested by the hesitant rhythm and beautiful imagery of the second line: "one bottle   amber   perfect   a hundred-year-old." Balanced against this is the despairing fifth line: "for living on this earth   in the winters of this climate." The hoped-for cure has no power beyond the imagination of its purchaser, yet there is in the perfection and persistence of the bottle evidence of a kind of faith that armed our ancestors against despair even if it could not cure their bodily ailments.

The example of Marie Curie is a more personalized symbol of the doubleness of power. The "perfect" bottle is replaced by the "purified" element, both of them elegant and full of promise. Curie knew first-hand the destructive power of the radioactive element she was working with, as it robbed her of her sight and touch, yet she persisted in her work with the "earth-deposits" (1) of pitchblende. Figuratively, she too was delving into the earth, divulging its secret powers. Her discoveries too were full of hope and disappointment. Much-honored, "famous," but doomed by the power she released, she had her "cure . . . for melancholy" (4), the denial that she was being destroyed by the source of her intellectual power.

The concluding four lines demonstrate the effectiveness of those hesitant spaces that sometimes replace punctuation, sometimes merely reinforce rhythms. The ambiguities of grammar are especially poignant: in line 14, the word "denying" might be taken as an absolute term, but it has a direct object, "her wounds" (15). The phrase is then altered and extended: at first she seemed a person in denial, then a person who denied that she had wounds, and finally a person who denied the cause of those wounds.

The symbols may also be read in the light of the poet's feminism to focus more pointedly on a woman's experiences, particularly when the last line concludes with the positive assertion that despite the self-destructive result, Curie found in uranium a source of her own power. "She died," but it was the death of "a famous woman" (14) who had triumphed in that male preserve, science. And though she shared her Nobel prize in chemistry with her husband, she also won the physics prize, the only woman ever to be doubly awarded by the Nobel committee. From this perspective, her power was the greater because of her sex. And of course the power of her discoveries has outlived her and grown greater through their further development.   TRA

Emily Dickinson   Because I could not stop for Death

(page 752)

Beyond doubt, this is the most discussed of Emily Dickinson's poems, and it has excited a wide array of interpretations. The literal content seems to offer few difficulties: a woman busy with her life is called away from it by a kindly gentleman (Death), who takes her for a carriage ride past the living, pauses at what must be her grave, and proceeds through centuries toward the destination "Eternity." There are many fine details characterizing the stages of life in stanza 3; stanza 4 emphasizes both the femininity of the speaker and the chilliness of her ride; stanza 5 mysteriously understates her burial; and the last stanza perpetuates the ride in Death's carriage beyond the human comprehension of time (the concept of eternity, as Keats says in the last stanza of "Ode on a Grecian Urn," teases us "out of thought").

There is little quarrel among the critics about these literal matters. The continuing question is what this little allegory *means*. Does it link death with sexuality (the gentleman come courting)? Does it pretend to render a judgment on posthumous experience? Does it define the values of life as they are discovered in the moment of dying? Does it celebrate the soul's entry into heaven? These suggestions, and several others, have been made by eminent critics and scholars. Furthermore, there is little agreement about the tone of the poem—is it confident? whimsical? terrified? triumphant? uninvolved?

What follows, then, is *one* interpretation that is both plausible and consistent with the poet's ideas. The teacher may wish to use this poem, and the references below, as an introduction to discriminating between critical approaches and interpretations.

Death is remarkably, and surprisingly, characterized in this personification as "kindly," a word that so violates normal expectations as to signal the need for interpretation. Death has traditionally been thought of as "kind" to the extent that it releases a person from a life of suffering or from the limitations imposed by mortality. Such a meaning might be implied by the fact that "Immortality" is included as a personified fellow-passenger in the carriage, but the images of life in the poem do not suggest a life of pain—it contains both labor and leisure, nonchalantly linked by alliteration, which are as easily put away as a basket of sewing; and it is represented by the playing children and the maturing grain. In fact, life and death seem equally attractive, and the speaker, pleased with Death's "Civility," apparently accepts his invitation with pleasure. The poem presents Death's visit not as an inevitable and unavoidable event, but as a polite invitation that the speaker finds attractive—an interpretation that divides the speaker form ordinary people.

The tone of the poem is governed by the speaker's willingness to accept Death's kind offer, and the key to the speaker's choice lies in the final stanza. Until then, the poem has been a retrospective recollection of events, reported from the speaker's present situation and colored by her perceptions and attitudes "Centuries" later. Although in real terms (calendar terms, sun terms) hundreds of years have passed since the beginning of the ride with Death, to the speaker this whole span of time *"Feels* shorter than the Day" she died. Now being dead, the speaker no longer shares the feelings or the ideas of the living. The word "surmised" (line 23) underscores this, for in mid-nineteenth-century America, and in several other poems by Emily Dickinson, the word had decidedly negative connotations; it meant to guess in error, or to guess without personal experience as a basis. The speaker guessed at the destination of her ride—eternity—but has not reached what the living suppose that implies, heaven. Instead, what she is now experiencing is an endless, cool, and detached journey toward an unknown destination. The speaker retains the power to remember her life, and retains her consciousness, but her present situation is undefinable. In this interpretation, the poem presents an allegorical dramatization of posthumous experience: it is neither hellish nor blissful, but only eternally conscious and emotionless.

The metrical anomaly in the fourth stanza is the reversal of expected line lengths in the first two lines. The first line should be tetrameter, the second trimeter. The importance of this alteration is that it points to the reversal of direction of the poem. The third stanza provides a brief chronology of life, from childhood through maturity to cessation, but the fourth stanza contradicts that last idea: rather than passing "the Setting Sun" (moving, that is, into the symbolic end of the journey), the carriage has been left behind by the passing day and is now in timeless darkness, as evidenced by the chilly dews. But the speaker has dressed in "Gossamer" and "Tulle," delicate and fine fabrics that are no protection against the endless, cold night. With this stanza, the poem ceases its pleasant, comfortable presentation of memories of life, and moves into the chill of death.

Among the important critical readings of the poem, the following offer much variety: Richard Chase, *Emily Dickinson* (New York: Sloane, 1951) 249–51; Theodore C. Hoepfner, "'Because I Could Not Stop for Death,'" *American Literature* 29 (1957): 96; Charles R. Anderson, *Emily Dickinson's Poetry: Stairway of Surprise* (New York: Holt, 1960) 241–46; Clark Griffith, *The Long Shadow: Emily Dickinson's Tragic Poetry* (Princeton: Princeton UP, 1964) 127–34; Richard B. Sewall, *The Life of Emily Dickinson* (New York: Farrar, 1974) 571–72, 717; Robert Weisbuch, *Emily Dickinson's Poetry* (Chicago: U of Chicago P, 1975) 113–17.   TRA

John Donne   Hymn to God My God, in My Sickness

(page 753)

Because of the personal reference in lines 28–30, we may not unfairly take Donne himself as the speaker in this poem. In stanza 1 he is preparing his soul ("I tune the instrument") for his entry into heaven, where he will become part of the holy choir that not only furnishes but is God's music.

In stanza 2 the dying poet initiates the extended geographical metaphor that governs the poem's four central stanzas—for which the first stanza and the last provide a frame. Lying flat on his sickbed, with his doctors bent over him trying to make a proper diagnosis and prescribe a suitable treatment, he compares himself to a flat map of Earth stretched out on a table with geographers bent over studying it. The explorers of Donne's day were fervently seeking a "Northwest Passage" or strait that would give merchants easier access to the treasures of the Orient. A strait is of course a narrow and difficult passageway connecting two larger bodies of water, and Donne makes it symbolize the confining, difficult fever through which he must pass in moving from this life to eternal life. In these straits, he sees his "west," a natural and traditional symbol for death (because it is there that the sun sets).

He is not afraid of death, however, for he is confident that it is closely followed or accompanied by resurrection. He illustrates this belief by reference to the map. On a flat map (containing, from left to right, eastern Asia, the Americas, Europe, Africa, the Middle East, and central Asia), if you trace a line *westward* from the right-hand edge of the map to the left-hand edge, you arrive finally again at eastern Asia or the Orient, at the same meridian from which you started, demonstrating that west and east are one. In the same way, Donne argues, death and resurrection are one.

Illustrating from the map again, he shows that its three principal straits all lead to places that, in one way or another, may be taken as symbols of heaven, the realm of resurrection. The Anyan (Bering) straits lead ultimately to the "eastern riches" (that is, the precious spices of the East Indies); the straits of Magellan lead from the stormy Atlantic Ocean to the peaceful "Pacific Sea"; and the straits of Gibraltar (entered from the Atlantic) lead through the Mediterranean to the Holy City, "Jerusalem." Moreover, the three straits lead to the three continents that were thought, in the medieval period, to constitute the whole world, and that were peopled (according to Christian legend) by the descendents of the three sons of Noah. The whole world and its riches, material and spiritual, in turn are symbols of the glories of heaven. The symbology here is rich and complex and perhaps needs a chart to clarify it:

Anyan Straits — "eastern riches" — Asia — Shem	} Riches	} Glories
Straits of Magellan — "Pacific Sea" — Africa — Cham	of the	of
Straits of Gibraltar — "Jerusalem"* — Europe — Japhet	world	Heaven

The biblical names in the last line of this fourth stanza provide a transition to the biblical and Christian geography of the fifth stanza. Speculative Christian writers had proposed that the Garden of Eden has been located at the same spot where Jesus was later crucified, thus giving a neat formal design to the Christian story. The place where Adam had sinned by eating the forbidden fruit was the same as that where Christ had redeemed mankind from the eternal consequences of that sin. Christ's "tree" (the cross) stood in the same place as Adam's tree (the tree of the knowledge of good and evil). This identification endorses the identification of the first Adam and the last Adam (Christ).

The last eight lines of the poem are a prayer. The first Adam, because of his sin, had been condemned by God to get his bread by the "sweat" of his face (Genesis 3.19); the last Adam (Christ) had redeemed that sin by shedding his blood on the cross. Donne prays that the Lord will find "both Adams" met in him. The anguish of his fever has brought beads of sweat to his brow, and he prays he may be saved by the blood of the Redeemer. "[P]urple" (a word that in Donne's day applied to any color between modern purple and crimson) was a metonymy or symbol for royalty (being the color of kings' robes), and was also the color of blood (compare "The Flea," page 814, line 20). Thus the poet wishes to be received by the Lord wrapped in Christ's "purple" (the blood of

---

*Jerusalem, as part of the Mediterranean world and a "center" for Christianity, was probably considered by Donne more European than Asian. It was certainly not oriental.

Christ the Redeemer and the robe of Christ the King). He also wishes to exchange the crown of thorns that had mockingly been put on Christ at the crucifixion (and which in Donne's case is a symbol of suffering) for Christ's "other crown"—the golden crown that Christ wears enthroned at the right side of God in heaven (and which for Donne is a symbol for salvation). The last three lines identify the speaker as the Dean of St. Paul's, who preached God's "word" to others' souls and now wishes to preach it to his own. As traditionally all sermons elaborate on a biblical text, he appropriately chooses for his sermon to himself a passage from Psalms, roughly paraphrased in the final line. It is an appropriate choice for Donne, for it repeats one of his favorite themes (compare "Batter my heart, three-personed God," page 766).

For a brilliant and much fuller discussion of this poem, see Clay Hunt, *Donne's Poetry: Essays in Literary Analysis* (New Haven: Yale UP, 1954) 96–117. There is also an excellent but shorter discussion in Charles B. Wheeler, *The Design of Poetry* (New York: Norton, 1966) 192–95.   LP

Chapter Seven

Figurative Language 3

Paradox, Overstatement, Understatement, Irony

Emily Dickinson Much Madness is divinest Sense

(page 757)

Emily Dickinson wrote many poems on madness or mental breakdown, incipient, current, and past; and John Cody, a practicing psychiatrist and a highly competent reader of poetry as well, has written an excellent book—*After Great Pain: The Inner Life of Emily Dickinson* (Cambridge: Harvard UP, 1971)—in which he examines these poems. This poem, however, quite properly is not one of them and, quite properly, is not even listed in his index, for the "madness" here belongs to a different category of meaning. This poem is not actually concerned with the examination of neurotic or psychotic states.

The issue in this poem is the individual versus society, or conformity versus nonconformity; its "Madness" is a metaphor for nonconforming genius, a nonconformity of self-reliance as advocated and practiced by Emerson and Thoreau. When a true genius appears among us, with ideas and beliefs quite different from our own, society ("the Majority") regards him or her as a dangerous lunatic who should be locked up in Bedlam and chained to the wall. Years later we may discover that this person, not the majority, was the one who had sensible ideas. The point may perhaps be illustrated by a brief consideration of the careers of Socrates, Jesus, Columbus, Galileo, and Dickinson herself.

The paradox of the poem is resolved when we see that "madness" is here a metaphor.   LP

John Donne   The Sun Rising (page 758)

Like many other Donne poems in this text, this presents the dramatic situation of a speaker addressing a second party (in this case, the personified sun) from an easily identified place and time: he is in bed, with his love, at break of day. Like "Batter my heart, three-personed God" (page 766), "The Flea" (page 814), and "Song: Go and catch a falling star" (page 958), the poem has a sense of immediacy arising from the speaker's apparent change of heart or mind as he is speaking, so that these poems have the effect of motivating their own conclusions out of the ideas with which they begin.

In the impertinent and colloquial opening lines, the speaker angrily chides the busybody sun for interrupting the lovers. Let him go elsewhere, remind other people for whom punctuality is a necessity (schoolboys, apprentices, courtiers, farmers) that it is time for them to be up and busy. Lovers, he says, are not governed by the sun with his "rags of time"—seasons, hours, days, months; his peeping through their curtains is improper and rude (as rude as is the speaker in addressing the interloper).

While the first stanza insists that this is neither the time nor the place for the sun to intrude, it does acknowledge the sun's power in keeping the world on time. But in the second stanza the speaker denies that the sun's beams do have the power to control mankind: he can shut them out merely by blinking, though he won't do so because that would mean not looking at his love. With a traditional overstated metaphor, he suggests that his love's eyes are so bright that they might blind the sun himself; but if they have not, then the sun should go off on his daily inspection of the world and return— tomorrow (as he inevitably will)—to report whether the East and West Indies, sources of spices and gold, haven't left their accustomed places to gather into the person of his love, here in the bed. And if the sun in his journey should ask for all the kings of the world, he will be told that they too have left their kingdoms, and are gathered into the person of the speaker.

The third stanza extends the metaphor of the world contracted into the one bedchamber. The woman is all the nations, the speaker all their rulers— and there is nothing left out there for the sun to shine upon. All those who call themselves princes are imitations, as are their honor and their wealth. Having reduced the world to that point, the speaker then pityingly tells the weary old sun that he can do his job of warming the world merely by shining on the two lovers, as he invites him to do.

Thus the initial attitude, chasing away the powerful sun, changes to welcoming his warmth and attention. What does the speaker really want, then? (And does he, literally, have any choice in the matter?) Most of all he wants his lady to overhear the extravagance of his praise for her and his claims of the importance of their love. The changes in attitude, from chiding the sun to denigrating his power to welcoming him into the chamber, while they are inconsistent, have in common the theme that he and his love are superior to the whole world, to the sun itself. The intellectual playfulness of his dialogue, the wide-ranging references, even the inconsistencies, mean "this woman means more to me than the whole world." The sprightliness of this "overheard" speech might have his lady laughing at his outrageousness, but she could not help being flattered by it.   TRA

Countee Cullen   Incident (page 759)

Good poetry may be simple or complex. This poem relates a simple incident simply, in simple stanza form, without elaboration of metaphor or simile. And yet, in twelve lines, it sums up the poignant tragedy of the black
experience in America—friendliness rebuffed, the childish hurt that leaves a
scar, happiness turned to ashes.

Simple as the poem is, we should not regard it as artless. Notice how the
four mouth-filling syllables *Heart-filled, head-filled* in line 2 are counterpointed against the five skipping syllables of *Baltimorean* in line 3. Because
the two hyphenated words are jammed with consonants and separated by a
comma, and because they spread two metrical accents evenly over four syllables, they take twice as long to pronounce as the five syllables and three
accents of *Baltimorean*. The emphasis is appropriate to their emotional importance and gives them the sense of *fullness* required by the meaning. Notice also how the climactic incident of the poem is set off by the rhythm. The
other lines of the poem are all to some degree end-stopped; even line 3 is followed by a natural pause. But lines 7 and 8 break in the middle, and line 7 is
the one line in the poem that demands that the voice rush on to the next
line without pause. Thus the contemptuous action and the contemptuous epithet are isolated by the rhythm. Finally, notice how the significance of the
incident is brought home by understatement. We are not told that the
speaker's glee was turned to pain, that the contemptuous epithet went
through him like a sword or rankled in his consciousness, or that he felt suddenly crushed and humiliated. We are told only: "Of all the things that happened there / That's all that I remember." Need we be told more?   LP

[Reprinted from Laurence Perrine and James M. Reid, *100 American
Poems of the Twentieth Century* (New York: Harcourt, 1966) 190–91.]

Marge Piercy   Barbie Doll (page 761)

Piercy satirizes contemporary American society's emphasis on physical
beauty as the major criterion of value for girls and women. The toy that became a twentieth-century icon of young girls' aspirations for their personal
appearance—a doll with slim figure, perfect face, and fashionable makeup
and clothing—is presented here as the symbol of false values that enforce
stereotypical thinking about females who cannot conform to the doll's image
and suffer terribly as a result.

The poem's verbal irony is its most notable technique for conveying this
theme. The young girl whose life Piercy charts was given numerous toys from
an early age, all of them gender-related and intended to shape the girl's thinking about herself and her future role in society: dolls that "pee-pee" like infants,
"miniature GE stoves and irons," and tiny lipsticks. But when a classmate

informs her that she has "a great big nose and fat legs"—in fatal contrast to Barbie's snub nose and slender limbs—the girl begins to feel her inadequacy. Her personal qualities are those normally praised in boys but unwelcome in girls: high intelligence, physical strength, a strong sex drive, and "manual dexterity." The seeming non sequitur after the list of these positive attributes— "She went to and fro apologizing"—indicates that the girl has internalized her society's false values and has suffered a near-total loss self-esteem.

As the girl grows older, presumably well-meaning adults advise her to compensate for her physical appearance by developing personality traits that might appeal to men: she should "play coy," "smile and wheedle." The poem's most inspired lines employ an unexpected simile drawn not from Barbie's ultra-feminine world but from the masculine realm of car parts: "Her good nature wore out / like a fan belt." Piercy uses an image here that the girl herself, with her manual dexterity and other stereotypically masculine traits, might well have appreciated.

Moving the poem into surrealistic allegory, the final stanza completes the death of the girl's spirit as she amputates the offending nose and legs, then lies in a casket wearing "undertaker's cosmetics" and thus managing the closest resemblance to Barbie she will ever achieve. Piercy's verbal irony grows almost savage in the final lines, as fatuous onlookers in the funeral home remark that the girl is now "pretty": "Consummation at last. / To every woman a happy ending."

This poem is discussed by Elizabeth G. Peck in "More than Ideal: Size and Weight Obsession in Literary Works by Marge Piercy, Margaret Atwood, and Andre Dubus" (*Platte Valley Review* 18, no. 1 [Winter 1990]: 69–75). Peck describes the poem as a critique of our culture's "size and weight obsession," which "as a cultural phenomenon, has moved out of the laboratory and into our literature as a thematic concern."   GJ

William Blake   The Chimney Sweeper (page 763)

Blake uses dramatic irony here for sympathetic rather than detractive purposes. In line 3 the boy, too young to articulate clearly, is calling out his trade in the streets—sweep, sweep, sweep, sweep—but the poet is telling us that we should weep over his pitiful plight. In lines 7–8 the innocent boy is genuinely trying to comfort his friend and does not recognize, as the poet does, the ironic discrepancy between the comfort he intends and the lack of comfort he actually offers, for not being able to have one's hair soiled is hardly consolation for having it shaved off! In line 24 the boy's words are an expression of a childlike trust that the poet, with more experience of the world, knows to be unfounded: the poem, in fact, is a protest against the harm that society causes its children by exploiting them for labor of this kind. In each case the dramatic irony arises from the poet's knowing more or seeing more than the child does, but also in each case the boy's ignorance testifies to his good heart and likable innocence.

The dream in lines 11–20 is obviously a wish-fulfillment dream, though Blake would not have been familiar with this Freudian terminology. It is also a miniature allegory, capable of two interpretations, one applying to this world, the other to the next. On the first level—most obviously the wish-fulfillment level—the "coffins of black" are the chimneys the boys work in; the "Angel" who releases them is a wise legislator or rich benefactor (like Oliver Twist's Mr. Brownlow) who releases them from the bondage of their labor with the key of social legislation or of wealth; the green plains represent a happier future. At this level, the dream represents only a wish or a hope. On the second and perhaps more relevant level, the coffins are real coffins and the Angel is one of God's angels who releases the boys into heaven with the key of death. At this level, the poet is saying that the only release for these boys, under the then existing conditions of society, is through death.   LP

Percy Bysshe Shelley   Ozymandias (page 764)

The central theme of "Ozymandias" is the vanity of the claims of human tyrants to enduring glory. It is brilliantly conveyed through irony of situation: the overturn of expectation by fulfillment. After reading the inscription on the pedestal, the second line of which may be paraphrased, "Look on my works, ye mighty (but lesser) kings, and despair of ever equaling them," one expects to look up and see a great imperial city with marble palaces, temples, hanging gardens, monuments, and fortified walls; instead, as far as the eye can reach, one sees only emptiness and sand.

Increasing the irony is the fact that the sole remaining work of this self-proclaimed "king of kings" is a huge broken statue (its hugeness manifesting his megalomania), carved by an artist who saw through the self-deluding ego-centrism of the ruler and recorded it in stone, mocking Ozymandias, as it were, to his face. In the "frown, / And wrinkled lip, and sneer of cold command," the sculptor knew that his imperceptive and arrogant master would see only the signs of his awesome authority and power whereas the more perceptive viewer would note the absence of joy, wisdom, compassion, and humility—the marks of true greatness—and see only crude ambition and cruel passions. The insight of the artist has outlasted the power of the conqueror.

The emptiness of Ozymandias's pretensions to everlasting fame is further increased by the fact that this whole account has been related to the speaker by "a traveler from an antique land." That is, the speaker would never have heard of Ozymandias at all had it not been for his chance encounter with a desert explorer. (And most of us, in our turn, would never have heard of Ozymandias had the poet Shelley, another artist, not written a poem about the incident.)

No English reader in 1817 could have read this poem without thinking of Napoleon, who had made himself conqueror and ruler of almost all of Europe before he was defeated at Waterloo in 1815 and exiled on the barren island of St. Helena in 1817. In more recent times we may be reminded of Hitler, Mussolini, Stalin, or Mao.

Except for the awkwardness caused by the separation of the transitive verb "survive" (7) and its objects "hand" and "heart" (8), the poem is brilliantly written. In "Nothing beside remains" (12), the word "beside" means both "beside" and "besides." The alliterating *b*s, *l*s, and *ss* of the last two lines put a heavy emphasis on the words that re-create the vast level emptiness, and the final unstopped vowel sound allows the voice to trail off into infinity.

Two pitfalls for the student: (a) The "hand" that mocked the passions of Ozymandias is the sculptor's; the "heart" that fed those passions was Ozymandias's. The passions depicted in the stone visage have outlasted both the artist and the tyrant. (b) The words on the pedestal were not composed by the sculptor. Ozymandias commanded the sculptor to inscribe them there. The sculptor "mocked" Ozymandias by his frank portrayal of the ruler's character in the sculptured visage.   LP

EXERCISES (page 765)

1. Paradox	4. Understatement	7. Paradox ("immortal" is ironic)
2. Irony	5. Paradox	8. Paradox
3. Overstatement	6. Overstatement	9. Paradox

John Donne   Batter my heart, three-personed God
(page 766)

In the first quatrain Donne metaphorically compares God to a tinker who is trying to mend a metal utensil such as a kettle. Donne (the kettle) cries out to God that he needs to be made anew, not just repaired. It is not enough for God to "knock, breathe, shine," He must "break, blow, burn," and batter. The parallel series of verbs reflect the three persons of the Trinity.

The verbs "knock" and "break" belong to the Father (representing Power); "breathe" and "blow" belong to the Holy Spirit (the word *spirit* comes originally from a Latin word meaning "to breathe"; cf. *respiration*); "shine" and "burn" belong to the Son, a concealed pun on *sun*.

In the second quatrain Donne compares himself to a town "due" to God but "usurped" by Satan (or sin), who has taken captive God's viceroy, Reason. The "enemy" (10) again is Satan (or sin).   LP

Elisavietta Ritchie   Sorting Laundry (page 767)

The opening stanza metaphorically links the "you" of the poem to clothes and other laundry. The word "Folding" (1) literally describes the speaker's handling of the laundry, and figuratively implies the loving actions that she has performed in making this man part of her life (including the ordinary domestic actions she is now engaged in, which also give her pleasure).

The catalogue of laundry that must be folded (stanzas 2–9) is witty and self-assured. The seams of their pillowcases are strong enough not only to preserve the cases for their ordinary use, but metaphorically also strong enough to preserve the dreams of the people who slept on them. The gaudy towels, bought on an impulse and not in keeping with the style of the household, refuse "to bleach into respectability." Shirts, skirts, and pants, as they go through the cycles of the washing machine, are recycled and recapitulate themselves. Socks that went into the machine two by two, like the beasts entering the ark, come out "uncoupled."

The poem turns at line 28 to a different kind of catalogue: objects that have neglectfully been put into the washer (a comment perhaps on the two people who aren't overly fastidious in cleaning out their pockets). The list is again of ordinary objects, until it reaches lines 39–40: "broken necklace of good gold / you brought from Kuwait." This token of love, a gift brought back to her from his distant travel to the wealthiest part of the Middle East, raises other associations for her—in particular, she notices "the strangely tailored shirt / left [behind] by a former lover" of hers (41–42). There may be a small drama in these two articles—perhaps the gold necklace was a courting gift, perhaps it tipped the balance in his favor and led her to dispense with her former lover.

(Because of events that have taken place since this poem was written— the invasion and spoliation of Kuwait by Iraq and the liberation of it by U.S. and allied forces—it will probably be necessary to remind students of what Kuwait represented before the events of 1990–91: a luxurious, oil-rich kingdom busy with foreign businessmen. It is to *this* Kuwait and what a gold necklace from there would call to mind that the poem makes reference.)

In any case, the rather tidily separated catalogues (first laundry, and then found objects) are mixed together in this stanza, and what follows is a surprising leap. A lover's gift and a recollection of a love affair broken off lead the speaker to the fearful thought: "If you were to leave me" (43). The consequence of such desertion would be shattering loneliness, expressed in a return to the opening metaphor. Folding clothes for two of them was an expression of her love; folding only her own clothes would leave a void so great that "a mountain of unsorted wash / could not fill / the empty side of the [king-sized] bed" (49–51).

The many references to pieces of laundry prepare the reader for the overstatement of the "mountain" of washing, as in its way does the reference to the former lover's shirt. This household is full of clothes and household items and everyday objects, including things that need discarding and clothes left behind by others. Like the constant use of plurals in naming things, less obtrusive overstatements earlier in the poem prepare for the "mountain": "giants" (6), "so many" (7, 16), "All" (19), "Myriad" (22), and "maelstrom" (37). The grammatical structure also contributes to this sense of fullness, as the lists are presented in noun phrases rather than complete sentences. Yet the speaker can be witty about them and enjoy her housekeeping, as long as she can keep her love with her. Her insight into how important her love is to her is the result of her "sorting," not only laundry but her life.   TRA

Billy Collins   The History Teacher (page 769)

The teacher's simple motive in sugar-coating his history lessons is "to protect his students' innocence" (1), a naïve wish that ignorance of harsh reality will keep them safe and secure. And so he minimizes the discomforts and dangers of the prehistoric eras, and tries to make them seem real and relevant to the students by framing them in familiar, contemporary terms— "sweaters" and gravel "driveways" (4, 6).

When he turns to historic events he uses the same technique. The word "Inquisition" (7), itself perhaps a euphemism, means no more than asking questions, being inquisitive, about everyday matters. The bloody dynastic war for dominance in Britain, symbolically named for the white and red roses adopted as emblems by the Lancastrians and Yorkists, is reduced to a squabble in a rose garden. The ferocious damage of the atomic bomb dropped on Hiroshima is reduced not only by the pilot's ironically naming his bomber after his dear mother, but by the teacher's ignoring the second bomb at Nagasaki and by his presenting the bomb itself as no bigger or more threatening than "one tiny atom."

But this euphemistic language creating a tissue of understatements is ironically undercut by the reality of lines 14–17. The real children, presumably protected from the violence, destruction, and injustice of the past, express those very impulses in their playground bullying. That they turn on "the weak / and the smart" (15–16) seems to strike directly at the kindly but misguided teacher who exhibits both the smartness of his education and the weakness of his control over their behavior.

The conclusion finds him wondering if he can get away with calling the Boers "bores" and so ignore the racist and colonialist realities of yet another war.

Instructors who wish to open up the ideas of this poem to further discussion might introduce questions about the effect of television violence—or the suppression of it—on young people. The poem might also be compared to Housman's "Terence, this is stupid stuff" (page 662), which takes up the mistake of avoiding life's unpleasantness.   TRA

Robert Frost   A Considerable Speck (page 770)

This gently humorous poem offers a glimpse of a writer at work who is distracted by a tiny mite crawling across his manuscript page. Though his first instinct is to destroy the mite with the tip of his pen, instead he finds his

poet's attention engaged by the mite's travails. Watching its erratic movements, the speaker comes to believe that "Plainly with an intelligence I
dealt" (15), since the speaker ascribes an intelligent instinct toward self-
preservation in the mite's strategies to escape the page.

Yet the speaker claims that he isn't a sentimental lover of natural creatures who might claim an equivalence between a mite and a human being: "I
have none of the tenderer-than-thou / Collectivistic regimenting love / With
which the modern world is being swept" (24–26). At the same time, the
speaker does not have the typical reaction to an annoying pest, asserting that
the mite "was nothing I knew evil of" (28).

Nonetheless the poem does suggest a link between the complex, intelligent
human being and the mite he observes. In a bit of hyperbole, he ascribes "mind"
to the mite's actions, since a mite in peril behaves in the same way as a human
being who finds himself in a difficult situation. Other language in the poem suggests that the speaker is using language playfully (this is a poem that is easy to
take too seriously). The line "It seemed too tiny to have room for feet" (16)
makes a pun on physical feet vs. poetic feet, just as "a period of ink" (5) connotes both a punctuation mark and the potential end of the mite's life. In the
final stanza, the speaker asserts that "No one can know how glad I am to find /
On any sheet the least display of mind" (32–33), suggesting his identity as a
reader who compares the movements of a mite to the "display" of words on a
sheet of paper that reveal a degree, however small, of literary intelligence.

Johannes Kjorven writes that "The focus in the comic-satirical fable 'A
Considerable Speck' on the activity of the mite on a white piece of paper is
a reminder that the essential Frostian man, however 'microscopic' his powers of mind, understands, or insists on reaching, some 'meaning'" (*Robert
Frost's Emergent Design* [Oslo: Solum Forlag, 1987] 105). According to Robert
Faggen, the poem "satirizes the grandiosity of human endeavors . . . the
analogies between man and mite in the poem suggest a belittling perspective
of man and God, creation and creator" (*Robert Frost and the Challenge of
Darwin* [Ann Arbor: U of Michigan P, 1997] 67).

Although "A Considerable Speck" is not one of Frost's major poems, and
is overlooked by most critical commentators on his work, it does show the
poet's mastery of tone (here, one of gentle irony) and his obsessive interest
in phenomena of the natural world.   GJ

W. H. Auden   The Unknown Citizen (page 771)

The title alludes to the "Unknown Soldier." It is ironic because *everything* is known about the "unknown" citizen—except, apparently, his name.
The information about him is filed under a code number. The citizen has
been reduced to a set of statistics. The loss of his name symbolizes the loss of
his individuality. The unknown soldier's *body* had been blown to bits; the unknown citizen's *soul* has been blown to bits.

In the old sense, a "saint" (4) was a person who served God. In the "modern" sense, he is a person who serves "the Greater Community." The old-fashioned saints, to serve God, often had to defy the world—and in doing so, they found their souls. The modern saint, to serve "the Greater Community," must only do everything he is told to do—and in so doing, he loses his soul. The things "necessary to the Modern Man" are purely materialistic things—"A phonograph, a radio, a car and a frigidaire"—and they are "necessary" not mainly to serve the man but to keep the economy going. The unknown citizen had no opinions of his own but adopted those of the state—that is, he accepted state propaganda. He "never interfered" with the education of his children: what his children really received was indoctrination, not education, and the unknown citizen never questioned the rightness of what his children were taught.

For Auden himself the questions "Was he free? Was he happy?" are the important questions, not absurd ones, and in his eyes *everything* was wrong. The answers to the questions are that the unknown citizen was *not* free, though he never realized his lack of freedom, and that he was neither happy nor unhappy, for it takes a *man*, with a soul, to be happy or unhappy—and to be a man, one must be free, at least in his soul. The unknown citizen did not live; he existed. He was not a man but a statistic, a comfortable conformist, a pliant tool in the hands of the state.

The satire in the poem is against several tendencies of modern life: its increasing demands for conformity, uniformity, and collectivization; its materialism; and its disposition to do everything by statistics, to exalt the "average," and to put life into the hands of social scientists and managers. The old-fashioned saint was an extraordinary man; the modern one is an average man—if he can be called a man.

Be sure to ask students, "*Was* he free? *Was* he happy?"   LP

Joyce Carol Oates   American Holiday (page 772)

The subject of this poem is American jingoism and boosterism, as expressed in the military celebration that attends an "American holiday." The ironic tone is established through the use of exclamation points and verb choices evoking violent action: "bombarding" (2), "plummeting" (4), "reddening" (6), and "darkened" (9). In the second stanza, the alliteration and the double meaning of "brassy" (5)—made of brass but also cheap and flashy—further communicate the ironic intent of the poem.

In the third stanza, the focus shifts from the typically American, loud and proud celebration to the vulnerable natural creatures—birds and human beings—and the effect of the celebration upon them. The birds are "scattered skyward" (8), shrieking, while the speaker and her fellow onlookers have "wet ashes" (11), an image of penitence and death, blown into their nostrils.

The subdued tone of the final stanza provides an effective closure. Whereas the holiday had been described in the first line, ironically, as a

"Military New Year's Eve!" (1), suggestive of a new year and new beginnings, the speaker admits in the penultimate line that it's "Only Monday"
(12). (Most American holidays, of course, such as Memorial Day and Veterans' Day, are celebrated on Mondays to provide a three-day weekend.) To
the speaker, who sees the negative characteristics of the holiday celebration—shrill jingoism, mindless self-congratulation, and a glorification of violence—there will be "A long week ahead" to ponder the ironies implicit in
American patriotic fervor.   GJ

Lucille Clifton   **in the inner city** (page 773)

The irony is verbal. The speaker is responding to the sociological/political
term that relegates the black experience to a ghetto of deterioration and decay.
The poem does not contradict that characterization: that ghetto is in fact "no
place" (10) that one would choose to inhabit. But rather than argue that the
inner city is somehow not so bleak as it is painted, the poem draws a contrast
between the vitality of life in such a blighted area and the lifelessness and regimentation of the white counterpart to "the inner city," "uptown." "[U]ptown"
is silent at night, without the buzz and activity of street life. Its planned development houses are stiff, rigid, "straight as dead men," not ramshackle and randomly arranged by patterns of living. "[U]ptown" the lights are "pastel,"
subdued and tinged with the color of elegant lampshades, not bare-bulb bright
or neon vibrant.
    Most of all, of course, the speaker ironically juxtaposes a social scientist's
term with the connotatively powerful "home" in the refrain lines that open
and close the poem. "You who want to pigeonhole and pity us who live here,"
she says in effect, "do not have any idea what really constitutes a home."
    A valuable discussion of other aspects of this poem is contained in
Shirley A. Williams's "Blue Roots of Lucille Clifton's 'in the inner city'"
(*Massachusetts Review* [1977] 550–52).   TRA

M. Carl Holman   **Mr. Z** (page 774)

M. Carl Holman was a black poet, and "Mr. Z" is the ironic portrait of a
black man who attains distinction in life by disowning his own racial and
cultural heritage and adapting himself to the manners and values of the
white world. He is apparently light-skinned, for he is able to do this quite
successfully, and he marries a white woman who, out of a similar motivation,
has disowned her Jewish heritage and is adapting herself to the manners and
values of the gentile world. The marriage is a marriage of convenience for
both of them, for through marriage, they are both enabled to shake off some
of the social stigma of their own backgrounds. There is also the suggestion
that neither of them could have acquired a purely white gentile mate of

respectable social pretensions: they have had to settle for the second best, which is nevertheless better, in their eyes, than marriage within their own cultures.

In giving Mr. Z only an initial, not a name, the poet suggests that Mr. Z has lost personal identity by disclaiming racial identity. In choosing the last letter of the alphabet for that initial, the poet suggests his own low opinion of Mr. Z. The satire of the poem is directed mainly at Mr. Z and the type of person he represents. But the satire also hits, secondarily, at the snob values of a WASP society that make people like Mr. Z and his wife possible. Mr. Z is clearly a person of considerable ability, and in a healthy society he could have remained himself and still have acquired the kind of recognition he needed.

The obituary notices cruelly reflect the false values of this society by making Mr. Z's distinction relative, not absolute. There is subtle though probably unconscious condescension in the statement that Mr. Z was " 'One of the most distinguished members of his race.' " (Implication: He did pretty well for a black person. Further implication: Blacks are inferior.) But the obituary notices are particularly cruel for Mrs. Z, for they implicitly reveal the fact that she and Mr. Z had labored all their lives to conceal. This is irony of situation.

There is muted irony throughout the poem: "perfect part of honor" (2), "Faced up" (7), "exemplary" (9), "profane" (10), "right" (17), "Not one false note" (23). The first ironic note is in the first line, and it might be labeled either verbal or dramatic. The reader realizes, as Mr. Z's "teachers" and Mr. Z do not, that an accident of birth cannot possibly be a "sign of error." (One infers, incidentally, that Mr. Z was lighter-skinned than his mother, and that his father may have been white.)   LP

Adrienne Rich   Afterward (page 775)

QUESTIONS

1. What does it mean "to give . . . back in kind" (4)?
2. What are the paradoxes in lines 9–10? Explore the situational irony of the poem.

This miniature portrait of pride undergoing its (inevitable?) fall rests on the situational irony of one who once boasted of superiority being reduced to shame by failure. Those "hopes" (1, 5) which the woman once held above her friends—hopes for a *"happiness / Above the asking of the crowd"* (6–7)—have come to nothing, and she now is resigned to being the object of pity for those to whom she condescended.

The poem has the potentiality of spitefulness as those who had to suffer the woman's pride now see her shamed and downcast. But they are characterized as people "who know limits," who are themselves resigned to life that does not grant wishes. The fellow-feeling of the gentle reproof in lines 3–5 suggests not "I-told-you-so" gloating but a tender regard for the unhappy woman who had hoped for too much.

The paradox of lines 9–10 involves spatial imagery as a representation of emotional conditions. Those who know themselves limited in their scope nevertheless yield space enough to "give room" to their friend, and she in turn who has been so grand in expectations is now so reduced in size that she will have to grow gradually until she can "fit her doom." The implication is that the total deflation of hopes may yet be reversed sufficiently to fill up the space of her limited reality. Knowing one's limits is better than the insubstantial confidence of grandeur, though it may take a shocking loss to teach the lesson.

A similar theme is expressed, with more pathos, in Kay's "Pathedy of Manners" (page 689).   TRA

Robert Browning   My Last Duchess (page 775)

Speaker: The Duke of Ferrara. Time: Late Italian Renaissance, probably mid-sixteenth century. Place: An upper room or corridor in the Duke's palace. Audience: An envoy from the Count whose daughter the Duke plans to marry. Occasion: The Duke and the Count's emissary have just concluded negotiations over the terms of the marriage and the dowry that the Duke expects to receive with his bride. (Students need to know that a duke of Ferrara was a supremely powerful figure, equal in status to a king.) On their way to join the company of guests and courtiers in the assembly hall below, they pass a portrait of the Duke's former Duchess, and the Duke pauses to display it for the emissary, engaging him now in what seems purely social talk.

The primary subject of the poem is the character of the Duke, but Browning is interested in his character also as it reflects his period in history (the pride and arrogance of the aristocracy, its system of arranged marriages, its enthusiasm for art and artists). A secondary and pendant point of interest lies in the character of the Duchess.

The Duke is characterized, first, by pride—pride of birth and station. He is a duke—let no one forget it!—and one with a "nine-hundred-years-old name"! His dissatisfaction with his former wife (but he refers to her always as his "Duchess") is that she forgot it. Instead of being lofty and reserved like himself, saving her smile only for him, thus enhancing the eminence of his station, she treated social inferiors as equals, blushed when they complimented her, was too visibly pleased when they did her favors. She did not comport herself like a duchess! And why didn't he try to correct her? Because to have done so would have been to "Stoop." Even if she had accepted his tutelage without making excuses or arguing back (the ultimate humiliation)—"E'en then would be some stooping; and I choose / Never to stoop" (42–43). A proud purchaser doesn't haggle over defects in the merchandise; he simply sends it back and demands replacement.

Second, the Duke is cruel. Were it not for the "stooping," the Duke would not hesitate to tell his wife "this . . . in you disgusts me" (37–38). But since he wouldn't stoop, he "gave commands; / Then all smiles stopped together" (45–46). What were the commands? Browning doesn't tell us, and doesn't need to, for the very tone in which the words are uttered sufficiently underlines the Duke's cruelty and arrogance. But probably they were to have the Duchess put to death. In the opening lines, "That's my last Duchess painted on the wall, / Looking as if she were alive," the subjunctive mood implies that she is no longer living—a suggestion repeated in line 47.

Third, the Duke is a connoisseur of art. There is no need to believe that his love of art is not genuine: love of art can coexist comfortably with egotism and cruelty in some natures (read *The Autobiography of Benvenuto Cellini*); and this was a time of great enthusiasm for art and artists. The Duke is a patron and collector of art. He speaks appreciatively of the merits of Fra Pandolf's painting and keeps a protective curtain in front of it, which he allows no one but himself to draw. Nevertheless, his love of art is not pure; it too reflects his pride. He is proud of having commissioned work from painters and sculptors of such eminence as Fra Pandolf and Claus of Innsbruck, and he carefully drops their names into his conversation ("I said / 'Fra Pandolf'" by design," 5–6). Part of the value of his Neptune taming a sea-horse is that it is "thought a rarity," and that Claus of Innsbruck cast it in bronze "for me!" (55–56).

Finally, the Duke is shrewd. He knows what he wants, and he knows how to get it. While apparently simply making pleasant conversation about the shortcomings of his former Duchess, he is indirectly informing the envoy what he expects in his new Duchess, knowing that the envoy will report it back to the Count. Primary evidence of the Duke's shrewdness is his skill in speech. His disclaimer of such skill (35–36) is part of the evidence for it, and should remind the reader of a similar disclaimer by Shakespeare's Mark Antony in his oration on Caesar, which serves a similar purpose. It is a rhetorical trick, designed to throw the listener off guard. The Duke's momentary gropings after words (21–23, 31–32) by no means support this disclaimer, for the words he eventually comes up with are exactly the right words, and the hesitation in his speech only serves to give them added emphasis. But the conclusive proof of the Duke's skill in speech is the beautifully modulated passage (48–53) in which he couches his demand for dowry. Clearly the dowry is his main motivation in this new marriage (he is driving a hard bargain: his rank and nine-hundred-years-old name for her money), but he is too polished to avow this openly, so he adds, "Though his fair daughter's self, as I avowed / At starting, is my object" (52–53). The words "I repeat" and "as I avowed / At starting" show that the Duke has mentioned both of these matters before, in reverse order; he is now driving them home in the order of their real importance, making sure he is clearly understood. The passage is a masterpiece of diplomatic circumlocution. Though the nature of the demand is made perfectly clear, it is gloved in a sentence softened by a double negative and by a skillfully tactful and euphemistic choice of diction: not *riches* but "munificence"; not *proves* but "Is ample warrant"; not *my demand* but "no just pretense / Of mine"; not *refused* but "disallowed" (49–51). The hard bargaining is thus enveloped in an atmosphere of perfect courtesy. The Duke's diplomatic skills are also shown throughout in his treatment of the emissary, which is subtly designed to flatter. After the business conference, he gives the emissary a private showing of his prized portrait and chats in a friendly manner about personal affairs. This courtesy, from the man who is accustomed to give commands and who objected to too much courtesy in his Duchess, is apparent throughout the interview: "Will't please you sit and look at her? . . . / Will't please you rise?" (5, 47). And when the envoy, having risen, waits respectfully for the Duke to precede him downstairs, as befits his eminence, the Duke tells him, "Nay, we'll go / Together down, sir" (53–54). And so the envoy walks side by side down the stairway with the possessor of a nine-hundred-years-old name who has just said, "I choose / Never to stoop." How can he do other than return a favorable report to the Count?

So much for the Duke; what about the Duchess? The Duke paints her as being frivolous, trivial, too free in manner, "too soon made glad." The reader's reaction to her, however, is controlled by the genuine pleasure she takes in compliments; by her graciousness to all, regardless of station; and especially by the simple things she takes delight in: the beauty of a sunset, a gift of a bough of cherries, a ride round the terrace on a white mule. Her response to these indicates a warm, sensitive nature that takes joy in natural things rather than in gauds and baubles or the pomp of position and power that attract the Duke.

The poem is a masterpiece of dramatic irony, a dramatic irony that is manifested chiefly in the whole tone of the poem rather than in specific passages. The Duke speaks all the words. He seeks to give a favorable impression of himself (and no doubt succeeds with the envoy, who belongs to his world and has not our advantage of perceiving him through the lens of art) and an unfavorable impression of his last Duchess. What Browning conveys to the reader is exactly the opposite.   LP

Chapter Eight

Allusion

Robert Frost "Out, Out—" (page 779)

A newspaper account would have given us facts—the boy's name, his age, the exact place and time of the accident. The poet, as omniscient narrator in this poem, is interested in communicating experience. The first six lines provide a vivid sense of the setting through combined images of sight (sawdust, "stove-length sticks of wood, . . . Five mountain ranges . . . Under the sunset," 2, 5, 6), of smell (the resinous scent of new-cut timber), and of sound (the onomatopoetic snarling of the buzz-saw as the timber is pushed through it, its onomatopoetic rattling as it waits for the next load). Vivid visual imagery continues through the poem (the boy holding up his injured hand, the boy under ether puffing his lips out with his breath). The poem also provides dialogue (as a newspaper account wouldn't except in the form of a witness's answers to a reporter's questions) and includes the poet-narrator's own comments ("Call it a day, I wish they might have said . . ."; "the saw, / As if to prove saws knew what supper meant, / Leaped out at the boy's hand . . ."; "No more to build on there," 10, 14–16, 33).

The role of chance is underscored in the poem in that the boy's death is really a double accident. The cutting of the hand is caused by a moment of inattention, but moments of inattention rarely have such a dire consequence. The boy's death is caused by shock, but fatal shock infrequently follows such a "minor" accident. The boy does not expect it. The attendants can't believe it. There is indeed a terrible situational irony involved in the swift progression from the boy's first reaction ("a rueful laugh," 19) to his perception that the accident may cost him his hand to the ending that no one anticipates.

The abruptness of the last line-and-a-half misleads some students into thinking the central theme of the poem identical with that of Housman's "Is my team plowing" (page 674), namely, that life goes on without us when we are gone just as it did before. To be sure, these lines do embroider the central theme with the truth that individual death does not bring human life to a halt. But Frost deliberately leaves the antecedent of "they" ambiguous, and he does not say how quickly "they . . . turned to their affairs" (34). We should not assume that the sister returned to the normal course of her life as quickly as did the doctor, or that the unseen parents immediately resumed their lives as if nothing had happened.   LP

William Shakespeare   From *Macbeth* (page 780)

The importance of recognizing Shakespeare's poetic rhythms is made clear in the punctuation and scansion of the third line of this passage. A prosaic reading, emphasizing the dictionary stresses only, sounds like this: toMORrow and toMORrow and toMORrow. But the commas fall between the syllables of iambic feet, throwing greater stress on the normally slurred syllable "and," to this effect:

$$\text{To-mor-} | \text{row, and} | \text{to-mor-} | \text{row, and} | \text{to-mor-} | \text{row.}$$

That boring, eventless regularity imitates the apathy that has hardened Macbeth's heart and poisoned his mind.   TRA

e. e. cummings   in Just– (page 782)

In this little poem about "Just- / spring"—that is, the very beginning of spring—cummings captures the perennial delight of the children in a world that is "mud- / luscious" and "puddle-wonderful" and in which they can again play outside at marbles and piracies and "hop-scotch and jump-rope." The setting is urban, and the whistle of the balloonman advertising his wares in the park or along the sidewalks brings the children running.

The description of the "little / lame balloonman" as "goat-footed" links him (or identifies him) with Pan, half-man, half-goat, the Greek god of nature and legendary inventor of the panpipes. When Pan blew on his pipes in the spring, all the little creatures of the field and wood came running. Thus cummings's city scene reenacts ancient ritual, and "the queer / old balloonman" ushers in the season that begins life anew as he has done each spring since the beginning.

Though the poem is written in free verse, it is organized into alternating four-line and one-line "stanzas" with a floating refrain in the thrice-repeated "balloonman whistles far and wee" each time preceded by an announcement that it's spring. The hyphenated adjectives "mud- / luscious" and "puddle-wonderful" express exuberance in the assonance of their principal vowel sounds and echoing *d*s and *l*s; the hyphenated nouns "hop-scotch" and "jump-rope" display assonance and consonance respectively; the lines "luscious the little / lame balloonman" glide on alliterating *l*s; and breathless *eddieandbill* and *bettyandisbel* echo each other in both vowel and consonant sounds. The whole builds up a celebration of spring and the children's delight in it. Cummings called it "Chanson Innocente."   LP

Countee Cullen   Yet Do I Marvel (page 783)

The allusions are to Tantalus and Sisyphus in Greek mythology. Both were condemned by Zeus to eternal torments: Tantalus suffered thirst and hunger while standing in a lake whose waters withdrew whenever he tried to drink, and a bough of fruit just over his head soared up whenever he tried to reach it. Sisyphus had to push a heavy rock up a hillside, and just as he neared the top it rolled back to the bottom and so he had to start again.

The "reason" for Sisyphus's punishment was a number of crimes, including ravishing his own niece, stealing, plundering, and killing. He was singled out by Zeus for accusing the god of abducting a mortal woman—Zeus had committed the crime but was angry at Sisyphus's tattling. Tantalus too incurred the god's ire by interfering with his authority. He is said to have stolen a favorite dog of Zeus, to have taken the food of the gods (ambrosia and nectar) and given it to mortals, and, most monstrously, to have killed his own son and served him to the gods for food.

These allusions are powerful because of the legendary cruelty of the punishments and because the criminals challenged the behavior of the god; they are appropriate in a poem that questions the motives of God.

The first line of the poem is verbal irony: the poem is rife with doubt about God's goodness and kindness. The second line continues the ironic tone with understatement by referring to God's high eminence with the words "stoop" and "quibble," terms more appropriate to snobbery than omnipotence.

The implied questions, in order, are: Why is the mole blind? Why must mankind be mortal? Why are Tantalus and Sisyphus condemned to endless suffering? And, after a third quatrain that shifts the rhyme scheme from alternatively rhyming lines (*ababcdcd*) to couplets, how can a man born black find joy and delight? The third quatrain offers its ironic answer to these questions—men are too engaged with "petty cares" (11) to comprehend the mind of God. As an answer the statement is ironically self-debasing, indicating that if we were not so trivial in our interests we might be able to ask the right questions (a question-and-answer catechism) and so reach the truth. Our distress is caused by our own weakness.

But limited as we are by our intrinsic nature, we can only "marvel" (13) at our own shortcomings. In this poem, God is emphatically *not* "good, well-meaning, kind" (1) for he has ordained the inscrutably ironic conditions of the Creation.

From the perspective of the speaker, I would say that the relative importance of the topics, in descending order, is: human mortality, the limits of human understanding, racial inequality, mythical examples of eternal suffering, and the blindness of a mole. However, by its positioning in the concluding couplet, the quandary of a black poet is most emphatic.   TRA

John Milton   On His Blindness (page 783)

The three parables grouped together in Chapter 25 of Matthew's Gospel teach the necessity of being prepared for the day of judgment, for the coming of the Lord. They emphasize chiefly two aspects of preparedness: that the Lord's arrival will be sudden and without warning, and that the actions of the waiting life are an enactment of the judgment to be made (and, as in the third parable, verses 31–46, that men cannot recognize the meanings of all their actions). The middle parable to which this poem alludes teaches that the state of being prepared for the Lord's return is an *active* state, which insofar as possible requires the servants to perform as their master has performed—even if, to their limited understanding, the master has seemed a sharp dealer more interested in profit than in justice.

The parable of verses 14–30 contrasts the behavior of servants of a lord who in his absence are entrusted with sums of money. Two of them employ the money as their lord had, in trade and usury, and double their sums, while the third buries the one talent he has been given. When the lord returns from his travels, the two who have doubled his money are rewarded, but the one who has only the single talent to surrender back is cast "into outer darkness." The parable has been interpreted to equate the talent with faith, and to mean that one must not merely possess faith, but employ it in the manner God intends. (Taken literally, of course, it seems to teach the value of investing and taking risks, and castigates the person who merely hoards and saves.)

Milton had begun going blind in the late 1640s; this sonnet has been dated variously from 1652 to 1656, while Milton was actively involved in his duties as Oliver Cromwell's "Latin Secretary" (a position roughly equivalent to secretary of state), explaining and justifying Cromwell's Puritan regime to the monarchies of Europe. In the sonnet he ponders his future life and work, contrasting the possible use of his literary talent (and his faith) in ways far different from writing public statements and pamphlets supporting the Cromwellian theocracy. The poem seems to report a crisis in his life, examining the alternatives for a writer who wants his gift to fulfill God's plan for him.

In his blindness (both physical and, momentarily, spiritual) Milton laments that he is not employing his talent, which he supposes useless to do the Lord's work, and fears that when he is confronted by his Maker and made to render his account, he will be cast away. He is foolishly about to ask how a man whose sight has been taken by God can be expected to do the same work as others. But his patience, personified, forestalls the question, telling him that his affliction is not a heavy burden and that his service to God may be merely to "stand and wait" (14) rather than to pursue a life of action.

The word "wait" has several relevant denotative meanings (this poem might be used as the occasion for students to learn to consult the *Oxford English*

Dictionary, with its full historical definitions). It may mean "to await"—that is, to stand in readiness for the master's arrival; or "to wait upon"—to attend to less active tasks than the "thousands" who range over the world carrying out the Lord's commands, as Milton figuratively is doing for Cromwell. In obsolete meanings current in Milton's time, it also meant "to hope" or "to expect," or—a definition that returns to line 1—"[to] consider." Patience is thus counseling him to accept his less spectacular tasks, to be ready for whatever God intends, to live in Christian hope and expectation of his salvation, and to return to the starting point of the sonnet—to consider again.

In the octave, Milton appears to misunderstand the meaning of the parable, thinking it unfair of God to expect "day-labor" (7) from one who has been deprived of eyesight. But like the verbal echoes of the language of trade, the objection to the parable is literal-minded; properly understood, as Patience instructs him, it teaches him to bear what he must, to stand in readiness, and not to believe that only great activities gain God's grace, for the best service is performed by those who accept their limitations and maintain an active faith.

The word "prevent" (8) is the hinge of the sonnet, occurring at the point separating the octave from the sestet. In its sense of "forestall" it reveals that the ideas of the sestet prevent him from voicing the foolish question to which his considerations have led him. In its further reference to the concept of "prevenience," it suggests that the advice of Patience is an action of God predisposing him toward performing God's will. In both senses, it reveals a circularity in the poem: "as I was about to murmur my complaint, Patience counseled me to consider again." This circularity is also suggested in the obsolete meaning of "wait"—"to consider." In effect the poem says that a reading of the parable momentarily led the poet to a misunderstanding of God's purposes, but God's prevenience checked him in time to see what those purposes really are. The half-rebellious mood of the octave never turns into open rebellion.

For further discussion of this sonnet, see Marjorie Nicolson, *A Reader's Guide to John Milton* (New York: Farrar, 1963) 152–55; E. M. W. Tillyard, *Milton* (New York: Collier, 1967) 160–62; and Macon Cheek, "Of Two Sonnets of Milton," reprinted in *Milton: Modern Essays in Criticism*, ed. Arthur E. Barker (New York: Oxford UP, 1965) 125–35.   TRA

Katharyn Howd Machan   Hazel Tells LaVerne (page 784)

This poem alludes to the fairy tale in which a young woman is asked to kiss a frog who is actually a disguised prince; her reward will be the elevation of her own status to that of a princess. Machan has fun with her allusion by making the speaker a cleaning woman who finds the frog in a toilet bowl she is scouring.

This ironic situation is well evoked through the poem's use of free verse; the short, conversational lines remind us of the title, which indicates that

Hazel is telling a friend of hers, probably another cleaning lady, about the incident. The use of non-standard English reveals the speaker's level of education and her colorful use of language. Her lively, distinctive voice is created by such locutions as "climb up the sida the bowl" (8), "sohelpmegod he starts talking" (10), and "I hitsm with my mop" (21).

The last two lines express the speaker's hard-edged realism, which precludes any indulgence in fantasy or a belief in fairy-tale scenarios.   GJ

Edwin Arlington Robinson   Miniver Cheevy (page 785)

"Miniver Cheevy" is a portrait etched in irony. Misfit and failure, unable to adjust to the present, Miniver escapes reality by dreaming of a romantic past and by drinking. Miniver longs for "the good old days" (or "bad old days"), which are more highly colored in his imagination than they were in actuality.

"Child of scorn" (1)—this deliberately ambiguous phrase suggests a mythological paternity. Miniver's father was scorn personified, and Miniver is his father's son. Miniver scorns the present: its art, its warfare, its materialistic aims, its drabness. But Miniver is also the target of scorn. His own scorn of the present is a rationalization of his failure to adjust to it, a defense against the scorn of others. The word "child" points up his essential immaturity.

The triteness of "days of old," "swords . . . bright," "steeds . . . prancing," "warrior bold" (5–7) signals the superficiality of Miniver's idealization of the past, and its source in romantic literature. The homely word "neighbors" next to "Thebes and Camelot" (11–12) makes Miniver's dream ludicrous, and the ironic juxtaposition of "grace" with "iron clothing" (23–24) sounds a clank. That Miniver, if he could have chosen, would have belonged to one of the wealthiest families of history—the Medici—reveals the falsity of his contempt for gold; that then he would have "sinned incessantly" (19) exposes the cheapness of all his values. Notice how the collocation of "ripe" and "renown" makes the first word suggest "overripe" and the second "notoriety." "[F]ragrant," because it follows, brings to mind not springtime and blossoms but fall and decaying fruit (13–14).

Robinson achieves his effect through form as well as diction. The repetition of Miniver's name at the beginning of each stanza reinforces the self-centeredness of his dreams. The short last line and feminine ending of each stanza furnish an anticlimax that jars Miniver's romantic idealization. The hissing *s* sounds in *assailed the seasons* and *sinned incessantly* echo Miniver's scorn and his evil glee in the prospect of sin. Robert Frost has expressed his delight in the second to last stanza: "There is more to it than the number of 'thoughts.' There is the way the last one turns up by surprise around the corner, the way the obstacle of verse is turned to advantage." The last "thought," of course, is the drop that overflows the bucket, emphasizing the futility of Miniver's thinking. In the final stanza the alliteration of key verbs—*kept, coughed, called, kept*—reasserts the continuance of the activity. The last line is brilliant poetic economy. Robinson first tells us that Miniver has been drinking by telling us that he "kept on" drinking. And the parallelism of "kept on drinking" with "kept on thinking" makes us supply a "drank, and drank, and drank, and drank" to match the previous repetitions of "thought."

Born too late? Miniver would have been "born too late" whenever he had been born.

For a fuller discussion, see *Colby Library Quarterly* 6 (June 1962): 65–74.   LP

T. S. Eliot   Journey of the Magi (page 786)

The traditional story tells of the three Magi, journeying from the East, following a star, bearing gifts of gold, frankincense, and myrrh, to worship the child in the stable. When the star stopped over Bethlehem, the Bible tells us, "they rejoiced with exceeding great joy." Eliot's poem undercuts our sentimental anticipation almost immediately. It doesn't mention the star; it says nothing of gold, frankincense, and myrrh; above all, it doesn't represent the experience as one of transforming joy.

Eliot's narrator, one of the Magi, is remembering the journey a long time after it happened, perhaps dictating it to be put in writing by a scribe (33–35). He begins with a description of the hardships of the journey: freezing weather, bad roads, refractory camels, unreliable camel men, hostile cities, unfriendly towns, dirty villages, high prices. Instead of following a star with unwavering confidence and joy, they are plagued by doubts telling them this journey is "all folly." As they near their destination, they encounter indications suggesting hope of something better—a temperate valley, a running stream, a white horse; but these indications are balanced by less hopeful ones—"six hands at an open door dicing for pieces of silver." (The images here anticipate events or symbols connected with the life and death of Christ—the three trees, the three crosses on Golgotha; the white horse, the first of the four horses of the Apocalypse, a symbol of Christ; the vine leaves and wine-skins, the wine of the Eucharist; the six hands dicing, the soldiers who diced for Christ's garments; the pieces of silver, the thirty pieces for which Judas betrayed Christ.) When they finally reach the stable, instead of presenting a glorified vision of a haloed Christ child surrounded by adoring shepherds and angels, the narrator can only say, "It was (you may say) satisfactory."

This poem is concerned with the experience of conversion, of spiritual rebirth. Conversion, as Eliot depicts it and as he knew it, is not necessarily a sudden transcendent experience accompanied by light from heaven and "exceeding great joy." It may instead be a slow painful process, accompanied by doubt of its validity, by spiritual agony and perplexity. It means destruction of one's former beliefs and way of life and their replacement by a new, more demanding way of life. "This Birth," the speaker says (he is referring both to the birth of Christ and his own rebirth), was "hard and bitter agony for us, like Death, our death." It made them no longer able to live comfortable lives among their people, whose beliefs they no longer shared. Yes, he would do it again, he says; but he does not say so eagerly. He yearns, in fact, for another death—physical death—to put an end to a difficult, demanding life.

[This commentary is adapted from Laurence Perrine and James M. Reid, *100 American Poems of the Twentieth Century* (New York: Harcourt, 1966), 133–34.]   LP

William Butler Yeats   Leda and the Swan (page 788)

What this sonnet describes is, quite literally, a rape. The action of the rape is indicated precisely. through sexual terms and symbols. The first quatrain describes the fierce assault and the foreplay; the second quatrain, the act of intercourse; the first part of the sestet, the sexual climax; the last part, the languor and apathy following the climax. But this is no ordinary rape: it is a rape by a god, by divine power temporarily embodied in the majestic form of a swan. And so it is described in terms that bring out awesomeness, not sordidness. The divinity appears as a "feathered glory" and its assault is a "white rush." It is also a momentous rape: it has large consequences for the future. And so the climax is described in terms that convey not only the experience of orgasm but also its remote consequences: the destruction of Troy, the death of Agamemnon. And then, after the moment of passion is over, and its results indicated, Yeats asks a question about the significance of the act: "Did she put on his knowledge with his power?"

Neither the word *swan* nor the name *Zeus* is mentioned in the body of the poem. We must rely on the title for our cues to the mythological event. Leda was a mortal princess by whose beauty Zeus, king of the gods, was smitten, and with whom he consummated his passion, having taken the form of a swan. There are several versions of this story, but in all of them Helen of Troy was one offspring of this union, and in the version used by Yeats, Clytemnestra was another. (See William Butler Yeats, *A Vision* [New York: Macmillan, 1956] 51.) The later abduction of Helen by the Trojan prince Paris from her husband the Greek king Menelaus led, of course, to the ten-year siege of Troy by Greek forces under the command of Agamemnon and to the ultimate defeat of the Trojans and the burning of Troy by the Greeks. On his return from Troy, Agamemnon was murdered by his wife Clytemnestra and her lover. (It matters little which version of the Leda story we know; the ultimate results are the same.)

In her union with the god, Leda clearly took on some of the power of the godhead, for she bore in her womb the forces that were to shape the future. Did she also take on his knowledge? The question can be formulated in different ways. Can human sexual passion ever foresee its consequences? Can power and wisdom coexist in human life? Can man ever combine the vitality and passion of youth with the knowledge and wisdom of age?

The question posed is left unanswered. Critics differ over whether an answer is implied. Some say the question is left open: that it is unanswerable. Others claim that it is the third of three rhetorical questions asked in the poem, all implying a negative answer (lines 5–6: "They can't"; lines 7–8: "It can't help but feel"; lines 13–14: "No"). Others suggest that power and knowledge can be combined in moments of artistic inspiration. This is a rich poem. For three provocative discussions, see Brian Arkius, *Builder of My Soul: Greek and Roman Themes in Yeats* (Gerrards Cross: Smythe, 1990) 98–101; Elizabeth Butler Cullingford, *Gender and History in Yeats's Love Poetry* (Cambridge: Cambridge UP, 1993) 142–64; and M. L. Rosenthal, *Running to Paradise: Yeats's Poetic Art* (New York: Oxford UP, 1994) 254–55.   LP

Adrienne Rich   I Dream I'm the Death of Orpheus

(page 789)

QUESTIONS

1. How do the allusions to the Cocteau film help us to understand the female speaker and her "certain powers" (2)? What is her "mission" (8) and what must be "obeyed to the letter" (9) by Orpheus?
2. In the dream-logic of the poem, the speaker usurps the role of the heroic poet. What is the outcome of the speaker's quest? What sort of triumph is suggested by the final two lines?

This is one of many poems in which Rich considers her own identity as a poet and, especially, her use of her own creative power.

She draws her imagery from the Jean Cocteau film about the ancient poet-singer Orpheus, imagining him as a mirror-image of her own artistic self. As a poet, the speaker must fight the cultural "authorities" (4) who would curtail her powers. To fight against the forces arrayed against her requires "the nerves of a panther" (10) and, as she notes sardonically, "contacts among Hell's Angels" (11)—one of the poem's many allusions to the underworld of the Orpheus myth.

Only by remaining "sworn to lucidity" (14) can the speaker remain true to herself and to her calling. Her job is a considerable one, since she must remain focused despite "the mayhem, the smoky fires" (15) of the harrowing underworld. The specifically feminist nature of her undertaking is made clear through the incantatory repetition of the phrase "a woman," and we are reminded of the title: in the dream-logic of this poem, the speaker replaces Orpheus, switching the gender of a cultural icon representing the art of poetry. Thus, in the last two lines, Rich's speaker becomes the negative image of the Orpheus figure, appearing "on the wrong side of the mirror" (17).

As Albert Gelpi remarks, "What the dream-poem traces out is the resurrection of Orpheus through the woman's determination to resist all depersonal-
izing forces—psychological, political, sexual—arrayed against the exercise of
her powers." ("Adrienne Rich: The Poetics of Change," in Barbara
Charlesworth Gelpi and Albert Gelpi, eds., *Adrienne Rich's Poetry and Prose*
[New York: Norton, 1975] 296). Claire Keyes calls the poem "a modern re-
shaping of the myth of Orpheus in the underworld. Taking its images from the
Jean Cocteau film, Rich's poem is overtly feminist and carries forth her theme
of the 'reconstruction of the mind.' In this poem, her psyche undergoes the
changes. In reading the poem, we participate in this reconstruction and observe
how Rich transforms the myth to suit her own purposes" (*The Aesthetics of
Power: The Poetry of Adrienne Rich* [Athens: U of Georgia P, 1986] 120).   GJ

Chapter Nine

Meaning and Idea

Anonymous   Little Jack Horner (page 791)

"Little Jack Horner," of course, presents an example of dramatic irony—a boy who sticks his thumb in a pie is *not* a good boy.   LP

A. E. Housman   Loveliest of Trees (page 792)

Robert Frost   Stopping by Woods on a Snowy Evening
(page 793)

"Loveliest of Trees" (*A Shropshire Lad*, 2) is a *carpe diem* poem expressing the philosophy that life is short and that one should therefore enjoy it fully while one can, wasting no moment that might be filled with pleasure. The pleasure proposed in this poem is the enjoyment of beauty, especially of natural beauty, as symbolized by the blossoming cherry tree.

In assuming that the natural life span of man is seventy years, the speaker *alludes* to the Old Testament (Psalm 90.10): "The days of our years are threescore years and ten." The speaker is twenty. Normally one would think of a young man at that age as having ample time left for pleasure and enjoyment. His "only" and "little" therefore come as small shocks of surprise, emphasizing how few fifty years really are for something so wonderful as the enjoyment of nature. This is not verbal irony (for the speaker means what he says), but irony of situation—a discrepancy between what the reader anticipates and what he actually hears.

"Snow" (line 12) is metaphorical, representing the masses of white bloom with which the cherry trees are hung at Eastertide. The critical argument concerning this point is summarized in Laurence Perrine, "Housman's Snow: Literal or Metaphorical?" *CEA Critic* 35 (1972): 26–27.

The speaker is not Housman but a Shropshire lad (for Housman was older than twenty when he wrote this poem), but he undoubtedly speaks *for* Housman, or one aspect of him. This aspect should be contrasted with other aspects, as expressed, for instance, by the speaker in "To an Athlete Dying Young" (page 971).

"Stopping by Woods on a Snowy Evening" is one of Frost's best-known poems. It is discussed further in Chapter 10, "Tone" (page 804), where an additional element of meaning is suggested in a symbolic reading of "sleep" as death. The conclusion drawn there is "that beauty is a distinctively human value that deserves its place in a full life but that to devote one's life to its pursuit, at the expense of other obligations and duties, is tantamount to one's death as a responsible being." One might also explore the many possibilities of the repeated last line, including that of dramatic irony suggesting that the speaker is in fact dozing off as the poem trails off in monotonous iteration. He wills himself to go on, but the poem doesn't present any forward motion. And dozing off on this "darkest evening of the year" in a frozen landscape may result in literal death.   LP, TRA

Ralph Waldo Emerson   **The Rhodora** (page 795)

Robert Frost   **Design** (page 796)

Emerson's and Frost's poems both begin with an observation from nature and end with an idea about God, but their conclusions are diametrically opposite. Both start out with the speaker recalling a discovery (using the identical phrase "I found") implying a questing search for meanings in the natural world, but one finds a benevolent "Power" while the other is horrified to discover a "design of darkness." Emerson looks at the early-blooming Rhodora showing forth its flower in obscurity, unobserved by less perceptive seekers than the speaker. What can be the purpose of such beauty being "wasted," far from the eyes of appreciative men? It is not wasted, because a "Power" guided the speaker to admire the flower that the "Power" had placed there for him to find. His confidence and optimism are reinvigorated by this chance encounter.

The connotations in Frost's poem work in two opposite directions. First, there is a series of words and images suggesting innocence—"dimpled," "heal-all," "morning," "right," "snow-drop," "flower," "blue," "innocent," and the five-times repeated "white." Second, there is an equally impressive sequence suggesting evil—"spider," "death," "blight," "witches' broth," "dead," "night," "darkness," "appall." The collocation of these two kinds of words seems to pose a question.

The design indicated by the title is formed by three things—a white heal-all, a white spider, a white moth. The heal-all, a wild flower with medicinal virtues, is usually blue. Spiders are ordinarily black or brown. What has brought together these three white things, two of them so rarely white? It would seem the work of a conscious artist. But what is the consequence of this artistry? Death. The white moth, lured by the usually protective kindred color of the heal-all, has been trapped by the spider and killed. It is held now "like a white piece of rigid satin cloth" (the image not only describes a dead moth exactly but suggests the lining of a coffin). The three white things are thus "Like the ingredients of a witches' broth." The suggestion that these ingredients have been mixed "to begin the morning right" (rite?) is ironical. There is irony also in the connection of the innocent color white with this sinister enterprise of death.

In the eighteenth century, a favorite argument for the existence of God was the so-called argument from design. The intricate construction of the universe, it was held, with all of its stars and planets whirling in mathematically chartable courses regulated by the law of gravity, testified to the existence of an infinitely wise creator, for how could there be design without a designer? As the Nineteenth Psalm so eloquently expresses it, "The heavens declare the glory of God, and the firmament showeth his handiwork."

Frost's title alludes to this famous argument in a grimly ironical fashion: the design in nature, Frost points out, is that of "a witches' broth." Thus the poem asks a terrible question: "What brought the kindred spider to that height, / Then steered the white moth thither in the night? / What but design of darkness to appall?—" (11–13). Perhaps the universe is governed, not by infinite goodness, but by infinite evil. The poem does not assert this proposition as an actuality; it merely suggests it as a possibility. And the suggestion is immediately softened, apparently, by the provision of another possibility—that perhaps design does not govern in a thing so small. But the afterthought, tossed in so casually, when examined closely turns out to be not very comforting either. If nature is not governed by design, then it is governed merely by chance, coincidence, anarchy, chaos—certainly not by the traditionally omnipotent, benevolent God who is concerned over the smallest sparrow's fall.

Cast in the sonnet form but confining itself to only three rhyme sounds (the title might refer to the pattern of the poem as well as the design made by the three white things in nature), Frost's brief poem chillingly poses the problem of evil.

Emerson's use of the verb "brought" (16) and Frost's of "steered" (12) make Frost's poem seem almost a reply to Emerson's. Both poems ask the purpose of the bizarre or unlikely natural object (Emerson even states his question in his subtitle, asking the source of origin of the flower), and they offer opposite answers. Emerson's poem is structured in two octaves rhyming *aabbcdcd* (a stanza break after line 8 would show this structure even more clearly). The first describes the rhodora and its setting and proffers two interpretive ideas—that the flower seems to exist "[t]o please" its isolated environment, and that its beauty enhances by contrast the natural surroundings. In the second octave, the poem introduces personification through apostrophe, moving the focus from observer to the object being observed. Here the speaker imagines "sages" who assume that the flower is "wasted" by being hidden away from popular gaze (9–10), an assumption that blinds them to the answer. The famous couplet, made more emphatic by its unique feminine rhymes, gives the gnomic answer:

> Tell them, dear, that if eyes were made for seeing,
> Then Beauty is its own excuse for being. (11–12)

This is, of course, not really an answer to the question why the rhodora is found only in such out-of-the-way places, blooming out of the flowering season. It means simply that beautiful things need no explanation.

The conclusion of the poem ironically contrasts the inquisitiveness of the "sages" with the speaker's "simple ignorance" (15), and the irony is made stronger by enlisting the "Power" (16) on the speaker's side of the contrast. By implication, the questioning mind is shown to be inferior to the intuitive, unschooled heart, the lover of beauty reaches deeper meanings than the analytical, scientific searcher for truth.

For discussions of the Frost poem, see Karen L. Kilcup, *Robert Frost and the Feminine Literary Tradition* (Ann Arbor: U of Michigan P, 1998) 214–16; and Jay Parini, *Robert Frost, A Life* (New York: Holt, 1999) 110–11.

Emerson's poem is analyzed by R. A. Yoder in *Emerson and the Orphic Voice in America* (Berkeley: U of California P, 1978) 81–82.

[Part of this commentary is adapted from Laurence Perrine and James M. Reid, *100 American Poems of the Twentieth Century* (New York: Harcourt, 1966) 46–47.]   LP, TRA

Emily Dickinson   I never saw a Moor (page 797)

Emily Dickinson   "Faith" is a fine invention (page 797)

The first, apparently simple poem offers a serene expression of religious faith, and as such forms a striking contrast to the second. Whereas the latter poem makes the sophisticated, witty point that scientific proof of religious principles may be necessary to a person who suffers spiritual "emergencies" or for whom faith does not come easily, the speaker of "I never saw a Moor" insists that "seeing" is not necessary to belief. She is not only certain that heaven exists—again, in contrast to other Dickinson poems that express formidable, often anguished doubt about orthodox Christian dogma—but claims she is as sure of its location as someone who has been given railroad tickets for a specific, known destination.

The poem has often been taken at face value, and in fact Dickinson's early editors gave it the title "Faith." Certainly the very simplicity of the poem, including its regular metrical pattern and unsophisticated diction, suggests a speaker unbothered by religious doubt. She argues that a reasonable person does not need to see earthly phenomena such as the moors or the sea in order to believe they exist, and that her faith in God and heaven operates on the same principle. Her position no doubt represents the kind of unwavering, forthright belief enjoyed by millions of churchgoers throughout the centuries.

Close inspection of the speaker's claims, however, has suggested to some critics (including this writer) that Dickinson is here employing a persona in order to satirize a blithe, unthinking acceptance of orthodox faith. The poem's regular meter, after all, verges on a sing-song, and in the first stanza the exact rhymes of "Sea" and "be," combined with the childish-sounding alliteration of "Billow be," hardly suggest a mature or hard-won viewpoint.

In *Emily Dickinson: Perception and the Poet's Quest* (University, AL: U of Alabama P, 1985) 57–58, I pursued this argument, claiming that the speaker employs "specious logic" in the second stanza: lines 5 and 6 are "analogous to the corresponding two lines of the first stanza, but with line 7 the speaker claims a 'certainty' that does not logically follow from her argument about the heather and the sea. While there are definite means through which she might have made 'certain' of those phenomena, we are left to wonder *how* the speaker has learned about the existence of heaven. Her blithely dispensing with the 'how' of religious quest marks her as immature and untrustworthy; and because the syllogism attempted by the poem is invalid, the speaker's argument collapses . . . . [S]he certainly lacks all the sophisticated intelligence other Dickinson speakers bring to bear upon this all-serious subject. All this, added to the speaker's assurance not only that heaven exists, but that she is 'certain . . . of the spot,' constitutes a stance so exaggerated that Dickinson's ironic intent becomes clear."

Critical commentary has reflected an attempt to reconcile this poem with Dickinson's characteristic skepticism. Edwin Moseley ("The Gambit of Emily Dickinson," *University of Kansas City Review* 16 [1949]: 17) finds that the poem's "calmness" suggests "the Puritan's concern with the practical." On the other hand, Clark W. Griffith calls the poem "a tinkling little credo" that is either ironic, or a kind of "whistling in the dark" (*The Long Shadow: Emily Dickinson's Tragic Poetry* [Princeton: Princeton UP, 1964] 4, 109–10).

In sixteen carefully chosen words, "'Faith' is a fine invention" gives witty expression to post-Darwinian religious skepticism. The poem's arch, mock-decorous tone pokes gentle fun at society's conventional "Gentlemen" who carry forward the tradition of religious orthodoxy, insisting that empirical evidence—of the kind obtained by microscopes—is necessary for anyone suffering a crisis of faith.

By placing "Faith" in quotation marks and calling it an "invention," the speaker underscores the limited ability of human ideas and language to create a convincing intellectual bridge to the unknowable realm of the spirit. In sharp contrast to "I never saw a Moor" this poem implies that scrupulous, responsible inquiry, not mere acceptance of inherited faith, represents the path toward knowledge. Whether training the microscope on the particulars of nature or of the self, the speaker insists—in a dry understatement—that it is "prudent" to rely on personal truth-seeking, not on a possibly spurious system of belief created by others.   GJ

John Keats   On the Sonnet (page 798)

Billy Collins   Sonnet (page 798)

The subject of Keats's sonnet is the sonnet form itself. The speaker seems to regret that poets write in such fixed forms, with their "dull rhymes" (1) and mechanical structures; at the same time, his own sonnet with its flowing rhythms, and its graceful combination of end-stopped and run-on lines, illustrates the way a good sonnet should be written.

Poetry, the speaker implies, should be uncontainable, but if it must be contained by a fixed form, then certain principles should be followed. Ideally a poem should be unfettered and free, like a naked foot, but if it must be clothed in a sandal, then a good poet should find "Sandals more interwoven and complete" (5) rather than mechanically rhymed and metered verses that constrain the meaning and spirit of a poetic idea.

The speaker further lectures the aspiring sonneteer to "weigh the stress / Of every chord, and see what may be gained / By ear industrious, and attention meet" (7–9). In other words, a good poet follows his own ear and weighs every syllable for its effect on sound and sense, rather than simply pouring the poem into the pre-ordained mold. Not a word or syllable should appear in the poem simply to effect a rhyme or round out a metrical scheme; these errors are like "dead leaves in the bay-wreath crown" (12).

Walter Jackson Bate notes that Keats's ideas on the sonnet were influenced by his reading of Shakespeare's sonnets: "the structure, cadence, and rhetorical devices were in his mind. If more than mere rhyme scheme were followed, the form would be a fresh if minor challenge" (*John Keats* [Cambridge: Harvard UP, 1963] 298).

In a contemporary reconsideration of this fixed form, Collins's "Sonnet" is a witty tribute to, and critique of, the conventions of the Petrarchan sonnet. As the speaker progresses through his fourteen lines, he employs imagery that irreverently illustrates techniques long used by sonnet authors. For instance, the deliberate cliché in line 3, "love's storm-tossed seas," satirizes the way in which a conventional poetic form has often led, in the hands of mediocre writers, to trite and unimaginative metaphors. In the next line, the image "rows of beans" implies that sonneteers must literally be "bean-counters," carefully keeping track of lines and syllables. The mostly monosyllabic string of words in this line effectively underscores its meaning.

The poem continues to use playful images as it proceeds. In line 6, the sonnet's characteristic use of iambic pentameter becomes "the iambic bongos" (6). Two lines later, the need to use rhyme at the ends of each line becomes a "station of the cross" (8), a hyperbolic suggestion that a poet suffers greatly to maintain the necessary rhyme scheme. In the final line, the funny image of Petrarch in his "crazy medieval tights" (13) effectively caps off this light-hearted riff on one of the most venerated poetic forms.   GJ

John Donne   The Indifferent (page 799)

John Donne   Love's Deity (page 800)

The irony in "The Indifferent" depends on a simple reversal of what human beings usually call vice and virtue. For the speaker, constancy in love is a vice, promiscuity is a virtue. Love's "sweetest part" is variety, not fidelity. In the speaker's "religion" any woman who is faithful to one mate is a "heretic." The

goddess of this religion is Venus (Aphrodite) who in classical mythology was
herself unfaithful to her husband Vulcan (Haephestus) through affairs with
Mars (Ares), Mercury (Hermes), Bacchus (Dionysus), and others, by one of
whom she was mother of Cupid (Eros). When Venus hears the speaker's complaint that modern women are guilty of heresy (that is, of fidelity to one man),
she forms herself into a one-person investigating committee and finds that the
report is greatly exaggerated—she has found two or three faithful women, but
no more, and she will punish them by giving them unfaithful mates.

The speaker in "Love's Deity" suffers from unrequited love and accuses
"Love's deity" (Cupid) of having overreached his assigned duties. He wishes
he could speak to the ghost of some lover who died before Cupid ("this
child") was born, in order to confirm his charges. He believes that the older
gods, who put Cupid in office, intended that his duties be restricted to assisting mutual lovers and bringing together young persons who could and would
reciprocate each other's love. But, like other ambitious bureaucrats, Cupid
has enlarged the powers of his office beyond its intended limits; he has tyrannically seized powers not meant to be his and aspires to powers equal to those
of Jove himself. Instead of presiding over and helping to create a realm of
harmonious and reciprocated feeling, Cupid has introduced obsession, lust,
intrigue, and betrayal into his domain. Worst of all, the speaker seems to feel,
Cupid has caused *him* to be in love with someone who does not return his
love. This is the burden of his complaint through the first three stanzas. In
the third stanza he becomes openly rebellious and blasphemous, proposing
that if humankind were sufficiently aroused "by this tyranny / To ungod this
child again, it could not be / I should love her who loves not me."

In the final stanza, however, shocked by the violence to which his
thought has risen, he returns to a more moderate dissatisfaction. Addressing
himself as "Rebel and atheist" (for wanting to "ungod" the child again), he
reproaches himself for complaining; as he realizes, there are two worse fates
that Love could have made him suffer. Love could have (a) made him cease
loving or (b) made her return his love.

But is this not an almost complete reversal of his previous thought? Indeed it is. Are these worse fates not paradoxically the very solutions he had
earlier been desiring for his problem? Indeed they are. How do we explain
them then? First, by understanding that the speaker, psychologically, must
give vent to his pain (as he does in the first three stanzas) before he can view
his situation more calmly and philosophically. Second, by absorbing the new
information (withheld until the final stanza) that the woman loved by the
speaker is already attached to another man (she is probably a married
woman; but at least she is fully committed elsewhere and was so before the
speaker fell in love with her).

What, then, are the philosophical beliefs or values that serve to moderate, though not to obliterate, the speaker's suffering? First, that there is value
in *all* loving. Although unrequited love involves deep anguish, there is a
richness of feeling in this anguish that makes it better to have experienced it

than never to have felt at all. Second, that infidelity in love is a grave moral deformity. "Falsehood [infidelity]," the speaker says, "is worse than hate." He would rather endure the pangs of unreciprocated love than enjoy the favors of a faithless woman.

[*Note:* Donne's favorite figurative devices are paradox and overstatement. It is probable that "hate" (27) and "scorn" (4) are both overstatements of her lack of responsiveness to any suit of adulterous love; or perhaps they literally express her feeling toward infidelity itself rather than her feeling toward the speaker.]

But now that we have resolved the contradictions and paradoxes in "Love's Deity," how do we resolve the contradictions between "Love's Deity" and "The Indifferent," both composed by the same poet? The speaker in "Love's Deity" regards fidelity in love as a virtue; the speaker in "The Indifferent" regards it as a "dangerous" vice. The two recommendations are polar opposites.

The easiest and best way of explaining the contradiction is simply to say that the two poems, though written by one poet, have two different speakers, neither one necessarily speaking for Donne himself. Donne in many of his poems seemed to be exploring different ways of regarding love by deliberately expressing disparate views through disparate speakers.

It should be noted that the speakers in these two poems mean different things by the word "love." The speaker in "The Indifferent" consistently uses the word to mean physical love—copulation. Nothing in the poem suggests that he recognizes any further dimensions of meaning for the word. The speaker in "Love's Deity" consistently means something more by the word: something perhaps combining warm affection, admiration, and physical desire. He makes a distinction, as the other speaker does not, between "love" and "lust."   LP

Billy Collins   My Number (page 801)

Edwin Denby   I had heard it's a fight (page 802)

These two witty poems personifying death seem at first reading not to take the topic seriously. In both cases, careful reading and analysis reveal an ironic distance between the superficial tone of the speaker and his genuine emotions.

Collins's title alludes to the trite, fatalistic phrase "your number is up." A similar phrase from wartime experience states that when your name is on the bullet, you are fated to be killed. The poem itself is (until the last line) a series of questions, as is appropriate when wondering whether one's number has been called. In the first ten lines the questions are wishfully evasive—asking whether personified Death might just be occupied elsewhere and so not interested in the speaker, or even whether the speaker is really important

enough to be found out by Death. In the first quatrain Death might be dealing personally and individually with a widow or a hiker; in the second, Death
might more generally be "making arrangements" (5) for larger devastation or
catastrophe involving multitudes. Part of the wittiness of the poem to this
point is derived from the specificity of "Cincinnati" and "British Columbia"
(2, 4), part from the colloquial and commonplace suggestions in lines 6–8 in
which ordinary accidents or a familiar disease are treated like purposeful
"arrangements" (5) made by Death.

At line 11 the poem drops its evasiveness to wonder whether the grim
reaper might be as near as the end of the lane leading to the speaker's cottage,
might have arrived in a "black car" (rather than on an apocalyptic pale horse),
might be putting on his traditional garb and retrieving his traditional fatal implement "from the trunk" (15). The hypotheses bring the fearful event closer
though the details of the personification seem more cartoon-like: the flippant
tone of the first ten lines gives way to an even more jocular caricature.

The closing couplet focuses the theme and means. Greeting his guest with
polite familiarity, the speaker forthrightly acknowledges to himself that he will
need even more effective verbal tricks to escape—or that the tactics employed
so far haven't really worked and that blarney may finally not avert fate.

Denby's poem creates a contrast between what the speaker "had heard"
about the approach of death and the near-death experience he has had. The
opening quatrain is both colloquial and melodramatic, a series of cliché
phrases that represent the physical event. The opening sentence, "I had
heard it's a fight," evokes a typical death-struggle and then the string of
clichés exaggerates the reality: "clammy touch," "kicks you / In the stomach,"
"clutch / At a straw," and "that will fix you" are all so trite that there is almost nothing of the genuine, fearful experience presented.

The second quatrain announces a doubt ("I don't know," [5]) and proceeds to a metaphorical representation of the real thing. Death is personified
as a seductress who overcomes the speaker's certain knowledge that to accept
her advances will send him to hell (as a sinner? at least, metaphorically)—
but "what the hell, why not?" he seems to ask himself. So he succumbs to the
temptation and has his "sweet" encounter that almost kills him.

Guilt ensues, the speaker reforms his life so as to avoid any more liaisons
with the fatal temptress—but he gets "a kick" (13) out of recalling that
moment when life was in the balance. The metaphor is extended by the
denotative puns of the last line: "dying" was a Renaissance metaphor for experiencing sexual climax, and "quick" denotes both rapidity and vitality,
meaning both "fast" and "alive." The "sweet thrill" (6) was too soon over, but
it was invigorating; it was like a loss of life, yet exhilarating.

As thematic contrasts, the more light-hearted poem by Collins does express a fear of death, while Denby's more serious, imaginative near-death experience suggests that death might be both a loss and a fulfillment.   TRA

Chapter Ten

Tone

Richard Eberhart   For a Lamb (page 806)

Emily Dickinson   Apparently with no surprise (page 806)

For a far different poem about a lamb see Blake's "The Lamb" (page 946), one that evokes the positive implications that Eberhart plays upon. In comparing them, note the contrasting poetic stances that contribute to their tones: Blake's speaker is a child who mirrors the innocence of the lamb and symbolically links himself to it; Eberhart's speaker is a mature realist who doesn't apostrophize but is imaginative enough to draw some larger consolation from the fact of universal mortality.

Dickinson's poem may profitably be compared with Frost's "Design" (page 796), for both poems raise similar issues, and both (like Melville in *Moby-Dick*) make the color white, usually associated with purity and innocence, take on exceedingly sinister connotations.   TRA, LP

Michael Drayton   Since there's no help (page 808)

From the first eight lines of this sonnet it seems apparent that the speaker (the male, as we shall see) and his beloved are breaking off their relationship. Does the speaker want to break it off? He asserts quite positively, perhaps too positively, that he does (3–4), but even in these first eight lines this assertion is undercut by the implication that he is acting under constraint ("Since there's no help") and by the suggestion that at any future meetings they may have difficulty disguising their still-existent feelings for each other. If any doubt remains that he does not really want to break off the relationship, it should be dissolved by the sestet, especially the last two lines, where he declares that she could still bring his love back to life, if she only would. He obviously hopes that she will. The rich allegorical and poetic language of the sestet (as opposed to the clipped, prosaic language of the octave) indicates that his true feelings come out here, and that he deliberately falsified the feelings in the octave.

Does *she*, then, want to break off the relationship? Although she is given no words in the poem (he is the speaker throughout), the "Nay" beginning in line 2 is a clear signal that this line is spoken in response to some gesture or word of protest made by her against his pronouncement in line 1. She does not want to "kiss and part." A further clue to her feelings is provided by his including her along with himself in his forecast of the difficulty *both* will have in concealing their feelings at future meetings.

But if neither of them *wants* to break off the relationship, *why* are they breaking it off? To answer this question, we must examine the allegorical death scene depicted in the sestet. When asked how many figures are involved in this scene, students initially answer four. But do we then have two dying figures, two deathbed scenes? Or are not "Love" and "Passion" two different names (suggesting the spiritual and the physical aspects) for one dying figure? Clearly they are one person, most fittingly called "Love/Passion." There is only one deathbed (11), and the dying figure is referred to by a single pronoun in each of the last four lines ("his," "his," "him," "him"). The masculinity of the pronoun suggests that the dying Love/Passion is *his* (the speaker's). The logic of the situation suggests that the two attendants at the bedside, Faith kneeling in prayer, Innocence pulling down the eyelids of the presumably dead figure, are *hers*. By a subtle associative logic these two attendants, ostensibly present to ease the death, are made to appear the causes of the death. Her innocence is closing up the eyes of his passion; her faith (religious scruple) is assisting at the bedside. Yet, he asserts, if she would, she might at the very moment of death—"Now," in an instant—bring his Love/Passion quite suddenly back to life. Surely, the situation is clear. Though the woman wishes to retain his love, she also values and wishes to preserve her innocence (her purity, her chastity); her faith tells her that fornication is a sin. He claims that, by refusing to satisfy his passion, she is causing both it and his love (they are one and the same) to die.

The relation of sound and sense in this sonnet is discussed on pages 864 of the text.   LP

William Shakespeare   My mistress' eyes (page 809)

This witty sonnet might serve as a model of courtship, if a lady were to be won by realistic honesty. The speaker at length rejects the customary (lying) praise of hyperbolic lovers, insisting that his lady is only a woman, not a "goddess," and yet she is "as rare" as any woman who has been praised with overstated comparisons. In other words, he loves her for what she is, and does not think she wishes to be lied to about qualities she does not possess. It is a different kind of praise he offers, a high estimate of her common sense and her delight in wit.

The object of his satire is the "false compare" of the Petrarchan sonnet tradition. The formalities of the tradition required that the poet begin by praising the lady's hair (usually as fine and bright as spun golden wire), proceed to her ivory or alabaster forehead, her eyebrows arched like Cupid's bow, her pearly teeth, cherry-red lips, and so on, moving down the various parts of her body (generally rather coyly below the waist) to her delicate light feet. But Shakespeare seems realistically to present the order in which a man might look at a woman whose inner worth is also important to him, moving from eyes to lips to breasts, then to hair, cheeks, breath, voice, and gait, and at each stop he realistically claims her to be less than ideal. To the modern ear, the least complimentary word in the poem is "reeks," but the word was not used to mean *stinks* until the eighteenth century, and Shakespeare's meaning is much less offensive—it means *exhales*. His tactic throughout the poem is not to substitute some other quality for the traditional overstatement, but just to say "she is not like *that*." What she *is* like is a woman, and for that he loves her.   TRA

Adrienne Rich   Miracle Ice Cream (page 810)

QUESTIONS
1. Does the interjected "yes" (3) set up the tone of "one piece of your heart" (4)?
2. Define the contrasts of tone between the company name "Miracle" (1) and the "fast-food miracles" (9); between the simile "like pearls" (2) and the metaphor "pearl of dusk" (7); between "dusk" (7) and "Late" (8); between "one piece of your heart" (4) and "the rest of your heart" (10).

Struck by the company name, the speaker meditates upon the contrast between the idea of miracles and the reality of "what's . . . given" (5). The opening quatrain conveys a memory of small miracles, the unexpected but pleasant sweetness of commingled sounds and flavors associated with summer treats in childhood. The experience is not a burst of joy but only feeling "happy / with one piece of your heart" (3–4). The interjection "yes" (3) even suggests some reluctance to acknowledge that such small things can touch her, a note also struck by the diminutive "little avenue" (1) and the limitation to "one piece" of her emotional life. Still, the arrival of the truck, with its jaunty tune and the promise of the delight of ice cream, is not denied—is even made more miraculous by the simile comparing the notes of the ragtime music to "pearls" being "strewn behind it," an appealing image of riches and beauty generously brought into the modest "little avenue" (1) of childhood.

The sestet begins with other beauties, realistic ones: "what's . . . given" involves other images: the "rich shadow," the gently swinging breasts, and the pale, translucent "pearl of dusk" dissolving earlier in the autumn evening than in childhood's summer (5–7). Many contrasts set apart the miraculous sweetness of the ice cream scene from the scene of "what's still given" (a phrase that suggests a reduction in the possibilities of happiness). Daylight gives way to dusk, outdoors to indoors, the exuberant movement of strewn pearls to the lightly swinging breasts, promises of pleasure to the dissolution and darkness of night coming on. And one should add: childhood gives way to maturity, a simple vision of miracles yields to darker, richer realities.

The concluding three lines move into another vision of reality. What fills "the rest of your heart" (10), that portion that has not been touched by childhood memories, is more disturbing and flatter in tone. After dusk, "late," the speaker must evaluate other realities such as those brought in by "the evening news," by the tawdriness of "fast-food miracles," by "ghostly revolutions," and by the knowledge that now occupies "the rest of [her] heart." Night has indeed come on. "[T]he evening news" (8) connotes television pictures of crime scenes, political squabbles, perhaps war reports—certainly not ragtime melodies and ice cream. "[F]ast food miracles" connote unsavory non-nutritional time-savers designed for the microwave, not the slow-paced ice cream truck stopping to delight little palates. And "ghostly revolutions" has haunting implications: "ghostly" may mean vague, ill-defined, frightening, as well as spiritual or religious. Positive revolutions are passionate, principled, and hopeful.

The tone of the poem thus displays a progressive shift from simple pleasure through realism to something like lassitude and despair.   TRA

Alfred, Lord Tennyson   Crossing the Bar (page 810)

Thomas Hardy   The Oxen (page 811)

Despite the fame and popularity of "Crossing the Bar," students often have difficulty with it, and it is well to make sure that they understand it. The two complementary sets of figures used to express approaching death are the coming of night and setting out on an ocean voyage. The moment of death in the first set is the disappearance of the last light of day: the arrival of "the dark." In the second set it is the moment of "crossing the bar": leaving the harbor, which belongs to the land, and setting out on the ocean. As the land represents temporal life, the ocean—"the boundless deep"—represents eternity. "[T]hat which drew from out the boundless deep" (7) is the soul: in Tennyson's thought the soul comes from eternity, takes fleshly embodiment during life, and returns to eternity upon death. Tennyson wants no "moaning of the bar"—no lamentation over his death—for his soul is returning "home," is passing on to eternal life, and will see its "Pilot" (God) "face to face" after death. The occasion should therefore be one for joy rather than for sadness.

The whole poem expresses Tennyson's faith in immortality. Despite its popularity, which stems largely from its message, the poem is a good one. An oversubtle cavil about the image of the pilot, raised by Brooks and Warren in their manual for *Understanding Poetry*, 3rd ed. (New York: Holt, 1960), is satisfactorily answered by G. Geoffrey Langsam in *Explicator* 10 (Apr. 1952): item 40. For a debate about the tone of the poem, see James R. Kincaid, "Tennyson's 'Crossing the Bar': A Poem of Frustration," *Victorian Poetry* 3 (1965): 57–61, and Laurence Perrine, "When Does Hope Mean Doubt?: The Tone of 'Crossing the Bar,'" *Victorian Poetry* 4 (1966): 127–31.

"The Oxen" divides exactly in the middle, the first two stanzas presenting a scene from the speaker's childhood, the second two, one from his adult life. If we take the speaker as Hardy himself, or as a contemporary of Hardy, the two scenes are divided by Darwin's *Origin of Species* (1859) and by the dramatic decline of religious faith that it accelerated. In the poem the superstition of the kneeling animals is symbolic of the whole system of Christian belief that Hardy was taught as a boy and that he gave up as a man, but that, like Matthew Arnold (see "Dover Beach," page 816), he never ceased to regret. Though he can no longer subscribe to Christian doctrine or to its worldview, he regrets the loss of the emotional security and comfort provided by that worldview.

In emotional tone the two halves of the poem differ sharply. In the first two stanzas, there is a sense of warmth, of comfort, and of community. Young and old sit "in a flock / By the embers in hearthside ease" (3–4), and the speaker uses the plural pronoun "we." In the last two stanzas, there is isolation and darkness. The speaker uses the singular pronoun, refers to the barton as "lonely," and with the word "gloom" describes not only the darkness of the night but also the spirit of the times—the desolation caused by the loss of religious faith. The superstition of the kneeling oxen—along with the divine birth and the resurrection—is dismissed as a "fancy," one that few people any longer accept, but that was nevertheless "fair" (attractive).

The word "hope" in Tennyson's poem and in Hardy's has opposite meanings relative to the expectations involved. Tennyson's *hope* expresses expectation without real doubt; Hardy's expresses a wish without real expectation. Tennyson's poem expresses confident faith that it will be so; Hardy's expresses a wistful yearning that it might be so. Hardy does not say that he would go out to the barton to see the oxen kneel. He says (in effect), "I *feel* I would go *if* someone asked me." But no one will ask him, and it doesn't occur to him to go alone. Moreover, if someone did ask him, he wouldn't really go. The feeling is an ephemeral one that would not survive the invitation. Hardy (or the speaker) is an intellectually sophisticated twentieth-century man who would feel himself a goose to go on such a fool's errand. To put this point across to a class, it might be useful to ask: Would Hardy go if someone asked him? Would *you* go? Today Linus may wait in the pumpkin patch on Halloween to see the Great Pumpkin, but he won't when he is five years older, and no one of high-school or college age in America today would be caught dead waiting for Santa Claus to come down the chimney. Hardy's "hope" is a wistful yearning, not a hope.

Reading Tennyson's poem aloud, one should read the word *hope* very quietly, without emphasis, for to emphasize it is to express doubt, and the serenity and beauty of the preceding imagery indicate absence of doubt. One need not, in reading Hardy's poem, put artificial emphasis on "hoping": the inversion of accent (a trochee instead of an iamb) forces an emphasis on it. Hardy's poem, in its own way, is as quiet and as beautiful as Tennyson's, but the quietness comes from resignation rather than from faith. (For further comment, see the discussion of "The Darkling Thrush," page 315, in this manual.)   LP

Emily Dickinson   ## One dignity delays for all (page 812)

Emily Dickinson   ## 'Twas warm—at first—like Us (page 813)

The theme of "One dignity delays for all" is that all of us, no matter how humble, will one day be honored and treated like nobility—namely, on the day of our burial. In the second stanza the funeral procession through the streets of the village is compared to the progress of a king, duke, or bishop through his domain. The hearse is a carriage, the casket is the royal chamber, the undertaker and his assistants are footmen, bells toll in the church towers, and crowds stop to watch on the sidewalks or follow behind the hearse. In the third stanza the procession stops at the graveside, the officiating clergy ("dignified Attendants") conduct a funeral ceremony (like a coronation ceremony or an official welcome to a visiting prince), and everyone takes off his hat as prayers are read and the casket is lowered into the grave. (The above account may be overspecific in its point-to-point comparisons, but the general meaning is valid.)

"[M]eek escutcheon" (15) combines oxymoron and metaphor. Metaphorically it represents our humanity. Just as a coat of arms entitles its bearer to ceremonial treatment on all occasions, so our common humanity entitles us to ceremonial treatment at death. We may all look forward to this moment of grandeur. It "delays" (waits) for all.

"'Twas warm—at first—like Us" describes the changes that take place in a body between death and burial. The poem begins its description at a point a split-second after the instant of death. Though still warm, the body has already become an "It," is no longer a *he* or *she*. Then, in almost clinical detail, are shown the loss of body warmth, the vanishing of expression from face and eyes, the stiffening of rigor mortis, the increasing and finally utter separation between the worlds of the dead and the living. In the final stanza, as it is lowered into the grave, the corpse is a mere thing, a weight, unable by any sign to assent or demur to what is happening. The final word "Adamant" underscores its stoniness.

Written in Dickinson's characteristic elliptical style, the poem demands for grammatical completeness that we supply an *it* at the end of line 2, an *if* after "As" in line 12, and a completing verb (*show? manifest? manage?*) at the end of line 12. But the meaning is clear without these additions. Dickinson's omissions simply compact her meaning.

There may be a latent irony in the fact that the "dignity" that "delays for all" does not occur till we can no longer be conscious of it, but in the poem this irony is muted. The tone of the poem is generally one of excited anticipation, marked by the exclamatory elation of the last two stanzas, and by words like "dignity," "mitred," "purple," "Crown," "state," "grand," "pomp," "surpassing," "ermine," and "escutcheon." Death in this poem is not the great democratizer, leveling all ranks, but the great "aristocratizer," elevating all to the status of nobility.

The tone of "'Twas warm—at first—like Us," on the contrary, is one of unrelieved and increasing horror. Concentrating not on the funeral ceremonials but on the physical facts of death, it projects not an elevation in status but a reduction in status, from human being to thing. Its tone is determined by words like "Chill," "frost," "Stone," "cold," "congealed," "Weight," and "dropped like Adamant." Instead of "pomp surpassing ermine," it presents us with a dead body crowding "Cold to Cold."   LP

John Donne   The Apparition (page 813)

John Donne   The Flea (page 814)

"The Apparition" has frequently been misread as an expression of hate and revulsion in which the motive of the speaker, a rejected lover, is revenge. It is, in reality, a poem of thwarted love and unspent desire in which the speaker is making a last desperate effort to obtain his lady's favors. In so doing, he adopts a new strategy. In the past, he has presumably tried and failed with all the usual methods—praising the lady's beauty, flattering her in various ways, declaring the strength and depth of his love for her, and so on. This time he attempts to *frighten* her into his arms. He works on various anxieties he *hopes* she may have. Instead of telling her how much he loves her, he tells her that his love "is spent." (By portraying himself as having slipped the hook, he may make himself seem more valuable in her eyes than when she was assured of his devotion.) He predicts that, if she rejects him, she will in the future have to settle for a much inferior lover. He attempts to frighten her with the prospect of his ghost appearing at her bedside, scaring her to death. Most of all, however, he tries to terrify her by threatening that his ghost will utter some unspecified but awful pronouncement or curse upon her, possibly capable of damning her soul for eternity, the nature and content of which he will not reveal to her now, because (he says) he wants revenge— and if he told her now, she would do anything necessary to avoid it.

But the speaker's assertion that his love (*desire* would be a more accurate term) "is spent" is undermined by the whole tone and intensity of the poem.

If he no longer cares about her, why should her "scorn" be killing him? Would it not be more logical for him to say he was "cured"? And why should he send his ghost to her bedside? Obviously he has intense feelings concerning her still.

Most misreadings of the poem misinterpret "feigned vestal" (5) as meaning "feigned virgin." But why should Donne use the fancier term if a simpler one means the same? The speaker, having unsuccessfully solicited the woman many times, has no personal grounds for doubting her virginity. What he accuses her of is not that she has falsely claimed to be a virgin, but that she falsely thinks herself capable of *sustaining* the state of virginity, as the vestal virgins did. Inferentially she has rejected his advances in the past by claiming that she wants to preserve her virginity or that she is by nature virginal. (The word "feigned," spelled *fain'd* in the manuscripts of Donne's poems, is a pun blending the meanings of *feigned* ["pretended"] and *fained* ["wished for"].) The speaker in effect is telling her, "Don't deceive yourself. You have the same strong carnal desires as I have, and if you do not take me, you will eventually settle for someone much less capable than I of satisfying your sexual needs." This "someone," tired out from their earlier lovemaking, will think, when she tries to wake him to protect her from the ghost, that she wants *more* lovemaking, and he will pretend to be asleep. Thus she will have to face the scary ghost alone. Trembling like an aspen tree and bathed in cold sweat, she will be "scared to death." Her "sick" candle will blink out, and she will become hyperbolically a "verier ghost" than her visitant. The "sick taper" is metaphorically her life (see "Out, out, brief candle" from *Macbeth*, page 780). It could be taken literally as well if we assume that a couple could go to bed leaving a candle burning by the bedside. It was commonly believed that a candle would dim in the presence of a ghost.

The speaker will not tell her what his ghost would say because, he says, he wants her to "painfully repent" her mistreatment of him, and if she knew *now* what it would say, that knowledge would "preserve" her and keep her "innocent." Innocent of what? Innocent of the one crime that has been alleged against her in the poem—that of being a murderess—of "killing" the speaker by her scorn. She can remain innocent of this crime only by ceasing to "kill" him—that is, by granting him her favors. What could the ghost say that would be terrible enough to accomplish this end? We do not know—nor does the speaker know. If he did, he would say it now. But he is gambling on the psychological principle that an unknown threat is more frightening than a known one. It is the darkness at the top of the stairs that daunts us. It is more frightening to hear a strange cry in the dark than to face five armed men by daylight. Thus the speaker does not reveal what the ghost will say, first because he does not *know*, and second because not telling will be more frightening than telling. In short, he *wants* her to remain "innocent" of the crime of "killing" him. He *wants* her to fulfill his unspent desires.

Donne here uses the cliché of Renaissance poetry which makes a woman "kill" a man by refusing to satisfy his desires, but he gives it an original twist by taking the metaphor literally and developing the whole poem on its literalness. It is important that the speaker accuses the lady of "killing" him, not having "killed" him. He is not yet "dead"; therefore there is still time for her to revive him and remain innocent of "murder."

In "The Flea" a young man attempts to seduce a young woman by the use of highly ingenious but highly sophistical reasoning. Basically, his argument is that losing her virginity will be no more damaging to her than a flea bite.

Before the first stanza, a flea has bitten the young man and then has jumped to the young woman and begun to bite her. The young man sees an opportunity and seizes it. He points to the flea and remarks that it has innocently mingled their bloods within itself, which is no more than what sexual intercourse does (according to a traditional belief), and yet is more than she will allow to him. (When he says "more than we would do," he means, of course, more than *she* would do, for he is eager enough himself.) His remark that the flea's action cannot be called a "sin" or "shame" or "loss of maidenhead" indicates that she is a virgin and wishes to preserve her virginity until she can surrender it without sin.

Between the first and second stanzas the young lady raises her finger to squash the flea. The young man protests, urging her to spare the flea, in which, because of their commingled bloods, they "almost, yea more than married are." With dazzling sleight-of-wit he has parlayed his claim that the mingling of their bloods within the flea is tantamount to a sinless act of sexual intercourse into a claim that it is tantamount to marriage. The flea is their "marriage bed" and "marriage temple." If she kills it, he claims, she will be destroying three lives—his, hers, and its—and committing three sins—murder, suicide, and sacrilege. (The line "Though use [habit] makes you apt [habitually disposed] to kill me" indicates that the speaker has already attempted many times to seduce the young woman and has failed. He is metaphorically playing with the poetic lover's traditional complaint that he is "dying" of his unrequited love and therefore that the lady is "killing" him by withholding her favors.)

But the young lady pays no attention to the speaker's protest. Between the second and third stanzas she has cruelly (according to the young man) killed the flea—has "Purpled [crimsoned]" her nail with "blood of innocence." The flea's only guilt, the speaker claims, was contained in the drop of blood it sucked from its murderess, and now she declares triumphantly to the young man that neither he nor she has been injured (let alone "killed") by the flea's death. With one quick stroke of her finger she has indeed thoroughly discredited the young man's "logic." But the young man is not for a moment discountenanced. Nimbly, he turns his defeat into a further argument for his original design. Because his fears proved false, he contends, *all* fears are false, including hers that she will lose honor in yielding to him. She will lose no more honor in submitting to his desires, he claims, than she lost life in killing the flea. This argument (a generalization from a single instance) is, of course, as specious as those that have gone before, yet we have to admire the young man's mental agility in turning the tables and putting the young woman on the defensive once again.

Though one cannot make a dogmatic statement about what action follows the conclusion of the poem, evidence favors the inference that this attempt on the young lady's virginity is as unsuccessful as those that have preceded it. We know from lines 2, 9, 14, and 16 (we are given the information four times) that the young lady has previously denied the young man, and not just once but many times. Presumably this young man has also tried with no success the ordinary tactics of seduction—protestations of adoration, lavish compliments to the lady's charm and beauty, and pleas for pity—so he now turns to witty casuistry. We also know on what grounds the young lady has turned him down. She would consider the loss of her chastity a "sin" and a disgrace (line 6); she is concerned for her "honor" (line 26). In addition we see that the young lady is not taken in for a moment by the young man's preposterous "logic" in stanza 2. She calls his bluff, kills the insect, and laughs in his face. True, the young man is undismayed by this refutation and turns it immediately to his advantage. But are we to believe that the girl suddenly turns gullible or loses concern for her honor just because the young man has made a clever answer? If we extrapolate from the evidence given *in* the poem as to her past behavior, her intelligence, and her morality, we must conclude that she is a sensible young lady, not at all deceived by the young man's sophistry, and that she is holding out for honorable marriage, whether with this young man or another. The young man may have "won" this skirmish between the sexes, but only at the verbal level.

In a previous manual I wrote that this poem is "not to be taken too seriously as a reflection of human life, but to be enjoyed for what it is—a virtuoso display of ingenuity and wit." On further reflection I would modify that statement. It may be truer to life than at first appears. We are given a situation where a young man has attempted many times to obtain the woman's favor but has always been refused. Yet the woman by all indications enjoys his company. She has never told him, "Begone, vile seducer. Never darken my doorway again!" And, indeed, why should she not enjoy the company of such a witty and clever young man? Is it not quite possible that the "seduction attempt" has become a little game they play? That after the first rejection or so, the young man has realized that her virtue is unshakable, yet keeps on inventing more and more preposterous reasons why she should yield to him, not expecting her to do so, but for the "fun" of the thing? A student of mine once declared indignantly that no man could ever win *her* heart with an analogy drawn from a *flea!* Exactly. But if we see the seduction attempt as a "game" that neither of its two players takes very seriously, it becomes quite believable.

Both "The Apparition" and "The Flea" present an often-rejected lover taking a new and "far-out" approach to winning a woman's favors. But in tone the two poems are radically different. In tone "The Apparition" is dark and menacing; "The Flea" is light and playful. The speaker in "The Apparition" attempts to attain his goal by threats, the speaker in "The Flea" by obviously specious reasoning. The speaker in "The Apparition" attempts to win his lady's favors by maximizing her fears of what will happen to her if she refuses. The speaker in "The Flea" attempts to win them by minimizing his lady's fears of what will happen if she consents. Fear is the weapon of a rapist. The methods used by the speaker in "The Apparition" are ingenious and sinister. The methods used by the speaker in "The Flea" are ingenious and witty. For a fuller discussion of these poems, see Laurence Perrine, "Explicating Donne: 'The Apparition' and 'The Flea,'" *College Literature* 17 (1990): 1–20.   LP

Matthew Arnold   Dover Beach (page 816)

Philip Larkin   Church Going (page 817)

"Dover Beach" is Arnold's lament over the decline of religious faith in his time. "The Sea of Faith," he tells us, was once "at the full," but now he only hears "Its melancholy, long, withdrawing roar" (21–22, 25), like the roar of waves receding or of the tide going out. Certainly, the mid-nineteenth century was a time of religious crisis—a time when vast numbers of thinking people were losing the simple Christian faith of their childhood teaching before the advance of scientific and rationalistic thought. The conflict and the agony are recorded in work after work of literature. Arnold's poem, first published in 1867 but possibly composed some ten or twelve years earlier, is surely one of the most eloquent expressions of despair ever written, combining profound pessimism with imperishable beauty.

The speaker is in a room overlooking the cliffs of Dover. He is so situated—where the cliffs curve—that not only can he look out over the English Channel and occasionally glimpse the coast of France (twenty-two miles away at this point) as it catches a gleam of moonlight, but he can also see, across the bay, the face of the cliffs themselves and the waves breaking on the shingle at their foot. In the room with him is a beloved woman (wife or sweetheart) to whom he unburdens his despair—not over any personal misfortune but about the state of the world.

The poem turns on a series of contrasts, of which the two most important are those (a) between the physical beauty of the world he sees outside his window and its actual spiritual darkness, and (b) between the full tide he sees outside the window and the ebbing "tide" of faith that he feels is responsible for the world's spiritual darkness.

Looking from his window, the speaker is first impressed by the beauty of the moonlit scene before him, and he summons his companion to the window to share its beauty with him. But then he becomes aware of the sound of the breakers crashing on the shingle, and this sound is a sad one. Being a person of broad intellectual culture, he is reminded by the sound of a passage in a Greek drama by Sophocles, who compared the ebb and flow of the sea to the ebb and flow of human misery. Then he thinks of his own time, and he is reminded by the sound of the ebbing of religious faith. This thought is so melancholy to him that he cries out to his beloved, "Ah, love, let us be true / To one another!" (29–30) for a loving human relationship seems the only value left in a world that has lost every other source of meaning—a world that, despite its illusory physical beauty, has "really neither joy, nor love, nor light, / Nor certitude, nor peace, nor help for pain" (33–34)—surely two of the most pessimistic lines in English poetry. The simile ending the poem gives concrete embodiment to this abstract statement and is deservedly one of the most famous in English poetry. As an image for complete meaninglessness in human life, it can hardly be surpassed. Words of negative connotation pile up—"darkling," "confused," "alarms," "struggle," "flight," "ignorant," "clash," "night"—to give a picture of utter confusion, blindness, cross-purposes, and uncertainty, in which warring armies cannot tell friend from foe and strike at both alike in the darkness. This uncertainty embodies the lack of "certitude" mentioned in line 34, which in turn stems from the ebbing Sea of Faith. The one remaining consolation—the possibility of a loyal personal relationship between two lovers, because of its positioning, seems a very frail one indeed. Instead of one person lost on a tiny raft at night in mid-ocean, we are left with two people on the raft clinging to each other out of desperation. The poem begins with light and ends in darkness.

Students must be made to see that the image in the last three lines is the figurative, not the literal, term in a simile. This poem is not about war, nor was it written during time of war—it is a poem about the loss of a common religious faith that once linked men together in a belief, hope, and some degree of brotherhood or community—a loss that has resulted in a world where men work only for self-advancement and at cross-purposes with each other.

It is also important to note that the poem was written, not by a believer blaming the rest of the world for its lack of belief, but by a poet who himself can no longer accept the stories and assumptions on which the old faith was based, and who regards its consolations and certainties as no longer possible for thinking men. If he had been himself a believer, he would have cried out, "O Lord! bring these people back to a belief in your eternal truth and loving overlordship!" Instead, his cry is to a human companion, "Ah, love, let us be true / To one another!"

The syntax in lines 7–14 is somewhat involved. The noun "roar" (9) is not the direct object of "hear" but the subject of the infinitives [To] "Begin," "cease," "begin," and "bring" (12–13). The direct object of "hear" is the whole infinitive phrase of which "roar" is the subject. In reading the poem one must reject the temptation to drop one's voice at the end of line 11.

Larkin's title "Church Going" may be interpreted in three ways: (a) the habit of church-going, of regularly attending Sunday services, a practice continued by diminishing numbers of people; (b) the visit to an old church by the speaker who is making the visit from motives far different from religious worship, but who ironically speaks of himself as a church-goer; (c) the historical

decline in importance of the Church in the lives of ordinary people and in affairs of state.

The speaker is taking a bicycle tour of his country. We know this because
he takes off his bicycle-clips after entering the church. What an economical
way of telling us! Have bicycle-clips ever been mentioned in a poem before?
Or since?

The speaker constantly undermines any pretense of self-importance. His
motivation seems mostly idle curiosity. He is not an expert in church architecture. Inside the church he wonders "what to look for" (21). Is the roof
new, cleaned, or restored? "Someone would know: I don't" (12). He wonders
who will be the last to enter the church for what it was. Will it be some
fanatic expert on church architecture, or someone addicted to Christmas
nostalgia who will not give it up? Or will it be someone like himself: "Bored,
uninformed" (46)?

But though he poses as a nonintellectual, and uses slangy speech, the
speaker entertains thoughts and questions about the future of the church
(and belief) that would not enter the thoughts of an ordinary man. Will it be
kept up as a tourist attraction or will it be turned into grazing ground for
sheep? Will it be a place to nourish superstition? Like Matthew Arnold's
speaker in "Dover Beach," this speaker believes that Christian belief is wan-
ing and will soon be gone; churches will fall "completely out of use" (22).
"But superstition, like belief, must die, / And what remains when disbelief
has gone?" (34–35). The church will be no more than "Grass, weedy pavement, brambles, buttress, sky" (36).

Though the assessments of the present and the future made in Larkin's
and in Arnold's poems are similar in their intellectual components, the two
poems differ widely in tone. Arnold's poem sounds the depths of human despair; Larkin's seems inspired more by idle curiosity.   LP

Gavin Ewart   Ending (page 820)

This sonnet of lost love calls upon traditional love-sonnet devices—
almost every line has at least one example of figurative language, and some
have several. But this is not a "traditional love sonnet," in either its theme
or its form. It is iambic tetrameter (not pentameter), rhymed in couplets
rather than in the forms of Italian or English sonnets. In fact, it may be
stretching the definition of the form beyond credibility to call this a sonnet,
unless one wishes to regard the 14-line length as an ironic allusion to the
sonnet and one of its traditional topics.

Here are the figures, by line numbers: 1. overstatement; 2. simile; 3. simile; 4. metaphor; 5. metaphor; 6. simile; 7. metonymy; 8. paradox ("running
slow") and metaphorical comparison to a clock, as well as a non-figurative
cliché in "running late"; 9. overstatement; 10. metaphor; 11. metaphor;
11–12. metonymy (while the sexual "parts" of the couple had "transmitted

joy," it is the two people and not their organs who are "reserved and cold and coy"); 13–14. personification.

Perhaps even more important to the tone and meaning of the poem is the constant use of situational irony to create bathos as exalted or overstated expectations are punctured by the commonplace and trivial. The first two lines set the tone, and it remains throughout.   TRA

Anonymous   Love (page 820)

There is a brief comment on these verses on page 820.   LP

Chapter Eleven

Musical Devices

Ogden Nash   The Turtle (page 823)

One might also ask why Nash chose to write about a turtle rather than a tortoise. The anatomical problem is the same for each.   LP

W. H. Auden   That night when joy began (page 825)

The two people in the poem have been disillusioned by their experiences with love. They have found that it is not lasting and that it ends in disappointment. They have been "burnt" by it. Thus they are deeply skeptical about their present affair. It begins, as have past affairs, in the joy of sexual excitement; they are prepared to find in the morning that their attraction has little or no other basis, but in the morning they are still in love; days pass, then weeks; they begin to realize that they have found a true human relationship, one rooted in something deeper than sexual attraction.

The basic metaphor presents two foot travelers cutting across fields that they hope are the public fields of love, where all may travel, but that they fear may be private lands where they will be shot or apprehended for trespassing. The metaphor in lines 3–4 beautifully combines the visual image of the sun's horizontal rays awakening them from their dream and the metaphorical idea of the landowner's shooting them for trespassing—that is, destroying their temporary illusion of love. But as they hike for additional miles (days), they outgrow their nervousness and begin to believe in spiritual peace, for they are not reproached for trespassing and they can see in the future (through love's field glasses) nothing that is not genuine and lasting love.

The rhyme pattern:

Lines 1 and 4 (of each stanza): alliteration and consonance
Lines 2 and 3 (of each stanza): alliteration and consonance
Lines 1 and 3 (of each stanza): assonance
Lines 2 and 4 (of each stanza): assonance

In line 10 the last syllable must be thought of as beginning with *r* rather than with *p* to preserve the integrity of this pattern, and in line 12 the final syllable must be thought of as including the final *s* (really a *z*) of *his*. The whole is ingeniously worked out, along with the extended metaphor; and the poet's pleasure (and ours) lies partly in the working out of this design.   LP

Theodore Roethke   The Waking (page 826)

In the villanelle "The Waking" the poet joyfully affirms his acceptance of a life in which the only constant is change. Though its tone is clear, the details of its meanings are not, and the following suggestions are made diffidently. Line 1: "I wake to sleep." Literally, this means, I wake in the morning only to have to sleep again at night. Symbolically it means, I am born to die—death is the inevitable concomitant of life. Nevertheless, the tone indicates a full acceptance of life on these terms. The speaker takes his waking "slow": he wishes to savor it fully. Line 2: The speaker feels his "fate" (change and death) in what he cannot fear (the life process). Line 3: He learns about life only through experiencing it. Line 4: "We think by feeling." Our deepest understandings come through intuition and emotion rather than through reasoning. Line 5: The speaker hears his being "dance from ear to ear": he is joyfully conscious of his existence. Line 7: He is conscious of other people and wishes to know about them. Line 8: He blesses the earth, which is the "Ground" of his existence and will be his place of burial. Line 10: Life is a mystery. The ultimate secret of how sunlight nourishes the tree, of how Light illuminates the "Tree of Life," or of how spirit enters matter, cannot be intellectually known. Line 11: Life is process. The worm climbs up the evolutionary scale of being: death constantly recurs in this evolutionary life cycle. Lines 13–15: Great Nature holds death and dissolution in store for all of us, so let us enjoy each moment while we may. "Lovely" may be construed as an adjective (paralleling "lively"), as an adverb (modifying "learn"), or as a noun of direct address to the "you" of lines 7 and 14. Line 16 (the most difficult of the poem's several paradoxes): Physical decay and the speaker's knowledge of constant change (degeneration and regeneration) in life's processes keep him resolved to make the most of life and to trust the goodness of the cycle. Line 17: The present falls away from us eternally; what falls away from us is permanence. Change and death are constantly "near" to us. Line 19: Take all the above suggestions with two pinches of salt. At best (like all paraphrase) they are reductive, and some may be flat wrong. For additional discussion, see Richard A. Blessing, in the *Ball State University Forum* 12 (Aug. 1971): 17–19, and Karl Malkoff, *Theodore Roethke* (New York: Columbia UP, 1966) 121–22.   LP

Gerard Manley Hopkins   God's Grandeur (page 828)

The theme of the poem might be stated in some such words as these:

The natural world is filled with the beauty and energizing power of its Creator. But men, ignoring God's authority,

through their commercial and industrial activities, have de-
spoiled and polluted this beauty and separated themselves from
its spiritually regenerating power. Nevertheless, the power is
never used up; through God's love for his world, nature's
beauty is continuously renewed.

How pale and flat this prose statement is as compared to the poem's
"grandeur"!

In line 1 the word "charged," because of its associations with electricity
and gunpowder, has many times the force of *filled*. In line 2 the image is of
crinkled metallic foil (gold, tin, silver, or lead) being shaken in the sun and
flashing light reflections from each of its multifold creases and facets. In line
4 "rod" is a metaphor or symbol for God's authority and chastening power.
In lines 7–8 the soil is "bare" because man has pitted it over with his heaps
of coal and iron ore and paved it over with streets and walks; and man cannot feel the grass underfoot anyway because his feet are cased in shoes. (We
need not assume that Hopkins denounces the wearing of shoes, though he
may indeed think it good sometimes to walk barefoot in the grass.) Pavement and shoe leather serve the poet here as symbols for man's twofold separation from nature. In lines 11–12 the image of the sun's light disappearing
in the west, only to reappear next morning in the east, is a symbol for the
perpetual renewal of nature. And this renewal springs from the love of the
Holy Ghost (third member of the Trinity) in His traditional metaphoric embodiment as a dove (symbol of gentleness and tenderness) brooding over the
world (as over a nest) with warm breast and bright wings. The word "bent"
means both that the earth is curved (as suggested by the preceding image of
the sun's apparent travel around it) and bent out of shape from man's mis-
use of it.

Just as the world is charged with the grandeur of God, so this sonnet is
charged with a rich verbal music appropriate to its subject. In its end rhymes
it follows the strictest and most demanding pattern for the Italian sonnet
(four rhyme sounds). Alliteration is apparent in almost every line, perhaps
most brilliantly in the three two-word clusters of line 14 ("*W*orld
*br*oods–*w*arm *br*east–*br*ight *w*ings"). Assonance is especially apparent in line
11 ("l*a*st–bl*a*ck," "W*e*st–w*e*nt") and line 13 ("H*o*ly Gh*o*st *o*ver"). Consonance is prominent in line 1, where each stressed syllable ends with a *d*
("worl*d*–charge*d*–grandeur–Go*d*"). In the question in line 4, where nine
short monosyllables (all but two of them stressed) are spat out in rapid succession like bullets from a machine gun, there is internal rhyme (*men–then*),
alliteration (*now–not, reck–rod*), and assonance (*not–rod, reck–men–then*);
except for the initial "Why," each stressed syllable in the series gets into the
act once, if not twice. In line 5 the triple repetition of a whole phrase ("have
trod") emphasizes the repetitiousness of the action described. In lines 6–7
two sets of internal rhymes (*seared–bleared–smeared; wears–shares*) combined
with three *sm-* alliterations (*smeared–smudge–smell*) put such an emphasis on

words of disagreeable meaning as to give one a feeling of almost physical revulsion. But we leave this analysis incomplete; the reader's patience will be
"spent" long before the poem's "music" is.

An interesting thematic comparison may be made between this sonnet
and Wordsworth's "The world is too much with us" (page 694).   LP

William Shakespeare   Blow, blow, thou winter wind

(page 830)

The contrasts are between the unpleasantness inflicted by people upon
each other (in the court, in this play—but by implication, in any urban setting) and the discomforts of living at the mercy of the weather in a natural
setting. The song clearly makes the case that social injuries are less bearable
than nature's pain. It focuses primarily on how men are "unkind" (2), that is,
in older definitions, "unnatural"—acting against their kind. Reminiscent of
King Lear's complaint against his ungrateful daughters, though much less
forceful, the song specifically isolates such "unkind" attitudes as "man's in-
gratitude" that leads him to forget "benefits" that he has enjoyed from others
(3, 13).

In their assaults on us, the wind and freezing weather are metaphorically
presented as animals that bite or sting sharply, but their wounds are less
painful because they are "not seen" and "not so sharp" (5, 15) as those inflicted by man upon man. One reason is that the weather, like the animals,
is not "unkind," turning against its own natural allies and friends. When
weather hurts us, it is not purposefully betraying but is only acting according
to its nature. Men who turn against men are unnatural.

There is much musicality in the poem, as befits a song. Most obvious are
the four repeated lines creating an extended refrain, but the rhyming throughout has a song-like effect. The rhyme scheme is *aabccbdddd*. (The rhymes
"*wind | kind*" and "*warp | sharp*" would have been exact rhymes in the pronun-
ciation of Shakespeare's English.) The four *d*-rhymes in the refrain are especially
pronounced because they are feminine and because they are preceded by assonant vowel sounds: "green *holly*" / "mere *folly*" in the first two lines and "-ho . . .
holly" / "most *jolly*" in the second two. The refrains also display a considerable
amount of alliteration: "*Heigh-ho . . . Heigh-ho . . . holly*," "*friendship . . . feigning . . . folly*," with repeats in the third lines "*heigh-ho . . . holly*." The alliterated
f-sounds of the second line in the refrain are picked up as consonance in the final line in the word "*life*," and the long *a* sound recurs not only in the repeated
"*heigh*" but in "*feigning*."

As to the meaning of the repeated "heigh-ho," the context would seem to
dictate that it be taken ironically, a pretended sigh of melancholy in this jolly
holly world. (And perhaps, the *OED* notwithstanding, it's the first usage of what
came to be the jolly song of Disney's dwarfs, "hi-ho, hi-ho.")   TRA

Gwendolyn Brooks   We Real Cool (page 831)

The placement of the pronouns in this poem gives its rhythm a syncopated effect appropriate to the jazz culture of the speakers.

The critic who called the poem immoral was oblivious to its dramatic irony (its tone). The poet does not share the opinion of the speakers that they are "real cool," nor does any moderately good reader, which obviously the critic was not.   LP

Maya Angelou   Woman Work (page 832)

The rhyming couplets of the first 14 lines catalogue the domestic chores assigned to many women in their roles as mother and house-keeper—as well as two not-so-domestic tasks in lines 11 and 14, "cane to be cut" and "cotton to pick." These extend the concept of "Woman Work" to include hard toiling in the fields outside the home (or "hut," in this case). These particular examples of agricultural work locate the poem in the South amidst the cane and cotton fields, and connote work on tenant or sharecropper farms, an economic level of bare subsistence at best. This inference is borne out by the last line of the poem with its statement that the speaker has in fact no personal possessions, or at least none to raise the spirit from the constant drudgery and labor of her daily life.

The within-doors tasks repeatedly circle around three subjects: the raising of children (lines 1, 6, 10), the care of clothing (lines 2, 9, 10), and providing food (lines 4, 5, 7). That the catalogue is arranged haphazardly and without organization suggests that the speaker does not really have control over her activities—they spring to mind not in orderly clusters but in the way that such chores press themselves on a person, one being finished (or almost finished) just as another springs up. The whole passage is literal as well as colloquial, with the implication that the speaker also doesn't have the time to find any sustenance for her imagination or the leisure to express herself in any but the most utilitarian terms. The varying refrain of the simple, colloquial subjects and verbs emphasizes the hard necessity of her tasks—"I've got" (1), "I got" (7), "I've got" (9), "I gotta" (12). There is in the whole passage little love and no joy, only "woman *work*."

With a shock of abruptness, the poem then shifts into a set of quatrains that express the deep yearning of the speaker for a life that has in it rest, comfort, and exaltation. The lines are still simple in their reference, still mostly literal, but replete with imagery. The desires they reveal evaluate the life of labor—desires for a cool brow, for rest and for rest again, and for a life that looks outward and upward to the beauties and powers of nature in contrast to the confinement and obligation she must live. With poignant irony, the speaker concludes that her only true possessions are sun, rain, sky, and the rest—but the emphatic desires embodied in the series of apostrophes that begin in line 15 sadly suggest that in fact she cannot really "call" them her "own." She yearns for the marvelous attention that nature might give her—but being forced to tend to her chores renders that all a hope and a dream. The second of the quatrains makes that all too apparent: no storm will in fact "blow [her] from here," nor is there a fierce wind that could "float [her] across the sky" to "rest again."   TRA

Sharon Olds   Rite of Passage (page 833)

In the order of their appearance, the musical devices include (1) alliteration: guests-gather-grade; smooth-small; jaws-jostling-jockeying; says-Six-seven-So-seeing; fold-frown; seven-says-six; turret-table; nutmeg-narrow; cheeks-chest; balsa-boat; guided-group; speaks-sake; (2) assonance: guests-men-men; hands-stand; jostling-jockeying; place-breaking; old-So; cake-table; seven-heavy-them-freckles-specks-chest; cheeks-keel; thin-him; day-they; (3) consonance: hands-stand-around; jostling-jockeying-breaking; dark-cake; up-group. And no doubt the sensitive ear will hear more, including the uncategorized effects of such echoes as clear-their-throats-room.

That the music virtually stops at line 22 is of course related to the sudden shift of tone and meaning as the boyish aggression of lines 12–13 ("I could beat you / up") leads to the chilling insight, "We could easily kill a two-year-old" (22). The reserve and proper behavior of the "room of small bankers" (11) shifts to brutal camaraderie when they agree—"like Generals"—that killing would be a simple matter. Once the boys have formed that potential bond they can then begin to play what boys play, "war" (26). And so they can celebrate life by mimicking what men do, destroying it.

The main poetic device is irony of situation. The mother has planned a party for her freckle-faced kid, provided the cake that resembles a turret, sees her son as fragile as the model boats he might construct, and then hears that sweetness, innocence, and vulnerability have been replaced by the destructive instincts of the pack.   TRA

Emily Dickinson   As imperceptibly as Grief (page 834)

The subject of the poem is ambivalence about seasonal change. The initial simile sets the tone: summer lapsed away imperceptibly, as "Grief" lapses imperceptibly; were the diminution of grief consciously perceived, its passing would seem to be a perfidious betrayal of the person for whom we grieve. So, the simile says, the passing of summer evokes an emotion that includes one's love and loyalty, the sadness of loss, and the consciousness of separation. But how can these emotions be identified with summer, the season of richness and growth, the apogee of the year to which spring climbs and from which autumn (in the distinctly American term) falls? If summer is like grief, what are we grieving *for*? "Spring" might be one logical answer—the loss in summertime of the exuberant excitement of that early time—yet the terms of the poem do not invite such a comparison.

The grief, rather, is associated with summer's relationship to us: it is summer that passes so imperceptibly that its betrayal *of us* is almost overlooked. This personification (overtly revealed in the feminine pronouns) and the constant tone of regret imply the imaginative act of the speaker: we long for the personal, permanent love for us of what we love. Why does the summer betray us by leaving us? The two middle stanzas present a series of appositives for the diminution of the season, presenting it in terms of its voluntary withdrawal and increasing alienation yet without showing any ill will toward those it leaves behind. These two stanzas also present a series of attempts to pinpoint or define the precise feelings excited by the imminent departure of summer: Is it like an intensification of "Quietness"? Has nature withdrawn from us as a person might shut herself up for a long quiet "Afternoon"? (The metaphor must be especially poignant when we recall Emily Dickinson's own sequestration.) The factual evidence is that both the coming on and the departure of night, at dusk and daybreak, seem strangely changed—an earlier darkness and a "Foreign" sunrise. The process resembles the ambivalence of a dear guest who "would be gone," whose gracious behavior is both full of courtesy and deeply distressing.

These attempts at definition reveal the ambiguities of feeling already noted in the simile of grief in line 1: the increased beauty of "Quietness distilled," the sense of being excluded mixed with an understanding approval of nature's sequestration, and most of all (placed in the climactic position), the paradoxical combination of "A courteous, yet harrowing Grace." But this is a poem about the "imperceptible," and it is to that quality that the poem returns for its conclusion. Without any of the "perceptible" (and humanly comprehensible) means of transportation, neither the wing of the bird nor the keel of the boat, two silent means of departing, "Summer made her light escape / Into the Beautiful." The guest, though gracious, does not live with us, but elsewhere, and finally manages to escape. The final line, "Into the Beautiful," has been criticized for its abstract vagueness, but the sense of an ideal, abstract realm of beauty as the proper "home" for this sojourning visitor, this sequestered captive, may be appropriate in its vagueness. If the process of its departure is "imperceptible," so too may be its destination.

The music of this poem is muted, as befits its subject. Approximate rhymes, subtle consonant links, delicately unobtrusive alliteration, and the poet's marvelous ear for related vowel sounds all reinforce the elegiac tone. For example, in the last stanza, the phrase *without a Wing* alliterates the *w* followed by the assonance of short *i*—but the effect is softened by the fact that the syllable *with-* is metrically unstressed, while *Wing* is stressed. The preponderant consonant sounds in the stanza are the sibilant *s* of "thus," "service," "Summer," and "escape," the crisp *t* of "without," "light," "into," and "Beautiful," and the *k* of "*k*eel" and "es*c*ape"—consonants that with the *w*s and *l*s underscore the quickness and lightness of the action being described.

But perhaps the most interesting example of the use of musicality is to be heard in the key term, *imperceptibly*, a word so proper to its purpose that the poet reiterates a form of it two lines later. The word has the flickering of its consonant sounds—*mp*, sibilant *c*, *pt*, and *bl*, all rapidly unobtrusive—and the light swiftness of its collection of short vowels. It also has an intrinsic rhythm that finds echoes throughout the poem in words with an elegiac "falling" rhythm: IM-per-CEP-ti-BLY and IM-per-CEP-ti-BLE both alternate stressed and unstressed syllables, and both occur in perfectly regular iambic lines. The stresses within the words, however, are not equal: in both, the syllable *-cep-* is more heavily stressed than the initial *im-*, and both of those syllables receive greater stress than the final stressed *-bly* or *-ble*. Both words, that is, are rapid in pronunciation (owing to their vowel and consonant combinations) and rise to a central stress before falling off in a final, very lightly stressed syllable.

This falling effect in a final light stress can be heard as well in such key words as PER-fi-DY and BEAU-ti-FUL; the elegiac tone is also reinforced by the high incidence of words that are individually trochaic in rhythm (though they usually function in regular iambic foot patterns): *Summer*, *Twilight*, *Nature*, *spending*, *earlier*, *Morning*, *foreign*, and so forth.   TRA

William Stafford   Traveling through the dark (page 835)

Line 3 makes clear that it is not unusual for dead deer to be found on the Wilson River road. The only inference to be drawn is that they are hit by autos as they cross the road on their way to the river, but that most drivers, after the impact, leave the carcass where it falls and drive on. That the speaker stops—even though he was not the one who hit the deer—shows him to be an unusually responsible person. He has carefully driven around in front of the animal, has turned down his headlights—another responsible action—but has left the motor running, hoping to make quick work of pushing the carcass over the edge, not stopping too long on the dangerous unlit road.

That he recognizes an ethical dilemma when he discovers the unborn fawn still living inside the dead doe particularly marks him out as a thoughtful person concerned with the preciousness of all life; and that he hesitates—thinking hard "for us all"—again reveals his deep sense of involvement. Who are the "us all" for whom the speaker thinks? Himself surely, the unborn fawn surely, other motorists traveling the Wilson River road and, beyond that, all humanity, perhaps all life forms, which need relationships with other forms of life in order to exist.

But what are his options? There is no way he can deliver the unborn fawn: he is hardly equipped to perform a Caesarean in the middle of the road. Nor could he mother the fawn, were it born. He must either take responsibility for killing the fawn by pushing its dead mother over the edge, or walk away and leave the dead doe there, endangering other lives—motorists who might be killed while swerving to miss the body. There is no choice, really. The second alternative would be equivalent to washing his hands of moral responsibility—like Pontius Pilate in the Bible. The fact that he hesitates, however—considering the options—makes us like him. That one "swerving" from what should and must be expeditiously done makes him fully human.

Many of the images have symbolic implications, though perhaps not of the kind that benefit from being pinned with a label and spelled with a capital S. The image of "Traveling through the dark" (how different in effect from "Driving at night"!) suggests the difficulties of living life and having to make moral decisions with only limited knowledge and with no certain moral guidance. The cold of the doe's body and the warm spot in its side are *signs*, not symbols, of death and life. The car, its steady engine purring, its parking lights "aimed ahead," suggests a kind of automated life that never hesitates, does not make decisions, and is always ready for action. Its purring engine contrasts with the stillness of the wilderness (and of the unborn fawn), which has its own claims on the speaker, and which seems to "listen" (16), as if for his decision. The red tail-light of the car is a conventional symbol of danger, and "the glare of the warm exhaust turning red" in which the speaker stands (15) almost symbolizes his dilemma. He must choose between spilling the warm blood of the unborn fawn over the edge of the canyon or endangering the lives of other human beings.

"[C]anyon" (3) is the only line-end in the poem without any correspondence in sound to another line-end in its stanza, and even it alliterates with the first line-end in the following stanza, just two lines away.   LP

Adrienne Rich   In Those Years (page 836)

QUESTIONS

1. In lines 1–9 the poem implies reasons for and against replacing the concepts "of *we, of us*" with "*I.*" By examining such phrases as "we lost track" (1), "reduced to" (4), "trying to" (7), "a personal life" (7), "and, yes" (8), and "the only life" (8), analyze those reasons.
2. Explore the metaphor of the birds and the weather (10–14). What judgment does it make of "saying I" (14)?
3. Locate examples of assonance and alliteration. In which of the two sections of the poem do these musical devices predominate?

Assonance and alliteration are more prominent in lines 1–9. Examples of assonance: "Years-people-we-meaning-we-we," "you-reduced," "found-ourselves," "trying-life-life." Examples of alliteration: "we-we-we-we-were-was-we-witness." The incidence of the repeated "we" in these two lists ironically reinforces the theme that social, collective consciousness has greater value than personal individuality. By contrast with the melodic, insistent repetitions of lines 1–9, the cacophonous repetitions of lines 11–14 are forceful and ominous. Assonance links "screamed-beaks," alliteration links "plunged-personal-pinions," and consonance (absent from 1–9) links "rags-fog."

The phrases listed in question 1 are trite and conversational, suggesting that following the intellectual fashion of placing oneself as number one, of thinking first of self-gratification and self-discovery and so neglecting communal obligations, is based on superficial thought and easy acceptance of popular modes of self-justification. Such self-absorption is, the poem says, reductive. The justification—that one's own experience is all one can "bear witness to" (9)—is apologetically offered as a tautology, introduced by the phrase "and, yes" (8).

The final five lines present the judgment of history upon those who fell prey to the habits of thinking defined in the first nine. While the speaker and her contemporaries stood befogged on the shore, still "saying I" (14), the great and threatening forces of the political world wildly "screamed and plunged" (10) past them "headed somewhere else" (12).   TRA

Marilyn Hacker   1973 (page 836)

The speaker recalls her 1973 pregnancy, which to her was a "delight" (1) and part of her general good fortune at the time, for she also felt secure at being "thirty, married, in print" (2) as a poet.

Her family's reaction to the pregnancy was not all that she could have wished, however. She was married to a black man, and instead of congratulating her, someone (presumably a parent) writes back, "I hope your child is white" (4). The speaker's reaction is rebellious and angry: she tears up the letter into tiny pieces and hopes her daughter will be "black as the ace of spades" (6).

The child turns out to be a "hybrid beige" (7), which pleases no one in the speaker's extended family. The father's mother complains that there is no trace of blackness in the baby's appearance ("No tar brush left" [12]) while the speaker's own mother self-righteously pronounces that the baby is Jewish and white.

The poem is cast in the form of a sonnet, which effectively contains and succinctly expresses the speaker's rage and disappointment at the various family members' unenlightened views on a mixed racial heritage. The speaker allows herself the last word: "She's Black. She is a Jew" (14). This line insists that the baby participates fully in the heritage of both her parents, an absolute and positive definition that the baby's grandparents, sadly, have not been able to acknowledge.   GJ

Robert Frost   Nothing Gold Can Stay (page 837)

The paradox in line 1 is to be explained by the fact that when leaves first bud in the spring, they have a yellow tint, more gold than green, which they lose as the leaves grow larger.

The paradox in line 3 has been explained by Alfred R. Ferguson as re-ferring to much the same thing: "The earliest leaf unfolds its beauty like a flower," but I believe it refers to something different. Some trees and shrubs blossom in the spring before they bear leaves (the plum, for example; also the redbud and some species of peach and cherry). In botanical language, how-ever, the term "leaf," in its broadest sense, includes all foliar structures of the higher plants, including the sepals, petals, pistil, and stamens of a flower: all parts of the blossom, technically, are modified leaves. For trees like the plum, therefore, it is literally true that the "early leaf's a flower." That it remains so only "an hour" is an overstatement, but the blossoming period of these trees is brief at best; then the flowers drop off and the ordinary leaves begin.

Frost's poem, then, lists four things that have an early but brief period of perfect beauty (or happiness): the foliage of trees; plants that blossom before they bear leaves; the course of human history (as storied in the Eden myth, or other myths of a "golden age"); and a day (which begins with the fresh gold-tinted air at sunrise). It ends with a generalization: "Nothing gold can stay." But by this time Frost's examples have assumed the force of symbols: they remind us as well of the year (which begins with spring), of the indi-vidual human life (which blooms in youth), and perhaps of love (most bliss-ful in its early stages). Frost's "gold" is a symbol of perfection, and his theme is that most things reach their moment of perfection early and retain it briefly. His poem is about the transiency of beauty, bliss, youth, spring, and the transport of early love.

For another treatment of this theme in Frost, see his poem "The Oven Bird" (page 965). For additional perspectives on "Nothing Gold Can Stay," see Lawrance Thompson, *Fire and Ice.* (New York: Holt, 1942) 169–70; Charles R. Anderson, *Explicator* 22 (Apr. 1964): item 63; Alfred R. Ferguson, in *Frost: Centennial Essays* (Jackson: UP of Mississippi, 1974) 436–39; and John Robert Doyle, Jr., *The Poetry of Robert Frost* (Johannesburg: Witwaters-rand UP, 1962) 174–76. For a possibly fuller analysis than you may want of the musical devices in the poem (and *their* perfection), see John A. Rea, "Language and Form in 'Nothing Gold Can Stay,'" *Robert Frost: Studies of the Poetry*, ed. Kathryn Gibbs Harris (Boston: Hall, 1979) 17–25.   LP

Chapter Twelve

Rhythm and Meter

George Herbert **Virtue** (page 843)

Three stanzas presenting sweet things that die are contrasted with a fourth presenting the one thing that does not die. The first three stanzas parallel each other: each is an apostrophe beginning with the word "Sweet" and ending with the words "must die." The fourth stanza, which is not an apostrophe, reserves "sweet" for the third position in the opening line, and ends with the word "lives." The first three stanzas are interconnected because the "day" of the first stanza may be thought of as containing the "rose" of the second, while the "spring" of the third stanza contains them both. The ordering is also marked by the opening words of the fourth lines: "For thou . . . ," "And thou . . . , " "And all . . . ."

In stanza 1, the day is presented in an apt metaphor as the "bridal" (wedding) of the earth and sky, uniting them in light; the metaphor connotes a beginning, brightness, and hope. The dew is fittingly chosen to mourn the death of the day because dew is associated with evening. The dew is both a personification and a metaphor, both the weeper and the tears that are wept. The words "to night" function both as an adverb and, because the hyphen has been omitted, as a prepositional phrase in which the noun is a traditional symbol for death.

In stanza 2, through a bold metaphor, the crimson rose is compared in color to the face of an angry man and, in an even bolder overstatement, is described as so bright that it causes tears in an observer who rashly gazes at it without shielding his eyes (like looking directly at the sun). Yet, despite this dazzling brilliance, it too is doomed to die. Its "root" is ever in its "grave" (a metonymy for earth). The rose's death is a condition of its birth: it dies back into the very soil from which it sprang; its root is "ever" there.

In stanza 3, the spring is compared metaphorically to a box where "sweets" lie compacted. (For the seventeenth-century reader the connotations would suggest, not a box of candy, but a box of perfumes—rose petals, lavender, cedar sprays, etc.) But the poet's "music" shows that the spring also has its "closes" and must die like the rest. The "music" may be read literally as well as metaphorically (Herbert was a musician as well as a poet). The word "closes" has three relevant meanings: the spring ends or terminates, the metaphorical box shuts, and a "close" in music is a cadence or concluding strain.

Stanza 4 presents a contrast. A "sweet and virtuous soul," it declares, is immortal. Like "seasoned timber" it never "gives" (*buckles* or *snaps*). Even should the whole world "turn to coal," it would survive. Spiritual in its origin, and having preserved its purity and strength through virtuous discipline, it will live even more intensely after the destruction of everything physical.

Two thoughtful, brief discussions of this poem, by Louis L. Martz and M. M. Mahood, may be found in *Metaphysical Poetry*, ed. Malcolm Bradbury and David Palmer (London: Arnold, 1970) 109–10 and 143–44. There is an extended discussion in Helen Vendler, *The Poetry of George Herbert* (Cambridge: Harvard UP, 1975) 9–24.   LP

EXERCISES (page 852)

   a. Blank verse.
   b. Rhymed iambic couplets: $aabb^4cc^5$ with a high incidence of metrical variation in the pentameter couplets.
   c. Free verse, with a few metric lines (1 is a seven-foot iambic line, 10 is iambic trimeter, 11 iambic pentameter), but these are so irregular in position and length that the iambics are scarcely heard.
   d. Free verse.
   e. Blank verse.
   f. Irregularly rhymed iambic, with varying lines lengths (pentameter predominates, but trimeter and tetrameter are frequent).
   g. Free verse, randomly rhymed (but with occasional metric lines—e.g., lines 4, 6, 9–11 are anapestic tetrameter).
   h. Blank verse.
   i. Blank verse.
   j. Free verse.

William Blake "Introduction" to *Songs of Innocence*

(page 853)

The child upon the cloud substitutes for the traditional Muse. The Lamb symbolizes innocence. The poet is first inspired by an emotion or idea (stanzas 1–2), then finds words to express that experience (stanza 3), then writes down or publishes his poems for all to read (stanzas 4–5). (In the poem he fashions a pen from a hollow reed and dyes water to make ink.) In this "Introduction" Blake indicates the source of inspiration for his poems—childhood; their subject matter—innocence; their intended audience—both children and adults (the last line indicates that "Every child" may joy to hear them; but line 14 indicates that the book is for "all" to read); and their tone—pleasant (2), merry (6), cheerful (6), happy (10), joyous (20). (Actually they are all these and more.)

Lines 1–2 and 9–10 establish a regular tetrameter pattern with accents on both the first and last syllables of the line. In scansion the pressure of the pattern forces us to promote the initial prepositions (*On, In*) and the conjunctions (*And, So, While*) to accented status. *Every* (20) is pronounced essentially as two syllables. Dividing the feet *after* the stressed syllables produces one monosyllabic foot and three iambs in each line. Dividing the feet *before* the stressed syllables produces three trochees and one monosyllabic foot in each line. It is obviously duple meter, but whether one calls it iambic or trochaic is a purely arbitrary decision: it is no more one than the other.   LP

Walt Whitman   Had I the Choice (page 854)

Robert Frost   The Aim Was Song (page 855)

Whitman voices the desire to be able to imitate the irregular rhythms of the sea—free verse rhythms, which he practiced in most of his verse. The verse form here, however, supports the statement of the poem: "Had I the choice," he says, to match even the great metrists, I would trade away that skill if only I could imitate the sea. *Has* he that choice? *Can* he imitate the sea? The poem implies not, for it is written not in his long-cadenced free-verse lines, but in duple meters. He's trying to capture sea-rhythms, and the irregular line lengths create the visual impression that he might have done so. But the poem is iambic, as a few sample lines reveal:

$$\text{Had I} \mid \text{the choice} \mid \text{to tall-} \mid \text{y great-} \mid \text{est bards,} \mid \qquad 1$$

$$\text{These, these,} \mid \text{O sea,} \mid \text{all these} \mid \text{I'd glad-} \mid \text{ly bar-} \mid \text{ter,} \qquad 6$$

$$\text{Or breathe} \mid \text{one breath} \mid \text{of yours} \mid \text{up-on} \mid \text{my verse,} \mid \qquad 8$$

$$\text{And leave} \mid \text{its o-} \mid \text{dor there.} \mid \qquad 9$$

In Whitman's poem even the greatest poetic art is seen as pale and inferior when set beside nature. The implication for poetry is that the most desirable poetry will be that which is most natural, most *like* nature. The further implication is that free verse is natural and that metered, rhymed verse is artificial. Still another implication is that metaphors, similes, and contrived paradoxes ("conceits") are artificial.

In Frost's poem successful poetry is seen as an improvement on nature. Though it uses natural materials, it orders them, imposes form on them, and thus gives them a power that they do not have in their natural state. In repeating the words "By measure" in line 13—and placing a period after them—Frost gives the phrase tremendous emphasis. Song, he insists, is "measured"; rather than taking form from nature, it gives form to nature. Thus nature is made humanly meaningful.

Readers must judge the two philosophies by their own standards. But the fact is that great poetry has been written both in meter and in free verse. LP, TRA

Adrienne Rich   The Knight (page 855)

QUESTIONS

1. What is the tone of the first stanza? How do connotative words establish it? What expectations does the tone set up?
2. How do you account for the changed tone in the second stanza? Has the knight changed, or the speaker's perspective, or both?
3. Contrast the attitude toward his armor in the first and last stanzas. What does the poem suggest about the relationship between external strength and inner frailty?
4. Is the poem free verse or metrical?
5. The only end rhymes are in the fourth and eighth lines of each stanza, but there is a sound pattern that also links the fifth and seventh lines of each. Identify other sound repetitions such as assonance, alliteration, and internal rhyme. What are the contributions of these musical devices to the tones of the poem?

This haunting, frightening poem explores contrasts between external strength and beauty and internal vulnerability and decay. The portrait in the first stanza is wholly devoted to the visual effect of the armor and the "crackling banner" (7) borne by the knight. All the language is positive and brilliantly visual. From the glittering "soles of his feet" (5) to helmet flashing sunlight, the knight is a vision of brightness, confidence, and beauty. Sound reinforces the imagery: assonance (knight-rides, gaiety-mail, flash-crackling-banner), alliteration (knight-noon, splintered-suns, gaiety-glitter, palms-reply), as well as the rhymes (mail-sail) and approximate rhymes (noon-sun-suns) and the feminine endings (glitter, banner). A glorious sight he is!

The second stanza reverses the emotional power by exploring what lies beneath the armor (and between the first and last lines, which retain the splendor of the first stanza). The knight seems already a corpse, except for that "lump of bitter jelly" (11), one of his eyes; if he is not yet dead, the only sign of life is that organ by which others viewed his gloriousness in the first stanza. There are still musical effects, but except for the repeated first line they call attention to what is harsh and painful. Alliteration now links such words as living-lump and metal-mask, assonance joins living-bitter, jelly-set-metal, and rags-tatters. The rhymes mask and casque emphasize the hard metal that encloses the head, and in the feminine endings (tatters, ribbons) there is an ironic contrast to the glitter-banner pairing in stanza 1.

These two stanzas thus ironically juxtapose superficial brilliance and a hideous, painful reality trapped inside it. The conclusion expresses the hope that this constrained and suffering being will be "unhorse[d]" and freed from the identity imposed by his role as a knight, with all its false panoply. The concluding four lines offer two alternatives—a gentle defeat, or a corpse still encased and "hidden" by the sight of "the great breastplate" (23–24). There

are examples of musical devices here as well, though after the positive rein-
forcements of stanza 1 and the negative implications of stanza 2, these seem
less emotionally connected. For example, alliteration does not seem to add
much meaning to the terms it links: *Who-unhorse, free-from,* and *hurled-
hidden.* Only in the climactic last line does sound again add to the ironic effect, calling attention to the splendor of his *great* breastplate that has concealed the grim reality and may yet continue to do so.   TRA

Sylvia Plath   Old Ladies' Home (page 856)

This poem deftly employs imagery, sound, and pattern to evoke the daily
routine of these "old ladies."

Constructed in stanzas containing seven lines and lines containing seven
syllables, the poem features imagery appropriate to old age, beginning with a
striking bit of wordplay. The opening lines express a meaningful paradox, for
the old women are simultaneously tough and frail: "Sharded in black, like
beetles" employs the zoological meaning of "shard"—the tough outer sheath
that protects a beetle's body; at the same time, "shard" suggests that the
women are fragments of their former selves, anticipating the next line describing them as "Frail as antique earthenware." The alliteration of *b-* and *sh-*
sounds in these opening lines reinforces the paradox with its blend of hard
and soft effects. The remainder of the first stanza emphasizes the women's
tenacious clinging to life as they "creep" out into the sun or lean their desic-
cated bodies against a stone wall for a "little heat." The imagery of black
clothing and stones in this first stanza hints at the women's nearness to death.

The second stanza describes their daily activities of knitting and talking
about their children and grandchildren. Yet the bleakness of this routine is
again emphasized by the mechanical quality of their talk ("Sons, daughters,
daughters and sons") and the suggestion that their families no longer visit
them, since the women's children are "Distant and cold as photos" and they
don't know their grandchildren. The stanza concludes with the observation
that their black clothing is worn with age; note the pun on "wears" ("Age
wears the best black fabric") and the images associated with decay, "Rust-red"
and "green as lichens" (lichens are scaly, crusty growths that attach themselves to rocks and trees).

The final stanza brings us to the end of the women's day, when they are
hustled off to their beds, which are described as "boxed-in like coffins." The
stanza is dominated and unified by *b-* and *n-*sounds, its pace slowed by internal
rhymes ("boxed-in/grin" and "Stalls in halls") that emphasize the closing-in of
death, the "bald-head buzzard." Plath achieves a similar effect by using only six
syllables in the final line, underscoring her point that the women's lives grow
shorter "with each breath drawn." The tone of the poem remains objective and
dispassionate, its imagery and technical virtuosity helping to create this impressive, macabre portrait of a houseful of old women awaiting death.   GJ

Claude McKay   The Tropics in New York (page 857)

The paradoxical nature of the title hints at the speaker's displacement. A man of color (Claude McKay was a native black Jamaican), he has stopped to admire a lush display of tropical fruits on a New York street. The description of these fruits in the first stanza leads to the "memories" (5) in the second of his native Caribbean island, where such fruit grows in profusion. In America, the fruit might be used in a competition "for the highest prize at parish fairs" (4), suggesting the commodification of natural beauty.

The second stanza's descriptive imagery—"low-singing rills" (6), "dewy dawns and mystical blue skies" (7), and "benediction over nun-like hills" (8)—invokes the sanctity of his memories of his native land and its natural abundance. By using this language, he suggests the natural as one with the supernatural in a tableau of pure innocence.

The final stanza describes the speaker's emotional reaction to the fruit display, which operates as a Wordsworthian memory that triggers an intense and painful reaction. The word "hungry" (11) is appropriate in the context of the succulent fruits he has been viewing, and his longing is so powerful that he can no longer look at them. Finally "The Tropics in New York" conveys the poignance of desire for a lost and irrecoverable past.

Although this poem is not discussed in critical works on McKay, some useful general studies of his poetry include the following: Tyrone Tillery, *Claude McKay: A Black Poet's Struggle for Identity* (Amherst: U of Massachusetts P, 1992); Heather Hathaway, *Caribbean Waves: Relocating Claude McKay and Paule Marshall* (Bloomington: Indiana UP, 1999); and Winston James, *A Fierce Hatred of Injustice: Claude McKay's Jamaica and His Poetry of Rebellion* (London: Verso, 2000).   GJ

Linda Pastan   To a Daughter Leaving Home (page 858)

The title creates the expectation that this poem will be concerned with that ambivalent moment when a child becomes an adult and leaves the protection and guidance of the family: ambivalent, because it is a beginning and an ending, a gain and a loss. However, Pastan's poem does not focus on that event, but rather on a much less decisive one, when a child learns a minor physical skill, bicycle riding. The bicycle lesson and its result are a symbol for the later, more significant breach that the title denotes.

There is a symbolic contrast between the two kinds of motion that the poem centers on. The speaker is expecting a circular motion, a return to the starting point ("home"), as reflected in the references to round and curved objects: "two round wheels" (6), "my own mouth rounding" (7), and "the curved / path of the park" (9–10). The speaker even anticipates (with mixed feelings) the abrupt cessation of the daughter's ride, the "thud" that will signal the end of it, an event that may injure the child but will also return her to her mother's care. But this bicycle lesson portends not a return but a departure, so that other images of motion point in lines leading directly away from the speaker. The daughter grows "smaller" (16) to the mother's sight as she grows stronger in her own competence and the delight of her freedom. The final image captures the essential poignancy of the symbolic meaning as the daughter's exertions culminate in her joy and her mother's grief.

The arbitrary line endings make a meaningful contribution to the poem in two ways. First, they afford opportunities for surprise (paralleling the speaker's surprised experience), as when a phrase *seems* to have ended with the line end, but then is extended or even reversed in meaning by the opening of the next line. Examples: extending the meaning, "my own mouth rounding / in surprise" (7–8), "I kept waiting / for the thud / of your crash" (11–13), "pumping, pumping / for your life" (18–19); reversing the expected meaning, "as you wobbled away / on two round wheels" (5–6), "while you grew / smaller" (15–16), "screaming / with laughter" (19–20).

The second contribution of the line endings is more meaningful because it helps to create emotional meaning. The need to pause at the ends of lines adds a hesitancy to the speech rhythms that reflects the speaker's difficulty in adjusting to this new independence in her daughter. This can be seen in some of the phrases already quoted (the sequence of lines 7–8 and 11–13, for example), but is most significant in the breathless pause between lines 13–14 ("as I / sprinted to catch up") and in the lump-in-the-throat pauses between lines 21–24:

> the hair flapping
> behind you like a
> handkerchief waving
> goodbye   TRA

Judith Ortiz Cofer   Quinceañera (page 859)

The quinceañera, a party marking a fifteen-year-old girl's birthday, is a rite of passage in Latin cultures. The poem focuses on the transition from girlhood to womanhood, especially as the transition effects changes in the girl's maturing body and in her fearful mind.

The tone of the poem is solemn to the point of suggesting that the speaker feels herself a victim of cultural and physical imperatives. Her childhood dolls have been "put away like dead / children" (1–2), and for the party her hair "has been nailed back" (7) to her skull, an image that hardly suggests light-hearted or pleasurable anticipation of her party. Not only has she suffered the nailed-back hair: her mother has "twisted / braids into a tight circle" (9–10), an image that suggests a narrowing rather than an expansion of the girl's life and prospects.

The middle lines of the poem continue the emphasis on physical transformation, specifically by referring to the girl's incipient menstruation. Again the images are negative and painful. From now on, the girl must wash her own clothes and sheets "as if / the fluids of my body were poison" (12–13). Rhetorically she asks, "Is not the blood of saints and / men in battle beautiful? Do Christ's hands / not bleed into our eyes from His cross?" (16–18). These references relate the girl's beginning endurance of menstruation to her cultural heritage of a violent, Gothic-hued Christianity.

In the poem's closing lines, the focus narrows to the girl's consciousness of her inevitable physical growth. The final two lines—"I am wound like the guts of a clock, / waiting for each hour to release me" (23–24) are particularly noteworthy. The simile of the clock reminds us that the girl is helpless in regard to the physical changes taking place in her body. Just as the blood has begun trickling out of her "guts," so will it take guts—personal courage—to endure the transformation that has begun. The final line again conveys the idea that she is a prisoner in her own body who is waiting for time to release her into the relative stability of mature womanhood.   GJ

Lawrence Ferlinghetti   ## Constantly risking absurdity
(page 860)

The poem compares the poet to a circus performer and entertainer—high-wire artist, acrobat, and clown ("a little charleychaplin man") who, apparently, will try to catch the leaping form of "Beauty" while balanced on the high wire of "truth"—an almost impossible feat. The extended simile (which includes metaphor and personification) emphasizes that the poet must be constantly entertaining (poetry must give pleasure), but that he is also concerned with such higher realities as truth and beauty. It also emphasizes that the poet's task demands the utmost skill and precision and involves constant risk: a false step by the high-wire artist can cause death; a slip by the poet in published work involves public exposure of ineptitude. The sublime and the ridiculous are often narrowly separated, but in their reviews critics are quick to flay the poet who strives for the first and falls into the second. Ferlinghetti shows his own agility as a performer with a constant flow of double meanings and "sleight-of-foot" tricks (the play upon "sleight-of-foot" is appropriate both for the high-wire artist who performs magic with his feet and for the poet who does it with metrical feet). Serious? Yes. Solemn? No.

The arrangement of words on the page, and the varying lengths of lines as a rhythmic unit (some swift, some slow, some smooth, some jerky) mimic the succession of short, hurried steps that the high-wire artist takes across the wire before pausing to balance himself anew—or rather, to *seem* to regain his balance. Much of the artistry on a high wire involves making the audience suppose that it is a frightening, herky-jerky contest with gravity when in fact the practiced tightrope walker is never really off balance. The poet, too, may create fictive effects.   LP, TRA

James Wright   A Blessing (page 861)

The predominant figure describing the ponies is personification, and as the poem develops it becomes a reflection or projection of the speaker's feelings. When at line 15 he begins to identify "the slenderer one" as a beautiful girl his attraction to her is brought into focus—not as some form of perverse bestiality but as a love so clear and delicate that his best expression of it requires him to imagine a lovely young girl.

The poem opens with a line so prosaic as to suggest no more than pointless factuality, but immediately the metaphor of line 2 bounces us into a poetic world of figurative language and experience in which figures are substituted for fact. "Twilight *bounds*" like a playful pony while the characteristic darkening that is twilight is transferred to the eyes of the ponies (3–4). These two examples of synesthesia prepare for the major transference of human emotion to the ponies. They come "gladly" (5) and "can hardly contain their happiness" (9), terms that in fact describe the emotions of the speaker. At lines 11–12, the transference seems complete and opens up one of the mysteries of human experience: "They love each other. / There is no loneliness like theirs." The "loneliness" is the result of the "love," for it cuts them off from other emotional attachments—they are alone together, and "have been grazing all day, alone," without the need for other intercourse.

But in her self-sufficiency "the slenderer one" does show concern and interest in the speaker, and he is deeply drawn. In another figurative transfer, "the light breeze" that ordinarily "caress[es]" one's skin moves the speaker to his own caress of the delicate ear/"girl's wrist" (21). So caught up in the experience of projection and transference, the speaker has the sudden, concluding insight: if he could somehow actually "step . . . out of [his] body" and surrender his literal, factual existence, he "would break / Into blossom" (23–24). Such a glorious transformation from human to plant would enable him to express his feelings in beauty and fragrance.

The more surprising run-on lines tend to coincide with the more elaborate examples of figurative transference. Lines 3–4 create the comparison of the ponies' eyes to twilight darkness; lines 9–10 include the speaker and his friend as part of the ponies' supposed happiness; lines 20–21 strikingly compare the delicacy of the "long ear" to the delicate "skin over a girl's wrist." Most exceptional is the 3-line sequence at the end:

> Suddenly I realize
> That if I stepped out of my body I would break
> Into blossom. (22–24)

The first of these lines cannot make sense without the continuation of thought in the second—a very strange thought indeed, if it is read without the third. And the third moves the idea into new and unexpected areas of meaning.   TRA

Alfred, Lord Tennyson   **Break, break, break** (page 862)

The tone and mood are established in the first two lines, through imagery, sound, and rhythm. In context each word in the image-bearing phrase "cold gray stones" has negative connotations that reinforce each other and give the reader a good notion of how to interpret the opening line with its three carefully spaced repetitions of the one word "break." Both good things and bad things can be broken, but the second line makes it impossible to read a cheerful note into the speaker's apostrophe. The tone will be sorrowful; and the repetitions of the opening line give the tone an emphasis that suggests that the speaker's sorrow may continue forever, as indeed the sea waves do. The sorrowful tone is given additional weight by the assonance of the long *o*'s in "cold–stones–O" and a lesser but still appreciable effect by the repeated long *a* sounds in "br*ea*k" and "gr*ay*."

We do not learn the source of the speaker's sorrow till halfway through the third stanza. There we learn that it is grief for some very beloved person who is irrevocably gone. The last two lines repeat and make more specific the source of this grief: "But the tender grace of a day that is dead / Will never come back to me" (15–16). This is an elegiac poem. The speaker's beloved is dead.

But if the poem is elegiac in tone, what purpose is served by the intermediate images (lines 5–10)? They symbolize progressive stages in human life. The "fisherman's boy" and his sister represent childhood at its careless innocent play. The "sailor lad" is late adolescence or early manhood singing at his work. The "stately ships" are maturity performing its necessary duties. By their happiness, their joy in their work, or their "stately" missions in life, they provide foils for the sorrow of the speaker. But, under the burden of his grief, their activities are meaningless to him.

Lines 6, 8, and 12 are perfectly regular anapestic trimeter, which I would call the basic meter of the poem despite the existence of two tetrameter lines (11 and 15). This is not free verse; it has a definite metrical beat throughout. The most obvious and most memorable departures from a strictly anapestic form are, of course, the monosyllabic lines that begin the first and last stanzas. What is more grievously broken than a broken heart? What is less likely than sea waves to be influenced in their motions by the bidding of a human voice?   LP

ADDITIONAL EXERCISE

The following passage, a scene in the Garden of Eden, is excerpted from Milton's epic *Paradise Lost*. The poem is written in blank verse, but the *visual* signs of its metrical form (line spacing, capital letters at line beginnings) are here removed. Using your ear and your knowledge of the poem's meter, decide where the line breaks occur, and indicate them with a slash mark. (In the text of the poem as properly printed, "Now came" begins a full line, and "threw" ends one.)

Now came still evening on, and twilight gray had in her sober livery all things clad; silence accompanied, for beast and bird, they to their grassy couch, these to their nests were slunk, all but the wakeful nightingale; she all night long her amorous descant sung; silence was pleased: now glowed the firmament with living sapphires: Hesperus that led the starry host rode brightest, till the moon rising in clouded majesty, at length apparent queen unveiled her peerless light, and o'er the dark her silver mantle threw.

ADDITIONAL EXERCISE ANSWER

Now came still evening on, and twilight gray
Had in her sober livery all things clad;
Silence accompanied, for beast and bird,
They to their grassy couch, these to their nests
Were slunk, all but the wakeful nightingale;
She all night long her amorous descant sung;
Silence was pleased: now glowed the firmament
With living sapphires: Hesperus that led
The starry host rode brightest, till the moon
Rising in clouded majesty, at length
Apparent queen unveiled her peerless light,
And o'er the dark her silver mantle threw.

PL 4.598–609

Chapter Thirteen

Sound and Meaning

Anonymous   Pease porridge hot (page 864)

This verse has been described as a "clapping game" for children.   LP

A. E. Housman   Eight O'Clock (page 866)

The place of execution is probably the courtyard of the town jail. The clock is one of those that plays a four-note tune at a quarter past the hour, extends it to eight notes at the half hour and twelve at three-quarters past, and then plays a full complement of sixteen notes before beginning the bong, bong that announces the new hour. The young man, strapped and hooded, with a noose around his neck, sees nothing, but he hears the sixteen notes (the four "quarters") of the clock's tune "tossed" down upon the town, then the noises of the clock machinery as it tightens its springs (almost literally collecting its strength) before beginning the series of eight monotone strokes, at the first of which the trap will be sprung beneath him, and he will drop the distance (carefully calculated according to his weight) sufficient to break his neck.

The stanzaic form is iambic $a^3b^5a^5b^2$, with the a-rhymes all feminine, but with considerable metrical variation. The second line, for instance, with its initial trochee and its very lightly accented *on* in the third foot, brings together a number of unstressed or lightly stressed syllables that give it a speed consonant with the indifferent brightness of the tune played by the chimes. In contrast, the two internally punctuated spondees that begin line 3 and the internally punctuated first foot of line 5, followed by an initially stressed trochee, slow these two lines dramatically in consonance with the subjective experience of the protagonist. Of particular importance is the series of sharp *k* sounds beginning in line 6: "counted–cursed–luck–clock collected–struck," and the heavy *str-* alliteration of "Strapped" (5), "strength," and "struck" (8). The syntactical displacement of "Its strength" from the expected position immediately following the verb places the alliterating monosyllables *strength* and *struck* together in the final line, where the final word *struck* culminates both the *str-* and *k* series of repetitions. In addition, the heavy metrical regularity of this line, with its internal comma isolating the final verb, gives *struck* enormous force (the result of alliteration, consonance, rhyme, syntax, meter, and punctuation), thus putting a heavy emphasis on its double meaning. Not only does the clock mechanically strike the hour, but it (or perhaps the whole clock tower), personified as an executioner, brings down its axe with a powerful blow on the neck of the condemned, striking out his life.

The use of "morning" and "nighing" (2, 5) as adjectives is unusual enough that one may detect a suggestion of *mourning* and *sighing* behind them.   LP

Alexander Pope   Sound and Sense (page 867)

Introducing his topic with the general observation that good writing is the result of art (it looks easy, but mastery is acquired only by long practice), Pope then states the thesis of his passage in line 4: in good writing "The sound must seem an echo to the sense." He elaborates and demonstrates this thesis (simultaneously) through a series of five examples, each included within an iambic pentameter rhyming couplet. When a poet writes about a gentle west wind and a smooth-flowing stream, Pope begins, the verse should also be soft and smooth. (The following scansions represent my sense, and may be modified to fit yours.)

Soft is | the strain | when Zeph- | yr gent- | ly blows, |

And the smooth | stream | in smooth- | er num- | bers flows. |

The reversal of stress in the first foot gives additional emphasis to *Soft*, which is the key word in the first line. Most of the words in the line are soft in sound, especially *Zephyr*, whose *z-f-r* combination of consonants is softer than the *w-st-w-nd* of *West wind*, despite the latter's alliterating *w*s. The *g* in *gently* is a *j*. The explosive *b* of *blows* is gentled by the following *l* and long vowel sounds. *Soft* and *strain* containing a gentling *f* and *n* respectively. In the second line the key word *smooth*, itself a smooth-sounding word, is emphasized (a) by the meter, which joins it with *stream* (also smooth in its long vowel sound and concluding *m*), and (b) by its repetition in *smoother*. The fourth foot contains the soft consonants *n* and *m*. The fifth combines the soft *fl-* with a long vowel. The repeated *ss* in these two lines (I suspect) take on the color of their surroundings.

But when | loud surg- | es lash | the sound- | ing shore, |

The hoarse, | rough verse | should like | the tor- | ent roar. |

It is arguable whether the key word *loud* is a loud sound (its vowel, of course, is a diphthong, and is the sound we use for a cry of pain—"ow!" or "ouch!"), but it is inarguable that the meter puts a stress on it appropriate to its importance in the sentence, and that its effect is intensified by its near-rhyme with *sounding*. The onomatopoetic *roar* is emphasized by its anticipation in *shore*, *hoarse*, and *torrent*. The alliteration of *loud* and *lash* and the consonance of *hoarse* and *verse* give emphasis and linkage to these two pairs of words. Though none of the words in these two lines sound particularly harsh (the roughness and hoarseness we may imagine in *rough* and *hoarse* disappear from *ruff* and *horse*), bringing three accents together in *hoarse, rough verse*, the meter puts extraordinary emphasis on words that are hoarse-meaning and rough-meaning, and pushes together three syllables that do not articulate easily. The grammatical pause contributes to this lack of articulation.

> When Á-jax strives some rock's vast weight to throw,
>
> The line too la-bors, and the words move slow.

It is not just the five stressed syllables in a row that slow down the first line and give it such a sense of strain and muscular effort; it is the impossibility of sliding these words easily off the tongue, the muscular effort required in the reading. The mouth has to be reshaped for each word in the series. Even in a single word like *strives*, effort is required, for we must pronounce five distinct consonant sounds (*s-t-r* and *v-s*) with only one vowel sound between them (*v-s* is harder than *s-t-r*). In the second line the two spondees, bringing three stresses together at two points in the line, slow the line down.

> Not so, when swift Ca-mil-la scours the plain,
>
> Flies o'er the un-bend-ing corn, and skims a-long the main.

In each of these lines the reader has the choice of stressing the first or the second syllable in the opening foot. I have elected to stress *Not* because (a) it signals the change from the grunting effort of Ajax to lift his rock to the effortless ease of swift Camilla running, (b) the two unstressed syllables following it speed up the line, and (c) the increased distance separating the first two stresses gives added emphasis to the second stress—*swift*—which is the key word in the couplet. The name *Camilla* (like *Zephyr*) fits Pope's purpose perfectly, so easily do the syllables flow together. (Contrast the effort and speed involved in saying the three syllables of *Camilla* and of *rock's vast weight*.) The assonant short *is* of *swift*, *Camilla*, and *skims* quicken these words, as well as link them in meaning. In the second line I stress the initial *Flies*, again because the reversed stress gives added emphasis to the more important word, and because the succeeding unstressed syllables add speed to the line. (The three unstressed syllables together were not allowed by the strict rules of Pope's day, however, nor the two consecutive vowel sounds in *the* and *un-*. Pope's unmodernized text—*th' unbending corn*—blends *the* and *un-* together in one syllable.) The notable variation here, however, is the introduction of a six-foot line (called an *Alexandrine*) into the pentameter pattern. The extra foot, making it possible to divide the line into two three-foot segments (separated here by a comma), gives the line additional light-ness (see discussion in Exercise 1, page 873).

Hear how | Tim-o- | theus' var- | ied lays | sur-prise,

And bid | al-ter- | nate pas- | sions fall | and rise!

With no other text than that before us, the reader with a sensitive ear can confidently declare that Pope put the accent on the second syllable of *alter-nate*. With the accent on the first syllable, the meter goes smash. When the accent is put on the second syllable, the line perfectly alternates unstressed and stressed syllables (it is the most regular line of the whole fourteen), thus echoing the alternation of passions of which Timotheus sings. (British usage, as opposed to American, even today stresses the second syllable of *alternate* when used adjectivally, as we do with the word *alternative*.)

Pope's passage is a brilliant display of technical virtuosity.   LP

Emily Dickinson   I heard a Fly buzz—when I died
(page 871)

Of the more than seventeen hundred poems in Dickinson's collected work, over five hundred are on the subject of death. Over and over she pictures or imagines what the experience of dying is like, and what, if anything, exists beyond it. Her solutions to these problems are as various as Donne's on sexual love. In this poem—one of her greatest—the poet projects her imagination into the future through a speaker who is recollecting the past—a technique she also uses in "Because I could not stop for Death" (page 752).

The poem presents a deathbed scene—a conventional motif in nineteenth-century fiction when people were part of large families and died more often at home than in hospitals. In these scenes the protagonist is shown on her deathbed, surrounded by relatives, neighbors, and friends, who have gathered to give comfort, to hear any last words, and to say farewell.

Some readers will regard the appearance of the fly as the first event of the poem because it is mentioned first, but the poem does not follow a strictly chronological order. (The answer to question 1 is *b, d, a, c*.) In line 1 the speaker announces her subject and theme, providing the poem's "topic sentence," as it were. She then goes back and relates what led up to it. (It's as if one said, "I shared a sandwich with our president once. Here's how it happened" or "Here's how it was.") Use of the past perfect tense in line 5 indicates that earlier there had been weeping and lamentation, but now the mourners have ceased weeping and are restraining external displays of feeling in preparation for witnessing the solemn moment of actual death. The "Stillness" (both of sound and motion) in the room is not a mere *absence* of speech and movement; rather, the atmosphere seems charged, like that lull in a storm when the air takes on a greenish tint and the silence is electric. The first "Heaves of Storm" had been the weeping and mourning of those gathered around the deathbed; the second will presumably accompany or immediately follow "that last Onset"—the moment of death itself. In stanza 3 the speaker is not literally making out her will. The formal conveyance of her larger properties (land, house, bank deposits, investments) would have been made, in the presence of a lawyer, long before. In the poem she is disposing of smaller items ("Keepsakes"), saying perhaps that she wants Cousin Lizzie to have her blue scarf, her daughter to have her favorite brooch, and her son to have the family Bible. The terms "willed" and "Signed away" are metaphorical.

It is at this moment ("and *then* it was"), when everyone is silently awaiting the moment of death, that the fly makes its appearance. Whether it has just arrived or has been present all along but unnoticed is an unanswerable and unimportant question. What *is* important is that the fly now dominates the dying woman's awareness and does so till her actual death in the poem's final line.

What are we to make of this fly—and of the poem?

The poem is structured on an ironic contrast between expectation and fulfillment. The imagery and language of the second stanza ("last Onset," "the King," "Be witnessed") indicate a confident expectation among the onlookers, and undoubtedly in the dying woman also, that some solemn and awesome event is about to occur. (Notice how much more formal and solemn is the phrase "Be witnessed" than "be seen.") The *King* will appear to carry off the soul of the dying woman. And who is "the King"? The king may well be Death itself, personified as a majestic figure. Perhaps more likely the king is God, or Christ, or the Angel of Death. But, for the speaker, all that appears is a small and rather nasty domestic insect—bluebottle or blowfly—trying to make its escape through the windows but continually bumping up against the glass, which it cannot see. It interposes itself between the light from the windows and the speaker. And perhaps the light also represents some special enlightenment the speaker had expected but failed to receive at the moment of death.

Some students will interpret the windows in line 15 as the eyes of the dying woman, but this interpretation is too allegorical. The "Room" is not allegorized, why should the windows be? The windows are literal windows, but as the speaker's vision blurs and dims, they become the last thing she can discern; and then they too go dark. It is her eyesight that fails, not the windows; but it fails in the sense that her literal eyes can no longer see the literal windows. In the final line, being dead, she can no longer see at all. She cannot see to see any illumination she might have hoped for from the windows, because of the interposition of the fly, or death.

At one level, the poem may be given a purely psychological interpretation about the experience of dying. One expects it to be a momentous and illuminating experience; but, the poem hypothesizes, death may turn out to be merely the diminution and final cessation of one's sensory and physical powers. Instead of illumination at the end, the dying person's consciousness in the final moments may be unable to focus on anything more significant than the sound and movement of a blowfly.

Most readers, however, will want to give the fly more than a purely literal significance and, indeed, one can hardly avoid seeing the fly as a symbol of death, coming not in the majestic form of a king but in the trivial and even repulsive aspect of a fly. However, if we stop with the simple assertion that the fly is a symbol of death, we will lose much of the richness of the symbol. For its fuller meanings we must examine all the connotations of the "Fly" in this context, especially as they contrast with those of "King." For fuller discussion, see Clark Griffith, *The Long Shadow: Emily Dickinson's Tragic Poetry* (Princeton: Princeton UP, 1964) 134–37; Robert Weisbuch, *Emily Dickinson's Poetry* (Chicago: U of Chicago P, 1975) 99–102; and Charles B. Wheeler, *The Design of Poetry* (New York: Norton, 1966)188–92.

In addition to the symbolic richness of this poem, we need also to appreciate the marvelous vividness with which the poet brings to life the actual, literal fly, especially in line 13 (one of the most magical lines in English poetry).

The basic rhyme scheme is *xaxa xbxb xcxc xdxd*, but the rhymes are perfect only in the final stanza. The one onomatopoetic word in the poem is *buzz* at the end of line 13. But notice how this buzz is brought into the poem and gradually intensified. In line 11, the final word, *was*, though unrhymed in its own stanza, and unrhymed in the formal rhyme scheme, nevertheless rhymes perfectly with *buzz* in the first line of the final stanza. In line 12 the word *interposed* continues the buzzing into the final stanza. In line 13 the vowel sound of *buzz* is preceded by the identical vowel sounds in "*u*ncertain" and "st*u*mbling," making three *u* sounds in close succession. Finally, the *b* sound in *buzz* is preceded in line 14 by the *b*s in "*b*lue" and "stum*b*ling." Thus, *all* the sounds in *buzz*—its initial and final consonants and its medial vowel—are heard at least three times in lines 11–13. This outburst of onomatopoetic effect consummates the aural imagery promised in the opening line, "I *heard* a Fly buzz—when I died." But line 13 combines images of color, motion, and sound. Though the sound imagery is the most important, the poem concludes with a reference to the speaker's dimming eyesight, and we may infer that she *saw* a blur of the bluebottle's deep metallic blue as well as hearing its buzz. The images of motion between "blue" and "buzz" belong to both the visual and aural modes of sensing. The speaker hears and imperfectly sees the "uncertain" flight of the fly as it bumbles from one pane of glass to another, its buzzing now louder, now softer. The meter of line 13, if the poem is scanned, is perfectly regular, but the two grammatical pauses help to give it an uncertain, irregular effect. Would it be too fanciful to say that the line itself stumbles over its three *b* sounds?   LP

EXERCISE (page 873)

The letter in parentheses indicates the superior version.

1. (a) ("Independence") The linkage in sound of "guide" and "guard" (alliteration and consonance) emphasizes their syntactical parallelism in an iambic pentameter

couplet. Version *b* takes more words (and an extra foot) to make a less forceful connection. (The biblical allusion is to Exodus 13.21.)

2. (b) (*Comus*) The blank verse passage, after the generalization in line 1, calls for harshness in line 2 and musicality in line 3. The three hard consonant sounds of "*crabbed*" crowding around one vowel are much harsher than the soft consonants in "*rough*" (pronounced *ruff*); in addition, two accents coming together on "dull fools" emphasize these words (as does their repetition of *l*s) and strain the meter (a monosyllabic foot replaces the expected iamb in the fourth position), whereas "foolish men" is pleasant in sound and regular in meter. The name "Apollo," with its final open vowel and its mellifluous *l*s (picking up *l*s in "musical" and "lute") is far more melodious than "Phoebus."

3. (b) ("Mid-Winter") The core of each version is "crows croak hoarsely" with its suggestion of raucous cawing. The three sharp *k* sounds in "crows croa*k*" are supported in version *b* in "out-cast" and "across"; and the hissing *s* of "hoarsely" is reinforced in "out-cast" and "across," and "whiteness" (with the addition of three sharp *t*s). In version *a*, "fleeing" and "over the snow" are rather pleasant in sound.

4. (b) (*Tristram*, 6) The gaps in "Your _____ how bells of singing gold / Would sound at _____ over silent water" must be filled with pleasant, musical sounds. In version *b* "low voice" is soft and lovely, "tells" provides an internal rhyme with "bells," and "twilight" a half-rhyme with "silent." In version *a* "talk attests" is noisy; "evening" is softly pleasant but provides no rhyme.

5. (b) (*The Princess:* "Come down, O maid") The blank verse of version *a* is metrically regular throughout. In version *b* the superfluity of unstressed syllables in line 1 (MYR-i-ads of RIV-u-lets HUR-ry-ing THROUGH the LAWN) gives the effect of speed; and the onomatopoetic words "moan" and "murmuring" are reinforced by the *m*s, *n*s, and *r*s in "*m*yriads," "immemorial," "elms," and "innumerable."

6. (a) (*Romeo and Juliet*, 3.5) The effect wanted is a harsh unpleasantness. The nasal "sings so" is less pleasant and less flowing than "warbles." The metrical irregularity of "STRAIN-ing HARSH DIS-cords" strains the meter and puts heavy emphasis on harshness, whereas the smooth regularity of "with HARSH dis-CORD-ant TONES" mutes it. "Unpleasing sharps" lacks the pleasant assonance of "tones" and "doleful."

7. (b) (*Don Juan*, 7.78) The flowing rhythm and euphonious sound of version *a*— its liquid *l*s, *r*s, and *m*s and its soft *f*- and *v*-sounds—make it beautiful to listen to; but this beauty is highly inappropriate to the subject. The sharp monosyllables, the clogged meter, and explosive *b*s and *d*s of version *b* make it far superior.

8. (a) ("Reconciliation") The repeated *s* sounds in "sisters," "incessantly," "softly," and "soiled" provide the repetition called for and perhaps even the sound of hands sloshing repeatedly in sudsy water.

9. (b) ("Elegy Written in a Country Churchyard") In line 1 "tolls," like "knell," is onomatopoetic. In line 2 a spondee appropriately slows down the line by bringing three accents together:

The low-́ ing herd́ wind slow-́ly o'eŕ the lea.́

In line 4 a slight accent on "and" in the fourth foot requires a slight compensatory pause before it (as if there were a comma after "darkness"), thus isolating the final pronoun and preparing for the meditative nature of the poem. (In version *a* lines 3 and 4 are absurdly swift for the solemnity of the subject.)

10. (b) ("Epistle to Dr. Arbuthnot") In line 1 the succession of short monosyllables with sharp endings ("let," "flap," "bug," "wings") spits out the spite of the speaker at the subject of his satire, and line 2 adds another ("child"). But the manifest superiority of version *b* is the superiority of "stinks and stings" to "smells and bites." The alliterating *sts*, the assonance of the short *is*, and the sharp final consonants link these verbs in sound as well as in syntax and give them a force that the soft word "smells" lacks (though "bites" has it).

Wilfred Owen   Anthem for Doomed Youth (page 875)

The octave has its geographical setting on the battlefield (since this is a World War I poem, in France). The sestet has a geographical setting back home (since Owen was an English poet, in England). The octave concerns the death of soldiers in battle. The sestet concerns the bereavement of friends and family back home. The imagery of the octave is primarily auditory. The imagery of the sestet is primarily visual. The tone of the octave is angry and indignant. The tone of the sestet is tender. (Line 8 is transitional: the "sad shires" are back in England. This line connects the deaths to the bereavement and shifts the geographical locus from battlefield to home.) Both octave and sestet are introduced by questions.

Octave and sestet are unified by the central metaphorical image of an Anglican funeral service. Neither the literal terms of this metaphor (battle and bereavement) nor the figurative term (church funeral service) is named, so this is a metaphor of the fourth form (see page 718). The terms of the central metaphor are arrived at, as it were, by adding up the subsidiary figures and drawing a total. In the octave, at least, the central metaphor emphasizes contrast more than similarity, for the point is that these soldiers will never have a church funeral. Instead of the items in the second column of the list below (the figurative terms), they will have only the items in the first column (the literal terms):

literal	*figurative*
Owen's poem	anthem
monstrous anger of the guns	passing-bells
rapid rifle fire	orisons
wailing shells	choirs singing
bugles calling	voices of mourning
glimmers of good-byes in boys' eyes	candles held by altar boys
pallor of girls' brows	pall-cloth on coffin
tenderness of patient minds	flowers
dusk coming each evening	drawing-down of blinds

The last metaphor on this list does not belong to the funeral service image, but it too is associated with the formal observance of death. (In addition to the metaphors, the octave uses considerable personification: guns are angry, rifles stutter and patter out prayers, shells wail and are demented, bugles call, shires are sad. Words like "monstrous," "stuttering," and "demented" suggest that the noises of battle are like those of a madman.)

Students will have their greatest difficulty with lines 10–11. Many will identify the "boys" with the "doomed youth" and read these lines as referring to the gleam in the eyes of the dying soldiers on the battlefield. Candles at a church funeral, however, are not held by the dead man but by attendants (altar boys). The logical organization of the sonnet, moreover, places this scene back home rather than on the battlefield. The boys and girls of the sestet are younger brothers, sisters, sweethearts, or other persons close to the dead.

The main point of the poem is that a church funeral service would be a "mocker[y]" for these dead soldiers. Funeral services are a means of ritualizing or giving dignity to human death. These soldiers, however, did not die a human death; instead, they were slaughtered like "cattle." The dignity of a funeral service would be inappropriate to the indignity of their death. Owen's poem, though a tribute (an "anthem") to the dead soldiers, is mainly a bitter attack on modern war. It expresses horror, indignation, and anger at the senseless slaughter of human beings by mechanical means. Modern warfare, it implies, is mass slaughter: a mockery of human dignity. Death in modern warfare is an animal death, not a human death.

In the octave, sound is adapted to sense chiefly by the use of words and phrases whose sounds imitate meaning. The onomatopoetic series *stuttering– rattle–patter* is reinforced by the *t*s in "cattle," "monstrous," and "hasty." The onomatopoetic *wailing* is reinforced by the *l*s in "bells," "shrill," "shells," "bugles," "calling." (*Bells* and *shrill* may perhaps themselves be considered onomatopoetic.) The phrase *rifles' rapid rattle* is given speed by its pronounced trochaic rhythm (the phrasing corresponding with the meter)* and by the alliteration of the liquid *r*s, but the hard *p* and *d* of *rapid* reinforce the staccato quality of *stuttering–rattle–patter.*

In the sestet, sound is adapted to sense chiefly by the linking together through similarity in sound of words logically connected in meaning, for example, *candles–hands, glimmers–good-byes, pallor–pall, dusk–drawing–down.*   LP

*The basic meter of the poem is iambic pentameter, and in *scansion* line 3 would be divided as follows:

$$\acute{O}n\text{-}l\breve{y} \mid \breve{the} \; st\breve{u}t\text{-} \mid \acute{t}er\text{-}ing \; r\acute{i}f\text{-} \mid \acute{l}es' \; r\acute{a}p\text{-} \mid \acute{i}d \; r\acute{a}t\text{-} \mid \breve{t}le.$$

In *reading* the line, however, we hear "rifles' rapid rattle" as three trochees.

Margaret Atwood   Landcrab (page 876)

A landcrab is one of a number of species that live mostly upon land, returning to the sea only for breeding—and thus violating expectations about the normal environment of crabs.

The reversal of sea and land in the habitat of this crab evokes thoughts of the origin of the land-dwelling human being, which, according to one theory, was the sea. Thus there may be a parallel: both crab and mankind have deserted their original environment.

The parallel is not an attractive one to the speaker, and she forthrightly denies the marine origin of people, preferring instead to infer some miraculous creation of humanity. However, the denial is rendered less forceful by the speaker's alluding to the fabulous Greek stories of Deucalion (who after the great flood was instructed to sow his mother's bones, and took that to mean the stones of the earth, which were transformed into men and women), and of Cadmus (who was instructed to sow dragons' teeth, which sprang up as armed warriors).

The speaker seems to be repulsed by the idea of kinship with the crab, since the descriptive details of lines 5–23, while accurate observations of appearance and behavior, are not humanly attractive. But there are vestiges of personification in these lines—"timid," "routine," and "dance"—which imply that despite her preference not to be identified with the crab, she does detect similarities. Lines 24–27 expressly attribute to the crab a human emotion, "contempt" for the comparative softness and vulnerability of mammals.

The speaker does concede that if she is more than a crab, it represents at least "a piece of what / we are." It displays for us some of our characteristics that, at those moments when we acknowledge them, are the materials of our nightmares. If the crab seems like "the husk of a small demon" (13), there is also something terrifyingly demonic in us—the true link between the species.

The free-verse rhythms established by the line-ends have a variety of emphasis and speed depending on end-stopping and run-ons and by syntactical units conforming to or violating expectations created by line-ends. One characteristic of some free verse is clearly illustrated here, the creation of a norm for the number of speech (or rhetorical) stresses per line. In this poem, the norm is two stresses, with some variations, as the second paragraph demonstrates. (Free verse cannot be scanned, of course; what I accentuate are the speech stresses, not the stressed syllables of metrical feet.)

HERmit, hard SOCKet
for a TIMid EYE
you're a soft GUT SCUTtling
SIDEways, a bone SKULL,
round BONE on the PROWL.
WOLF of treeroots and gravelly HOLES,
a MOUNT on STILTS,
the HUSK of a small DEmon.

The contribution of cacophony and euphony is more pronounced than the rhythm. In the lines just quoted, alliteration, assonance, and consonance draw attention to key words and emphasize the distaste that the speaker feels for her subject: *soft gut scuttling* has assonance in the short *u* sound and consonance in the repeated terminal *t* sounds in the first three syllables. That *t* is found throughout the paragraph, both in the terminal sound and elsewhere: hermi*t*, socke*t*, *t*imid, *t*reeroo*t*s, moun*t*, s*t*il*t*s.

Lines 22–25 (mentioned in the study questions) display both euphony and cacophony as the harsh sounds are used to present the landcrab while more melodious sounds describe the mammals. The crab is characterized by *k* and *t* sounds (*coupling, quick, clatter, rocks*), while the mammals are presented with *m, l,* and *b* (*mammals, lobes, bulbs*). Lines 26–27, in which the crab's dismissive scorn for mammals is stated, combine harsh sounds (*scruples, contempt*) with a phrase that begins with the euphony of mammals but ironically and abruptly closes with one of the "crab" consonants: *warm milk.*   TRA

John Updike   Recital (page 877)

This playful, near-nonsensical poem derives its charm almost wholly from its manipulation of sound. The speaker, reading in the *New York Times* that a man named Roger Bobo has given a tuba recital, imagines that Eskimos, barracuda, and "Men of every station" (5) are attuned to the recital.

The diction is chosen wholly for its sound effects, as in the rhyming of "Manitoba" (1) and "Aruba" (2) with "tuba" (4). The examples of men of every station—"Pooh-Bah, / Nabob, bozo, toff, and hobo"—are chosen purely for the musical effects of assonance (the long o-sounds) and alliteration (the *b*-sounds). In fact, throughout the poem a clever use of assonance and alliteration mimics effectively the brassy, forthright sound of a tuba.

There is a final bit of playfulness in the division of the words "Indubi- / Tably" (7–8) and "nobo / Dy" (8–9), which again emphasize sound over sense.

This delightful poem can be used in the classroom as an argument that poetry need not always be serious or "dark." Even poets who normally write more thematically substantial poems than "Recital" can often exhibit a playful side.   GJ

Adrienne Rich   Aunt Jennifer's Tigers (page 878)

QUESTIONS

1. Vocabulary: *screen* (1), *topaz* (2). Describe the picture sewn on the screen.
2. Explore the contrasts between Aunt Jennifer and the needlework she creates. How does line 10 sum up her life? What "ordeals" can you infer? What is implied by line 7?
3. Scan the poem, locating anapestic substitutions in lines 1, 2, 5, 6, and 9. How do these create a "prancing" (12) rhythm? How does that rhythm support the contrasts you explored for question 2?
4. Anapestic and iambic feet may create "rising" rhythms, while dactylic and trochaic may contribute to "falling" rhythms, both patterns subtly reinforcing emotional meanings. But sometimes individual words themselves may have rising or falling rhythms. Consider the rhythmic contributions of the following words: "Jennifer's" (1, 5, 8), "fluttering" (5), "ivory" (6).

By means of a contrast between a woman and the subject of her artistic creation, the poem portrays her life—the opposite of "prancing, proud and unafraid" (12), she was mastered by the ordeals she faced (10). Her hands were "terrified" (9), her fingers fluttered (5) as she sewed her needlepoint, and she was weighed down by her role as wife or widow.

What she sewed was a picture of a tiger hunt in far-off India, the tigers prancing in their green world fearlessly unaware of the men lurking beneath a tree ready to attack them. The scene is an ironic contrast to the life of its creator. Sleek, self-assured (yet moving toward their destruction), her tigers symbolize the life she could not live, free and dangerous, "Bright topaz denizens of a world of green" (2). We cannot know whether Aunt Jennifer longed for such a life for herself, but we can recognize in her artwork an expression of what life did not literally afford her.

The meter of the poem is itself "prancing," an iambic with enough anapestic substitutions to create a free, rollicking rhythm that itself is ironically juxtaposed to the apparently humdrum world of Aunt Jennifer. This is particularly pronounced in lines 5–6, both of which contain a pair of anapestic feet:

Aunt Jen-ni- fer's fin-gers flut-ter-ing through her wool

Find e-ven the I-vor-y need-le hard to pull.

The meter in these lines is anapestic (each has three iambic feet and two anapestic, a sufficient proportion to create the effect of anapestic). But interestingly, the rhythms seem more dactylic, since the words tend to echo the rhythm of the aunt's name

Jen-ni-fer flut-ter-ing I-vor-y.

With this as a clue, we can see that while the meter retains a rising pattern either in duple or triple meters, many individual words display the falling rhythms we associate with dactyllic, not only those quoted from lines 5–6, but also *denizens* (2), *certainty* (4), *heavily* (8), *terrified* (9). The effect is to counterpoise the pathos of Aunt Jennifer's plain and unremarkable life to the sprightly, rollicking rhythms that might be associated with the excitement of the prancing tigers. It is also interesting that the needlepoint screen captures the tigers just before they are to be hunted down, so that the artifact preserves that "proud and unafraid" moment in their lives as a representation of Aunt Jennifer's projected but unrealized vivacity and freedom. Neither the aunt nor the tigers can outlive the reality that will overcome them, but it is a brave moment for both that she preserves.   TRA

John Donne   At the round earth's imagined corners

(page 878)

The first eight lines vigorously cry out for the trumpet call of Doomsday and the assemblage of resurrected souls and bodies at the place of judgment before God. There are actually two commands here, one for the sounding of the trumpets and the other for the gathering of the "infinities / Of souls." Why the speaker should so earnestly be asking for the destruction of the world is not anywhere evident within the poem. Two possibilities suggest themselves, but neither has much force. He includes among those going to judgment those "whose eyes / Shall behold God and never taste death's woe" (7–8). Since he is still living he may be pleading to be one of those who will avoid the pangs of death; but that motive seems too petty and selfish in this context. Furthermore, he does not include himself specifically, for his apostrophe is directed to "you" who will never suffer death, not "we." On the other hand, when he reverses himself and asks that Doomsday be postponed, he offers two reasons: that the other souls may continue at their rest and that he may continue to "mourn a space" (9). Is some great personal grief or loss the reason for wishing for all life to cease (including his own), some mourning that he wants to end and yet wants to continue?

Most commentators skip over this issue, assuming simply that a devout Christian must at some time or other meditate upon the end of the world and its glorious consequences—salvation of the good, damnation of the wicked. The allusion to Revelation 7.1 in the opening image is taken to be the starting point for a meditation that is elaborated and made concrete through the first eight lines, which then gives way to a less philosophical contemplation of the idea as the speaker examines the condition of his own soul and its lack of preparedness for that climactic event.

Certainly we can see a clear contrast between the tone of the opening octave and the concluding sestet. The bombastic apostrophes of the octave are suddenly stilled as the personal unworthiness of the speaker leads him to petition for grace and repentance "[h]ere on this lowly ground" before he is led to the seat of judgment "there" in heaven (12). The metrical irregularity of line 12 forcefully draws the contrast between "there" and "here," with a caesura inserted before the trochaic substitution for additional emphasis:

When we are there. ‖ Here on this low-ly ground,

The caesura is given even more weight by the absence of any rhetorical or grammatical pauses in the preceding line.

The scansion of lines 1–8 reveals the insistent and pounding rhythm, particularly in the catalogue of those summoned to judgment:

All whom the flood did, and fire shall, o'er-throw,

All whom war, dearth, age, a-gues, tyr-an-nies,

Des-pair, law, chance hath slain, and you whose eyes

Shall be-hold God and nev-er taste death's woe.

(I have been more liberal here in marking spondees than may be necessary, so as to call attention to the drumbeat of rhythm that seems to accompany the trumpets of doom.)

Three of the more valuable comments on this well-known sonnet are Louis L. Martz, *The Poetry of Meditation* (New Haven: Yale UP, 1954) 50–52; George Williamson, *Six Metaphysical Poets* (New York: Farrar, 1967) 84–85; Stanley Archer, "Meditation and the Structure of Donne's Holy Sonnets," *ELH* 28 (1961): 140–41.   TRA

Galway Kinnell   Blackberry Eating (page 879)

In this brief poem Galway Kinnell uses gustatory imagery with gusto. The taste of those "fat, overripe, icy, black blackberries" (2) is conveyed from the speaker's tongue to the reader's imagination so vividly as almost to make the reader's mouth water. The vivid gustatory image is compounded with visual imagery ("fat," "black") and tactile imagery ("icy"). There is tactile imagery also in "the stalks very prickly" (4) where the repeated *k*-sound (which also picks up the *k*s of "blac*k*" and "brea*k*fast" in the preceding line) reinforces the prickliness. Then, since the speaker is a poet as well as a blackberry-eater, he notes that the "ripest berries / fall almost unbidden to [his] tongue, / as words sometimes do" (7–9). The poet slyly uses the word "tongue" in two senses here, first as an organ of taste and then as an articulator of speech. Notice that blackberries (like raspberries, dewberries, and loganberries; unlike blueberries, cherries, and grapes) are composed of many smaller parts (called drupelets). The words that he especially loves, like the blackberries, come in "fat" little lumps: they are "one-syllabled" but "many-lettered" (11). The words *strengths* and *squinched* (10), both containing nine letters, are according to authorities the longest monosyllabic words in the language (*squinch*, to be found only in an unabridged dictionary, is a dialect word meaning "to twist"). But notice that the speaker demonstrates his love for such words not only by his two examples but by choosing three seven-lettered monosyllabic words ("squeeze," "squinch," and "splurge," 12) for his verbs in the final clause of the poem.

The speaker's favorite word in this poem, however, is "black." It occurs three times by itself and four more times as part of "blackberries." We may profitably examine its three solo appearances. In its initial use, "black blackberries" (2), it may at first seem redundant, but it is not, for unripe blackberries are green, and the speaker is emphasizing that these berries are ripe or overripe. The poet must have chuckled to himself when the next phrase fell "almost unbidden" to his tongue. He was so charmed that he invented a whimsical myth to go with it. The blackberry stalks were given their prickles as a penalty for knowing "the black art of blackberry-making" (5–6)! This myth obviously lacks the magnitude of the myth of Adam and Eve in the garden, which inspired Milton to write *Paradise Lost* (the prickles are a "penalty," not a punishment), but it is perfectly sized for the brief poem Kinnell puts it in, and is a delightful spin-off from the phrase "the black art." The black arts are ordinarily the arts practiced by witches and conjurors for unauthorized and wicked purposes, but in Kinnell's poem the phrase is stripped of all of its negative implications. The art of making blackberries is a black art only in that it produces black berries; the word is placed in a context where it means only good, not bad. Finally, in its last two lines, the poem gives us a "black language of blackberry-eating," thus completing the metaphorical comparison between blackberries and words—both of them good. The image of "black language" may summon up for the reader the image of black words printed on white paper; but in any form it calls up an experience of pleasure and delight.   LP

Mark Doty   Golden Retrievals (page 880)

This playful, joyous sonnet in the voice of a golden retriever says that a dog's life might have some advantages over a man's. The dog has at least this limitation/superiority—he doesn't think about the past or "tomorrow," but exists "here, / entirely, now" (10, 14). No doubt that could be a limitation, but the way in which past and future are presented in lines 7–10 suggests that a man might be better off not "thinking of what you never can bring back" or lost "in some fog" wondering what the future holds (8–9).

By contrast, the dog is "entirely" concerned with what can "capture [its] attention / seconds at a time." The human invents games of "[f]etch" and "[c]atch" which the dog may or may not be interested in; certainly the man thinks he will be, that these games are the kind of play that the dog enjoys. But the dog really takes pleasure in pursuit of rabbits, leaves that seem animate, and squirrels, and he loves the deep scents of decaying, "thrillingly dead thing[s]" (6).

The dog conceives of his "work" as keeping his supposed master in the reality of the here and now, unraveling the "warp (and woof!)" of the orderly, neat fabric that time seems to present to "haze-headed" men (11–12). Spontaneity, instinct, and down-to-earth reality are the lesson this canine "Zen master" can teach. Does the human master learn? The poem doesn't stop to say, though the implication is that what the dog advocates is really much more appealing than worrying in a haze about yesterday and tomorrow.

The rhythms of the poem are delightfully jerky, an imitation of the bounding dog's indirect zigging and zagging. The poem is in form a sonnet, but substitutes 10-syllable free verse lines for iambic pentameter, and contrives a unique rhyme scheme: *abba ccdd efef xx*. None of the quatrains has the same pattern, and the couplet lacks rhyme altogether. This dog is no slave to formal patterns of behavior or of poetry.

Onomatopoeia obviously occurs in the "bow-wow, bow-wow, bow-wow" of the last line, and the "woof!" of the pun in line 11. Less obvious are "bark" (12) and "gong" (13).   TRA

Richard Wilbur   **A Fire-Truck** (page 880)

An erudite poet who makes frequent use of literary allusion, Richard Wilbur notes that the eighth line of this poem, *"Thought is degraded action!"* deliberately "echoes a notion entertained by Henry Adams in his 'Letter to American Teachers of History' (1910)." Donald L. Hill writes that "A lesser poet would have got only so far as to have the bell proclaim the glory of action, while he himself compared it cleverly with second-best thought. To give the bell the whole proposition is a characteristically bold and delightful stroke of wit" (*Richard Wilbur* [New York: Twayne, 1967] 159).

The seven lines introducing this abstract thought, however, are a triumph of imagery, making the sight and sound of the fire-truck palpably vivid in the reader's imagination. Note the abruptness of the opening two lines, their lack of punctuation evoking the bold, sudden appearance of the truck; likewise, the alliteration of "street," "siren-blast," "sends," and "else skittering" (the *s*-sounds continue into the third line, along with repeated *b*- and *r*-sounds that anticipate the crucial "Blurring" in line four) stressing the powerfully unified, single effect upon the senses of the truck's color, noise, and movement. The second stanza repeats the pattern of the first in the initial two lines' headlong motion, uninterrupted by punctuation, and in its similar alliterative pattern.

The poem's rhythm shifts dramatically after the eighth, italicized line, shifting the focus from the physical reality of the truck to the intellectual response of the speaker. In its extraordinary string of adjectives, each separated by a comma, the ninth line forms a sharp contrast with the rapid motion of lines 1–2 and 5–6, suggesting the speaker's halting attempt to capture the truck in words. The truck's loud, stunning physicality, a phenomenon so powerful it has rendered the speaker's "mind a blank," gives way (as it howls "beyond hearing") to a living image in the speaker's imagination, a "phoenix-red simplicity, enshrined / In that not extinguished fire." Ultimately the poem privileges the powers of mind over the things of this world, since like the phoenix of mythology the fire-truck will be reborn again and again in the speaker's memory, a sacred relic "enshrined" in his consciousness; similarly, the fire toward which the truck headed becomes an image of imaginative power that lives not to destroy but to recreate the sensual vividness of the truck itself.

The poem is discussed further in Michael Hulse, "The Poetry of Richard Wilbur," *Quadrant* 25, no. 10, (October 1970): 49–52, and in Paul F. Cummins, *Richard Wilbur: A Critical Essay* (Grand Rapids, Mich.: Eerdmans, 1971) 14–15. Regarding the technical effects of the poem, Cummins notes: "In the third stanza, the rhyming of 'blank' with 'thank' reinforces the central theme of the poem. . . . [The speaker's] mind has been purged of its prior troubles and reduced to an unthinking, 'blank' state, and for this he wishes to 'thank' the truck. In the last stanza, the 'mind-enshrined' rhyme summarizes the meaning of the poem. Thoughts, images, and feelings once perceived by the *mind* are lasting; they become *enshrined* in our memories."   GJ

William Carlos Williams   The Dance (page 881)

The repetition of the first line of the poem as its last line gives the poem a circularity of form, which is emphasized internally by the repetition of the word "round" (2, 2, 5), "around" (3), and its rhymes "impound" (6), "Grounds" (9), "sound" (10), plus the assonant "about" (8). The poem lacks end rhyme but is rich in internal rhyme, exemplified in the above; in "prance as they dance" (11); and in such approximations as "squeal"–"tweedle"–"fiddles" (3–4), "tipping"–"thick"–"hips" (5–7), "bellies"–"balance" (7), "about"–"butts" (8–9), etc. The abundance of participial verb forms—"tipping," "kicking," "rolling," "swinging," "rollicking"—contributes also to the sense of vigorous motion. The triple meter gives this motion speed, but is subject to occasional jolting irregularities (as in 5, 6, 8) which remind us that these are thick-shanked, big-bellied, heavy-butted peasants dancing, not a graceful group of nymphs on Mount Olympus. The great majority of the lines are run-on (only the last ends with a full stop, and 1 and 6 with partial stops), thus giving the poem a sense of continuous motion, especially when the lines end with such traditionally unlikely words as "and," "the," and a hyphenated "thick-," where the reader is thrown forward into the next line without even a pause to observe the line-ending. This fact is further enhanced by the fact that all but three of the lines (5, 6, 11) have feminine endings, so that the meter as well as the grammatical incompleteness throws the reader forward. A highly unusual feature of this poem is that all but three ("around," "impound," and "about") of the words of more than one syllable (there are twenty-six of them) are accented on the first syllable; and this also contributes to the sense of continuous motion. The exceptions to the foregoing observations occur just frequently enough to keep the reader a bit off-balance, like the peasants themselves.

Three onomatopoetic words provide the music for all this motion—the "squeal," "blare," and "tweedle" of the bagpipes, bugle, and fiddles.   LP

Chapter Fourteen

Pattern

George Herbert **The Pulley** (page 884)

In this simple-seeming parable, God bestows on His creature man the blessings of physical strength and beauty, mental wisdom, spiritual honor, and the pleasures that can be derived from these gifts. These constitute most of "the world's riches" (4), but there is one more: "rest," that particular pleasure that God Himself enjoyed on the seventh day of creation. Having given His creature all but that, God decides to withhold it as an additional spur to man's loving his creator. In that way, if God's "goodness" (19) fails to direct man to love God, then the need for rest will "toss him to [God's] breast" (20).

Throughout the poem, as in the parables of the Bible, spiritual values are expressed in worldly, material terms. So God's gifts are "riches" and "treasure," rest is a "jewel," God's goodness is expressed in "gifts," and if man fails to adore God for Himself, both God and man will sustain losses (4, 9, 12, 13, 15). In keeping with this metaphorical context, a physical engine (the pulley) provides the climactic image: man's full love of God may require not only the weight of God's manifest goodness in bestowing so many treasures but also the additional weight of man's "weariness" (19).

As we also may find in even the most serious religious poems of the Metaphysicals, Herbert's contains wordplay and puns—intellectually invigorating verbal gestures that delight as well as convey meaning. "Rest" (10) means both the ability to indulge in relaxation but also the remainder—rest is the rest of God's treasure. "[R]epining restlessness" (17) combines in an alliterative phrase both fretful agitation and a spiritual depression resulting from the lack of rest—man will desire to rest, and express that desire in restless activity.

The form Herbert has chosen consists of five-line stanzas rhyming *ababa*; the iambic lines are trimeter in the first and fifth, pentameter in the second, third, and fourth. The pattern is thus $a^3bab^5a^3$. There are few variations in the iambic meter, so those that do occur stand out. The second and third stanzas show one pattern of variations that draws attention to meanings: in both stanzas, the *b*-rhymed lines have feminine rhymes resulting from extrametrical syllables at the end. This is most striking in the rhythmic result in line 7, where all four of the capitalized words have falling rhythms—Beauty, Wisdom, Honor, Pleasure, even though, except for the additional unstressed syllable at the end, the line is regular:

Then Beau– ty flowed; || then Wis– dom, Hon– or, Pleas– ure.

The feminine rhyme also emphasizes the antithesis expressed in line 14:

And rest in Na– ture, || not the God of Na– ture.   TRA

John Keats On First Looking into Chapman's Homer

(page 886)

The octave is concerned with exploration, the sestet with the experience of discovery.

The octave is an extended metaphor in which traveling is the figurative term for reading, and "the realms of gold" the figurative term for literature. The "goodly states and kingdoms" are various kinds of literature, and the "western islands" are specifically poetry, the domain of Apollo, god of poetry and inventor of the lyre (from which the word *lyric* is derived). Though geography should not be pressed too hard, these islands are probably called "western" to associate them with the West Indies, where many of the early English and Spanish explorers sought gold.

The sestet consists of two similes conveying the thrill of discovery. First, the speaker compares himself to an astronomer looking through his telescope when "a new planet swims into his ken." Anyone who has looked through a good astronomical telescope can testify to the swimming or quaking motion that an observed celestial body has as it enters the field of vision. The word "ken" is also beautifully effective here because it not only means "range of vision," it is also associated with knowing or knowledge; and the excitement here is generated by the astronomer's discovering a planet—a whole new world—previously unknown to man.

The second simile partly derives its force from the fact that the early explorers, seeking a shorter route to the East Indies and Cathay, at first thought they had found it and did not realize that what they had actually found was a new continent separated from their destination by another whole sea. Balboa's discovery of the Pacific thus came as a surprise and vastly expanded European ideas about the size of the Earth. Keats captures the exact awestruck moment when the explorer and his men first encounter this vast, shining, and unguessed-at new ocean while crossing the mountains of a land they did not know to be an isthmus.

One would prefer poets to be historically accurate, and it would be folly to pretend that nothing is lost when they are not. Yet Keats's subject is not history but human experience, and when one contemplates the consequences of substituting the three syllables of *bal-BO-a* for the three syllables of "STOUT COR-tez," one may even be glad for the blunder. (The name "Cortez" in Spanish is accented on the second syllable, but common British pronunciation reverses the accents.) The first loss is the adjective "stout," which, along with "eagle eyes," gives strength and stature to the discoverer. The second loss is one of sound and rhythm, which support his strength. "STOUT COR-tez" with its three *t*s, sharp *k* sound, and two stresses, gives the adventurer just that needed intrepid quality, while *bal-BO-a* softens its *b*s with a liquid *l* and trails off into two vowel sounds suggestive more of grace than of strength. The heroic description of the discoverer matches the heroic verse and voice ("loud and bold") of Chapman's translation, which for Keats first captured the heroic qualities of Homer's epic narratives.

But if this poem were only about Keats's discovery of Chapman's translation, it would be of limited interest. What gives it enduring value is Keats's transformation of his discovery into a symbol for all discovery, his magnificent success in conveying the excitement that may attend any discovery, made by any of us, whether it be of universal or only personal significance.   LP

William Shakespeare   That time of year (page 887)

In this sonnet an aging speaker, constantly aware of his approaching death, addresses a beloved person considerably younger than himself.

The structure of thought in the sonnet is perfectly matched to the formal divisions marked out by its rhyme scheme. In each of the three quatrains the speaker makes a metaphorical statement of his increasing age and nearness to death, and in the concluding couplet he makes a counterstatement of his beloved's increased love for him. This structure is formally expressed in the language of the poem. Its opening line contains the words "thou mayst in me behold"; the second and third quatrains each begin "In me thou see'st"; the concluding couplet, before making its counterstatement, summarizes what has preceded in its opening words "This thou perceivest."

In the opening quatrain the speaker compares himself to "That time of year" (late autumn or early winter) when "yellow leaves, or none, or few" hang upon the trees. In the second stanza he compares himself to the dusk of day, fading from sunset into night. In the third he compares himself to a sinking fire, whose glowing embers are about to be extinguished by the ashes of the fuel that once "nourished" it. Though the quatrains (each a sentence) make parallel statements, they are arranged in a climactic order and could not be rearranged without loss. First, they are concerned with diminishing periods of time (a year, a day, the length of time that a fire will burn), and thus they bring us metaphorically closer and closer to the thought of death (weeks, hours, minutes). In addition, the first quatrain emphasizes coldness ("[b]are" boughs "shake against the cold"); the second emphasizes darkness (twilight fading into "black night"); the third combines cold and dark in the image of the sinking fire, which is losing both warmth and light. Finally, the first quatrain looks backward in time to what has been lost, the second looks forward to what will be lost, and the third combines references to past and future.

Each central metaphor is complicated by an additional metaphor or metaphors. In the first, the tree's leafless boughs are called "Bare ruined choirs." A choir is that section of a church or chapel containing wooden choir stalls, and the sight of bare ruined choirs would have been familiar to every reader of Shakespeare's time because of the confiscation of Roman Catholic monastic properties throughout England by Henry VIII some half-century earlier and the subsequent spoliation of the monasteries by Reformation landowners. Through this association of thought the "sweet birds" become not only the songbirds that have migrated south for the winter, but also the choir singers who once sang in the now-ruined monastery churches. The image of desolation is thus intensified. In the second quatrain, "black night," because of its association with sleep, is called "Death's second self"— a kind of twin or surrogate of Death "that seals up all in rest." In the third quatrain, the ashes of the fire become the deathbed on which the fire's personified youth is expiring, paradoxically "consumed" (in a third metaphor) by the food that once "nourished" it.

Against the three quatrains with their metaphorical statements of declining life and approaching death, the speaker opposes a concluding counterstatement concerning love. He throws human love, as it were, into the teeth of death. That the couplet is a counterstatement is metrically signaled by the inversion of stress in the opening foot. It begins, however, as a summarizing statement—"This thou perceivest"—where "This" refers for its antecedent to all of the images in the preceding quatrains (that is, to the grammatical objects of the verbs indicating *seeing* or *beholding*). The speaker then asserts his belief that the friend addressed throughout the sonnet loves the speaker all the more intensely because of the friend's realization that the speaker must soon die. The friend's increased love compensates for the speaker's impending death. Death's negative is countered by an affirmation of love.

Or so it would seem, on a first reading. On a second reading, we may be less sure of the strength of the affirmation. The speaker, we notice, is a person who needs to be loved. He does not conclude: "This thou perceivest, which makes my love more strong, / To love that well which I must leave ere long." That is, he is not primarily concerned with giving love but with receiving it. We may then ask what evidence he has for his final assertion and perhaps question whether he is asserting a belief, expressing a hope, or making a plea. We may also begin to wonder whether he is actually as old as the metaphors in the quatrains suggest, or whether he does not mix considerable overstatement with these metaphors, perhaps as a play for the beloved's sympathy. The poem, seemingly simple on the surface, becomes increasingly complex and ambiguous as we delve into it. Some readers will read it for moral profundity; others will find it more notable for psychological profundity. (The questions raised here are more likely to rise in the mind of a reader who has read more of Shakespeare's sonnets than in that of a beginning student who reads the sonnet out of context. Such a student, however, may be asked to recall Sonnet 138— "When my love swears that she is made of truth" [page 688], where the speaker, surely not far past thirty, also refers to himself as "old" and quite clearly feels insecure in his relationship with a younger beloved.)   LP

Dylan Thomas   Do Not Go Gentle into That Good Night (page 889)

In form this poem is a villanelle. Its nineteen lines utilize only two rhyme sounds (based on night and day); its alternating refrains rhyme *night* and *light*. Many villanelles are charming, graceful, light poems, characteristic of society verse. Thomas here gives the villanelle a force and intensity it had never had before—though many poets have tried to match it since. ("Do Not Go Gentle into That Good Night" is perhaps a turning point in the history of the villanelle.)

As shown by the concluding section, the poem is addressed to the poet's father. In some respects a fierce militant most of his life, the elder Thomas in his eighties went blind, became ill, and showed a tendency to turn soft and gentle. The son was dismayed by this change. He wanted his father to die as he had lived, to maintain his salty individuality to the last. Though the poet was something of a pantheist in his religious belief and felt that death was "good," he still considered it right and natural that men should resist death, put up a struggle against it, not die placidly. "[W]ise men . . . Good men . . . Wild men . . . Grave men," he tells his father in separate stanzas (punning on the word *grave*), have all for good reasons raged against their approaching deaths. In the last section (where his tenderness toward his father is manifest), he prays his father (paradoxically) to "curse" and "bless" him with his "fierce tears" and to "not go gentle into that good night." ("Good night" is both a metaphor for death and a pun for farewell.)   LP

EXERCISE (page 890)

1. Structure. First four lines in each stanza describe scenes; last four in each constitute a refrain, with two lines continuing the description by repetition, and the final two lines indented to emphasize the irony.
2. Structure. Three verse paragraphs devoted to the three parts of the argument.
3. Structure. Division into questions and answers, with climax in a separate line with italic font.
4. Structure. Two voices in a dialogue, one spoken (the employer) flush left, the other unspoken (the servant) indented.
5. Rhythm and structure. Phrases divided or jammed together for rhythmic effects and emphasis.

6. Arbitrary division into triplets (the first three consisting of a single sentence each, but thereafter no pattern).
7. Structure and meaning. First two quatrains set off by spacing, sestet breaks and indents in the middle of line 11 (rather than the expected space between 11 and 12) to emphasize the shift from description to analytical questions.
8. Structure. Each of three stanzas presents an action; indented lines plead the lover's case as a response to the actions of the beloved.
9. Structure. Cadenced phrases moving left to right, possibly in imitation of high-wire artists' short, hurried steps and pauses for balance on the wire.
10. Structure. Indented lines constitute refrains.

William Shakespeare   From *Romeo and Juliet* (page 891)

Since *Romeo and Juliet,* except for a few brief prose passages, is written throughout in iambic pentameter, and since much of it also rhymes (the lines rhyming sometimes alternately and sometimes in pairs), it is not surprising that 14 lines from a total of more than 3,000 should fall into the rhyme pattern of an English sonnet. That this excerpt does so from design, rather than from coincidence, however, can be definitively demonstrated.

1. The passage has four kinds of unity: grammatical, situational, metaphorical, and tonal. First, the passage begins at the beginning of a sentence and ends at the end of a sentence. It is grammatically self-contained. Second, the passage covers a self-contained episode or situation: it begins with the first words of Romeo and Juliet and ends with their first kiss. Third, the passage is unified by a single extended metaphor, one in which a pilgrim, or palmer, is worshiping at the shrine of a saint. Fourth, the religious nature of this metaphor—employing words like "profane," "holy," "shrine," "sin," "pilgrims," "devotion," "saints," "palmers," "prayer," and "faith"—combines with the delicious punning wit of the dialogue to give the passage unity of tone: a tone of earnest delicacy and delightfully charming gravity, which forces us to take seriously an episode we might otherwise take cynically. Romeo, we feel, is not simply a fresh young man on the make and Juliet an easy mark: this is genuine love at first sight. "[D]ear saint, let lips do what hands do" is tonally a great deal different from "Gimme a little kiss, won'cha?"

2. In structure as in form, the excerpt is organized into three quatrains and a final couplet. In the first quatrain Romeo, initiating the basic metaphor, apologizes for taking Juliet's "holy" hand in his unworthy one, but humbly offers to make up for the offense by giving the hand a gentle kiss. In the second quatrain Juliet reassures Romeo, telling him that he has done no wrong but has only shown mannerly devotion in taking her hand, for pilgrims quite properly touch saints' hands, and pilgrims "kiss" by clasping hands. She thus simultaneously encourages Romeo to hold her hand but with maidenly delicacy indicates that there is no need for him to kiss it. In the third quatrain, however, emboldened by this reassurance, Romeo decides to play the long shot and ask for a kiss on the lips. But he puts the request

delicately and charmingly. Do not pilgrims and saints have lips as well as hands? he asks. Translated, this means, why should we not kiss with our lips instead of merely with our hands? Juliet, still modest, yet keeping to the metaphor, replies that pilgrims' lips are for praying with. Then Romeo brilliantly seizes his opening: "let lips do what hands do." The line has two meanings. Hands not only kiss, they also pray. Lips not only pray, they also kiss. So Romeo, shaping his hands into the attitude of prayer, prays also with his lips; but what he prays for is a kiss. In the final couplet Juliet, not unwillingly defeated in this contest of wit (for what can a saint do when a faithful pilgrim prays to her?) gracefully surrenders: she grants the kiss, thus answering Romeo's prayer. The first quatrain is Romeo's apology; the second is Juliet's reassurance; the third is the plea; and the couplet is the plea granted. Structure follows form.

3. In Shakespeare's time the sonnet form was used primarily for the treatment of love. His play concerns a pair of "star-crossed lovers." The episode in the excerpt concerns their first meeting and their first kiss. What could be more appropriate than that Shakespeare should deliberately cast the episode into the form of an English sonnet?

This discussion is abridged from the essay "When Form and Content Kiss, / Intention Made the Bliss," in Laurence Perrine, *The Art of Total Relevance: Papers on Poetry* (Rowley, MA: Newbury, 1976) 75–77.   LP

John Donne   Death, be not proud (page 892)

This tightly constructed sonnet matches structure to form while producing some surprises for those acquainted with both the English and Italian sonnet forms. There are three quatrains and a couplet (as in the English sonnet), but the rhyming pattern is not *abab cdcd* etc., but *abba abba cddc aa*: the Italian quatrain is used in the English rhetorical structure, and the English closing couplet returns to the *a* rhyme, thus implying circularity.

These formal elements are in harmony with the structure of thought. The sonnet, an extended apostrophe, consists of these rhetorical units: an opening quatrain that makes an assertion (based on faith) denying that death is either mighty or dreadful; a second quatrain offering "proof" that death is not dreadful; a third offering "proof" that it is not mighty; and a couplet that returns to faith and faith alone as a support, and to the rhyming sound of the opening line. While the speaker attempts to use reason and logical proof to shore up his opening remark, he unwittingly reveals the weakness of his reasoning, the falseness of his premise, and the desperation that would lead a man to such an undertaking: he reveals a man stating a deep wish as if it were an easily demonstrable truth.

The opening quatrain, in a tone of forced bravado, uses only two techniques of argument, neither logically admissible: the simple insistence that what "some" have said is not true, and the condescending tone of "poor

death." If it is a *fact* that people overthrown by death "die not," then the final phrase of the quatrain is valid, for the syllogism is clear: death cannot kill
men; I am a man; therefore, death cannot kill me. What is not established
here, of course, is the universality of immortality, so the syllogism, though
valid, is based on an unproved major premise.

It is important to bring formal logic into the discussion of this poem, for
the patent illogicality of the speaker is what makes the poem so moving. In
his desperate need to reassure himself, the speaker is nevertheless the butt of
dramatic irony, an example of the futility of attempting to prove an article of
faith by means of reason—and so intensely in need of such proof that he argues fraudulently.

The second quatrain attempts to prove that death is not to be feared. But
the two "proofs" are fallacious: lines 5–6 argue by analogy (death is like sleep;
sleep gives pleasure; therefore death gives pleasure), while line 7 employs the
favorite device of advertisers, the "endorsement" of "our best men." The
third quatrain, intended to prove that death is not powerful, opens with two
illogical devices: name-calling ("slave," because death is caused by other
agents) and the aspersion of dwelling with evil neighbors. It returns to argument by analogy, insisting that drugs or spells induce a better sleep than
death does, and then closes with another belittling condescension.

The concluding couplet, in a tone of triumph, asserts that the case has
been proved and that eternal life is our universal destiny. It does so in paradox, the death of death, which requires the only possible resolution, the faith
of a believer in Christian salvation.

The key to further meaning in the poem may be found in the speaker's
apparent unawareness of what he is additionally revealing about himself and
his feelings about death. When in the second quatrain he attempts to disprove death's dreadfulness, he inadvertently uses death's might as his evidence: death is *more* powerful than "rest and sleep," and it has the power to
deliver the soul from the captivity of the body. When in the third he attempts to disprove death's power, he calls to witness its dreadfulness: in line
9, the frailty of human life makes us subject to a frightening array of powerful killers, and in line 10 the neighbors of death are a catalogue of dread. Perhaps even more telling is the speaker's ambiguity about "sleep," death's analogue. In the second quatrain, rest and sleep are the sources of "Much
pleasure," though not so much as death can give. Yet in the third, the sleep
induced by drugs or charms is "better" than the sleep of death—and in the
couplet, what is most desired is eternal wakefulness, not rest or sleep. The
great victory is that both sleep and death "shall be no more."

The speaker knows what he wants—the eternal bliss of salvation—but
he is vainly trying to prove through logical argument that he can receive it.
That attempt is doomed, as theologians and philosophers have long demonstrated, and the speaker's own desperation is vividly shown by his failure. Finally, he rests where he began—and where according to the scriptures he can
find his much-desired certitude. He accepts and triumphs in the paradoxes of

his faith, which defy logical or rational analysis, but which assure him that "the last enemy that shall be destroyed is death" (1 Cor. 15.26), that "death is swallowed up in victory" (1 Cor. 15.54), and that "death and hell [will be] cast into the lake of fire" (Rev. 20.14).   TRA

Claude McKay   The White City (page 893)

This sonnet is a strongly worded expression of the "hate" (3) of a black man for a large city, presumably New York, that is populated mostly by whites. (McKay was a black Jamaican who lived as an adult in New York City.) The first line insists that he will not compromise with the city's racist attitudes, but instead continues to bear his hatred "nobly" (4). Paradoxically, it is his hatred that enables his personal salvation as a human being, his ability to make "my heaven in the white world's hell" (7).

In the concluding lines, he evokes images of the city—the trains, towers, and wharves—and claims they are "sweet like wanton loves because I hate" (14). As he had expressed earlier in the poem, the city enables his "vital blood" (8) by inspiring his intense emotion.

An interesting feature of the poem is its form: a Shakespearean sonnet. The form is associated with love poetry, but here McKay has written an effective hate poem instead, implying an appropriation of the white culture's poetic form for his own uses.

One critic writes that the poem "emphasizes themes of isolation and independence, and reinforces a distinct separation between speaker and reader, between individual and group struggle": Heather Hathaway, *Caribbean Waves: Relocating Claude McKay and Paule Marshall* (Bloomington: Indiana UP, 1999) 44. Other discussions of the poet's racial themes may be found in Tyrone Tillery, *Claude McKay: A Black Poet's Struggle for Identity* (Amherst: U of Massachusetts P, 1992); and in Winston James, *A Fierce Hatred of Injustice: Claude McKay's Jamaica and His Poetry of Rebellion* (London and New York: Verso, 2000).   GJ

Adrienne Rich   Final Notations (page 893)

QUESTIONS

1. Who or what are the repeated "it" and "You" (9–12)? How is the "You" different in reference from "your" (2–3, 5–8, 13)? Explain the poem as a "Final Notation."
2. What is the effect of repetition in the poem? The concluding couplet contains three phrases repeated from the opening quatrain. How have the meanings of the phrases been enriched by the time of their final usage?
3. Explain the meaning and effect of the one phrase in the couplet that is not repeated.
4. What *formal* aspects of a sonnet does the poem display, and in what ways is the poem unlike a sonnet? What *structural* aspects of a sonnet do you detect?

Except for being written in free verse rather than iambics, this laconic poem is structured as a Shakespearean sonnet—three quatrains and a couplet—with the "turn" of a Petrarchan sonnet between lines 8 and 9. Its form is precisely that of a sonnet, in the first two quatrains describing death in the third person as "it," then turning in the third to direct address. The first two establish a relationship between "it" and the second person "your," while the third describes an even more intimate relationship between "you" (death) and "us," human beings.

The opening quatrain, echoed in the couplet, is full of abstractions—*time, thought, heart, breath* (the latter two metonymies rather than literal references to cardiac or pulmonary functions). The second quatrain is more explicitly physical—*ribs, heart, flesh*—and the reference to "thought" has more explicit meaning than in the first quatrain. The two similes in the third line develop the concept of occupation with two examples, both spatial and both emotionally evocative.

The turn accomplished by the third quatrain personifies death as "you" and develops the simile of death as occupying one's bed. The occupation is not only of a death-bed but also of a love-bed, comparing the act of dying to a sexual act (and perhaps recalling the Renaissance denotation of dying).

The couplet adds only one phrase to those quoted from the opening quatrain: "it will become your will." The phrase radiates meanings, from the future tense of "to be" to the willing of property to the willing of one's own extinction. Death will of necessity come to you, its inevitability will at some point detach you from all your worldly possessions, and as it gnaws away at ribs, heart, and flesh it will become what you most desire.

The theme of the poem is stated directly and repetitiously—dying will be a complex but brief experience. This is a "notation" that is most certainly "final" (title).   TRA

Martha Collins   The Story We Know (page 894)

The poem departs from the strictness of its chosen form by varying the two refrain lines, which should be identical in language (if not in syntactical function or meaning). Its maintenance of the proper rhyme scheme for a villanelle is emphasized by the high incidence of monosyllables as rhyme words, seeming to insist that we notice the perfect rhyming. That kind of self-consciousness about form and its fitness to subject (which is often the tone adopted in lighter verse) is parodied in line 2, which presents a bouncing iambic regularity in the monosyllables of an empty social encounter, mimicking the shallowness of the occasion in the monotony of rhythm. Line 2 is also one of only three perfectly iambic pentameter lines, and is the only one of them to punctuate pauses precisely between all of its feet, to reinforce its sense of empty repetition (the other two, lines 4 and 16, vary the rhythm to avoid such regularity).

The metrical norm in the poem, however, is anapestic pentameter, as determined by the relative frequency of the triple foot, and particularly by the meter of the two refrain lines:

The way | to be-gin | is al- | ways the same. | Hel-lo,   1

and Good-bye | at the end. | That's ev- | er-y sto- | ry we know,   3

This meter is well suited to such society verse as the villanelle, and Collins plays ironically with the expectations aroused by this traditionally light, polite form. In fact, part of the poem's force comes from setting up a shallow, blasé expectation in both reader and speaker, for if we are conditioned to the superficial pleasantries of social verse, so the speaker in her ennui seems to have conditioned herself to expect only superficiality in her relations with other people. She "knows" how all relations begin and end: a social "Hello," "and Good-bye at the end" (1, 3), a pattern of uninvolved pairing with all the expected accoutrements of love affairs without love—external things that take the place of feelings. It is, as she says, a boring sequence, "a story we know / so well we don't turn the page" (9–10). But on this occasion, something more meaningful takes place, not only a mutual dependency but a shared fear of death. The social routine of hello/goodbye comes to symbolize the physical reality of mortal life, "the way we all begin and end" signaled to the speaker by the "cold white sign" (18, 17) of snow obliterating both the air and the pine.

Blasé sophistication, so aptly captured in the form of light verse, turns out to have a darker implication, as the speaker learns that the pattern of her personal social life, full of empty beginnings and endings, is also the pattern of mortal existence.   TRA

Wendy Cope **Lonely Hearts** (page 895)

"Lonely" is of course the common thread linking the five separate personal ads. Each of the "writers" is "in search of something" (7) or rather someone who will match his or her personality and interests, but each of them has reached a point of desperation as indicated by placing a personal ad. All of them have a "simple wish" (1), to find someone to be with, whether sexually, merely for companionship, or for that submerged hope, that "it may lead" somewhere once it has begun. None of these five ad-writers would be a suitable match for any of the others, intensifying the sense of hopelessness that all this wishing implies.

The form of the villanelle is appropriate in two distinct ways: in its origins, implying a witty but trivial elegant social setting, it reinforces the superficiality of a two-line definition of oneself and one's hopes as well as the charm of the word-dance that the refrains create. Secondly, by the repeated refrains it links all of these desperate people into an equivalency that may even suggest that their desperation is a potentially universal condition: over and over, different types with different desires present themselves as needing help, in a list that seems as if it could go on and on, as the columns of the personal ads do.

The two refrains are in themselves interesting. The first understates its urgency by using the phrase "simple wish" to represent something much deeper. The second reveals a possible cause for these people's loneliness: they are restricting their hopes and their activities to a limited area, "North London." While that may be large enough to embrace the several types in the poem, it is still a restricted area. We may well wonder: don't people who live in North London get out much? Is each of them hemmed in not only by the narrow range of interests by which they define themselves, but also by the streets and neighborhoods that are familiar to them?   TRA

Thomas Hardy   The Ruined Maid (page 896)

In this satire on Victorian moral and sexual attitudes, two girls from the country meet in London. One, Amelia, has been "ruined" since coming to London to escape the drudgery, lassitude, and constriction of living on a farm, and now has the clothes and appearance of a "la-dy" (15). Her un-named friend, still coarse and ill-spoken, "a raw country girl," marvels at how Amelia has risen in the world, and wishes that she could wear such "feathers [and] a fine sweeping gown," but Amelia tells her that such elegance only comes with being ruined.

Obviously, the term "ruined" is misplaced, for Amelia has in any worldly sense been raised up, not thrown down, by her sexual experience. It is her friend who is still at the bottom of the social scale and who ironically envies the one whose disgrace has brought her so much. Hardy is satirizing several things here. A woman's reputation rests on how she is defined by others rather than by any absolute standard. Some use the term "ruined," yet her sit-uation is clearly above her friend's. When she repeatedly uses it to explain her social advancement, Amelia is herself using verbal irony. The situational irony is that the moral standard that condemns her bears little relevance to her actual existence.

But has she in some deeper sense lost her moral standing by becoming (presumably) a courtesan? The poem doesn't imply that. All she seems to have lost is the life of difficult toil and the depressing ignorance that her wide-eyed friend still shows. Her sophistication and vivacity make her supe-rior to her virginal friend.

The rhythm and meter of the poem are suited to light-hearted, comical verse. The meter is anapestic tetrameter, with the usual sprinkling of iambic substitutions. The rhythm is emphatically stressed, as the hyphenated words of the country girl clearly show by drawing out their final syllables as if they were in Gilbert's lyrics for Sullivan—they could as well be spelled "prosperitee," "companee," "ladee," "melancholee," an effect made even more audible by their rhyming with the refrain phrase "said she."   TRA

Robert Frost   Acquainted with the Night (page 897)

At a purely literal level this poem says merely that the poet has taken many walks at night through the city and is thoroughly familiar with its nighttime aspects. But clearly the poem is meant to be read symbolically. The chief symbol is the night, which suggests the darker aspects of existence. But to grasp anything like its full significance, we must examine the details of the poem. The following discussion does not pretend to exhaust their implications.

That the poet has walked out and back in rain indicates that he has endured physical discomfort. That he has walked beyond "the furthest city light"—beyond the city limits—may suggest that he has "transgressed"—gone beyond legal or moral limits. His having looked down "the saddest city lane" indicates that he has seen the poverty and misery of the city's slum areas. His unwillingness to explain to the watchman what he is doing out so late at night suggests feelings of guilt or embarrassment. The "interrupted cry" across houses from another street—possibly a scream of terror cut short by strangulation—suggests violence and evil. That the cry is not directed toward him suggests his loneliness. The illuminated clock, which seems detached from the earth and at "an unearthly height" (because its tower is blotted out by darkness), may at first seem like something supernatural, but is really only a man-made instrument able to "proclaim the time" but not to judge it. It thus suggests a universe without moral or divine oversight—a universe indifferent to man.

The night in Frost's poem is thus a remarkably subtle and evocative symbol for hardship, guilt, sorrow, loneliness, evil, desolation, and isolation at the personal, social, and cosmic levels. The clock against the sky, man-made but "at an unearthly height," strikingly proclaims the absence of authoritative moral direction, human or superhuman, in an indifferent universe.

And how does the poet respond to this dark perception of the universe? The calm, matter-of-fact tone of voice in the first and final lines counters the dark experience of the intervening lines with a quiet refusal to be daunted. The final line is indeed an understatement. The poet has been more than "acquainted" with the night—he has explored it thoroughly; but his tone of voice says, in effect, "I can take it."

Though the poem resembles a sonnet in containing fourteen lines of iambic pentameter, its rhyme scheme is that of *terza rima*, made famous by Dante's use of it in *The Divine Comedy*, of which the *Inferno* is the best-known section.

Some critics have read the "luminary clock" as a metaphor for the moon. But (a) one cannot easily tell time by the moon, as one can by the sun; it rises at a different hour every day and is often observable in full daylight; (b) this is a city poem and its imagery is city imagery; (c) if the clock *were* the moon, then the phrase "at an unearthly height" would be literal, obvious, and uninteresting; (d) Frost has himself identified the clock as a tower clock in Ann Arbor (see *Frost: Centennial Essays* [Jackson: UP of Mississippi, 1974] 521; and *Frost: Centennial Essays III* [1978] 296).

There are excellent discussions of this poem in Reginald L. Cook, *The Dimensions of Robert Frost* (New York: Rinehart, 1958) 107–108; and in Reuben A. Brower, *The Poetry of Robert Frost* (New York: Oxford UP, 1963) 126–29.   LP

Emily Dickinson   These are the days when Birds come back (page 898)

The time of year is "Indian summer," an unseasonably bright and warm spell of weather that may occur after autumn has begun. This phenomenon is particularly marked in Emily Dickinson's region, New England. (The adjective "Indian" is a racial slur derived from the stereotyped notion that American Indians were untrustworthy—as in "Indian giver.")

The poem begins by asserting what is not a fact in nature: migrating birds do not return to their northern summer haunts if the autumn weather turns briefly summerlike. It is important to see that the poem creates a division between what is true in nature and what the speaker sees, feels, and believes. One can account for the opening assertion in these terms: once autumn has set in, people tend to spend less time outdoors enjoying the weather, but do venture forth for the occasionally balmy day. At that time, they will notice birds—the nonmigratory birds, of course—and it will seem *to them* that there are more birds around. This mistaken assertion sets up the speaker as one who can be defrauded—or can defraud herself—by what nature presents, an important factor in interpreting stanzas 3–4.

The second stanza reports on the similarity between this moment in autumn and the weather in June, for in both the skies are brilliantly blue and the sun is golden. But it presents June as an example of "old, old sophistries," a phrase of negative reverberations: June has for ages and ages been cleverly deceitful, creating in us some sense of being cheated or lied to. Line 6 ambiguously calls both Indian summer and June a "mistake." In order to understand this, we must notice that the poem posits change and permanence as opposites, and that the speaker desires permanence and continuity. The "sophistries" of June are emotional: we enjoy that season so enormously that we are led by our desire into wishing that it will not pass. When it inevitably does, we feel cheated. And what affects us over the long period of summer is now concentrated into a few days of autumn's mistaken fine weather.

The first two stanzas establish the desire that nature's delights be never-ending. The second two stanzas evoke the intellectual, judging mind of the speaker: those feelings were fraudulent, there is no permanence as the falling leaf and "ranks of seeds [bear] witness" to the true time of year. The diction of stanza three represents the power of the mature rational faculty in Latinate sophistication: "Almost thy plausibility / Induces my belief" (8–9). The wisdom of Solomon may be demonstrated with simple natural devices, but its dicta are not simple and childlike.

Still, the speaker wishes that she did not know what she knows. The concluding two stanzas turn away from what the rational faculty has so clearly discerned in order to voice a yearning for the impossible. In ritualistic apostrophe, she prays to be allowed to share with nature this "sacrament of summer days" and like a child to be taken into full communion in this requiem of the year. The symbols of Christian communion and the promise of eternal life express her profound wish for what is unchanging and immortal. But beyond that desire stands the fact: as stanzas 3–4 have so clearly shown, she is not "a child," nor can she be sustained by self-deception. Despite all the appeal of an immortality analogous to the cycle of seasons, that cycle of change is the reality. To share in the resurrection that nature has is not to become immortal but to succumb to death and be replaced by other mortals. Such is the testament of seeds and leaves.

The form of this poem is most obviously established by the three two-stanza units that comprise it. That the rhyme scheme of the first two stanzas does not precisely match that of the remainder, and that approximate rhymes are characteristic of these first stanzas, supports the sense that the speaker is striving to find the explanation for her feelings. Once the form is established in stanzas 3–4, the stanzas in which rationality predominates, that form continues into the last stanzas (the *join–wine* rhyme would have been less approximate in Dickinson's time and place). The structure of the poem follows this division into three two-stanza units, as it presents the speaker's emotional response to the weather (1–2), her rational judgment of reality (3–4), and her wish that she could transcend the reality (5–6). The form and structure are also attuned in the use of refrains in the two outer pairs of stanzas, "These are the days when" (1, 4) and the ecstatic yearning of "Oh . . . Oh" (13–14) and "Thy . . . Thy" (16–17).   TRA

Maxine Kumin Woodchucks (page 899)

The speaker of this poem is a farmer whose crops have been attacked by woodchucks, requiring her to seek desperate measures to get rid of them. (The poet lives on a farm in New Hampshire and often writes about the satisfactions and travails of farm life.)

Yet the woodchucks are hardy creatures, and have burrowed deeply enough in the ground to avoid her attempt to gas them to death; they have also proved immune to cyanide poisoning. Finally the speaker decides she must shoot the creatures with a .22 rifle.

Throughout the poem, however, there are suggestions that the speaker feels guilty over her attempts to kill these natural creatures, who after all are simply foraging for food. In the first stanza, for example, she uses the punning phrase "the case we had against them was airtight" (4), suggesting that the jury may still be out. In the third stanza, she describes herself as "righteously thrilling / to the feel of the .22" (13–14), claiming that the woodchucks are taking the food from her mouth and those of the members of her family. Yet the phrase "righteously thrilling," like her description of herself as "puffed with Darwinian pieties for killing" (16), suggests the morally dubious posture of one who must convince herself, and not wholly successfully, that she is doing the right thing.

A tone of guilt enters the poem and deepens as it proceeds. The first animal she kills is the "littlest" (17) woodchuck, evoking the image of an adult woman firing on a tiny, helpless creature. A similar emotion is evoked when the next woodchuck she kills is the baby's mother. By humanizing the woodchucks in this way, the speaker intensifies the portrait of herself as an unjust killer rather than a pragmatic farmer.

By the penultimate stanza, the speaker refers to herself as a "murderer" (23), and her guilt is further suggested by the fact that she dreams of killing the last woodchuck, an "Old wily fellow" (25) that has so far eluded her. Clearly, she is bedeviled by her own conscience. By the last couple of lines, her guilt is so intense that she compares herself to a Nazi: "If only they'd all consented to die unseen / gassed underground the quiet Nazi way" (29–30). In other words, if her initial attempt to gas the woodchucks had worked, she would not have had to confront them face to face and feel the guilt that arises when she shoots them.

The poem is rendered in carefully patterned stanzas, six-line units with the rhyme scheme *abcacb*. This pattern lends the poem its qualities of thoughtfulness and technical control, appropriate to a poem that takes a complex attitude toward the killing of animals.

Wesley McNair writes of this poem: "Kumin shows us how dark the narrator's obsession really is and how far from the hermit's ideal of coexistence the speaker has taken us" ("Kumin's Animal Confederates," in Emily Grosholz, ed., *Telling the Barn Swallow: Poets on the Poetry of Maxine Kumin* [Hanover, NH: UP of New England, 1997] 124).   GJ

Robert Herrick   Delight in Disorder (page 900)

"Wantonness" (2) may be defined in this context in two ways: playfulness and extravagance. It should not be construed as lewdness or cruelty, two potential denotations that the context denies because the speaker is praising the kind of dress that attracts and delights, not that seduces and betrays.

The structure of this little poem follows that of much Petrarchan verse in praise of a beloved woman as the eye of the beholder moves from top to toe. After the introductory statement of the subject, the poem moves from shoulders to waist to wrists to skirt to feet—but it is wittily contrasted to the Petrarchan norm, which focuses on the physical attributes of the woman herself, while Herrick's poem looks only at the apparel. Where we expect such a poem to travel from hair to eyes to lips and then downward to breast, and so forth, this one moves from scarf to "stomacher" to "cuff . . . petticoat . . . shoestring." Shakespeare makes a joke about such poems in *As You Like It* when Jaques ridicules the lover who writes "A woeful ballad / Made to his mistress' eyebrow" (2.7.147–48). How much more ludicrous to write about her "shoestring"! (Shakespeare's playful irony about such poetry can also be found in "My mistress' eyes," page 809).

Herrick's point is clear enough: too much precision, too much artfulness in dressing is less attractive than a few touches of carelessness in appearance. They make the woman seem less calculating, even less "wanton" in the other senses of the word. She's human, subject to error, perhaps more delightfully vulnerable; perfection may be very cold. Ironically, of course, his description is precise in its rhythms and rhymes: iambic tetrameter couplets (tetrameter calling more attention to its rhyming than the longer pentameter line), and in this case all the couplets are closed with punctuation. The trochaic substitutions at the beginnings of lines 2, 4, 8 are the only metrical substitutions, and coming where they are in those lines have a much slighter effect than if they were placed later in the lines. He advocates a certain careless insouciance, but writes carefully about it.

But don't miss one further irony: the "sweet disorder" (1) that he advocates is itself carefully contrived to give the impression of carelessness.   TRA

Michael McFee   In Medias Res (page 901)

A playful lament on the physical aging of the male body, "In Medias Res" features a pattern of lineation that graphically represents its meaning.

Like an extended belly, the increasingly longer lines describe a speaker whose thickening waist creates comical inconveniences; the humorous tone is enhanced through the use of such puns as "breathtaking" and "cinch." Pants the speaker wore to his wedding now seem breathtakingly small; they would also take his breath away literally if he tried now to squeeze into them. A belt that was once "a cinch" to fasten now represents a struggle as he tries to cinch his increasing girth. Similarly, the title has a double reference in that the speaker is literally "in the middle of things"—that is, his life—and his prominent waist is at the midpoint of his body.

For all its wry surface humor, however, the poem does have a serious undertone in discussing advancing age in the context of mortality and natural processes. He compares his body to a house loosening from its foundation; his list of startlingly disparate items subject to decay—"loose-filled graves and families / and stars"—emphasizes the ruthless and universal effects of time's power. The metaphor "entropy's dike" implies that human efforts to stay the forces of natural change are temporary and ultimately futile.

The poem closes by returning to the speaker's main concern: his own aging process. He acknowledges his decline in sexual attractiveness and potency in a reference to his "zipper's sneer," and closes by portraying his enlarged belly as an animal: "hibernation- / soft, ready for / the kill." But instead of a virile young hunter prepared to pit himself against nature, the overweight speaker anticipates his own future health problems and views himself as the ultimate "kill." Though describing a man "in medias res," the poem ultimately contemplates last things.   GJ

Chapter Fifteen

Evaluating Poetry I

Sentimental, Rhetorical, Didactic Verse

Anonymous   God's Will for You and Me (page 906)

Gerard Manley Hopkins   Pied Beauty (page 907)

The poetic deficiencies of "God's Will for You and Me" are not far to seek. Its literal language is trite ("when things go wrong," "God knows best"). Its figurative language is trite ("willing feet," "our daily key"). Its remaining imagery is feeble ("child," "song," "dark or bright"). Eight of the poem's fourteen lines repeat the phrase "Just to" ten times, followed by "be." These three words constitute almost 40 percent of the poem. The rest is mostly a string of abstract adjectives—"tender," "true," "glad," "merciful," "mild," "trustful," "gentle," "kind," "sweet," "helpful," "cheery," "loyal"—strung together in no particular order and often duplicative or overlapping in meaning (*kind–helpful, glad–cheery, gentle–tender–mild*). Worst of all, the poem's tripping triple meter and childish repetition of "Just to be" make God's will for you and me seem simple, undemanding, and easy to carry out. In truth, no man could do it successfully for one whole day. The poem not only fails to create experience; it falsifies it.

Though both poems concern God, their themes are quite different. "God's Will for You and Me" is didactic verse instructing us how God wishes us to live our lives; "Pied Beauty" is, first, a hymn of praise to God for the variegated, changing beauty of the natural and human worlds and, second, a contrast between this variegated, changing beauty of the created world and the uniform, unchanging beauty of the Creator. (This theme has its biblical base in James 1.17: "Every good gift and every perfect gift is from above, and cometh down from the Father of lights, with whom is no variableness, neither shadow of turning.")

The first theme is stated in the title and first line of the poem and is developed and exemplified in the next eight. "Glory be to God," the poet exclaims, for the beauty of things that are pied, dappled, couple-colored, brinded, stippled, plotted and pieced, fickle, or freckled. With one exception these terms all apply to things that are of more than one color. The exception, "fickle," referring to variation in time rather than space, ties in with "swift, slow" and reminds us that this varying beauty is in constant motion and is constantly changing. The white clouds move and change in shape across a brightening or darkening blue sky; the decoratively rose-mole-stippled trout swim in a changing current. In line 5, which introduces human activities into the poem, farmers alter the landscape by laying it out in plots of grazing, fallow, and plowed land.

The concluding two lines of the poem summarize the first theme and introduce the second. The praise for this diverse, changing beauty is due to a Creator whose beauty is "past [beyond] change." The poem thus brings into contrast multiplicity and unity, constant change and changelessness, plenitude and amplitude, with the implication that the latter are greater. If the wonders of the created world (a world that varies "who knows how?") pass understanding, how much more so must the beauty of their Creator!

The achievement of the poem lies, first, in its packed, vivid imagery. Line 4, for instance, in six words introduces three separate vivid images (two literal, one figurative). There are "finches' wings" (black and gold) and "chestnut-falls" (fallen chestnuts beneath a tree, glowing in mahogany browns), these latter compared by a compound adjective to fresh firecoals glowing golden and umber in a grate. Though the imagery of the poem is chiefly visual, the opposition of "sweet, sour" reminds us that the world is variegated in its appeal to the other senses as well. Second, the poem is remarkable for its rich use of sound: patterned end rhyme; paired alliterations linking words parallel or opposed in meaning (*swift, slow; sweet, sour; adazzle, dim*), or simply the complex orchestration of such a line as 4 (with the alliteration of *Fresh–fire–fall–finches*; the assonance of *fresh–chestnut* and *finches' wings*; the *l* consonance of *coal–falls*). Third, the poem is remarkable for its concentration. In line 4 every word is image-bearing; in line 9 all words but the initial "With" carry a full freight of meaning (contrast such lines with the slackness of "Just to be tender, just to be true"). Finally, "Pied Beauty" is notable for its freshness of diction. The four adjectives in line 7 are all apposite yet unexpected; the adjectives in "God's Will for You and Me" are as predictable as those in the Boy Scout oath.   LP

William Blake   A Poison Tree (page 907)

Granfield Kleiser   The Most Vital Thing in Life (page 908)

One might almost judge these poems from their titles alone. The first title presents an image; the second is an abstract phrase, more suitable for an essay or sermon than for a poem.

The second poem is abstract from beginning to end. It has no dramatic situation. The poet addresses the reader directly. His message—that the most vital thing in life is to control one's feelings—is stated baldly and re-peated over and over. The reader is told to "curb resentment," to "maintain a mental peace," to "learn to keep strict silence," to "keep [his] mental bal-ance." The tone is preachy and didactic. There is no development: the good advice simply comes out in a string of platitudes. The poem is without im-agery. Its one metaphor is the utterly trite one of a "battle" (13). The poet mixes formal diction ("defrauded") and colloquial diction ("peeved") with-out purpose and without any sense of impropriety. His meter (iambic-anapestic trimeter, with feminine endings in the odd-numbered lines) is much too swift and bouncy for so serious a theme. A number of words seem included simply to sustain the meter: "quite" (4), "mental" (6), "All" and "simply" (8), "Be assured" (23). This is didactic verse, not poetry; it conveys advice, not experience.

"A Poison Tree" also has a message, but it is conveyed through a parable or extended metaphor rather than explicitly stated. The poem has a begin-ning, a middle, and an end, and could not be rearranged in its presentation, as could "The Most Vital Thing in Life."

The speaker (who is not the poet) sets up the basic contrast and theme of the poem in the first stanza. To tell one's wrath is to end it. To conceal one's wrath is to cause it to grow and become destructive. The speaker pre-sents two episodes from his life: one in which he was open and candid about his feelings, the other in which he suppressed his feelings. The first episode is presented briefly, for it ended quickly. The second occupies the rest of the poem, for it is of slow development. It is related in a sustained metaphor, which begins in the last phrase of the first stanza. The speaker has buried his wrath like a seed, and like a seed it begins to "grow." In the second stanza the speaker nurses his anger. He waters it with fears of his foe and with tears of rage and frustration. He suns it with hypocritical, deceiving smiles. The seed has sprouted. In the third stanza the seed-become-tree bears an apple, poiso-nous because it is the fruit of wrath, but bright and shiny on the outside be-cause the wrath has been concealed. The speaker's "foe" sees and covets it, and in the final stanza steals and eats it. The speaker finds his foe dead be-neath the tree, and is "glad." Thus the consequences of concealed wrath are shown to be horrifyingly destructive, for they include not only the death of the "foe" but the moral perversion of the speaker. The most chilling aspect of the conclusion is released by the word "glad." It touches emotional centers never approached in "The Most Vital Thing in Life." The speaker has de-stroyed not only his "foe" but himself. (It is here we see that the speaker is not the poet. Where the speaker is "glad" for the death of his foe, the poet is appalled, and makes us feel appalled. Dramatic irony is at work.)

Note the simplicity and economy with which this tale is told. The seed–sprout–sapling–tree development does not need stating; it is implied in the verbs of the poem. The facts that the apple is poison (stanza 3) and that the foe has been killed by eating it (stanza 4) also need no statement; they are implied by the title and the sequence of events.

Blake's message has been embodied in a simple but powerful and moving poem; Kleiser's message remains a versified message.

And what about the messages themselves? Blake's poem advocates expressing one's wrath. Kleiser's recommends suppressing it. Which advice is more valid? One may wish to hedge a little here and to suggest that it depends on circumstances (the occasion for the anger, its intensity, and one's relationship to the person causing it). One can agree with Kleiser that it is unwise to express irritation over every petty annoyance or to tell strangers exactly what one thinks of them. But Blake is talking about "wrath" and about wrath felt toward persons with whom one is in daily association. Kleiser's maxims are tepid, conventional, and often questionable. (Is controlling one's temper really "the most vital thing in life"? More important than love? More important than standing up for justice? Is it really true that "to win a worthwhile battle / Over selfishness and spite, / You must learn to keep strict silence / Though you know you're in the right"?) Blake's advice is bold and unconventional and in fact anticipates by over a century some of the insights of Sigmund Freud. In short, Blake's poem presents a poet who is both feeling and thinking deeply; Kleiser's presents a poet who is doing neither.

A further question remains about the interpretation of Blake's poem. Does the speaker *plan* the death of his "foe," or is he merely pleased when it occurs? Is this poem about revenge? The answer, certainly, is that the speaker does not plan the death from the beginning. The central issue of the poem is not between forgiveness and revenge but between the expression and concealment of anger. Suppressed anger, the poet believes, festers and turns poisonous. At some point it turns into hate and the hate *possibly* into planned revenge. The question cannot be answered with certainty and is ultimately unimportant. The speaker's gladness at his foe's death fully reveals his moral perversion whether the death has been plotted or not. A good case can be made, indeed, for the contention that the speaker's "foe" is his foe *because* the speaker conceals his anger from him, rather than vice versa. If "friend" and "foe" were interchanged in the first stanza, would not the "foe" become a friend and the "friend" turn into a foe?   LP

Robert Francis   **Pitcher** (page 908)

George E. Phair   **The Old-Fashioned Pitcher** (page 909)

The first poem celebrates pitching as an art, the second as a feat of endurance. This is their difference of intention at the literal level, but the second poem has only a literal level.

"The Old-Fashioned Pitcher" is a familiar exercise in sentimental nostalgia for "the good old days." Its one cleverness lies in its imitation of a more famous poem of the same sort, "The Bucket" by Samuel Woodworth (1785–1842).

Woodworth's first stanza begins "how dear to my heart are the scenes of my childhood" and ends by referring to "The old oaken bucket, the iron-bound bucket, / The moss-covered bucket which hung in the well." Comparison of their stanzaic pattern, and of their opening and concluding lines, shows that Phair's poem is a conscious allusion to Woodworth's. Aside from this element of parody, "The Old-Fashioned Pitcher" has little to recommend it. The adjective "old" before "village green" (2) is an obvious sentimentalism designed to elicit a stock response of warm affection for former times. The phrase "ducks from the scene" (4) is trite and slangy. Line 7 is a blatant example of "padding" (the use of unnecessary words to fill out the metrical requirements of the line): "that is the reason" could be reduced to "that's why" or "therefore"; "hanker and long for" uses two verbs where one would suffice. The nouns "hurler" and "twirler" are used so often in sports pages simply as variations for "pitcher" that it is difficult to know whether the poet here intended to differentiate them. They can be differentiated, of course. A "hurler" relies upon strength and speed simply to "fire" the ball past the batter. A "twirler" puts a spin or twist on the ball, causing it to curve or break in a manner deceptive to the batter. The former relies upon strength, the latter on skill. Since throwing curve balls puts a greater strain on the muscles than throwing fast balls, the "twirler" suffers more often from a sore arm than the "hurler." Does the poet recognize this distinction? Does he mean to confess "I prefer strength to skill—Goliath to David"? Or is he not rather saying simply that "men aren't what they used to be"? Evidence favors the latter surmise. If the old-fashioned pitcher was "iron-armed," what need had he to be "stout-hearted"? It seems unlikely that this poet was thinking about such distinctions. Sentimental gush and critical thought are seldom bedfellows.

"Pitcher" celebrates the skill and subtlety of the good pitcher. His "art" is to be off-center. His "aim is / How not to hit the mark he seems to aim at"— the batter's bat, or the dead center of the strike zone (directly over the center of the plate and halfway between the batter's knees and shoulders). (Notice how the two "aim's" vary slightly in meaning.) He must "avoid the obvious"— the pitch that goes exactly where it seems to be going—but he must "vary the avoidance" lest the batter learn what to expect. The other players on the team—infielders and outfielders—throw to be understood (the shortstop throwing to first base does not want to fool the first baseman); but the pitcher throws "to be a moment misunderstood" by the batter (so that the batter will swing too low or too high, or too soon or too late, hitting an easy pop-fly or an easy grounder or missing the ball altogether). Yet "not too much. Not errant, arrant, wild"—the three adjectives are not redundant (like "hanker and long for") but are skillful variations of meaning; no good pitch is "errant" (wandering or deviating from his intention), "arrant" (flagrantly and shamelessly wide of the mark), or "wild" (out of control). The pitcher does not want to walk the batter, cause his catcher to drop his pitch, or throw so wide of the plate that the catcher can't reach it (allowing baserunners, if any, to advance). Rather "every seeming aberration" is "willed" (intended, under perfect control). He wants "Not to . . . communicate" (not to hit the batter's bat squarely) yet (here is the paradox) he *wants* "to communicate": he wishes the batter to understand his intention but "too late" to make a base hit.

The poet exemplifies in his own verse the subtle skill he celebrates. He varies "the avoidance" of the obvious, not only in his choice of words ("errant, arrant, wild") but in the very form of his poem. It consists of five pentameter couplets, each different in its "rhyming." The first pairs "aim" with "aim at." The second couples two three-syllable words with only the hissing of a final sibilant to connect them in sound. The third pairs two four-syllable participles ending in *-d,* but throws things off a bit by shoving the subject of the second of the two parallel sentences up to the end of the first line. The fourth pairs "willed" and "wild" (alliteration and consonance). The fifth has perfect rhyme.

So—at the literal level alone—the first poem is clearly superior. But obviously (however, in this context, it won't be obvious at all to many students) the first poem is symbolical. The poet is speaking not only about pitcher and batter but about poet and reader. (The clues are words like "art," "passion" "technique," "comprehended," "communicate," and "understand"—words more often found in discussions of poetry than of baseball.) The poet wants to be understood by his reader—but not too easily. If he is too obvious (literal, or trite), the reader will find his work dull and uninteresting; if he is not, sometimes, "a moment misunderstood," the reader will not return for a second reading. The poet, after all, is not writing directions for how to assemble a piece of furniture. He wants to communicate with the whole reader. To do this he must throw a few sliders and curve balls—must use figurative language (like paradox and symbol) and other devices of indirection. As Emerson says of the poet, he "must mount to paradise / By the stairway of surprise."   LP

Malcolm Cowley   The Long Voyage (page 909)

Sir Walter Scott   Breathes there the man (page 910)

"The Long Voyage" arises from a specific situation. The poet, or speaker, is on a ship rapidly taking him away from his native country. As is natural in such a situation, a powerful feeling of nostalgia, even of homesickness, arises in him for the land he loves and is leaving. The emotion is convincing, first, because it is expressed through images, concretely—hills, trees, birds, seasons—not abstractly; second, because it is uttered in a quiet voice—the poet does not rant about the emptiness in his heart, the tears in his eyes, the anguish in his soul; third, because he doesn't make exaggerated claims about his country, which he says is like "almost . . . any country": its pines are no darker, its dogwood no brighter, its birds no swifter. Nevertheless, this is *his* country, and that makes the difference. He knows "its face, its speech." The very water folding back against the prow reminds him of his country's earth breaking against the plow—an excellent simile—and the foam on the water reminds him of his country's dogwood. The emotion is not strained or exaggerated; the poem expresses a universal feeling arising from a specific situation.

"Breathes there the man" does not arise from a specific situation. It talks about no specific man. The poet is expressing not his own feeling for his country but scorn for some other (hypothetical) man who has no such feeling. There are no images in the poem—no sharply defined pictures, sounds, or smells. The language is abstract. It is spoken not quietly but shrilly, at the top of the poet's voice. The tone is oratorical, as established by the diction and the construction of the sentences ("Breathes there the man," "go, mark him well," "High though his titles," "foreign strand" [for "shores"], "power, and pelf" [for "money"], "fair renown," and so forth). The poet climbs up the ladder of his own eloquence till he calls his hypothetical victim a "wretch, concentered all in self" who "doubly dying, shall go down" to "vile dust." The poet has lashed himself into a frenzy of virtuous indignation, and the sentiment is strained and exaggerated. Surely, if a person lacks a love of country, it is more his misfortune than his crime; he deserves compassion, not consignment to the "vile dust." Love cannot be compelled. Moreover, such a person is not necessarily a "wretch, concentered all in self." Surely men who have voluntarily left the country of their birth and found other places to live that they liked better—whose hearts have not "burned" when they returned to the original country—have lived decent lives, loved their families, been kind to babies, enjoyed life, and been mourned by friends when they died. The poet has exaggerated and oversimplified the facts of life, has whipped himself up by means of words to an artificial state of feeling. The emotion does not well up naturally. The poem rings resoundingly, but it also rings hollowly, like a drum.

Sir Walter Scott was a good man who wrote good novels and some good poetry, but this poem is "rhetorical." It is taken from the opening of Canto 6 of *The Lay of the Last Minstrel,* which is sung by the ancient minstrel who tells the story. In context it has a certain dramatic propriety, but it is not clearly distinguished from an utterance that might not be Scott's own—that is, there is no detectable dramatic irony. It is, of course, usually reprinted out of context as a patriotic set piece.   LP

Ella Wheeler Wilcox   **The Engine** (page 910)

Emily Dickinson   **I like to see it lap the Miles** (page 911)

As the simile in line 13 of "The Engine" reveals, this poem elaborates on the cliché "iron horse" as a metaphor for a railroad engine. The true subject of the poem is identified in the title, so that its elaboration resolves no mystery. However, it does present real difficulties because the characterization of a horse is intermittent and wavering, and other comparisons intervene to blur its focus. For example, "panting breath" *might* characterize a galloping horse, but "startled scream" (2) is distinctly out of character. "Swift as a bird" is an overstatement, and "Darts" seems inappropriate for an engine speeding along its tracks.

The first stanza tries to find figurative terms for literal facts about the engine and winds up mixing and distorting its figures. The chugging sound is compared to someone (or some animal) panting in exhaustion—but *do* engines seem exhausted? The whistle is personified as a "startled scream"—but a train whistle is not an instinctive and unexpected reaction; it is planned and purposeful. The "sudden flight" of a bird as it "Darts" is not an apt comparison for a train smoothly rolling along its tracks.

Such inappropriateness continues throughout the poem. The "[a]wful dangers" represented by "[r]ocks and chasms" (5–6) past which it steams pose no threat to the engine on its tracks. Trains moving between "[r]ocks and chasms" do not move in a "straight" line but must curve as they follow the bend of the road carved out of such a landscape. It isn't possible to discern which actual aspects of a steam engine are supposed to be represented by the personification of lines 9–10—what "[t]errible thoughts"? what "fierce desires"? in what sense is the heart of the engine "mad"?

These weaknesses of figurative language and distortions of the actuality of a steam engine (along with trite phrases like "deep, dark night," "panting breath," "swift as a bird," "sudden flight," and predictably exact rhyme) mark this as an inferior poem.

By comparison, and in its own right, Dickinson's presentation of the "iron horse" is vivid, exciting, and exact, and displays a marvelous control of the relationship of sound to meaning, showing how poetic genius can take a commonplace or trite figure and make it new. Once again, the basic metaphor of the poem compares a train to a horse, though neither train nor horse is named in the poem. The subject is a train because it laps up miles and valleys, feeds itself (takes water) at tanks, peers (with its headlight) into shanties by the sides of roads, hoots (with its whistle), is punctual, and stops "docile and omnipotent" (obedient to the engineer but tremendously powerful) at its "stable" (station or roundhouse). It is a horse because it laps, licks, feeds, steps, peers, has ribs, crawls, complains, chases itself, neighs, and stops at a stable. It is a whole train rather than just a locomotive because it "chase[s] itself down Hill."

The most unusual technical feature of the poem is that both of the first two stanzas ends with a run-on line. These run-on lines give the poem, or the train, a continuous forward motion (there are no full stops until the end of the poem), a forward motion that finally grinds to an abrupt halt on the word "Stop" (line 16). The stop—it must be a strong one to stop a train—is made strong in a number of ways: first, the word *stop* itself stops suddenly, ending with an explosive consonant; second, though in a normally unstressed position, the

word receives a strong metrical stress (with the partial exception of the preceding line, which slows the train down, this is the only line in the poem
stressed on the initial syllable); third, it is followed and preceded by grammatical pauses; fourth, it is followed and preceded (on the other side of the grammatical pauses) by stressed syllables, with one of which it has assonance and
with the other of which it alliterates. All these features emphasize or isolate the
word *stop* in a remarkable way. The phrase that follows—"docile and omnipotent"—is a beautiful expression of power at rest.

     But before the train comes to a stop, it makes a variety of motions and
sounds. In the first two lines the regular meter and the predominance of *l*s
give the train speed, while at the same time the monosyllabic words ending
in *p* or *k*, found throughout the first stanza, give it the clippety-cloppety-
clackety sound of iron wheels going over joints in the rails. In line 4 the big
word *prodigious* slows the line down as the train slows down to "step" around
a curve—an effect that is repeated in line 6. The division of what would normally be line 9 into two lines again slows the train down, this time to a crawl,
as it goes through a tunnel, tooting its whistle each inch of the way. The
three trochaic words in succession—*horrid—hooting stanza*—convey the regularity and repetition of the whistle's sound, intensified by the narrow walls
of the tunnel. The onomatopoetic word *hooting* sounds like *tooting* but alliterates with *horrid*, thus emphasizing the repetitiveness of the sound while
also retaining the metaphoric sense that this is a creature rather than a
machine.

     This brief analysis by no means exhausts the adaptation of sound to sense
in this poem, but it perhaps indicates the chief features.   TRA, LP

Coventry Patmore   **The Toys** (page 911)

Eugene Field   **Little Boy Blue** (page 912)

     "Little Boy Blue" is an appealing poem. Its melody is pleasing, and so are
its rhymes. The word order is natural and unforced, and so are the words
themselves. The poem makes effective use of alliteration and other musical
devices. The picture it presents of the loyal toy soldier and dog awaiting the
return of their Little Boy Blue is touching. The poem is skillfully done, and
it has been much beloved by the American public. It is nevertheless a sentimental poem, manipulating its materials to draw tears from the reader, subtly falsifying life by dimming the darker colors and brightening up the
warmer ones. It aims at being sweetly sad.

     Its title is sweet. The boy who dies is not Bobby, or Peter, or Donald; he
is "Little Boy Blue"—the name has nursery rhyme associations. And he has
not only a sweet name but a sweet disposition. He played nicely with his toys
on the evening of the night he died (though he must have been sick, and most
children are short-tempered and hard to manage when sick), and then he

toddled sweetly off to bed at the appointed time, without a single protest, quite contrary to ordinary boy-nature. If Boy Blue ever had fits of ill temper or disobedience, they are not mentioned; only his pretty actions, such as kissing his toys, are mentioned. In describing Boy Blue and his possessions, the poet uses the adjective "little" eleven times in twenty-four lines. Not only is Boy Blue "little," his hands are "little," his face is "little," his chair is "little," his toys are "little." Most of these *littles* are quite superfluous; the word is being used only to manipulate the reader's sympathies, to evoke a stock response. Also, instead of telling us that Little Boy Blue *died*, the poet says that he was "Awakened" by "an angel song" (14, 13). It is a sweet way of describing death; the uglier features are avoided, and death becomes a gentle and sweetly sad experience, like a song. (Some students will have difficulty with the "angel song" metaphor and think that Little Boy Blue grew up—apparently rather suddenly—leaving his childish toys behind.) This death occurred many years ago, but the little toys are still true.

But now, three questions. First, how does the poet know that Little Boy Blue "dreamt of the pretty toys" if he died in his sleep? Second, in what sense are the toys "True"? Do they really wonder what has happened to Little Boy Blue "Since he kissed them and put them there"? Or is this not an example of what Ruskin called "the pathetic fallacy"—the fallacy of attributing human emotions to inanimate objects? That is, has not the author sentimentalized not only the little boy but even also his toys? And third, why, after all these years, are the toys still where Little Boy Blue left them? (Here is a question that the poet did not intend us to ask. If the toys are still in the chair where Boy Blue left them, his parents must have closed up his room when he died and resolved to leave everything just as he left it. People occasionally do such things, to be sure, but only very rarely; and we usually feel that such a reaction to death is excessively sentimental or even morbid, not healthy. Quite understandably, the poet glosses over this aspect of the situation and concentrates our attention instead on the supposed fidelity of the toy dog and the toy soldier, as though this quality was what really kept them there.) In short, the author is not treating death seriously; instead he is playing with us and with our emotions.

"The Toys," at first view, may seem a slightly crude poem beside "Little Boy Blue." The meter is not so lilting, the rhyme is not so regular, there is no stanza pattern, and even the syntax may at times seem slightly strained.* But the meter is such as to keep our attention focused constantly on the content; it does not set up a separate tune or by a pretty lilt soften and sweeten a pathetic subject matter. Moreover, the treatment of the subject matter is honest. Having once described his son as "little," the poet drops the adjective and does not use it as a spurious means of attaching sympathy to his subject.

---

*Actually the syntax in lines 3–6 is skillfully arranged so that "dismissed" may take either "him" or "His Mother" as its object, both meanings being appropriate. By one construction "His Mother" is the subject of an absolute phrase; by the other it is the object of the verb.

He does not idealize the behavior of little boys. Though his son is grave, quiet, and thoughtful, he is also, like most boys, sometimes willful and disobedient. The father's behavior, as contrasted with that of the parents of Little Boy Blue, is normally human. He loses his temper, strikes the boy and scolds him, then later feels remorse and worries about what he has done. But the boy, though he has been sobbing, is not so grief-stricken that he cannot sleep, as a sentimentalist might have made him. He is deep in slumber, and beside his bed, to console himself, he has arranged his treasured collection of toys. These toys are enumerated and described: they include "a red-veined stone," "A piece of glass abraded by the beach," and "two French copper coins." The imagery is fresh and precise. We are not told, moreover, that the boy kissed these toys before going to sleep, or that he is dreaming of them, or that they, on their part, are faithfully waiting for him to wake up. The incident is moving because it has been honestly treated. Moreover, the poet has effectively used the incident to communicate, by analogy, a larger truth about life. We are all children, ultimately, and have our childish ways. We grown-up children have our grown-up toys no less foolish really than the contents of a child's pocket. And we too disobey the Commandments of Our Father and stand equally in need of forgiveness.

In referring to his son's having disobeyed "the seventh time" (3), the poet enriches his meaning by a biblical allusion to Matthew 18.21–22. When Peter asked Jesus how often he should forgive his brother's sinning against him, Jesus answered, not seven times, but "seventy times seven."

[This discussion is abridged from the essay "Are Tears Made of Sugar or of Salt?" in Laurence Perrine, *The Art of Total Relevance: Papers on Poetry* (Rowley, MA: Newbury, 1976) 125–29.]   LP

John Keats   When I have fears that I may cease to be
(page 913)

John Keats   O Solitude! (page 913)

Written shortly after Keats turned twenty, "O Solitude!" was his first published poem; though it makes skillful use of the sonnet form, it employs conventional diction and rhythms and could probably have been written by any of a dozen now-forgotten poets of his era. But a mere two years later, having undergone perhaps the most rapid and astonishing poetic development in literary history, Keats had transformed himself from a competent poet into a great one, composing the magnificent sonnet "When I have fears that I may cease to be" a few months before his culminating achievement in the great odes.

Apart from its conventional language and imagery, "O Solitude!" expresses a city-dweller's nostalgia for the countryside in a tone that verges on self-pity. The apostrophe in the first line strikes a self-dramatizing pose; the "crystal" river and "flowery" slopes are stock images evoking little authentic emotion. The yearning for an idealized companion with her "innocent mind" is likewise stereotypical. The poem depends more on predictable rhetoric for its effects than on original, articulate expression.

By contrast, "When I have fears that I may cease to be" is poetry of a different order altogether. As Walter Jackson Bate remarks in *John Keats* (Cambridge: Harvard UP, 1963) 291, Keats in this sonnet "breaks deliberately not only with those he has written before but also with the sonnet as conventionally used in this period." Here the speaker's solitude is clearly the poet's own: considering the possibility of an early death, he suffers the writer's anxiety that he will not live long enough to complete his work. The alliteration ("gleaned," "garners," "grain"; "high-pilèd," "Hold," "Huge," "high") helps knit the lines into an eloquent unity, and the *l* and *n* sounds repeated throughout the poem create a mournful undertone of regret and longing. The originality of phrasing—"high-pilèd books, in charactery," "Huge cloudy symbols of a high romance," "the magic hand of chance" contrasts sharply with the stale diction of the earlier sonnet. What had been an abstract "innocent mind" in "O Solitude!" here becomes the "fair creature of an hour," stressing Keats's mature themes of mutability and imminent death. And here the speaker's solitude is personal and deeply felt, not abstract and stylized: the poem recalls the joy of erotic union as "unreflecting love," one of those Keatsian miracles of phrasing that captures his yearning for a passional life unconstrained by intellect or artifice. Ending this sonnet with a couplet that uses enjambment to avoid a mechanical or sententious conclusion, the poem finally expresses that most terrible solitude of a man who fears that his life—both his love and his celebrated work—might come to nothing.

This and other Keats sonnets composed around the same time often have been compared to those of Shakespeare (whose work he was rereading), a comparison that testifies to their verbal energy and emotional power. At the same time, they display a restrained but virtuosic lyricism, particularly a mastery of sound, that is all Keats's own and that marks this sonnet as one of his finest short poems.   GJ

Chapter Sixteen

Evaluating Poetry 2

Poetic Excellence

John Donne The Canonization (page 916)

Useful discussions of this poem may be found in Cleanth Brooks, *The Well Wrought Urn* (New York: Reynal, 1947) 10–17; Clay Hunt, *Donne's Poetry* (New Haven: Yale UP, 1954) 72–93; Doniphan Louthan, *The Poetry of John Donne* (New York: Brooleman, 1951) 110–18; Patricia Garland Pinka, *This Dialogue of One* (University, AL: U of Alabama P, 1982) 126–32.   LP

John Keats Ode on a Grecian Urn (page 918)

Keats's great odes have been the subject of much critical study. The following are useful introductions to this rich area: Walter Jackson Bate, *John Keats* (Cambridge: Harvard UP, 1963) 510–20; Harold Bloom, *The Visionary Company: A Reading of English Romantic Poetry* (Garden City, NY: Doubleday, 1961) 406–410; Robert Gittings, *John Keats* (Boston: Little, 1968) 318–21; David Perkins, *The Quest for Permanence: The Symbolism of Wordsworth, Shelley, and Keats* (Cambridge: Harvard UP, 1959) 233–42; Helen Vendler, *The Odes of John Keats* (Cambridge: Harvard UP, 1983) 111–52. A useful group of articles is collected in Walter Jackson Bate, ed., *Keats: A Collection of Critical Essays* (Englewood Cliffs: Prentice, 1964).   TRA, GJ

Emily Dickinson There's a certain Slant of light
(page 920)

This universally praised poem is mentioned in almost every extended treatment of Dickinson's work, and many of them include an index to poems that are analyzed in the text. The following citations should be regarded as preliminary and suggestive; it may be useful to know that there is little disagreement about this poem, so that sampling a few should be sufficient for classroom presentation.

Charles R. Anderson, *Emily Dickinson's Poetry: Stairway of Surprise* (New York: Holt, 1960) 215–17; Sharon Cameron, *Lyric Time: Dickinson and the Limits of Genre* (Baltimore: Johns Hopkins UP, 1979) 100–103; Jane Donahue Eberwein, *Dickinson: Strategies of Limitation* (Amherst: U of Massachusetts P, 1985) 142–43; Clark Griffith, *The Long Shadow: Emily Dickinson's Tragic Poetry* (Princeton: Princeton UP 1964) 26–29; Greg Johnson, *Emily Dickinson: Perception and the Poet's Quest* (University, AL: U of Alabama P, 1985) 110; Inder Nath Kher, *The Landscape of Absence: Emily Dickinson's Poetry* (New Haven: Yale UP, 1974) 80–81; Vivian R. Pollak, *Dickinson: The Anxiety of Gender* (Ithaca: Cornell UP, 1984) 110; Yvor Winters, *In Defense of Reason*, 3rd ed. (Denver: Swallow, 1960) 293–98; Cynthia Griffin Wolff, *Emily Dickinson* (New York: Knopf, 1986) 312.

Among periodical treatments of the poem the fullest is Donald Thackrey, "Emily Dickinson's Approach to Poetry," *University of Nebraska Studies*, 13 (Nov. 1954): 76–80. A useful collection of excerpted studies is included in Thomas M. Davis, *14 by Emily Dickinson* (Chicago: Scott 1964), 31–41.   TRA, GJ

Robert Frost   Home Burial *(page 921)*

The three critics paraphrased in question 8 are (a) John F. Lynen, *The Pastoral Art of Robert Frost* (New Haven: Yale UP, 1960) 114; (b) George W. Nitchie, *Human Values in the Poetry of Robert Frost* (Durham: Duke UP, 1960) 129–30, 166–67, 223; and (c) John C. Kemp, *Robert Frost and New England* (Princeton: Princeton UP, 1979) 118–19, 155–56. Of these, Lynen seems to me furthest from the truth. Against Nitchie it may be argued that on a previous occasion of emotional conflict between them, the young wife *had* left her husband (39), and had either come back to him voluntarily or been persuaded by him to come back, and that her last action in the poem is to open the door wider. The husband accepts the fact that she is leaving ("Where do you mean to go?"), and threatens that *this* time he will bring her home "by force."

The most remarkable critical discussion of this poem is Randall Jarrell's illuminating line-by-line analysis, "Robert Frost's 'Home Burial,'" *The Third Book of Criticism* (New York: Farrar, 1969) 191–231; also in *The Moment of Poetry*, ed. Don Cameron Allen (Baltimore: Johns Hopkins UP, 1962) 99–132. If, after reading Jarrell, you want to read more, the following may be worth your perusal: Blaine Barry, *Robert Frost* (New York: Ungar, 1973) 75–78; Frank Lentricchia, *Robert Frost: Modern Poetries and the Landscape of Self* (Durham: Duke UP, 1975) 62–65; and Richard Poirier, *Robert Frost: The Work of Knowing* (New York: Oxford UP, 1977) 12–35.   LP

T. S. *Eliot*   The Love Song of J. Alfred Prufrock

(page 925)

"Prufrock" is one of the most discussed poems of the twentieth century. Of the mass of commentary that has accumulated concerning it, some of the following may be particularly helpful: Roy P. Basler, *Sex, Symbolism, and Psychology in Literature* (New Brunswick: Rutgers UP, 1984) 203–21; Cleanth Brooks and Robert Penn Warren, *Understanding Poetry*, 3rd ed. (New York: Holt, 1960) 386–99 (also in earlier editions); Elizabeth Drew, *T. S. Eliot: The Design of His Poetry* (New York: Scribner's, 1949) 34–36; Paul Engle and Warren Carrier, *Reading Modern Poetry*, rev. ed. (Glenville, IL: Scott, 1968) 148–55; Laurence Perrine and James M. Reid, *100 American Poems of the Twentieth Century* (New York: Harcourt, 1966) 110–12; Grover Smith, *T. S. Eliot's Poetry and Plays* (Chicago: U of Chicago P, 1956) 15–20 *et passim*; and Morris Weitz, *Philosophy of the Arts* (Cambridge: Harvard UP, 1950) 94–107, 145.   LP

Wallace Stevens   Sunday Morning (page 930)

"Sunday Morning" is almost universally celebrated as the great poem of Stevens's early career and has therefore been very widely analyzed. Among the published essays devoted to it in whole or in major part, the following are useful: R. P. Blackmur, "Wallace Stevens," *Language as Gesture* (New York: Harcourt, 1952); Price Caldwell, "'Sunday Morning': Stevens' Makeshift Romantic Lyric," *Southern Review* 15 (1979): 933–52; J. V. Cunningham, "Tradition and Modernity," *Tradition and Poetic Structure* (Denver: Swallow, 1960); Frank Lentricchia, "Wallace Stevens: The Ironic Eye," *Yale Review* 56 (1967): 336–53; Carol Kyros Walker, "The Subject as Speaker in 'Sunday Morning,'" *Concerning Poetry* 10 (Spring 1977): 25–31; Yvor Winters, "Wallace Stevens, Or the Hedonist's Progress," *In Defense of Reason* (New York: Swallow, 1947); Michael Zimmerman, "The Pursuit of Pleasure and the Uses of Death: Wallace Stevens' 'Sunday Morning,'" *University Review* 33 (1966): 113–23.

Among the many book-length studies of Stevens's poetry, the following have illuminating readings of this poem: Harold Bloom, *Wallace Stevens: The Poems of Our Climate* (Ithaca: Cornell UP, 1976) 27–35; Merle E. Brown, *Wallace Stevens: The Poem as Act* (Detroit: Wayne State UP, 1970) 157–63; Joseph Carroll, *Wallace Stevens' Supreme Fiction* (Baton Rouge: Louisiana State UP, 1987) 48–55; David M. LaGuardia, *Advance on Chaos: The Sanctifying Imagination of Wallace Stevens* (Hanover, NH: UP of New England, 1983) 45–49; A. Walton Litz, *Introspective Voyager: The Poetic Development of Wallace Stevens* (New York: Oxford UP, 1972) 44–53; Robert Rehder, *The Poetry of Wallace Stevens* (New York: St. Martin's, 1988) 65–86; Herbert J. Stern, *Wallace Stevens: Art of Uncertainly.* (Ann Arbor: U of Michigan P,

1966) 87–104; Henry W. Wells, *Introduction to Wallace Stevens* (Blooming-ton: Indiana UP, 1964) 52–57.   TRA

Langston Hughes   The Weary Blues (page 934)

This poem, one of Hughes's best-known, conveys the sound and impact of a black blues player in New York City.

Since the blues is a musical art form largely evolved in the African-American musical tradition, Hughes stresses the race of the blues player, his "ebony hands" (9) and the distinctly black vernacular of his song. Written in alternating long and short lines, the poem helps communicate through its form the motion of the piano player "Swaying to and fro" (12) and the mu-sical punctuation of his song. The rhymes and repetition serve a similar func-tion, suggesting the rhythmic and soulful intensity of his playing.

The two verses quoted from the song itself are significant. In the first, the player asserts that he intends "to quit ma frownin' / And put ma troubles on the shelf" (21–22). In the second, however, he repeats that he has the weary blues and feels a "wish that I had died" (30). These contrasting lyrics suggest the dual function of the blues: the cathartic expression of pain and the real-ity that the pain still exists.

The speaker keeps himself in the background of the poem, functioning as a sympathetic observer. By the closing lines, the speaker identifies so strongly with the piano player that he can imagine what happens to the man after he has gone home for the night: "the Weary Blues echoed through his head. / He slept like a rock or a man that's dead" (34–35). The implication is again dual and contrasting: the player may sleep like a man who has suc-cessfully purged his sorrow, or he may mimic the death wish he had expressed in the second quoted lyric of the song.

Steven C. Tracy writes: "Hughes presents the flip-side of the romantic vaudeville blues image of the wild and celebrated jazz player, good-timing his way through life. . . . [The musician] is one of the main practitioners living the unglamorous life that is far more common than the kinds of lives the most successful blues stars lived" (*Langston Hughes and the Blues* [Urbana and Chicago: U of Illinois P, 1988] 220–22). In another discussion, by Milton Metzler, the critic observes that the poem's "subtly syncopated rhythm shows an innate musical sense. The poem is jazz in words, the heartache music [Hughes] heard coming out of the people he grew up with" (*Langston Hughes: A Biography* [New York: Crowell, 1968] 88).   GJ

Elizabeth Bishop   The Fish (page 936)

This most anthologized of Bishop's poems has also received considerable critical attention, and is at least mentioned in all book-length studies of the poet. Those that are most useful are Anne Colwell, *Inscrutable Houses: Metaphors of the Body in the Poems of Elizabeth Bishop* (Tuscaloosa: U of Alabama P, 1997), David Kalstone, *Becoming a Poet: Elizabeth Bishop with Marianne Moore and Robert Lowell* (New York: Farrar, 1989), and Thomas J. Travisano, *Elizabeth Bishop: Her Artistic Development* (Charlottesville: U of Virginia P, 1988). All three are well indexed for their several references to this poem, as is an important collection of reprinted essays, Harold Bloom, ed., *Elizabeth Bishop* (New York: Chelsea, 1985), which contains a seminal discussion of the poem, Willard Spiegelman, "Elizabeth Bishop's 'Natural Heroism.'" Another earlier periodical essay is R. F. McFarland, "Some Observations on Elizabeth Bishop's 'The Fish,'" *Arizona Quarterly* 38 (Winter 1982): 364–76.   TRA

Adrienne Rich   Diving into the Wreck (page 938)

QUESTIONS

1. Vocabulary: *assiduous* (10), *floss* (20), *crenellated* (48), *haunters* (70), *vermeil* (80).
2. What does the poem tell us about the speaker? Why is she contrasted with Jacques Cousteau in line 9?
3. Does this poem function as an allegory? Why or why not?
4. What is the nature of the "wreck" into which the poet-speaker dives? What is the purpose of her quest? Why does she take with her a book of myths, a camera, and a knife?
5. Why does the speaker refer to herself as both a "mermaid" (72) and a "merman" (73)? How does the line "I am she: I am he" (77) help elucidate the themes of the poem?
6. Technically considered, line 89 in the final stanza—"the one who find our way"— is grammatically incorrect. Why is this usage deliberate and appropriate in this context?

Here Rich creates her own mythic descent into the underworld, where her purpose is to explore the sunken wreck of modern civilization.

The speaker is well prepared for her quest, "having read the book of myths" (1) and brought both a recording instrument (a camera) and a defensive weapon (a sharp knife). She emphasizes the solitary nature of her journey, contrasting herself against the most famous of male underwater explorers, Jacques Cousteau, who was aided by an "assiduous team" (10) who represent the material and psychological support the culture affords to male questers but that is denied to the woman poet.

As the speaker descends, she stresses the awkwardness of her journey and her own physical smallness: "My flippers cripple me, / I crawl like an insect down the ladder" (29–30). Once she is underwater, she emphasizes the solitary nature of her small, questing self within the vastness of the sea: "I have to learn alone / to turn my body without force / in the deep element" (41–43).

Acclimatized to the underwater environment, she recalls her purpose and the tools her poet-self has at her disposal: "I came to explore the wreck. / The words are purposes. / The words are maps" (52–54). She seeks to create an objective assessment of the wreck, tallying the damage done but also what is still valuable among the wreckage. As the poem nears its conclusion, the speaker imagines herself as an androgynous being—"I am she: I am he" (77)—who will presumably be free of the age-old gender biases which, it is implied, helped to wreck the culture in the first place. Moreover, the speaker draws the reader into the poem as part of the process of reassessment and recovery: "We are, I am, you are / by cowardice or courage / the one who find our way" (87–89). Thus the poet-speaker is, unlike a self-glorifying male quester, the tentative but determined leader into a process that is ultimately communal, focused not on individual demarcations but on cultural unity and cohesion.

Alice Templeton observes that "the poem actually offers very little analysis of the wreck and quite a bit of explanation of how the wreck is approached, how the inquiry is carried out, and how the explorer understands the mission and her/himself" (*The Dream and the Dialogue: Adrienne Rich's Feminist Poetics* [Knoxville: U of Tennessee P, 1994] 44). See other discussions of the poem in the following: Craig Werner, *Adrienne Rich: The Poet and Her Critics* (Chicago: American Library Association, 1988) 172–76; Claire Keyes, *The Aesthetics of Power: The Poetry of Adrienne Rich* (Athens: U of Georgia P, 1986) 152–55; and Barbara Charlesworth Gelpi and Albert Gelpi, eds., *Adrienne Rich's Poetry and Prose* (New York: Norton, 1975) 280–81, 298–99.   GJ

Poems for
Further Reading

Matthew Arnold   To Marguerite (page 943)

"To Marguerite" (the poem was given various titles by Arnold) develops an explicit symbol: human beings are symbolized as single islands, forever both linked and separated by a sea that clasps them to itself and estranges them from each other, while they eternally yearn to be merged into "a single continent" (16). This predicament is made more painful because the islands can share and communicate a sense of the beauty of the world (stanza 2), yet that beauty serves only to create "a longing like despair" (13) and the desire for a union that can never be.

The last stanza asks the reasons: why should they be subjected to the "fire" of desire that will immediately cool, and why should they at the same time feel "deep desire" and yet know that it is in vain? The answer is that "a God" has so created these feelings. While the capitalization suggests the Christian God, a more appropriate identification would be the god of love, Eros.

The speaker of this poem is percipient, and his symbolic expression is both emotionally powerful and intellectually comprehensible. He speaks definitively, in the plural, without pushing his private feelings to the front. The imagery is valid (especially in lines 7–14), and the language has freshness and power—who can read the poem carefully and not be haunted by "The unplumbed, salt, estranging sea" of life?

An extended analysis of "To Marguerite," exploring not only its themes but also its debt to tradition, is Kathleen Tillotson's "'Yes: in the Sea of Life,'" *Review of English Studies* 3 ns (1954): 346–64.   TRA

Margaret Atwood   Siren Song (page 943)

In mythology, only one man who heard the sirens' song survived—Odysseus, who had himself tied to the mast of his ship with his ears wide open so that he could not leap overboard to go to the sirens, while his mariners were required to block their ears so as to avoid the ravishing sounds. Odysseus listened to the song, but does not report its words, only the allure of the music.

Atwood invents her own myth to reveal how a siren seduces men to their destruction. First she promises to disclose the secret of the "irresistible" song if the mariner will free her from her bondage—the bondage of having to be disguised with a bird's body and of having to sing the "fatal and valuable" song. She is herself, then, a victim in need of the help of a male. She then promises the mariner that he alone will be the man to whom the secret will be revealed, and that in his uniqueness he can answer her cry for help. And thus she seduces him into coming closer, to his death, for to get closer he will "leap overboard."

The myth is allegorized in this way to point to an ulterior meaning having to do not with sailors and sirens, but with men and women, with the powers and weaknesses of each sex. The female is dangerous to the male because she knows exactly what his weaknesses are: he is egotistical, he wishes to think himself "unique," he wants to be strong and to rescue the helpless female. She in turn is bound by the limitations placed by men on her sexuality: they wish her to be alluring yet weak, dangerously beautiful and ultimately possessed of some secret that they cannot penetrate. So she plays out the role, "boring" as it is to her, luring men to their destruction without any more satisfaction than she gains from knowing her power will always work.

The ironies of the poem are played against the expectations created by Homer: the ravishing song is not supernal but really quite mundane, a direct appeal to masculine egotism. The verbal ironies employed by the siren are all designed to flatter and stroke that ego, as she pretends to be disgusted with her role and to need to be rescued, when in fact she possesses the power in their game. There is a delightful structural irony at the moment of the climax (23–25) as well, for the siren sings to the sailor, "Only you, only you can / you are unique / at last." The phrase "at last" both completes the statement of her longing—"at last, the unique man who will rescue me"—and announces the fulfillment of her plan: "at last" she has destroyed him.   TRA

W. H. Auden   Musée des Beaux Arts (page 944)

The poem descriptively alludes to three paintings by Pieter Brueghel the Elder (prints might be shown to students): lines 5–8, *The Census* (or *The Numbering at Bethlehem*); lines 10–13, *The Massacre of the Innocents*; and lines 14–21, *Landscape with the Fall of Icarus*. The title of the poem may be derived from the name of the museum in Brussels where the Icarus painting hangs, the Musées Royaux des Beaux Arts, though it simply means "Fine Arts Museum," a title general enough to include all three "Old Master" paintings.

The poem is in free verse and has an irregular rhyme scheme. In the opening verse paragraph the following lines rhyme: 1/4, 2/8, 5/7, 6/13, 9/11, 10/12, and there is no rhyme for line 3. The concluding verse paragraph, while not regular, tightens up the rhymes somewhat, in keeping with the single focus of the subject: 14/15, 16/20, 17/21, 18/19. The two sets of rhymed couplets begin to suggest some more explicit closure of meaning for the poem, but the last two lines return to the more random pattern, reinforcing the understated meaning—that something as momentous as a boy falling out of the sky does not signal a definitive event, but only a momentary amazement to the men who continue on about their business. The apparently irrelevant or random rhyming may thus be seen as a reinforcement of the theme, that great events seem irrelevant or not personally significant to the mass of self-involved people.

The sequence of the pictured events may also be seen as reinforcing the theme: they move from the birth of Christ, to the slaughter by Herod of the first-born sons, to the mythical story of Icarus—events that would seem to the modern picture-viewer of decreasing personal significance, even if the last of them did originally symbolize a very human problem, the danger of rashly pursuing a superhuman aspiration.   TRA

D. C. Berry   On Reading Poems to a Senior Class at South High (page 945)

The poet begins by assuming, from their orderly appearance in rows of chairs, that the students are "frozen" (4) and incapable of a living response to his poetry. But as he reads, planning "to drown them" (13) with his words, the power of poetry floods the room, and the surprised poet and class metaphorically swim together until the ringing of the school bell, which breaks the enchantment. All of them, students and poet, then go on to other more normal pursuits, back to their ordinary lives. The experience, however, has transported the poet beyond himself, and it takes his domesticated, imaginatively named cat to bring *him* back to normal.

The poet's defensive condescension—his prejudice that these students are cold to poetry, his fear that his poetry may not move them—is washed away by the mutual experience, to the extent that he himself must be restored to his human form. The poem wittily converts the pejorative image of "frozen fish" into the vital image of "thirty tails whacking words" (19) and his plan of drowning his audience converts into the water in which, for the time, the poet and students have a medium they can share. Both "frozen fish" and "drown" are used metaphorically, apparently as the poet's self-conscious device for asserting his superiority, but both come so vitally to life that even after the experience the poet feels fins at the end of his arms. Ironically it is his cat who restores him from his fishy condition.   TRA

William Blake   The Lamb (page 946)

William Blake   The Tiger (page 947)

"The Lamb" was first published in *Songs of Innocence* (1789) and "The Tiger" in *Songs of Experience* (1794). Blake described these two volumes as "Showing Contrary States of the Human Soul." Though the poems in *Songs of Experience* are generally darker in tone than those in the earlier book, Blake is not necessarily suggesting that innocence is better than experience. Rather, each state shows the incompleteness or the inadequacy of the other.

In the "Introduction" to *Songs of Innocence* (page 853), Blake was bid by his muse to "Pipe a song about a Lamb." This is it. The central question asked in this poem is "Little Lamb, who made thee?" The central question asked in "The Tiger" is "Did he who made the Lamb make thee?" "The Tiger" was obviously written to complement "The Lamb." Together the two poems make a poetic diptych.

In "The Lamb" the speaker is a child, and the chief effect of the poem is a childlike simplicity, produced by the use of a simple vocabulary—mostly monosyllabic, end-stopped lines—one statement to a line, a songlike meter (six four-beat lines in each stanza, framed at beginning and end by a pair of three-beat lines), paired rhymes, and frequent repetitions. The situation and content of the poem also express this childlike simplicity. The child talks to a lamb, asks it a question and answers the question himself, and in his answer shows his trustful, unquestioning acceptance of the Christian story he has been taught. The lamb was created by Christ, who in the New Testament is called "the Lamb of God," and who through his incarnation became "a little child." The child and the lamb are thus one with Christ in name as well as in gentleness and love, and the poem appropriately ends, "Little Lamb, God bless thee."

In "The Tiger" the speaker is an adult, possibly the poet; he does not literally speak to the tiger, he apostrophizes it; and the central question of the poem is left unanswered.

The image in the first two lines is one of the most vivid in English poetry. Primarily we are meant to see two eyes glaring in the dark (see line 6); but if we think of the orange and black stripes of the tiger's body, we also have a flamelike image. The tiger is associated with images of fire throughout the poem. He is imagined to have been made in a cosmic smithy ("forged," "hammer," "chain," "furnace," "anvil"), and his creator is personified as a powerful smith. But is this smithy in "distant deeps or skies"—in hell or heaven? And was the smith Satan or God? And, having created the tiger, did the smith "smile" to see what he had made? These are the questions urged on the reader insistently, like the blows of a hammer on an anvil (the interrogative "what" is used thirteen times during the poem), and in a meter whose accents fall also with the force and regularity of hammer blows. The tiger is described as awesome—that is, as arousing both fear and admiration in the beholder. Its "fearful symmetry," the burning brightness of its eyes, its twisted sinewy heart, the "deadly terrors" of its brain—these qualities suggest beauty, strength, fierceness, and violence. But if the tiger is awesome, its creator is even more so. He is "immortal" (3, 23), daring (7, 8, 24), winged (7), strong (9–10), "dread" (12, 15), and an artist (9).

The difficult lines 17–18 have been explained in too many ways to go into here—in terms of astrology, as metaphor for dawn and dewfall, as symbolic of love and pity, as an allusion to the war in heaven between the good and the rebel angels depicted in Milton's *Paradise Lost*, as an allusion to symbols in Blake's private mythology, as an image for showers of sparks sent out from the cosmic forge and of the water used to temper the glowing metal, and so on. Perhaps, in their broadest and simplest sense, they can be taken to suggest, "When even the stars wept, did the creator of the tiger smile?"

No answer to its central question is stated in the poem. Is one implied? A survey of Blake criticism produces no consensus. About half of the critics say that the question is rhetorical, intended by Blake to be answered "Yes." The creator of the Lamb was also the creator of the Tiger, and He looked on his work and found it "good." The power of the poem is the power with which it expresses this mysterious paradox in the nature of God, creator of both the rainbow and the whirlwind. But the other half say that the question is unanswerable, and was not intended by Blake to be answered one way or the other—that Blake's poem is about the mystery and ambiguity of the universe, which is ultimately beyond man's understanding. (And one lonely voice—Kathleen Raine, in *Encounter* 2 [1935]: 48—declares boldly: "The answer is beyond all possible doubt, 'No'; God, who created the lamb, did not create the tiger.")

A greater variety of answers is produced by the question, What do the lamb and the tiger symbolize? But here we welcome a variety of answers, for the symbolism is rich and permits a range of meanings. (The poems obviously call for symbolic reading. We are being asked much more than whether the same god created the aardvark and the camel.) Among the answers suggested are good and evil, God's love and God's wrath, gentle meekness and powerful energy, innocent purity and strong sexuality, peace and war, mercy and justice, pardon and punishment.

Textual note: The text of "The Tiger" used here differs in line 12 from that published by Blake in *Songs of Experience* ("What dread hand? And what dread feet?"). In the original manuscript this line is followed by a discarded stanza of which the first line is "Could fetch it from the furnace deep?" The cancellation of the stanza left line 12 syntactically incomplete, and Blake seems to have been dissatisfied with it, for in a copy later given to a friend he altered the line in ink to "What dread hand formed thy dread feet," and another friend, perhaps on Blake's authority, printed the poem in a book of memoirs with "forged" in the place of "formed." I have used the version that seems to me best, and the one that may have represented Blake's final intention.   LP

David Bottoms   Sign for My Father, Who Stressed the Bunt (page 948)

In poems about parent–child relationships, a common theme is the difference between children's and adults' attitudes toward their parents. The theme is visible in such different but comparable poems as Langston Hughes's "Cross" (page 693), Theodore Roethke's "My Papa's Waltz" (page 997), and David Bottoms's "Sign for My Father, Who Stressed the Bunt."

Bottoms's speaker recalls his boyhood focus on his father's bunting lessons; though he admired his father's "style" and skill, he was more interested in hitting dramatic home runs than in learning a strategic technique for sacrificing a turn at bat that allows another player to advance and score. Bottoms's skillful wordplay emphasizes the contrast between youthful, ego-driven aspirations and mature teamwork. The speaker's father could bunt the ball "like a seed" down either baseline, implying the adult's role as a nurturer and his willingness to put aside his own ambitions in favor of his son's future blossoming. As a boy, the speaker was interested primarily in transcending "the bank" that served as the center-field fence in their makeshift ballpark; a suggestion of baseball as a metaphor for poetry is present in the speaker's assertion that later he "could homer / into the garden beyond the bank," fulfilling his heroic/Homeric aspirations to move beyond his father's position as a mere worker in a world of capitalist limitation (the bank as fence) into an Edenic garden of art and achievement.

Yet the focus of the poem is praise of the father, not the son. Part of the speaker's maturity has been to recognize the nobility of what he once considered—in another notable pun—his father's "whole tiresome pitch" about the importance of bunting. Continuing the implied metaphor of baseball as poetry, the speaker concludes with a poignant comparison of the poem he is writing to the secret signs employed to direct upcoming plays in baseball: "Like a hand brushed across the bill of a cap, / let this be the sign / I'm getting a grip on the sacrifice." As Michael Cass observes of this poem, "Bottoms does his part in attempting to revive the serious pun in American poetry" ("Danger and Beauty: David Bottoms' 'In a U-Haul North of Damascus,'" *The Southern Review*, 20, iii [Summer 1984]: 745).

Finally the speaker has learned what his father had sacrificed for him, and its expression is this belated but moving acknowledgment of his father's patient life-lessons.   GJ

Gwendolyn Brooks   Sadie and Maud (page 948)

"Sadie and Maud" is a compact narrative poem that compares the lives of two African American sisters.

The sisters make different choices for their lives, Maud going to college for intellectual pursuits while Sadie "stayed at home" (2) and quickly became embroiled in a turbulent but vital existence. As the speaker puts it, "Sadie was one of the livingest chits / In all the land" (7–8).

Sadie's choices don't please her family, however. She has two children out of wedlock, which scandalizes her parents and her sister. Ultimately Sadie dies young, presumably from her fast, hard living, and her two daughters leave home to seek their own fortunes. Sadie had left them nothing but the "fine-tooth comb" (16) with which, as the speaker reported earlier, she had scraped life for all its substance and complexity.

The final stanza returns to Maud, describing her as "a thin brown mouse" (18) who finished college but has now outlived the rest of her family and lives alone in their house. The poem suggests that Maud, despite her "respectable" choices, has not really lived at all. Rather the poem sympathizes with the vibrant, colorful Sadie, who made mistakes but did not neglect to live her life to the fullest.   GJ

Gwendolyn Brooks   a song in the front yard (page 949)

This is the song of a good girl longing to be a little bit naughty. Her mother has strict rules ("in at quarter to nine" [12]) and sneers at the speaker's wish to "have some wonderful fun" (10) though the girl doesn't seem to know exactly what Johnnie Mae will be doing as "a bad woman" (14). The speaker seems pre-pubescent, unaware of what behavior "brave stockings" and "paint" (19–20) connote. For her, the contrasts begin between front and back yards, weeds and roses, her economic security and the life of "charity children" (on public assistance, presumably). Outside the bounds of her mother's rose garden and propriety and morality there is a tempting world of good times, wonderful fun, staying out late. The price to pay for such fun is a reputation as "bad," or even "Jail soon or late," but the allure of "night-black lace," wearing makeup and "strut[ting] down the streets" seems worth the price (18–20).

The child-like tone of the poem is created by the girl's wishes and her vagueness about what bad people actually do. To suppose that George's theft of the "back gate" is what will point him toward jail indicates the limits of her imagination. (The back gate, closing off the back yard from the alley where "the charity children" have "a good time" is a symbol of the mother's protection of her child. We may certainly presume that it has been replaced since "last winter" when George stole and sold it.) This tone is reinforced by the form of the poem. While the lines are not regular in length, they contain enough anapestic feet to define that as its meter. Here are a few examples:

Where it's rough | and un-tend- | ed and hun- | gry weed grows | 3

How they | don't have | to go in | at quar- | ter to nine | 12

That George'- | ll be ta- | ken to Jail | soon or late | 15

And wear | the brave stock- | ings of night- | black lace | 19

And strut | down the streets | with paint | on my face | 20

This meter often occurs in verse meant to sound unsophisticated and even childlike. "A Visit from Saint Nicholas" ("'Twas the night before Christmas and all through the house") is a familiar example. In this book Hardy's "The Ruined Maid" employs this meter to emphasize the simplicity of the country girl.   TRA

Lucille Clifton   good times (page 950)

Occasions for joy in the lives of the poor are few and far between, but when they come they are likely to be jollier, more spontaneous, and more festive than the pleasures of the well-to-do. The joyousness of the occasion is in direct proportion to its rarity. Lucille Clifton, a black poet, here presents just such an occasion in the lives of a poor black family. The first stanza states the causes for celebration, the second stanza presents the celebration itself. For once the rent, the insurance premiums, and the electric bill have all been paid, and uncle Brud has "hit / for one dollar straight" (4–5)—that is, his one-dollar ticket in a lottery or numbers game has won the whole prize; it does not have to be divided among several winners. The result is that the mother has baked homemade bread, Grampaw has come to visit, and there is spontaneous dancing and singing in the kitchen, with a bottle of liquor to add to the gaiety.

The speaker is one of the children in the family, possibly the eldest one. She is so deeply impressed by the "good times," which are in such contrast with their usual life of debt and privation, that she ends each stanza with three lines devoted to proclaiming them, and then adds a two-line coda in which she instructs her younger sisters and brothers to "think about the / good times." Lay them up in your memory, for you may not experience many more.

The irony in the poem is that the "good times" being celebrated in this poem are what a middle-class observer would call hard times.   LP

Judith Ortiz Cofer   Women Who Love Angels (page 950)

This poem is a graceful depiction of certain women who live their entire lives more on a spiritual than on a physical plane.

Such women have little physical appetite, so they remain "thin" (1); they lack sexual desire, so they "rarely marry" (2). They live an exalted life that resembles a movie set, "spacious rooms, French doors / giving view to formal gardens" (4–5). They are devoted to the most bodiless of art forms, music, playing their pianos with heads tilted "at a gracious angle / as if listening / to notes pitched above / the human range" (11–14).

The poem implies a critique of these women, for in their love of the spiritual, they neglect to live in, or even acknowledge, the rough-and-tumble physical world. The setting also suggests a class issue, since the women clearly have the money and privilege that enable a spiritually focused existence.

Yet we cannot deny that the women's lives are appealing. They always live "long lives" (3), in fact, presumably because they are exempt from the stresses and mishaps that befall less exalted mortals. Even their deaths are graceful, "their spirits shaking gently loose / from a hostess too well bred / to protest" (19–21).   GJ

Samuel Taylor Coleridge   Kubla Khan (page 951)

The first publication of this poem included a lengthy note by Coleridge attributing its inspiration to a combination of having taken a prescribed dose of opium for an illness he was suffering, and then reading a seventeenth-century travel book about the Chinese ruler; he claims that in his "reverie" he had composed between two and three hundred lines of verse, but as he was beginning to write them down he was interrupted by a visitor, and returning to his work discovered that he had forgotten the rest. (The account is available in any collection of Coleridge's works and need not be quoted here.) Whether this was literally true is less important than the effect Coleridge had in mind in reporting it; the account was written some fifteen years after the poem, and seems to have as its purpose emphasizing the air of magic and mystery of the poem itself, as well as promoting the Romantic ideal of poetry as spontaneous, impulsive, and free of narrowly rational thought.

But as many commentators have shown, the poem itself is highly crafted, not likely the product even of a practiced poet unless he is paying close attention to his effects. Elisabeth Schneider analyzes at length the assonance, consonance, alliteration, and internal and end rhymes of just the first five lines, demonstrating the "half-caught echoes, correspondences of sound felt but too complex to be anticipated or to remain tabulated in the mind even after they have been analyzed."

Through line 36 the poet describes the site of Kubla Khan's pleasure dome: a landscape of contrasts and opposites, with a river bursting forth with great force from a fountain in a "romantic chasm," meandering through a pleasant valley, then sinking once again into a cavern leading to the "sunless sea." The dome itself is built over "caves of ice," and the dome is surrounded by gardens and forests, bounded by walls and towers. The scene combines wildness with gentleness, heights with depths, explosive creative force with calm obliteration, warmth with coldness, holiness with demonism, tumult with lifelessness, artifice with nature, the momentary present with an ancestral past, light with dark, and a peaceful scene with prophecies of war. It is, says Harold Bloom, a "vision of creation and destruction, each complete." It presents "the balance of reconciliation of opposites" that for Coleridge was "the mark of the creative imagination."

At line 37 the poem turns to a different scene, a "vision" the poet once had of another distant and exotic moment, of a singing maiden (playing on an antique instrument) whose song seems to him to have corresponded to Kubla Khan's pleasure-dome. If he could revive within himself the feelings aroused by this vision, he too would be able to create "in air" what Kubla did on earth—and his creation would mark him off from the multitudes, who would see in him a holy man of magical powers.

His desire is to create poetically the totality that was expressed in Kubla Khan's achievement; as he phrases it, however, this is only a wish, something beyond his powers. Yet as Bloom points out, what the poem "Kubla Khan" does is precisely that.

This intriguing poem has excited much commentary, among the best of it the following: Walter Jackson Bate, *Coleridge* (New York: Macmillan, 1968) 75–84; Harold Bloom, *The Visionary Company* (Garden City: Anchor/ Doubleday, 1963) 229–33; G. Wilson Knight, *The Starlit Dome* (London:

Methuen, 1968) 90–97; Elisabeth Schneider, "Kubla Khan" from *Coleridge, Opium and Kubla Khan*, repr. in *Coleridge: A Collection of Critical Essays*, ed. Kathleen Coburn (Englewood Cliffs: Prentice, 1967) 88–93.   TRA

Stephen Crane   War Is Kind (page 952)

Crane employs the subjects and language of sentimental and rhetorical poetry in creating this ironic dirge to the fallen dead. The "maiden" grieving for her lost "lover" (the word does not imply a sexual relationship, as "maiden" makes clear), the child in grief for its dead father, and the "humble" mother grieving over the casket of her son—all these are stock characters of sentimentality. Rhetorical poetry abounds in such phrases as "[T]he unexplained glory flies above them" (9), "[s]wift blazing flag" (17) and "bright splendid shroud" (24). Both the sentimental and the rhetorical are forms of ironic overstatement in this poem, the means of exaggeration for the sake of truth.

The truth Crane has to tell is that war is *not* kind but cruel, both to those who fight and to those who cherish them. The title (which Crane gave to the book as well as to this individual poem in it), repeated as half the refrain, is verbal irony. The contrasts between the celebratory war stanzas and the personal responses are situational irony. This irony is augmented by contrasts in the levels of diction. At one level we find *thirst, drill, corpses, gulped,* and *button;* at the other, *affrighted, unexplained glory, swift blazing flag,* and *bright splendid shroud.* These are not restricted to the sentimental first, third, and fifth stanzas, nor to the other two, but occur in both sorts. The indentation of two stanzas creates a structure of alternating materials—the sympathetic advice to the mourners, and the glory and waste of war.

The indented stanzas share another feature: the repetition and rhymes of their third and sixth lines, which are ironically juxtaposed to the celebrations of war. Along with the repetitions of the last two lines in the other stanzas (made more emphatic by their being so short) and the repetition with variation of the first line to open stanzas 1 and 3, the poem achieves an incantatory tone in addition to the predominating irony. One unusual feature in these patterned repetitions is the absence in the final stanza of a variant of line one. Where we might have expected "Do not weep, mother, for war is kind," we have only silence.

Daniel G. Hoffman provides a suggestive commentary on the poem in his *The Poetry of Stephen Crane* (New York: Columbia UP, 1957) 189–90.   TRA

Frank A. Cross, Jr.   Rice Will Grow Again (page 953)

This Vietnam war poem ironically juxtaposes the fragility of human life with the continuity of one of the food staples of that region. The random and pointless killing of the farmer at his life-sustaining task now haunts the killer

even in the safety of Kansas as he dreams of the farmer still planting rice all
around his bed.

The scene of the killing is rendered in small, realistic details. The two
men are on patrol, "walking / On the dikes / Like damn fools" (1-3), presumably because they are in an exposed position. They are mindful not to
step on potentially dangerous unexploded ammunition, but they are "steppin
light" (5), which suggests a kind of light-heartedness. That suggestion extends as well to the casualness with which Mitch shoots the farmer.

There is a terrible ambiguity in the reported shooting:

> Mitch saw the farmer's hand
> Going down again
> With another
>   Shoot (17–20).

The farmer is planting his rice shoots; Mitch shoots him. The word "shoot,"
set off in its own indented line, points to both the seedling and to the burst
of gunfire. The dying man is presented in matter-of-fact details, though the
word "bubbled" (32), so accurate for the event, also suggests "babbled." The
farmer's last words (translated for the foreign intruders) look to the future:
damning his killer, the farmer invokes that time when the rice fields will
again be rice fields rather than killing fields. This literal fact is then transformed into the nightmare that burdens his killer.   TRA

Countee Cullen   For a Lady I Know (page 955)

Students will need little help in grasping the ironic humor in Cullen's
clever quatrain. Sometimes criticized by other members of the Harlem Renaissance for his lack of "race anger" and bitterness, Cullen preferred to han-
dle race issues with a relatively light touch, employing traditional meter and
rhyme rather than the jazz-inspired improvisatory verse of his contemporary
Langston Hughes.

The "lady" of the title, so irremediably racist that she imagines her
whiteness will give her privileged status in the spiritual realm, is the object
of satiric scorn, which is given sharper point by the rhyme of her "snores"
with the busy "chores" to be performed by black servants, even in heaven,
while she sleeps. The poem's delightful humor, however, does not obscure
Cullen's implication that a certain type of upper-class individual in early
twentieth-century America could never conceive of racial equality; and that
a Caucasian-dominated Christian religion apparently had done nothing to
disabuse such an individual of a racist view of humanity.   GJ

Emily Dickinson   A Light exists in Spring (page 955)

There is in the fourth stanza a submerged military metaphor that reveals the
speaker's difficulty in capturing the meaning of her experience. The peculiar

light of spring, she says, is as brisk in its going as a marching horizon or as noon being called away to duty (or perhaps, exploding), but the briskness is immediately denied some of its force by being robbed of the defining "Formula of sound" (15) so that the effect is simply of swift departure. In the personifications that lead up to this stanza, the poet faintly implies a military aspect for the light, posting it on sentry duty as it "stands abroad / On Solitary Fields" (5–6) or as it "waits" and points out distant objects.

The military quality of the light is kept subdued and faint because Dickinson does not want to suggest extraneous connotations of soldiering, the glorious but confused sounds, and the regularity of military maneuvering; her light is vigorous and brisk, but it is also silent, distant, and unpredictable. Its presence is the occasion for an incomprehensible exhilaration, but its passing leaves a nostalgia, not for exuberance, but for contentment. The effect of this light is plainly more than the speaker can define.

The opening statement is almost flatly descriptive, running over the first two lines and coming to a full stop after the third. The effect is very nearly prosaic and serves as a foil to the excited personifications that follow. These lines contain the only factual data available, and they are meager: the light is peculiar to early March, a time in New England only anticipating spring. Beyond the bare identification in time, the poem employs various figures to represent the speaker's feelings and, oddly, there is nowhere an attempt to render this light in a visual image. Although the light "exists," that is, is there for any who look, it is only presented in the objects of the landscape; the real subject of the poem is how the speaker reacts, and these reactions are none too clear to her.

For example, in the second stanza she explicitly states that the color is incomprehensible ("Science cannot overtake" it), and that it is only known by one's feelings. The description of the place where the light shines is curiously mixed: the color "stands abroad," self-sufficient and claiming some distinction for itself—a positive image suggesting the masculine vigor of a sentry; but it is located "On Solitary Fields," which suggest isolation and loneliness. Which impression is it that "Human Nature feels," then? Similarly, in the third stanza, the light is distant, deferential, and powerful enough to reveal "the furthest Tree / Upon the furthest Slope you know," yet it also seems intimate and wise enough about the ways of nature to speak to you.

In both these stanzas, and more particularly in stanza 4, the concluding lines of the quatrains thrust the meaning back upon the human observer who is, successively, sensitive to the quality of light, intensely curious about its meaning, and deeply affected by its departure. Each time it seems to invite understanding and each time its secrets are withheld.

The final stanza attempts to define the terms of the experience, first by definition and then by means of simile. The presence of the light has inspired a contentment similar to that of a "Sacrament," and its passing produces "A quality of loss." However, the words "Content" and "Sacrament" are rather surprising, for the speaker has been suggesting not mild contentment or piety but exuberance and briskness. Apparently, this light elicits *all* these responses: it is vigorous and strong, yet produces nostalgic longing and the feeling that its message (if it were to speak) would content us; it is sacramental because it combines the ecstasy of communion with the longing for the real union that communion represents and promises.

These are difficult paradoxes, but beyond them the poem dramatizes explicitly the larger emotional response evoked by these separate reactions: "It passes and we stay" (16). Whatever apparently confused and contradictory feeling the speaker may have about the light, she knows that its passing touches her sense of loss, and the loss is intense enough to require the power of a blasphemous image. The frustration of being repeatedly offered what seems a defining and meaningful experience only to have it snatched away is the theme. The sense of separateness from nature and its possible meanings is complete; there is only loss, frustration, and an overwhelming sense of inability.

There are many readings of this poem in print. The fullest and most reliable is in Clark Griffith's *The Long Shadow: Emily Dickinson's Tragic Poetry* (Princeton: Princeton UP, 1964) 85–101.   TRA

Emily Dickinson   A narrow Fellow in the Grass (page 955)

The subject of the poem is snakes and the (male) speaker's fear of them, and this is vividly rendered through Dickinson's effective use of visual, tactile, and visceral imagery and through her consistently surprising but precise word choices.

The word "Fellow" (twice used for the snake), when contrasted with "Nature's People" (17), suggests someone of inferior class and breeding. The adjective "narrow" is exactly right for a snake, but whoever used it to describe one before? "[R]ides" suggests effortless motion, without legs. But the characteristic of the snake principally emphasized in the first two stanzas is the suddenness of its appearance. (The departure from normal word order in line 4 not only provides an oblique rhyme for line 2 but gives unusual emphasis to "sudden.") One is not aware of the snake's presence until the grass parts unexpectedly at one's feet and one catches a fleeting glance of "A spotted shaft"; then the grass closes again and opens farther on, this time without revealing the snake. (The grass is not that of a mown lawn, but the ankle- or calf-deep grass of a field.)

Stanzas 3–4 indicate how alien to man is the snake's habitat and emphasize the suddenness of the snake's *disappearance*. Though "Occasionally" snakes come out to forage in a field or enjoy the sun, their preferred habitat is the swamp, land too wet and cool for man to use even for agricultural purposes. Yet the speaker "more than once" when "Boy, and Barefoot" (thus vulnerable to snakebite) had come across one basking in the sun and, mistaking it for a discarded "Whip lash," had stooped to pick it up, when it suddenly "wrinkled" and vanished.

The first two pairs of stanzas indirectly suggest the power of the snake to startle the speaker, whether by sudden appearance or disappearance. The last two stanzas, partly through effective contrast with each other, reveal the snake's power to inspire deep fear in him. With several of "Nature's People" (e.g., squirrels, birds) he has struck up an acquaintance, and he feels for them "a transport / Of cordiality." But he has never met "this Fellow" (the snake), either alone or in the company of friends, "Without a tighter breathing / And Zero at the Bone." The images in the final two lines strike home with the shock of pure terror. "[T]ighter breathing," with its unexpected adjective, is precisely accurate for that feeling of constriction in the chest that makes it difficult to breathe. And to contrast with "cordiality" (warmth of heart) in stanza 5, we are given—not just a chill, or cold, or even freezing—but "Zero" (the lowest point on the centigrade scale), and not at the heart but at the "Bone" (cold piled upon cold).

Many students will have difficulty with the image of the "Whip lash / Unbraiding in the Sun," the participle suggesting motion to them. But the basking snake is motionless. A whiplash of braided leather left out in the sun too long will begin to dry out and disintegrate, its thongs loosening and cracking. The snake, with its mottled leather back, has a similar appearance. When the boy stoops to pick up what he thinks is a whiplash, it suddenly comes to life and hurries off.   LP

Emily Dickinson   I died for Beauty—but was scarce

(page 956)

In a letter, Emily Dickinson once listed John Keats among her favorite poets, and his influence is apparent here in the allusion to the famous last lines of Keats's "Ode on a Grecian Urn" (page 918): "Beauty is truth, truth beauty,—that is all / Ye know on earth, and all ye need to know." But Dickinson's macabre poem slyly undercuts Romantic claims to the primacy and immortality of art—and of artists' reputations.

Characteristically, Dickinson employs a deceased persona who is "adjusting" to her existence after death and locating her mortal existence within the context of eternity. In this respect, the poem can be usefully compared with "Because I could not stop for Death" (page 752) and "I heard a Fly buzz—when I died" (page 871). But unlike the isolated speakers in those poems, the persona here finds a "kinsman" who is lain in the tomb next to hers. Dickinson's speaker, asked by her companion why she died, claims pridefully that she died "For Beauty"; the companion, replying that he died "for Truth," insists they are "Brethren," co-martyrs for the highest values in human existence. One might even assume that Dickinson, the American late-Romantic, is wistfully imagining a conversation with Keats himself, but then providing in her poem's last stanza a harsh corrective to her own romantic leanings. For a discussion of this poem's relationship to Keats's, see Joanne Feit Diehl, *Dickinson and the Romantic Imagination* (Princeton: Princeton UP, 1981) 120–21. Diehl notes that "Dickinson refuses to embrace Keats's hard-won vision, for she prefers to remain in the dark—still questioning, torn by doubt."

If Dickinson's poem ended with the second stanza, it could be considered a redaction, in her own distinctive style, of Keats's poetic argument. Yet her final stanza allows the speaker and her companion only a temporary sense of triumph in their having died in the pursuit of such high callings. In the end, nature triumphs over art, mindless natural process over human ideals; above all, the poem critiques the notion of an artist's personal immortality, since the "Moss" not only silences the voices of the two interlocutors but finally eradicates their names. In a macabre stroke worthy of Edgar Allan Poe, Dickinson uses disturbingly physical imagery here by picturing, as in a nineteenth-century adumbration of a horror film, a relentlessly growing moss reaching the speakers' mouths and presumably garbling, then stopping altogether, their proud self-congratulations, and ultimately covering even their gravestones ("our names") as well. As in the other Dickinson poems mentioned above, the only redeeming note is that the speaker of the poem, in the poem itself, *does* speak; for all the horror implicit in Dickinson's postmortem lyrics, her habit of casting them into the first person insists that a kind of selfhood does survive mortal life, though she insists that the pretensions and achievements of that life ultimately come to nought, giving way to a new and usually—as in this poem—unknowable mode of being, beyond representation in language.   GJ

Emily Dickinson **I like a look of Agony** (page 957)

A shocking first line is one of Dickinson's signature effects, as in "I heard a Fly buzz—when I died" (page 871) and "I felt a Funeral, in my Brain," (page 705). Here the shock is the initial impression of sadistic relish, modulated in the second line to an insistence that the speaker likes to witness agony because she knows it is *honest*. People may pretend to a variety of emotions for a variety of reasons, presenting a false show of happiness, or indifference, or even pain. But the ultimate in pain, true "Agony," cannot be feigned.

One of this poem's most interesting features is the relationship between the first and second stanzas, for the second begins with its own shock; the poem focuses not on survivable anguish but on the death agony. The lack of transition is telling, implying an analogy so inarguable in the speaker's mind that it needs no rhetorical elaboration: just as agony is an absolute extreme of physical experience, death is the crux of human destiny in a larger, spiritual context. As Robert Weisbuch notes, the capitalized "Agony" may suggest "the word's biblical sense, Christ's foreknowledge of his crucifixion" (*Emily Dickinson's Poetry* [Chicago: U of Chicago P, 1975] 97). For Dickinson, extreme suffering strips away human pretenses, revealing the ineluctable fact of mortality. Like "Agony," the capitalized "Beads" has a religious implication, suggesting rosary beads as well as the droplets of sweat on the dying sufferer's forehead. While an accomplished actor might feign anguish, including a convincing show of tears, these "homely" beads of sweat are evidence of genuine suffering, genuine experience. This poem's directness of expression—one might even call it bluntness—and its forthright, unvarnished language effectively reinforce its meaning.   GJ

John Donne   The Good-Morrow (page 957)

As the title announces, this poem is a morning greeting addressed by the speaker to his love. The questions in the opening lines colloquially declare a parallel between this morning's awakening and an awakening to life that took place when they began to love. All time before then was like infancy, or like a miraculous two-century sleep. The controversial quality of these lines continues throughout the poem, producing the kind of syntactical and elliptical problems found in line 5: "but this, all pleasures fancies be" means "with the exception of this (our love), all pleasures are merely imagined ones." The mock innocence of the first three lines is elaborated on in lines 6–7: the speaker has in the past had his share of sexual experiences, but to his innocent sleeping soul they were only prophetic dreams of the love he now shares.

Pursuing his reference to other love exploits, the speaker assures his lady that there can be no cause of jealousy between them. He puns on the words "watch" and "wake," synonyms in Donne's time, to insist that the alertness to each other that this morning has brought is not for fear of loss, because (he logically says) their mutual love rules out the possibility of loving others. Each of them is the whole of the other's society, just as the room they share is equivalent to all other places. The elliptical syntax of lines 12–13 extends this spatial reference. "Let" in these lines means both "let us concede" and "let us ignore." For other people whose sense of the spaciousness of the world derives from traveling, explorers and map-makers are necessary, but these two lovers in themselves contain all worlds. (Line 14 alludes to the Renaissance theory that each individual human being is a microcosm, a little world that parallels the greater universe and contains all its elements. Each of the lovers is thus a world, and being joined by their love, each *has* a world.)

The third stanza further extends the geographical metaphor, but it begins with a Renaissance commonplace, that the face of the lover is mutually mirrored in the eye of the partner, both of them being simultaneously a mirror and the image in the other's mirror. Line 16 momentarily returns to the theme of jealousy, as the speaker assures his love that their mirrored faces reveal the honesty in their hearts. They are themselves like the hemispheres of the newly explored and mapped Earth—but better, since they do not have the sharp coldness of the north, nor the sinking sunset of the west. Lines 19–21 employ another Renaissance notion, that mortality and decay are the result of the mixture of unequal or dissimilar elements in the body. Donne concludes that since the two of them are not dissimilar (being "one" in their love), or, at least, since they are completely "alike" in the intensity of their feelings, they need not fear death.

The rich allusiveness of the poem, with its hyperbolic declarations balanced against recurrent denials of any need for jealousy or the fear of infidelity, make this a more complicated poem than its declarative statements suggest. The speaker insists on the perfection and permanence of their mutual love, but this idealism is presented in a context that acknowledges the probability of change. The references to new geographical discoveries attest to the temporal nature of human knowledge, just as the opening stanza shows that individual human beings develop and change. Despite the insistence in the last three lines, death is a certainty for these perfect lovers, and if the real hemispheres of Earth contain "sharp north" and "declining west," the microcosm of the lovers' united being will ultimately be subjected to the same vicissitudes. At the same time that the poem declares the permanence of this love, it alludes to the actual impossibility of it.

The fullest analysis of this poem is by Clay Hunt, in *Donne's Poetry: Essays in Literary Analysis* (Hamden, CT: Archon, 1969) 53–69, a repr. of the Yale UP 1954 ed. Other valuable comments may be found in Wilbur Sanders, *John Donne's Poetry* (Cambridge: Cambridge UP, 1971) 64–68, and Judah Stampfer, *John Donne and the Metaphysical Gesture* (New York: Simon, 1970) 142–46.   TRA

John Donne   Song: Go and catch a falling star (page 958)

In content this poem expresses an extremely disillusioned and cynical view of human life and particularly of feminine virtue. The speaker, addressing an unidentified interlocutor, bids him in the first six lines to perform a series of tasks that share the common characteristic of being impossible. The implication is that the task he commands in the last three lines of the stanza is equally impossible: to find any condition of life that favors the advancement of "an honest mind." (In modern idiom, "Nice guys finish last.")

In the second stanza the speaker zeroes in on his true target—women's lack of virtue. If, he tells his companion, you are a person with a gift for seeing miraculous events or things invisible to the ordinary eye, go on a journey, ride "ten thousand days and nights," do not return until you are old; no matter how wide or long your search, even with your gift for seeing wondrous things, you will be unable to find a woman who is both beautiful and faithful in love. (He may perhaps find some faithful ugly ones, but those women with opportunities to be unfaithful will take them.)

In the third stanza the speaker seemingly retreats half a step from this extreme conclusion. *If* you find one, he tells his companion, let me know, for it would be sweet to make a "pilgrimage" to see such a saint. But then he retracts this injunction, showing that he has not really retreated at all. Do not tell me, he says, for even were she still true when I received your letter, still, by the time I could complete my journey, were it only next door, she would have proved unfaithful to two or three lovers. His "pilgrimage," he is convinced, would turn out to be a fool's errand. It is as impossible to find a woman both "true and fair" as to catch a falling star.

How seriously are we to take this poem? Should we imagine the speaker or poet as a man extremely embittered from a series of personal betrayals? Possibly. But it is called a "Song," and was indeed written to an "air" already in existence. Its meter is songlike (tetrameter, except for two monometer lines in each stanza). Its rhyming is copious (alternating in the first four lines, then a couplet of feminine rhymes, then three rhymes on one sound). More-over, its images and overstatements are so extreme, or so witty and charming, and its progress so amusing, that it is hard to take the poem gravely. It seems more playful than disenchanted, more entertaining than sad. The poet, one decides, has adopted a fashionably cynical pose and tried to see how ingen-iously and entertainingly he could deal with it. In short, the poem—and its speaker—are too lively to be lugubrious.   LP

John Donne   The Triple Fool (page 959)

The speaker is (a) a poet and (b) a rejected lover. The complaint of a spurned lover was one of the commonest subjects for poetry in Donne's time; but, as so often in his poetry, Donne here takes a thoroughly conventional subject and gives it a thoroughly original treatment. Part of his originality is that, instead of complaining about his lady's coldness, he turns the blame for his unhappiness on himself, calling himself a "triple fool." Another part of his originality is his exploitation of the modern idea that writing about one's suf-fering in a structured form has therapeutic value for the poet. But the origi-nality is also manifest in finer details of the poem; for instance, in the choice of the unusual epithet "whining" attached to "poetry" (is he characterizing *all* poetry with this epithet or just the kind that complains about the cruelty of the poet's beloved?), and in the use of a "scientific" analogy for explaining the healing effect of expressing his grief in verse: ocean water (grief), he claims, is purged of its salt (bitterness) in its passage through narrow, crooked, under-ground ways ("rhyme's vexations") to freshwater lakes and streams (psycho-logical health). (The word "rhyme" may be read literally here but is more prof-itably taken as a metonymy for verse in general; "rhyme's vexations" are the difficulty of finding words that exactly fit the writer's meaning and at the same time fulfill the requirements of both meter and rhyme.) But the main power of the comparison lies in the implicit link between the salt of ocean water and the salt of tears. In speaking of grief Donne mentions neither tears nor salt, but he knows that his readers will make the connection. Having admired Donne's analogy, how do we judge it when we learn that Donne's "science" is false? Although Donne used the standard scientific explanation of his time for the difference between salt water and fresh water, we now know that the real explanation is almost the opposite of his: the salt in the ocean is deposited there by streams that dissolve it from the earth on their way from the lakes to the seas. How does this knowledge affect the worth of the poem? The differences between scientific truth, historical truth, and poetic truth must at some time be confronted. They are germane to other poems in our study, such as Donne's "A Valediction: Forbidding Mourning" (page 729) and Keats's "On First Looking into Chapman's Homer" (page 886).

It is important in reading this poem to determine with some accuracy how serious the poet or the speaker (are they the same?) is in calling himself a "triple fool." A careful reading reveals, I think, that the tone of the poem is relatively light. The speaker bears his follies lightly, humorously exaggerating each of his three claims for being a fool. He is not in despair. First, he claims that he is a fool for loving someone who does not return his love: "she" (the beloved woman) denies him; consequently, he asserts, he suffers pains and grief. But he reneges on this assertion before he has finished making it, by saying, in lines 4–5, "But where's the wiseman that would not be I / If she did not deny?" This purely rhetorical question pays extravagant tribute to the beloved, implying that she has so many desirable qualities that nowhere in the world could a wise man be found who would not want to trade positions with the speaker if the woman did not "deny" him. The speaker's folly is thus substantially diminished. He can hardly be thought too great a fool for seeking the love of so desirable a woman.

Second, he claims that he is a fool for expressing his grief in "whining poetry" (3). But nothing he says in the rest of the first stanza supports this initial declaration. He develops the idea of the therapeutic value through a beautifully apt and ingenious comparison. The poet ends the stanza with a direct statement of his belief in the power of poetry to alleviate grief: "Grief brought to numbers cannot be so fierce, / For he tames it that fetters it in verse" (10–11).

Third, he claims he is a fool because some musician may set his poem to music and sing it in a public concert. This song, while delighting other members of the audience, starts the poet's grief flowing again. But at this point he makes the most illogical statement in the poem. Love and grief are proper subjects for poetry, he claims, but not if it is *good* poetry—not if it pleases when it is heard; for then the triumph of love and grief over him are published abroad, and he becomes a "triple fool": first, for loving a woman who does not return his love; second, for expressing his grief in verse, which alleviates the pain; third, for thus opening the possibility that his poem may be set to music and sung publicly, thereby (a) arousing once more his grief and (b) subjecting him to the embarrassment of letting the whole world know of his "folly."

The poem ends with a generalization: the biggest fools are not congenital idiots, but those who are "a little wise"—wise enough, perhaps, to

perceive their folly. The speaker, basing this generalization on his own experience, has been wise enough to choose an extremely attractive and virtuous woman to fall in love with, is gifted enough to write a good poem
about his grief, but is unlucky enough to prompt a gifted composer to set
his words to music and sing them in public. We must quarrel, however,
even with this last assertion. If he really is grieved and embarrassed by this
third event (no act of his own), why does he write *this* poem ("The Triple
Fool"), which can only make his follies even more widely known? Is he not
sucking pleasure out of his grief?   LP

Keith Douglas   Vergissmeinnicht (page 959)

The setting is probably the North African desert where British forces under General Montgomery fought a prolonged and bitter campaign against
German forces under General Rommel ("The Desert Fox") during World
War II. The speaker, a British soldier, accompanied by one or more fellow soldiers, has returned, three weeks afterward, to the site of a particularly fierce
engagement. They find, still sprawled under the barrel of his antitank gun,
the body of a German soldier who had made a direct hit on the speaker's tank
before being killed. In the gunpit spoil the speaker finds a photograph of the
dead German's sweetheart, signed with her name and the German word for
"Forget me not." The poem is based on a series of ironies: the inscription
"Forget me not" addressed to a soldier incapable now of memory; the fact
that the dead soldier's war equipment is still "hard and good," while its user
is "decayed"; the horrible contrast between the living man loved by the girl
and the corpse with its burst stomach and dusty eyes; the dual nature of man
that makes him capable of both love and killing; the fact that the shot aimed
at the soldier had "done the lover mortal hurt" (an ironic understatement).
What the speaker discovers in the dead German is a man once much like
himself. His tone expresses neither enmity, hate, nor triumph, but only pity
and shared humanity. The poem may be usefully compared with Hardy's
"The Man He Killed" (page 670).   LP

W. D. Ehrhart   Guns (page 960)

The speaker (like the poet) is a veteran of the Vietnam war. At the age
of eighteen he "killed / a ten-year-old" boy (21–22) and is still haunted by
the sight (lines 22–24 are in the present tense because the horrifying fact remains vividly present to him). The speaker is now the father of a four-year-
old daughter who, in all simplicity, tells her father that using a gun is
"'dumb'" (11), and he agrees with her but refrains from telling her exactly
why that is true. He was indeed ignorant at the time of the killing—"I didn't
know" (22) he admits to himself, though what it was he didn't know is not

clear. Was it that there was a boy in his line of fire? That the target was not a man as he supposed but a boy? That shooting someone showed him for the first time "what steel can do to flesh" (16)? Or, as time seems to have taught him, that using a gun was intrinsically wrong?

He knows that at some time he will have to explain to her to keep her from going "into the world / wide-eyed and ignorant" (28–29) as she now is and he was then. He must do that to protect her from the shattering realization that he had. Whatever it was he didn't know before the terrible event he will have to teach her, because he sees that "another war in another place" (32) will have the same effect on the young that he had to suffer. "[A]nother generation" (33) will go into that next war as ignorant as he was because "their fathers never told them" (35).

Despite the difference in tone and detail, this poem says much the same thing as Owen's "Dulce et Decorum Est" (page 651), and could profitably be compared to it as a writing assignment on tone.   TRA

Carolyn Forché   The Colonel (page 961)

The country is El Salvador, as we know from the context in which it appears—Forché's book *The Country Between Us* (New York: Harper, 1981), in which perhaps a third of the poems stem from visits to El Salvador made over a two-year period. Since the students do not have that context, perhaps they should be told beforehand which country is referred to. On the other hand, there may be value in asking them to identify as nearly as possible the locale of the poem. There are sufficient clues to identify the locale as a small Latin American country dominated by American culture and governed by a military regime, against which there is considerable opposition.

The precise date appended at the end suggests that the poem is based on an actual incident. Does this mean that the poem is factual, not fictional? It is written in prose, not verse. How does it differ, then, from a reportorial account? In many ways. No names are named, either of persons or places. The poem is addressed to a particular reader (a "you"), not to a general reader. The poem uses images that would not ordinarily be found in a newspaper account: "The moon swung bare on its black cord over the house." Perhaps most important, the last two sentences are surrealistic. They take us into a fantasy world. How distant they are from the first two!

The first two sentences reveal that the poem is a reply to a friend back home. The friend has asked some such question as "Is it true, as I heard on a news report, that you have been to Colonel __'s home?" The speaker replies, "I was in his house." The failure to give the "his" an antecedent in the poem, plus the fact that the friend knows his name, suggests that the colonel is well known outside his country and is important within it. His name has appeared in the newspapers. He may be the military dictator; he is at least a member of the ruling military junta. What does he mean when he talks of "how difficult it had become to govern"? What would he consider the signs and purposes of good government?

The central point in this poem lies in the shocking contrast between the civility and the brutality implied by the colonel's lifestyle. The tray of coffee and sugar, the daily papers, the pet dogs, the TV set, the good dinner—all suggest a style of civilized and gracious living such as many in our country enjoy. But the pistol on the cushion, the broken bottles embedded in the walls, the bag of human ears, and the colonel's angry outburst against "rights"—all suggest something quite different.   LP

Robert Frost   Birches (page 962)

Birches have white bark on the trunk and black bark on the branches and on the junctures where the branches join the trunk. They are such slender trees (unlike oaks) that they are easily bent over during "ice-storms": sometimes the weight of the ice carries their tops clear to the ground (to "the withered bracken") and freezes them there. When the ice melts, their tops are released, but the trees seldom resume their original straightness: they lean at all angles across the straighter, darker trees.

Though written in continuous form (no stanza or paragraph breaks), the poem may be divided roughly into three equal parts or "movements." The first twenty lines describe the appearance of the trees and their thawing after an ice-storm that bends the birches down "to stay." And what a beautiful and yet accurate description it is! But this is what the speaker calls the "matter-of-fact" (22) about birches.

In the second movement (21–41) the poet moves away from fact into fancy. Although he knows that ice-storms are what bend the birches, he likes to imagine that they were bent down by a farm boy who had no companions and so had to invent his own amusements. He fancies such a boy getting his best play by swinging on birches; that is, by climbing the trees up into their topmost branches where they can no longer bear his weight but bend over gracefully and allow him to drop to the ground. This fancy becomes so vivid in the speaker's imagination that he seems to be describing a real boy—one who played this game with great skill. "He learned all there was / To learn" about doing it well, climbing to exactly the right height and releasing at exactly the right moment for experiencing the maximum thrill. The poet's use of the past tense here abets the feeling of reality. It almost seems to the poet himself that the boy had bent down all the birches on his father's land. We have forgotten the "matter-of-fact" that "swinging doesn't bend them down to stay / As ice-storms do."

If the second movement takes us away from "matter-of-fact" into improbable fancy, the final movement (41–59) takes us even further, into impossible fantasy. The first line of this section ("So was I once myself a swinger of birches") might be taken as literally true, but in the next line the speaker begins to "dream" of becoming one once again. Swinging birches at this point becomes a symbol for getting away from earth (literally, the ground; symbolically, life) for a while and then coming back to it. This wish, of course, is impossible to fulfill, but the poet likes to indulge himself with it when his life "is too much like a pathless wood" and he is "weary of considerations" (of having to make countless practical and moral decisions about problems in his life). At such points he'd "like to get away from" life for a while, and then come back, and he imagines himself doing it with the same grace and skill as he attributed to his imaginary farm boy. "That would be good both going (getting away from his troubles) and coming back" (returning to the persons and activities that he has loved).

One other symbol must be explicated to get to the whole meaning of the poem. As the speaker climbs his imaginary tree (54), he is pointed "*Toward* heaven"; but he does not want to get there: "Earth's the right place for love: / I don't know where it's likely to go better." Such a statement could hardly be made by anyone with a strong belief in the traditional Christian concept of heaven as the perfect place that the righteous go to after death. "[H]eaven" here is not a place, but a perfection of life or art that man can aspire to in this life. The imagined farm boy who "learned all there was / To learn" about swinging birches and who

> always kept his poise
> To the top branches, climbing carefully
> With the same pains you use to fill a cup
> Up to the brim, and even above the brim

is appealing because Frost has endowed him with the desire and the ability to do the thing skillfully. Frost always admires the person who has learned to perform a task or a game with conscious skill, whether it be swinging birches, chopping wood, building a load of hay, or writing poetry.

Frost writes poetry well. "Birches" is written in blank verse. The first four lines are perfectly regular, establishing the meter for the reader. After that, though there is no deviation from the pentameter, there is considerable variation in the iambs, principally to enhance the conversational quality of the verse ("But I was going to say . . ."), but also to reinforce meaning. The best example of this is probably to be found in lines 39–40:

$$\text{Then he flung} \mid \text{out- ward,} \mid \text{feet first,} \mid \text{with a swish,} \mid$$

$$\text{Kick-ing his} \mid \text{way down} \mid \text{through the air} \mid \text{to the ground.} \mid$$

Frost also makes effective use of onomatopoeia (*click, cracks, swish*); of alliteration (*cracks and crazes, climbing carefully*); of consonance (*left and right, feet first*); of assonance (*Shattering and avalanching*); and even of internal rhyme (*cup, Up*). The figurative language employed in the poem is homely yet highly original—the most important figures: metaphor, *broken glass*; similes, *inner dome of heaven, girls on hands and knees, fill a cup, a pathless wood;* personification, *Truth;* and understatement, *One could do worse than be a swinger of birches.* These open a whole new area for discussion and exploration; however, an instructor's manual cannot touch all the bases, even in a poem that mentions baseball.

However, one allusion in the poem demands attention because of its importance to theme: the motif of the half-fulfilled prayer in lines 50–52.

> May no fate willfully misunderstand me
> And half grant what I wish to snatch me away
> Not to return.

In the *Iliad,* 16, Achilles prays that his friend Patroclus may recapture the Greek ships from the Trojans and return safe. In Pope's translation:

> Great Jove consents to half the chief's request,
> But heaven's eternal doom denies the rest;
> To free the fleet was granted to his prayer;
> His safe return, the winds dispersed in air.

Patroclus frees the ships, but is slain by Hector in the process. In the *Aeneid,* 11, the Trojan Aruns makes a similar request: he prays to Apollo that he may slay the leader of the foe's cavalry and return safe home. In Dryden's translation:

> Apollo heard, and granting half his pray'r,
> Shuffled in winds the rest, and toss'd in empty air.

Alexander Pope, in his mock epic *The Rape of the Lock,* 2, exploits the tradition by giving his hero the ambition to clip a favorite lock of hair from his heroine's head. He prays to the goddess of Love to help him

> Soon to obtain, and long possess the prize.

But the event is now predictable:

> The pow'rs gave ear, and granted half his pray'r,
> The rest, the wind dispers'd in empty air.

Frost makes it very clear that he wants no half-fulfillments of his wish. If he has to choose between climbing birches and staying back, he will choose staying back, because "Earth's the right place for love." The central theme of "Birches," and of Frost's poetry in general, is life's livability. Is life worth living or not? Sometimes he gives a dark answer, sometimes a bright one, but the most characteristic answer gives a slight edge, often a very slight edge, to the affirmative. Check this generalization with the other Frost poems in this book and see if you agree. "Birches" is one of his most popular and most anthologized poems; first, because it is excellent poetry, and second, because it seems more optimistic than it really is. The description of the thawing ice is a beautiful phenomenon beautifully described. The account of the imaginary farm boy swinging birches is appealing in many ways. The assertion that "Earth's the right place for love" is what we'd all like to believe. The sunniness of these passages is so brilliant that we overlook or forget the passage about life's being "like a pathless wood," so terrifying and painful that we would like to get away from it, not by climbing a tree with a "snow-white trunk" but, perhaps, by plunging into a stagnant pool that we cannot climb out of. If "Birches" is a poem of beauty and love, it is also a poem of terror.   LP

Robert Frost   Mending Wall (page 963)

At first reading this poem will seem to be about walls and about two New England farmers who have opposite philosophies concerning them. Each philosophy is stated twice: the speaker's in the first line and in line 35: "Something there is that doesn't love a wall"; the neighboring farmer's in line 27 and in the final line: "'Good fences make good neighbors.'" But as we dig into the poem a little deeper we may conclude that the poem is less about walls and opposed philosophies concerning them than it is about opposed kinds of mental habit. The neighboring farmer's philosophy is clear and definite, and we know exactly where he got it. He got it from his father, who got it from his father, who got it. . . . In short, it is a traditional piece of folk wisdom, a proverbial saying that he has accepted as dogma without questioning its meaning or validity. The speaker, on the other hand, states his philosophy more tentatively: "*Something there is* that doesn't love a wall." He seems not quite certain what that "Something" is, though. As a matter of fact, he knows exactly what "spills the upper boulders in the sun" over the winter months. It is "the frozen-ground-swell" underneath the wall: the expansion of the earth caused by the freezing of the moisture always present in the ground. Nature causes the wall to crumble. But he is inclined to think there may be more to it than that: not just nature but something *in* nature or in the nature of things "doesn't love" a wall. He hasn't put a label on it. But not only is he more tentative in his thinking than his neighbor, he is also more reflective, thoughtful, and flexible. He has a questioning habit of mind. Of his neighbor's proverbial saying he asks, "'*Why* do they make good neighbors? Isn't it / Where there are cows?'" ("*Why*" is the kind of question his neighbor has never asked.) But in asking this question, or rather these two questions, he confesses that there is some truth in his neighbor's position, and he identifies exactly the source of that truth. When one or both neighbors own livestock, the wall prevents contention between them by keeping the livestock in their proper fields and keeping one farmer's cows from eating the other's crops. (A "good neighbor," as defined by the proverb, is one whom you can live next to without friction.) The neighbor's attitude toward walls, like most proverbial wisdom, contains a half-truth. ("Look before you leap" and "He who hesitates is lost," though contradictory, both state half-truths; that is, each is true in some situations, neither is true in all situations.) It is now apparent that the speaker's attitude toward walls is not so diametrically opposed to his neighbor's as at first appeared. He recognizes

the necessity, the desirability, of *some* walls. Indeed he has all by himself on occasion gone out and "made repair" after hunters have completely torn down
part of a wall. Still, the desirability of a wall depends upon the situation, and
"'here there are no cows.'" Before *he* built a wall he'd ask what he "'was
walling in or walling out.'" He continues to think that there is "'Something'"
that "'doesn't love a wall, / That wants it down,'" but he is not himself opposed to all walls, just unnecessary ones, and especially those that wall in or
wall out something that ought not to be walled in or out. However, he is flexible. *He* is the one who contacts his neighbor "at spring mending-time" to let
him know when he is available. He knows what his neighbor's attitude toward
walls is, and he knows that to stay on neighborly terms with him, he must
honor that attitude even while trying to argue him out of it.

But there is much more to the contrast between these two farmers than
simply their attitudes toward walls. The speaker is observant: he can tell the
difference between the gaps made by the frozen-ground-swell in winter and
those made by hunters in other seasons. He knows how handling rocks all day
can wear one's fingers "rough." He has imagination, a playful, whimsical turn
of mind, and a sense of humor. Some boulders, he observes, are so round that
they "have to use a spell to make them balance: / 'Stay where you are until our
backs are turned!'" He compares the process of mending wall to "just another . . . game, / One on a side." He anticipates his point about the cows by
saying: "My apple trees will never get across / And eat the cones under [your]
pines." His perceptiveness is apparent when he thinks about how to explain
what the "Something" is that doesn't love a wall. Whatever it is (Love perhaps? Some principle of community or brotherhood?), the speaker knows
that, to reach his neighbor's understanding, he must communicate the idea in
concrete terms, not in abstractions. He fleetingly thinks of "elves" because his
fancy has a fondness for elves and because elves (if one actually believes in
them, as the speaker almost surely doesn't) are a physical agency that the
neighbor's mind could grasp—and might accept if he were an Irish peasant
rather than a New England farmer. But the speaker immediately realizes the
absurdity of this explanation and casts it aside, for "it's not elves exactly, and
I'd rather / He said it for himself." This last remark shows the speaker's grasp
of an important principle of education: that the learner will be much more
likely to grasp and accept a concept that he has figured out for himself than
one he has merely had *explained* to him (if you want a fancy name for this
method of teaching, it's *heuristic*). Thus we find in the speaker a mind that is
probing, perceptive, and critical, but also imaginative, whimsical, and playful,
though possibly a little indefinite in its inability to define that "Something"
even to itself. In the neighbor we see a matter-of-fact, uncritical mind that accepts traditional wisdom unquestioningly and holds on to it dogmatically. It is
this contrast of minds that provides the central interest of the poem. In the
speaker's perception his neighbor "moves in darkness"—the darkness of ignorance and uncritical acceptance. He sees his neighbor there, "Bringing a stone
grasped firmly by the top / In each hand, like an old-stone savage armed." The

implications of the simile are: first, that an unquestioning habit of mind is primitive, like that of paleolithic man; second, that there is something potentially menacing about such a habit of mind. No doubt the speaker and his neighbor will continue to get on amicably enough, and not start throwing rocks at each other: the neighbor is conscientious and hard-working, and both men want to be "good neighbors" in some sense of the term. Nevertheless, it is people shouting slogans, clinging to half-truths dogmatically, who rush into wars against each other and go on holy crusades. It is this kind of mental set that creates unnecessary "walls" between men, that "Something" (Love? Reason? Brotherhood?) "wants . . . down."

Such, at least, is my reading (a fairly old-fashioned one) of what has become one of Frost's most controversial poems. On one axis, the range of opinion goes from Robert Graves's statement "If anyone asks: 'But what is the something that doesn't love a wall?' the answer is, of course, 'frost'—also its open-hearted namesake, Robert Frost," to Elizabeth Jennings's assertion that "Good fences make good neighbors" is the moral of the poem. On another axis, opinion ranges from Carson Gibbs's assessment of the speaker as "witty, tolerant, and reasonable" to Donald Cunningham's that he is "hollow, vain, and foolish." For varying viewpoints, see Elaine Barry, *Robert Frost* (New York: Ungar, 1973) 109–12; Marie Boroff, *Language and the Poet* (Chicago: U of Chicago P, 1979) 24–30; Donald Cunningham, "Mending a Wall," in *Gone into If Not Explained*, ed. Greg Kuzma (Crete, NE: Best Cellar, 1976) 65–73; Carson Gibbs, "Mending Wall," *Explicator* 20 (Feb.1962): item 48; Robert Graves, "Introduction," *Selected Poems of Robert Frost* (New York: Holt, 1963) xiii; Elizabeth Jennings, *Frost* (New York: Barnes, 1966) 24; John C. Kemp, *Robert Frost and New England* (Princeton: Princeton UP, 1979) 13–26; Frank Lentricchia, *Robert Frost* (Durham: Duke UP, 1973) 104–107; John F. Lynen, *The Pastoral Art of Robert Frost* (New Haven: Yale UP, 1960) 27–31; Marion Montgomery, "Robert Frost and His Use of Barriers," *South Atlantic Quarterly* 57 (1958): 349–50; Richard Poirier, *Robert Frost: The Work of Knowing* (New York: Oxford UP, 1977) 104–106; Charles N. Watson Jr., "Frost's Wall: The View from the Other Side," *New England Quarterly* 44 (1971): 653–56.   LP

Another author speaks

"'Good fences make good neighbors'" may be the most famous phrase in all of Frost's poetry. Like many famous quotations, it is misleading when quoted out of context or when it is offered as Frost's "philosophy."

The poem is narrative, restricting itself to the speaker's attitudes. It poses the narrator against his neighbor, as men of two opposing philosophies, and, as can be the case when we report our experiences, the narrator is given the privilege of considering his position the correct one. The neighbor is only permitted to speak his famous line, twice; what *he* thinks of the speaker is altogether missing from the poem. It can be instructive to ask a class to imagine exactly what the neighbor might be thinking about the speaker—what a man who "will not go behind his father's saying" (or so the speaker claims) thinks about a man who first informs him it is time to mend the wall, and then wants to ask what walls are for, and who seems to believe in some vague "'Something . . . that doesn't love a wall.'"

A proper reading of the poem requires taking into account the limitation and the implicit prejudice that results from one participant's report of a debate, and that naturally renders the resolution suspect: the speaker clearly thinks he has "won" because he is a thinking man who wants "to go behind" rural lore, while his neighbor "moves in darkness" of the mind. The reader also needs to understand the dialectic opposition of the two points of view. The speaker is a man who wants to know the reasons for his actions, who investigates and meditates, who likes to believe (probably thinking himself only whimsical) in the vague "Something," in using spells to balance the stones, even—almost—in elves. That is, he is a compound of rationality and a desire to find something beyond rationality. He is also a man of apple orchards, of domestication, of playing games according to equitable rules, who takes pride in being civil and civilized.

Stripped of the prejudiced reporting of the speaker, the neighbor is a man who accepts traditional teachings, who shares in the responsibility of maintaining private property, and whose land is in its natural state, a pine forest. He also believes in neighborliness and the soundness of workmanship. What the speaker's attitude contributes to the portrait of the neighbor reveals more about the speaker than about his opponent in the game of wall-mending. Because of the neighbor's taciturnity, the speaker thinks him shallow-minded, ignorant, primitive, unable to think or investigate. That is, he interprets the neighbor's attitude as further evidence of his own superiority. The man who is different from him is the man who is inferior to him. Does the neighbor go so far in interpreting the speaker's difference?

John F. Lynen points out that the poem presents an unresolved question: "Should man tear down the barriers which isolate individuals from one another, or should he recognize that distinctions and limitations are necessary to human life?" Attempting to answer this question, many readers have tried to pin down the poem to a simple set of paired opposites—liberal and conservative, rational and instinctive, civilized and primitive, and many more. But although the terms of the poem teasingly invite the search for an easy symbolic reading and also tease the reader into supposing that the speaker is "right," no easy symbols or easy solutions are available. The poem is memorable for the irresolution that keeps us searching.   TRA

Robert Frost   Never Again Would Birds' Song Be the Same (page 965)

Time, place, situation: Adam in the Garden of Eden before tasting the forbidden fruit, expressing his love for Eve and drawing conclusions about her effect on the world and about God's purpose in creating her—to add forever some quality of her beauty to nature. There is probably no example of dramatic irony in this book that is more total and central to the meaning of the poem—for Adam has got it completely wrong and, moreover, in his praise for Eve, he is displaying the primacy of his love for his wife that will cause him to join her in tasting the fruit. (The allusions in this poem are to full accounts of Adam's Fall, such as Milton's in *Paradise Lost*, rather than to the bare story in Genesis.)

Several details of the poem are especially ironic in light of the events that followed. The fact that her "eloquence" could only produce its effect on the birds "when *call* or laughter carried it aloft" (6, 8) predicts in part the grief and lamentation, and the harsh recrimination, which move both Adam and Eve after the Fall. That the sound of Eve's voice "never would be lost" (12) from nature may look toward the permanent change of the natural world as well as the human world caused by the Fall, the coming of death into the world. And the confident last line, asserting that the purpose of Eve's creation was to make the world better, makes fullest use of irony, for the opposite was the result.

Yet for all the darker implications, we should not overlook the genuineness of this loving statement, the praise that expresses Adam's nature as well as Eve's beauty. No man can foresee the future, and there is a hint of self-knowledge on that point in the opening line and in the concession to fact implied in such words and phrases as "Admittedly" (6), "Be that as may be" (9), and "probably" (12). Consequently, when Adam declares his conclusions so forcefully, even while he concedes to some uncertainty, he reveals the depth and grandeur of his love. It is a statement of love that wills itself to ignore or push aside contradictory possibilities, a universal human trait.   TRA

Robert Frost   The Oven Bird (page 965)

The bird of which Frost writes is common in New England; it is so named because it builds an oven-shaped nest (a dome with an entry hole) of twigs and leaves on the floor of the forest. Properly called ovenbird, it has two distinct kinds of song: at mating season, it warbles melodically; but through the rest of the year in the north before it migrates, its song is said to be a harsh repetition of the syllables "tea-CHER," accenting the second syllable, which it repeats with increasing volume but in the same tempo. Unlike many songbirds whose singing is limited to mating and territorial songs that seem to fade away as the summer proceeds, the ovenbird continues to announce his presence—and seems to insist on his pedagogical purpose and his centrality.

This information is supplied because in fact not "everyone has heard" the ovenbird, not even all New Englanders. The overstatement of the first line should strike the reader as claiming universality when reality is something else; the overstatement in effect signals that the poem is not really a naturalist's description but an imaginative and meaningful symbol. The first three lines sound boastful, the bird laying claim to power and position and demanding universal attention.

"He says," the poem repeats (4, 6, 10), personification that reiterates his role as teacher. *What* he says is that as the summer runs on, it is less luxuriant, less joyful, less beautiful than spring, and when the autumnal leaves imitate the springtime petals in falling from the trees, the bird points out how all of nature has been tainted by humanity and its works.

This bird not only "says," he also "knows" (12)—he knows that this is no world for joyous singing, that his lesson is not beautiful but must be delivered. But at last he is not really sage or speaker—he concludes by asking not in language but by his persistent presence "what to make of a diminished thing" (14). His loud song has seemed to have power and perhaps even some healing force: he "makes the solid tree trunks sound again" (3) as they echo soundly, the reverberating forest taking on some of the health and vigor of early summer. But the reality is that as time passes during the year there is a diminution of natural vitality, and the more we hear the ovenbird as he outsings the other birds, the more that fact is impressed upon us.

The poem thus takes as its subjects the downward slope of the year and the emotions it evokes, and the intrusive presence of humanity that also diminishes the natural world. There is a further dimension suggested by line 9, "And comes that other fall we name the fall." The immediate and literal contrast is between "early petal-fall" (6) of springtime and the fall of leaves in the autumn. However, "we" are introduced once again, "everyone" as line 1 says, and the naming of the season "the fall" is our doing. We also have named another Fall, the disjunction between man and Creator that brought death into the world and made us and all creation to suffer "the penalty of Adam, / The seasons' difference" (*As You Like It*, 2.1.5–6). The actions of man have had two results, then: building our highways taints nature, and falling from grace spoils the perfect world. Thus the evidence of the ovenbird symbolizes an array of "diminished things."

The form of the poem supports these themes. Like a sonnet it contains 14 lines of iambic pentameter (line 2 is freely varied), but its rhymes do not conform to any sonnet scheme and it is not divided into quatrains and couplet nor octave and sestet. Yet there are intriguing reminiscences of sonnet forms: the last four lines do form a quatrain *abab*, the opening two lines are a rhymed couplet, and there is a "turn" after line 8 when the fall from Eden is introduced. Not to be too literalistic about formal matters, this may be called a "diminished" sonnet.   TRA

R. S. Gwynn   Snow White and the Seven Deadly Sins

(page 965)

Fancifully mingling fairy tale, Christian lore, and modern life, this poem exuberantly lavishes its irony on all three. Its underlying allegory posits a "Good Catholic girl" in bondage to sins but maintaining her virtue through hard work, prayer, and the instructions of her church. At the end, presented with a fairy-tale possibility of escape into a more acceptable kind of bondage, marriage to a "charming . . . *Male*," she chooses instead to withdraw from both sin and the role assigned to women in scripture, and to immure herself in a convent. There is a meaning there, but to state it in this way seems far too ponderous for the delightful wittiness of this poem.

One important twist that Gwynn gives to the "Seven Deadly Sins" rests in the modern setting. These seven are certainly not tempting or alluring (what sin is *supposed* to be), but rather coarse, contemporary versions. *Pride* is not spiritual pride but narcissism; *Lust* is into pornography and sado-masochism; *Gluttony* is a besotted beer-guzzler; *Avarice* expresses himself in poker games; *Envy* is cheap but brand-conscious; *Sloth* is a lazy slob; and *Wrath* is a physical brute. Allegories of the sins traditionally tend to portray them either as seductive or as monsters; Gwynn's are entirely human por-traits, reminding us that the grandeur of evil (Milton's Satan, Shakespeare's Iago) is much less prevalent than debased humanity.

"Impeccably" as an adverb for the charming prince's speech is wonder-fully right: from the Latin, he is exempt from the possibility of sinfulness.

Gwynn's poem alludes primarily to the Disney version of the tale, which it employs both for witty contrast and as an ironic butt—such happily-ever-after visions of reality don't contain much human truth apart from our desire for wishes to come true. The Disney dwarfs cannot be identified with these sins except perhaps for Grumpy (Wrath?) and Sleepy (Sloth?); there is no corresponding sin for Doc, Happy, Dopey, Sneezy, or Bashful. Disney's jolly work song ("Hi ho, hi ho, it's off to work we go") is answered by "*Ho-hum. Ho-hum. It's home from work we come.*" And the episode of Snow White's eat-ing of the poisoned apple and being awakened by her Prince Charming is turned upside down as the "Good Catholic girl" wards off both an evil spell and a bridegroom.   TRA

Rachel Hadas   The Red Hat (page 967)

The poem recounts one of the minor and uncountable phases in a par-ent's permitting a child to move toward maturity and independence. The son is "officially" (2) allowed to walk to school alone—officially, because that is what should formally be taking place, the mother knows, although "[s]emi-alone" (3) is the actual fact, for one or the other of the parents is permitted (by the boy) to trail along behind him on the other side of the street until he reaches the point when they are not allowed by him to follow farther.

The mother recalls that only "two weeks ago" (13) he was taken to school, led by the hand, and would "dawdle, dreamy, slow" (14), in a show of childish incapability and inattentiveness that certainly did not promise a sudden ca-pacity to go alone to school or anywhere else without parental pushing and pulling. But once released, he is now "striding briskly" into self-sufficiency. The power that pulls him forward toward school is "far more powerful than school," for it is the pull of independence.

The subject of the poem is the emotional response of the parents toward an inevitable and even "officially" welcomed change. Their boy is growing toward manhood. But having to stand back, to allow him to move into places where he can make mistakes for himself and learn by his own volition, is painful. The summary second paragraph metaphorically compares the difference between then and now to being adrift in a flimsy boat in dangerous seas—but ironically, although one might have expected the mother to draw a comparison between her newly launched son and a small craft "wavering in the eddies" (20) of his new environment, she compares the parents to the "empty, unanchored" boat. "The red hat" of the child has sailed away from them, leaving them to feel bereft and directionless. It is an unexpected conclusion, but once considered, a truth that any parent will feel either sooner (as in this case) or later, when children have shown their true independence and leave their parents behind without that stabilizing mission of protection and control.   TRA

Donald Hall   My Son, My Executioner (page 967)

Hall's brief, eloquent lyric expresses a young father's heightened awareness of mortality after the birth of his son. Before becoming parents, the speaker and his wife gloried in the youthful delusion that they might "live forever," but their child brings a new, chastened perspective; now it is their son who represents "enduring life," while the parents begin "to die together." The poem turns on the paradox that new life emphasizes the fact of natural process toward death; the speaker is aware that his baby's "cries and hungers document / Our bodily decay."

The poem's language contains another paradox as well: though the son is described, in the startling first line, as the speaker's "executioner," he is also an "instrument / Of immortality," since his life will remain as a testament to the parents' existence after they are gone. The tone is one of quiet pathos; the insight brought by the child's birth inspires neither anger nor resentment on the speaker's part, but rather a hushed, awed awareness of his changing role in the natural cycle of love and regeneration.   GJ

Thomas Hardy   Channel Firing (page 968)

Hardy's dating of this poem may make it seem prophetic, since World War I broke out in August 1914; but it was a prophecy almost anyone could have made, for the event referred to in line 1 was well known: the Royal Navy was conducting gunnery practice in the English Channel, and the guns could be heard many miles inland. (Hardy is reported to have been surprised, in fact, that the war began only a few months afterward.)

The speaker in the poem is one of the dead, presumably a clergyman buried within the chancel of his church where the clergy were usually interred; he is familiar with the altar, chancel windows, and "glebe cow" (9), and seems to be in the habit of having chats with others buried nearby, including "Parson Thirdly" (31). The folklike simplicity of the poem, achieved through its tetrameter quatrains and simple diction, makes the whole experience seem rustic and unsophisticated, the material of a ballad. The dead have been awakened by the great guns ("loud enough to wake the dead," we might say), and at first they suppose that "Judgment-day" has come. The noise has even terrified the hounds, the churchmouse, the worms, and the cow—not because they anticipate the apocalypse, of course, but because they instinctively fear loud sounds.

God, however, sardonic but comforting, tells the dead to return to their sleep: it's only men threatening men, not a divine event. Although many men *deserve* to go to hell, God has not destroyed the world, nor does he seem to want to anytime soon, for he takes pity on mankind's need for "rest eternal" (24).

Parson Thirdly's reaction to this news in the penultimate stanza is pragmatic: if God is not going to separate the sheep from the goats, it might have been more pleasant to have "stuck to pipes and beer" (32) instead of depriving himself for the sake of piety.

The tone of the poem shifts markedly in the last stanza. Instead of the folk narrative of the speaker and the paternal chattiness of God, the last stanza turns to brooding lyricism. Alliteration, consonance, and assonance ("roaring–readiness"; "again–guns"; "hour–roaring"; "readiness–avenge") pack the first two lines. The last two abound in *st* and *t* sounds: "*St*ourton Tower," "Camelot," "*st*arlit Stonehenge"; and the last two feet in this iambic poem are trochees, mysteriously trailing off in the mournful music that the theme demands. The bulk of the poem has been whimsical, folksy, and not particularly alarming—ironically, since the subjects have included naval bombardment, skeletons, damnation and piety, and God's potential wrath; but the theme is the persistence among men of aggression, violence, and the recurrence of military conquest to establish and maintain civilization. God (who tends to speak in clichés, the rustic father of his rustic flock) puts it directly: "'The world is as it used to be'" (12).

A "glebe cow" is pastured in the parcel of land allotted to a clergyman as part of his benefice; like the land and the parsonage, it is provided for his use but is not his private property. The name "Parson Thirdly" may allude to the Holy Trinity; a Parson Thirdly is a character in Hardy's novel *Far from the Madding Crowd*. The spelling "Christès" (15) is archaic, in keeping with the ballad style and the time references implicit in the last stanza.

For further discussion see Babette Deutsch, *Poetry in Our Time* (Garden City, NY: Anchor/Doubleday, 1963) 9–10; John Crowe Ransom, "Introduction" to *Selected Poems of Thomas Hardy* (New York: Macmillan, 1961) x–xii; Cleanth Brooks and Robert Penn Warren, *Understanding Poetry*

(New York: Holt, 1976) 45–48; J. O. Bailey, *The Poetry of Thomas Hardy: A Handbook and Commentary* (Chapel Hill: U of North Carolina P, 1970) 262–64.   TRA

Thomas Hardy   The Darkling Thrush (page 969)

The end of the day, the end of the year, and the end of the century symbolically unite with the bleakness of the imagery in the first two stanzas of this poem to evoke a mood of utter desolation and hopelessness. The contrast between this desolation and the apparently unlimited joy of the thrush's song is the pivot on which the poem turns, and the contrast is so striking that it leads many students to read into this poem an optimism that is in fact not there. Conditioned by earlier experience with more cheerful poets and with sentimental cliché, they see in this poem the dark cloud with a silver lining, the tale of woe with a happy ending, darkness giving way to light, despair overcome by hope.

What the poem actually presents is subtler and less cheerful. The speaker is overcome with wonderment at the joy of the thrush's song, and momentarily—but only momentarily—he is prompted to wonder whether the bird may not know of some "blessed Hope." But, notice, he does not say that the thrush knew of some "blessed Hope." He does not even say, "I thought [did think] . . . he knew," but only, "I *could* think. . . ." That is, it's *as if* the bird sang out of some "blessed Hope." The speaker *could*—but didn't—think so. The thought has crossed his mind, but transiently, too swiftly to take up residence there. The speaker, after all, sees no cause for joy or hope "written" on the world around him. In the last line he flatly states that he is unaware of any hope. The bird sings, really, out of instinct, not out of knowledge, and basically the speaker knows this. The poem concludes, then, not with hope, but only with the wistful wish that there *were* some reason for hope, and with wonderment at the mystery of the bird's joyous song. The conclusion of "The Oxen" (page 811) evokes a similar mood and presents a similar interpretive problem.

Image and mood blend perfectly in this poem. The simile of the "tangled bine-stems" that score the sky like "strings of broken lyres" is marvelously effective, both visually and emotionally exact, giving a sense of music destroyed, of something else come to an end—like the day, the year, the century.   LP

Thomas Hardy   Hap (page 970)

Hardy's sonnet expresses an eloquent complaint against a random universe that is wholly indifferent to human happiness. Since a sonnet requires precisely the kind of formal unity and complex structure whose absence in the universe at large the speaker rails against, "Hap" may be seen as a kind of self-consolation (what Robert Frost called "a momentary stay against confusion") that responds to universal chaos with an example of artistic order.

The speaker insists that randomness is more unbearable than an actively malicious deity would be. If his sufferings were caused by a "vengeful god," he could at least take comfort in his own innocence and suffer the "ire unmerited." But rather than a malicious god, the speaker identifies "Crass Casualty" and "dicing Time" as the source of his pain. The abstraction "Casualty" suggests both the random, or casual, nature of human experiences, and the damaging accident that a human life becomes when subjected to the meaningless flux of nature; "dicing" has a similarly double meaning with its implication that time gambles with human fate and brings cutting pain to the human spirit. In the poem's best-known phrase, the speaker calls Casualty and Time a pair of "purblind Doomsters"; violent, gangster-like forces that are purblind, or partly blind, seem to the speaker the worst possible kind, since (unlike a vengeful god) it would seem possible that the luck of life's draw could just as easily have provided "blisses" to the speaker instead of his present suffering.

Hardy's clarity of vision and his use of such poetic techniques as, for example, the rhetorical question (in lines 9 and 10) and alliteration ("pilgrimage" and "pain" suggesting that the speaker's religious seeking has given way to modern despair), are the poet's only weapons against the indifferent universe he confronts.

For an extended discussion of this poem—including Hardy's employment of a persona, his use of religious allusion, and his skill in employing the sonnet form—see William E. Buckler, *The Poetry of Thomas Hardy: A Study in Art and Ideas* (New York: New York UP, 1984) 90–93.   GJ

A. E. Housman   To an Athlete Dying Young (page 971)

The speaker is a fellow townsman of the dead athlete, possibly (though not necessarily) one of the pallbearers carrying his coffin to the cemetery for burial. The athlete had died within months of winning the annual race for his town. The poem is an extended apostrophe addressed by the speaker to the athlete.

The parallelism of action and language between the first two stanzas beautifully underscores the ironic contrast in situation. After his victory in the race, the townspeople had "chaired" him (borne him in triumph on their shoulders) through the "market-place" to his home. Now, less than a year later, they bring him "home" again, again "Shoulder-high." But the meaning of "home" has changed between the two stanzas. In the second it is a metaphor for the grave. The "road all runners come" is death, and the youth is being borne "Shoulder-high" in his coffin. The "town" to which he now belongs ("stiller"—an understatement—than that which noisily "cheered" just a few months ago) is the cemetery or necropolis (city of the dead).

The chief ironic shock of the poem, however, comes in the third stanza. Most people would consider the death of a young athlete at the peak of his ability an occasion for lamentation; the speaker considers it one for congratulation. "Smart lad," he says (not "Poor lad,") and proceeds to praise the young athlete for dying "betimes." Except for his hyperbolic use of the word "Smart" when he literally means "fortunate" (the athlete did not commit suicide), the speaker is perfectly serious, and speaks for the poet; that is, the irony involved here is neither verbal nor dramatic but situational. Both speaker and poet regard the athlete as fortunate; the irony lies in the discrepancy between our expectation (initiated by the title and sustained through the first two stanzas) that the athlete's death will be regarded by the poet as pathetic or "tragic" and our discovery that it is regarded quite otherwise.

In the rest of the poem the speaker supports this attitude and is not undercut by the poet. The athlete has slipped away from "fields where glory does not stay." It is better, the speaker believes, to die when everyone is singing your praises than to die in obscurity years later (as so many once-celebrated athletes do). The "fields where glory does not stay" are literally athletic fields, symbolically earth or life in general; "glory" is fame and the pride of triumph. The "laurel" is the symbol, not just of victory (the ancient Greeks awarded a laurel wreath or "crown" to victors in the Pythian games) but of fame. The "rose" is traditionally a symbol for a girl's beauty. Though athletic fame is won by young men at an early age, the speaker declares, its duration is even shorter than a young woman's beauty. This runner, who sets a new record for the course he ran, will not be alive to see his record broken; the silence that would have greeted his future athletic decline will sound "no worse than cheers" (an ironical understatement: he will be aware of neither) now that he is dead. In stanza 5 the speaker praises the athlete for having won (metaphorically) one more race: he has raced his fame to the grave and has arrived there first (has died while his name is still unforgotten). In stanza 6 the speaker again speaks to the athlete as if he had some choice in the matter, and urges him to set his "fleet foot on the sill of shade, / And hold to the low lintel up / The still-defended challenge-cup." The "sill of shade" is the threshold of the door to the tomb, the "low lintel" is the crosspiece over it. The "still-defended challenge-cup" (his trophy) is the kind that has the winner's name inscribed on it each year. The winner is allowed to keep the cup until he is defeated, when it passes into the hands of the new winner. This athlete has died with the challenge-cup still in his possession.

The last stanza contains a sophisticated literary allusion that supports some identification of the speaker with the poet (Housman was a celebrated classical scholar). In Book 11 of the *Odyssey*, when Odysseus visits the Greek underworld (Hades), he is surrounded by shades of the "strengthless" dead. Since these shades are depicted as peculiarly impotent—strengthless and senseless—Housman is not predicting here some kind of immortality for the dead athlete, but simply making one more contrast between what he was in life and what he will become in death, "strengthless" and senseless. Nevertheless these shades will find "unwithered" on his head the laurel "garland [fame] briefer than a girl's" rose garland (beauty). The last two lines of the poem allude to the symbols of stanza 3.

Housman in this poem dwells on the transience of youth, fame, and beauty, and on the desirability of dying while one still has them rather than after they are lost. It is a theme that appears elsewhere in his poetry (see especially *A Shropshire Lad,* 23 and 44—"The lads in their hundreds" and "Shot? so quick, so clean an ending?"). It reflects one part of Housman's mind but not the whole of it, as can be seen from "Terence, this is stupid stuff" (page 662) and "Loveliest of Trees" (page 792).   LP

Langston Hughes   Aunt Sue's Stories (page 972)

This childhood reminiscence delicately and poignantly brought to the speaker what was apparently his first awareness of slavery and racism. The scene is simple and gentle, conjuring up a warm sense of love and security:

Summer nights on the front porch
Aunt Sue cuddles a brown-faced child to her bosom
And tells him stories. (3–5)

"Stories" are fictions, fairy tales, and anecdotes about people long ago and far away. Aunt Sue maintains the tone appropriate to telling a child "stories" but includes in them truths that do not come "out of any book at all" (20). She tells of slavery, sorrow, and "dark shadows" (15). She doesn't frighten the child, telling her stories "softly," but the dark shadows of meaning spread not only across her stories but over the boy a well. In a subtle shift of language indicating his growing perception, the "brown-faced child" becomes "the dark-faced child," that shadow of a cruel reality impinging on him—presumably for the rest of his life. Truth, even when softly told, is powerful, though Aunt Sue purposely tells her stories mildly and gently so as not to arouse fear or hatred.   TRA

Langston Hughes   Theme for English B (page 972)

In simple, prosaic language befitting the speaker's status as a young college student, Hughes's poem uses a white teacher's English composition assignment to probe a black student's racial awareness in white-dominated America.

The student questions his instructor's contention that if the page he writes comes out of himself it will necessarily be "true," implying that truth depends on social context and may be defined differently by blacks and whites. Stating the facts of his upbringing, his likes and dislikes, the speaker can say at most that "being colored doesn't make me *not* like / the same things other folks like who are other races." By the end of the poem, the speaker admits that he and the instructor are connected, partly by virtue of being American; but at the same time he insists on a racial divide that can never be eradicated. This paradox of the student's sense of oneness with white culture, combined with a separateness partly desired and partly enforced, controls his argument and gives the poem its consistent tone of gentle, thoughtful irony.

For all the poem's apparent simplicity, Hughes makes unobtrusive use of rhyme, alliteration, and careful selection of detail to emphasize his theme. The situation of the student being in a "class" under the authority of a white "instructor" itself mirrors his situation in society at large as a "class-B" citizen. The alliteration of "Bessie, bop, or Bach" illustrates the mix of white and black cultural influences in his sensibility. The internal rhyme of "page"/ "age" linking stanzas 1 and 2, the "write"/ "white" rhyme beginning the third stanza, and especially the "me"/ "free" / "B" rhymes of the last few lines knit the poem into a quiet unity. The end of the poem reinforces its paradoxical theme by expressing the student's awareness that the instructor is "somewhat more free" than he is; and, in the free-standing last line, by adopting a tone of mock docility as a good student obediently turning in his assignment. The poem as a whole convincingly and movingly portrays a young black man's self-awareness in mid-twentieth-century America.

Further discussion may be found in James A. Emanuel, *Langston Hughes* (New York: Twayne, 1967) 54–55; and in Gary F. Scharnhost, "Theme for English B," *Explicator*, 32 (December): item 27.   GJ

Ted Hughes   Thistles (page 974)

The thistles symbolize the persistence of unyielding, stern, and violent qualities in man and nature—a dogged prickliness. Hughes finds this quality both in the ineradicable thistle and in the marauding Viking of old—and links them fancifully by imagining the decayed bodies of the Vikings as the nutrient source of the thistles. He even identifies physical resemblances: the spikes of the thistle are like spears or swords; the fine hairiness of the blossom is like that of the blond Scandinavian, and its redness recalls both a decorated helmet and blood bursting from a head wound; and the autumnal change from green to woody grey is like the greying of hair and of flesh tones.

The opening line invites an investigation of musical devices, starting the poem with the assonance of *rubber tongues* and the alliteration of *hoeing hands*, but the primary sound effect comes from repeated harsh consonants: *k, sp, st, p, f,* and guttural *g*. Appropriately, these reinforce the spikiness of the central symbol.   TRA

Randall Jarrell   The Death of the Ball Turret Gunner

(page 974)

The poem captures both the terror and the ironic humor of its subject in the phrase "washed me out," which takes literally the euphemism for the failure to qualify for military duty. Rather than failing to measure up to training standards, the speaker has been so mutilated that his body must be flushed from his turret by a water hose.

The poem refers explicitly to the U.S. Army Air Corps in World War II. The B-17 and B-24 bombers had a gunner's glass turret on the belly of the fuselage, and airmen wore fur-lined leather jackets; antiaircraft shells were called "flak" as an acronym for the German word *Fliegerabwehrkanone*, though the shorter word sounds like an onomatopoetic imitation of the noise of the explosion; and the bombers were attacked by squadrons of fighter planes.

The first three lines of the poem abound with musical devices, chiefly alliteration (*sleep–State, loosed–life, feel–fur–froze*) and assonance (*mother's–hunched, fell–belly–wet, sleep–dream*). These culminate in the internal rhyme *black flak*, whose flat *a* and harsh *k* sharply bring to a halt such devices. After this rhyme, the only musical device is the concluding and horrifying rhyme *froze–hose*. This pattern of sounds reinforces the irony of the poem's conclusion.

The metaphors of the first two lines create a parallel between the position of the unborn child in his mother's womb and the man's position in the "belly" of the bomber. The movement from one to the other is ominously referred to as falling, and the animal processes of generation and birth are obliquely implied in "my wet fur." The speaker seems to pass directly from the moment of birth to his place in the gun turret, and his existence is governed by the dreams of his mother (for her child's success, happiness, and safety) and the subsequent dream of the "State" (for its own safety and its national ideals). These dreams are both shattered when, flying above 30,000 feet, he is shocked by the shells of antiaircraft guns to the opposite kind of dream, the nightmare of attacking fighter planes. He awakens from idealistic dreams to discover that reality is a nightmare, but his wakefulness lasts only a moment.   TRA

Jenny Joseph   Warning (page 974)

Although it does not present serious obstacles, some of the British slang usage in the poem might be glossed for students:

doesn't go (2) means isn't proper or suitable
pavement (5) is sidewalk
shops (6) are stores or markets
public railings (7) are iron fencework along the front of houses
    and buildings marking the public boundary of property
at a go (13) means at one time or sitting
pickle (14) is a generic term for any pickled condiments such as
    chutney, pickle relish, cocktail onions, etc.
beermats (15) are pasteboard coasters provided in pubs to
    absorb spilt beer or ale.

It is important for students to recognize the British urban setting, in any case, because the behavior that the speaker expects to evince represents the violation of standards of propriety inculcated in British children for whom adults "set a good example" by their own proper actions. The national stereotypes of reserve and propriety are an essential background for the ironies of the poem.

The speaker announces to her husband (apparently) that when she is "an old woman" (1) she will become an eccentric who purposely sets out to shock by her perverse disobedience of standards of propriety. Her eccentricities include dressing in bad taste and in colors that do not become her, wasting money on expensive drinks and frivolously ostentatious clothes, sitting down wherever she pleases when she feels tired, rudely eating up samples of food set out for customers in food stores, pressing buttons that say "in case of emergency, press here," running along the railings that border the sidewalk dragging a stick against them to make a racket, risking her health by wearing "slippers in the rain" (9), stealing flowers, and spitting in public. In short, in her old age she will do all the things that she had been trained in the "sobriety of . . . youth" (8) to refrain from doing. She will enjoy a second childhood—having had her first one thoroughly suppressed by those who taught her to behave properly.

Her husband she will also permit to join her in the self-indulgence that good manners prohibit. He will be allowed to dress as inappropriately as she, to give up his healthy diet and indulge in his favorite foods without stinting, and to do in his old age what boys love to do, collect useless objects and hide them away.

For now, however, as she says in the third paragraph, they must maintain the standards that proper middle-class morality demands: sensible clothing, financial responsibility, good training for the children, and social and intellectual conformity. Still, she suggests that it would be right "to practice a little now" (20) some of her future outrageous behavior so as not to shock people when she suddenly adopts it later.

The central ironic butt is of course all those standards of propriety that the speaker proposes violating, some of them pointless, some of them having a serious purpose (sobriety vs. drinking, observing rights of property vs. stealing, accepting certain eating restrictions vs. endangering one's health). But for the most part, the proposed eccentricities do little more than shock by being unrestrainedly self-satisfying. At a deeper level, however, the speaker's target is self-repression. Many people follow the "good example" set by grown-ups to the point of being unable to imagine acting independently or from impulse. These are the people whose shock is connoted by the garishness of purple clothes and a red hat, for the speaker goes beyond saying that she will be a little naughty—she will be loudly naughty, a "red" revolutionary, an ordinary woman who adorns herself in the purple hue of royalty. Repression deserves an opposite, strong liberation.   TRA

John Keats   La Belle Dame sans Merci (page 975)

Vocabulary: *sedge* (3), *haggard* (6), *meads* (13), *zone* (18), *manna* (26), *grot* (29), *thrall* (40), *starved* (41), *gloam* (41).

Even with full explication, this literary ballad retains its air of melancholy mystery, because the meaning of the encounter between the knight and the faery lady is never made explicit. This sense of an unresolved riddle is characteristic of many folk ballads, and it may be that Keats was after no more in the poem than a narration of fairyland and dream omens. When the knight concludes "this is why I sojourn here," the reader might very well reiterate the narrator's opening question, for the events reported by the knight don't seem to account for his despair, his physical debility and suffering, which are what the narrator has asked about.

The three opening stanzas ask the question—"what can ail thee?"—and describe the landscape and the knight. Both are incongruous, the speaker reports: knights should be hearty, purposeful, strong, not pale and feverish; they should be in quest of adventure, not "loitering" beside the dried marsh grass at a lakeside; it is early winter, and the natural creatures have withdrawn either to more congenial climates or to their stored winter hoards. This is no place for a knight nor, despite his armor, does this man seem heroic.

The tale of the knight's encounter with the faery connects her with the fullness of nature: like an animal, light-footed and wild-eyed, she is met in a meadow, and the knight bedecks her with nature's flowers, and, as if rescuing a lost maiden, sets her on his horse, rapt with her beauty and her song. (But lines 19–20 ambiguously report her initial response to him: does "as" mean *while*, or does it mean *as if?*) Like a goddess of nature, the lady repays his adoration with nature's plenty, and speaks to him an unknown language; surely, he supposes, she is saying she loves him. Strangely, once she has taken him to her cave, her "sweet moan" becomes weeping and sighing, and he must tame her by kissing her "wild wild eyes"; again, as if in repayment, she lulls him to sleep, but that sleep turns to nightmare with a dream that began in the cave and continues to be repeated here on the "cold hill's side" where he awakens and the narrator finds him. The dream is apparently of his precursors, vigorous kings, princes, and knights, now in the paleness of death as he will be, warning him that he has been enslaved by "La Belle Dame sans Merci."

Obviously, what a reader wants to know is "who *is* this beautiful woman without pity, and why has she done this to the man?" Does what happened to the knight have any relevance to our lives? Does the poem do more than warn us against sexual indulgence? One plausible (but by no means the only or inevitable) interpretation links the poem with the processes of nature and human attitudes toward them. The first three stanzas establish a sense of appropriate behavior as the seasons change, and of appropriate actions for people: in winter, squirrels, birds, even grasses retreat before the coldness and dryness, and wandering knights with their manly strength should be leading their active lives where they can perform their heroic deeds. But this man has fallen in love with the beauty and wildness of nature, supposes that she loves him, and that he can tame her and live with her. What his horrid dream discloses is that this is illusion, and that by loving her he has become her thrall. His fate is the fate of all men—death—but he must also languish in despair because he has set his heart on what must always be changing.   TRA

John Keats   Ode to a Nightingale (page 977)

The thematic elements of this great poem are at the heart of Keats's work: poetry, human misery, time and change, and the power of sensations. The speaker, moved by the beauty of a nightingale singing, wishes he could join with the bird and escape "The weariness, the fever, and the fret" of human existence. At first he supposes that wine might be the vehicle, but then decides that the poetic imagination will serve him better; and no sooner has he said so than he feels himself transported on "viewless wings of Poesy" to be with the bird. Unable to see in the darkness, he can only guess by scent at the richness of nature, all of it partaking of the "Fast fading" intensity of growth and decay. Still listening in the dark, he recalls his repeated wish to escape the world through death, and that desire seems even more intense as he is ravished by the beauty of the bird's song.

But the nightingale is a bird of life, not of death—it is immortal in the sense that nightingales flourished in ancient days, in biblical days, and even in legends and fairy tales. Yet through all the past and in fiction, the word "forlorn" has existed, as the speaker discovers to his chagrin when his imagination leads him to re-create an image out of fairyland. He discovers as well that though the imagination can cheat us out of our grasp of reality for a time, the power to think and understand will once again intrude. To use the word "forlorn" in imagining a fairy world is to invite the analytic mind to see that one is not in fact "with" the bird, but alone, a "sole self." Returning to one's own reality also leads to the recognition that the song of a nightingale is the creation of a living thing, and it too will fade, move away, and finally die away, "buried deep" in another valley.

The poem ends in a state of puzzlement: was the experience a vision (revealing a supernatural reality) or a "waking dream" of what can never be? Without the actual stimulus of the singing bird, without its music, the speaker is left to ask which is the true state of awareness—this present, grasping the literal reality of existence, or that moment of poetic transport?

This brief outline of the poem does not pretend to exhaust its richness, nor even to touch upon all its complex concerns. Many valuable comments have been written, of which the following are recommended. The most helpful single volume for study of this poem is *Twentieth-Century Interpretation of Keats's Odes*, ed. Jack Stillinger (Englewood Cliffs: Prentice, 1968). Besides Stillinger's excellent introductory essay, the book contains the essays by Brooks and Fogle separately listed below and a note by Anthony Hecht.

Additional useful references include Harold Bloom, *The Visionary Company* (New York: Anchor, 1961) 427–32; Cleanth Brooks and Robert Penn Warren, *Understanding Poetry*, 3rd ed. (New York: Holt, 1960) 44–47; Douglas Bush, *John Keats: His Life and Writing* (New York: Macmillan, 1966) 132–38; Morris Dickstein, *Keats and His Poetry* (Chicago: U of Chicago P, 1971) 205–21; Richard Harter Fogle, "Keats's Ode to a Nightingale," *PMLA* 68 (1953): 211–22; F. R. Leavis, *Revaluation* (New York: Norton, 1963) 244–52; H. M. McLuhan, "Aesthetic Pattern in Keats's Odes," *University of Toronto Quarterly* 12 (1943): 175–79; David Perkins, "The Ode to a Nightingale" in *Keats: A Collection of Critical Essays,* ed. Walter Jackson Bate (Englewood Cliffs: Prentice, 1964) 103–11, repr. from David Perkins, *The Quest for Permanence* (Cambridge: Harvard UP, 1959) 244–57; Stuart M. Sperry, *Keats the Poet* (Princeton: Princeton UP, 1973) 262–67; and Helen Vendler, *The Odes of John Keats* (Cambridge: Harvard UP, 1983) 77–109.   TRA

Maxine Kumin   The Sound of Night (page 979)

The metrical form is highly varied iambic tetrameter, with a hexameter line to open each stanza.

The stanzaic form is three rhymed tercets (*aaabbbccc*) primarily achieved through approximate rhyme, most often consonance. Lines 1–3 share only the concluding voiced *-s* preceded by contrasting vowel sounds; 4–6 share *-t*, and 4 and 6 in addition have an unvoiced *-s*; lines 7–9 share *-nk*, while 8 and 9 have exact rhyme. There are some random links between tercets, as in stanza 2 where the terminal *-k* of the first tercet carries over into the fourth and fifth lines (*blankets, Crickets*), although the rhyme sound of this tercet is in the terminal *-t*. (Note that a *t* rhyme characterizes the middle tercet of each stanza.)

The most striking variations occur in the last stanza. The first three lines are linked by alliterated *s-* while the first and third lines have exact rhyme as well. The terminal *-t* of the second tercet is repeated in the final tercet at the same time that exact rhyme joins these tercets together (*light–tight–night*). This last variation of the pattern occurs at the climactic point, for the theme of the poem contrasts light with night, and the final two lines state the theme most directly.

That theme: that "day creatures" may luxuriate in the sounds of night and delight in their variety and vitality; but they will always find these sounds mysterious and a little threatening.   TRA

Philip Larkin   Aubade (page 980)

The *aubade* of the troubadours was a bittersweet dawn song as the coming of sunrise with its joyous connotations was the signal for a lover's departure from his beloved paramour, lest their illicit affair be discovered. Larkin's ironic use of the term is painful: his dawn song is not wistful about separating from a mistress, but terror stricken at the prospect of the inevitable parting from life itself.

Larkin does not make that life attractive, but tedious and mundane. It is a life of work, offices, and telephones, with only drink and "People" to relieve the boredom or the lurking fears of death. The emphasis is not on beauty or pleasure or love, all to be lost in the obliteration of death, but on the fear of nothingness. The images associated with life provide the only defense against the thoughts of death, and they are images of social connection, culminating in the last line: "Postmen like doctors go from house to house." All of us, that is, share in the disease of fearing death, and the cure comes in links with other people. But communication is a temporary cure, an alleviation of the *fear*, but certainly no defense against death itself or the knowledge of its inevitability.

The time of the poem, four o'clock in the predawn morning, is a time of total darkness and silence. Staring into "soundless dark" (2) is like staring at death, for the two primary senses of hearing and sight have been lost. Deprived of physical sense, the speaker must "see" what his mind knows, "the total emptiness forever, / The sure extinction" (16–17).

Neither the rich, elaborate fabric of religion—now tattered and "motheaten" (23)—nor the fallacious plausibility of the plainer fabrics of rationalism is sufficient to hide the naked fact of fearfulness; rich or plain, these are mere covers or garments, incapable of disguising the reality at such a time as this.

And "Courage is no good" (37) at such times, because it cannot alter the fact the speaker is staring at. Since he defines life in its social connections, "to love or link with" (29), courage seems only a matter of social behavior that has value in the impressions one gives to other people. "It means not scaring others" (38) with the horrifying truth that the speaker understands and faces. He does display another kind of courage, though—the courage to acknowledge to himself his fears and to look into the darkness with honesty.

The final stanza, in which the dawn slowly comes, restores the speaker's physical senses and leads him to project the resumption of daylight activities. The terror subsides and the fact of "what we know," though it is as plain and as familiarly unremarkable as a piece of furniture, may be ignored in the workaday world. The knowledge that he has faced when alone can be put aside; the dilemma of knowing that "we can't escape" (43) death and "Yet can't accept" (44) it can be postponed another day.

The poem carries the additional richness of its verbal echoes of two well-known passages from Shakespeare, Hamlet's soliloquy beginning "To be, or not to be" (3.1.55–89) and the conclusion of Jaques's speech on the seven ages of man (*As You Like It*, 2.7.162–65). The allusions to Hamlet's speech occur in lines 8, 17, 18–19, and 30, and to Jaques's in lines 27–28. These allusions in effect reopen the questions raised in Hamlet's meditation, and in several other themes in that play—courage, friendship, even drink—as if Larkin's speaker were being forced to reexamine Hamlet's condition for himself. What he finds, in his modern (and more squalid) experience is a similar dilemma: although being alive is fraught with pain and misery, chiefly because of fear and loneliness, the alternative "not to be" is worse, and so like Hamlet he will have to live with his "indecision."

Because these allusions are only faintly signaled, by little more than a single word or phrase, Larkin is relying on a reader's thorough recall of the Hamlet soliloquy and of the whole play, and most students are not likely to make the connection for themselves. If the instructor wishes to use the poem for a further lesson in allusion, the class should probably be supplied in advance with copies of the Shakespeare passages, and asked to find the verbal echoes.   TRA

Larry Levis   L.A., Loiterings (page 981)

In two brief vignettes, this poem suggests the seedy, rather heartless ethos of Los Angeles at night.

The first vignette, "Convalescent Home," portrays the old people in the home as "High on painkillers" (1) and, like furry animals, in the process of "licking / themselves good-bye" (6–7). The striking final metaphor pursues the idea that the old have become, or are treated as, less than human as they are shuttled toward death: "They are the small animals vanishing / at the road's edge everywhere" (8–9).

The second vignette captures economically the life of a "go-go girl" (10) at work in a night club. Her hair has turned green from the cheap hair dye her mother has stolen from a discount store; emotionally, the girl is not really present, "her eyes are flat / and still as thumbprints" (15–16). As in the first vignette, deathliness is emphasized. The girl's eyes are also compared to "dead presidents pressed / into coins" (17–18), and finally she is like "the screen flickering in / an empty movie house / far into the night" (20–22).

Both vignettes convey the bleak, soulless solitude of individuals observed by the "loitering," omniscient speaker.   GJ

Edna St. Vincent Millay   Pity Me Not (page 982)

In this highly rhetorical but gracefully lyrical sonnet, the speaker repeatedly insists (she is addressing a former lover) that she does not want pity. The passing of a day, the vanishing of natural beauty, the departure of the moon or the tide—these are all accepted with philosophical resignation.

Her true subject is introduced in the second quatrain of this Shakespearean sonnet, in which she asks that she not be pitied because "a man's desire is hushed so soon, / And you no longer look with love on me" (7–8).

She does not need pity because she has always known that love is fleeting. She compares its evanescent nature to wind-blown blossoms and, again, to the shifting tides of the sea.

Her resignation and acceptance, however, are intellectual rather than emotional processes, as the concluding couplet makes clear. Here, in a surprising reversal, she does ask for pity: "Pity me that the heart is slow to learn / What the swift mind beholds at every turn" (13–14). Accepting the loss of love is a difficult process, emotionally, though the sonnet suggests—in its calm tone and its careful deployment of imagery—that the speaker has progressed beyond the period when she suffered the "fresh wreckage" (12) of loss, and has achieved at least a measure of acceptance.   GJ

Joyce Carol Oates   Loves of the Parrots (page 983)

The subject of Oates's poem is the rapacity of nature, whose emblem here is a group of parrots in the Yucatán. The speaker focuses on parrots because the poem as a whole suggests that the birds are "parroting" a fact of human nature—namely, rapacious sexual urges.

Irony pervades the poem, beginning with the title. Of course, parrots cannot "love" in any meaningful sense of the word. In the opening stanzas, they are preening in the sun, the image of their "arterial red" (4) coloring suggesting incipient violence. Searching for lice in their feathers and "Picking / their toenails" (6–7) are the mundane activities of which the birds are described as inordinately proud. The pettiness of their activity contrasts ironically with the splendor, beauty, and "imperial" (7) nature of their appearance.

Thus the poem has suggested the delusiveness of a sexual imperative disguised as "love." In the third stanza, further violent images convey this distinctly non-romantic view of mating, the male bird being "galvanize[d] . . . like an electric shock" (8–9) and the female birds responding fearfully to his shrieking demands. When the male is ready to mate, the female is simply commanded to obey.

In the fourth stanza, the violent imagery becomes even more explicit and dire: the birds' eyes are described as "Mad" (15), and during the mating process "bloody breast feathers go flying!" (18). The final line expresses the theme that the birds' behavior—and again, by implication, human sexual behavior—has illustrated: "Love, not death, is the bitter thing" (21). Love is bitter because in its preening romantic pretensions it attempts to disguise a self-regarding and violent lust.   GJ

Sharon Olds   I Go Back to May 1937 (page 983)

The title is slightly misleading: "I go back to" implies that I was there at that time, and am reminiscing about my experience. But in fact 1937 was five years before the birth of the poet/speaker, and the incident she reports occurred before her parents were married. As the poem develops, we revise our thinking about the title: it means "I go back" in my imagination and conjure up a scene I could never have witnessed.

The first 12 lines of the poem vividly create that imagined scene with a wealth of specific detail: two "dumb . . . innocent" kids, "about to graduate . . . about to get married" (10–12). Their innocence is profound and optimistic: they know that "they would never hurt anybody," certainly including each other. However, there are ominous tones in the detailed description. The speaker's father stands in front of "red tiles glinting like / bent plates of blood" (4–5), while the portrait of her mother includes a "wrought-iron gate" with "sword-tips black in the May air" (8–9). These images are presages of the violence to come. These two know nothing about life or the consequences of their actions and have no real sense of what the future will bring.

In her imagination, the speaker would like to warn them of the terrible guilt and suffering that their marriage will bring, the destruction of their own happiness, the pain that they will bring to their children. She pities them in their ignorance and innocence, but cannot in fact or in imagination stop them. Because she wants to be born, their marriage must be allowed to take place, so she sees herself "bang them together / at the hips" to "strike sparks from them" (27–29). Her final warning is that once they have done their damage to each other and to their children, she "will tell about it" (30).

Exactly what they will do is left for other poems to express. For now, there are the vague terms "do bad things," "suffer," "want to die" (17–19).   TRA

Sharon Olds   The Victims (page 984)

The title becomes ambiguous in its reference as the poem proceeds. At the outset it clearly refers to the mother and all "her / kids" (among them, the speaker) who for years "took it" from the father until she "kicked [him] out." But the sequence of losses suffered by the husband, which fill his ex-wife and children with glee, gradually transform him into a victim, both of their hatred and vengefulness, and of his business circumstances. The "bums in doorways" constitute yet another set of victims, arousing the pity of the speaker and an implicit revaluation of her father as victimizer. And we may see the speaker herself as the final victim—of her mother who taught her to hate and take it until revenge became possible.

This last victimization expresses the central theme of the poem, which recalls that of Blake's "A Poison Tree" (page 907). The sequence of abuse, acceptance, revenge, and spiteful pleasure at the father's suffering now haunts the speaker as she observes other men whose lives may have been blighted in similar ways. She comes, at the end, to question the implications of the slangy phrase with which the poem opens: if the family "took it" (referring to some sort of abuse or perceived affront), then the father must have "given it"—but what was he giving? What kinds of giving and taking are funda-mentally at stake here? The bums who now have "nothing / left" but their pitiable destitution arouse these questions. What was the family taking from the father—his abuse? his humanity? or both?

The language of the first ten lines is casual, colloquial, and realistic. The question that begins in line 11 introduces the first figures—the metaphors of dark suits hanging like "carcasses" and of the toes of shoes like noses "with their large pores" (like an alcoholic's nose?). These grotesque comparisons have the effect of representing the distorting hatreds of the speaker. The sec-ond set of figures arouses disgust and pity, implying a changed perception on the part of the speaker. The description of the bums, their bodies metaphor-ically transmuted into "white / slugs," their torn suits so filthy that they ap-pear to be constructed from "compressed silt," their hands like the flippers of marine mammals, and in particular their eyes paradoxically looking like fire underwater, moves the speaker to begin "wondering" about men so trans-formed and abused, and about their families and associates who might share the responsibility for their dehumanization.   TRA

Robert Phillips Wish You Were Here (page 985)

The title ironically quotes the postcard cliché sent home by people on vacation; it implies that the writer is having so much fun that he would like to share it with those who have stayed at home—and has the further impli-cation that the writer is more fortunate than the person who receives the postcard.

The irony is both verbal and situational. The writer does not really wish to share his vacation experience, and the vacation has turned out miserably. The opening simile is apt: a spinning top is a toy, and represents play and fun, but just as tops slow down and fall over once the spin has stopped, the fun of this vacation is spent. The poem presents a family in a rented vacation house or cottage by the sea in an area full of other tourists in search of the same beach enjoyment. (There is "sand underfoot" [3], and a drawer or cupboard with a tangle of "hardware I don't even own" [10] needs sorting as a means of doing something constructive since playing is impossible.) The cause of the misery—"[r]ain six days / running" (2–3)—has them housebound or searching for a movie they haven't seen. The young children are "frantic" (4) with boredom and frustration, but there are so many similarly afflicted tourists that parking at the movie is impossible.

So back in the house they try to occupy themselves with things that kill time until "[c]ocktails at five, too much looked forward to" (11), as an anodyne. The speaker even telephones an "old flame" as a possible diversion and escape from family annoyances. The last stanza caps off the experience with nightmares of fear, shame, and inadequacy, a fitting if disturbing self-assessment. In the first, the clean-shaven speaker (even shaving twice in one day) is unexpectedly thrown out of work by his opposite, a "bearded boss." This dream may be con-nected to the wasted expense of this vacation as well as to the idleness forced on him by the weather. In the other nightmare, the speaker is back in high school (perhaps where he had met his "old flame") playing on a junior varsity football or baseball team—but just as this vacation is not fun and games, in his dream he fails by dropping the ball.   TRA

Marge Piercy   A Work of Artifice (page 985)

This symbolic parable might have taken its point of origin from the adage "as the twig is bent, so grows the tree," but it seems rather to be the re-sult of literal observation. As the poem says, a bonsai is a tree that might have grown to full height except that it was constantly pruned from its first sprouting, nipped and shaped over years into a miniature replica of the tree it might have been. This tree in its natural growth "could have grown eighty feet tall" in its natural habitat, and might have been destroyed by a natural force like lightning.

But the bonsai is not allowed its nature; it is "a work of artifice" (the title has positive connotations that a synonymous phrase such as "artificial work" would not have had). Through the tedious work of crippling and maiming the tree, the gardener "croons" (to it? to himself?) a song about *his* definition of its natural quality. The song opens up the symbolism of the poem, as the gardener trains the bonsai to think that its nature is to be miniature, "small and cozy, / domestic and weak," like a dependent wife with her mastering husband. The bonsai has the good fortune to have a provider who keeps it in a pot; a wife is lucky to be financially taken care of in her domestic habitat.

The last eight lines move from the single bonsai to generalizations about "living creatures" and how they must be trained to remain miniature. The creatures are of course women, as the details demonstrate: "the bound feet" (20) alludes to the practice in some cultures of maiming women by binding the feet of females to inhibit growth; "the crippled brain" (21) may refer to any social practice that relegates women to an uneducated place; "the hair in curlers" (22) calls to mind most specifically the uncomfortable and unnatural habit of dressing women's hair to create varieties of coiffure; and the last two lines quote an advertising slogan for a popular beauty cream.

What these details share in common is a variety of "artifices" created for women with the purpose of pleasing men (the *you* in the phrase "the hands you / love to touch" is a man for whom a woman wants to be attractive). The poem has shifted, by the last statement, to acknowledge that the dwarfing of a woman's spirit has been completed—it is she, not the man who prunes her, who voluntarily chooses to employ hair curlers and skin creams. She has been persuaded that being "small and cozy, / domestic and weak" is her true identity. That is the irony the poem presents.   TRA

Sylvia Plath   Mad Girl's Love Song (page 986)

An eager student of poetic tradition as well as, toward the end of her career, a notably innovative poet, Sylvia Plath attempted a startling variety of
established patterns, composing numerous sonnets, villanelles, and other
fixed forms during her apprenticeship. "Mad Girl's Love Song"—written
when the poet was an undergraduate, originally published in *Mademoiselle*
magazine, and later printed in the afterword to Plath's novel, *The Bell Jar*—
was the poet's own favorite among her villanelles. It effectively combines her
distinctively somber subject matter with the characteristic humor and playfulness often associated with the villanelle form; its blend of a seemingly
light, even jaunty tone with an underlying dark message anticipates later,
more famous Plath poems such as "Daddy" and "Lady Lazarus."

Like the protagonist of *The Bell Jar*, the speaker here is one who is
viewed, by others and perhaps by herself, as a "mad girl," and the source of
her madness is the same excess of isolation and subjectivity imaged by the
"bell jar" itself. The speaker, like most "mad" people, is unable to distinguish
clearly between her subjective fantasy life—as evinced by the repeated line
"I think I made you up inside my head"—and such fixed markers of external
reality as nature (the stars overhead) and religious concepts (God and Satan), which the speaker recasts in her own vibrant but eccentric terms. Her
refusal to accept a reality in common with others is stressed in the other repeated line, "I shut my eyes and all the world drops dead." In her sealed-off
inner world, she can dismiss the stars and welcome an "arbitrary blackness";
she can imagine the male figure to whom she addresses this lyric as a demon-
lover who "sung me moonstruck, kissed me quite insane." Even God "topples
from the sky" as the speaker embraces her fierce subjectivity.

The final two stanzas clarify the situation: the girl has been abandoned
by her lover, and her shut eyes are her way of coping with the pain of aban-
donment. She prefers entering a realm of private myth, where she can "grow
old" and forget the lover's name, and where she imagines having loved "a
thunderbird" instead of a man. Yet the villanelle's characteristic repetitions
and circularity emphasize the mad girl's delusions, her self-defeating logic:
she goes nowhere, ending where she began. Edward Butscher notes: "The
poem is important for the thematic emphasis placed upon madness as a congenital human condition. . . . There is none of the awkward straining after
verbal showmanship common to other early works." He adds that the refrains
"represent madness refined to purest self; the empiric world is distilled until
it has no tangible value" (*Sylvia Plath: Method and Madness* [New York:
Pocket Books, 1977] 79–80).

The villanelle, a "closed form," is thus perfectly suited to this depiction
of a closed inner world of subjectivity taken to the extreme of madness. Yet
the poet's playfulness should not obscure our awareness of the speaker's
doomed isolation.   GJ

Sylvia Plath   **Spinster** (page 987)

The "plot" of this narrative poem involves a "particular girl"—meaning both *specific* and *fastidious*—who is "afflicted" by the random disorder of a "burgeoning" spring, feels a nostalgia for the exactness and precision of winter's austerity, and chooses to withdraw from both springtime and love into spinsterhood.

The poem establishes two contrasting sets of values through the symbols of spring and winter. To use the diction of the poem, spring is irregular, tumultuous, unbalanced, uneven, rank, slovenly, unruly, vulgar, treasonous, giddy, insane, mutinous. Winter is scrupulous, austere, orderly, disciplined, exact. Connotatively, the terms used for spring are negative, those for winter are positive—but we must look behind the language to determine the poem's central purpose, for it displays an ambivalence that must be taken into account. To the "particular girl," whose sense of threat and danger results in a series of overstatements, all the negative terms seem appropriate; to the poet, the matter is not so simple—as the pejorative title might lead us to see.

What develops is a portrait of a woman who protests too much, whose rejection of all that disorder brought on by April betrays an unacknowledged desire and fascination. The point is made clearest at the end, where the link between springtime and a man's dangerous desire is brought into final focus. The second stanza had shown him as part of the slovenliness of spring; lines 28–30 transform him and his love into a violent threat—a man trying to break through her "barricade" by means of "curse, fist, threat"—or, what she really fears most, "love." To see love only as the driving force felt by men is to be limited by more than a "frosty discipline." The poem suggests that *love*, if she could allow herself to feel it, might lead her to new perceptions and a fuller life.   TRA

Sylvia Plath   **Wuthering Heights** (page 988)

Plath's poem recalls the setting of the English moors in Emily Brontë's famous novel. By emphasizing the confrontation between a solitary speaker and the forbidding landscape, the poem illustrates the fragility of life within a death-haunted portrait of nature.

The first stanza establishes the chilly and delusive nature of a world whose horizons "only dissolve and dissolve / Like a series of promises, as I step forward" (8–9). There is nothing to warm the speaker; the sky is "pale" (7) and seems to possess an oppressive, threatening weight. The emphasis on a pervasive deathscape intensifies in the second stanza, where the speaker finds "no life higher than the grasstops / Or the hearts of sheep" (10–11). She fears that if she scrutinizes the details of what she is seeing too closely—e.g., "the roots of the heather" (17)—then she, too, will feel a perhaps irresistible invitation to leave the realm of the living and join the dead.

The third stanza offers a semi-comical description of the previously mentioned sheep, but still there is a subtle emphasis on the landscape's deathly indifference to the speaker's life. Earlier she had felt the wind trying to "funnel my heat away" (16), and now, looking into the "black slots" (22) of the sheep's eyes, she feels that "It is like being mailed into space, / A thin, silly message" (23–24). Again the speaker stresses the delusive and ungiving traits of this natural world, since the sheep are standing about "in grandmotherly disguise" (25) and their bleating noises are "hard, marbly" (27).

The remainder of the poem continues the well-established deathliness of the speaker's surroundings with such images as "solitudes / That flee through my fingers" (29–30); "Hollow doorsteps" (31); "black stone" (36); and "valleys narrow / And black" (43–44). Again the speaker feels herself anomalous as a living creature, "the one upright / Among all horizontals" (37–38). She identifies with the living grass, which unlike the sheep seems "too delicate / For a life in such company" (40–41).

The poem ends with a sudden shift in perspective: looking beyond her own immediate surroundings, she notes in the far distance those black and narrow valleys, where "house lights / Gleam like small change" (44–45). Again the poem suggests how little life matters in this world, the emblematic lights of human habitation representing, as the pun "small change" has it, something of little value and something unable to effect much change within the surrounding world.   GJ

Dudley Randall   To the Mercy Killers (page 989)

This sonnet presents a case against euthanasia, a subject on which students will all have an opinion. In discussing the poem, it is important to notice that Randall does not raise the question to the level of a universal issue. He does not contend that euthanasia is wrong; he says only that he does not want it for himself. Can we infer any ethical attitude in what he says? He certainly does not impugn the motivations of those who might "conspire" (3) to end his suffering. They are "kindly" (2), and are motivated by mercy. Nevertheless, the word "conspire" has negative connotations, and even more so does the word "murder" in line 1.

The most effective lines in the poem are those in which he lists what he might become. Line 6, a series of monosyllabic nouns (*stub, stump, butt, scab, knob*) preceded by those in line 5 (*clot, clench*) and followed by those in line 7 (*pain, stench*) with their two multisyllabic adjectives (*screaming, putrefying*), all held together by alliteration, assonance, and consonance—like links in a chain or boxcars in a freight train—are a powerful *tour de force*. But there is an important consideration that the speaker has not taken into account: the consequences for other people. He adopts a heroic stance in his determination to experience the full range of human life, but other lives besides his own will also be affected. He will need doctors, nurses, caretakers; and who among them, performing their duties, will find pleasure in attending "a screaming pain, a putrefying stench"?   TRA

John Crowe Ransom   Bells for John Whiteside's Daughter (page 990)

A child's death is a dangerous subject for a poet. It invites sentimentality. Though the occasion is one for genuine grief there is always a temptation to "hoke" it up a bit, to sweeten it, to picture the child as a little angel and to soften the harsher contours.

In this poem, the speaker is an adult attending the funeral of a dead child. He is specifically a friend and neighbor of the child's father, named in the title. This title has a double meaning. The "Bells" refer to the church bells that ring for the funeral in the final stanza; they also suggest that the poem itself is a tribute, a chiming of rhymes, composed in the dead girl's memory.

The poet-speaker finds it difficult to believe that the child he knew is dead. She was so rapid in her movements, so fleet of foot, so loud and boisterous in her play, that her stillness now is almost beyond belief. Rather than pretend that she is merely playing, however, he speaks of her as being in a "brown study" (a state of somber, abstracted brooding). But such a state is so uncharacteristic of the child that it "Astonishes" the speaker and the other adults gathered for her funeral.

The child in this poem is clearly not a "little rose" but a real child— active, noisy, and often vexatious in her play. Indeed, her games are metaphorically described as "wars," whose clamor reached the adults in their "high window," and whose tyrannies disturbed the geese whom she woke from their "noon apple-dreams" and harried into the pond. The term "little / Lady" applied to her is ironical rather than sentimental in intention and effect (her "rod" is both scepter and prod). The one long sentence comprising the three central stanzas has a freshness of imagery and imagination, and gives us a vivid impression of the child at her play. The geese—lazy, sleepy, proud—serve both as victims of the child's play and as a character-contrast to the child herself, yet the poet's whimsy of having them speak "in goose" is appropriate to the kind of imaginative play that a child might engage in.

In the last stanza, however, the speaker is brought back to the present reality. The bells ring for the funeral service, and the adults who have been "sternly stopped" by the child's death are "vexed at her brown study, / Lying so primly propped." If they had been sometimes "vexed" by her play in life, they are more "vexed" to see her here, lying "so primly" (who was never prim in life), "propped" rigidly in her coffin (who had such "speed" in her body and such a "tireless heart" in life). "[V]exed" is an inspired word here; while pointing up ironic contrasts, it expresses genuine grief through understatement. For additional comment on Ransom's poem, see Robert Heilman, in

The Pacific Spectator 5 (1951): 458–60; Thornton H. Parsons, John Crowe Ransom (New York: Twayne, 1969) 53–55; and Robert Penn Warren, "Pure and Impure Poetry," Kenyon Review 5 (1943): 237–40.   LP

Adrienne Rich   Delta (page 990)

In this very short poem, Rich's message is clear: the poet cannot be contained by the definitions and expectations of her audience.

The speaker employs the symbol of the delta to suggest her past accomplishments as a poet, but in the first stanza she warns that these "fragments" (2) no longer represent her, since she has moved out of the delta into new territory that is "deeper into the heart of the matter" (4).

In the second stanza, she adds the image of a human hand to the mix, insisting that the reader cannot "grasp" (5) her through simplifying or generalizing definitions of her past achievements. As a poet, she is a protean force that moves in many directions like a hand "with its five fingers spread" (8).

Alice Templeton asserts that this poem recognizes "the power of poetry to break open the new and the possible. . . . In 'Delta' the poet warns the reader and critic not to assume a complete knowledge, of the poet, or of the subject, that poetry can never deliver" (The Dream and the Dialogue: Adrienne Rich's Feminist Poetics [Knoxville: U of Tennessee P, 1994] 140).

The poem is characteristic of Rich in insisting on the autonomy and freedom of the poet's creative power.   GJ

Adrienne Rich   Dreamwood (page 991)

Poets are sometimes distracted from the work at hand by the physical realities of their writing situation and then find that the distraction itself can be an inspiration for poetry. Robert Frost's "A Considerable Speck" (page 770) is an example, since in that poem the speaker is distracted by a mite crawling across his manuscript page. Similarly, in "Dreamwood," Rich's speaker finds her attention taken by the typing stand on which she works, seeing in the cheap wooden surface "a landscape, veined" (2) which suggests to her the possibilities of the poetic imagination.

As in other Rich poems, the speaker is fascinated by maps and journeys, which are metaphors for poetic investigation. The wood-grain of the typing stand reminds the speaker of such journeys, and she sees in the wood "a map of variations / on the one great choice" (12–13)—that is, her choice to devote her life to poetry. She notes further that poetry isn't an end but a means, not "revolution but a way of knowing / why it must come" (17–18).

Having taken her inspiration from "this cheap, massproduced" (18) typing stand, she is further emboldened to insist that poetry is more than the daydreaming of which she has accused herself in the poem's opening lines.

Rather, her inspiration proves that "the material and the dream can join" (23) in a single, ongoing, revolutionary process that is limited only by the poet's own imagination.

Alice Templeton summarizes the poem thus: "As the poet, writing the 'last report' of the day, sees a 'dream-map' in the woodgrain of her typing stand—as the material world leads the poetic imagination—so might the dream impress itself on the material world" (*The Dream and the Dialogue: Adrienne Rich's Feminist Poetics* [Knoxville: U of Tennessee P, 1994] 154).   GJ

Adrienne Rich   The Fact of a Doorframe (page 991)

This poem states the speaker's hopes that she can write a poetry that is solid and authentic—as solid and authentic, the poem's major image implies, as a doorframe, which also serves as an image for access and entry into a distinctive poetic world.

The speaker emphasizes the difficulty of her task throughout the poem. In the first stanza, she pictures herself "thrusting my forehead against the wood" (3) as an image of suffering. Yet it is this suffering for art that proves its authenticity: "music is suffering made powerful" (8).

The second stanza alludes to Grimms' fairy tale of the goose-girl, again an image of redemptive suffering and loss. (In the tale, a virtuous princess is undone by a devious lady's maid, who usurps her role as the bride of a handsome prince and forces the real princess into the menial task of tending geese. Because the princess had a horse, named Falada, who could speak, the lady's maid in her newly powerful role requests that the horse's head be cut off, and "the goose girl" then asks that the horse's head be nailed to the arch of a doorframe where she can always remember it.) Using the fairy tale likewise stresses what the speaker calls in the third stanza the "ancient and stubborn poise" that poetry represents throughout the ages. Poetry, according to the speaker, should be "violent, arcane, common" (18), paradoxically accessible and difficult at once. As Willard Spiegelman remarks, "Words fail, words support: a doorframe steadies and also gives one leave to thrust one's 'forehead against the wood'" ("'Driving to the Limits of the City of Words': The Poetry of Adrienne Rich," in Barbara Charlesworth Gelpi and Albert Gelpi, eds., *Adrienne Rich's Poetry and Prose* [New York: Norton, 1975)] 393).

The poem ultimately exalts the difficult but necessary striving of the poetic enterprise.   GJ

Adrienne Rich   Our Whole Life (page 992)

This poem deals with the noble but difficult effort, described so frequently in Rich's poetry, to use language and poetry as a means of truth-telling.

In the first half of the poem, she diagnoses the problem of inauthentic language, the "permissible fibs" (2) and the "knot of lies" (3), a poetic problem but also a political one, since the lies are translated "into the oppressor's language" (9). In the second half, she uses the politically charged image of an Algerian who came from his village "burning / his whole body a cloud of pain" (12–13), but unable to articulate his suffering. As the speaker dryly notes, "there are no words for this / except himself" (14–15).

As Emily Dickinson often does, Rich here states a principle (in the first nine lines) and then uses a specific example (in the remaining six lines) that illustrates the principle. The poem is effective because the political rhetoric of the opening lines is illustrated scorchingly in the closing lines about the Algerian. Language is more than a political or intellectual concept, the poem implies; it affects the lives of real people who have "no words" (14) with which to fight back against political oppressors.

"At perhaps the most terrifying point in her intellectual/emotional process," Craig Werner writes, "Rich creates the image of a burning Algerian, the victim of cultural solipsism as manifested in global imperialism. . . . The 'whole body' of the Algerian, like the 'whole life' of the title, transcends definition; as an emblem of the need for a language adequate to that experience, the Algerian challenges readers to accept their relationship both to his experience as victim and to the culture which victimizes him" (*Adrienne Rich: The Poet and Her Critics* [Chicago: American Library Association, 1988]: 65).

Willard Spiegelman discusses the poem's verbal technique: "The seeming randomness of the technique—the absence of punctuation, the participial nature of phrases, the infrequent verbs—makes the poem, like so much else in Rich's work, seem entirely provisional. . . . The horror of pain is its permanence: it takes no verbs. Any translation is like a photograph, immortalizing a reality of which its form is an inadequate imitation and that its articulating can hardly hope to cure" ("'Driving to the Limits of the City of Words': The Poetry of Adrienne Rich," in Barbara Charlesworth Gelpi and Albert Gelpi, eds., *Adrienne Rich's Poetry and Prose* [New York: Norton, 1975] 371). Alice Templeton summarizes the poem briefly: "the poet desires the untranslatable image and recognizes its revolutionary power to expose and shame previous lies" (*The Dream and the Dialogue: Adrienne Rich's Feminist Poetics* [Knoxville: U of Tennessee P, 1994] 15).   GJ

Alberto Ríos   Nani (page 993)

The *sestina*, of which this is the only example in this book, is a highly contrived fixed form making use of the patterned repetition of six end words through six stanzas, followed by a three-line *envoi* in which the six words are repeated in the middles and at the ends of lines. Ríos has slightly disguised the fact that his poem is a sestina by not providing stanza breaks except between what the pattern defines as the third and fourth stanzas, and before the envoi.

But if we do not recognize the form for what it is, the poem is nevertheless hypnotic in the repetition of end words that in themselves are emblematic of the poem's theme: *serve, me, her, words, more,* and *speak* (to list them in the order of the first stanza). These words display a variety of sound links, including the assonance of *serves–her–words* and *me–speak* and the alliteration of *serves–speak* and *me–more,* which increase the feeling of repetition and reinforce their significance in the poem. Essentially Ríos presents a small domestic scene in which a man is being served food by his grandmother, "the absolute *mamá*" (*nana* and *nani* are diminutive nicknames for a grandmother in the Spanish of America). Her serving, and then her smiles, and climactically her wrinkles, are her means of communication, and they speak wordlessly about her love for the speaker and for her dead husband, and finally about her children and all the ties of love. The speaker has lost two-thirds of his ability to speak or understand Spanish, so even when his grandmother speaks, it is to him as if her words dribble down her chin; but mostly she does not speak words, only gestures, looks, wrinkles, though she is so eloquent in these that when she cooks something at the stove it is as if she were doing "something with words." The "me–her" relationship is tenuous, not held by language but by a deep sense of closeness. As "the absolute *mamá*," nani speaks by serving, loves by feeding, and expresses the rich heritage of the family by the accumulated wrinkles of a long life of service and love. To the grandson who has lost the spoken language, the question is how much of this heritage he will be able to maintain: "I wonder just how much of me / will die with her, what were the words / I could have been, was." Yet the nani goes on serving, serving love.   TRA

Edwin Arlington Robinson   The Mill (page 994)

"The Mill" was first published in 1920. Its setting is earlier, sometime during the Industrial Revolution, probably late in the nineteenth century. The miller's remark (5) means that individual millers are no longer able to make a living: they are being replaced by industrialization.

Certainly, Robinson has not been at pains to be perfectly clear about what happens in this poem. The miller's remark (5) is cryptic. We are not told "What else there was" (13) in the mill, or "what was hanging from a beam" (15), or where the miller's wife went (16), or what kind of "way" (19) she is thinking of, or what ruffles the water (23). But surely this story of a double suicide gains in power exactly *because* it is not at first perfectly clear. Readers feel a growing horror as its meaning gradually dawns on them, as bewilderment shifts to suspicion and suspicion to certainty. If we change "what was hanging from a beam" to "his body hanging from a beam," the poem is made clearer, but its effect is greatly weakened. We no longer experience the terror of the half-seen.

Obscurity in a poem may arise from various causes, including the poet's ineptitude. It is not always as integral a part of meaning as it is here. But it can be. The point can be driven home by analogy to the person who spoils a joke by explaining it. A joke, too, is a small work of art. It must not be made so clear that its effect is destroyed.

This poem is briefly discussed by Wallace L. Anderson in *Edwin Arlington Robinson: A Critical Introduction* (Boston: Houghton, 1967) 103–104.   LP

Edwin Arlington Robinson   **Mr. Flood's Party** (page 994)

Few poems balance so precisely on the point between comedy and pathos, tears and laughter, as "Mr. Flood's Party." For the poet to have poised it so was a triumph in the management of tone.

The drunk has always been a figure of comedy, and Mr. Flood, as he drinks and sings with himself, "With only two moons listening," is richly comic. The similes enhance the humor. Mr. Flood with a jug at his lips and the ghost of a warrior with a horn at his lips may be visually similar, but the discrepancy between their emotional contexts makes the comparison ludicrous. Mr. Flood setting his jug down may resemble a mother laying down her sleeping child, but the incongruity between the drunk's solicitude for his jug and a mother's solicitude for her baby again is ludicrous. But the fun is not supplied entirely by the poet; it is supplied also by Mr. Flood himself. The grave solemnity, the punctilious courtesy, with which Mr. Flood goes through the social ritual of greeting himself, inviting himself to drink, welcoming himself home, and cautioning himself against a refill ("No more, sir; that will do")—all show a rich vein of humor that makes us laugh with Mr. Flood as well as at him. This is a lovable drunk—though he is not loved. With two Mr. Floods, and two moons, we are almost prepared ourselves to believe that "the whole harmonious landscape rang" (it takes two people to create harmony) until we realize that this is only the heightened sense of appreciation that every drunk has for the beauty of his own singing.

But the things that make Mr. Flood ludicrous also make him pathetic. The allusion to Roland winding his horn calls up one of the most famous and moving episodes in all literature, in *The Song of Roland*, and the comparison, though ludicrous, is also plangent and moves us with emotions more profound than comedy. Roland was sending out a call for help, and Mr. Flood needs help too; but we know that no help came for Roland in time to save him. The comparison to the mother and her sleeping child, in much the same way, reminds us of the familial relationships and gentleness and love that are missing from Mr. Flood's life. These two images, with the help of the silver moon, lay a veil of tenderness and soft emotion over the poem, which moves us to compassion as well as laughter. Mr. Flood, after all, is not a mere ne'er-do-well. He has a delightful sense of humor and an old-fashioned courtesy. He was once honored in the town below and had many friends there. He has an educated man's acquaintance with literature: in speaking of the fleetingness of time, he can quote from *The Rubáiyát of Omar Kháyyám* ("The

Bird of Time has but a little way / To flutter—and the Bird is on the Wing")
and then use the quotation wittily and gracefully to propose a toast. The reference to *The Song of Roland,* though made by the poet, reinforces our sense
of Mr. Flood as a sensitive and educated man. The song he sings—"'For auld
lang syne'"—has added force because Mr. Flood can look only backward for
better times; he can't look for them in the present or the future. Mr. Flood is
old: the husky voice that wavers out, and the trembling care with which he
sets down the jug are signs of age as well as of drink. His loneliness is stressed
throughout the poem: he climbs the hill "alone" (1), there is "not a native
near" (6), he speaks "For no man else in Tilbury Town to hear" (8), he must
drink with himself (9–16), he stands "Alone" (17), the moonlight makes a
"silver loneliness" (45), he is "again alone" (52), he has no friends in the
town below (54–56). A ghost in the moonlight, Mr. Flood sends out his call
for help, and he is answered only by other ghosts—"A phantom salutation of
the dead"—old memories.

We are not told why Mr. Flood has been cast out from the town below,
why he is no longer honored, for what social sin or error he has lost his place
in society. We only know that he is old, alone, friendless, dishonored, deserving of compassion but getting none. The "strangers" who would have
shut their doors to him in the town below are probably many of them literal
strangers, but some are former friends from whom he has been estranged. The
final note of the poem is not one of laughter, but of heartbreak.

[Reprinted from Laurence Perrine and James M. Reid, *100 American Poems of the Twentieth Century* (New York: Harcourt, 1966) 7–8.]   LP

Edwin Arlington Robinson   Richard Cory (page 996)

Despite the popularity and apparent simplicity of this poem, it is often
badly misread by students, who reduce it to the platitude that "great wealth
does not guarantee happiness." Such a reading ignores nine-tenths of the
poem. What the poem actually says is much more terrifying: that good birth,
good looks, good breeding, good taste, humanity, *and* wealth do not guarantee happiness. The poem establishes all these qualities as being Cory's, and
the "people on the pavement" thought that Cory "*was* everything" (not *had*
everything) to make them wish that they were in his place. This larger meaning must be insisted on. "Richard Cory" may not be as great a poem as, say,
Robinson's "Mr. Flood's Party," but it is a genuine poem, neither superficial
nor cheap.

The word "gentleman" is used both in its modern sense of one who is
well behaved and considerate of others and in its older sense of one who is
well born. The first meaning is established by Cory's courteous and uncon-
descending "Good-morning" to the "people on the pavement" and by his being "admirably schooled in every grace." The second meaning is established
by a constellation of words that, by their primary or secondary meanings,

suggest aristocratic or royal privilege: "crown," "favored," "imperially," "arrayed," "glittered," "king," "grace," "fine" ("crown" here means *top of the head*, but is also a symbol of royalty; "Clean favored" means *clean-featured*, but "favored" is also *privileged*; "grace" means a *social nicety*, but it is also the term used for addressing a duke; "in fine" means *in sum*, but "fine" implies also a quality of character and dress. Notice how the adverb "quietly" before "arrayed" imbues Cory with good taste: he dresses finely but unostentatiously).

Cory's first name has as its first syllable the word *rich* and is the name of several English kings, including the gallant Richard Coeur de Lion. His last name has a sonorous sound and is a good English name such as might belong to the New England landed gentry. It is in addition suggestive of such French words as *cor*, hunting horn; *coeur*, heart; and *cour*, royal court.

"[P]avement" is an appropriate word not only because it alliterates with "people." A pavement is lower than a sidewalk; it establishes the commonness of the "people" in contrast with the higher status of Cory; it has the "people" looking up at him.

The surprise ending is not there for its own sake. By setting up an ironic contrast, it suggests a number of truths about life: that we cannot tell from outside appearance what may be going on inside a person; that often the people we envy have as many troubles as we, or more; that, as has been said above, birth, wealth, breeding, taste, and humanity do not ensure a happy life.

There is an excellent discussion of this poem in Norman C. Stageberg and Wallace L. Anderson, *Poetry as Experience* (New York: American Book, 1952) 188–92. I expand slightly on the present discussion in *The Art of Total Relevance: Papers on Poetry* (Rowley, MA: Newbury, 1976) 97–99.   LP

Theodore Roethke   I knew a woman (page 997)

This poem is a tribute of praise and gratitude from a middle-aged poet to a younger woman whose eager sexual expertise taught him in fullest measure the delights of sensual love. The verb in the title may be understood in both its ordinary and its biblical sense. The imagery of the poem throughout emphasizes physical movement and the attractions of the body. The woman was "lovely in her bones," and "when she moved, she moved more ways than one." The "bright container" (4) is her skin. The tribute paid in lines 6–7 is both humorous and deeply meant, for "English poets who grew up on Greek" would include such favorites of Roethke's as Sir John Davies, Ben Jonson, and Andrew Marvell. In stanza 2 the terms "Turn," "Counter-turn," and "Stand" are the English equivalents of the Greek words *strophe*, *antistrophe*, and *epode*, indicating the movements made by the chorus in Greek drama while chanting a choral ode. The metaphor in lines 12–14 compares the woman to the curving sickle that cuts the grass in harvesting and the speaker to the straight rake that gathers it up. Moving in synchronism they produce a "prodigious mowing." Although the metaphor hardly needs further explanation, it is not irrelevant that the verb *to mow*, in Scottish dialect, means to have sexual intercourse, and that the noun *rake* refers not only to the harvesting tool but to a sexually oriented male. Stanza 3 continues the poem's tribute to the sexual talents of the woman. The "mobile nose" in the whimsical mixed metaphor of line 20 suggests that of a rabbit (or other animal) sniffing the air.

Stanza 4 is difficult, for the poet here turns philosophical, and his transitions are abrupt. But if the precise meanings are puzzling, the tone is not. Clearly the poet sees no contradiction between "eternity" and enjoyment of the sensual life. He swears his lady cast a "white" shadow, not a dark one. Perhaps such pleasure as she afforded him is a foretaste of eternity. If he is a "martyr to a motion not [his] own" but hers, he has been a willing martyr, and his old bones still "live to learn her wanton ways." "To know eternity" is the important thing, "But who would count eternity in days?" The question is rhetorical; the answer is, No one but a fool; eternity may be tasted in a minute. The poet himself measures time "by how a body sways." The first line of the stanza seems to refer to the natural process of the human life cycle from conception to death, but also to glance back at the sexual metaphor in lines 12–14. The simile "white as stone" calls up the image of a white marble gravestone, a marker separating life from eternity. The use of the past tense in the first three stanzas and the switch to the present in the fourth may indicate that the woman is dead (and the poet himself is certainly older). But the last two lines indicate that he has not forgotten the lessons she taught him. The poem ends, as it began, as a celebration of sensual love.

For additional suggestions, see discussions in *Explicator* by Virginia L. Peck, 22 (Apr. 1964): item 66; Helen T. Buttel, 24 (May 1966): item 78; Nat Henry, 27 (Jan. 1969): item 31; and Jenijoy LaBelle, 32 (Oct. 1973): item 15.   LP

Theodore Roethke   My Papa's Waltz (page 997)

This reminiscence of a boy's relationship with his father packs considerable verbal complexity and meaning into a small poetic space.

The poem conveys both the pleasure and the fear of the speaker's nocturnal dances with his drunken father. Language implying a pleasurable experience ("waltzing," "romped," "held") is counterbalanced with phrases denoting pain and terror ("hung on like death," "scraped," "You beat time," "clinging"). As one critic observes, "This love dance, a kind of blood rite between father and son, shows suppressed terror combined with awe-inspired dependency" (Peter Balakian, *Theodore Roethke's Far Fields: The Evolution of His Poetry* [Baton Rouge: Louisiana State UP, 1989] 62). Throughout the poem, this verbal ambivalence reflects the speaker's conflicting emotions toward his father: his boyhood love of his "papa," his mature disapproval of his father's drinking.

The central comparison of the father and son's drunken cavorting to a waltz, the most graceful of dances, establishes a tone of gentle irony that— like the first stanza's understated phrase "Such waltzing was not easy"—controls the poem. Far from a harsh indictment or attack on the father, the poem describes carefully what happened without rendering judgments; in fact, there is a suggestion that the speaker disapproves of his own mother's protective disapproval when he recalls, in a less than flattering description, that her "countenance / Could not unfrown itself." Typical of this poem's concise use of language is the pun on "countenance" (permission and face) and the word's suggestion, in both its meanings, of a small-minded pomposity in the mother's attitude. In contrast to her Mrs. Grundy-like demeanor, the father is sympathetically portrayed as a working man whose hands are "battered" and "caked hard by dirt," someone perhaps deserving of a release through a few drinks and a Dionysiac bonding with his son.

At the same time, the inchoate violence of the "waltz"—during which the boy gets dizzy, scrapes his ear, and has his head used as a drum—gathers force as the poem proceeds, culminating in the powerfully ambivalent concluding image of the boy "clinging" to the father's shirt. This single word, with its equivalent stressing of desperate affection and desperate fear, encapsulates the speaker's ambivalent attitude toward his father. One major source of the poem's power, in fact, is his refusal to "resolve" this ambivalence, allowing the poem to mirror convincingly the often paradoxical conflicts inherent in family ties.   GJ

Sherod Santos   Driftwood (page 998)

This sonnet, arranged into two septets, describes a piece of driftwood held by the speaker's son in a fishing boat, and the meaning the speaker draws from it.

The driftwood shows evidence of a long and turbulent life, "a history of fells and sailroads, of flare-ups" (5); it has been bathed in salt and partly eaten by worms. The use of alliteration in the first stanza, especially the "l" and "r" sounds, helps convey the rolling lilt of the driftwood's past movement through water and bruising obstacles.

In the second stanza, the driftwood is described as "Stripped from the tree of reckoning, arrayed / against the world's unpunished harms" (8–9). The speaker is clearly comparing the driftwood's many travails since it was torn from its original tree to the slings and arrows of human fortune.

In the closing lines, the speaker shifts into considering what the emblematic driftwood may mean for his son. He hopes it will "bolster / the peacemaker's heart in him" (10–11), and steer him safely around the inevitable obstacles life will cast in his way.

Though the speaker's son is young, the aged piece of driftwood forces the speaker to think about "the end-all meaning" (14) of his son's life; the reference to "folktales" (13) unites the father and son with all of humanity that must, like the driftwood, suffer a perilous "journeying" (14) through life.   GJ

Anne Sexton   The Abortion (page 998)

According to her biographer, Diane Wood Middlebrook, Anne Sexton confessed in a letter to a friend that she had undergone an abortion, an experience that helps give this poem its authentic-sounding tone of somber guilt and sorrow.

Following the poem's thrice-repeated refrain, "*Somebody who should have been born is gone,*" are lines featuring Sexton's gift for the unexpected metaphor. The first set of three-line stanzas describes a woman driving to Pennsylvania for her abortion, then returning home again. Her observations of the landscape as she drives employ metaphors evocative of the child she decided not to bear: the land "puckered its mouth"; the mountains' "green hair" is "like a crayoned cat." The undulating landscape itself "humps on endlessly," a sexual image evoking excessive generative urges, and a sunken road is compared implicitly to the speaker's own womb: "the ground cracks evilly, / a dark socket from which the coal has poured."

The poem gains in emotional power as the speaker continues to employ childlike, whimsical imagery to communicate the pathos of her own adult emotions during this crisis. The living grass of the landscape she passes appears "bristly and stout as chives," yet makes her wonder "how anything fragile survives." She describes the abortion doctor as a "little man," but one not like the fairy tale character Rumpelstiltskin, who was able to spin straw into gold; the doctor, she implies, engages in a reverse process, changing something potentially precious into blood, taking away "the fullness that love began." As she returns home after the abortion, the lush landscape gives way to a thin sky and a flat road, suggestive of barrenness and the speaker's bleak mood as she calls herself, in the harsh concluding stanza, a "coward," and explicitly mourns "this baby that I bleed."

A. R. Jones calls this last image "brilliantly horrible," and argues that "the *persona* driving back from the abortionist rationalizes her sense of guilt and loss and concludes by turning upon herself" ("Necessity and Freedom," in Linda Wagner-Martin, ed., *Critical Essays on Anne Sexton* [Boston: G. K. Hall, 1989] 35).   GJ

Anne Sexton   Her Kind (page 999)

In "Her Kind," Sexton defines one of her most characteristic personae: a woman who suffers frequently from mental illness and suicidal longings, and who is viewed by her society as unwomanly or as frankly evil, a "witch." The poem's brilliant images and deft use of rhyme, rhythm, and repetition lend structure and significance to its turbulent subject matter.

Though the speaker seems to internalize her society's scapegoating of the mentally ill, calling herself "a possessed witch" indulging in the nocturnal habit of "haunting the black air" and "dreaming evil," she is actually employing the witch image for her own purposes, creating a persona who is neither repellent nor ugly but who is portrayed, as the poem proceeds, as vulnerable and undeniably human. The second stanza takes a surprising turn toward domestic metaphors, following the witch as she fills caves with "skillets, carvings, shelves," nurtures other feared creatures ("the worms and the elves"), and enjoys "rearranging the disaligned." Essentially, then, she is a good witch, though fatally "misunderstood." The final stanza describes her fate as she is driven off in a cart, waving her "nude arms at villages going by," to be burned at the stake.

The repeated refrain, "I have been her kind," indicates the speaker's sympathy and identification with the mentally ill "witch." As Diane Wood Middlebrook observes, "Through the use of an undifferentiated but double 'I,' the poem sets up a single persona identified with madness but separated from it through insight." Steven E. Colburn calls attention to the poem's structural division into "three brief episodes" in which "this legendary figure of women's power is cast into a variety of situations by the storyteller that illustrate by turns the fortune of her character as rebel, servant, and victim."

These and other extended remarks about this much-discussed poem may be found in Middlebrook, *Anne Sexton* (Boston: Houghton Mifflin, 1991) 114–15; in Colburn, "'This Is My Tale Which I Have Told': Anne Sexton as Storyteller," in Linda Wagner-Martin, ed., *Critical Essays on Anne Sexton* (Boston: G. K. Hall, 1989) 167–79; and in Greg Johnson, "The Achievement of Anne Sexton," in Linda Wagner-Martin, ed., *Critical Essays on Anne Sexton* (Boston: G. K. Hall, 1989) 85–86.   GJ

William Shakespeare   Fear no more (page 1000)

Both the tone of this dirge from the fourth act of *Cymbeline* and the dramatic situation which is its occasion are characteristic of the late romances of Shakespeare. This is sung or spoken by two young men who suppose their adopted stepbrother is dead; but not only is the stepbrother only in a drugged sleep, "he" is really a princess who has had to flee the tyranny of the court—and the two singers who have been raised as Welsh shepherds are in actuality her long-lost princely brothers. These plot details contribute little to interpreting this song as a poem. But they make it, in its place in the play, a reinforcement of the mysterious powers of goodness that defeat the malevolent plotting of the villains in Shakespeare's last plays. Since everything works out for the best, despite all odds, a funeral lament like this emphasizes

escaping life's pains and fears, not the grief of the mourners. Their love is expressed not in joy that the dead person has gone to heavenly bliss (the play
is set in pre-Christian Britain), but in the consolation that he is now safe
from danger and is sharing in a universal fate.

The "fears" that beset the living are of two kinds: natural (summer heat,
winter cold, lightning and thunder) and social, with the greater emphasis on
the latter. Although they personally know nothing of court life, these young
men describe the conditions of a capital city, where ordinary people have to
work for food and clothing, and where social disparities ("chimney-sweepers"
with their grueling and miserable lives contrasted to "Golden lads and girls")
subject people to the frowns of their superiors and the cruelty of tyrants as
well as to slander and rash censure. There is some "joy" in such a life, however slight: there is love, momentarily alluded to in line 17. But the prepon-
derance of experience has been "moan," and death's release is to that extent
to be welcomed.

The universality of death, encapsulated in the repeated rhyme "must . . .
come to dust," contrasts the equality of the dead to the social hierarchies and
injustices that govern the living. Rich and poor, mighty and weak, learned
and ignorant, all "must . . . come to dust," and the inequities of society will be
obliterated. Death is the great deliverer and equalizer.   TRA

William Shakespeare Let me not to the marriage of true minds (page 1001)

This sonnet makes an interesting contrast to "My mistress' eyes" (page
809). The subject here is a union of minds, while "My mistress' eyes" is a
poem about physical attraction; this sonnet is idealistic, the other realistic.
The opening sentence refers to the marriage ceremony in the Anglican *Book
of Common Prayer*: ". . . if either of you do know any impediment why ye may
not be lawfully joined together in matrimony . . . confess it." This reference
is made emphatic by the extreme metrical irregularity of the first line, and
made more vivid by the regularity of the first three feet of the second line.

The first quatrain proceeds negatively: I do not admit impediments; love
is not love if it alters or bends. The second quatrain reverses the rhetoric,
positively insisting that love is permanent and fixed; and the third returns to
the negative, "Love's not Time's fool" and again, "Love alters not." In effect,
the three quatrains describe what intellectual love is not, what it is, and
again what it is not. (One scholar discovers in this, and in other details of the
poem, that this sonnet is "protesting too much," and that it must be seen as
ironic overstatement. While the poem may seem too hyperbolic when laid
beside "My mistress' eyes," there is really little within this poem to suggest
less than sincerity.)

The examination of the three quatrains as rhetorical parallels reveals a
frequent pattern of Shakespeare's sonnets: they are repetitive, offering three

different contexts to make the same statement. In the first quatrain, the context resembles a courtroom or public debate, as the echo from the marriage ceremony implies question and response. Here, the response is suitably intellectualized, a matter of defining terms that is appropriate to the subject of "minds." The diction reinforces the effect, being rational and legalistic ("Let me not," "Admit impediments," "alters . . . alteration," "remover to remove").

The second quatrain develops two two-line images, the "ever-fixèd mark" of a beacon or lighthouse unshaken by storms, and the pole star by which navigators steer, both images sharing the context of nautical travel, its dangers and its safeguards. Line 8 states our inability to know the exact value of the star, even though we can make use of our instruments to steer by its steadfastness, and it contrasts the "wandering" of human life with the star's immobility. True intellectual love preserves us in danger, and guides us when we wander.

The third quatrain continues to develop single images in two-line statements linked together in a common context. "Time's fool" is the toy or plaything of personified time, having no value to him. This is "Father Time," who dispassionately destroys the "rosy lips and cheeks" of the young (this is the only reference to physical beauty in the poem—*it* is "Time's fool"). Time with his sickle is linked to the "grim reaper" who at the day of "doom" will finally destroy all life, and only then will the "marriage of the true minds" be dissolved.

The couplet returns the poem to the courtroom of the opening quatrain. The poet invites disproof of his testimony, and employs as his witnesses two incontrovertible facts: since I have written (this poem proves that), and since certainly at least one man has loved, then my statements must be true. The couplet seems irrefutable, except that its conclusion is not necessarily valid: while it claims that these self-evident facts prove that the argument of his sonnet is also self-evident, there is no real connection. The "proof" is rhetorical rather than logical (and like the opening quatrain, couched in negative rhetoric).

This justly popular poem has been much analyzed. Among the most interesting commentaries are the following: Edward Hubler, *The Sense of Shakespeare's Sonnets* (Princeton: Princeton UP, 1952) 92–93; Kenneth Muir, *Shakespeare's Sonnets* (London: Allen, 1979) 107–108; Paul Ramsey, *The Fickle Glass: A Study of Shakespeare's Sonnets* (New York: AMS, 1979) 157–58; Katharine M. Wilson, *Shakespeare's Sugared Sonnets* (London: Allen, 1974) 301–303.   TRA

Karl Shapiro   **The Fly** (page 1001)

This extended apostrophe is very nearly a literal portrait of this most-loathed insect. The few instances where the fly is given human qualities or attitudes stand out—its "comic mood" that leads it to a mid-air sex act (7–8), its surprising coyness (10), its courageous and chivalrous hand-kissing (19), its begging to be freed from flypaper (30).

In the first three stanzas, the fly is placed in its environment: in the decaying flesh of cat or man, on a plate of food, in a compost heap, crawling on a hand. All of these descriptions (beginning with the metaphor and comparison of the first line) use witty language to present disgusting and abhorrent actions. Stanzas 4–6 place the fly in juxtaposition to those humans who directly assault it: children, who for fun try to capture and hold buzzing flies in their hands; "wives" who employ pesticides and flypapers to keep them out of the house; and "a man" who feels he must resort to physical violence of various sorts in order to kill, crush, disembowel, and tear the pest, and in his gigantic superiority to the minute corpses strides triumphantly through them.

Unlike other insect poems in this book, Shapiro's is most nearly simply a portrait sketch, with the secondary purpose of describing how we treat its subject. For contrasting uses of insects as subjects, see Donne's "The Flea" (page 814) and Dickinson's "I heard a Fly buzz—when I died" (page 871).   TRA.

Dave Smith Little Ode to the Wheelchair Boys (page 1002)

The speaker in "Little Ode" has stopped his car next to a schoolyard where three boys in wheelchairs are having a race organized by their special-ed teacher. The teacher is "like Psyche," the personification of the soul, and she tries to give the boys "something like courage" (9). The speaker emphasizes the touching awkwardness of the boys' race, their "heads bobbing as each scopes / The line they race for but cannot see" (4–5).

In the second stanza, the speaker relates the boys' effort at the race with incipient erotic desire; they want to please their beautiful teacher with her "fine legs" (10) and "young woman's breast" (11). Yet the speaker emphasizes that the wheelchair boys have little chance at winning in the larger game of life, since they must compete with "those who run and jump and shriek to win" (17).

Finally the poem stresses the boys' courage in pursuing the race "fearless as men who give / Their one life for a cause" (19–20). Again the teacher, "this tall gold girl" (26), spurs their desire, though the speaker again recognizes the boys' unhappy fate in the context of their healthy classmates.

The poem carefully avoids the maudlin or the sentimental. It offers a bleak but touching view of courageous human striving in the face of formidable obstacles; but it finally emphasizes an equally formidable desire to succeed.   GJ

Cathy Song   The Youngest Daughter (page 1003)

A native of Hawaii, Cathy Song here writes about her sense of the cultural difference between herself and her mother. At the same time, the poem suggests the intimacy and affection of the mother-daughter bond.

At several points in the poem, the speaker highlights the literal difference in the two women's skin color, the mother's having been darkened out in the fields while her own skin has remained "pale as rice paper" (4); this simile aptly suggests her island heritage. Similarly, in the second stanza she refers to her skin as "aspirin colored" (12), another appropriate image since here she describes her own problems with migraine headaches and the role of her mother in massaging her face and thus lessening the pain.

In the third and most vivid stanza, the speaker describes the ritual of bathing her mother, who is ill with diabetes. Again she highlights the older woman's maternal role, calling attention to her breasts "floating in the milky water" (23) and thinking to herself: "six children and an old man / have sucked from these brown nipples" (28–29).

In the final stanza, the mother prepares a snack for them both: tea, rice, and gingered fish, foods that again suggest the mother's Hawaiian heritage; but the mother also includes "a slice of pickled turnip, / a token for my white body" (44–45). The poem's tribute to the speaker's mother ends effectively with a "toast to her health" (49) and an abrupt, unexpected vision of transcendence: "a thousand cranes curtain the window, / fly up in a sudden breeze" (51–52). This emblem of quiet but breathtaking triumph brings effective closure to this moving tribute to the bonds between mother and daughter.   GJ

Gary Soto   Small Town with One Road (page 1005)

The speaker, now a man whose "easy" job is "only words" (26, 27) (poet? professor?), has returned to the cotton farming valley where he was reared. He is accompanied by his small daughter, and as they "suck roadside / Snowcones in the shade" (30–31), he meditates on his beginnings. He recalls being a barefoot kid, leaping across the black asphalt highway to spend dimes for red candies, and a home life busy with dogs, cats, chickens, beans for supper: "It's a hard life where the sun looks," for "Okie or Mexican, Jew that got lost" (18, 17). The memories are of a life of manual labor, sweating in the hot sun, dreaming "the money dream" of relief from "shovel, / Hoe, broom" (19, 27–28).

And yet there is a vividly sensuous side to this reminiscence, a richness captured in images of sight, sound, feeling, taste—captured particularly well in line 6—"Sweetness on their tongues, red stain of laughter"—where the color of candy or snowcone is transferred to the tongue in a synesthetic mingling of taste and color, so that the pleasure of the taste is transferred to the color, and that in turn is the color of laughter. Soto intensifies what might be a prosaic description (open-mouthed laughing kids reveal the candy's red dye stain on their tongues) through the concentration of metonymy and metaphor. The leaps of meaning in this phrase are like the leaping kids themselves.

The tone of the poem is thus complex: the speaker is pleased that he is no longer trapped in the "hard life" (18), fearful that the success he has had in escaping it might disappear, and concerned for his worrying, serious daughter. Yet as he recalls himself (and then in line 33 sees himself in the "brown kid" standing and then leaping as he had done), he feels nostalgia for the rich exuberance that he has lost—and probably a little regret that his daughter will not experience it for herself.   TRA

Wole Soyinka Telephone Conversation (page 1006)

This ironic clash between cultures by the Nigerian Nobel Literature laureate portrays a man who has learned much about the appearance and behavior of whites in London but is nevertheless dumbstruck by the overt racism of the landlady. He knows that there are prejudiced people—and wants to avoid wasting his time going to her building if she will object to his dark skin. As he awaits her response to the news that he is African, he hears in her silence a loss of her "[p]ressurized good-breeding," that is, the artificial politeness and indirection that make him imagine her lipstick and gold cigarette holder. Her questions when they come are rudely abrupt: "'HOW DARK?'" and "'ARE YOU LIGHT OR VERY DARK?'" (10–11). The questions are so blatant as to make him check on the reality of his surroundings.

He in turn is "ill-mannered" in his "silence" (15), unable to answer such simplistic questions. When he does reply it is to ask for a further simplification, offering her the colors of milk chocolate and dark chocolate as examples. When she assents that that comparison would do, he becomes more elaborate (and puzzling to her): "'West African sepia'" (22). His final description, which leads her to hang up noisily, not only tells her of color variations on the palms of his hands and soles of his feet, but also includes his "raven black . . . bottom" (32), a feature that he offers to show her for her edification.

The pretended gentility of both the landlady and the speaker is at the end blown away.   TRA

Edmund Spenser One day I wrote her name upon the strand (page 1007)

This sonnet in the rhyme scheme of the Shakespearean form shares structural patterns with both that and the Petrarchan form. Clearly there is a division into three quatrains and a couplet, but there is also a major "turn" at line 9 recalling the octave-sestet structure.

The opening quatrain is divided into pairs of lines repeating the act of writing the beloved's name in the sand and its subsequent obliteration, first by the action of waves, and then more emphatically by being engulfed by the rising tide. The lover's writing her name in the sand is slightly silly, the act of a lovesick boy (like Orlando carving Rosalind's name in the bark of trees in *As You Like It*). There is some playfulness in this, too, as obviously the woman is watching him write—a seaside game that doesn't immediately call up ideas of "immortaliz[ing]" her (6).

It is the woman who introduces the more serious subject, contrasting what is "mortal" and subject to "decay" to what is immortal. She analogizes: just as her name is easily destroyed by water if it is written in sand, so her mortal body will "decay," and with the loss of her life even that name will be forgotten.

The stock answer is that time may destroy the "baser things" (9), including her own mortal flesh, but his poetry will give her an immortality (fame) as his beloved that will outlast the destruction of the world itself. The tone of the third quatrain and the couplet is contrasted to that of the opening quatrain, as eternity and resurrection are juxtaposed to the playful name-writing pastime. In the dialogue it is the woman who introduces the serious subject of mutability, and the replies of the poet transform that into claims of immutable, eternal life.

This poem could provide a fruitful lesson in the management of sound and music as these are linked to the three parts of the argument. The first quatrain abounds in decorative devices: assonance (day-name-came-waves-away-again-came-made-pains-prey); alliteration (waves-washed-away, pains-prey); and consonance (strand-second-hand, tide-made). These joined to the repetitive, playful action give the quatrain some of its lightheartedness. There are far fewer examples of musicality in the second quatrain—a continuation of the long *a* sound picked up in the rhyme and repetition of line 5 (vain-vain-assay), the repetitive *mortal-immortalize* of line 6, and the consonant *l*-myself-like-wipèd-likewise in 7–8.

In the remaining six lines, when the dialogue returns to the poet in a more serious vein, once again there is much music, but it functions less as decoration than as emphasis. For example, the *v*-sound that achieves a climax in line 14 (Our love shall live) occurs at least once in every line but the thirteenth—devise-live-verse-virtues-heavens. The sounds here reinforce meanings by joining important words, especially "verse," "virtues," and "heavens," and of course "love" and "live."   TRA

Wallace Stevens   **The Death of a Soldier** (page 1007)

This poem has both a specific and a general subject, and it might best be read as a symbolic statement: it presents what the title says, but the meaning expands from the specific issue of the death of a soldier on a battlefield to encompass human death in general. The "soldier" is only an extreme example whose death invites certain special responses not always associated with the deaths of ordinary people—chiefly, those traditional attitudes that are so easily evoked by apologists for war, by national holiday commemorators, by politicians and patriots: those who die in war "have not died in vain," but have served some national (or religious, or universal) purpose. Stevens has chosen a soldier so as to excite such stock responses, which he subjects to situational irony: a military death is apparently the most meaningful death in a secular, nontheist society—but in actuality it is no more meaningful than the changing of the seasons.

Death in this poem is part of a natural process, linked in simile twice to the change of season in autumn, just another "fall." It is not the occasion for imposing upon survivors the duty of memorials or funereal pomposity. Its apparent uniqueness—that something in particular has stopped, a singular human life—is compared to the momentary cessation of wind, a stillness that is deceptive in the larger context of climatic motion. No human life is important, no human death is important, not even those that a secular, patriotic nation celebrates.

Such nihilism is not pleasant to contemplate, yet this poem has a shapeliness and rhetorical power that make the ideas less repugnant. There is, after all, a kind of beauty in the stark, simple, and unadorned presentation of the idea: an individual human death is no more important than the change of the seasons, and the impersonal physical processes of the world will go on, "nevertheless," in the impassive reality of absolute truth. ("[N]evertheless" is a marvelously evocative word, in this context, for in its double negation it emphasizes Stevens's point: mere human life or death can *never* make any *less* the reality of a world of factual truth.)

Formally, the poem reflects its reductive philosophy in its structure. The free verse stanzas have a syllabic pattern made visible by the printing. The norm is an opening line of about 10 syllables, a second line of 8, and a final line of 4 (the last stanza offers this variation: 7 in line 2; 5 in line 3). The stanzas themselves, that is, seem to dwindle down toward immobility and silence, "As in a season of autumn, / When the wind stops. . . ." Yet, as the stanzas repeat the pattern and thus imply continuity, the clouds (and poetry) will "go, nevertheless."   TRA

Wallace Stevens   Disillusionment of Ten O'Clock
(page 1008)

At first glance, this seems a zany and extravagant collection of images, a surreal poem with little but emotional effect. It is in fact social satire directed at pallid people who have neither overt nor secret excitements in their lives. Like ghosts of the truly living, they haunt their own houses (which, in double meaning, are their only haunts). They do not dress imaginatively, nor do they even possess subconscious dreams of things odd or exotic. They don't "dream of baboons," or of "periwinkles" (another double denotation: the word "periwinkle" means both a garden ivy and a sea snail; the wild diversity of the word emphasizes the extravagance that they *don't* dream about). And they are already in their nightgowns and in bed at ten o'clock: dull, unimaginative, unexciting, plain people.

All that relieves this vision of domestic drabness is an occasional sailor, passed out drunk in the street or barroom, whose dream reveals a vital, overimaginative psyche. But the poem doesn't even say he's dreaming: although he is "drunk and asleep in his boots" (13), his imagination is so lively that he actually "*Catches* tigers / In red weather" (14–15). The tigers and the weather are as "strange" (7) as the sleepers are ordinary.   TRA

Wallace Stevens   The Snow Man (page 1008)

The single sentence constituting this poem is ambiguously framed, either offering advice or a definition: in its barest statement, it can be paraphrased, "only a person as cold-minded as a snow man would not think such a cold place implies misery." Is the speaker advocating such lack of emotion as appropriate to the surroundings and as a defense against despair? Or is he lamenting the inhumanity that would be necessary to escape such emotions? The last two lines provide a partial answer: the reality of the situation is that this observable landscape contains "the nothing that is," and that it has no further dimensions of meaning beyond its mere physical existence. To "think of misery" therefore is to add a false meaning, one derived not from reality but from an observer's emotional reaction.

These last two lines may echo *Hamlet*, 3.4, when the Ghost appears to Hamlet in Gertrude's closet but remains invisible to her. Hamlet asks his mother, "Do you see nothing there?" and she replies, "Nothing at all; yet all that is I see" (131–32). Stevens's snow man is an unemotional, practical realist, unable to see anything but actuality, and able to see that the actuality implies nothing beyond itself. Neither ghosts nor implications of meaning are available to him.

The only way a person can avoid thinking of misery in such a barren place is to be, like the snow man, "nothing himself," a person without feeling. The first three stanzas create the visual scene, in details that seem quite forbidding. The trees have been subjected to wintry transformations, "crusted" and "shagged" and made "rough" in appearance by the weakness of the distant sun. Stanzas 3 and 4 add the effect of the "sound of the wind," which to an emotional observer would imply misery. The defense against such feeling is "a mind of winter," coldly unemotional and in total harmony with the surroundings.

While this is the overt statement of the poem, there remains a third alternative to either misery or emotional coldness: the visual imagery implies the possibility of perceiving beauty in the chiaroscuro of shapes and textures. The three types of evergreen trees have distinctly different shapes, and the winter has given them three distinct textures. The crusted pines tower above with their foliage at the tops of their tall trunks; the shaggy junipers sprawl flat and disorderly in their low branching; and the conical Christmas tree–shaped spruces are roughened but glittering. Although the scene is not inviting, it nevertheless possesses stark beauty. The snow man's coldly analytical philosophy is a defense against misery and a definition of reality, but it does not comprehend esthetic responses.

For two slightly different interpretations of this much-discussed poem, see A. Walton Litz, *Introspective Voyager: The Poetic Development of Wallace Stevens* (New York: Oxford UP, 1972) 99–100, and Daniel Fuchs, *The Comic Spirit of Wallace Stevens* (Durham: Duke UP, 1963) 69–70.   TRA

Leon Stokesbury   Listening to My Mother's Comic Banter with Sackboys and Servers (page 1009)

The adult speaker in "Listening" describes his aging mother's habitual "comic banter" with grocery store sackers and fast-food workers, a banter in which he hears a confirmation that "there is no god" (2).

The mother's banter is pure cliché, "often beginning with something / along the lines of 'working hard,' / then straight to 'hardly working'" (20–22); or she exclaims about the hot weather. Despite the banality of his mother's words, the speaker sees an "ascension" (34) to spiritual concerns inside them: "I observe my mother's eyes / shifting from her daily dull to a fine / acetylene shine: opaque proof / perhaps, of linkage to some / living thing outside herself" (35–39).

At this point, the poem shifts to the speaker's imagining that his mother, as a young woman, had glimpsed a spiritual emptiness at the heart of the world. Though his mother's banter suggests her intellectual limitations, and the speaker says outright that she "would not even know / how to say so" (45–46), he claims that his mother had sensed that there is no governing power in the universe. To cover her resulting anxiety, the speaker asserts, his mother indulges in her comic banter and depends on "the kindness / of strangers" (58–59) to get her through the day.

Apart from its serious content, the poem is noteworthy for its frequently comic depiction of the mother as, in some ways, a stereotypical older Southern woman. The poem suggests a touching connection, too, between mother and son, since the son has reached the same atheist conviction that he claims to hear in his mother's words.   GJ

Dylan Thomas   Fern Hill (page 1010)

"Fern Hill" is Dylan Thomas's evocation of the delight, the wonder, the long carefree rapture of boyhood summers spent on a farm in Wales. The reader is made to share his pleasure in the barns and fields and orchards, in the farmhouse itself, in the animals both wild and domestic, in afternoon and night and morning. In the fourth stanza the poet compares this boyhood experience to the experience of Adam and Eve in Eden. Like theirs, its chief characteristics were joy and innocence and a feeling of timelessness. Like theirs, his experience came at the beginning of life and, like them, he felt it would last forever. But the theme of the poem is the transience of youthful joy and carefree innocence. All the time that he is heedless of time, he is bound by its chains, which hold him "green and dying." Just as Adam and Eve were thrust out of Eden, so the boy is to be thrust out of the garden of childhood.

The boy is the protagonist of the poem. Time is the antagonist—unseen, unfelt, and unheeded by the boy, but comprehended clearly by the mature poet looking back. The boy, "happy as the grass was green," feels that he has forever. But, inexorably, in its alternation of afternoon and night and morning, Time is carrying him out of the enchanted realm, "out of grace," toward age and death. The boy who is "prince of the apple towns" (6)—and described with such aristocratically connotative adjectives as "Golden" (5), "honored" (6), "lordly" (7), and "famous" (10), who feels himself master of all he surveys—is at the same time, though unaware of it, a slave, held by "Time" in "chains" (54).

Thomas has a talent for refurbishing clichés and getting new or double meaning out of them, both the old and the new. "[H]appy as the grass was green" (2) and "happy as the heart was long" (38) both remind us of the commoner expression "Happy as the day is long" and gather its meaning into fresher expressions. "[O]nce below a time" (7) gathers up the meaning of "Once upon a time" and bends it to the use of the poem's theme—that the boy is really a slave of time, not master of it. In "All the sun long" (19) and "all the moon long" (25) the poet freshens the familiar phrases by substituting metonymies for the expected "day" and "night." In "Adam and maiden" (30) Thomas substitutes for "Eve" a noun that represents her in her innocence and at the same time sounds like "Eden," thus tripling its significance.

If you have to beg, borrow, or steal, get a recording of Thomas reading this poem and play it for your class. Thomas's voice is as "golden" as his poetry. Mary C. Davidow in the *English Journal* 58 (Jan. 1969): 78–81, and Sister M. Laurentia, in *Explicator* 14 (Oct. 1955): item 1, offer further interesting and useful observations about this poem.   LP

Chase Twichell   **Blurry Cow** (page 1012)

Reminiscent of William Carlos Williams's "The Red Wheelbarrow" (page 661), although with a slighter theme, this poem presents a snapshot of a scene which is revealed (in line 6) to be observed from the window of a passing train. Lines 1–5 seem no more than a picturesque view of cows "transfixed" and motionless as if posing to be photographed in "black and white" (an ambiguous phrase that may refer to monochromatic photography or the coloring of Holstein cattle or both), the only motion the stamping occasioned by an insect's sting. But after the line space the scene opens up and the true perspective is revealed.

Because the viewer is passing the scene rather than stopping to observe, the cow's hoof will be lifted "forever" and its haunches will remain as balanced as the pans of a scale—immobilized in a single glimpse. "The rest" of the action of the cattle "is lost," also "forever" (10, 7), for the scene shifts as the train moves. The cow's head is now not "transfixed" but "a sudden slur" as it passes from sight (1, 11). (The noun "slur" does not have its common meanings of an insulting remark or garbled speech but the rarer denotation of a smeared or blurred impression in printing—a visual rather than audible slur, as suits a poem involved with appearances.)

Once the cows are out of sight the attention goes to the farm with its "loping" dog almost keeping up with the train's motion and with another slurred sight, "a woman [who] *wavers* / in her *mirage* of laundry" (14–15). (Again, two precisely used visual terms: *wavering* when referring to light means flickering or flashing, and a *mirage* presents an illusory or unsubstantial sight.) As the train hurries away, the images become less and less precise.

The theme of the poem is a natural consequence of images rapidly passing away. In "the mind's eye" (17) the visual sights are blurred, and seem to have their own power to "stray" into the memory to form "the afterimage / of this day on earth" (17–19). Williams's poem combines ideas about seeing with questions about values, and leaves the reader knowing that a great deal "depends upon" how one looks at and interprets the visual details. Twichell's poem concentrates on how the eyes work as they register the appearances of things, and how the memory, apparently beyond conscious control, selects out and holds one such appearance as representing the whole experience.   TRA

John Updike   **Telephone Poles** (page 1013)

Updike uses a commonplace fact of the twentieth-century landscape to launch a meditation on changing contemporary attitudes toward nature and religious faith.

In a tone of quiet, understated irony, the first stanza places the telephone poles in the context of ancient mythology and initiates an extended comparison of the utilitarian but unsightly poles to once-living trees. Modern human beings see the poles "like the eyes of a savage sieving the trees / In his search for game" and they are such an accustomed sight that they "blend" into the landscape, fading "into mere mythology." In an ingenious conflation of mythology and technology, Updike imagines that these bearers of electrical currents are "Each a Gorgon's head, which, seized right, / Could stun us to stone."

One critic argues that the poem "celebrates the ingenuity of man's ability to fulfill his needs by placing his mark on the natural world" (Donald J.

Greiner, *The Other John Updike: Poems/Short Stories/Prose/Play* [Athens: Ohio UP, 1981] 21). But Updike's use of first-person plural suggests that the speaker(s) in this poem represent a generalized contemporary viewpoint, and the key phrase in the first stanza refers to the human observers as "washed clean of belief." A Christian writer, Updike instead is employing dramatic irony to satirize contemporary humankind's complacency and approval as nature gives way to technology and as a rich mythological and religious tradition yields to a sterile, self-congratulatory rejection of human spirituality.

In the second stanza, the trumpeting of modern achievement ("Yet they are ours. We made them.") is undercut by the description of the poles as dead trees "roughened" by linemen's cleats and tortured by "spikes" that have "been driven sideways at intervals handy for human legs." While the speakers' attention is on the manifestations of human cleverness, the reader's attention is drawn to the blithe destruction—the imagery suggests a crucifixion—of natural beauty. While acknowledging that the poles/dead trees provide "thin shade," the speakers insist on the advantage of defeating natural processes: "there is not that tragic autumnal / Casting-off of leaves to outface annually. / These giants are more constant than evergreens / By never being green."

Updike's subtle use of dramatic irony predicts that technology ultimately will erode the human connectedness to nature that gave rise to mythology (by implication, to literature itself) and to religious faith. He posits a world in which we have replaced natural beauty with "electrical debris," our formerly responsive and percipient human sensibilities coarsened beyond redemption.   GJ

Mona Van Duyn   What the Motorcycle Said (page 1013)

With its playful use of personification and sound effects, "What the Motorcycle Said" recalls the counterculture hipster era of the 1960s.

The motorcycle's voice conveys unbridled, youthful ego: the repeated syllable "Am" (1, 13, 28) that forms part of its revving noises articulates the motorcycle's unabashed pride in its own existence, especially in its loudness and physical power.

The first few stanzas clarify the rebellious stance the motorcyle represents: it hates riders who wear protective helmets, it proudly zooms past "phonies in Fords" (7), it claims the ability to bypass history itself. In the middle stanzas, it reinforces its hatred of middle-class bourgeois values ("hate middle-class moneymakers" [17]) and glorifies living in the present moment: "It's Nowsville, man" (19).

The penultimate stanza contains a witty reference to Walt Whitman's *Leaves of Grass*, with a pun on "grass" as marijuana (in the preceding stanza, the motorcycle had confessed to being "stoned" [24]): "Passed a cow, too fast to hear her moo, "I rolled / our leaves of grass into one ball. / I am the grassy

All" (25–27). Included here is also an allusion to Marvell's "To His Coy Mistress," specifically to these lines: "Let us roll all our strength and all / Our sweetness up into one ball" (page 730). In addition, Van Duyn's lines slyly poke fun at the counterculture's pretensions of oneness with nature; another of the noises the motorcycle makes, "OM" (1, 28), serves the same purpose, recalling the Buddhist mantra that became part of popular culture in the 1960s.

Students will respond to the brash, comical braggadocio of the motorcycle's "sayings," whose intellectual thinness is suggested by the poem's last line: "the world's my smilebutton" (30). The poem has effectively communicated both the exuberance and shallowness of extreme youth by personifying the motorcycle as a self-glorifying hipster.   GJ

Derek Walcott   The Virgins (page 1014)

For a brief discussion of "The Virgins" and several similar Walcott poems, see James Wieland, "Adam's Task: Myth and Fictions in the Poetry of Derek Walcott," in *The Ensphering Mind* (New York: Three Continents, 1988) 165-88. Book-length studies of Walcott's poetry include Stewart Brown, ed., *The Art of Derek Walcott* (Mid Glamorgan, Wales: Seren, 1991) and Rei Terada, *Derek Walcott's Poetry: American Mimicry* (Boston: Northeastern UP, 1998).   GJ

Walt Whitman   When I Heard the Learn'd Astronomer
(page 1015)

This poem expresses a conflict that may seem even more cogent today than when Whitman wrote it: precise scientific knowledge is an assault on the cherished mysteries of the universe. Feelings similar to Whitman's were voiced in the wake of man's first steps on the surface of the moon on July 20, 1969; as the cameras of rocket probes send back close-up photographs of the more distant planets in our solar system, the skies may seem to lose their appealing wonder.

Whitman's ironic contrasts are readily perceived because of their directness and abundance, and though it may be a violation of his attitude toward "charts" and "columns," they may be indicated as paired lists:

crowd in lecture room	individual man
much applause	silence
mathematical counting	"unaccountable" feeling
lighted room	dark night
indoors	outdoors
approving audience	tired and sick poet
sitting	rising and gliding, wandering
scientific precision	random looking, "from time to time"
scientific thought	poetic feeling

These ironic contrasts make the speaker's decision seem more natural, more attractive, more human. The initial repetition of "When" in the first four lines has a hypnotic sameness, imitating the poet's boredom with the regularity of scientific proofs; and the redundancy of "proofs," "figures," "columns," "charts," "diagrams" and "add, divide, . . . measure" reinforces the sense of repetitiousness and—for the speaker—the meaninglessness of such data about the universe. The phrase "perfect silence" in the last line ironically comments on the supposed perfection of scientific knowledge: genuine perfection is not mathematical or measurable, but is the harmonious response of perfect feeling to perfect stars.

The poem presents Whitman's distaste for precise, rational knowledge and his love of emotional, instinctive wonder at the mysteries of nature. His choice of the word "mystical" rather than *mysterious* extends his preference into a claim that his experience surpasses the astronomer's knowledge in a religious sense as well. His insight into the wonders of heaven seems to him to penetrate the merely mysterious and to reach to supernatural wisdom.   TRA

William Carlos Williams   Danse Russe (page 1015)

In 1916 Williams (like so many Americans) was deeply impressed by Diaghilev's famous Ballet Russe in its New York appearance. His poetic response to the power of the performance seems ironic, yet for all its "grotesque[ness]" (8) the scene in the poem has a power of its own.

The scene is at first glance merely ludicrous: on a summer afternoon when the family is napping, a man takes the opportunity of being alone to dance nakedly in front of his mirror, quietly singing a celebration of his loneliness and proclaiming himself "the happy genius of [his] household" (19). What makes this more than a self-deprecating effusion is the complexity suggested by the title which connotes grace, exuberance, and above all a professional artistry that took the world by storm. Against the high expectations created by the title, Williams presents first a lazy domestic situation, with wife, baby, and (presumably) housemaid all napping. The natural world outside the house is by contrast extreme in its glorious brightness, reminiscent more of a staged scene than of nature itself. The speaker "in [his] north room" with the brightness of a summer sun partially dimmed by "the yellow drawn shades" (7, 17) performs his dance, a solo number not marked by grace or artistry but by "grotesquely" exaggerated motions like "waving [his] shirt round [his] head" (8, 10).

Imagine the Ballet Russe introducing a Stravinsky ballet with its brilliant movements and garish colors dancing to sold-out houses—The Firebird, for example—as the backdrop for summer's indolence, blindingly bright sunlight, and a not-very-athletic naked man alone in his room waving his shirt about! What do those "shoulders, flanks, buttocks" (16) have to do with balletic perfection? How does the celebration of loneliness reflect the éclat of the great ballet company? Is there any comparison between the speaker's relation to his "household" and creativity of the eccentric genius Diaghilev directing his renowned company?

The answers are in William's deep faith in American individuality and vital potency. The speaker is all the "genius" his family needs, in two important senses of the word: he has the necessary intellectual and artistic power to direct his own world, and he is the presiding spirit over it, its defining characteristic. A man who can face the fact that he was "born to be lonely" (13) and turn it into a lyric and energetic expression is a kind of genius. In an improved version of the cliché "a man's home is his castle," Williams shows us that a man's household is his fulfillment and his creation.

And do not miss the way Williams hedges his assertion: the whole experience is couched as a hypothesis. "If . . . if . . . If," then "Who shall say" otherwise? Who indeed, since the whole episode, if it takes place at all, takes place behind "the yellow drawn shades," a dance to a mirror rather than an audience.   TRA

William Carlos Williams   **Poem** (page 1016)

This famous gem is not as rich in theme as "The Red Wheelbarrow" (page 661), but it is a fine example of the poet's control of form and structure in a minimal space. The event reported is simple, domestic, familiar: a cat in its curious prowl around the house, apparently going nowhere in particular, is observed in its graceful and delicate movement. But with situational irony, the animal for all its care and precision winds up with its two right feet in an "empty / flowerpot," leaving the observer with an amused smile: cats will go *anywhere*, no matter how inexplicable or incongruous the result. The irony is an anticlimactic revelation of a cat-truth and a false human expectation, contrasting the personifying assumptions behind the word "carefully" and the humor of the final picture.

The structure and form of the poem seem to imitate those careful steps, one precise and measured stanza for each movement (but we must be careful not to be too literal about this: four stanzas, four paws, but moving paws are the focus of only the two middle stanzas). The normal line length is three syllables, with variations, and the slight pauses required for line ends provide just the right hesitation, particularly in the lines ending in prepositions (2, 3, and especially 10). In the book cited below, Henry M. Sayre calls our attention to the "careful manipulation of certain consonants . . . c, f, t, and p." Every line but the eighth contains one or more of these sounds, and as Sayre says they occur in the stressed words in a line: "cat," "climbed," "top," "jamcloset," and so forth. It is in the climactic last stanza that these sounds flourish (except for the c as in "cat," a sound that disappears after "carefully"): "pit, "empty," and especially the piling on of these aspirated consonants in "flowerpot."

Is it too fanciful to point out that "pfft" is a sound made by angry cats in comic strips? or that "pfft" came into the American language in the first half of the twentieth century as a slang term to indicate an abrupt ending? Perhaps.

This poem receives a slightly different reading in Sayre's *The Visual Text of William Carlos Williams* (Urbana, IL: U of Illinois P, 1983) 79.   TRA

William Carlos Williams   Spring and All (page 1017)

The title might lead the reader to expect joy and exuberance, something to pair with cummings's "in Just—" (page 782). In Williams's poem, spring is barely newborn and isn't mentioned until line 15 when its *approach* is announced. In fact, the poem focuses on what we could call the phenomena of springtime only in lines 20–24. For the most part, spring is still down the road (to use a metaphor from the poem), and most details point to winter death rather than spring birth.

The opening paragraph consists of two imagistic sentence fragments providing locale and feeling. The first consists of two prepositional phrases ("By the road . . ." and "under the surge . . .") followed by a noun phrase: "a cold wind." The second sentence fragment looks as if it will be another prepositional phrase, but "[b]eyond" is being used as an adverb that locates the following pair of noun phrases. Structurally, then, the opening of the poem may seem as frustratingly distant from declarative statements as the poem is distant from its title.

For three paragraphs, the poem creates images of death and decay, the "leafless" and "[l]ifeless" (13–14) aftermath of winter's destruction. The morbidity is increased by the particular road the speaker is traveling, the "road to the contagious hospital" where presumably those with deadly diseases are isolated to keep the community safe. The visual images are vivid and forbidding, and primarily display horizontal flatness with some bare remnants of vertical growth, "standing and fallen" (6) in the phrase of the poem. There is almost no physical movement, only "the surge of the . . . / clouds driven [by] a cold wind" (2, 3–4)—but it is up in the sky; here in this "waste" the only motion seems to be that of the observer's eyes as they move from still object to still object (in lines 1–13, all noun phrases that stress immobility).

The central two-line paragraph promises movement to come, but line 14 seems at first only to be continuing the imagery of the preceding lines until we notice that "dazed spring," not the landscape, is "[l]ifeless in appearance, sluggish." Thus the mood is maintained, and spring is no more vital at this point than the winter it supplants.

Lines 16–19 call to mind not the "contagious hospital" but its opposite, the maternity hospital. The imagery is still not heartening, though, as it turns from visual to tactile and emphasizes the chill of entering "the new world naked, / cold, uncertain" (16–17). As King Lear says to Gloucester, "Thou know'st the first time that we smell the air / We wawl and cry" (4.6.179–80).

There is again some grammatical frustration as the pronouns "they" and "them" (16, 18) have no antecedents but refer to the "objects" named in the next paragraph.

That is where, at last, some semblance of spring is presented, but in contrast to what has preceded, there is very little imagery, only "the stiff curl of wildcarrot leaf" (21). For the rest, the statements are abstract, one way of reminding us that these things have not yet actually made their appearance. They *will* come, "But now [there is only] the stark dignity of / entrance" (24–25) and the assurance that beneath this "waste of broad, muddy fields" (5), in the roots of the vegetation, there is a "profound change" (25). To replace this horizontal world, there will be a thrusting upward of leaf.

Two readings that explore contrasting symbolic meanings of this poem are Hugh Kenner, *A Homemade World* (New York: Knopf, 1975) 62–63, and James Paul Gee, "Structure of Perception in Williams' Poetry," *Poetics Today* 6 (1985): 375–97.   TRA

Ralph Tejeda Wilson   **Henzey's Pond** (page 1017)

As suggested by its subtitle, "Henzey's Pond" is a memory piece, inspired partly by Brueghel's famous painting *Hunters in the Snow*.

The memory conveyed here is the speaker's childhood hockey-playing in a Catholic parochial school. The poem opens with its central image, "the smooth stone disc of the pond" (3) on which the children are skating and "inscribing" (3) their fleeting texts, an idea taken up in the next few lines by references to the literal texts of the phonics worksheets and Baltimore catechisms the children carry in their bookbags.

Religious imagery pervades the poem, from the hockey sticks "like flattened bishop's crooks" (8) and the "nun-dark puck" (9); to the nuns' rosary beads and the children's mild oath *"Hail Mary!"* (12); to their uniform ties embossed with images of the Holy Ghost "like rude coronals" (18). By the end of the poem, the children's white shirts are "like billowing wings" (22), an angelic image suggesting their youthful innocence in a world already demarcated into strict categories of good and evil. Though they are playing hockey "at the edge / of blasphemy with hell's own bells" (13–14), they have not crossed over the edge, and the bell image is a witty reminder of the school bell that will ring to stop their activity.

In its closing lines, the poem comes full circle to describe again the frozen pond, this time as a "sheening / glass outbrightened" (23–24). The children are remembered as racing across this glass "without reflection" (24), punning on "reflection" to convey the mirror-like surface of the pond and their own childlike lack of mature reflection. Furthermore, "reflection" likewise has a religious connotation, suggesting the adult speaker's infusion of spiritual meaning into his memory of an ordinary childhood hour of sport and fun.   GJ

William Wordsworth   Composed upon Westminster Bridge, September 3, 1802 (page 1018)

The poet's sister Dorothy recorded the occasion of this sonnet in a journal entry:

> We left London on Saturday morning at half past five or six, the 31st of July. . . . We mounted the Dover coach at Charing Cross. It was a beautiful morning. The city, St. Paul's [Cathedral], with the river, and a multitude of little boats, made a most beautiful sight as we crossed Westminster Bridge. The houses were not overhung by their cloud of smoke, and they were spread out endlessly, yet the sun shone so brightly, with such a fierce light, that there was something like the purity of one of nature's own grand spectacles.

Wordsworth was traveling with his sister to Dover to catch the boat to Calais, to say farewell to his former mistress (he was to marry Mary Hutchinson on October 4) and to meet for the first time his ten-year-old illegitimate daughter. Obviously, the trip was fraught with emotional meaning, and perhaps the scene that Dorothy describes was colored for him by the purpose of his mission. Perhaps, too, when he affixed the incorrect date to this sonnet he was thinking of the paradoxical feelings of that trip, and wanted to place this vision of London nearer his wedding.

Whatever the psychological motives, the sonnet is unusual for Wordsworth because it is in praise of an urban scene. However, the terms of that praise are equivocal and even (some would say) paradoxical. What is beautiful about London is that it is unlike London: it is made beautiful by the sun, and all of its normal busy life is abnormally still. That is, he is praising it for an appearance it rarely has. Its more usual condition is revealed in the contrasts he develops. It is usually neither "fair" nor "touching"; it is usually not "silent, bare . . . bright and glittering"; its air is usually smoke-filled; it is not characterized by "a calm so deep"; and the river normally is choked with traffic and does not seem to glide freely through its channel.

The time of day recorded by Dorothy must have some effect on this brilliant impression, too: Westminster Bridge crosses the Thames on an east–west line, and to go from Charing Cross toward Dover they would have been heading directly into the rising sun when the low angle of light was aimed and reflected into their eyes—"such a fierce light," Dorothy calls it. Perhaps whatever was busy at that time of day was partially blocked from view by the brightness.

The height of praise in the poem comes at the opening of the sestet, lines 9–10:

> Never did sun more beautifully steep
> In his first splendor, valley, rock, or hill.

Here, Wordsworth grants the city parity with nature insofar as the sun's splendor is concerned. Note that this effect is credited to the sun, not to the city, and that this rare "beauty of the morning" (5) is compared to a garment spread over the city, another implication that what is underneath the garment may not be so beautiful. Still, if only for a moment sunlight has the power to transform, it must be acknowledged that the city can take on a beauty on a par with nature's.

The poem works with two contradictory attributes, the power that is implied by the words "majesty" and "mighty" (3, 14) and is suggested by the energy generated by smoky industry, and the calm immobility of the scene. "[T]ouching . . . majesty" (3) is perhaps an apt oxymoron capturing these contrasts, the noun connoting awe-inspiring power, the adjective connoting what is gentle, poignant, vulnerable. Some interpreters would carry this further into a contrast between life and death, suggesting that in its lifeless state the city has beauty, but when it springs to life it is the opposite. One will have to decide whether the last line has the literal force of "dead," or is a metaphorical extension of the simile "seem asleep" in the preceding line.   TRA

William Wordsworth   I wandered lonely as a cloud
(page 1019)

The subject is typically Romantic and Wordsworthian: the speaker in an idle moment, alone in nature and feeling detached from it and from the social world, comes upon a natural event that moves him so deeply that his future life is shaped by it, and the memory of it can spontaneously return to him, to renew the emotion of the original experience. But why *should* a scene of natural beauty have such an effect? Is there more to this than the portrayal of the emotional response of a sensitive person? Does he *do* anything or only passively receive a gift from nature?

First, the speaker's condition before the event: wandering alone, but also "lonely," an emotional state in which he regrets his isolation, and yet in his simile also glories in it—"lonely as a cloud / That floats on high" (1–2), superior to the valleys and hills on Earth. And the simile contains another figure as well, personification, so that the opening situation is an example of poetic perception: the self compared to a cloud, the cloud given two human attributes, loneliness *and* superiority. So the speaker sets out from a point of poetic creativity even while he feels himself to be idly uninvolved.

As soon as the daffodils are visible, the poetic imagination shifts into a higher gear. The first impression, "crowd," is immediately and spontaneously revised into a more reverberative "host," the daffodils are "golden" in more than color, the rhythm takes on a lilt as the tetrameter line is broken in half with "Beside the lake, beneath the trees" ("Beside" and "beneath" establishing a different spatial relationship from "high o'er"), and the daffodils are given costume and dance motions. What we might judge to be a serene and dispassionate emotional state in lines 1–2 suddenly leaps into creative energy that continues through line 14.

The major figure of the second stanza is overstatement, revealing the speaker's need to capture the intensity of his excitement—the flowers seemed infinite, heavenly, brilliant, "never-ending"; the speaker's sensitivity enabled him to see "Ten thousand . . . at a glance." They seemed all to be dancing in unison, and the waves seemed to mimic (but of course fell short of) them in dancing.

At line 15, the submerged self-consciousness that has been implied by the spate of poetic devices finally comes to the fore: the "poet" must examine both his response and the external stimulus to it. He discovers that despite his reluctance ("could not but be" implies that he has tried to avoid it—perhaps that's what he was consciously doing by wandering "lonely as a cloud"?), he feels cheerful being in the "jocund company" of the daffodils. Unlike the "sparkling waves," he does not try to dance with them, but only gazes and gazes, storing up the emotion of the moment without knowing or thinking that the "golden daffodils" brought him more wealth than the single experience.

The additional wealth is the ability to relive that experience, not only as a memory, but as an emotion, even—what he did not do when he actually saw them—to the extent of letting his heart figuratively dance "with the daffodils." But notice again the emotional straits that he is in when they come to him: alone, lying on his couch, "In vacant or in pensive mood," looking into himself with "bliss" that comes from solitude—then once again, unbidden and unexpected, the merry daffodils "flash upon that inward eye."

But what is really flashing is his own creative power—for, in fact, the daffodils cannot be jocund, cannot feel glee, do not dance. The lively, bright beauty of a surprising natural sight was the starting point for a poet's imaginative creativity; *that* is what can fill his heart with pleasure.   TRA

William Wordsworth   The Solitary Reaper (page 1019)

The poem relates the awakening of the speaker's imaginative response to an experience of wordless expression and the extended effect of the experience on him. Apparently on a walking tour in the Highlands of Scotland, the speaker sees and hears a girl gathering grain while she sings a native song. Moved by both her solitude and the sorrowful melody, the speaker tries to find correspondences between the unintelligible song and other human experiences, but finally acknowledges that whether he understands it or not, it has moved him deeply enough to live on in his memory.

In accordance with his theories about poetry as the "spontaneous overflow of powerful feelings," a power which he attributes to the singing girl, Wordsworth frequently strives to give his poems both immediacy and the sense of personal experience. In this case, however, his starting point was not at all personal; the poem is based on a passage from a friend's manuscript account of a Scottish tour. Thomas Wilkinson had written: "Passed by a female who was reaping alone, she sung in Erse as she bended over her sickle, the sweetest human voice I ever heard. Her strains were tenderly melancholy, and felt delicious long after they were heard no more." The poem reports this (with direct quotation and verbal echo) as if it had happened to the speaker, achieving immediacy in the first three stanzas by using the present tense.

The opening lines emphatically establish the solitariness of the girl and awaken parallel feelings in the speaker: "single" (1), "solitary" (2), "by herself" (3), "Alone" (5). He has, or imagines, companions whom he exhorts to "Behold" and "listen," demanding excited attention; yet this he balances against the injunction to remain quiet so as not to disturb the girl's song and to preserve her sense of being alone. What strikes him most in the opening stanza are her solitude and the "melancholy" nature of her song, which seems to overflow the deep valley in which she works (the Scottish Highlands are for the most part barren and sparsely inhabited, with arable land restricted to the valleys).

In the second and third stanzas, as he listens to the music in a foreign tongue, the speaker imaginatively searches for corresponding situations that will explain the emotions with which he responds. The second stanza offers two comparisons, both suggesting relief from the hardships of natural surroundings. The singer is like two very different kinds of birds in two contrasted geographical locales, implying the universality of the experience: the nightingale singing in an oasis in the parched Arabian desert, promising cool comfort to exhausted travelers; or the cuckoo signaling the coming of spring to the stark, rocky islands battered by the seas in the northern-most reaches of Scotland. Both scenes are isolated, forbidding, and lonely; both are momentarily relieved; and both imply that the speaker feels himself isolated, wandering in a wholly uncongenial natural setting, momentarily restored by the beauty of the song he hears.

The third stanza moves from geographical extremes to contrasts of time and social rank. The song might be a traditional lament expressing grief for ancient, heroic battlefield defeats or it might refer to the "natural sorrow, loss, or pain" of ordinary daily life in the present. Just as loneliness and weariness were universalized in stanza 2, stanza 3 universalizes melancholy here and everywhere, now and in the past.

The third stanza has asked for intelligible fact: what is she singing about? In the final stanza, the poem suddenly shifts into the past tense, in its first line denying the possibility (or even the necessity) of understanding exactly what the girl was saying. As it turns out, the speaker's inability to understand the meaning of the song has been an advantage. He has found in the melody and in the singer's isolation the occasion for his own imagined creation of the universal themes of loneliness and melancholy. Looking back on this experience, he has discovered that his imagination was revitalized, and that his profound feelings have persisted even after he has mounted up from the scene of her singing.

A full, suggestive reading of this poem is in Geoffrey H. Hartman's *Wordsworth's Poetry, 1787–1814* (New Haven: Yale UP, 1964) 3–18.   TRA

Judith Wright   Portrait (page 1020)

The poem consists of two iambic pentameter stanzas, each five lines in length, and each having four lines with end rhyme, either perfect or approximate. The two stanzas are balanced against each other by similarity and contrast. The stanzas are separated in time by the break between them.

The first stanza is dominated by present-tense verbs, the second by past-tense verbs. The first line in the first stanza and the last line in the second stanza both contain the word "game" and the phrase "when it began." These are the two non-rhyming lines in their two stanzas, but some critics would say that they rhyme with each other (inventing a category called *identical rhyme*). Certainly their singularity in their own stanzas and their resemblance to each other, plus the fact that they are the first and last lines in the poem, give them special emphasis in the formulation of theme.

Put together, the poem is the "Portrait" of an ordinary housewife at two stages in her life. In the first stanza, soon after her marriage, she performed her routine duties (cooking, cleaning, mending) cheerfully. Because she was motivated by love, she regarded these chores as permanencies and performed them without complaint. In the second stanza she performs them out of "old habit," cleaning the house that *looks* "like home" and dressing herself for the periodic visits of her grown children in a way that *looks* "like love." We may now notice that the rhymes in the first stanza are both perfect rhymes, while those in the second are both approximate rhymes. The latter are spelled so that they *look* like perfect rhymes, but in fact are pronounced differently.

The speaker blames no one for these losses; she merely reports sadly that too often what starts out with the eager enthusiasm of a child's game ends up as sterile ritual in which the real warmth of marriage and family life is absent.   LP

William Butler Yeats   Sailing to Byzantium (page 1021)

In his book *A Vision*, Yeats wrote that if he could be given a month of antiquity and leave to spend it where he chose, he would spend it in Byzantium about the year A.D. 525. Byzantium (later known as Constantinople and presently as Istanbul), the eastern capital of the Holy Roman Empire, was in that period notable for the flowering of its art: painting, architecture, mosaic work, gold and silver metalcraft, book illumination, and so on. For this reason, it represented for Yeats a holy city of the imagination.

The title "Sailing to Byzantium" would seem to indicate that the poem is about a voyage; but line 1 ("*That* [not *This*] is no country for old men") together with lines 15–16 (". . . therefore I have sailed the seas and come / To

the holy city of Byzantium") indicate that the voyage has already been completed. It is an imaginary voyage, of course, for it has been made not just
across space, from Ireland to Byzantium, but backward through time, from
the twentieth century to the sixth. The important considerations, therefore,
are not the voyage itself, but why the poet made it; and not Ireland and
Byzantium, but what they represent.

The poem deals with the antitheses of the physical and sensual world
versus the world of intellect and imagination, the moral versus the eternal,
nature versus art. Modern Ireland represents the first term in these opposi-
tions, Byzantium the second. The poet, growing old (he was 63 when this
poem was published) can no longer engage fully and unreflectively in the life
of the senses, and longs for something beyond the life of the senses, for the
life of the senses is mortal and dies. He finds what he is looking for in works
of art ("Monuments of unaging intellect"), which are eternal. The poem may
be looked on as a kind of prayer: let me leave this country of the young, the
unreflective, the sensual, and the dying, and sail to the city of imagination
and unaging intellect. There let my next incarnation be as an artificial gold-
and-enamel singing bird that cannot decay as my body is decaying now but
that will exist eternally. Let me be a work of art rather than a man!

Yeats thus seems to be elevating art above nature, the eternal above the
mortal. But there is a catch here. What will this gold-enameled bird sing
about? It will sing of "what is past, or passing, or to come"—a line that echoes
line 6: "Whatever is begotten, born, and dies." Art celebrates the mortal
world—the world of process, change, decay, and death. The poem thus has a
circular movement in which the last line returns us to its beginning. The
poet presents us not with a preference but with a dilemma. He wishes to escape from life into art, but as a work of art he will celebrate life. Art is both
superior and inferior to life. Though not subject to decay, it is an "artifice,"
without life. The dilemma is comparable to that presented by Keats in "Ode
on a Grecian Urn" (page 918).   LP

William Butler Yeats   The Second Coming (page 1022)

In 1919, the year this poem was published, Ireland was in the midst of a
bloody civil war; World War I had only recently ended (November 1918);
and Russia was engaged in civil war following its Revolution of 1917. All
these events portended for Yeats the approaching end of the Christian era,
the historical cycle begun almost two thousand years earlier with the birth of
Christ. In Yeats's historical theory the transition from one historical era to
another was always marked by an epoch of violence and disorder.

The poem is divided into two sections. The first gives the poet's impression of the present. The second presents an apocalyptic vision of the future.

His description of the present is terrifying. The opening two lines present
a symbol of a world out of control. In the ancient art of falconry the falcon

was trained always to return to the wrist of the falconer upon a signal. But in Yeats's image the falcon has flown beyond the hearing of his master's signal. The adjective "Mere" (4) here retains its obsolete meaning of absolute, entire, sheer. "[C]eremony" (6) had for Yeats particular value as connected with orderly and civilized living (see "A Prayer for My Daughter," which followed immediately after "The Second Coming" in Yeats's *Collected Poems*). The closing lines of this section describe a familiar crisis situation where good people, by nature moderate and tolerant, are uncertain what should be done, whereas the bigots, the terrorists, and the assassination squads are full of "passionate intensity"—all too certain in their ignorant minds that they know exactly what is needed.

The opening lines of the second section seem to sound a note of hope. "Surely," the poet declares, "some revelation is at hand"—the word "revelation" suggesting a divine manifestation; "Surely the Second Coming is at hand"—the words "Second Coming" reminding us of the Second Coming of Christ prophesied in the Bible. Things can hardly get much worse; therefore these violent actions must be auspices of change, signs of the shifting from one historical era to another. No sooner has the poet uttered the words "Second Coming" than he has a vision. An image arises to consciousness (not just from his own unconscious but from the racial unconscious underlying it) of the stone sphinx in the Egyptian desert slowly coming to life and "moving its slow thighs." The vision is vivid. Yeats depicts not only its gaze, "blank and pitiless as the sun," but the reactions of the desert birds to this amazing phenomenon. In indignant clamor they "Reel" in circles above the slowly awakening sphinx; but Yeats with marvelous poetic economy depicts them only through their shadows (thus giving us in one picture the shadows, the birds that cast them, and the bright desert sun that causes them). The vision is brief, but now Yeats knows (or claims to know) that "twenty centuries of stony sleep [the sphinx's] / Were vexed to nightmare by a rocking cradle" (19–20) (a metonymy for the infant Christ), and he also knows what "rough beast, its hour come round at last, / Slouches towards Bethlehem to be born." The vision is a vision of horror. The new era, its time come to replace the old one, is symbolized by a "rough beast." (The question asked in the last two lines is rhetorical, as shown by the ambiguous syntax of the sentence, in which "And" indicates the presence of parallelism but in which "what" can logically be linked only with "That" in line 19 ["I know that . . . and what . . ."], making "what" not an interrogative but a relative pronoun calling logically for a period at the end of the sentence. But when was logic ever the most direct way to poetic power?)

Our expectation, set up by the title and by lines 9–10, that the poem would concern the Second Coming of Christ, is shattered by the last two lines of the poem. It is the coming of Antichrist that is prophesied. Legends tell us that Antichrist will be born in Bethlehem, and Antichrist is referred to recurrently in the New Testament as the "beast." It is Yeats, however, whose genius has assimilated Antichrist with the desert sphinx and given him new dimensions of horror and evil by his use of the adjective "rough" and the verb "slouches."

Surely, this poem derives its greatness from the feeling of evil and horror it so powerfully evokes. Yet the most controversial critical question regarding the poem occurs just here. Scholars familiar with Yeats's historical theories (expressed most fully in his book *A Vision*) have pointed out that the era Yeats expected to follow the Christian one was more amenable to him than the Christian era, and that therefore the advent of the "rough beast" is to be welcomed.   LP

William Butler Yeats   The Wild Swans at Coole (page 1023)

Both his theory and his practice point to the need to read an individual poem by Yeats in the context of the rest of his poetry and of his life. A full understanding of this poem requires at least a reading of Donald A. Stauffer's analysis in *The Golden Nightingale* (New York: Macmillan, 1949) 48–79. But even without the richness of the Yeatsian context, the poem has beauty and power that are available to the sensitive reader.

Both actually and superficially it is a meditation on nature and on the passage of time, which alters the human observer but leaves nature essentially unchanged; it thus resembles Wordsworth's "Tintern Abbey" and Keats's "Ode to a Nightingale" (page 977), poems in which the response of the man is both intensely present and also intensely subjective and retrospective. External natural facts elicit feelings and memories and desires, and time present is contrasted with time past, human and natural. Nature undergoes cyclical changes and keeps returning to its same condition; the human being undergoes progressive changes that include decay and death, but also memories of earlier states. Nature is permanent and always in the present, man is transient but contains his own past, his sensitive present, and his predictions of the future.

The elegiac tone of this poem is established in the first stanza—autumn, dryness, twilight, stillness. But paradoxically the poem also contains terms that contrast with these: beauty, mirror-like clarity, brimming water, clamorous wings. Yeats maintains the tone, and also the contrasts, throughout the poem, summing up his inability to understand the swans in the simple declaration that they are "Mysterious, beautiful" (26). Although he attributes much to them, they cannot be wholly captured in his language or his imagination, justifying the recurring Yeatsian strategy of the conclusion—a rhetorical question. For other examples, see "Leda and the Swan" (page 788) and "The Second Coming" (page 1022). The questions in these poems are not really questions, for the poem has implied the answer, as it does here. The speaker does not really wonder where the swans will be (in fact, they will most probably be where they are now, in the streams and lake of Coole Park, and if not these particular swans then their indistinguishable offspring). Nor does the question really mean "what other men will be delighted by them," for any man who sees them will be delighted. Nor does it mean "where will *I* be when 'I awake some day / To find they have flown away'" (29–30), for the answer to that is implicit too: since the swans represent to him the continuity and permanence of the natural world, any awakening that discovers them gone will be an awakening out of nature into death.

The number "nine-and-fifty" (6), phrased archaically and with an implied hint of magic, first introduces the mystery of the swans: although they seem paired "lover by lover" (19), the number is odd. The mystery of this number is augmented by the other one, nineteen; both are prime numbers, both end in nine, and both sound so very precise that a reader inevitably asks their significance. Is there a meaningful link between 59 and 19? The speaker has carefully kept track of the number of years he has been returning to this spot, and has carefully counted the swans, year after year—and yet, as he reports, even on that first count he had not finished counting before they took flight. How can he know their precise number? As they suddenly mounted into the air, perhaps disturbed by his presence, perhaps even reluctant to be numbered, they scattered (suggesting random motion) yet wheeled; they flew in rings but the rings were "broken" (11). What this succession of images suggests is a precise but uncountable number, a patterned movement that remained incompleted: a contrast between the human desire to discover number and geometric shape, and nature's reluctance to be comprehended in such intellectual undertakings.

From this perspective, we can see that the qualities attributed to the swans in the remainder of the poem are human interpretations: their wings beat like bells (tolling the passage of time, to the observer?), they are lovers, the water is "Companionable," they are "Unwearied" (21, 19), their hearts do not grow old, and—a clear indication that the qualities are not inherent in the swans—"Passion or conquest" *attend* them (23–24). They are therefore genuinely mysterious, for the poem has not penetrated their mysteries, but seen in them parallels and contrasts to the human condition, revealing the impossibility of understanding them for what they are.

The natural world, then, is impenetrable to the human observer. What remains in the poem is the situation in which this places him—seeing the swans in their continuity, recognizing in himself the changes that time brings, confessing the pain that these changes have caused, and projecting further loss in the future. As the final question indicates, there will be other men to fill his place (as in fact there have been other swans to replenish the flock), but there is no consolation for the man in that fact, nor does his verbal tactic of thinking of his future as an awakening lessen the sense of loss.   TRA

Drama

The Elements
of Drama

Chapter One

The Nature of Drama

Susan Glaspell   **Trifles** (page 1033)

See the commentary on "A Jury of Her Peers" on page 45 of this manual.

The main difference between the texts of the play and the short story is that the story more explicitly defines the emotions of the characters—and in particular, of Mrs. Hale (given the name "Martha" in the story but not in the play). Mrs. Hale is the point-of-view character in a limited third-person story. Her feelings and her motives are explored, and she is more clearly presented as a person with internal conflicts having to do with her sense of guilt for the lonely life of Minnie Wright and complicity in the crime she committed. She is initially mistrustful of Mrs. Peters, a woman who has not known Minnie and who by definition is "married to the law." She must therefore be more hesitant in working up her defense of the woman who committed the murder.

In the play, the women approach their task more as "peers" than as characters with a personal conflict. This is shown most clearly in one passage in which Glaspell reverses the roles of these women. The story (page 389) assigns to Mrs. Peters a discovery that Mrs. Hale makes in the play (page 1039). In the story, Mrs. Peters finds the clumsily sewn quilt piece (an indication of Mrs. Wright's "nervous" lack of concentration on her sewing, and thus evidence of a state of mind that could be linked to the murder of her husband). In both play and story, Mrs. Hale begins to pull out the bad sewing, to Mrs. Peters's consternation. Again, reversing their roles, in the story it is Mrs. Peters who wonders what made Mrs. Wright nervous, and Mrs. Hale who defends her: "I don't know as she was nervous. I sometimes sew awful queer when I'm just tired." In rewriting the play as a story, Glaspell decided to make the case that Mrs. Peters discovers this evidence, and that Mrs. Hale not only destroys it by pulling out the bad stitches (as she had done in the play) but also denies that the sewing is a sign of distress. Mrs. Peters in the story is at this point like her husband—investigating and analyzing clues—while Mrs. Hale is attempting to cover up for her old girlhood friend. In the play, they were mutually engaged in detection and defense.

Mrs. Peters also does not display "timid acquiescence" in her "thin voice," does not have a "frightened look" and "a voice that seem[s] to shrink away from the subject," "a flurried voice" when she first confronts her husband after the discovery of the dead canary. These are all qualities in her that are added or emphasized in the story and that change its focus from that of the play. In "Trifles," Mrs. Peters and Mrs. Hale mutually arrive at the same position, helping each other determine that although Minnie Wright is legally guilty of murder, she is not to be convicted on the evidence they have found. In "A Jury of Her Peers" Mrs. Hale is the indubitable protagonist, helping and directing Mrs. Peters to share that position.

In the play, the two women are joint protagonists, one more experienced than the other, but no more contrasted than they are in the initial stage direction: Mrs. Peters "is a slight wiry woman, with a thin nervous face. Mrs. Hale is larger and would ordinarily be called more comfortable looking, but she is disturbed now and looks fearfully about as she enters." They are different, but neither of them dominates their growing relationship. As if to emphasize this, Glaspell concludes that stage direction: "The women have come in slowly, and stand close together near the door." They are "close together," not far apart.

This aspect of the play more clearly focuses one of the themes that both works share, the conflict between the men and the women. There are differences of personality but not of philosophy or purpose between the women in the play. They are aligned against the men in two ways, one trifling, the other immediately consequential. They are concerned with what Sheriff Peters laughs at, "the insignificance of kitchen things" (story), the manifold cares of women in a rural life, particularly the sewing, the cleaning, the cooking, the constant labor that to their husbands seems not labor but play. This the women wryly allow the men to condescend to them about, knowing better but not challenging the patronizing jokes. These are the "trifles" of the play and the story. The title of the story points to the other, more significant alignment of the women against the men: they will undercut the attempt to bring the law of the male-dominated society to bear upon Minnie Wright. They will judge her—and on the evidence they have, they find her guilty of justifiable homicide, and they pardon her. Thus with a diminished area of conflict between the two women, the play more directly focuses on the conflict between the sexes and its two expressions, minor and major in nature. The women will allow the men to patronize them; that is the price they pay for their sympathetic forgiveness of Minnie Wright's crime.

There are other differences between play and story that exploit the strengths of both genres. In the story, the author freely interprets Mrs. Hale's feelings and ideas, and allows her to interpret those of the other characters. This too strengthens the position of this character as protagonist, for she emerges as the most sensitive, and the one most open to self-examination and the resolution of inner conflicts. As the point-of-view character in the story she is also the most perceptive, so that we easily trust her interpretations—Mr. Hale is not vicious in belittling the women but speaks "with good-natured superiority" (page 395), the county attorney is "disdainful" when he pushes at the dirty pans under the sink (page 396), she notices the "flurried voice" of Mrs. Peters when the attorney is "too preoccupied to notice" it (page 404), and so forth. Mrs. Hale's perspective controls our reading and directs our sympathies.

In the play, without such interpretive remarks, the characters are more immediate and direct in presenting themselves. They are not filtered through Mrs. Hale's consciousness, but stand alone, unique and believable human beings. The playwright offers stage direction to assist the actors in their interpretations (and the written text thus allows readers some insight by that means), but much of the effect of the play will depend on the abilities of the acting ensemble to feel their way into these characters, to sense the conflicts and congruences of them as integral individuals working together to create the totality of dramatic effect. There is a great burden upon the actors, and an even greater one on the reader who does not see a staged presentation, to interpret and intuit the reality of these people. But if we are competent in doing so, we are more immediately in touch with them, and if the play is staged effectively, we will be able to achieve that sense of reality without the moderating imposition of an author's definitions and descriptions.   TRA

Joyce Carol Oates   The Interview (page 1045)

The confusion of an old man longing for death or companionship, the confusion of a young man engrossed in his own ego, and the confusion of a young woman struggling to escape her own ignorance and inexperience— these are the materials for a pathetic confrontation. But the playwright so broadens their characterization and actions that the play ironically undercuts the potential pathos, and the result is semi-realistic farce.

The interviewer is a smug, early-success man whose smattering of information, gleaned from a public relations sheet, leads him to presume upon the solitude and confusion of a very old man. Having as his assignment to capture the thoughts of a presumed member of the French Academy, a distinguished writer, about the imminent millennial shift, he barges into the room of the wrong man, identifies him as the "immortal" he has been sent to interview, and proceeds to badger the old man until his younger assistant tells him he's in the wrong hotel. His interview consists of having the old man autograph the books of the writer he supposes him to be, pressing him with questions about his sexual history, knocking out and then breaking his hearing aid, using a flash camera that stuns him, and finally denouncing him when the confused old man identifies him as "Death." When his assistant arrives to send him to the hotel of the actual man he was to interview, he dashes away.

The interviewer's ineptitude and brash egotism make him a comic antagonist to the old man. But the "immortal" is no less ironically presented. He is senile but pompous, whimpering but silly. His inability to respond except to imagine his dead wife and repeat his Nobel acceptance speech places him so fully in the past that any suggestion he might have about what the twenty-first century might bring would be useless—and he has no suggestion.

And Kimberly, the assistant, is obviously working to get on the same fame train as her boss, though her malapropisms and ignorance make success unlikely. The only quality she seems to share with the interviewer is her insensitivity to the real needs of her subject, though she does try to offer him kind concern (in exchange for room-service lunch).

As the footnotes suggest, the play is full of misinformation, not only Kimberly's thinking that "Nabokov" is "Nureyev" but the anachronisms linking this "immortal" to Colette, Franz Liszt, Pirandello, and Nabokov. This welter of false information is part of the farcical representation of the play, as important as the physical slapstick in undercutting the seriousness. Perhaps the central irony is directed at the concept of a writer being proclaimed "immortal" during his lifetime—and possessing nothing of the power, authority, or wisdom that the label implies.   TRA

Edward Albee   The Sandbox (page 1056)

In an introduction to his play "The American Dream," Edward Albee writes, "The play is an examination of the American Scene, an attack on the substitution of artificial for real values in our society, a condemnation of complacency, cruelty, emasculation and vacuity; it is a stand against the fiction that everything in this slipping land of ours if peachy-keen." Elsewhere he tells us that in writing "The Sandbox" he extracted several characters from "The American Dream," which he was working on at the time, and "placed them in a situation different than, but related to, their predicament in the longer play." We may assume, therefore, that his dramatic purposes in "The Sandbox" are similar to, though not identical with, his purposes in "The American Dream."

The play belongs, of course, to the "Theater of the Absurd," a modern dramatic genre in which the logical absurdity and meaninglessness of the events presented on the stage reflect an absurdity and meaninglessness which the playwright sees in life. But the meaninglessness of the events presented does not mean that the play is meaningless. "The Sandbox," indeed, is a brief summation of a life and a death; a dramatic synecdoche. What it shows is a life emptied of content and value. Life, as presented here, is vapid, barren, and sterile, and death is without dignity.

The play works largely by means of symbols, many of them multiple symbols. The sandbox itself, for instance represents (a) a beach; (b) Grandma's second childhood (she plays in it with a toy pail and shovel); (c) the grave (she buries herself in it); and (d) the barrenness of modern civilization, which T. S. Eliot presented as a desert in "The Waste Land." The bareness of the stage reinforces the symbolism of emptiness and sterility. The toy shovel, like the sandbox, is a childhood symbol, but simultaneously a gravedigger's spade.

The Young Man, too, is a multiple symbol. Young, athletic, and a movie actor, he embodies those three popular idols of American life: youth, sports, and Hollywood. More comprehensively, he represents illusion. Handsome and friendly on the outside, he is empty on the inside. Though he greets everyone with a "Hi!" and a smile, he doesn't know what his name is, he forgets his lines, and his smile is vacuous. As a movie actor, his trade is illusion. The worship of such illusions is equivalent to spiritual death; and the Young Man is also the Angel of Death. But the death he brings is as empty and meaningless as the life he represents.

Mommy and Daddy have a marital relationship all too common in modern life, though exaggerated in the play. They call each other by pet names, but there is no affection between them. Mommy is the emasculating female: dominant, scornful, mocking, reproving, impatient, sarcastic. She gives the orders. Daddy, though he has fulfilled his social function by getting rich, is humanly a cipher, completely subjugated by Mommy. Toward Grandma they observe all the proprieties: they give her a place in their house, they give her a "decent" burial with music and the appearance of mourning. In life, however, they really buried her alive, and on stage they literally do so. Beneath conventional expressions of grief ("the time has come for poor Grandma . . . and I can't bear it!"), Mommy is eager to get Grandma out of the way and be done with her.

Grandma is the most authentic character in the play: she says what she thinks, doesn't wrap her feelings in pious ceremonial. She is also the most perceptive character: she knows what's going on, sees through the Young Man's imbecility, is capable of using metaphor. But Grandma has been soured by her life, rendered disagreeable, cranky, difficult, and even sub-human ("Graaa!").

The life that Albee has depicted in "The Sandbox" is absurd and meaningless, and so, he implies, is much of modern American life.   LP

David Ives   Time Flies (page 1063)

This brief play is full of jokes, puns, and wisecracks. Its chief source of humor is the presentation of two insects as a pair of human beings meeting (and mating) for the first time. The inventiveness of the play in providing them with food, drink, furniture, and the other accoutrements of a human dating situation is hilarious. Gnats are offered (in a variety of preparations) as hors d'oeuvres, the drinks range from stagnant water to insect-related mixed drinks, grasshoppers and stingers, the lights at May's apartment are fireflies, her record collection consists of groups named for insects or other animals, and when they consult the TV Guide all the shows contain insect references.

The thematic center of the plot is presented in its title, and in the Latin phrase that is repeated, "carpe diem." For these mayflies, time really does fly past, and if they are to have any meaning or pleasure in their lives, they will certainly need to seize the day—the only day of their lives. But this serious point is embroidered with puns and jokes. For example, Horace has mistaken May's name for "April," and when she corrects him he comments "Later than I thought, huh?" When May mistakenly calls him "Vergil" and he corrects her, we see the relevance of two Latin poets' names to the "carpe diem" theme.

These hijinks surround a simple story: meeting, mating, and dying, as the television presenter David Attenborough says, and the emotions presented in the lives of the mayflies are predictable in that sequence—some shyness at first, some awkwardness as they grow more familiar, the climax of sexual mating, and then the anger, resentment, and finally acceptance as they face their early death.

The antagonist is the television voice of David Attenborough describing the brief and apparently meaningless lives of mayflies, providing them with information about themselves that they had not imagined. In addition there are the threatening voice of the frog (a predator for insects, but also the source of some joking about the French) and the song of the cuckoo that reminds them that their time is quickly passing. But it is time and mortality that really threaten.

The play combines nonrealistic fantasy with realism. The fantasy arises from the treatment of insects as humans, the realism from the literal presentation of a television personality and the "facts" that he introduces. The theme, that life is brief and therefore must be lived to its fullest, is made both more intense and more funny by being embodied in the mayflies. It is also the theme of the British film *Brief Encounter* (1945) alluded to when loss is inevitable. The film told the story of a love between two people who meet only for an afternoon, and who face their separation with the same brave reticence as May and Horace who imitate the characters' British reserve.

TRA

Chapter Two

Realistic and Nonrealistic Drama

Henrik Ibsen   A Doll House (page 1079)

It may be difficult, both for the instructor and for students, to look at so famous and influential a play without being dazzled and misled by what it represented in its own time ("the door slam heard round the world") in the cause of women's rights and by what contemporary readers and producers do to keep it relevant to "women's issues." Perhaps the most important corrective that can be applied is Ibsen's own statement twenty years after the play opened, when he was saluted by the Norwegian Association for Women's Rights as "the creator of Nora":

> I have been more of a poet and less of a social philosopher than most people have been inclined to believe. . . . I can't claim the honor of ever having worked consciously for women's rights. I'm not even sure I know what they are. To me it has seemed a matter of human rights. (Quoted in Shafer, 61).

This disclaimer is important because it broadens the theme rather than denying that Nora's situation makes a statement on the position of women. Nora is certainly the protagonist, but as Ibsen implies, that does not mean that she alone carries the themes of the play. Study questions 3 and 9 may be used to open up this issue. The title: with the permission of the translator, I have used the title that scholars now generally agree is most appropriate, although it is not the one Professor Reinert used nor the traditional ones used for most English translations, A Doll's House and The Doll's House. A Doll House, referring to a child's miniature model of a home, complete with furnishings, is the literal meaning of Ibsen's words, and more accurately reflects the situation in which Nora, Torvald, their children and servants, and to some extent their visitors exist: a prettified imitation of a home and a marriage. Of the options offered in study question 3, A Doll's House seems to imply that Nora is alone the creator and possessor of the falseness of this home. While her noble, criminal act and the lies it necessitated have presumably made it possible for Torvald to survive and even thrive, not even Nora supposes that she is the possessor of the home (clearly, when she departs, she wants to take nothing of Torvald's with her).

As to who is responsible for the doll-house condition of their marriage, we must recognize that it is a mutual creation. After criticizing her financial irresponsibility, Torvald insists "I don't want you any different from just what you are—my own sweet little songbird" (page 1082); Nora is no less conscious of the pretenses required to maintain their play family when she tells Mrs. Linde that she might tell Torvald of her life-saving act "when I'm no longer young and pretty . . . I mean when Torvald no longer feels about me the way he does now, when he no longer thinks it's fun when I dance for him and put on costumes and recite for him" (page 1089). They are both aware that their marriage is founded on childish role-playing, but at the opening of the play neither wants to change that—and it seems, with Torvald's business success, they will never need to do so. But there are stirrings in Nora as she tells Mrs. Linde that someday she would like to tell Torvald of her sacrifice for him, and as she tells her and Dr. Rank that like a mischievous child she wants Torvald to hear her say a naughty word. These stirrings toward growing out of her child's world provide the impetus for the plot.

That plot gets under way as a consequence of one of the many ironies that fill the play: Torvald's promotion, which promises the happiness that money is presumed by the Helmers to buy, motivates both Krogstad and Mrs. Linde to become involved in the life of this house, and these two influential outsiders precipitate Nora's self-examination and her final decision. Both of them enter the action with good intentions and with financial difficulties, paralleling Nora's situation of years before: Krogstad needs to improve his position in the bank and rehabilitate his name for the sake of his growing children, and Mrs. Linde needs a job and a sense of being useful to others. Krogstad's villainy develops as he is thwarted and then scorned, while Mrs. Linde's desire to help leads her to push Nora toward the full revelation of the past so that her marriage can be re-established on firm ground. Both characters contribute to the fall of the house, and then, by marrying, resolve their own situations and remove themselves from the Helmers' lives.

Much of the action of the play involves Nora's efforts to maintain her secret, a secret that puts her in conflict with Mrs. Linde's principle of honesty and at the mercy of Krogstad's blackmail. She thus creates a dilemma for herself out of her two desires (to outgrow her child-bride role and show that she has been mature and responsible, and to maintain her presumed innocence and mask the crime). The role of Dr. Rank in this action is to shed light on the dilemma Nora faces. As friend and confidant he is a pillar of the household, both Torvald's best friend and the person with whom Nora can talk of her hopes and affections. But under the pressure of Krogstad's demands, Nora desperately but playfully turns to Dr. Rank for financial help—and her coquetry leads him to declare his love, which makes it impossible for her to pursue their intimacy. On the other hand, the doctor's fatal illness cuts him off from further friendship with Torvald (Rank knows that his friend is too immature to stand up to the ordeal of watching death). With their only friend gone, the Helmers are forced into the intimacy of the final scene.

Is Nora's transformation from child to adult too sudden to be plausible? In one sense, as suggested by the second study question for *Othello* (page 1356), the question is impertinent: we should ask instead, does her change represent a vital, human truth? Her change occurs in the space of three hours in a theatrical performance, in the space of about 36 hours of elapsed time in the dramatized action, and at a rather late point in the life of a woman with three children—but those three "clocks" by which we measure this dramatic event all have in common a literalism about the relationship of personality to action. They ask, that is, for an examination of literal psychological causalities rather than for an analysis of a realistic drama. For we must not confuse "realistic" with "real" or "literal." In a realistic play, these should be the pertinent questions: Do people make self-discoveries that change the course of their actions? Is Nora sufficiently characterized to explain how the events that are dramatized (and those from the past that are called into the present action as influences) can account for a change in her? Does her change result in an effective dramatic climax? Does her change embody Ibsen's themes? The answer to *these* questions is "yes."

And what does the future hold for Nora and Torvald? This, too, is an impertinent question, for of course there is no future after the final curtain. We should ask, rather, with what feelings Ibsen leaves the audience. Do we want Torvald to discover himself and the errors that have led him to his isolation? Do we believe that Nora has the courage to seek out the meaning of her life without the comfortable hypocrisies she deserts? Does this play sadden or exhilarate us? Or both? Does it achieve anything of the double emotion of a tragic ending?

Much has been written about this play, but the indispensable source for any teacher of the play, to be used more or less extensively depending on the amount of time one has, is Yvonne Shafer, ed., *Approaches to Teaching Ibsen's A Doll's House* (New York: MLA, 1985)

Two excellent film versions (both made in 1973) starring Claire Bloom and Jane Fonda are available on videocassette, and a BBC television production with Juliet Stevenson was made in 1991. Claire Bloom also appears on an audio recording of 1971.   TRA

Tennessee Williams   The Glass Menagerie (page 1143)

On a realistic-nonrealistic scale, *The Glass Menagerie* lies perhaps midway between *A Doll House* and "The Sandbox." Its principal (though not only) nonrealistic elements lie in the use made of (a) a narrator, (b) lighting, and (c) music.

(a) Tom combines the roles of narrator, stage manager, and character. As narrator he tells us, "The play is memory." He clearly means his own memory, and the play may be said to assimilate the first-person and dramatic points of view. It is not realistically consistent, however, for in all or part of some scenes (2, 6, 7) Tom is not present, and these scenes could not logically come from his memory.

(b) "Being a memory play," Tom informs us, "it is dimly lighted, it is sentimental, it is not realistic." Lighting is indeed used for emotional and sentimental effects. At the climax of the quarrel between Tom and Amanda in scene 3, the upstage area is "lit with a turgid smoky red glow," while in scene 7 the new floor lamp, with its rose-colored silk shade, throws a soft light on Laura's face, bringing out its "fragile, unearthly prettiness." Williams skillfully handles his plot so that the inopportune-opportune electrical failure in scene 6 not only underlines Tom's preparations for leaving home by using the light bill money to pay dues to the Merchant Seamen's Union but also requires the final romantic scene, between Laura and Jim, to be played out by candlelight. Laura's final blowing out of these candles both ends the play and symbolizes the extinction for her of any hope for a fulfilling life. Lighting is also used for ironical effects, as when the outsize photograph of Tom's father suddenly lights up in scene 4.

(c) "In memory everything seems to happen to music," says Tom. The "fiddle in the wings" playing the Glass Menagerie theme adds poignance and delicate beauty to the scenes featuring Laura. The music from the Dance Hall turns ominous when some cruel revelation is about to be made. But the music, like the lighting, is also used for ironic effects, as when in scene 5 the music from the Dance Hall—"All the World Is Waiting for the Sunrise"—is counterpointed against Tom's remarks about the thirties, when "All the world was waiting for bombardments," or as when, later in that scene, Tom tells his mother they are going to have "a gentleman caller," and this "annunciation" is "celebrated with music."

Williams's original script called for a fourth nonrealistic feature, the "Screen Device," by means of which magic-lantern slides were to be projected on one wall bearing titles and images such as *Où sont les neiges d'antan* when Amanda talks about her former beaux in scene 1, or a picture of blue roses to introduce scene 2, in which Laura tells about her high-school crush on Jim O'Connor. The screen device was not used in the immensely successful first Broadway production of the play, and critics have found it distracting and gimmicky, seemingly designed "to reduce all the scenes—even the tenderest—to ludicrous parodies" (Gerald Weales, *Tennessee Williams* [Minneapolis: U of Minnesota P, 1965] 33). Of the two editions of the play—the Library Edition (New Directions) and the Acting Edition (Dramatists Play Service), the former includes the "Screen Device," but the later does not. The text of the play used here is that of the Library Edition with the screen device omitted.

Williams also makes an impressionistic use of time. The domestic drama and the illusions of the "American dream" are played off by Tom against the social realities of the thirties throughout the play; yet we get into trouble if we try to be precise in dating it. In the last scene Jim speaks of having visited the Chicago World's Fair (1933–1934) "summer before last," but Tom in his narration refers to the bombing of Guernica (1937) and the Munich Pact (1938), and in scene 5 he reads a newspaper with the enormous headline "Franco Triumphs" (1939).

Whatever its nonrealistic features, which include the poetic prose spoken by Tom as narrator, the dialogue of the play is completely realistic, and real as granite, and the characters rendered through it are solid and unforgettable.

Whose play is it—Tom's, Laura's, or Amanda's? A strong case can be made for each. Tom is both the narrator and the trapped young artist struggling to break away from a stultifying environment. Of the three main characters he is the one who takes positive action to break out of illusion and pursue his goal, though apparently to no effect, for in his first appearance he is still dressed as a merchant sailor and his final narration indicates he has done little but travel a great deal. The negative imagery ("The cities swept about me like dead leaves") enforces a feeling of futility. Instead of pursuing, he is "pursued"—by the memory to his sister Laura. —Is it then Laura's play? The play's title refers to her; she is the focus of the action, which, according to Williams's opening notes, consists of two parts—preparation for the gentleman caller, and appearance of the gentleman caller; it is she who brings the curtain down by blowing out the candles. Yet Laura is almost entirely a passive character, a figure of pathos, acted upon rather than acting. She has her brief moment of hope and disappointment, and at the end is the same wistful, pathetic creature she was at the beginning. —Is it then Amanda's play? Certainly, Amanda is the most rounded, fully developed character in the play; her role would demand the most talent from a player taking her part; and the actress taking her part would receive top billing on the theater marquee. She is all that Williams says she is in his opening note—heroic, foolish, tender, unwittingly cruel, lovable, laughable, pitiable, and, above all, vital—a unique dramatic creation.

The chief symbol of the play is the glass menagerie, the dream world which Laura retreats to and which, in its delicate and fragile beauty, is a symbol for Laura herself. When Tom, in scene 3, quarrels violently with his mother, tries to leave, has trouble with his coat, and hurls it across the room shattering several of the figurines and drawing a cry of wounded pain from Laura, we see his dilemma. His quarrels with his mother distress Laura, and he cannot leave without damaging her. Of all the figurines in the collection, the glass unicorn most symbolizes Laura, because its horn, like her shyness, separates it from the normal world and makes it unique. When Jim, during the dancing, temporarily overcomes her shyness, and accidentally breaks off the horn, Laura is not distressed. "It doesn't matter. Maybe it's a blessing in disguise." But when, after kissing her, Jim draws himself up short and reveals his previous commitment, Laura gives the broken figurine to him to keep as a souvenir, and withdraws forever from the world of normality.

The principal primary sources for investigation of the biographical backgrounds of the play are *Remember Me to Tom* by Edwina Dakin Williams (the playwright's mother) as told to Lucy Freeman (New York: Putnam's, 1963) and Tennessee Williams's *Memoirs* (New York: Doubleday, 1975). The former reveals how much Edwina had in common with Amanda beyond a liking for jonquils. The latter, weaving back and forth in time, mingles family recollections with a very explicit history of Williams's sexual experiences and homosexual activities; it is not recommended for incautious assignment.   LP

Three versions of the play are available on video or DVD. The 1950 version stars Gertrude Lawrence, the original Amanda Wingfield, and is more freely adapted to cinematic techniques. A 1987 version stars Joanne Woodward and John Malkovich, and is more faithful to the text. Recently, the Broadway Theatre Archive released a 1973 television version starring Katharine Hepburn.   TRA

Luis Valdez   Los Vendidos (page 1197)

This bizarre satire combines elements of realistic and nonrealistic conventions. The realistic include the following characterizations: a government functionary seeking an "affirmative action" or "politically correct" representative of a minority group to make a public display of the government's lack of prejudice; a salesman whose glib patter echoes the familiar pitches of car salesmen; recognizable but exaggerated representations of the minority group. In addition, the play includes literalistic references to actual political figures (Governor Reagan and Senator Murphy) and to historical realities such as the crop-workers' strikes, the provision of inadequate housing for them, and the activist group the Brown Berets. (This play was first performed at a Brown Beret rally.)

The nonrealistic elements include Honest Sancho's direct address to the audience at the play's opening; the machine-like figures who are automatons activated by a snap of the fingers; the drawn-out parallels between men and automobiles in Sancho's sales pitches; and to some extent the formulaic structural principle with its echo of folk tales or children's tales, as the plot introduces a sequence of characters, each rejected for some inadequacy so that the next can be brought in. And, of course, the surprise ending in which the four automatons (who have been posing as machines) step forward as humans, and Sancho is revealed to be a machine, provides a brilliantly ironic nonrealistic conclusion.

This mingling of conventions is one source of humor in this dark comedy, for it introduces opportunities for unexpected and surprising shifts in tone. If the role reversal of Sancho and his models at the end is the most striking, we should notice that smaller surprises occur throughout the play. Some of these are the result of Sancho's "used Mexicans" failing to satisfy the needs of the Secretary. Thus the Farmworker who seems to be perfect for her purposes—inexpensive, cheap to run, versatile, compact, and so greasy that he can slide easily through tangled vines and branches—is disqualified because he is unable to speak English. As Valdez clearly implies, what makes him fit to serve as the Secretary's demeaning definition of the ideal Mexican is the result of a lack of education, so that his disqualification is a concomitant of his suitability. (When at the end the Mexican-American complains that he always has to act that role, Johnny tells him that it's his education that suits him for that stereotype.)

Similarly, the urban Johnny Pachuco seems right for the job (though the English that he knows, "Fuck-you," doesn't exactly fit), since he will be docilely victimized and tormented at will, and thus will provide sadistic pleasure to police and others. But he is only economical to maintain because he can steal, and he tries to prove it by snatching the Secretary's purse. Her rejection of him contains another of the little surprises, as she says, "We can't have any *more* thieves in the State Administration" (emphasis added). Then the Revolutionario is disqualified by virtue of the one presumably essential characteristic: he's Mexican, not an "American product," a rather strange shortcoming considering that Miss Jimenez has come shopping at "Honest Sancho's Used Mexican Lot." That leaves only the Mexican-American, who again starts out seeming to be just the ticket. But after she has paid cash for him, he begins spouting revolutionary rhetoric, as a result of "bugs from the factory," while the other three models join in menacing the Secretary until she flees, leaving behind her money.

It is clear that Valdez's satire cuts in many directions. The Secretary is certainly one of the sell-outs ("Vendidos") as she reveals from her first entrance when she insists on an anglicized pronunciation of her name. She has done her best to distance herself from her Mexican heritage and only lets slip a "Chihuahua" when she is startled by the Farmworker's working speed. Her selling out is the primary target of the play, for it has led her to espouse all the values of a repressive and dismissive government. What they want is a "model" with a pleasing skin color, docile actions, and correct attitudes: the metaphor of the automobile-model automatons captures the total disregard for human individuality that would fulfill the purposes of the Secretary and the administration she works for.

The four models seem also to represent sell-outs, striving as they do to fit the mold that the government presents to them, and Honest Sancho is certainly a sell-out as he panders his wares. The surprise ending of the play, however, shifts the situation. The supposed automatons are not sellouts but role-players who adapt themselves to the prejudices of the Anglo establishment in order to live off it, and who enjoy their gains with macho robustness. In this reversal, the true sell-outs are the Secretary and *dis*-honest Sancho, she the creature of the state and he the instrument of his actors.   TRA

Chapter Three

Tragedy and Comedy

Sophocles **Oedipus Rex** (page 1216)

For the beginning student of drama, this play is of course made more difficult by the conventions of classical tragedy—the use of choruses, the non-realistic set speeches, the "static" stage action, the (translated) poetry, the reporting of off-stage actions by messengers. But this particular example of Greek tragedy is made even more difficult by the apparent importance to the story of incidents that precede the play. Almost without exception, students asked to recount the plot will begin not at the beginning of the play, but at the beginning of Oedipus's career or even at the point of the first oracle to Laïos predicting a parricidal, incestuous son. The distinction between the action *on stage* and antecedent events must be made very clear if the nature of this play is to be properly understood.

A city wracked by plague turns to its king for relief, trusting that his almost superhuman wisdom will save them. Oedipus, however, has already begun the task, for he is awaiting the return of Kreon, his wife's brother and a prince of Thebes, from the oracle; the message is that the murderer of the former king, living unpunished in the city, is the cause of the plague. Oedipus lays a curse on the murderer ("that that man's life be consumed in evil and wretchedness," 1.234) and begins his search for the identity of the guilty person. At Kreon's suggestion he consults the blind seer Teiresias and forces him to divulge what he is reluctant to reveal: that Oedipus is the pollution in the city, the murderer of Laïos, and is living "in hideous shame with those / Most dear" (11.351–52). Enraged at what seems an incredible lie, Oedipus accuses Teiresias of plotting with Kreon so that the latter may gain the crown. Teiresias leaves, pronouncing further that Oedipus is "to her / Who bore him, son and husband" (11.443–44).

Kreon's denial of a plot against Oedipus is logical and prudent: since he already has the rights and powers of the kingship, why would he want to add the anxieties and responsibilities of the crown? When Queen Iokastê tries to patch up the quarrel between her husband and her brother, Oedipus reports to her Teiresias's accusation of murder, and to dispel his anger she skeptically offers him proof that soothsayers and oracles are not trustworthy: she and

Laïos had been told that her son would kill his father and marry his mother—yet as everyone knows, Laïos was murdered by a band of marauders at a place where three highways meet. Oedipus uneasily recalls that he had received a similar prophecy, and fleeing from the home of his supposed parents to avoid such guilty acts, he had killed a man at just such a place. He begins to realize that he may indeed have been Laïos's murderer—that his own curse may alight on himself. But he takes hope from the report that the king had been killed not single-handedly but by a group. He sends for a shepherd, the lone survivor of Laïos's party, to hear the true circumstances of the murder.

A messenger from Corinth arrives to announce that Oedipus's presumed father Polybos has died of age and illness, thus apparently disproving the oracle's prophecy that Oedipus would kill him, but Oedipus is unwilling to return as king of Corinth because his mother Meropê still lives. When he tells the messenger of the prophecy that had driven him from home, the messenger offers him the good news: he need not fear, for he was not in fact the son of Polybos and Meropê. Tending his flock near Mount Kithairon, this very messenger had received from a Theban shepherd an infant who had been exposed to die on the mountain and had taken him to Polybos, who raised him as his son. Iokastê tries to dissuade Oedipus from further questioning, having deduced from this news the whole horrid truth: she is the mother of her husband, who has killed his father.

The shepherd appears who has been with Laïos at his death and is recognized by the Corinthian as the man who had given him the infant. He reveals that the baby was said to be a son of Laïos and was sent to be exposed on the mountain for fear of the prophecies. Now Oedipus possesses the whole truth and rushes into the palace, from which another messenger emerges to report that the queen has hanged herself and that Oedipus has stabbed himself in the eyes with her brooches to blind himself to all the horror and misery he has unknowingly created. Being led forth from the palace, he acknowledges that although Apollo brought his "sick, sick fate" upon him, "the blinding hand was [his] own!" (11.1287–88). He summarizes his life in a powerful lament, asks Kreon to care for his children, bids his daughters farewell, and begs for the fulfillment of the curse he has pronounced on Laïos's murderer, banishment from Thebes.

This rehearsal of the actions of the play demonstrates several important dramatic points: the only causal effect of the oracle in the action is Oedipus's vow to discover and punish the murderer; the whole movement of the plot is toward knowledge, first the discovery of the identity of the murderer, and then the discovery of Oedipus's true parentage. Confusing discussions of the causal role of the gods and oracles are not necessary, even though they are tempting: we are presented with what Oedipus *is*, not with what he was; we share with him his quest for the truth, not his flight from Corinth to avoid a prophecy, not his defensive murder, not his glorious achievement of the throne nor the early years of his marriage. All those come forth as he searches for the truth of his past, but it is important to accept what the king is at the beginning of the play ("not one of the immortal gods, . . . [but] the man surest in mortal ways / And wisest in the ways of God," 11.35–38). In the justified pride of his position, he undertakes the actions that will save the country and then unflinchingly goes on when others beg him to stop. The search for enlightenment is rewarded with knowledge of the most horrid kind, too horrid for a mere mortal to look upon, and yet he presses for the execution of the sentence he has pronounced upon himself.

Recognizing the boundaries of the action within the time of the play also clarifies the question of Oedipus's tragic flaw. It is not the rashness of having killed a group of men who attacked him on the highway, nor is it the arrogance of supposing he could avoid the prophecy by fleeing from Corinth. The pride he displays within the action is justified: as a wise king, he must take the responsibility of ridding the city of its pollution; in undertaking the search for the murderer, he is following the instructions of the oracle. His rage at Teiresias and his suspicion of Kreon's plot are motivated by his certainty that he did *not* kill the king and an intelligent inference based on the fact that Kreon had recommended consulting the soothsayer. His flaw— the traditional term is an unfortunate one—is his insistence on learning the truth, extending his knowledge to discover himself fully. The sight/blindness, light/dark ironies that abound in the play point in this direction, toward an enlightenment too great for a man to bear.

The chorus has several important functions in this drama: it comments, in a slightly obtuse, conservatively pious way on the actions it has witnessed, acting in part as a surrogate for the audience; and its songs (and dances) reinforce the moods created by the actions. By interrupting the action, it also makes the passage of time between events more dramatically credible. The links between the choral songs and the preceding actions are not always immediately clear, and students usually need to have them pointed out. The parodos is a prayer for divine intervention in the plague, springing directly from the news that the oracle is being consulted. Ode 1 comments on the oracle's warning that Laïos's murderer is still in the city, but rejects as impossible Teiresias's pronouncements against Oedipus—the chorus is thus torn between belief and disbelief in the messages from the gods. Ode 2 is a shocked response to Iokastê's protective and impious skepticism about oracles. Ode 3, after the revelation that Oedipus had been rescued from exposure on the mountain, ignores Iokastê's newfound awareness that her husband will discover himself to be the most miserable of men, and instead is a hymn to Kithairon and the gods who attended Oedipus's rescue, as if the chorus cannot bring itself to face the situation being revealed. Ode 4, after the full revelation of Oedipus's past, grieves for the fall of so great a man, "Majestic Oedipus! / . . . now of all men ever known / Most pitiful is this man's story" (11.1147–51). In the Exodos, the chorus joins with Oedipus in a "commos," a responsive song or chant, as an introduction to the lament in which he looks back on his life; and the chorus concludes the play with a moral which is not exactly the central theme of the action but is appropriate to the insight of the chorus.

Are the gods just to Oedipus? Has he deserved his catastrophic fate? Too much has been written on this subject already, but we might well remember that these are not the questions we usually ask about great interpretive literature—they mean "has poetic justice been served, have the good been rewarded and the wicked punished?" We might as well also ask "does suffering always bring wisdom?" and "does wisdom always bring happiness?" Perhaps rather than asking for poetic justice or for philosophic truisms, we need to bear always in mind that although Oedipus is *almost* godlike in wisdom, he is human, and that although his sufferings are terrifying, he bears them with courage and determination that are themselves *almost* god-like (for which, in another play about the end of his life, he is rewarded with elevation to the status of immortal demi-god). Sophocles is not writing a play about the acts of gods—just or unjust—or about an intrinsic relationship between suffering, wisdom, and happiness. Rather, his subject is a great man who loyally does his duty to others and to his own need to know himself. Such men are not always happy.

Just as this note cannot mention even most of the topics the play includes, so the following brief bibliography should be regarded as only introductory: S. M. Adams, *Sophocles the Playwright* (Toronto: U of Toronto P, 1957); C. M. Bowra, *Sophoclean Tragedy* (Oxford: Clarendon, 1944); Bernard M. W. Knox, *Oedipus at Thebes* (New Haven: Yale UP, 1957); Richmond Lattimore, *The Poetry of Greek Tragedy* (Baltimore: Johns Hopkins UP, 1958); A. I. A. Waldock, *Sophocles the Dramatist* (Cambridge: Cambridge UP, 1951); and Cedric H. Whitman, *Sophocles; A Study of Heroic Humanism* (Cambridge: Harvard UP, 1951). A convenient selection of essays and excerpts from full-length studies is included in *Oedipus Tyrannus*, eds. Luci Berkowitz and Theodore F. Brunner (New York: Norton, 1970).

A faithful videotape production is available in the Films for the Humanities series. It is called *Oedipus the King* and stars Michael Pennington as Oedipus, Claire Bloom as Iokastê, and John Gielgud as Teiresias.   TRA

William Shakespeare   Othello, the Moor of Venice
(page 1263)

Of the many "problems" that have been analyzed in the extensive criticism of this play, the one that most intrigues beginning students is explicitly voiced by Othello when he asks about Iago in act 5, "Why he hath thus ensnared my soul and body," to which Iago retorts, "What you know, you know," and vows silence (5.2.301–302). Iago's motivation is a central issue because he himself so often talks about it, and no doubt also because Coleridge famously pronounced that the soliloquy that concludes act 1 reveals "the motive-hunting of motiveless malignity," a fiendish lack of human motivation in a character who continually attempts to find in himself the motives that other men do have. At one point or another, Iago credits himself with ambition, spiteful envy of Cassio's promotion, sexual jealousy because Othello has cuckolded him, profit from robbing Roderigo, the pleasure of deceiving Roderigo and Othello, jealousy that Cassio too has slept with Emilia, love for Desdemona, hatred of Cassio's handsomeness, and mere hatred of Othello; and the careful critic will have no difficulty in finding other implied but not stated motives. That these do not sufficiently define Iago may be seen in disparities between stated motives and action: why, if he loves Desdemona, does he conspire in her death? Why, if he wants the lieutenancy, does he destroy the man who could give it to him? Why, since Roderigo can so easily be robbed of cash, does he kill him? Why, if he is so jealous of his wife, does he malign and finally kill her? While the changing circumstances of the play may answer some of these questions, it is this sort of arithmetic of motive and action that makes Coleridge's conclusion so attractive. Intelligent, cunning, capable of tempting and controlling the characters around him, Iago nevertheless does not use his powers to achieve his stated goals, but in fact renders those goals unattainable.

Like Milton's Satan, Shakespeare's antagonist fascinates, drawing the attention of the reader to himself and in part robbing the protagonist of the attention due him. The more we notice Iago, the less we notice Othello, whose commanding presence in any stage performance may, by contrast, be reduced in reading and analyzing the play. The result is what Shakespeare certainly does not intend, that Othello is read merely as Iago's victim, as passively susceptible as are Roderigo, Desdemona, and Cassio. If only Coleridge's word could be taken, we might more easily focus our interest not on Iago and what makes him tick, but on the great central figure, the tragic hero.

Othello's greatness is nearly a definition of the Shakespearean tragic hero: his weaknesses or "flaws" are virtues carried to excess. He loves, but "too well," too intensely and totally; he trusts, but too much, and too indiscriminately; he has so great a sense of moral virtue and of his own honorable responsibility that he makes of himself an agent of divine justice to extirpate sin; his sensitive, poetic imagination leads him to vivid, pictorial fantasies of his wife and her lover. Iago in his soliloquies provides a partial catalogue, though of course he sneers at the general's virtues: "The Moor is of a free and open nature / That thinks men honest that but seem to be so" (1.3.375–76); "The Moor, howbeit that I endure him not, / Is of a constant, loving, noble nature" / (2.2.264–65). And Lodovico, spokesman for the Venetian government, can only grieve to witness Othello's abuse of Desdemona: "Is this the noble Moor whom our full Senate / Call all-in-all sufficient? This the nature / Whom passion could not shake? Whose solid virtue / The shot of accident nor dart of chance / Could neither graze nor pierce?" (4.2.247–51).

The thematic center of the play is the perversion of Othello's goodness by the evil workings of his mind, and the chief concern is Othello's fall from greatness, not as victim but as the agent of his own destruction. By insinuation and apparent reluctance to speak, Iago forces Othello to draw from him his suspicions, and excites Othello's visual imagination into picturing scenes of Desdemona's lustful acts; and then, once he has administered this small dose of poison, Iago urges Othello onward into a deeper conviction by pretending to argue against the certainty of Desdemona's guilt. The growth of Othello's jealousy is the result of his own energies, the strength of his love and his desire for perfection driving him to take up the sword of divine justice.

Is Othello gullible? Does he succumb too quickly, too easily to Iago's temptation? While these questions may arise from an inappropriately realistic approach to the play, what they mean is "How wrong is it to be honest and frank and to believe that your old friends are too?" Do we admire cynical suspiciousness or vulnerable trust? Shakespeare created Roderigo (not a character in Cinthio's novella "Tale of the Moor of Venice," the source of the play) to provide a parallel whose gullibility answers these questions. Roderigo is indeed what Othello calls himself in act 5 after he has learned of Desdemona's innocence: fool, dolt, a man without honor. Roderigo's willingness to wait his turn to enjoy the woman he "loves," the ease with which Iago can manipulate him into the cowardly attempt on Cassio's life, the whining stupidity which makes him so easy a prey—these are explicitly contrasted to Othello's true love and noble nature. Iago marks the contrast in his first soliloquy when he apologizes to himself for wasting time gulling such a "snipe" as Roderigo ("sport and profit" excuse the waste) and sets as his real target a man of "free and open nature" to be led (he hopes) as easily as such "asses" as Roderigo. Like Satan's, Iago's cunning is in leading people into self-destruction, not merely in duping them—and his skill is great, for no one in the play has the least suspicion of him (until Roderigo in act 4), not even the two people who must know him best, his wife Emilia and his battlefield companion Othello. If Othello is vulnerable to him, so are Cassio, Desdemona, and Roderigo, and even Montano and Lodovico: everyone to whom he lies believes him (a statistical demonstration that Othello is not to be considered especially susceptible), and ironically almost everyone turns to him for advice.

Structurally, *Othello* moves toward its catastrophe inexorably, with an increasing narrowing of focus. The first act, in Venice, has the breadth of three parallel situations—the gulling of Roderigo, the military danger of the invasion of Cyprus, and the private conflict between Brabantio and the newly married general and his wife. The subplot of Roderigo is maintained right up to the fifth act, repeating again and again Iago's ability to manipulate the young man's sensual ambitions for his own profit and the pleasure of watching him squirm. In terms of development, the Iago-Roderigo action is less a subplot than a recurring situation, a reminder of what Iago can do to lesser men whose "love" is only lust. The great public issue of a Turkish invasion, which in act 1 vies in importance with the private affair of the "unnatural" marriage, is removed at the opening of act 2 when the enemy fleet is "banged" and dispersed by the storm (no doubt Shakespeare's audience would recall the similar fate of the grand Armada), constricting the action to Iago-Othello-Desdemona. The last we hear of the Turks is the proclamation in act 2 that links their loss with the celebration of Othello's nuptials as the double occasion for general holiday. The cashiering of Cassio raises Roderigo's false hopes and sets up Iago's plan to make Othello suspect the motives of his wife as she generously pleads for the lieutenant's reinstatement.

Othello's downfall commences in act 3, after the play has amply established the many virtues in his character. As the poisonous suspicion grows in him, we witness a deterioration of his free, open, and trusting nature, as he commits himself to one act after another that undercuts his greatness: he sets Emilia to spy on Desdemona, he deputizes Iago to take vengeance on Cassio, he stoops to eavesdropping as Iago interviews Cassio, he subjects Desdemona to verbal and then to physical abuse, he lurks in the darkness observing the ambush of Cassio, and then finally murders his innocent wife. But this deterioration is all the while accompanied by the perplexing and paradoxical constancy of his love, for although he is convinced of Desdemona's guilt, he cannot refrain from loving her. This is shown clearly in 4.1, when he exclaims on the "pity of it" after Iago draws him back from thoughts of her sweetness, delicacy, gentleness, and beauty. As he approaches the murder in the last scene, he has managed to subdue whatever hatred he had displayed in abusing her and thinks of himself as the abstract agent of divine justice—but simultaneously, he is drawn by the beauty of her skin, her balmy breath, the "cunning'st pattern of excelling nature," to kiss her again and again, even to wish that he could preserve her physical perfection and love it after her death. Like the loving God who must punish his beloved creature for her sin, he must strike the one he loves and pities.

After the murder, as the unwinding mysteries reveal to him the extent of his injustice, Othello's character sinks lower. For a moment he is willing to hide his crime behind Desdemona's dying words (5.2.121–26), but then pulls himself up to denounce her lie (5.2.128–29). His lowest moral point comes in the speech at 5.2.258, in which he gives way to self-pity, blames his act on "fate" and the stars, and cries out for punishments of hell to remove him from the sight of what he has done—all without acknowledging that he has been personally responsible. This is counterbalanced by his final speech, when once again he resumes his noble, moral character: he yields up his pride as a great commander, asks only for an honest, plain report of his character, and then reorienting himself in the wide geographical world he had inhabited, he accepts both his guilt and his responsibility to the state. Recalling his defense of Venice against her enemies, he identifies himself both with the Turk who "beat a Venetian and traduced the state" and with the hero who brought him to justice. He began the last scene in ignorant usurpation of the role of divine justicer; he ends his life in an enlightened act of human justice and final farewell to his beloved.

Of the plethora of critical works dealing with the play, the following may be noted: John Bayley, *The Characters of Love* (New York: Basic Books,

1961); A. C. Bradley, *Shakespearean Tragedy* (1904, repr. New York: St. Martin's, 1964); G. R. Elliott, *Flaming Minister: A Study of Othello as Tragedy of Love and Hate* (Durham, NC: Duke UP, 1953); Helen Gardner, *The Noble Moor* (London: Oxford UP, 1956) and "*Othello*: A Retrospect, 1900-1967," *Shakespeare Survey 21*, ed. Kenneth Muir (Cambridge: Cambridge UP, 1968); Harley Granville-Barker, "Preface to *Othello*," *Prefaces to Shakespeare*, Vol. II (Princeton: Princeton UP, 1947); Robert B. Heilman, *Magic in the Web: Action and Language in* Othello (Lexington, KY: U of Kentucky P, 1956); G. Wilson Knight, *The Wheel of Fire*, 5th rev. ed. (New York: Meridian, 1957); Marvin Rosenberg, *The Masks of Othello* (Berkeley: U of California P, 1961); Arthur Sewell) *Character and Society in Shakespeare* (New York: Oxford UP, 1951); E. E. Stoll, *From Shakespeare to Joyce* (New York: Doubleday, 1944); and *Othello: An Historical and Comparative Study* (Minneapolis: U of Minnesota P, 1964). Convenient collections of articles and excerpts from books are Leonard F. Dean, ed., *A Casebook on* Othello (New York: Crowell, 1961); Harold Bloom, ed., *Iago* (New York: Chelsea, 1992) and *William Shakespeare's* Othello (New York: Chelsea, 1987); and Linda Cookson and Bryan Loughrey, eds., *Critical Essays on* Othello (Harlow, Essex: Longman, 1991).

Among the several versions of the play available on videotape and DVD, the most wholly satisfactory is that directed by Trevor Nunn for the Royal Shakespeare company and distributed by Films for the Humanities.

A note on Othello's race

There can be no serious question about Othello's race. Iago, Brabantio, and Roderigo all refer disparagingly to it ("thick-lips," "sooty bosom"), and Othello himself states plainly "I am black." The word "moor" was used in Shakespeare's time to identify black Africans as well as practitioners of the Muslim religion. But Othello is black and, insofar as his religion is identified, a Christian.

His race is thematically important, particularly as it would have provided a prejudiced point of departure for Shakespeare's audiences. Brabantio's attitude toward it may be taken to represent the common attitude: his daughter is "unnatural" in loving a black, her action so extreme as to make him suppose that magic or witchcraft is the cause (and Desdemona herself acknowledges that her elopement was "downright violence and storm of fortunes"). Common prejudices of the time would have presumed the black man to be less rational, more passionate and lustful, less civilized, and—at the extreme—inherently evil (as the play indicates, the devil himself was thought to be black in hue). Against these assumptions Shakespeare creates a noble, Christian, virtuous man of great imagination, calm self-control, frankness, and honesty, and he bestows on white Iago the qualities of a devil. An audience perceives not only the literal color contrast between the protagonist and antagonist, but the contrasting inversion of the moral qualities symbolically associated with their colors. As he so often does, Shakespeare achieves intense dramatic effects by demonstrating that common prejudices are opposite to the truth.

A note on teaching Shakespeare

For the inexperienced student, reading a Shakespeare play can be a most difficult task, for the conventions of Elizabethan drama are polar opposites of those of the realistic drama for which such students have had most of their training (chiefly through television and film). Not only do Shakespeare's characters speak verse, in an older vocabulary and syntax, with such conventions as the soliloquy and aside, but the plots present unrealistic patterning of action and feeling, great emotional sweeps from pathos to terror to low comedy, extremes that could not even be considered in a realistic drama. There are few stage directions to aid the visual imagination, and students toiling through unfamiliar speech patterns and vocabulary will find it extremely difficult to visualize the scene or "hear" the dialogue. Such aids as are available on film, DVD, videocassette, and sound recordings, while often tending to pull the plays toward more realistic conventions, should be employed to help students imagine the sights and sounds of drama that are implied in the script they are reading. Even a brief sampling of recorded dialogue can encourage students in the necessary exercise of the imagination.

Perhaps most difficult of all lessons is the distinction between action and character, because Shakespeare's characters may seem so psychologically alive that students will be drawn to the assumption that the intention of the plays is to present fully rounded personalities. But as E. E. Stoll rightly points out, a Shakespeare play is not "what we call drama as it is ordinarily practiced today. It is as in Aristotle—situation first and motivation or psychology afterwards, if at all. The effect is emotional, with which psychology or even simple narrative coherence often considerably interferes" ("Source and Motive in *Macbeth* and *Othello*" from his *From Shakespeare to Joyce*, New York: Doubleday, 1944). It can be useful to offer students an analogy to a dramatic form that is familiar to many of them—musical comedy. There they will find parallels in nonrealistic plotting, appreciation of musical effects analogous to the poetic effects of Shakespeare's verse, versions of the soliloquy represented in musical solos, the acceptance of an emotional effect at the expense of realistic "psychology or even simple narrative coherence," and in general an appreciation by the audience of nonrealistic conventions. Students familiar with opera, of course, will have an even tighter analogy available to them. (I have found that merely playing for them a recording of the concluding duet of the second act of Verdi's *Othello*, derived from *Othello*, 3.2.434–69, excitingly impresses this point upon students.)   TRA

Molière   Tartuffe, or The Impostor (page 1358)

Like Molière's other masterpiece of the same period, *The Misanthrope* (1666), *Tartuffe* is a comedy with dark overtones. In the later play, the protagonist Alceste is a man with an obsession for honesty and plain speaking that nearly destroys him. His excessive insistence on that virtue in himself and in others brings him to the brink of losing his love and his liberty. In the earlier, Orgon too is obsessed, but the object of his passion is not so clearly a virtue. His religious zeal makes him the dupe of a hypocritical con-artist, so that what might be considered adherence to a valuable belief system is distorted into a feverish adoration of the embodiment of his beliefs. He is thus doubly obsessed, with his religion and with a pretended purveyor of the faith. When the play opens he already seems to have completed transferring his confidence from Christ to Tartuffe.

Orgon's first scene (1.4) occurs as he returns from a two-day visit to his country estate. He brushes aside the friendly greeting of his brother-in-law Cléante to ask about the family—and about Tartuffe, his live-in spiritual adviser. The maid Dorine reports that his wife Elmire was badly stricken with headaches, chills, and fever, and was unable to eat. But Orgon ignores this news, and continually presses Dorine to tell him about Tartuffe, who in contrast was "bursting with health, and excellently fed," devouring pheasant and mutton, downing beakers of port, and snoring away in his bed while others watched over Elmire's sickbed. Because Orgon has not responded to anything she had told him about Elmire, Dorine concludes the scene with sarcastic verbal irony: "I'll go and tell *Madame* that you've expressed / Keen sympathy and anxious interest" (1.4.35–36). But the scene displays more than the fact that Orgon's infatuation with Tartuffe has displaced his affection for his young wife. It has also created in him a kind of blindness to reality. For one thing, he has not even noticed what Cléante has to tell him in the opening line of the next scene (1.5), that Dorine was "laughing in [his] face" with her irony. Even more blindly, he was not hearing what she had said about Tartuffe, the only object of his interest! As she is describing the luxuriant pleasures of Tartuffe's bed and table, Orgon repeatedly interjects "Poor fellow!" His first encounter with the man has so possessed him that he cannot see or hear what Tartuffe is actually doing. That blindness is the basis of the plot, and is the key to Orgon's character. Tartuffe does not actually have to deceive him, because Orgon is bent on self-deception.

The play opens with a scene displaying another representation of that kind of blindness. Orgon's mother Madame Pernelle is denouncing all the members of the household who have not been "Tartuffified." All of them in the house, she declares, "break in and chatter on and on" (1.1.11), a remark that sets up the comedy of her own refusal to allow any of them to speak or defend themselves until Damis introduces the name of Tartuffe. Her complaints are that no one will take her "good advice," that Dorine is too "saucy" for her position as lady's-maid, that Damis is a "foolish . . . dunce," that

Mariane's demureness is a sign of secretive hypocrisy, that Elmire is an over-dressed spendthrift, and that Cléante indecently counsels them all in their worldly ways. Most of all, of course, they do not obey Orgon and love Tartuffe. When they are allowed to proffer their arguments—that Tartuffe is a hypocrite, bigot, and fraud—she accuses them of lying because Tartuffe has wounded them by the truth of his condemnation. As she departs from the house, she displays the shallowness of her own Christian beliefs, slapping her maid Flipote for moving too slowly.

These two scenes, which I've summarized in reverse order, typify the seriocomic tone of much of the play. In both, we see traditional comic behaviors carried to the point where they cause a shudder of fear. Madame Pernelle is a railing termagant whose verbal abusiveness and intolerance of other points of view are comic. She is rigid and automatic in her thoughts and feelings, and probably should be played for the laughs that such a shrew can elicit—and then her verbal assaults become physical as she arbitrarily and pointlessly takes out her frustration on a defenseless person. She is a petty tyrant who departs from her son's domain because it is too loosely controlled. At home with Flipote as her subject, there is no doubt how total her control will be.

In the case of Orgon's first scene, the comedy resides in the inappropriateness of his concern for his gluttonous mentor as he is being told of his wife's illness. That this is represented by mechanical repetition ("Ah, And Tartuffe? . . . Poor fellow!" repeated four times) drives the satiric joke home. We cannot miss it, any more than we could miss Madame Pernelle's heavy-handedness in cutting off other people's speaking. It is not only the incongruity of Orgon's concern for Tartuffe at such a time, but also the rigid and mechanical means of displaying it, that makes these actions comic. What is seriously threatening in this scene is what Madame Pernelle's made overt and obvious: this obsession can extend to physical danger. (We have a comic version of maid-slapping in 2.2, when Orgon threatens and then vainly tries to slap Dorine, who is too agile and clever to suffer his blows.)

The first act also makes it clear that the members of the family arrayed against Tartuffe are correct in their judgment of him. It is Orgon who unwittingly reveals that zealot's hypocritical conniving when he tries to describe to Cléante the fervent piety of the man as he first saw him, impoverished but devout, in church. The clues are there, but Orgon missed them: Tartuffe would humbly kneel *nearby*, and start to pray.

> He'd *draw* the eyes of everybody there
> By the deep fervor of his heartfelt prayer;
> He'd sigh and weep, and sometimes *with a sound*
> *Of rapture* he would bend and kiss the ground.
> (1.5.26–30; italics added)

The ostentatiousness of this performance is obvious to all but Orgon (he's certainly told this story before, as Dorine hints when she defends

Valère's presumed apostasy: "Would you have him go [to church] at the same hours as you, / And kneel nearby, to be sure of being seen?" [2.2.71–72]). Cléante correctly judges what has happened to Orgon—he has lost his common sense, his ability to make clear-eyed judgments. How far Orgon has gone down that road he himself defines in paraphrasing the text that Tartuffe has no doubt been preaching to him:

> Under his tutelage my soul's been freed
> From earthly loves, and every human tie:
> My mother, children, brother, and wife could die,
> And I'd not feel a single moment's pain.
>
> (1.5.18–21)

Tartuffe's texts have been Matthew 10.35–37 and the harsher version of that teaching, Luke 14.26 ("If any man come to me, and hate not his father, and mother, and wife, and children, and brethren, and sisters, yea, and his own life also, he cannot be my disciple"), which also counsels taking in beggars from the street.

The denial of family ties and adoration of his model are already ingrained in Orgon at the outset of the play, and all that follows is built upon them. The attempt to marry Mariane to Tartuffe, the disinheriting of Damis, and the flat refusal to believe that Tartuffe propositioned Elmire are all of a piece: the truth is with Tartuffe, and all others are plotting against him. His mind having been overpowered, Orgon surrenders everything to the "poor fellow." Once Tartuffe has Orgon completely in his control, he readily gives up his imposture, for there is no more to be obtained from him. In his triumph Tartuffe does suffer two losses—the hand of Mariane, and the body of Elmire—but that they are lost to him seems to be inconsequential to his delight. He has been in quest of power and property, and believes he has achieved them.

Ironically, Orgon's motives have also been for power and control. Like his tyrannizing mother, he wants to direct the lives of his household. He is, luckily, less adept at the power game than Tartuffe, for though Mariane's timidity and spinelessness make her seem an apt subject for his commands, his plan unravels when Tartuffe drops his mask. Disinheriting Damis is another tyranny that almost succeeds, and Elmire manages finally to overcome his incredulous denial of her. In going for control over this family, Orgon has given himself into the control of Tartuffe, but the power game concludes most fortunately with the highest earthly power prevailing through the agency of the king's officer.

Power and authority, in fact, have the sway in this comedy, not good sense and good intentions. Cléante argues cogently, points our Orgon's mistakes, counsels moderation both when Orgon is in his pious fits and when his disappointment with Tartuffe leads him to denounce all religion, but Cléante has no effect whatever. It is good for the audience to have a mouthpiece for rationality and kindness, but it is not so comforting for him to be impotent.

Dorine also makes a stab at reining in Orgon, and while she can adroitly avoid being slapped, and can get away with many ironic jabs, her plan to save Mariane's marriage is not working. Audiences also like to see witty servants who can manipulate their masters into doing the right things, but Dorine only reminds us that in *some* plays there are such rescuers, although not in this one.

The fact is that Orgon's disease—the uncontrollable obsession that makes him so easy a prize for Tartuffe—is not curable by the pat methods of comic drama. Only the intervention of what one critic calls *rex ex machina* (an appropriate pun, since the king is given the godlike ability to see into men's hearts) can rescue Orgon from the consequences of his folly. In many plays, the unmasking of the villain is sufficient to produce the comic resolution when he is stripped of his power. But Tartuffe's power over Orgon is increased when he shows his plain face because he now has the motive of revenge added to his desire to acquire Orgon's property, and both civil and criminal law are on his side: he has a deed of property and he has evidence that Orgon is a traitor to the king.

The subtitle "The Impostor" is in fact more appropriate than the title Molière used in the lost earlier version of the play, "the hypocrite." Tartuffe's villainy is not pretended piety; he only employs that as one of his weapons. As the Officer explains, the all-seeing

> King soon recognized Tartuffe as one
> Notorious by another name, who'd done
> So many vicious crimes that one could fill
> Ten volumes with them, and be writing still.

(5.7.63–65)

He is a manifold criminal, an impostor whose sins extend far beyond hypocrisy (we actually hear of sins enough—lechery, gluttony, envy, pride, to name a few). Such men do more than dupe the gullible, and more than good sense and judgment is required to fend them off.

For further discussion, see the following: Percy A. Chapman, *The Spirit of Molière* (Princeton: Princeton UP, 1940); Lionel Gossman, *Men and Masks: A Study of Molière* (Baltimore: Johns Hopkins UP, 1963); W. D. Howarth, *Molière: A Playwright and His Audience* (Cambridge: Cambridge UP, 1982); Gertrud Mander, *Molière* (New York: Ungar, 1973); Martin Turnell, *The Classical Moment* (New York: New Directions, 1948).

Two versions of the play adapted for television are available on VHS or DVD. The earlier one (1978), starring Victor Garber and Donald Moffat, from the "Broadway Theatre Archives" series, is distributed by Kultur (www.kultur.com). It uses the Richard Wilbur translation in a production based on a stage performance and is quite faithful to the text. The other from 1984 is a Royal Shakespeare Company production for BBC. The translation is by the contemporary English playwright Christopher Hampton, and the starring roles are taken by Anthony Sher and Nigel Hawthorne. Despite some questionable interpretive adaptations, this version can also be useful for classroom discussion.   TRA

Anton Chekhov   The Boor (page 1415)

Rude and rumpled misogynist meets pretty, dimpled widow sworn to perpetual mourning. Delicate femininity meets boorish masculinity. It appears to be a mismatch made in hell, yet within a quarter of an hour or so they are in each other's arms, after he has turned soft and sentimental and she has brandished a pistol demanding a duel.

Mme. Popova has been widowed seven months, a period she has devoted to seclusion and deep mourning. She has totally withdrawn from the social world, and even contemplates entering a convent to complete her break from worldliness and the distractions of society. But unless she finds a very liberal-minded abbess, she is not a likely candidate, for her "vocation" has nothing to do with religion. The desire to withdraw is (she believes) based on her undying love and her rejection of any kind of happiness that she might find in an ordinary life.

It is this really unnatural sequestration that is the subject of Luka's admonitory monologue in the opening moments of the play. She has neglected her social duties and allowed the estate to deteriorate from idleness, and she is also neglecting the chance for happiness with the young soldiers of the local regiment. As he says, she may be as pretty as "peaches and cream" now, but her youthful beauty will fade and then there'll be no chance for a "life of pleasure" when she desires it.

But this dedication to the memory of her late husband is really shallow posturing, based on delusion about the proper behavior of a widow, and has almost nothing to do with a genuine grief. Mme. Popova makes this obvious when she tells Luka her true motives for vowing never to stop mourning: she will show her husband's "shade" that she is faithful to his memory, even though Luka knows full well that he was "often unjust . . . , cruel, and . . . even unfaithful" to her. She will demonstrate to him how true and faithful a spouse should be. In effect, her isolation is based less on her love and loss than on her desire to demonstrate her finer spirit. It is the opposite of selfless dedication; it is self-indulgence, and when an exsoldier intrudes upon it, it melts away.

Smirnov the misogynist has his own self-indulgent definition of his role. Worn down by his fruitless efforts to collect debts in order to pay off his own debt, he is certainly boorish in charging into Mme. Popova's drawing room—and he knows it, and even prides himself on his boorish ways. He has given up all respect for women and their ways, and he scorns the beauty of dimples and feminine moods. He has, he claims, been jilted by nine women, jilted twelve, and fought three duels over women. His wide experience of women's ways (he says) has turned him against all of them, and in particular has made him furious with their air of believing that only women can have "tender feelings." This history of his love life clearly implies that he has had as little experience of genuine love as Mme. Popova, and further implies that his boorish misogyny is as self-indulgent as her dedicated bereavement. They are equally matched: neither will have anything to do with the opposite sex.

(Chekhov is famously reticent about psychological analysis of his characters: he reports realities without speculating about their origins. If we were to indulge in such speculation, we might conclude that both Smirnov and Mme. Popova are desperately defending themselves against further emotional injury by retreating into secure positions of invulnerability. But perhaps such speculation is too heavy for this hilarious "vaudeville.")

Structurally, *The Boor* exemplifies a plot based on reversal. The paradoxical action, of antagonists falling in love, is reminiscent of many longer romantic plays in which attraction grows from enmity. Chekhov's handling of the plot shows the stripping away of the poses adopted by the two protagonists under the pressure of their mutual antagonism and attraction. Their conflict—ludicrously exaggerated into a threatened duel with pistols—is the catalyst for their mutual growth.

Such exaggeration is characteristic of farce, a genre with which this play has much in common. Other farcical elements include the shouting matches (each of them is too sensitive and distraught to be able to bear the shouting of the other), the physical comedy of Smirnov's breaking two chairs with his intense grip, and the virtual mauling of the poor horse Toby, that for sentimental reasons is to be given extra oats and then as a symbol of Mme. Popova's rejection of the dead Popov is to be given no oats at all.

But the play is also an example of satirical comedy, for it displays two characters whose selfish posturing makes them ridiculous and who in the end seem to drop their rigid rejections in order to find some natural or normal relationship.   TRA

Plays for
Further Reading

Christopher Durang   For Whom the Southern Belle Tolls
(page 1431)

Rich Orloff   Oedi (page 1526)

These two parody plays are included chiefly for the "fun" they provide (to quote Orloff's comment on "Oedi"). They probably will make little sense to anyone who is not at least minimally familiar with the two masterpieces that they spoof, Sophocles's *Oedipus Rex* and Tennessee Williams's *The Glass Menagerie*.

Durang's satiric target is more narrowly focused on Williams's play, and if it has a serious intent it is to deflate the self-indulgence of Williams's pretentions that his themes are of universal significance. The transformations here are less light-hearted than Orloff's. Amanda is less concerned with the misery she foresees in the life of her younger child than she is with getting Lawrence off her hands. Lawrence is not dreamily pathetic but whining and slightly "moronic," Tom is not torn by his hopes and despairs but merely selfish, and the "gentleman/feminine caller" Ginny is just a caricature with the running gag of elocutionary loudness and an actual hearing defect. Durang brings to the foreground the homosexuality of Tom/Tennessee who picks up sailors at the movies, and emphasizes it both by Amanda's blindness to it and Ginny's lesbianism. The play is as much an in-joke as it is parody, but for those who do find Williams's play taking itself too seriously, it does apply the corrective of a lampoon.

"Oedi" updates the great tragedy to contemporary times but preserves enough of the original references to make its echoes transparent and its gags both satiric and funny in their own right. The "town crier" (perhaps a vestige of the Chorus) announces the news as if on a spot-news TV channel, even including the "teaser" aspect of asking listeners to hear the full story on the 11 o'clock news. Jocasta's "Jewish-mother" schtick parodies the maternal concern of a modern mother. Oedipus's concern with political polls and public image turn the king of Thebes into a modern elected official, complete with his spin doctors Creon and Tiresias. When Oedipus manages to talk himself into a weepy speech of apology instead of blinding himself, the transformation works through gradual stages of self-mutilation from blinding to castrating to amputation of an arm or just a finger, each stage less drastic—and tragic—than the last.

Instead of the exaltation of human potentiality that tragedy brings us, Orloff shows the self-absorbed degradation of a modern world and its politics. If there is a serious point here, that would be it.   TRA

Arthur Miller   Death of a Salesman (page 1445)

Miller's play perches between realistic and nonrealistic drama, with stage directions that call for visual changes as lights focus on different playing areas, walls appear and disappear, surrounding apartment buildings emerge or give way to leafy greenness, and musical motifs punctuate and interpret the actions. The scene changes often coincide with movements into the past or with imaginary entrances of the dead brother Ben, or with movements into scenes not observable by the protagonist, Willy Loman. Such fluidity of time and place is more characteristic of the novel than of the drama, and, except for Ben's entrance into the "present" when the dead man appears to urge Willy to suicide, could easily be accommodated to the most realistic cinema techniques. The lack of dramatic realism in the staging is almost entirely due to what in a novel would pass for psychological realism, the author's ability to enter into the mind of the character so as to bring memories or imagining vividly into the present.

Death of a Salesman shares with *The Glass Menagerie* the sense of being largely "a memory play," but without so obvious a device as a narrator, and with a stricter sense of the present time from which to view the past. And it shares with *Oedipus Rex* the sense of the present as the culmination of past actions, and the revelation to the audience of the past as it comes to light in the present. But the differences between Miller's play and these others are great. In Williams's play, the device of Tom's narration is less rigid in its focus, particularly insofar as it suggests that Tom is the center of attention (see the discussion on page 383 of this manual). The memory scenes in Miller's play are restricted to Willy's recollections. Willy's rival for the role of central character, Biff, has no scenes dependent on his memory—even the scene in the Boston hotel, revealing the major conflict between father and son as Biff discovers Willy's adultery, is presented through Willy's point of view when he suffers his breakdown in the restroom of the restaurant.

Miller provides a realistic motivation for these memory journeys: Willy's feverish desperation, his "exhaustion," has slightly unhinged his brain, a condition familiar to Linda and Happy, but news to the visiting Biff. The sequence of flashbacks begins as present thoughts of the car lead Willy to begin a car-polishing conversation with the boy Biff, and then the boys appear as a literal, visual representation of Willy's memory; the past comes to life in the present. In the course of the play, we learn much about Biff's development, but chiefly as a manifestation of Willy's influence on him. Both sons are Willy's spiritual heirs, dividing his attributes between them. Like Willy, Biff is a petty thief, is manually adroit, and is full of restless hopes for the great accomplishment that will mark him a success; Happy has inherited Willy's charm and his habitual mendacity. But neither of them shows any sign of the goodness that Linda sees in her husband (her judgment in that matter may be questioned, of course: she says to her sons, "You're both good boys, just act that way, that's all," suggesting that the goodness she sees in Willy may also be a matter of loving faith rather than an ethical or moral fact).

Unlike Williams, Miller is concerned with a realistic motivation for the memories, and with their direct relevance to the protagonist. Unlike Sophocles, Miller does not imply that the incidents of the past are newly discovered by the protagonist. Willy has known these things and has evaded their implications and lied to himself and others about their truth. Willy is not searching the past to explain the present; rather, in the misery and mental confusion that afflict him from the first scene, the past seems to be forcing itself into his consciousness, as if to offer him the chance to revalue his life. But his final imaginary conversation with his lucky brother Ben implies no alteration in his values: the world is still a dark jungle; there are diamonds there for the bold man's taking, and defrauding an insurance company is a proper and courageous means to obtain them. Willy's sacrifice of his life is an act of love—for Biff, not for Linda, who is absent from his last speeches—but it is guided by the same principles that governed his life. He wants Biff to be "magnificent," to be a hero by making an impression on "all kinds of people." The voyage into memory has not shown Willy the hollowness of his values.

Biff's claim to be the protagonist of the play rests mainly on two things: his return to new York opens his eyes to his father's deterioration under the pressures of his failures; and this experience leads him to some self-awareness, for in the Requiem he judges Willy ("He had the wrong dreams. All, all, wrong. . . . He never knew who he was") and asserts to Happy, "I know who I am, kid." Though this seems a positive development, especially in contrast with Happy's reaffirmation of Willy's dream, it is difficult to know what genuine gain Biff has made. Presumably he will return to his wandering life in the West, sustaining himself by manual toil, following the self-reliant dream of his pioneer grandfather who deserted wife and sons to fulfill his own dream. Except for the rural setting, which Willy himself had sought in buying a house that was later swamped by apartment development, this self-reliant notion is merely an older, more idealistic (and more selfish) version of the dream that Willy followed. It may be that Biff will be more honest with himself and others in the future, which would certainly be an improvement; but a different setting, with the wife he hankers for, doesn't necessarily imply a different set of values.

Willy's values are all based on the "American dream" of success, and some critics have seen them as the twentieth-century debasement of Emerson's doctrine of self-reliance—a term that Willy himself uses, but in a sense far different from Emerson's meaning. For Willy, the dream has been of fame, one's name in the paper, riches. His father seems to embody an earlier version of the dream—the free-spirited wanderer, the pioneer in the wilderness carving his way (literally), the success through "Yankee ingenuity," an irresponsible Ben Franklin. Willy's father, that nineteenth-century flute maker and flute player (Thoreau played the flute in his cabin at Walden Pond) provides the recurring musical motif that opens and closes the play "telling of grass and trees and the horizon," the old simplicities of rural America where possibilities were limitless. In Willy's case, however, the dream has taken on the sentimental falseness of Horatio Alger and has been used to mask ethical and moral shortcomings. The center of Willy's philosophy is to be "well liked," to achieve success as a salesman through charismatic personality. The measure of success is material possession, and Willy has allowed himself to believe in advertisements, to buy "brand name" cars, a washing machine, a vacuum cleaner (his mistake with the refrigerator was in buying an off-brand). He has always looked to the future to bring fulfillment and happiness (he's "never so happy as when he's looking forward to something"), not only to his hopes for Biff but even to his own funeral. The past he tries to remember with nostalgia about the rustic setting of the house; the future has always seemed ready to open up on those horizons of possibility. But these dreams have assumed such importance in his life that they have justified the petty deceits employed in trying to achieve them—the lies about his sales records, the pilfering of sand and lumber to improve the house, the encouragement of Biff's cheating for the sake of a college scholarship, as well as the not-so-petty adultery that destroyed his son's respect for him, and the suicide made to look accidental to defraud the insurance company. Success at any cost was Willy's program for himself and Biff, but the result of that philosophy is self-destruction.

As the comparison with Sophocles suggests, I am not among those who classify this play as a tragedy—but it is not necessary that a play satisfy the definition of tragedy to be great. Miller's achievement is genuine and important, embodying a serious theme and defining a serious flaw in a modern, materialistic world. For Willy Loman, modest hopes and minor dishonesties became a way of life, and Miller shows how understandably they arose, how temperamentally they persisted, and how pathetically they concluded.

Useful articles on Miller and the play are contained in the following: Robert W. Corrigan, ed., *Arthur Miller: A Collection of Critical Essays* (Englewood Cliffs, NJ: Prentice, 1969); Robert A. Martin, ed., *Arthur Miller: New Perspectives* (Englewood Cliffs, NJ: Prentice, 1982); James J. Martine, ed., *Critical Essays on Arthur Miller* (Boston: Hall, 1979); and Gerald Weales, ed., *Death of a Salesman: Text and Criticism* (New York: Viking, 1967).

Two versions of the play adapted for television are available on DVD. The earlier one (1966) stars Lee J. Cobb and Mildred Dunnock from the "Broadway Theatre Archives" series and is distributed by Kultur (www .kultur.com). The other from 1987 stars Dustin Hoffman and Kate Reid, and is available from a number of sources.   TRA

William Shakespeare   A Midsummer Night's Dream

(page 1538)

This may be the most beloved of Shakespeare's comedies because of its variety, exuberance, and delight. It is also probably the most frequently produced, in our time, of the romantic comedies. Yet it is not the simplest, and its multiple plots, so apparently effortless in their interweaving, make it one of the most structurally complex. Its unity is thematic, all six of its plots offering some explication of the central theme enunciated by Lysander, "The course of true love never did run smooth" (1.1.134).

The first of the love plots, and the simplest, is announced in the opening exchange of speeches between Duke Theseus of Athens and his betrothed Amazon queen, Hippolyta. They have been battlefield enemies, yet ironically by conquering her with his sword Theseus has captured her heart as well. This strange origin of their love certainly underscores the maxim pronounced by Lysander: there could hardly be a rougher road to true love than out-and-out physical combat. But we must not misunderstand this relationship and see in Hippolyta an abject or even truculently unwilling bride (as some productions do, presumably to make her position less feminine in the old-fashioned gender stereotyping that this play mocks). Hippolyta is Theseus's equal, as we witness in their two major conversations. In act 4 the royal couple have gone to the woods of Athens (where by comic coincidence they stumble across the four sleeping lovers) to carry out some May Day ritual, to be followed by some hunting with his hounds. Their discussion is the smallest of small talk, a comparison of the qualities of Theseus's Spartan hunting hounds to those that Hippolyta has hunted with in the past—a minor conflict between them based on my-dog-is-better-than-your-dog.

The significance is not that they are in conflict, but that it is over such a trivial matter, and that they confront each other openly and directly, and in tones directly opposite to those of the four lovers in their nightlong quarrel. The royal couple are mature and self-confident, and their love is not at all challenged by a difference of opinion or experience. In fact, symbolically, their descriptions of Spartan hounds reflect the deep harmony of their own relationship, as both Hippolyta and Theseus comment on the musicality of the hounds' baying. It is, she says, a paradox that the noisy clamor of the dogs produces "So musical a discord, such sweet thunder" (4.1.117). And so it is with their love—out of the thunder and discord of warfare, a sweet music has emerged.

Hippolyta is so far from being Theseus's thrall that she overmatches him in their next extended conversation. In the opening of act 5, they are musing over the tale told by the four young lovers about their night in the woods. To Hippolyta the story is "strange," but Theseus dismisses it in a famous speech comparing lovers, poets, and lunatics—all of them completely subject to their imaginations, none of them able to report their experiences with the "cool reason" that he so prizes. But Hippolyta's answer corrects him: while the tale appears improbable and fanciful, it was told with such certainty and is so consistent, there must be a truth to it that reason cannot comprehend. Like the course of their own love, or the jangling of the hounds, heard aright the story has its own beauty and harmony.

The central plot is of course that of the four lovers whose tangled courtship fills the woods of Athens with discord and danger. Theirs is presumably the "midsummer night's dream" (though Bottom's experience with Titania would be a good match for the title). And the dreams they share run the gamut, from nightmare to wish-fulfillment, even including the predictive dream that Hermia has about Lysander smiling as a snake devours her heart. The lovers get into their pickle as a result of two classic obstacles in love's path—the ancient plot device of a blocking father who wants his daughter to marry the man of his choice, and the equally ancient device of mismatched feelings—external and internal sources of frustration and conflict. When Egeus demands that Hermia marry Demetrius (who loves her), though she prefers Lysander (who also loves her), we see that Egeus is merely adding a sharp edge to a classic love-triangle. Shakespeare goes him one better, of course, creating a love-quadrangle by adding Helena's love for Demetrius. So, at the outset both men love Hermia, she returns Lysander's love, and Demetrius's hopeless love for Hermia is balanced by Helena's hopeless love for Demetrius. Under the potent spell of pansy juice (a symbolic representation of love at first sight and the changeableness of human feelings), the two men switch their love from Hermia to Helena. At the height of this nightmare, the men are ready for a duel to prove who loves Helena more truly, while Hermia and Helena, bosom friends since childhood, are engaged in scrapping and threatening. Puck is ordered to make one final intervention by Oberon, who throughout the night had tried to make things work out for the four: the pansy spell is lifted from Lysander's eyes so that he will return to Hermia while Demetrius can remain spell-struck for Helena. Then Puck puts them into a deep sleep from which they will awaken in the right pairings. As he says, "Jack shall have Jill; / Naught shall go ill" (3.2.461–62).

This strange eventful night contains two more of the six plots, one contingent upon the other. The king and queen of the fairies are passionately opposed, a quarrel that reveals them to be nature deities as their discord has the power to turn nature topsy-turvy, change the seasons around, cause flooding and diseases and all manner of problems for the mortal world. This prodigious effect springs from trivial causes. Each of them is jealous of the favoritism shown by the other for Hippolyta or Theseus (the feeling cannot extend to sexual jealousy, since Oberon charges Titania only with leading Theseus from one mortal mistress to another). Furthermore, Titania has adopted an orphaned child, and keeps him for the sake of his mother, a former companion of hers. Oberon wants him as part of his train (presumably, males serve in his court, females in hers), but when she is adamant, he plans revenge. He causes her to fall in love with some mortal creature—the worse the better, as far as he is concerned.

As it happens (comic coincidence still working well), she awakens from her drugged nap to hear the singing of Bottom the weaver, and to see him in all his beauty, wearing the ass-head prop that Puck has mischievously put on him. Thus begins the ludicrous love plot of fairy queen and gross, disfigured craftsman, in which her dotage is matched by his smug arrogance and pretentiousness. Of all the plots, this one most clearly demonstrates that love can overpower any improbabilities and harmonize any discords. It ends as abruptly as it began, with Oberon's removing the spell from his queen once he has obtained the boy from her (her passion for Bottom having cancelled out other affections) and has taken his pleasure in chiding and taunting her. Once she is awakened, the fairy king and queen are majestically reconciled in a passage that combines the harmonious grace of poetry, music, and dance (4.1.82–101). They proceed with their trains to bless the marriages of Theseus, Hippolyta, and the four lovers.

The final love plot in A Midsummer Night's Dream is the performance in act 5 by the craftsmen of the tragic tale of Pyramus and Thisbe. This story of star-crossed lovers doomed by family enmities and destroyed by a calamitous misunderstanding is diametrically opposite the plots of love's fulfillment after trouble and turmoil. That is, this plot acts as a contrasting foil to the central theme displayed by the others, that overcoming obstacles will lead to the bliss of marriage. But no one who sees or reads the play can possibly feel as much pity for these lovers as Hippolyta expresses for Bottom in his grief, for the whole spectacle is ridiculous. It offers us one more way to find comedy in love, by recognizing in the foolishness and stupidity of the amateur actors an unflagging source of laughter.

In addition to illuminating in many ways Lysander's maxim about "the course of true love," A Midsummer Night's Dream also defines an ultimate human dream. As might be expected in so rich a play, the title is reflected in a number of ways. Dreams of all sorts run through it, from Hermia's prophetic dream of Lysander's delight at her misery to Bottom's dream (as he recalls it) of an erotic affair with the fairy queen to Titania's equally preposterous "vision" of having fallen in love with an ass. As Oberon predicts of the four lovers, when they awaken in the morning they will recall their night as no more than "the fierce vexation[s] of a dream" (4.1.68), a nightmare of confusion, conflict, hatred, and frustration. (We should probably note that in the nonrealistic conventions that govern this play, not to be in love is to be in hate, as all four of the lovers have no middle ground for their emotions.)

But the greatest dream is the one implied in Puck's jingle: when Jack and Jill find each other, nothing can go wrong. This is not a sleeping dream but the most beautiful aspiration, that permanent happiness will come from finding and marrying the perfect mate. This is the dream to which all the mortals subscribe, and which the play celebrates structurally as it brings together all the characters for the ritualistic fifth act celebrating marriage. That is the culmination of the "smiling comedy" of the play, the cheerful assurance that characters for whom we have developed some affection are able at the last to find their happiness.

However, A *Midsummer Night's Dream* also displays traces of scornful or satiric comedy, not only in the comic portrayals of the inept but pompous craftsmen but also in the overbearing father Egeus, and especially in the one enduring marriage of the play, that of Titania and Oberon. While all the others are striving to reach the well-defined goal, the fairy spouses have been there and back. It is one of the ironies of the play that we learn considerably more about the true tribulations of the mortal world from the actions and speeches of the fairies. Such information encompasses not only Puck's brisk definition of all mortals as fools, but the list of jests that he plays on them as he takes credit for old ladies dribbling their drinks and falling off their stools and other minor accidents that befall us all. And we should recall the more somber implications of Titania's narration of the consequences of fairy quarrels (2.1.81–117), where we learn of discomfort, disease, and death. It is Titania who reports the death in childbirth of the Indian boy's mother (2.1.135), and it is Oberon who blesses the marriage beds by warding off threats of marital discord, misfortunes, birth defects (5.1.398–415). Experience and observation have taught the fairies that the mortal world is beset with difficulties large and small, and in their actions they demonstrate one central problem with love's dream: from trivial causes may spring resentment, jealousy, vengefulness, shame. With time, these feelings may be overcome in reconciliation, but they will inevitably come to all who try to live that dream.

As a dream play, A *Midsummer Night's Dream* is of course nonrealistic in its presentation of these themes. The actor who plays Puck in the epilogue (5.1.418–33) makes that point very clear. If any in the audience, he says, have taken any offense at what the characters (mere "shadows" of reality) have done on the way to the happily-ever-after resolution of all love problems, they should think that what they observed was only a "dream" that came to them as they dozed through the performance. The conjuration is multi-dimensioned. What we have seen is that the "dream" of permanent bliss through marriage can indeed be reached after many rough moments; realists among us, with an eye on Titania and Oberon for examples of wedded bliss, might rightly scoff at that. "Shadows" of humanity cannot possibly be real. And even less credible to the realist, some of those "shadows" represent supernatural beings. The preposterousness of plot, character, and theme might well offend someone who (like Theseus) prefers "cool reason" to flights of fancy.

The epilogue is a joke, of course. No one entered the theater supposing that it was Athens, nor that the people on the stage were the actual characters of myth or legend, nor did we expect some literal version of reality. Throughout the play, in fact, Shakespeare plays with details that enhance the nonrealistic conventions. There are almost palpable distortions of clock and calendar that keep us off balance. What can "cool reason" make of the fact that the play is a "midsummer" dream, yet Theseus and Hippolyta cele-brate the rites of May on the eve of their wedding? Or that we are emphati-cally told that the "new moon" and the royal marriage will occur on the fourth day from the opening scene, yet only two and a half days elapse before that happy occasion? And is it only an inability to read the almanac that per-suades the craftsmen that the full moon will shine that night, or are new moon and full moon thoroughly conflated on a night when fairies, lovers, and craftsmen manage to navigate through the not-very-dark woods?

The point is that these distortions of literal reality are not mere slips of the pen, but are consistent with both the theme and the structure of the play. Its nonrealistic conventions (verse dialogue, comic coincidence, exaggerated characterization, and the rest) are supported by flagrant violations of reality. But for 400 years, the consensus seems to be that anyone who could take of-fense at this representation of reality would be more an ass than Bottom.

So complex a play has naturally been copiously studied. A few interest-ing analyses are to be found in: C. I. Barber, *Shakespeare's Festive Comedy* (Princeton: Princeton UP, 1959); K. M. Briggs. *The Anatomy of Puck* (Lon-don: Routledge, 1959); Robert W. Dent, "Imagination in *A Midsummer Night's Dream*," *Shakespeare Quarterly* 15 (1964): 115–29; Northrup Frye, *Northrup Frye on Shakespeare,* ed. Robert Sandler (Markham, Ont.: Fitzhenry, 1986); David P. Young, *Something of Great Constancy: The Art of A Midsummer Night's Dream* (New Haven: Yale UP, 1966).

There are several versions of the play on video and DVD. I still recom-mend the Royal Shakespeare Company production directed in 1968 by Peter Hall, which among many other glories boasts three of Britain's great actresses—Dame Judi Dench, Dame Diana Rigg, and Dame Helen Mirren. TRA

August Wilson   Fences (page 1600)

At the beginning of the play, Troy has been hardened by his experiences and has hardened himself against further pain and injury. He doesn't want Cory to be like him, to suffer as he has suffered from the prejudice of the white world, and so he refuses to let his son think of sports as a means of suc-ceeding since he was not allowed to succeed in that way. The world has changed, but Troy cannot see it. His hard life has left him few pleasures—Friday night drinking with Bono and sex with Rose. He feels stagnant in his "clean . . . hard . . . useful life," a man who was "born with two strikes" against him who has found a loving wife, a son, and a "halfway decent job" (page 1641). He is, at the outset, "safe." How he reached this impasse is disclosed by a summary of his life to this point reconstructed from realistically scat-tered conversational remarks:

In 1904, Troy Maxson was born in rural Alabama, the son of a cotton sharecropper and one of eleven children, including his brother Gabriel who was born in 1911. Like Troy in 1957, his father was trapped by his situation and could only concern himself with "getting them bales of cotton in to Mr. Lubin," the owner of the farm. He accepted his responsibility to his family, but he was a hard man, "just as evil as he could be" (page 1631), and when Troy was eight his mother deserted the family; she promised to return for Troy but she never did. His father then lived with a succession of women, all of them deserting him sooner or later. In 1918 when Troy was fourteen, his father found him "fooling around" with a girl when he was supposed to be plowing, and whipped him. Then the father in turn commenced to enjoy the girl, and in his turn Troy began whipping his father. The result was that he was severely beaten, so he left home, walked the 200 miles to Mobile, and then joined a group heading north.

He arrived in Pittsburgh, but couldn't find a job and lived in a shack along the river. For about five years he lived by stealing, then met and married Lyons's mother. When the baby came (1923), he tried to accept his responsibility by stealing more. One day, a man he was robbing shot him and Troy killed him with his knife, then spent fifteen years (1923–38) in the penitentiary.

There he met his best friend, Jim Bono, and learned to play baseball. When he was released in 1938 Lyons's mother had left him and taken their son. Troy felt himself a reformed man, and in 1939 he met and married Rose, who bore their son Cory in 1940. Troy played ball in the Negro Leagues, one season batting .432 and hitting 37 home runs facing such legendary opponents as Satchel Paige. By the time that Jackie Robinson became the first black player in the major leagues, Troy was 43 years old. He claims that the color ban still kept him from being accepted, but Bono and Rose insist that it was his age.

Troy nearly died from pneumonia in the summer of 1941. At 37, he was too old to be drafted when the Second World War began later that year, though his younger brother Gabriel served and was severely wounded and mentally disabled. Troy had Gabriel move into their house (using his $3000 veteran's bonus to purchase it), where he lived for more than ten years until renting his own rooms in 1957.

When his baseball career ended at some time in the early forties, Troy found work as a municipal garbage collector. He and his friend Bono still work as pick-up men at the back of a truck driven by a white driver.

As the play opens Troy has created a crisis in his job: he has requested to be made a driver and has been told to report to the Commissioner's office. His future is uncertain, though he claims to be confident that they cannot fire him for simply asking. In fact, he is given the promotion (though as Bono points out, he has no driver's license) and moves up to the front of his truck. In the course of the play, his promotion leads to his being assigned to a white part of the city and begin separated from Bono. The solitude of his assignment makes his advancement less appealing, and not working beside Bono leads to their gradually drifting apart. Their customary Friday evening drinking sessions come to an end, and Bono finds other ways to relax. But more than that, a rift grows between them, because Troy has begun an affair with a woman named Alberta. Bono disapproves, and tells him so; and Troy begins spending all his evenings with Alberta, having no time either for Bono or for his wife Rose.

Troy at length tells Rose of his affair, and of Alberta's pregnancy, for he feels he must accept responsibility for her and her child as well as continue to maintain Rose and their son Cory. Rose is deeply hurt and angered—this is, in fact, the first time that Troy has been unfaithful to her, and she had assumed that they would grow old together in a stable and unchanging life. When he tries to explain to her that Alberta offers him a new sense of himself, a man who has laughter in his soul, Rose can only remind him of how much she has submerged her own identity in him. Alberta's death in childbirth leads to a new accommodation in the relationship of Troy and Rose: she will help him by rearing the child and so fulfilling his obligation, but she will never be intimate with him again.

Troy's other climactic conflict occurs between him and Cory, who is being recruited for a football scholarship by a college in North Carolina. Troy's frustration with is own career in sports, having been barred from the success he should have had in the major leagues because of his color, makes him cynically reject the chance that seems to be opening up for Cory. Troy does not believe that the whites will really accept and reward Cory for his athletic ability, and he concludes that the boy will only be hurt and rejected as he himself was: "The white man ain't gonna let you get nowhere with that football noway" (page 1621). His ambition for Cory does not include a college education but what he thinks is more realistic, training and hard work that will lead to slow but gradual advancement—working as an auto mechanic or as a builder, some trade that will surpass such a service job as his own.

When Cory lies to him about a job arrangement at the A & P supermarket that will permit him to practice football and keep his job part-time, Troy has him removed from the football team. In their confrontation, Cory asks him why he doesn't "like" his son, and Troy defines for him his sense of paternal duties: he fully accepts his responsibility for the boy's physical well-being, but "I ain't got to like you." Troy's position is that a man who thinks he can get what he wants by being "liked" is a fool—"Don't you try and go through life worrying about if somebody like you or not" (page 1623); rather insist that you are paid what you earn. Life, Troy has come to believe, is a sequence of debts to be paid when you incur them, and of obligations to be returned by those who owe you. His code is keep your word to others and require others to keep theirs to you.

In his baseball metaphor, Troy counts the strikes against his son. Cory's first strike is when he lies to Troy about the job and football. His second comes when Troy is hurting Rose as they quarrel about Alberta, and Cory knocks Troy down trying to protect his mother from abuse. The third strike, and the end of their relationship, occurs when Cory denounces his father for his betrayal of Rose and for taking Gabriel's money and then getting rid of him. When Troy advances on his son, Cory grabs his baseball bat and threatens Troy with it, then loses it as they struggle over it. Troy checks himself and does not strike Cory with it, but throws him out of the house. Cory enlists in the Marines, and does not see his father alive again.

So in the years 1957–58, Troy Maxson sees his life fall apart as he confronts his major conflicts. He breaks through a color barrier at work, but the success cuts him off from his best friend. He finds another kind of love in his life, and through it loses both of the women who satisfy his needs. He confronts his son and tries to force him into a way of life that will be safe and secure, but loses him forever. And he boldly confronts death, and loses.

The title provides a recurring thematic comment. It refers first of all to the little wooden fence that Rose wants Troy to build around their front yard. As Bono says, "Some people build fences to keep people out . . . and other people build fences to keep people in. Rose wants to hold on to you all. She loves you" (page 1636). Rose also sings her prayer to Jesus, "be a fence all around me every day . . . protect me as I travel on my way" (page 1613). As the representative of stability, Rose wants a fence to function in both of Bono's definitions, to ward off outside dangers as well as to keep her loved ones within. It is ironic that the literal fence is completed for her after her safe haven has disintegrated through Troy's infidelity, and then functions as the boundary of the yard from which Troy banishes Cory.

In addition to the literal fence there are a number of fencelike barriers, literal and figurative, in the play. Troy has overcome two of them, the outfield fence over which he hit his 37 home runs and the fence that kept him from a promotion in the white man's hierarchy. Unfortunately, both of these triumphs turn to ashes for him, for his baseball career ended in frustration and his work as a driver has made him lonely and unhappy. Troy's life has been filled with obstacles, and more often than not overcoming them creates equivocal victories. Beginning fenced in by the economic system in Alabama, his escape led to criminality in the oppressive system he found in Pittsburgh. Within prison walls, he found a good friend and a new opportunity with baseball, but both are lost to him over time once he is outside the bars. His need to establish a stable home life and to help his disabled brother led to using Gabriel's pension for a house payment for which he is haunted by guilt and taunted by his son. He tries to break free of the constrictions of his domestic obligation and to find "a different understanding" of himself: "I done locked myself into a pattern trying to take care of [Rose and Cory, and] I forgot about myself" (page 1640). His experience with Alberta does give him a new sense of himself as a man taking risks and living more fully—but the consequences are catastrophic.

Troy Maxson is a tragic figure, for his mistakes arise from attempts to overcome barriers to a better, fuller life, and they destroy what he has achieved. It is instructive to compare him to Willy Loman, a man with parallel conflicts with his children, his wife, and the terms of his life, and at whose death the survivors present a concluding "epilogue" evaluating him. Willy does his best to avoid looking straight at his situation—he's evasive, self-deceptive, and incapable. Troy strives to help and support, to understand and to enlarge his life, to overcome both external and internal barriers.

Fences is perhaps the most realistic play in this collection. Its structure is linear, each scene building on the results of the preceding one, and its expository method is wholly naturalistic. The facts we learn about Troy's past are revealed at times when such facts would reasonably come out (for example, he speaks of his boyhood and early manhood to his son Lyons, as a way of telling him about obligations between father and sons when Lyons attempts to defend Cory). The passage of time is conventionally established as occurring between scenes, so that what we witness is a sequence of episodes each with its own naturalistic duration. And most emphatically, the life we glimpse is an entirely credible world of a defined social and intellectual nature, honest and true to the experience of its people and its place, captured in vigorous and beautiful dialect.

August Wilson has said this about his play:

> At the end of *Fences* every person, with the exception of Raynell, is institutionalized. Rose is in a church. Lyons is in a penitentiary; Gabriel's in a mental hospital and Cory's in the marines. The only free person is the girl, Troy's daughter, the hope for the future. That was conscious on my part because in '57 that's what I saw. (Quoted in David Savran, *In Their Own Words: Contemporary American Playwrights* [New York: Theatre Communications Group, 1988] 301.)

In a televised interview with Bill Moyers (available on PBS video), Wilson makes the important point: although this play is directly concerned with the experience of African Americans at the time and in the place in which it is set, its themes are not restricted to those specifics. It is about relationships between a father and his sons, between a wife and her husband, between fast friends, between a man and his social and economic environment, as well as about the situations of black people in an America of shifting racial barriers and attitudes.   TRA